THE
PREACHER'S
OUTLINE & SERMON
BIBLE®

EZRA – ESTHER

THE
PREACHER'S
OUTLINE & SERMON
BIBLE®

OLD TESTAMENT

KING JAMES VERSION

Leadership Ministries Worldwide
Chattanooga, TN

Library of Congress Catalog Card Number: 96-75921
ISBN Softbound Edition: 978-1-57407-201-3

Printed in the United States of America

DEDICATED

To all the men and women of the world
who preach and teach the Gospel of
our Lord Jesus Christ and
to the Mercy and Grace of God

&

- Demonstrated to us in Christ Jesus our Lord.

  "In whom we have redemption through His blood, the forgiveness of sins, according to the riches of His grace." (Ep.1:7)

- Out of the mercy and grace of God, His Word has flowed. Let every person know that God will have mercy upon him, forgiving and using him to fulfill His glorious plan of salvation.

  "For God so loved the world, that he gave His only begotten Son, that whosoever believeth in Him should not perish, but have everlasting life. For God sent not his son into the world to condemn the world, but that the world through him might be saved." (Jn.3:16-17)

  "For this is good and acceptable in the sight of God our Saviour; who will have all men to be saved, and to come unto the knowledge of the truth." (1 Ti.2:3-4)

The Preacher's Outline & Sermon Bible®

is written for God's servants to use in their study, teaching, and preaching of God's Holy Word...

- to share the Word of God with the world.
- to help believers, both ministers and laypersons, in their understanding, preaching, and teaching of God's Word.
- to do everything we possibly can to lead men, women, boys, and girls to give their hearts and lives to Jesus Christ and to secure the eternal life that He offers.
- to do all we can to minister to the needy of the world.
- to give Jesus Christ His proper place, the place the Word gives Him. Therefore, no work of Leadership Ministries Worldwide will ever be personalized.

ACKNOWLEDGMENTS AND BIBLIOGRAPHY

Every child of God is precious to the LORD and deeply loved. And every child as a servant of the LORD touches the lives of those who come in contact with him or his ministry. The writing ministries of the following servants have touched this work, and we are grateful that God brought their writings our way. We hereby acknowledge their ministry to us, being fully aware that there are many others down through the years whose writings have touched our lives and who deserve mention, but whose names have faded from our memory. May our wonderful LORD continue to bless the ministries of these dear servants—and the ministries of us all—as we diligently labor to reach the world for Christ and to meet the desperate needs of those who suffer so much.

THE REFERENCE WORKS

Aharoni, Yohanan, Michael Avi-Yonah, Anson F. Rainey and Ze'ev Safrai, Editors. *The MacMillan Bible Atlas*, 3rd Ed. Jerusalem: Carta, The Israel Map and Publishing Company, 1993.

Albright, W.F. *History, Archaeology and Christian Humanism*. New York: McGraw Hill, 1964.

Archer, Gleason L. *A Survey of Old Testament Introduction*. Chicago, IL: Moody Bible Institute of Chicago, 1974.

———. *Encyclopedia of Bible Difficulties*. Grand Rapids, Michigan: Zondervan Publishing House, 1982.

Atlas of the World. Hammond Concise Edition. Maplewood, NJ: Hammond Inc., 1993.

Baker's Dictionary of Theology. Everett F. Harrison, Editor-in-Chief. Grand Rapids, MI: Baker Book House, 1960.

Barker, William P. *Everyone in the Bible*. Westwood, NJ: Fleming H. Revell Co., 1966.

Benware, Paul N. *Survey of the Old Testament*. "Everyman's Bible Commentary." Chicago, IL: Moody Bible Institute of Chicago, 1993.

Bromiley, Geoffrey W., et al, Editors. *David*. "The International Standard Bible Encyclopedia." Grand Rapids, MI: Eerdmans Publishing Co., 1988.

Brown, Francis. *The New Brown-Driver-Briggs-Gesenius Hebrew-English Lexicon*. Peabody, MA: Hendrickson Publishers, 1979.

Cruden's Complete Concordance of the Old & New Testament. Philadelphia, PA: The John C. Winston Co., 1930.

Dake, Finis Jennings. *Dake's Annotated Reference Bible, The Holy Bible*. Lawrenceville, GA: Dake Bible Sales, Inc., 1963.

Douglas, J.D. Editor. *New Bible Dictionary*. Wheaton, IL: Tyndale House Publishers, Inc., 1982.

Easton's 1897 Bible Dictionary. Database NavPress Software, 1996.

Enhanced Nave's Topics. Database NavPress Software, 1991, 1994.

Frank, Harry Thomas, ed. *Atlas of the Bible Lands*. Maplewood, NJ: Hammond Incorporated, 1977.

Freedman, David Noel, Editor, et. al. *The Anchor Bible Dictionary*. New York: Doubleday, 1992.

Funk & Wagnalls Standard Desk Dictionary. Lippincott & Crowell, Publishers, 1980, Vol.2.

Geisler, Norman. *A Popular Survey of the Old Testament*. Grand Rapids, MI: Baker Book House, 1977.

Gill, Dr. A.L., Compiler. *God's Promises For Your Every Need*. Dallas, TX: Word Publishing, 1995.

Good News Bible. Old Testament: © American Bible Society, 1976. New Testament: © American Bible Society, 1966, 1971, 1976. Collins World.

Good News for Modern Man, The New Testament. New York, NY: American Bible Society, 1971.

Goodrick, Edward W. and John R. Kohlenberger, III. *The NIV Exhaustive Concordance*. Grand Rapids, MI: Zondervan Publishing House, 1990.

Grun, Bernard. *The Timetables of History*. 3rd ed. New York: Simon & Schuster, 1991.

Harrison, Roland Kenneth. *Introduction to the Old Testament*. Grand Rapids, MI: Eerdmans Publishing Co., 1969.

Holman Bible Dictionary. Nashville, TN: Broadman & Holman Publishers, 1991. Database NavPress Software.

Hooper, Jerry L., Editor. *The Holman Bible Atlas*. Philadelphia, PA: A.J. Holman Company, 1978.

ISBE. Grand Rapids, MI: Eerdmans Publishing Co., 1988.

Jauchen, John S., Editor, et. al. *NIV Thompson Student Bible*. Indianapolis, IN: Kirkbride Bible Company, 1999.

Josephus, Flavius. *Complete Works*. Grand Rapids, MI: Kregel Publications, 1981.

Kaiser, Walter C. *A History of Israel*. Nashville, Tennessee: Broadman and Holman Publishers, 1998.

Kipfer, Barbara Ann, Ph.D. *Roget's 21st Century Thesaurus*. New York, NY: Dell Publishing, 1992.

Kohlenberger, John R. III. *The Interlinear NIV Hebrew-English Old Testament*. Grand Rapids, MI: Zondervan Publishing House, 1987.

Kouffman, Donald T. *The Dictionary of Religious Terms*. Westwood, NJ: Fleming H. Revell Co., 1967.

Life Application® Bible. Wheaton, IL: Tyndale House Publishers, Inc., 1991.

Life Application® Study Bible. New International Version. Tyndale House Publishers, Inc.: Wheaton, IL 1991, and Zondervan Publishing House: Grand Rapids, MI, 1984.

Lindsell, Harold and Woodbridge, Charles J. *A Handbook of Christian Truth*. Westwood, NJ: Fleming H. Revell Company, A Division of Baker Book House, 1953.

Living Quotations For Christians. Edited by Sherwood Eliot Wirt and Kersten Beckstrom. New York, NY: Harper & Row, Publishers, 1974.

Lockyer, Herbert. *All the Books and Chapters of the Bible*. Grand Rapids, MI: Zondervan Publishing House, 1966.

———. *All the Kings and Queens of the Bible*. Grand Rapids, MI: Zondervan Publishing House, 1961.

———. *All the Men of the Bible*. Grand Rapids, MI: Zondervan Publishing House, 1958.

———. *All the Miracles of the Bible*. Grand Rapids, MI: Zondervan Publishing House, 1961.

———. *All the Parables of the Bible*. Grand Rapids, MI: Zondervan Publishing House, 1963.

———. *The Women of the Bible*. Grand Rapids, MI: Zondervan Publishing House, 1967.

Luckenbill, Daniel David. *Ancient Records of Assyria and Babylonia*, 2 vols. (ARAB) London: Histories and Mysteries of Man Ltd., 1989.

Martin, Alfred. *Survey of the Scriptures*, Part I, II, III. Chicago, IL: Moody Bible Institute of Chicago, 1961.

McDowell, Josh. *Evidence That Demands a Verdict*, Vol.1. San Bernardino, CA: Here's Life Publishers, Inc., 1979.

Miller, Madeleine S. & J. Lane. *Harper's Bible Dictionary*. New York, NY: Harper & Row Publishers, 1961.

Nave, Orville J. *Nave's Topical Bible*. Nashville, TN: The Southwestern Company. Copyright © by J.B. Henderson, 1921.

Nelson's Complete Book of Bible Maps & Charts. Nashville, TN: Thomas Nelson Publishers, Inc., 1996.

New American Standard Bible, Reference Edition. La Habra, CA: The Lockman Foundation, 1975.

New American Standard Bible, Updated Edition. La Habra, CA: The Lockman Foundation, 1995.

New Bible Dictionary, 3rd Edition. Leicester, England: Universities & Colleges Christian Fellowship, 1996.

New International Version Study Bible. Grand Rapids, MI: Zondervan Bible Publishers, 1985.

New Living Translation, Holy Bible. Wheaton, IL: Tyndale House Publishers, Inc., 1996.

Orr, William. *How We May Know That God Is*. Wheaton, IL: Van Kampen Press, n.d.

Owens, John Joseph. *Analytical Key to the Old Testament,* Vols.1, 2, 3. Grand Rapids, MI: Baker Book House, 1989.

Payne, J. Barton. *Encyclopedia of Biblical Prophecy*. New York, NY: Harper & Row, Publishers, 1973.

Pilgrim Edition, Holy Bible. New York, NY: Oxford University Press, 1952.

Ridout, Samuel. *Lectures on the Tabernacle*. New York, NY: Loizeaux Brothers, Inc., 1914.

Silverman, David P. ed. *Ancient Egypt*. New York: Oxford University Press, 1997.

Smith, William. *Smith's Bible Dictionary*. Peabody, MA: Hendrickson Publishers, n.d.

Stone, Nathan J. *Names of God*. Chicago, IL: Moody Press, 1944.

Strong, James. *Strong's Exhaustive Concordance of the Bible*. Nashville, TN: Thomas Nelson, Inc., 1990.

_____. *The Tabernacle of Israel*. Grand Rapids, MI: Kregel Publications, 1987.

Strong's Greek and Hebrew Dictionary as compiled by iExalt Software. Database NavPress Software, 1990-1993.

The Amplified Bible. Scripture taken from THE AMPLIFIED BIBLE, Old Testament copyright © 1965, 1987 by the Zondervan Publishing House. The Amplified New Testament copyright © 1958, 1987 by The Lockman Foundation. Used by permission.

The Evangelical Dictionary of Theology. Elwell, Walter A., Editor. Grand Rapids, MI: Baker Book House, 1984.

The Hebrew-Greek Key Study Bible, New International Version. Spiros Zodhiates, Th.D., Executive Editor. Chattanooga, TN: AMG Publishers, 1996.

The Holy Bible in Four Translations. Minneapolis, MN: Worldwide Publications. Copyright © The Iversen-Norman Associates: New York, NY, 1972.

The Illustrated Bible Atlas, with Historical Notes by F. F. Bruce. Grand Rapids, MI: Kregel Publications, 1994.

The Interlinear Bible, Vols.1, 2, 3. Translated by Jay P. Green, Sr. Grand Rapids, MI: Baker Book House, 1976.

The International Standard Bible Encyclopaedia, Edited by James Orr. Grand Rapids, MI: Eerdmans Publishing Co., 1939.

The NASB Greek/Hebrew Dictionary and Concordance. La Habra, CA: The Lockman Foundation, 1988.

The Nelson Study Bible, New King James Version. Nashville, TN: Thomas Nelson Publishers, Inc., 1997.

The New Compact Bible Dictionary. Edited by T. Alton Bryant. Grand Rapids, MI: Zondervan Publishing House, 1967. Used by permission of Zondervan Publishing House.

The New Scofield Reference Bible. Edited by C.I. Scofield. New York, NY: Oxford University Press, 1967.

The New Thompson Chain Reference Bible. Indianapolis, IN: B.B. Kirkbride Bible Co., Inc., 1964.

The New Unger's Bible Dictionary. Chicago, IL: Moody Press, 1998. Database NavPress Software, 1997.

The NIV Study Bible, New International Version. Grand Rapids, MI: Zondervan Publishing House, 1985.

The Open Bible. Nashville, TN: Thomas Nelson Publishers, 1975.

The Quest Study Bible. New International Version. Grand Rapids, MI: Zondervan Publishing House, 1994.

The Zondervan Pictorial Encyclopedia of the Bible, Vol.1. Merrill C. Tenney, Editor. Grand Rapids, MI: Zondervan Publishing House, 1982.

Theological Wordbook of the Old Testament. Edited by R. Laird Harris. Chicago, IL: Moody Bible Institute of Chicago, 1980.

Unger, Merrill F. & William White, Jr. *Nelson's Expository Dictionary of the Old Testament*. Nashville, TN: Thomas Nelson Publishers, 1980.

Vine, W.E., Merrill F. Unger, William White, Jr. *Vine's Complete Expository Dictionary of Old and New Testament Words*. Nashville, TN: Thomas Nelson Publishers, 1985.

Walton, John H. *Chronological and Background Charts of the Old Testament*. Grand Rapids, MI: Zondervan Publishing House, 1978.

Webster's Seventh New Collegiate Dictionary. Springfield, MA: G. & C. Merriam Company, Publishers, 1971.

Wilmington. Harold L. *The Outline Bible*. Wheaton, IL: Tyndale House Publishers, Inc., 1999.

Wilson, William. *Wilson's Old Testament Word Studies*. McLean, VA: MacDonald Publishing Company, n.d.

Wood, Leon. *A Survey of Israel's History*. Grand Rapids, MI: Zondervan Publishing House, 1982.

Young, Edward J. *An Introduction to the Old Testament*. Grand Rapids, MI: Eerdmans Publishing Co., 1964.

Young, Robert. *Young's Analytical Concordance to the Bible*. Grand Rapids, MI: Eerdmans Publishing Co., n.d.

Zondervan NIV Bible Library. Version 2.5. Grand Rapids, MI: Zondervan Publishing House.

THE COMMENTARIES

Adeney, Richard, H. *Ezra and Nehemiah*. Minneapolis, MN: Klock & Klock Christian Publishers, Inc., n.d.

Baldwin, Joyce G. *1 & 2 Samuel*. "The Tyndale Old Testament Commentaries." Downers Grove, IL: Inter-Varsity Press, 1988.

_____. *Esther*. "Tyndale Old Testament Commentaries." Downers Grove, IL: Inter-Varsity Press, 1984.

Barnes' Notes, Exodus to Esther. F.C. Cook, Editor. Grand Rapids, MI: Baker Book House, n.d.

Boice, James Montgomery. *Nehemiah, Learning to Lead.* Tarrytown, NY: Fleming H. Revell Co., 1990.

Braun, Roddy. *1, 2 Chronicles.* "Word Biblical Commentary," Vol.14. Waco, TX: Word Books, 1986.

Breneman, Mervin. *Ezra, Nehemiah, Esther.* "The New American Commentary," Vol.10. Nashville, TN: Broadman & Holman Publishers, 1993.

Brueggemann, Walter. *1 Kings.* "Knox Preaching Guides." Atlanta, GA: John Knox Press, 1982.

———. *2 Kings.* "Knox Preaching Guides." Atlanta, GA: John Knox Press, 1982.

Burroughs, P.E., D.D. *Old Testament Studies.* Nashville, TN: Sunday School Board, Southern Baptist Convention, 1915.

Carpenter, Eugene E., Eugene H. Merrill, Victor P. Hamilton, Donald A. Johns. *Ezra, Nehemiah, Esther.* "The Complete Biblical Library: The Old Testament," Vol.9. Springfield, MO: World Library Press Inc., 2000.

Chafin, Kenneth. *The Preacher's Commentary on 1, 2 Samuel.* Dallas, TX: Word Publishing, 1989.

Crockett, William Day. *A Harmony of Samuel, Kings, and Chronicles.* Grand Rapids, MI: Baker Book House, 1985.

Denton, Robert C. *The First and Second Books of the Kings. The First and Second Books of the Chronicles.* "The Layman's Bible Commentary," Vol.7. Atlanta, GA: John Knox Press, 1964.

DeVries, S.J. *1 Kings.* WBC. Waco, TX: Word Books, 1985.

Dilday, Russell. *The Preacher's Commentary on 1, 2 Kings.* Dallas, TX: Word Publishing, 1987.

Evans, Mary J. *1 and 2 Samuel.* "New International Biblical Commentary." Peabody, MA: Hendrickson Publishers, Inc., 2000.

Farrar, F.W. *The First Book of Kings.* Minneapolis, MN: Klock & Klock Christian Publishers, Inc., n.d.

———. *The Second Book of Kings.* Minneapolis, MN: Klock & Klock Christian Publishers, Inc., n.d.

Fensham, F. Charles. *The Books of Ezra and Nehemiah.* "New International Commentary on the Old Testament." Grand Rapids, MI: Eerdmans Publishing Co. 1982.

Gill, John. *Gill's Commentary*, Vol.2. Grand Rapids, MI: Baker Book House, 1980.

Gray, John. *I & II Kings.* Second, Fully Revised, Edition. "The Old Testament Library." Philadelphia, PA: The Westminster Press, 1970.

Henry, Matthew. *Matthew Henry's Commentary*, 6 Vols. Old Tappan, NJ: Fleming H. Revell Co., n.d.

Hertzberg, Hans Wilhelm. *I & II Samuel.* Philadelphia, PA: Westminster Press, 1964.

Hobbs, T.R. *2 Kings.* "Word Biblical Commentary," Vol.13. Waco, TX: Word Books, 1985.

Holmgren, F.C. *Ezra and Nehemiah.* Grand Rapids, MI: Eerdmans Publishing Co., 1987.

House, Paul R. *1, 2 Kings.* "The New American Commentary," Vol.8. Nashville, TN: Broadman & Holman Publishers, 1995.

Ironside, H.A. *Ezra, Nehemiah, Esther.* Neptune, NJ: Loizeaux Brothers, Inc., 1914.

Kaiser, Walter C., Jr. *A History of Israel.* Nashville, TN: Broadman & Holman Publishers, 1998.

Keil-Delitzsch. *Commentary on the Old Testament*, Vol.3. Grand Rapids, MI: Eerdmans Publishing Co., n.d.

Kidner, Derek. *Ezra and Nehemiah.* "The Tyndale Old Testament Commentaries." Downers Grove, IL: Inter-Varsity Press, 1979.

Maclaren, Alexander. *Expositions of Holy Scripture*, 11 Vols. Grand Rapids, MI: Eerdmans Publishing Co., 1952-59.

McGee, J. Vernon. *Thru the Bible*, Vol.2. Nashville, TN: Thomas Nelson Publishers, 1981.

Morgan, G. Campbell. *Living Messages of the Books of the Bible*, Vol.1. Old Tappan, NJ: Fleming H. Revell, 1912.

Newsome, James D., Jr. *1 Samuel, 2 Samuel.* Atlanta, GA: John Knox Press, 1982.

Payne, D.F. *I and II Samuel*, DSB. Philadelphia, PA: Westminster Press, 1982.

Payne, J. Barton. *1, 2 Chronicles.* "The Expositor's Bible Commentary," Vol.4. Grand Rapids, MI: Zondervan Publishing House, 1988.

Poole, Matthew. *Matthew Poole's Commentary on the Holy Bible.* Peabody, MA: Hendrickson Publishers, n.d.

Provan, Iain W. *1 and 2 Kings.* "New International Biblical Commentary." Peabody, MA: Hendrickson Publishers, Inc., 1995.

Redpath, Alan. *Victorious Christian Service.* Westwood, NJ: Fleming H. Revell Co., 1958.

Roberts, Mark. *The Preacher's Commentary on Ezra, Nehemiah, Esther.* Dallas, TX: Word Publishing, 1999.

Rust, Eric C. *The First and Second Books of Samuel.* "The Layman's Bible Commentary," Vol.6. Atlanta, GA: John Knox Press, 1961.

Sailhamer, John. *First & Second Chronicles.* "Everyman's Bible Commentary." Chicago, IL: Moody Bible Institute of Chicago, 1983.

Seume, Richard H. *Nehemiah: God's Builder.* Chicago, IL: Moody Bible Institute of Chicago, 1978.

Spurgeon, C.H. *Spurgeon's Sermon Notes. Genesis to Malachi.* Westwood, NJ: Fleming H. Revell Co., n.d.

The Interpreter's Bible, 12 Vols. New York, NY: Abingdon Press, 1956.

The Pulpit Commentary. 23 Vols. Edited by H.D.M. Spence & Joseph S. Exell. Grand Rapids, MI: Eerdmans Publishing Co., 1950.

Walvoord, John F. and Roy B. Zuck, Editors. *The Bible Knowledge Commentary, Old Testament.* Colorado Springs, CO: Chariot Victor Publishing, 1985.

Wiersbe, Warren W. *Be Committed.* Colorado Springs, CO: Victor Books, 1993.

———. *Be Determined.* Wheaton, IL: Victor Books, 1992.

Williamson, H.G.M. *1 & 2 Chronicles.* "The New Century Bible Commentary." Grand Rapids, MI: Eerdmans Publishing Co., 1982.

Wiseman, Donald J. *1 & 2 Kings.* "The Tyndale Old Testament Commentaries." Downers Grove, IL: Inter-Varsity Press, 1993.

Yamauchi, Edwin. *Ezra, Nehemiah.* "The Expositor's Bible Commentary," Vol.4. Grand Rapids, MI: Zondervan Publishing House, 1988.

Youngblood, Ronald F. *1 Samuel. 2 Samuel.* "The Expositor's Bible Commentary," Vol.3. Grand Rapids, MI: Zondervan Publishing House, 1990.

ABBREVIATIONS

&	= and		O.T.	=	Old Testament
Bc.	= because		p./pp.	=	page/pages
Concl.	= conclusion		Pt.	=	point
Cp.	= compare		Quest.	=	question
Ct.	= contrast		Rel.	=	religion
e.g.	= for example		Rgt.	=	righteousness
f.	= following		Thru	=	through
Illust.	= illustration		v./vv.	=	verse/verses
N.T.	= New Testament		vs.	=	versus

THE BOOKS OF THE OLD TESTAMENT

Book	Abbreviation	Chapters	Book	Abbreviation	Chapters
GENESIS	Gen. or Ge.	50	Ecclesiastes	Eccl. or Ec.	12
Exodus	Ex.	40	The Song of Solomon	S. of Sol. or Song	8
Leviticus	Lev. or Le.	27	Isaiah	Is.	66
Numbers	Num. or Nu.	36	Jeremiah	Jer. or Je.	52
Deuteronomy	Dt. or De.	34	Lamentations	Lam.	5
Joshua	Josh. or Jos.	24	Ezekiel	Ezk. or Eze.	48
Judges	Judg. or Jud.	21	Daniel	Dan. or Da.	12
Ruth	Ruth or Ru.	4	Hosea	Hos. or Ho.	14
1 Samuel	1 Sam. or 1 S.	31	Joel	Joel	3
2 Samuel	2 Sam. or 2 S.	24	Amos	Amos or Am.	9
1 Kings	1 Ki. or 1 K.	22	Obadiah	Obad. or Ob.	1
2 Kings	2 Ki. or 2 K.	25	Jonah	Jon. or Jona.	4
1 Chronicles	1 Chron. or 1 Chr.	29	Micah	Mic. or Mi.	7
2 Chronicles	2 Chron. or 2 Chr.	36	Nahum	Nah. or Na.	3
Ezra	Ezra or Ezr.	10	Habakkuk	Hab.	3
Nehemiah	Neh. or Ne.	13	Zephaniah	Zeph. or Zep.	3
Esther	Est.	10	Haggai	Hag.	2
Job	Job or Jb.	42	Zechariah	Zech. or Zec.	14
Psalms	Ps.	150	Malachi	Mal.	4
Proverbs	Pr.	31			

THE BOOKS OF THE NEW TESTAMENT

Book	Abbreviation	Chapters	Book	Abbreviation	Chapters
MATTHEW	Mt.	28	1 Timothy	1 Tim. or 1 Ti.	6
Mark	Mk.	16	2 Timothy	2 Tim. or 2 Ti.	4
Luke	Lk. or Lu.	24	Titus	Tit.	3
John	Jn.	21	Philemon	Phile. or Phm.	1
The Acts	Acts or Ac.	28	Hebrews	Heb. or He.	13
Romans	Ro.	16	James	Jas. or Js.	5
1 Corinthians	1 Cor. or 1 Co.	16	1 Peter	1 Pt. or 1 Pe.	5
2 Corinthians	2 Cor. or 2 Co.	13	2 Peter	2 Pt. or 2 Pe.	3
Galatians	Gal. or Ga.	6	1 John	1 Jn.	5
Ephesians	Eph. or Ep.	6	2 John	2 Jn.	1
Philippians	Ph.	4	3 John	3 Jn.	1
Colossians	Col.	4	Jude	Jude	1
1 Thessalonians	1 Th.	5	Revelation	Rev. or Re.	22
2 Thessalonians	2 Th.	3			

HOW TO USE
The Preacher's Outline & Sermon Bible®
Follow these easy steps to gain maximum benefit from The POSB.

① SUBJECT HEADING

② MAJOR POINTS

**③ SUBPOINTS
&
SCRIPTURE**

④ COMMENTARY

---

1 CORINTHIANS 13:1-13

CHAPTER 13

D. The Most Excellent Quality of Life: Love, Not Gifts, 13:1-13[DS1]

1. The great importance of love
  a. Verdict 1: Tongues without love are meaningless
  b. Verdict 2: Gifts without love are nothing
    1) Prophecy is nothing
    2) Understanding all mysteries & knowledge are nothing
    3) Faith is nothing
  c. Verdict 3: Giving without love profits nothing
    1) Giving one's goods
    2) Giving one's life—martyrdom

2. The great acts of love

Though I speak with the tongues of men and of angels, and have not charity, I am become *as* sounding brass, or a tinkling cymbal.
2 And though I have *the gift of* prophecy, and understand all mysteries, and all knowledge; and though I have all faith, so that I could remove mountains, and have not charity, I am nothing.
3 And though I bestow all my goods to feed *the poor,* and though I give my body to be burned, and have not charity, it profiteth me nothing.
4 Charity suffereth long, *and* is kind; charity envieth not; charity vaunteth not itself, is not puffed up,
5 Doth not behave itself unseemly, seeketh not her own, is not easily provoked, thinketh no evil;

6 Rejoiceth not in iniquity, but rejoiceth in the truth;
7 Beareth all things, believeth all things, hopeth all things, endureth all things.
8 Charity never faileth: but whether *there be* prophecies, they shall fail; whether *there be* tongues, they shall cease; whether *there be* knowledge, it shall vanish away.
9 For we know in part, and we prophesy in part.
10 But when that which is perfect is come, then that which is in part shall be done away.
11 When I was a child, I spake as a child, I understood as a child, I thought as a child: but when I became a man, I put away childish things.
12 For now we see through a glass, darkly; but then face to face: now I know in part; but then shall I know even as also I am known.
13 And now abideth faith, hope, charity, these three; but the greatest of these *is* charity.

3. The great permanence of love
  a. It never fails, never ceases, never vanishes

  b. It is perfect & complete

  c. It is maturity—mature behavior

  d. It is the hope of being face-to-face with God—possessing perfect consciousness & knowledge

4. The great supremacy of love

DIVISION VII

THE QUESTIONS CONCERNING SPIRITUAL GIFTS, 12:1–14:40

D. The Most Excellent Quality of Life: Love, Not Gifts, 13:1-13

(13:1-13) **Introduction**: there is no question, what the world needs more than anything else is love. If people loved each other, really loved each other, there would be no more war, crime, abuse, injustice, poverty, hunger, starvation, homelessness, deprivation, or immorality. Love is the one ingredient that could revolutionize society. Love is the greatest quality of human life. Love is the supreme quality, the most excellent way for a man to live.
  1. The great importance of love (vv.1-3).
  2. The great acts of love (vv.4-7).
  3. The great permanence of love (vv.8-12).
  4. The great supremacy of love (v.13).

DEEPER STUDY # 1
(13:1-13) **Love**: throughout this passage, the word used for love or charity is the great word *agape*. (See DEEPER STUDY # 4, *Love*—Jn.21:15-17 for more discussion.) The meaning of *agape love* is more clearly seen by contrasting it with the various kinds of love. There are essentially four kinds of love. Whereas the English language has only the word *love* to describe all the affectionate experiences of men, the Greek language had a different word to describe each kind of love.
  1. There is *passionate love* or *eros love*. This is the physical love between sexes; the patriotic love of a person for his nation; the ambition of a person for power, wealth, or fame. Briefly stated, *eros love* is the base love of a man that arises from his own inner passion. Sometimes *eros love* is focused upon good and other times it is focused upon bad. It should be noted that *eros love* is never used in the New Testament.
  2. There is *affectionate love* or *storge love*. This is the kind of love that exists between parent and child and between loyal citizens and a trustworthy ruler. *Storge love* is also not used in the New Testament.
  3. There is an *endearing love*, the love that cherishes. This is *phileo love*, the love of a husband and wife for each other, of a brother for a brother, of a friend for the dearest of friends. It is the love that cherishes, that holds someone or something ever so dear to one's heart.
  4. There is *selfless and sacrificial love* or *agape love*. Agape love is the love of the mind, of the reason, of the will. It is the love that goes so far...
  • that it loves a person even if he does not deserve to be loved
  • that it actually loves the person who is utterly unworthy of being loved

---

① Glance at the **Subject Heading**. Think about it for a moment.

② Glance at the **Subject Heading** again, and then the **Major Points** (1, 2, 3, etc.). Do this several times, reviewing them together while quickly grasping the overall subject.

③ Glance at **both** the **Major Points** and **Subpoints** together while reading the **Scripture**. Do this slower than Step 2. Note how these points sit directly beside the related verse and simply restate what the Scripture is saying—in Outline form.

④ Next read the **Commentary**. Note that the *Major Point Numbers* in the Outline match those in the Commentary. A small raised number (**DS1, DS2, etc.**) at the end of a Subject Heading or Outline Point, directs you to a related **Deeper Study** in the Commentary.

Finally, read the **Thoughts** and **Support Scripture** (not shown).

As you read and re-read, pray that the Holy Spirit will bring to your attention exactly what you should preach and teach. May God bless you richly as you study and teach His Word.

The POSB contains everything you need for sermon preparation:

1. **The Subject Heading** describes the overall theme of the passage, and is located directly above the Scripture (keyed *alphabetically*).

2. **Major Points** are keyed with an outline *number* guiding you to related commentary. Note that the Commentary includes "*Thoughts*" (life application) and abundant Supporting Scriptures.

3. **Subpoints** explain and clarify the Scripture as needed.

4. **Commentary** is fully researched and developed for every point.

  • **Thoughts** (in bold) help apply the Scripture to real life.

  • **Deeper Studies** provide in-depth discussions of key words.

---

*"Woe is unto me, if I
preach not the gospel"*
(1 Co.9:16)

TABLE OF CONTENTS
EZRA, NEHEMIAH, ESTHER

---

* A comprehensive chart of all Biblical Prophets—their times and places of ministry, their messages and practical application—may be found in *The Preacher's Outline & Sermon Bible®*, *Isaiah* Volumes 1 and 2. The Prophets Chart is also available as a separate booklet to compliment all POSB volumes, especially those containing a book or books written by these dear servants of God. It is our hope that you will access this invaluable tool as you preach, teach, or study about any of God's true prophets.

THE BOOK OF

EZRA

THE BOOK OF
EZRA

AUTHOR: no direct claim of authorship is made within *Ezra*. However, Jewish and Christian tradition have held that Ezra the priest wrote the book bearing his name. Although many theories have been proposed concerning authorship, the following evidence supports the position that Ezra—a priest and the leader of the great reformation following the exile—is the author:

1. The book of *Ezra* was written from the perspective of a priest, a Levitical leader. It is an inspiring account of the Jews' great determination to rebuild the temple, to reestablish the worship of the only living and true God, and to reestablish the nation. When writing, the author had two specific objectives in mind: first, to show the steadfast faithfulness of the returned exiles and, second, to show the right path to purity of worship, the worship of the one true God. This highly motivated the Jews to be faithful in worshipping the only true God once they had resettled in the land and rebuilt their nation. These facts point toward a priest's having written the great book of *Ezra*. Ezra 7:1-6 identify as Ezra as a priest and a scribe.

2. The book of *Ezra* was apparently written no later than 400 B.C., but no earlier than the return from captivity (458 B.C.), for the rebuilding of the temple is discussed. Sources available to Ezra (other than his personal experiences) were: the family records from the different tribes (2:1-70; 8:1-14) and priests (10:18-44), personal contact with Nehemiah (Ne.8:9; 12:26); and seven official Persian government documents, which were:

⇒ the decree by King Cyrus for the Jews to return to Judah to rebuild the temple (1:2-4)
⇒ the inventory of the articles for the temple (1:9-11)
⇒ the recorded accusations against the Jews by a group of enemies led by Rehum, the military commander (4:11-16)
⇒ the reply by King Artaxerxes I (4:17-22)
⇒ the report from Governor Tattenai (5:7-17)
⇒ the decree by King Darius that rebuilding of the temple by the Jews. In addition, the decree declared that the project would be financed and protected by Persia (6:1-12)
⇒ King Darius' letter of authorization for Ezra to restore the temple utensils and for sacrifices to begin again at Persia's expense (7:11-24).

3. The historical facts contained in the book were known to Ezra personally from his own experiences as well as from contact with the other Jews (7:1-10:16; Ne.8:1-12:36).

4. The words "This Ezra" (7:6) seem to be referring to the author of the book.

5. Jewish and Christian tradition actually say that Ezra is the author of the book of *Ezra*.

6. The end of *Chronicles* (2 Chr.36:22-23) is the same as the beginning of *Ezra* (Ezr.1:1-3a). And Ezra is believed to have written *Chronicles*. Also, throughout the book of *Ezra*, the style, choice of words, and thinking of the author match that of a priest.

Although the human author cannot be known for certain, the Divine Author is clearly known. The Holy Spirit of God *breathed* or *inspired* the great book of *Ezra*. Through His inspiration, the Holy Spirit has given to the world an inspiring account of the very events God wanted recorded about the Jews' history. These events include the Jews' return from captivity, their steadfast determination to rebuild the temple, their successful restoration of true worship, and the rebuilding of their nation. Studying these events shows us our constant need for devotion to the Lord and for a lasting and close relationship with the Him...

- Who is worthy of all worship
- Who always fulfills His promises
- Who gives us favor and authority
- Who has His hand upon all believers who trust in Him
- Who gives us mercy and protection to complete our assigned tasks

The inspiring account of the book of *Ezra* was written as both a warning and a promise to every reader.

DATE: about 450 B.C., after Ezra's main work of temple and spiritual restoration. It was also before the final of the three great returns, which was led by Nehemiah in 445 B.C. This was the time of the great Persian Empire. Three groups of Jews returned to Jerusalem from exile. All three groups of returnees were from the southern kingdom of Judah. No group returned separately to the promised land from the northern kingdom of Israel. Thereafter, the exile returnees for which *First* and *Second Chronicles*, *Ezra*, and *Nehemiah* were written were known simply as the Jews.

There were three groups of Jews who returned to Jerusalem from exile. However, this fact is important to note: all three groups of original exile returnees were from the Southern Kingdom of Judah. As far as is known, no organized group from the Northern Kingdom of Israel—the Israelites who had been exiled by Assyria—ever returned to the promised land. Thus the exile returnees, for whom *First* and *Second Chronicles*, *Ezra*, and *Nehemiah* were written, were the Jews from Judah.

THE FIRST GROUP RETURNED UNDER ZERUBBABEL'S LEADERSHIP

In 539 B.C., the Persians and Medes under King Cyrus defeated the Babylonians in a fierce battle for world domination. Just as the prophet Daniel had predicted, the Babylonians were so soundly defeated that the capital Babylon opened its city gates to the Persians without a fight (Da.5:1-31).

Like the Babylonians, the Persians adopted a wise policy of incorporating captured exiles into the society of the nation to which they were deported. These captives were given the right to rebuild their lives despite being exiled to a strange, foreign land. They had the right to secure personal employment, hold property, build homes, and start businesses. Of course, this policy strengthened the nations of Babylon and Persia both economically and militarily. But the Persian king Cyrus went a step further.

INTRODUCTION TO EZRA

One year after his conquest of Babylon (538 B.C.), King Cyrus proclaimed himself as the *Liberator of the People*. He allowed any exile who wished to return to his or her homeland to do so. Among those released were the Jews who had been taken captive at the fall of Jerusalem in 586 B.C. At this first release, Cyrus appointed Zerubbabel governor over Judah and the returning exiles. Almost 50,000 exiles were released to return to their homeland in Judah. When they arrived, the very first work undertaken by Zerubbabel was the building of an altar to offer sacrifices to the LORD. Soon thereafter, he and the returning exiles undertook the construction of the temple. However, opposition soon arose from the enemies of the Israelites, those of surrounding tribes and peoples who did not want to see Jerusalem and the temple rebuilt. The opposition was successful in stopping the work for a number of years. But in 520 B.C., the building of the temple was resumed. It was completed four years later (516 B.C.) (Ezra 4:1-6:22; Zec.6:16-22).

But, tragically, these first returnees under Zerubbabel soon drifted back into apostasy. Just as their fathers had done, they too turned away from the LORD, committing sin after sin, such as:

⇒ intermarriage with unbelieving neighbors (Mal.2:11; Ezr.9:1-2)
⇒ neglecting the worship of the LORD (Mal.1:6-14)
⇒ failing to offer sacrifices to the LORD as commanded by Him
⇒ participating in witchcraft and sorcery (Mal.3:5)
⇒ committing adultery (Mal.3:5)
⇒ bearing false witness and using profanity (Mal.3:5)
⇒ oppressing and stealing from people, even the wages due widows and orphans (Mal.3:5)
⇒ mistreating people (Mal.3:5)
⇒ failing to fear and show reverence for the LORD (Mal.3:5)
⇒ disobeying the commandments of the LORD (Mal.3:7)
⇒ stealing the tithe that belonged to God (Mal.3:8-9)

THE SECOND GROUP RETURNED UNDER EZRA'S LEADERSHIP

About 80 years after the first exiles returned to Judah, Ezra secured permission from the Persian king Artaxerxes to lead a second and smaller band of exiles back to Jerusalem. It was the year 458 B.C., and Ezra's purpose for returning to Jerusalem was to carry out spiritual and religious reforms, to stir a revival among the new nation of Israel. Revival and reformation were desperately needed because of the people's wickedness. They had slipped and turned away from the LORD. In stating his purpose for returning, Ezra clearly says that he had prepared his heart, that he was determined to study and obey the law of the LORD and to teach the law and commandments of God to the people (Ezr.7:10). Only about 1,800 Jewish exiles chose to return with Ezra. Leading the small band of exiles, he and they struck out and traveled over 900 miles, reaching Jerusalem some four months later (458 B.C.).

THE THIRD GROUP RETURNED UNDER NEHEMIAH'S LEADERSHIP

In 445 B.C., Nehemiah was visited by one of his brothers and a number of other men who had just returned from Judah. Interested in how the exile returnees were doing, Nehemiah asked about them. When they reported that things were not going well, that the returned exiles were suffering severe affliction and reproach from the surrounding people and nations and that the wall and gates of the city had been destroyed, Nehemiah was heartbroken. Scripture actually says that he wept and mourned for days, fasting and praying before the LORD.

Nehemiah held an official position in the royal court of the Persian king. He was the *cupbearer* to King Artaxerxes (Ne.1:11; 2:1). The cupbearer was a royal official who personally served wine to the king and who was sometimes required to taste the wine before serving it in the event an assassination attempt was being made upon the king. The *cupbearer* was a man who was greatly trusted by the king, a man in whom the king put a great deal of confidence. Thus, a close relationship was sometimes formed between a ruler and his cupbearer, which was obviously the case with Nehemiah and Artaxerxes.

The heartbreaking news about the returnees had a devastating effect upon Nehemiah. Grief and sorrow gripped him for days. In fact, the next time Nehemiah served wine to the king, he still exposed a sad countenance or appearance—so much so that the ruler asked him why he was so sad. Using the opportunity to share the affliction and distress of his people back in their homeland, he requested permission to personally return to Jerusalem. He expressed the desire to rebuild the wall and to make other improvements to the capital city. Having been granted permission, Nehemiah returned to his homeland.

After spending three days in Jerusalem, he privately surveyed the wall of the city at night in order to study the situation and determine what needed to be done. The next day, he called a meeting with the rulers of Jerusalem and shared with them how God had moved upon his heart when He heard about their distress. After sharing the decree of the king with the local rulers, he organized them to rebuild the wall of the city. Under his capable and courageous leadership, the construction project was, surprisingly, completed in 52 days (Neh.6:15). Throughout his stay in Jerusalem, Nehemiah supported the efforts of Ezra to stir revival among the people and to reform temple worship. In particular, Nehemiah supported Ezra's efforts to teach the law and commandments of the LORD to the people (Neh.8:1-18).

A quick glance at the chart on the page 4 will help the reader grasp the returns of the three different groups of Jewish exiles.

TO WHOM WRITTEN: the Jewish exiles who had returned from Babylonian captivity in particular, and to the human race in general. The exiles, who were allowed to go back to their homeland were full of zeal for the work of the LORD. While in Babylon, they had learned the futility of trusting in false gods and worshipping idols. They had put aside their idolatry and turned back to the LORD. Nonetheless, when the Jewish captives were released and allowed to return to the promised land, they still faced difficult times. They had to be strong to reestablish proper worship and to rebuild their society and nation. Would their spiritual fervor continue? It would if they listened to the message of the Book of *Ezra*. It was to the three groups of people returning from captivity that the great book of *Ezra* was written. The returnees needed to know that God had not forgotten them, not in the least. His sovereign hand would guide and protect them. Their task was to remain faithful in their personal and corporate worship of the LORD as they rebuilt their nation.

PURPOSE:
1. The *Historical* Purpose:
   a. To document both the return of the Jews from captivity and the rebuilding of the temple.
   b. To show the importance of the temple—how it was rebuilt and how it was the proper center of worship.
   c. To show how the Northern and Southern Kingdoms merged into one nation during the captivity.
   d. To trace the genealogy of the returned exiles.
   e. To show that God had preserved the lineage of the Messiah.
2. The *Doctrinal* or *Spiritual* Purpose:
   a. To point out that God's plan for Israel was not void. God, in His sovereignty, stirred the hearts of kings to allow His people to be released and to rebuild the temple. God would still allow His Name to be in Jerusalem. He would still honor the covenant He had made with Abraham and King David. And God's presence would still dwell in the midst of His people.
   b. To teach that believers must be united in their efforts to serve the LORD. Those who do the LORD's work must be willing to work diligently to overcome all opposition by the enemy. They must faithfully perform even undesirable jobs, fighting through exhaustion and staying totally committed to the task at hand.
   c. To teach that God's guiding hand is with the believer in all situations, good and bad.
   d. To teach that repentance and obedience always bring God's blessing. Peace, provision, protection, hope, victory, safety, the fullness of God's presence and more are available to the genuine believer who follows the Lord.
   e. To inspire all readers to remain faithful in their personal and corporate worship, stirring them to be fully committed to the Lord, to allow His blessings to continually flow upon them.
   f. To teach that there is spiritual rest and assurance for all who trust in the Lord. Just as God's blessings to the Jews included dwelling safely in the promised land, the eternal rest and reward of heaven awaits a life of faithful service.
3. The *Christological* or *Christ-Centered* Purpose: Jesus Christ, the Savior of the world, came through David's family line. The animal sacrifices offered up in the temple where God's Holy Presence dwelled were a symbol of the sacrificial death of Jesus Christ for our sins. All true worship in Old Testament times celebrated forgiveness of sins. Therefore, all true worship pointed forward to the sacrifice Christ so willing made on the cross, where He shed His life's blood to free us from sin. The faithful service of the Jews in *Ezra* and their commitment to reestablishing true worship both point to one critical fact: Jesus Christ is worthy of all worship. We are to worship God and God alone, the Eternally Existent One, existing in three Persons—Father, Son, and Holy Spirit.

SPECIAL FEATURES:
1. *Ezra* is "The Great Book That Shows God's Sovereignty." God moved on the hearts of King Cyrus and King Darius to support the Jews, allowing them to return to the promised land, complete the temple and worship God (1:1-11; 6:1-15).
2. *Ezra* is "The Great Book That Lists Those Returning from Captivity" (2:1-70; 8:1-14).
3. *Ezra* is "The Great Book That Describes the Laying of the Foundation for the Temple and the Restoration of Worship" (3:1-13).
4. *Ezra* is "The Great Book That Shows the Jews Were Unwilling to Compromise with the World" (4:1-3).
5. *Ezra* is "The Great Book That Warns the Believer That There Will Be Opposition in the World" (4:4-24).
6. *Ezra* is "The Great Book That Demonstrates God's Faithfulness in Providing What We Need to Complete Our Assigned Tasks" (5:1-17).
7. *Ezra* is "The Great Book That Describes the Completion of the Temple and the Great Revival Among God's People" (6:1-22).
8. *Ezra* is "The Great Book That Shows Ezra's Strong Leadership" (7:1-28).
9. *Ezra* is "The Great Book That Warns Us to Prepare for Heaven" (8:1-36).
8. *Ezra* is "The Great Book That Shows That We Constantly Need Spiritual Renewal" (9:1–10:44).

400 SILENT YEARS

	FIRST RETURN UNDER ZERUBBABEL	SECOND RETURN UNDER EZRA	THIRD RETURN UNDER NEHEMIAH
BIBLE REFERENCE	Ezra 1-6	Ezra 7-10	Nehemiah 1-13
DATE	537 B.C.	458 B.C.	445 B.C.
PERSIAN KING	Cyrus	Artaxerxes	Artaxerxes
EXILES RETURNING	46,697 (Ezr.2:64-65)	1496 Men 38 Levites 220 Servants 1754 plus women and children (Ezr.8:21)	Unknown
PURPOSE	To resettle in the land and rebuild the nation and temple: Under Persian rule	To teach God's law, stir revival and reformation, and renew temple worship	To rebuild the wall of Jerusalem and support Ezra's efforts of reformation
RESULTS	Oppression by neighbors; rebuilt the temple, but slipped away from the LORD (Ezr.9:1-2; Mal.1:6-14; 2:11; 3:5)	Reformed temple worship and stirred revival, teaching God's Word to the people (Ezr.9:1-10:44; Neh.8:1-10:39)	Rebuilt the wall and worked with Ezra in his reformation and teaching ministry (Ne.8:1-10:39)

GAP 57 YEARS

GAP 12 YEARS

Malachi (450–430 B.C.)(?)

432 B.C.

444 B.C.

456 B.C.

458 B.C.

515 B.C.

538 B.C.

Haggai (520 B.C.)
Zechariah (520–518 B.C.)

CAPTIVITY 70 YEARS
(605 – 536 B.C.)

4

OUTLINE OF EZRA

THE PREACHER'S OUTLINE AND SERMON BIBLE® is *unique*. It differs from all other Study Bibles and Sermon Resource Materials in that every Passage and Subject is outlined right beside the Scripture. When you choose any *Subject* below and turn to the reference, you have not only the Scripture but also an outline of the Scripture and Subject *already prepared for you—verse by verse.*

For a quick example, choose one of the subjects below and turn over to the Scripture; you will find this to be a marvelous help for more organized and streamlined study.

In addition, every point of the Scripture and Subject is *fully developed in a Commentary with supporting Scripture* at the end of each point. Again, this arrangement makes sermon preparation much simpler and more efficient.

Note something else: the Subjects of *Ezra* have titles that are both Biblical and *practical*. The practical titles are often more appealing to people. This *benefit* is clearly seen for use on billboards, bulletins, church newsletters, etc.

A suggestion: for the *quickest* overview of *Ezra*, first read *all the Division titles* (I, II, III, etc.), then come back and read the individual outline titles.

OUTLINE OF EZRA

I. **THE FIRST RETURN OF EXILES FROM CAPTIVITY AND THEIR RESETTLEMENT—LED BY ZERUBBABEL, 1:1–6:22**

   A. The Release and Return of the Exiles (After 70 years of Captivity): Hope Fulfilled, Being Freed from Captivity and Returning to the Promised Land, 1:1–2:70
   B. The Major Tasks of the Returned Exiles: Becoming Established, Settling Down, Reviving True Worship, and Building the Temple, 3:1-13
   C. The Continued Opposition Faced by the Returned Exiles: Being Attacked, Persecuted for One's Faith, 4:1-24
   D. The Completion of the Temple by the Returned Exiles: Four Pictures Demonstrating God's Faithfulness, 5:1–6:22

II. **THE SECOND RETURN OF EXILES FROM CAPTIVITY AND THEIR REFORM—LED BY EZRA, 7:1–10:44**

   A. Ezra's Royal Commission to Return to the Promised Land: The Picture of a Strong and Dedicated Leader, 7:1-28
   B. Ezra's Preparations and Return to the Promised Land (Almost 60 Years After the Completion of the Temple): A Picture of Preparing for the Promised Land (a Type of Heaven), 8:1-36
   C. Ezra's Confrontation with the People Over Their Evil Associations: A Picture of Genuine Revival, 9:1–10:44

DIVISION I — EZRA

THE FIRST RETURN OF EXILES FROM CAPTIVITY AND THEIR RESETTLEMENT— LED BY ZERUBBABEL, 1:1–6:22

(1:1–6:22) **DIVISION OVERVIEW**: after many years of captivity in the land of Babylon, the Persian conqueror King Cyrus issued a decree allowing any Jews who wished to return to Jerusalem to do so. There would eventually be three groups to return to the promised land from captivity. But this division of the book of *Ezra* concerns the first return led by Zerubbabel. Obviously, as with any group of freed captives who set out to return home, the exiles were rejoicing from the depths of their hearts. Yet four difficult tasks still lay out before this first group of returnees:

⇒ they were to reestablish the worship of the only true God, the LORD Himself
⇒ they were to rebuild the temple
⇒ they were to resettle the land
⇒ they were to rebuild the nation

The returnees were not only reestablishing themselves as a nation, but also reestablishing their religion and the proper worship of God. The tasks were hard, so the decision to be diligent had to be even more firm. Zerubbabel would prove a worthy leader and righteous example before the people. He and his brother rose up with zeal to build the altar of the LORD (3:2). From there, Zerubbabel and the priestly leadership continued to lead and inspire the Jews to success.

Ezra, being a scribe, was careful to record the official government documents important to the story. Moreover, Ezra was a priest; therefore, he was also careful to focus his writings on the importance of remaining faithful to the LORD. Each returnee needed relentless determination to complete the awesome task that lay ahead. They were to face fierce opposition. But because of their dedication and strong stand for the LORD, the foundation of the temple was laid (3:11) and the temple itself was finished (6:15). At last, proper worship was restored, beginning with the celebration of the Passover and the Feast of Unleavened Bread. This was a glorious moment, the height of all that the returnees had worked so hard to achieve.

Remember that Ezra was writing primarily to the exiles who had returned from Babylonian captivity and then to the succeeding generations. When the exiles had first returned, they found their nation in ruins. Now that they had rebuilt the temple and the nation, above all else they had to remain faithful to the LORD. If they and the generations to come were faithful, genuinely trusting in the LORD and living righteously, God would continue to guide and protect them. He would also continue to bless them with the richness of the promised land. The Jews had learned a hard lesson: the blessings of the promised land were directly tied to their relationship with God.

As the reader studies the first return of the Jews from captivity under the direction of Zerubbabel, he should keep this fact in mind: the LORD keeps His promises to His people. The Jewish people lived on; the nation flourished again; the lineage of the Messiah was preserved; the Messiah, the Savior of the world, Jesus Christ, did come.

"Whoever there is among you of all His people, may his God be with him! Let him go up to Jerusalem which is in Judah and rebuild the house of the LORD, the God of Israel; He is the God who is in Jerusalem" (Ezra 1:3).

THE FIRST RETURN OF EXILES FROM CAPTIVITY AND THEIR RESETTLEMENT— LED BY ZERUBBABEL, 1:1–6:22

A. **The Release and Return of the Exiles (After 70 years of Captivity): Hope Fulfilled, Being Freed from Captivity and Returning to the Promised Land, 1:1–2:70**

B. **The Major Tasks of the Returned Exiles: Becoming Established, Settling Down, Reviving True Worship, and Building the Temple, 3:1-13**

C. **The Continued Opposition Faced by the Returned Exiles: Being Attacked, Persecuted for One's Faith, 4:1-24**

D. **The Completion of the Temple by the Returned Exiles: Four Pictures Demonstrating God's Faithfulness, 5:1–6:22**

EZRA

CHAPTER 1

I. THE FIRST RETURN OF EXILES FROM CAPTIVITY & THEIR RESETTLEMENT—LED BY ZERUBBABEL, 1:1–6:22

A. The Release & Return of the Exiles After 70 Years of Captivity: Hope Fulfilled—Being Freed from Captivity & Returned to the Promised Land, 1:1–2:70

1. **The proclamation to free or release the captives: A striking fulfillment of prophecy, Is.44:28; 45:1, 13; Je.25:11-12; 29:10**
   a. The date: The first year of Cyrus's reign over Babylon
   b. The cause: God moved the heart of Cyrus

   c. The king's royal proclamation
   1) Acknowledged the LORD as the God of heaven & the Source of his power
   2) Claimed the LORD had appointed him to build a temple in Jerusalem
   3) Allowed any Jewish exile who wished to return & resettle in Jerusalem & Judah to do so
   4) Ordered the returning exiles to rebuild the temple

   5) Encouraged the Jews who did not return to give financial support to the returning exiles

2. **The preparation by the captives for returning to the promised land: A striking picture of being spiritually & materially prepared to serve God**
   a. Their motivation: The LORD stirred the hearts of some to go

   b. Their material provisions
   1) Neighbors gave them financial aid, supplies, & livestock as well as freewill offerings for the rebuilding of the temple

   2) King Cyrus returned all the temple furnishings & articles that Nebuchadnezzar had plundered, 2 K.24:13;

Now in the first year of Cyrus king of Persia, that the word of the LORD by the mouth of Jeremiah might be fulfilled, the LORD stirred up the spirit of Cyrus king of Persia, that he made a proclamation throughout all his kingdom, and *put it* also in writing, saying,
2 Thus saith Cyrus king of Persia, The LORD God of heaven hath given me all the kingdoms of the earth; and he hath charged me to build him an house at Jerusalem, which *is* in Judah.
3 Who *is there* among you of all his people? his God be with him, and let him go up to Jerusalem, which *is* in Judah, and build the house of the Lord God of Israel, (he *is* the God,) which *is* in Jerusalem.
4 And whosoever remaineth in any place where he sojourneth, let the men of his place help him with silver, and with gold, and with goods, and with beasts, beside the freewill offering for the house of God that *is* in Jerusalem.
5 Then rose up the chief of the fathers of Judah and Benjamin, and the priests, and the Levites, with all *them* whose spirit God had raised, to go up to build the house of the LORD which *is* in Jerusalem.
6 And all they that *were* about them strengthened their hands with vessels of silver, with gold, with goods, and with beasts, and with precious things, beside all *that* was willingly offered.
7 Also Cyrus the king brought forth the vessels of the house of the LORD, which Nebuchadnezzar had brought forth out of Jerusalem, and had put them in the house of his gods;
8 Even those did Cyrus king of Persia bring forth by the hand of Mithredath the treasurer, and numbered them unto Sheshbazzar, the prince of Judah.
9 And this *is* the number of them: thirty chargers of gold, a thousand chargers of silver, nine and twenty knives,
10 Thirty basons of gold, silver basons of a second *sort* four hundred and ten, *and* other vessels a thousand.
11 All the vessels of gold and of silver *were* five thousand and four hundred. All *these* did Sheshbazzar bring up with *them of* the captivity that were brought up from Babylon unto Jerusalem.

CHAPTER 2

Now these *are* the children of the province that went up out of the captivity, of those which had been carried away, whom Nebuchadnezzar the king of Babylon had carried away unto Babylon, and came again unto Jerusalem and Judah, every one unto his city;
2 Which came with Zerubbabel: Jeshua, Nehemiah, Seraiah, Reelaiah, Mordecai, Bilshan, Mizpar, Bigvai, Rehum, Baanah. The number of the men of the people of Israel:
3 The children of Parosh, two thousand an hundred seventy and two.
4 The children of Shephatiah, three hundred seventy and two.
5 The children of Arah, seven hundred seventy and five.
6 The children of Pahath-moab, of the children of Jeshua *and* Joab, two thousand eight hundred and twelve.
7 The children of Elam, a thousand two hundred fifty and four.
8 The children of Zattu, nine hundred forty and five.
9 The children of Zaccai, seven hundred and threescore.

25:13-17; 2 Chr.36:7-10, 18; Je.27:16; 52:17-23; Da.1:2; 5:1-4
3) Persia's treasurer, Mithredath, counted the temple articles & turned them over to the leader of the returning exiles, Sheshbazzar

- Gold trays (dishes) — 30
- Silver trays (dishes) — 1000
- Silver knives or censers or pans — 29
- Gold bowls — 30
- Silver bowls — 410
- Other major articles — 1000
- Total number of temple articles returned — 5400

4) Sheshbazzar & the exiles returned from Babylon to Jerusalem & Judah, the promised land

3. **The list of captives who returned to Jerusalem & the other towns of Judah: A striking commitment to the LORD & to the land promised by Him (heaven) after being taken captive by sin & the world**

   a. The leaders
   1) Zerubbabel: The governor
   2) Jeshua: The High Priest, 5:2; Ze.3:1
   3) Nine others

   b. The number of men from Israel's various clans or families, the people of Israel

c. The number of men from various cities & towns

d. The priests

10 The children of Bani, six hundred forty and two.
11 The children of Bebai, six hundred twenty and three.
12 The children of Azgad, a thousand two hundred twenty and two.
13 The children of Adonikam, six hundred sixty and six.
14 The children of Bigvai, two thousand fifty and six.
15 The children of Adin, four hundred fifty and four.
16 The children of Ater of Hezekiah, ninety and eight.
17 The children of Bezai, three hundred twenty and three.
18 The children of Jorah, an hundred and twelve.
19 The children of Hashum, two hundred twenty and three.
20 The children of Gibbar, ninety and five.
21 The children of Bethlehem, an hundred twenty and three.
22 The men of Netophah, fifty and six.
23 The men of Anathoth, an hundred twenty and eight.
24 The children of Azmaveth, forty and two.
25 The children of Kirjatharim, Chephirah, and Beeroth, seven hundred and forty and three.
26 The children of Ramah and Gaba, six hundred twenty and one.
27 The men of Michmas, an hundred twenty and two.
28 The men of Bethel and Ai, two hundred twenty and three.
29 The children of Nebo, fifty and two.
30 The children of Magbish, an hundred fifty and six.
31 The children of the other Elam, a thousand two hundred fifty and four.
32 The children of Harim, three hundred and twenty.
33 The children of Lod, Hadid, and Ono, seven hundred twenty and five.
34 The children of Jericho, three hundred forty and five.
35 The children of Senaah, three thousand and six hundred and thirty.
36 The priests: the children of Jedaiah, of the house of Jeshua, nine hundred seventy and three.
37 The children of Immer, a thousand fifty and two.
38 The children of Pashur, a thousand two hundred forty and seven.
39 The children of Harim, a thousand and seventeen.
40 The Levites: the children of Jeshua and Kadmiel, of the children of Hodaviah, seventy and four.
41 The singers: the children of Asaph, an hundred twenty and eight.
42 The children of the porters: the children of Shallum, the children of Ater, the children of Talmon, the children of Akkub, the children of Hatita, the children of Shobai, in all an hundred thirty and nine.
43 The Nethinims: the children of Ziha, the children of Hasupha, the children of Tabbaoth,
44 The children of Keros, the children of Siaha, the children of Padon,
45 The children of Lebanah, the children of Hagabah, the children of Akkub,
46 The children of Hagab, the children of Shalmai, the children of Hanan,
47 The children of Giddel, the children of Gahar, the children of Reaiah,
48 The children of Rezin, the children of Nekoda, the children of Gazzam,
49 The children of Uzza, the children of Paseah, the children of Besai,
50 The children of Asnah, the children of Mehunim, the children of Nephusim,
51 The children of Bakbuk, the children of Hakupha, the children of Harhur,
52 The children of Bazluth, the children of Mehida, the children of Harsha,
53 The children of Barkos, the children of Sisera, the children of Thamah,
54 The children of Neziah, the children of Hatipha.
55 The children of Solomon's servants: the children of Sotai, the children of Sophereth, the children of Peruda,
56 The children of Jaalah, the children of Darkon, the children of Giddel,
57 The children of Shephatiah, the children of Hattil, the children of Pochereth of Zebaim, the children

e. The Levites, including the Levite singers & doorkeepers
1) The Levites
2) The singers

3) The gatekeepers

f. The temple servants & Solomon's servants
1) Descendants of various clans

2) Descendants of Solomon's servants

g. The number who had no record that they were descendants of Israel, 59-63 1) The Babylonian towns from which they came	of Ami. 58 All the Nethinims, and the children of Solomon's servants, *were* three hundred ninety and two. 59 And these *were* they which went up from Tel-melah, Tel-harsa, Cherub, Addan, *and* Immer: but they could not shew their father's house, and their seed, whether they *were* of Israel:	thousand three hundred *and* threescore 65 Beside their servants and their maids, of whom *there were* seven thousand three hundred thirty and seven: and *there were* among them two hundred singing men and singing women.
2) The three families or clans from which they descended	60 The children of Delaiah, the children of Tobiah, the children of Nekoda, six hundred fifty and two.	66 Their horses *were* seven hundred thirty and six; their mules, two hundred forty and five;
3) The priests who had no record to prove they were true priests	61 And of the children of the priests: the children of Habaiah, the children of Koz, the children of Barzillai; which took a wife of the daughters of Barzillai the Gileadite, and was called after their name:	67 Their camels, four hundred thirty and five; *their* asses, six thousand seven hundred and twenty. 68 And *some* of the chief of the fathers, when they came to the house of the LORD which *is* at Jerusalem, offered freely for the house of God to set it up in his place:
• Were excluded from the priesthood	62 These sought their register *among* those that were reckoned by genealogy, but they were not found: therefore were they, as polluted, put from the priesthood.	69 They gave after their ability unto the treasure of the work threescore and one thousand drams of gold, and five thousand pound of silver, and one hundred priests' garments.
• Were not given the priests' share of sacred food until their priesthood was established: Determined by seeking the Lord through casting sacred lots h. The totals 1) The exiles or captives	63 And the Tirshatha said unto them, that they should not eat of the most holy things, till there stood up a priest with Urim and with Thummim. 64 The whole congregation together *was* forty and two	70 So the priests, and the Levites, and *some* of the people, and the singers, and the porters, and the Nethinims, dwelt in their cities, and all Israel in their cities.

	2) The servants
	3) The singers
	4) The livestock
	i. The offerings given for rebuilding the temple: Most likely given as a thanksgiving offering for their safe journey
	1) 61,000 gold coins
	2) 6,300 pounds of silver
	3) 100 robes for priests
	j. The settlement of the returning exiles: Settled in the towns from which their families had been taken captive & exiled to Babylon

DIVISION I

THE FIRST RETURN OF EXILES FROM CAPTIVITY AND THEIR RESETTLEMENT—LED BY ZERUBBABEL, 1:1–6:22

A. The Release and Return of the Exiles After 70 Years of Captivity: Hope Fulfilled—Being Freed from Captivity and Returned to the Promised Land, 1:1–2:70

(1:1–2:70) **Introduction**: being enslaved to someone or some thing is bound to be one of the most traumatic experiences of human life. Similarly, being set free or liberated from captivity is bound to be one of the most joyful experiences of life. Prisoners of war can give testimony to this fact, as can whole races of people down through history. Genuine believers also know what it is like to be set free from the captivity of sin, liberated by the power of Jesus Christ. Most of us at one time or another have been held in bondage by the chain of some sin, unable to break the bond ourselves. But when Jesus Christ set us free, He broke the chain of sin. And the sin that we had so often committed lost its power over us. No longer do we walk as captives of sin; instead we walk in the liberty of Jesus Christ. We walk toward the promised land of heaven, where we will live in the presence of God for all eternity. In that glorious day we will be perfected and freed from all the bondages and enslavements of this world, including the bondage of death. This is the practical message of the present Scripture.

As background to the present Scripture, remember: 70 years earlier the fall of Jerusalem had taken place and the people had been exiled to Babylon (2 K.25:1-30). Isaiah the prophet had warned the Jews: if they continued in their sin, rejecting God and engaging in false worship, they would be conquered and taken captive by Babylon (Is.39:5-7). The prophet Jeremiah had also warned the people, warned them for over 40 years (Je.20:4-6; 21:7-10). But the people had refused to listen to the warnings of the prophets. As a result, Babylon had attacked under the leadership of King Nebuchadnezzar. In 597 B.C., he invaded and laid siege to Jerusalem, eventually raiding the royal palace and temple. He stripped the city of all its wealth. He also deported a total of 10,000 people to Babylon: 7,000 soldiers, 1,000 skilled workers, and 2,000 others, including the prophet Ezekiel (2 K.24:10-16; Eze.1:1-3). But even this chastisement from the LORD did not arouse the people to turn from their sins and false worship. Thus 11 years later, in 586 B.C., the LORD used the Babylonians to utterly destroy Jerusalem and the temple. They then took the rest of the Jews into captivity and scattered them throughout the Babylonian Empire (2 K.25:1-21). Now, 70 years later, the Jews are being freed from their captivity. This is: *The Release and Return of the Exiles After 70 Years of Captivity: Hope Fulfilled—Being Freed from Captivity and Returned to the Promised Land*, 1:1–2:70.

1. The proclamation to free or release the captives: a striking fulfillment of prophecy, Is.44:28; 45:1, 13; Je.25:11-12; 29:10 (1:1-4).
2. The preparation by the captives for returning to the promised land: a striking picture of being spiritually and materially prepared to serve God (1:5-11).
3. The list of captives who returned to Jerusalem and the other towns of Judah: a striking commitment to the LORD and to the land promised by Him (heaven) after being taken captive by sin and the world (2:1-70).

1 (1:1-4) **Freedom, Decree of, Issued by Cyrus—Liberty, Secured by, the Jews—Captivity, Set Free from, the Jews—Exiles, Jewish, First Returned—Cyrus, King of Persia, Freed the Jewish Captives—Jews, Captivity, Set Free**: the Persian *Proclamation of Freedom* to release the Jewish captives was issued after 70 long years in captivity. At last, the Jewish exiles were allowed to return to their homeland. Both Isaiah and Jeremiah had predicted this phenomenal event (Is.44:28; 45:1, 13; Je.25:11-12; 29:10). And now the day of their freedom had finally come. Cyrus, king of Persia, issued the *Proclamation of Freedom* that gave any Jew who wished to do so the right to return to the land of Israel. The Jewish captives were set free. They could now shout out, "Thank God Almighty. I'm free—free at last." Ezra gives an account of the wonderful event:

OUTLINE	SCRIPTURE	SCRIPTURE	OUTLINE
1. The proclamation to free or release the captives: A striking fulfillment of prophecy, Is.44:28; 45:1, 13; Je.25:11-12; 29:10 a. The date: The first year of Cyrus's reign over Babylon b. The cause: God moved the heart of Cyrus c. The king's royal proclamation 1) Acknowledged the LORD as the God of heaven & the Source of his power 2) Claimed the LORD had	Now in the first year of Cyrus king of Persia, that the word of the LORD by the mouth of Jeremiah might be fulfilled, the LORD stirred up the spirit of Cyrus king of Persia, that he made a proclamation throughout all his kingdom, and *put it* also in writing, saying, 2 Thus saith Cyrus king of Persia, The LORD God of heaven hath given me all the kingdoms of the earth; and he hath charged me to build him an house at Jerusalem, which *is* in Judah.	3 Who *is there* among you of all his people? his God be with him, and let him go up to Jerusalem, which *is* in Judah, and build the house of the LORD God of Israel, (he *is* the God,) which *is* in Jerusalem. 4 And whosoever remaineth in any place where he sojourneth, let the men of his place help him with silver, and with gold, and with goods, and with beasts, beside the freewill offering for the house of God that *is* in Jerusalem.	appointed him to build a temple in Jerusalem 3) Allowed any Jewish exile who wished to return & resettle in Jerusalem & Judah to do so 4) Ordered the returning exiles to rebuild the temple 5) Encouraged the Jews who did not return to give financial support to the returning exiles

a. The date of the proclamation was 538 B.C., the very first year of Cyrus' reign over Babylon. He had conquered Babylon in 539 B.C. and freed the slaves the very next year. However, this was not the first year Cyrus had reigned as a king; he had ruled over other territory for more than 20 years. A quick glance at the following events is helpful in understanding the background that led up to the *Proclamation of Freedom*:

⇒ In 559 B.C., Cyrus became king over Anshan, a small territory in modern Iran.
⇒ In 550 B.C., Cyrus took control of both the Median and Persian nations, ruling as king over the whole Persian Empire. Throughout the years he enlarged the empire in all directions.
⇒ In 539 B.C., Cyrus conquered Babylon (modern Iraq), which extended the Persian Empire over the huge territory that is known today as Syria, Iraq, Iran, and Israel.
⇒ In 538 B.C., Cyrus issued the *Proclamation of Freedom* that released the Jewish captives, allowing the exiles to return to their homeland (Ezra 1:1-4).

Secular sources record how Cyrus brought relief to all the captives of Babylon, allowing the exiles from all conquered nations to return to their homeland. The famous *Cyrus Cylinder*, a clay inscription found in excavations at Babylon in 1879-82, records this fact. Thus King Cyrus allowed not only Jews but also captives of other foreign nations to return to their homeland if they so wished.

b. What caused King Cyrus to issue the *Proclamation of Freedom*, to release the captives? Most commentators suggest two reasons. First, by allowing all exiles to return to their homeland, Cyrus would build public loyalty for his regime. He would also build a strong buffer zone between him and surrounding nations that might be a threat, especially Egypt.

Second, part of the inscription on the Cyrus cylinder says this:

"May all the gods whom I have resettled in their sacred cities daily ask Bel and Nebo for a long life for me." [1]

---

[1] John F. Walvoord and Roy B. Zuck, Editors. *The Bible Knowledge Commentary, Old Testament.* (Colorado Springs Co: Chariot Victor Publishing, 1985), p.654.

However, a few commentators think Cyrus became a true believer in the only living and true God. Their conclusion is based upon the wording of the proclamation of King Cyrus and the fact that the prophet Daniel was a Prime Minister in the court of Cyrus. Matthew Henry says this:

> It should seem, his mind was enlightened with the knowledge of Jehovah (for so he calls him), the God of Israel, as the only living and true God, the God of heaven, who is the sovereign Lord and disposer of all the kingdoms of the earth: of him he says (v.3), he is the God, God alone, God above all.[2]

In his series *Thru the Bible*, J. Vernon McGee says this:

> Daniel was a Prime Minister in the court of Cyrus and evidently led him to a knowledge of the living and true God. Cyrus knew what he was doing when he made a decree proclaiming that the nation of Israel could return to their land. We are told that the will of the LORD was fulfilled in that act. Here is prophecy that was indeed fulfilled.
> It was during the reign of Cyrus that Daniel gave some of his greatest prophecies, including the 70 weeks prophecy concerning Israel.[3]

Several major prophecies were fulfilled by King Cyrus. Amazingly, Isaiah had even predicted that a ruler named *Cyrus* would set the Jews free from captivity. Cyrus was actually named in Scripture 140 years before he issued the decree that freed the Jews—an astonishing fact that shows the truth of God's Holy Word, that God will fulfill all that He says. Listen to Isaiah's prophecy, predicted over 100 years before Cyrus was even born and 140 years before he freed the Jews:

> **"That saith of Cyrus, *He is* my shepherd, and shall perform all my pleasure: even saying to Jerusalem, Thou shalt be built; and to the temple, Thy foundation shall be laid. Thus saith the LORD to his anointed, to Cyrus, whose right hand I have holden, to subdue nations before him; and I will loose the loins of kings, to open before him the two leaved gates; and the gates shall not be shut....I have raised him up in righteousness, and I will direct all his ways: he shall build my city, and he shall let go my captives, not for price nor reward, saith the LORD of hosts" (Is.44:28–45:1, 13).**

Josephus, the first century Jewish historian, says that it was the prophecy of Isaiah that aroused Cyrus to free the Jews. He states:

> When Cyrus read this [Isaiah's prophecy], and admired the divine power, an earnest desire and ambition seized upon him to fulfill what was so written; so he called for the most imminent Jews that were in Babylon, and said to them, that he gave them leave to go back to their own country, and to rebuild their city Jerusalem, and the temple of God, for that he would be their assistant, and that he would write to the rulers and governors that were in the neighborhood of their country of Judea, that they should contribute to them gold and silver for the building of the temple, and, besides that, beasts for their sacrifices.[4]

The source from which Josephus got his information is not known. But since Daniel was a Prime Minister for Cyrus, it is certainly possible that Daniel showed the king the prophecy of Isaiah. Also being a strong witness for the LORD, Daniel most likely did all he could to lead the king to a knowledge of the only true and living God.

In addition to the Isaiah prophecy given above, note other prophecies by Isaiah and Jeremiah concerning the freeing of the Jewish exiles:

> **"Who raised up the righteous *man* from the east [Persia], called him to his foot, gave the nations before him, and made *him* rule over kings? he gave *them* as the dust to his sword, *and* as driven stubble to his bow....I have raised up *one* from the north [Persia], and he shall come: from the rising of the sun shall he call upon my name: and he shall come upon princes as *upon* morter, and as the potter treadeth clay" (Is.41:2, 25).**
> **"And this whole land shall be a desolation, *and* an astonishment; and these nations shall serve the king of Babylon seventy years. And it shall come to pass, when seventy years are accomplished, *that* I will punish the king of Babylon, and that nation, saith the LORD, for their iniquity, and the land of the Chaldeans, and will make it perpetual desolations" (Je.25:11-12).**
> **"For thus saith the LORD, That after seventy years be accomplished at Babylon I will visit you, and perform my good word toward you, in causing you to return to this place. For I know the thoughts that I think toward you, saith the LORD, thoughts of peace, and not of evil, to give you an expected end. Then shall ye call upon me, and ye shall go and pray unto me, and I will hearken unto you. And ye shall seek me, and find *me*, when ye shall search for me with all your heart. And I will be found of you, saith the LORD: and I will turn away your captivity, and I will gather you from all the nations, and from all the places whither I have driven you, saith the LORD; and I will bring you again into the place whence I caused you to be carried away captive" (Je.29:10-14).**
> **"Thus saith the LORD; Behold, I will raise up against Babylon, and against them that dwell in the midst of them that rise up against me, a destroying wind....Make bright the arrows; gather the shields: the LORD hath raised up the spirit of the kings of the Medes: for his device *is* against Babylon, to destroy it; because it *is* the vengeance of the LORD, the vengeance of his temple" (Je.51:1, 11; see vv.1-11).**

---

2 Matthew Henry. *Matthew Henry's Commentary,* Vol.2. (Old Tappan, NJ: Fleming H. Revell, n.d), p.1030.
3 J.Vernon McGee. *Thru the Bible*, Vol.2. (Nashville, TN: Thomas Nelson Publishers, 1981), p.479.
4 Flavius Josephus. *Complete Works. Antiquities of the Jews*. (Grand Rapids, MI: Kregel Publications, 1981). Book 11, p.228.

Whether Daniel showed all these prophecies to King Cyrus is not known. Neither can we know if Cyrus ever turned to the LORD. But Scripture does say this: when it was time for God's prophecy to be fulfilled, Cyrus' decision to free the Jews did not just happen. The LORD God Himself "stirred," "moved" the heart of Cyrus to free the Jewish captives (v.1).

c. The royal *Proclamation of Freedom* was decreed 70 years after the Babylonian captivity (v.2). Just as Jeremiah had so clearly predicted 70 years earlier, after the Jews had been exiled from the promised land, King Cyrus allowed them to return. The first deportation had begun in 605 B.C. during the reign of Jehoiakim (Da.1:1). And after Cyrus' decree of freedom in 538 B.C., the first exiles began to return in 536 B.C. Including the time it took the Jews to return, settle down, and build the altar for worship, the 70 years were fulfilled.

Being stirred by the Spirit of God, King Cyrus issued his *Proclamation of Freedom*. Whether Cyrus knew the fact or not, the Proclamation included five points:

1) King Cyrus acknowledged the LORD as *the God of heaven* and as the source of his power and rule as king over the Persian Empire (v.2). The title *God of heaven* means that He is in heaven, and rules over the universe from heaven. He is *the LORD, the God of heaven,* who rules over all, including King Cyrus. It was the LORD who had given King Cyrus his power and rule. The title *God of heaven* is used 22 times in the Old Testament, 17 times in Ezra, Nehemiah, and Daniel.

2) Cyrus claimed that the LORD had appointed him to build a temple in Jerusalem (v.2). Even if Cyrus was not acting out of conviction and personal conversion to the LORD, he was being moved by the Spirit of God to free the Jews. He allowed them to return and rebuild their nation and temple in Jerusalem—just as Isaiah and Jeremiah had prophesied.

3) Cyrus allowed any Jewish exile who wished to do so to return to Jerusalem and Judah (v.3). He was not forcing them to return, only giving them the *right* to return. They were free to decide. They could decide to remain where they were, in exile and captivity.

4) Cyrus ordered the returning exiles to rebuild the temple of the LORD (v.3). Their rebuilding the temple—the house of worship—was essential, for the temple represented the very presence of the LORD. And the presence of the LORD was an *absolute essential* if the people were to rebuild their nation and lives. They had been exiled because they had rejected the LORD, turning to false gods and false worship. If they wished to return to the promised land and be assured of remaining there in peace and security, they would have to refocus their lives totally upon the LORD. This necessitated the rebuilding of the temple and the establishment of true worship.

5) Cyrus encouraged the Jews who did not return, to give financial support to the returning exiles (v.4). Remember that Jerusalem and the other cities of Judah had been utterly destroyed by the Assyrians and Babylonians. Rebuilding the land would be a costly project. A long and difficult task lay ahead of the returning exiles with many hours of exhausting labor and many days of suffering for some of the returnees. They would need a huge amount of financial aid (silver and gold), supplies, livestock, and any other freewill offerings the Persian public was willing to give them. Knowing this, King Cyrus encouraged the Jews who were remaining behind and other neighbors to help those who were returning to their homeland.

Thought 1. Several prophecies had been made predicting that King Cyrus of Persia would free the Jews from captivity, setting them free to return to their homeland. Even his name, Cyrus, had been predicted some 100 years before his birth. Amazingly, the prophecies were fulfilled exactly as predicted.

God's Word is always fulfilled: every prophecy, every promise, and every judgment. Every prediction concerning past history has been fulfilled. And every prediction concerning future history will be fulfilled.

(1) The prophecies concerning the return of Jesus Christ will take place. Jesus Christ will return.

> **"Let not your heart be troubled: ye believe in God, believe also in me. In my Father's house are many mansions: if *it were* not so, I would have told you. I go to prepare a place for you. And if I go and prepare a place for you, I will come again, and receive you unto myself; that where I am, *there* ye may be also" (Jn.14:1-3).**

> **"For the Lord himself shall descend from heaven with a shout, with the voice of the archangel, and with the trump of God: and the dead in Christ shall rise first: Then we which are alive *and* remain shall be caught up together with them in the clouds, to meet the Lord in the air: and so shall we ever be with the Lord. Wherefore comfort one another with these words" (1 Th.4:16-18).**

(2) The promise that the believer will receive eternal life is true. Quicker than the eye can blink, when a believer dies, he or she will be immediately transferred into heaven to live with the LORD eternally.

> **"And as Moses lifted up the serpent in the wilderness, even so must the Son of man be lifted up: That whosoever believeth in him should not perish, but have eternal life. For God so loved the world, that he gave his only begotten Son, that whosoever believeth in him should not perish, but have everlasting life" (Jn.3:14-16).**

> **"He that believeth on the Son hath everlasting life: and he that believeth not the Son shall not see life; but the wrath of God abideth on him" (Jn.3:36).**

> **"For he that soweth to his flesh shall of the flesh reap corruption; but he that soweth to the Spirit shall of the Spirit reap life everlasting" (Ga.6:8).**

> **"And the Lord shall deliver me from every evil work, and will preserve *me* unto his heavenly kingdom: to whom *be* glory for ever and ever. Amen." (2 Ti.4:18).**

(3) The prophecies of a new heavens and earth will be fulfilled.

> "But the day of the Lord will come as a thief in the night; in the which the heavens shall pass away with a great noise, and the elements shall melt with fervent heat, the earth also and the works that are therein shall be burned up. *Seeing* then *that* all these things shall be dissolved, what manner *of persons* ought ye to be in *all* holy conversation and godliness, Looking for and hasting unto the coming of the day of God, wherein the heavens being on fire shall be dissolved, and the elements shall melt with fervent heat? Nevertheless we, according to his promise, look for new heavens and a new earth, wherein dwelleth righteousness. Wherefore, beloved, seeing that ye look for such things, be diligent that ye may be found of him in peace, without spot, and blameless" (2 Pe.3:10-14).
>
> "And I saw a new heaven and a new earth: for the first heaven and the first earth were passed away; and there was no more sea" (Re.21:1).

(4) The prophecies concerning the coming judgment of God will take place. Every human being will stand before God to give an account for what he has done, whether good or bad.

> "For the Son of man shall come in the glory of his Father with his angels; and then he shall reward every man according to his works" (Mt.16:27).
>
> "When the Son of man shall come in his glory, and all the holy angels with him, then shall he sit upon the throne of his glory: And before him shall be gathered all nations: and he shall separate them one from another, as a shepherd divideth *his* sheep from the goats: And he shall set the sheep on his right hand, but the goats on the left" (Mt.25:31-33).
>
> "And as it is appointed unto men once to die, but after this the judgment" (He.9:27).
>
> "The Lord knoweth how to deliver the godly out of temptations, and to reserve the unjust unto the day of judgment to be punished" (2 Pe.2:9).
>
> "Behold, the Lord cometh with ten thousands of his saints, To execute judgment upon all, and to convince all that are ungodly among them of all their ungodly deeds which they have ungodly committed, and of all their hard *speeches* which ungodly sinners have spoken against him" (Jude 14-15).
>
> "And I saw the dead, small and great, stand before God; and the books were opened: and another book was opened, which is *the book* of life: and the dead were judged out of those things which were written in the books, according to their works" (Re.20:12).

(5) The prophecies of God—every word He has ever predicted—is absolutely trustworthy.

> "For verily I say unto you, Till heaven and earth pass, one jot or one tittle shall in no wise pass from the law, till all be fulfilled" (Mt.5:18).
>
> "And it shall turn to you for a testimony" (Lu.21:13).
>
> "God *is* faithful, by whom ye were called unto the fellowship of his Son Jesus Christ our Lord" (1 Co.1:9).
>
> "Know therefore that the LORD thy God, he *is* God, the faithful God, which keepeth covenant and mercy with them that love him and keep his commandments to a thousand generations" (De.7:9).
>
> "And now, O Lord GOD, thou *art* that God, and thy words be true, and thou hast promised this goodness unto thy servant" (2 S.7:28).
>
> "Blessed *be* the LORD, that hath given rest unto his people Israel, according to all that he promised: there hath not failed one word of all his good promise, which he promised by the hand of Moses his servant" (1 Ki.8:56).
>
> "For I *am* the LORD: I will speak, and the word that I shall speak shall come to pass" (Eze.12:25).

---

2 (1:5-11) **Service, Preparation for—God, Stirring Lives, for Service—Power, of God, to Stir Lives—Stirring, of God, for Service—Captives, Jewish, Returned from Exile—Exile, Jewish, Returned to Jerusalem—Promised Land, Return of Exiles—Returnees, Jewish, from Persia**: there was the preparation of the captives to return to the promised land. News of the *Proclamation of Freedom* was bound to spread like wildfire throughout the Jewish settlements of the Persian Empire. And joy over the prospect of freedom surely flooded the hearts of thousands. They could now be liberated, set free to return to their homeland. But for many this would be a difficult decision. Remember: it had been 70 years since the captivity of the Jews, 70 years since they had been deported into Babylon. This being the case, many were born and reared in Babylon. It was the only home they had ever known. No doubt many of these had become settled in Persia and were comfortably living in a prosperous, affluent society. Many owned their own homes, property, and businesses, and lived rich social lives, engaging in pleasurable and recreational activities. To return would mean giving up all of this. They would be sacrificing all they had built up and secured over the last 50 plus years. Returning to the promised land of God not only meant sacrificing all they had worked for but also giving it all up for a life of extreme hardship. If they chose to return, they would have to start building their lives all over again, for Jerusalem and the other cities of Judah had been totally destroyed by the Babylonians. Thus, the Jews had to rebuild their homes as well as all the communities, cities, businesses, economy, and political system of the nation. Because of these and other weighty factors, the decision to return was extremely difficult for many of the Jewish exiles.

Nevertheless, almost 50,000 Jews decided to return (49,897 to be exact; see 2:64-65). But note what was behind their decision to return.

OUTLINE	SCRIPTURE	SCRIPTURE	OUTLINE
2. The preparation by the captives for returning to the promised land: A striking picture of being spiritually & materially prepared to serve God a. Their motivation: The LORD stirred the hearts of some to go b. Their material provisions 1) Neighbors gave them financial aid, supplies, & livestock as well as freewill offerings for the rebuilding of the temple 2) King Cyrus returned all the temple furnishings & articles that Nebuchadnezzar had plundered, 2 K.24:13; 25:13-17; 2 Chr.36:7-10, 18; Je.27:16; 52:17-23; Da.1:2; 5:1-4 3) Persia's treasurer,	5 Then rose up the chief of the fathers of Judah and Benjamin, and the priests, and the Levites, with all *them* whose spirit God had raised, to go up to build the house of the LORD which *is* in Jerusalem. 6 And all they that *were* about them strengthened their hands with vessels of silver, with gold, with goods, and with beasts, and with precious things, beside all *that* was willingly offered. 7 Also Cyrus the king brought forth the vessels of the house of the LORD, which Nebuchadnezzar had brought forth out of Jerusalem, and had put them in the house of his gods; 8 Even those did Cyrus king	of Persia bring forth by the hand of Mithredath the treasurer, and numbered them unto Sheshbazzar, the prince of Judah. 9 And this *is* the number of them: thirty chargers of gold, a thousand chargers of silver, nine and twenty knives, 10 Thirty basons of gold, silver basons of a second sort four hundred and ten, *and* other vessels a thousand. 11 All the vessels of gold and of silver *were* five thousand and four hundred. All *these* did Sheshbazzar bring up with *them of* the captivity that were brought up from Babylon unto Jerusalem.	Mithredath, counted the temple articles & turned them over to the leader of the returning exiles, Sheshbazzar • Gold trays (dishes) 30 • Silver trays (dishes) 1000 • Silver knives or censers or pans , 29 • Gold bowls 30 • Silver bowls 410 • Other major articles 1000 • Total number of temple articles returned 5400 4) Sheshbazzar & the exiles returned from Babylon to Jerusalem & Judah, the promised land

a. The LORD *moved* (*uwr* or *ur*) their hearts (v.5). The Hebrew word means to awaken, arouse, stir, raise up. The Jews were aroused, constrained by the LORD to return to the promised land. The Spirit of God worked in their hearts, stirring them to make a concrete decision to return. Note their purpose for returning: to rebuild their homeland and the temple of God. The Jews were the followers of the only living and true God. Through the Jews, God gave to the world...
- the knowledge and worship of the only living and true God (Jn.4:22)
- the Messiah or Savior of the world, the Lord Jesus Christ
- the written Word of God, the Holy Bible
- the wonderful hope of the promised land, a type of heaven and of living with God eternally in a perfect world and environment

Who exactly were these 50,000 courageous people? Who demonstrated such a *strong faith in* the LORD and the wonderful promises He had given to Abraham and the descendants of faith (Ro.4:11-12, 16)? They were primarily from the tribes of Judah and Benjamin, along with some religious leaders from among the priests and Levites. Note that no exiles from the ten tribes of the Northern Kingdom are mentioned as returning. However, other Scripture tells us that some Jews from the northern tribes of Ephraim and Manasseh did return from captivity (1 Chr.9:3). In addition to these, some had earlier fled to Judah at the fall of the Northern Kingdom (2 Chr.11:16). Although some people refer to the *10 lost tribes of Israel,* Scripture clearly indicates that some believers from all the tribes returned to the promised land and are represented in the *Honor Roll of Believers* being kept by the LORD (1 Chr.9:3; 2 Chr.11:16; Ac.26:7; Js.1:1).

The point to note is the returnees' *strong, unwavering faith* in the LORD and His promises. *The Expositor's Bible Commentary* says this in quoting W.F. Albright:

> Commenting on the tenacious faith that inspired the Jews to return to Palestine under the Persians and again in the twentieth century. W.F. Albright...perceptively notes:
> But how could the Jews have been so filled with the conviction that Israel would indeed be restored, even after complete destruction, unless there were prophecies of Restoration to believe? The rationalistic attempt to do away with prophecy raises new problems which are much more difficult to solve than acceptance of the uniform early tradition presented by our Biblical sources. So far as we know, no people except Israel has ever been restored to its native land after such a clean break. If there were any remaining doubt, surely it would be removed by the close analogy which we now have in the second restoration of Israel, after twenty-five more centuries! No one can dispute that fact that it was the firmly held rabbinic belief in their ultimate return as a nation to Palestine that brought the Jews back to their ancient home in recent generations.[5]

b. Remember, Cyrus had encouraged the Jews who were remaining to give financial support to those who were returning (1:6; see v.4). This they did. And they gave liberally. Their neighbors willingly gave them financial aid, supplies, and livestock, as well as freewill offerings. Their gifts were to be used for the rebuilding of the homes, society, and temple of the nation. Note how this giving of financial aid to the departing Jews parallels the experience of the Israelites during the exodus under Moses (Ex.12:35-36). In both cases some of the wealth given by their neighbors was used to build

---

5 W.F. Albright. *History, Archaeology and Christian Humanism.* (New York: McGraw Hill, 1964), pp.59-59. Quoted in Edwin Yamauchi's *Ezra, Nehemiah.* "The Expositor's Bible Commentary," Vol. 4. (Grand Rapids, MI: Zondervan Publishing House, 1988), pp.603-604.

God's house of worship, which was the *Tabernacle* for the Exodus Jews and the *Temple* for the exiles now returning to Jerusalem.

A significant contribution of wealth was made by King Cyrus himself. He returned all the temple furnishings and articles that Nebuchadnezzar of Babylon had plundered (7–11; also see 2 K.24:13; 25:13-17; 2 Chr.36:7-10, 18; Je.27:16; 52:17-23; Da.1:2; 5:1-4). Persia's treasurer, a man named Mithredath, counted the temple articles and turned them over to the leader of the returning exiles, Sheshbazzar (v.8-10). These items or articles were to be placed in the temple after its construction. Obviously, the articles included the dishes, bowls, pans, knives, and other utensils or items needed in the slaughtering of sacrifices and in the other functions of worship. Only 2,499 items are listed in Scripture, but the total number of items given by Cyrus is said to be 5,400 (v.11). Obviously, the items listed were the major ones and the other items were of less value.

Note that Sheshbazzar is said to be the prince or leader of Judah (v.8). Just who he was is disputed, for Zerubbabel is also said to be the governor or leader of Judah, the leader who supervised the rebuilding of Jerusalem and the temple. Some commentators think the two names refer to the same person, with Sheshbazzar being the Persian name and Zerubbabel being the name by which the Jews called him. This seems to be a correct conclusion. For Scripture says in one place that Sheshbazzar laid the foundation of the temple (5:16), but it says in two other places that Zerubbabel laid the foundation (3:8-13; Zec.4:9). However, it should be noted that other commentators think the two names represent two different leaders, but that, for some unknown reason, Sheshbazzar passed from the scene and Zerubbabel took over the reigns of leadership for the returnees.

Thought 1. The preparation for the returning exiles is a striking picture for us. Their preparation shows us how we must be prepared to serve the LORD.

(1) We must be prepared *spiritually* to serve God just as they were prepared *spiritually*. God's Holy Word gives us at least seven ways to prepare ourselves for service:

(a) We must first be saved through the Lord Jesus Christ.

> **"But after that the kindness and love of God our Saviour toward man appeared, Not by works of righteousness which we have done, but according to his mercy he saved us, by the washing of regeneration, and renewing of the Holy Ghost; Which he shed on us abundantly through Jesus Christ our Saviour; That being justified by his grace, we should be made heirs according to the hope of eternal life" (Tit.3:4-7).**

(b) We must ask the Lord to create a clean heart and to renew a right spirit within us.

> **"Create in me a clean heart, O God; and renew a right spirit within me" (Ps.51:10).**

(c) We must put off the old man and put on the new man.

> **"That ye put off concerning the former conversation the old man, which is corrupt according to the deceitful lusts; And be renewed in the spirit of your mind; And that ye put on the new man, which after God is created in righteousness and true holiness" (Ep.4:22-24).**
>
> **"And have put on the new *man*, which is renewed in knowledge after the image of him that created him" (Co.3:10).**

(d) We must present our bodies as a living sacrifice to the Lord and not be conformed to this world.

> **"I beseech you therefore, brethren, by the mercies of God, that ye present your bodies a living sacrifice, holy, acceptable unto God, *which is* your reasonable service. And be not conformed to this world: but be ye transformed by the renewing of your mind, that ye may prove what is that good, and acceptable, and perfect, will of God" (Ro.12:1-2).**

(e) We must obey God and follow His leadership, the stirrings of His Spirit within our heart.

> **"Howbeit when he, the Spirit of truth, is come, he will guide you into all truth: for he shall not speak of himself; but whatsoever he shall hear, *that* shall he speak: and he will shew you things to come" (Jn.16:13).**
>
> **"What? know ye not that your body is the temple of the Holy Ghost *which is* in you, which ye have of God, and ye are not your own? For ye are bought with a price: therefore glorify God in your body, and in your spirit, which are God's" (1 Co.6:19-20).**
>
> **"Wherefore, my beloved, as ye have always obeyed, not as in my presence only, but now much more in my absence, work out your own salvation with fear and trembling. For it is God which worketh in you both to will and to do of *his* good pleasure" (Ph.2:12-13).**
>
> **"And thine ears shall hear a word behind thee, saying, This *is* the way, walk ye in it, when ye turn to the right hand, and when ye turn to the left" (Is.30:21).**
>
> **"And I will put my spirit within you, and cause you to walk in my statutes, and ye shall keep my judgments, and do *them*" (Eze.36:27).**

(f) We must seek those things that are above, the heavenly things of God.

> "If ye then be risen with Christ, seek those things which are above, where Christ sitteth on the right hand of God. Set your affection on things above, not on things on the earth. For ye are dead, and your life is hid with Christ in God. When Christ, *who is* our life, shall appear, then shall ye also appear with him in glory. Mortify therefore your members which are upon the earth; fornication, uncleanness, inordinate affection, evil concupiscence, and covetousness, which is idolatry: For which things' sake the wrath of God cometh on the children of disobedience….Put on therefore, as the elect of God, holy and beloved, bowels of mercies, kindness, humbleness of mind, meekness, longsuffering; Forbearing one another, and forgiving one another, if any man have a quarrel against any: even as Christ forgave you, so also *do* ye. And above all these things *put on* charity, which is the bond of perfectness" (Co.3:1-6, 12-14).

(g) We must pray continually, seeking the Lord for strength and waiting upon Him to renew our strength.

> "Ask, and it shall be given you; seek, and ye shall find; knock, and it shall be opened unto you" (Mt.7:7).
> "Seek the LORD and his strength, seek his face continually" (1 Chr.16:11).
> "But they that wait upon the LORD shall renew *their* strength; they shall mount up with wings as eagles; they shall run, and not be weary; *and* they shall walk, and not faint" (Is.40:31).

(h) We must put on the whole armor of God so that we can stand against all temptations and trials.

> "Finally, my brethren, be strong in the Lord, and in the power of his might. Put on the whole armour of God, that ye may be able to stand against the wiles of the devil. For we wrestle not against flesh and blood, but against principalities, against powers, against the rulers of the darkness of this world, against spiritual wickedness in high *places*" (Ep.6:10-12; See also vv.13-18).

(i) We must trust the Lord with all our heart and acknowledge Him in all our ways.

> "Trust in the LORD with all thine heart; and lean not unto thine own understanding. In all thy ways acknowledge him, and he shall direct thy paths" (Pr.3:5-6).

(2) We must be prepared *materially* to serve the Lord. Finances are an absolute essential in order to take the gospel to the world, to meet the needs of hurting people, and to support the church and God's servants worldwide. Listen to what God's Holy Word says about supporting His work throughout the world.

> "Give to him that asketh thee, and from him that would borrow of thee turn not thou away" (Mt.5:42).
> "But seek ye first the kingdom of God, and his righteousness; and all these things shall be added unto you" (Mt.6:33).
> "Go ye therefore, and teach all nations, baptizing them in the name of the Father, and of the Son, and of the Holy Ghost: Teaching them to observe all things whatsoever I have commanded you: and, lo, I am with you alway, *even* unto the end of the world. Amen" (Mt.28:19-20).
> "And he said unto them, Go ye into all the world, and preach the gospel to every creature" (Mk.16:15).
> "I have showed you all things, how that so labouring ye ought to support the weak, and to remember the words of the Lord Jesus, how he said, It is more blessed to give than to receive" (Ac.20:35).
> "Distributing to the necessity of saints; given to hospitality" (Ro.12:13).
> "Every man *shall give* as he is able, according to the blessing of the LORD thy God which he hath given thee" (De.16:17).
> "If thine enemy be hungry, give him bread to eat; and if he be thirsty, give him water to drink" (Pr.25:21).
> "*Is* not this the fast that I have chosen? to loose the bands of wickedness, to undo the heavy burdens, and to let the oppressed go free, and that ye break every yoke? *Is it* not to deal thy bread to the hungry, and that thou bring the poor that are cast out to thy house? when thou seest the naked, that thou cover him; and that thou hide not thyself from thine own flesh?" (Is.58:6-7).

---

3 (2:1-70) **Commitment, Example of, Exile Returnees—Promised Land, Commitment to, Example of—Jerusalem, Returned to, by Exiles—Judah, Returned to, by Exiles—Lists, Exile Returnees—Returnees, Exiles, Lists of**: what follows is a list of captives who returned to Jerusalem and the other towns of Judah. This is a list that is often skipped by the reader. But several facts about this list of names need to be kept in mind. First, these were the people who genuinely believed God and His promises, in particular, the promise that He had truly given them the promised land as their permanent possession.

Second, these were the people who were to continue carrying out God's purposes for the human race. These purposes were threefold: (1) the sending of God's Son Jesus Christ to the world; (2) the preservation of God's Word and, (3) the preservation of the promised land (heaven) for the world.

Third, these were the individual Jews who trusted the LORD and the promises given to Abraham. They believed the promises of God enough to sacrifice all they had to return to the promised land.

Fourth, these were the people who in most cases could prove their genealogy and ancestry, who could prove their claim to family property and their right of inheritance in the promised land. Some of the returnees did not have proof of their Jewish ancestry. Nevertheless, they were allowed to settle in the land, but were only given the rights of foreigners (Ex.22:21; 23:9; Le.19:33-34; De.10:18-19; 14:27-29). Any person who claimed to be a priest but could not prove his ancestry was excluded from the priesthood (vv.61-63). They were excluded, however, only until their claim could be proven by a true priest seeking the LORD's validation through the *Urim* and *Thummim*.

The long list of names and brief comments here and there are broken down into 10 points by the outline of the Scripture. The outline points are sufficient to understand the points being covered by the Scripture.

Thought 1. The captivity of the Jews and their returning to the LORD and the promised land are striking examples for us. If we turn away from the LORD and become captured by sin or the world, we too must make a renewed commitment to the LORD. We must repent of our sin, turning back to the LORD and beginning a renewed walk toward the promised land of heaven. But if we continue to walk in sin, we will destroy any hope of living fruitful and victorious lives. We will lose the assurance of pleasing God and of living with God eternally, lose the God-given strength to conquer the trials and temptations of this life. And when we come face-to-face with a terminal disease or with death itself, fear and regret will grip our hearts.

But there is a *Proclamation of Freedom* offered to every one of us. Even if we are gripped by sin and worldliness, we can be set free, liberated. All we have to do is repent, turn away from the land of sin and captivity and turn to God and the hope of the promised land of heaven. Committing our lives to God will set us free, liberate us to live eternally with Him. Listen to what God's Holy Word says about commitment to the LORD:

"Then Peter began to say unto him, Lo, we have left all, and have followed thee" (Mk.10:28).

"And he said to *them* all, If any *man* will come after me, let him deny himself, and take up his cross daily, and follow me" (Lu.9:23).

"So likewise, whosoever he be of you that forsaketh not all that he hath, he cannot be my disciple" (Lu.14:33).

"Then spake Jesus again unto them, saying, I am the light of the world: he that followeth me shall not walk in darkness, but shall have the light of life" (Jn.8:12).

"Then said Jesus to those Jews which believed on him, If ye continue in my word, *then* are ye my disciples indeed" (Jn.8:31).

"For if ye live after the flesh, ye shall die: but if ye through the Spirit do mortify the deeds of the body, ye shall live" (Ro.8:13).

"I beseech you therefore, brethren, by the mercies of God, that ye present your bodies a living sacrifice, holy, acceptable unto God, *which is* your reasonable service. And be not conformed to this world: but be ye transformed by the renewing of your mind, that ye may prove what is that good, and acceptable, and perfect, will of God" (Ro.12:1-2).

"Yea doubtless, and I count all things *but* loss for the excellency of the knowledge of Christ Jesus my Lord: for whom I have suffered the loss of all things, and do count them *but* dung, that I may win Christ" (Ph.3:8).

"Nevertheless we, according to his promise, look for new heavens and a new earth, wherein dwelleth righteousness. Wherefore, beloved, seeing that ye look for such things, be diligent that ye may be found of him in peace, without spot, and blameless" (2 Pe.3:13-14).

"My son, give me thine heart, and let thine eyes observe my ways" (Pr.23:26).

1. **Task 1: To get settled, laboring diligently to take care of one's family**
2. **Task 2: To establish regular worship**

   a. The religious & civil leaders—the High Priest Jeshua & the governor Zerubbabel along with their associates—rebuilt the altar
      1) Rebuilt it as instructed by God's law, His Word, Ex. 20:25; 27:1-8; 38:1-7; De.27:5-6
      2) Rebuilt it at the old site
      3) Rebuilt it despite fearing the hostile local residents who were unbelievers
      4) Offered the daily burnt sacrifices to the LORD

   b. The people celebrated the Feast of Tabernacles: A reminder of God's protection during the wilderness journeys

   c. The people instituted all the regular worship services & sacrificial offerings, Le.23:1-44
      1) Instituted on the first day of the seventh month
      2) Instituted all services & worshipped the LORD even without a temple
3. **Task 3: To begin building God's house of worship, laying a solid foundation**
   a. The preparations
      1) Hired skilled laborers: Masons & carpenters
      2) Made a trade agreement with Sidon & Tyre: To

CHAPTER 3

B. The Major Tasks of the Returning Exiles: Becoming Established, Laying a Firm Foundation for Life, 3:1-13

And when the seventh month was come, and the children of Israel *were* in the cities, the people gathered themselves together as one man to Jerusalem.
2 Then stood up Jeshua the son of Jozadak, and his brethren the priests, and Zerubbabel the son of Shealtiel, and his brethren, and builded the altar of the God of Israel, to offer burnt offerings thereon, as *it is* written in the law of Moses the man of God.
3 And they set the altar upon his bases; for fear *was* upon them because of the people of those countries: and they offered burnt offerings thereon unto the LORD, *even* burnt offerings morning and evening.
4 They kept also the feast of tabernacles, as *it is* written, and *offered* the daily burnt offerings by number, according to the custom, as the duty of every day required;
5 And afterward *offered* the continual burnt offering, both of the new moons, and of all the set feasts of the LORD that were consecrated, and of every one that willingly offered a freewill offering unto the LORD.
6 From the first day of the seventh month began they to offer burnt offerings unto the LORD. But the foundation of the temple of the LORD was not *yet* laid.
7 They gave money also unto the masons, and to the carpenters; and meat, and drink, and oil, unto them of Zidon, and to them of Tyre, to bring cedar trees from Lebanon to the sea of Joppa, according to the grant that

they had of Cyrus king of Persia.
8 Now in the second year of their coming unto the house of God at Jerusalem, in the second month, began Zerubbabel the son of Shealtiel, and Jeshua the son of Jozadak, and the remnant of their brethren the priests and the Levites, and all they that were come out of the captivity unto Jerusalem; and appointed the Levites, from twenty years old and upward, to set forward the work of the house of the LORD.
9 Then stood Jeshua *with* his sons and his brethren, Kadmiel and his sons, the sons of Judah, together, to set forward the workmen in the house of God: the sons of Henadad, *with* their sons and their brethren the Levites.
10 And when the builders laid the foundation of the temple of the LORD, they set the priests in their apparel with trumpets, and the Levites the sons of Asaph with cymbals, to praise the LORD, after the ordinance of David king of Israel.
11 And they sang together by course in praising and giving thanks unto the LORD; because *he is* good, for his mercy *endureth* for ever toward Israel. And all the people shouted with a great shout, when they praised the LORD, because the foundation of the house of the LORD was laid.
12 But many of the priests and Levites and chief of the fathers, *who were* ancient men, that had seen the first house, when the foundation of this house was laid before their eyes, wept with a loud voice; and many shouted aloud for joy:
13 So that the people could not discern the noise of the shout of joy from the noise of the weeping of the people: for the people shouted with a loud shout, and the noise was heard afar off.

secure the best cedar logs
   b. The construction date: Second month of the second year, which was April–May (c.536 B.C.)
   c. The project supervisors
      1) The two appointed superintendents: The governor Zerubbabel & the High Priest Jeshua or Joshua
      2) The project foremen: Levites 20 years old & older

      3) The three chief foremen: The family heads of three clans
         • Jeshua oversaw his sons & brothers
         • Kadmiel oversaw his sons
         • Henadad oversaw his descendants
   d. The dedication service celebrating the completion of the foundation
      1) The priests dressed in their priestly robes, secured their trumpets, & took their places
      2) The Levites secured their instruments & took their places
      3) The musicians played & sang songs about God's goodness & His covenant, 1 Chr.16:34; 2 Chr.5:13; 7:3; Ps.106:1; 136:1; Je.33:10-11
      4) The people shouted out praises to the LORD

      5) The deep emotions shown by the whole assembly
         • The older folks who remembered Solomon's temple wept: Was not as magnificent, Hag.2:1-9
         • The younger folks shouted for joy

         • The commotion of the weeping & shouting was so loud that it could be heard far away

DIVISION I

THE FIRST RETURN OF EXILES FROM CAPTIVITY AND THEIR RESETTLEMENT—LED BY ZERUBBABEL, 1:1–6:22

B. The Major Tasks of the Returning Exiles: Becoming Established, Laying a Firm Foundation for Life, 3:1-13

(3:1-13) **Introduction**: if anyone or anything is to last a long time, to grow, to prosper, to endure, to withstand the trials of life, it must be built upon a firm foundation. Whether an individual, a house, or a business, any entity without a solid foundation will collapse. If a person stands on shaky ground, he will sway back and forth and eventually fall.

⇒ A relationship built upon lies or unfaithfulness will be severed, but a relationship built upon truth and faithfulness will endure.

⇒ A person who lives a slothful, indifferent, and unmotivated life will fail, but one who diligently labors will be rewarded.

⇒ A person whose behavior is careless and undisciplined will be easily swayed by any wind that comes along; but a person whose behavior is disciplined will not be enslaved by the evils of this life, such as pornography, immorality, stealing, gluttony, lying, addiction to drugs, tobacco, alcohol, and a host of other enslavements.

Laying a firm foundation for their lives and their society was the concern of the exiles who had just returned to their homeland in Judah. Everything needed to be rebuilt: the cities, homes, businesses, economy, military, and temple. To rebuild their nation and temple was a mammoth task, for their nation had been utterly destroyed by the Assyrians and Babylonians. Nevertheless, it was for this purpose that they had returned. The awesome work that lay ahead for them is the subject of this Scripture. This is, *The Major Tasks of the Returning Exiles: Becoming Established, Laying a Firm Foundation for Life, 3:1-13.*

1. Task 1: to get settled, laboring diligently to take care of one's family (v.1).
2. Task 2: to establish regular worship (vv.1-6).
3. Task 3: to begin building God's house of worship, laying a solid foundation (vv.7-13).

1 (3:1) **Family, Duty Toward—Care, Duty, to Family—Diligence, Duty—Returned Exiles, Tasks of—Exiles, Returned, Tasks of—Returnees, Exile, Tasks of**: upon returning home, the first task of the exiles was to get settled, laboring diligently to take care of their families.

OUTLINE	SCRIPTURE	SCRIPTURE	OUTLINE
1. Task 1: To get settled, laboring diligently to take care of one's family	And when the seventh month was come, and the children of Israel *were* in the cities, the	people gathered themselves together as one man to Jerusalem.	

Apparently, the journey to Judah took about four months, for the distance would have been about 900 miles. This is the time it took the second group of returnees who came with Ezra (7:9). Nothing whatsoever is shared about the difficulties suffered by the travelers during the long days of their journey. They pressed on through every hardship and overcame every danger. Mile by mile they stayed on the roadway until they reached their destination.

After the returnees reached Judah they dispersed, each traveling the land to find his or her own home and property. The first task of every individual and family was to secure the basic necessities of life: housing, food, and water. Imagine what these first returnees found. Remember that the cities and Jerusalem had been totally destroyed, including Jerusalem's stone walls. A scene of utter devastation greeted the returnees. No building in Jerusalem—not a single home—was left standing. Heaps of debris were piled everywhere. On the outskirts of the former city, there may have been a few homes built by those who had escaped deportation by the Babylonians. But these were bound to be insignificant in comparison to the utter devastation of the former great city. Rebuilding the city and temple would involve cleaning up the debris before construction could begin. Of course, they would use what stone and other materials they could recover, but the task confronting them—cleaning up the debris and rebuilding the city—was enormous.

However, before construction of the city and temple could be undertaken, the returnees had to secure water either by digging wells or locating springs or uncontaminated streams. After being desolate for 70 years, the land had to be cleared and cultivated for crops and food. Temporary shelter—whether tents or huts—had to be erected until they could build their homes. Thus, providing the very basic necessities of life for their families was the first task of the exiles who had returned to Jerusalem and Judah.

Thought 1. Providing for and taking care of our families should be one of the first tasks of every family head. Our families are to be continually nurtured and strengthened, for God has appointed the family to be the primary structure of society. Every family member has a responsibility to strengthen other members of the family and the family unit as a whole. Listen to what God's Holy Word says:

(1) Husbands and wives are to love, respect, and submit to one another.

"**Submitting yourselves one to another in the fear of God. Wives, submit yourselves unto your own husbands, as unto the Lord**" (Ep.5:21-22).

"**Husbands, love your wives, even as Christ also loved the church, and gave himself for it**" (Ep.5:25).

"**Nevertheless let every one of you in particular so love his wife even as himself; and the wife *see* that she reverence *her* husband**" (Ep.5:33).

(2) Parents are to teach, nurture, and provide for their children.

> **"For the children ought not to lay up for the parents, but the parents for the children" (2 Co.12:14).**
> **"And, ye fathers, provoke not your children to wrath: but bring them up in the nurture and admonition of the Lord" (Ep.6:4).**
> **"And these words, which I command thee this day, shall be in thine heart: And thou shalt teach them diligently unto thy children, and shalt talk of them when thou sittest in thine house, and when thou walkest by the way, and when thou liest down, and when thou risest up" (De.6:6-7).**
> **"Train up a child in the way he should go: and when he is old, he will not depart from it" (Pr.22:6).**

(3) Children are to honor and obey their parents.

> **"Children, obey your parents in the Lord: for this is right. Honour thy father and mother; (which is the first commandment with promise;) That it may be well with thee, and thou mayest live long on the earth" (Ep.6:1-3).**
> **"Honour thy father and thy mother: that thy days may be long upon the land which the LORD thy God giveth thee" (Ex.20:12).**

(4) God's warning to parents is very strong: if a parent fails to take care of his or her family, he or she will face a worse judgment than an infidel (unbeliever).

> **"But if any provide not for his own, and specially for those of his own house, he hath denied the faith, and is worse than an infidel" (1 Ti.5:8).**

(5) God's Word to disobedient children is very strong.

> **"For the wrath of God is revealed from heaven against all ungodliness and unrighteousness of men, who hold the truth in unrighteousness....Backbiters, haters of God, despiteful, proud, boasters, inventors of evil things, disobedient to parents" (Ro.1:18, 30).**

---

2 **(3:1-6) Worship, Established - Instituted, Example—Worship, Renewed by Returned Exiles—Services, Worship, Established - Instituted—Exiles, Returned, Worship Established—Returned Exiles, Worship Established**: the second task of the returned exiles was to establish regular worship among themselves. As soon as they had settled down at their home sites, all the returnees assembled for worship in Jerusalem. For the faithful this was the moment for which their hearts had longed, the moment when God's people would once again be able to worship the LORD in freedom. And they were able to worship at the temple site in God's Holy City. The words *as one man* indicate that a strong sense of unity existed between the returnees. They were bound together by the Spirit of God for three great purposes: to restore the worship of the LORD, rebuild His temple and their nation. Significantly, they assembled in the most sacred of month for the Jews, the seventh month, Tishri, (September or October). On the first day the Jews celebrated the Feast of Trumpets; on the tenth day the Day of Atonement from the fifteenth to the twenty-first day the Feast of Tabernacles (see outline and notes—Nu.29; Le.23 for more discussion). Scripture gives a detailed description about how they reestablished worship at the site of the temple:

OUTLINE	SCRIPTURE	SCRIPTURE	OUTLINE
2. Task 2: To establish regular worship	And when the seventh month was come, and the children of Israel were in the cities, the people gathered themselves together as one man to Jerusalem.	evening.	
		4 They kept also the feast of tabernacles, as *it is* written, and *offered* the daily burnt offerings by number, according to the custom, as the duty of every day required;	b. The people celebrated the Feast of Tabernacles: A reminder of God's protection during the wilderness journeys
a. The religious & civil leaders—the High Priest Jeshua & the governor Zerubbabel along with their associates—rebuilt the altar	2 Then stood up Jeshua the son of Jozadak, and his brethren the priests, and Zerubbabel the son of Shealtiel, and his brethren, and builded the altar of the God of Israel, to offer burnt offerings thereon, as *it is* written in the law of Moses the man of God.	5 And afterward *offered* the continual burnt offering, both of the new moons, and of all the set feasts of the LORD that were consecrated, and of every one that willingly offered a freewill offering unto the LORD.	c. The people instituted all the regular worship services & sacrificial offerings, Le.23:1-44
1) Rebuilt it as instructed by God's law, His Word, Ex.27:1-8; 38:1-7; 20:25; De.27:5-6			
2) Rebuilt it at the old site	3 And they set the altar upon his bases; for fear *was* upon them because of the people of those countries: and they offered burnt offerings thereon unto the LORD, *even* burnt offerings morning and	6 From the first day of the seventh month began they to offer burnt offerings unto the LORD. But the foundation of the temple of the LORD was not *yet* laid.	1) Instituted on the first day of the seventh month
3) Rebuilt it despite fearing the hostile local residents who were unbelievers			
4) Offered the daily burnt sacrifices to the LORD			2) Instituted all services & worshipped the LORD even without a temple

a. The first step taken in reestablishing worship was the rebuilding of the LORD's altar. The people longed to approach the LORD through the substitute sacrifice; therefore, an altar was the first requirement (v.2). It was actually the religious and civil leaders, led by the High Priest Jeshua and the governor Zerrubbabel, who built the altar. Note several facts:

1) In anticipation of the worship assembly, the leadership evidently built the altar before the people arrived and constructed it exactly as God's Word dictated (Ex.27:1-8; 38:1-7; 20:25; De.27:5-6). Because the altar was large, it would no doubt have taken days to construct.

2) Great care was taken to rebuild the altar on the very site where the former altar had sat. Scripture actually says that the very same foundation was used (v.3).

3) The people worshipped despite the fact that they feared the local residents and other people who lived in the surrounding villages. These people were unbelievers who were hostile toward the Jews (v.3). They were foreigners who had been deported to Palestine by the Assyrians. Through the years the local residents and foreign deportees had intermarried and become known as the Samaritans (See DEEPER STUDY #2, *Samaritans*—Lu.10:33). They were worshippers of false gods who resented the Jewish returnees and were antagonistic toward them. Despite the animosity of their neighbors, the Jews overcame their fear and faithfully worshipped the LORD.

4) The daily burnt sacrifices were the first offerings presented to the LORD (v.3). This included both a morning and an evening sacrifice (Nu.28:2-4). Remember: the sacrifice symbolized the death of Jesus Christ, His sacrifice for us. He died for us, in our place, as our substitute. By dying for our sins, He frees us from sin and imperfection, which makes us acceptable to God (Jn.1:29; 1 Pe.2:24; 3:18).

b. The second step in reestablishing worship was celebrating the Festival of Tabernacles (v.4). During this particular festival, the people lived for seven days in tents or easily assembled booths. This feast celebrated God's care and protection over the Exodus Jews throughout their wilderness journey to the promised land of God. God loves and cares for His people; consequently, He overshadows them during times of hardship. No doubt, the significance of this festival was very meaningful and spoke to the hearts of these first returnees. They, like the Exodus Jews, had just been freed from captivity and returned to their homeland.

c. Through the following months, the returnees reinstituted the New Moon or monthly sacrifices (Nu.28:11-15), all the appointed feasts, and the freewill offerings. The first day of the seventh month was a monumental moment in Jewish history, for it was the day the returned Jews reestablished worship at the temple site and began to offer sacrifices to the LORD (v.6). They worshiped the LORD even without a temple.

Thought 1. A person who truly believes in the LORD is given a permanent relationship with Him. God's Spirit is placed within the heart of the believer, giving assurance of God's presence, love, care, guidance, protection, and provision. To keep this relationship alive and close, the believer worships the LORD, praising Him and seeking His strength to conquer all the trials and temptations of life. The genuine believer develops His relationship with the LORD through both personal and public worship.

(1) Listen to what God's Word says about personal worship, that is, prayer and personal Bible study.

"**Ask, and it shall be given you; seek, and ye shall find; knock, and it shall be opened unto you**" (Mt.7:7).

"**For ye have the poor always with you; but me ye have not always**" (Mt.26:11).

"**If ye abide in me, and my words abide in you, ye shall ask what ye will, and it shall be done unto you**" (Jn.15:7).

"**Study to shew thyself approved unto God, a workman that needeth not to be ashamed, rightly dividing the word of truth**" (2 Ti.2:15).

"**All scripture *is* given by inspiration of God, and *is* profitable for doctrine, for reproof, for correction, for instruction in righteousness**" (2 Ti.3:16).

"**Is any among you afflicted? let him pray. Is any merry? let him sing psalms**" (Js.5:13).

"**As newborn babes, desire the sincere milk of the word, that ye may grow thereby: If so be ye have tasted that the Lord *is* gracious**" (1 Pe.2:2-3).

"**Seek the LORD and his strength, seek his face continually**" (1 Chr.16:11).

"**He shall call upon me, and I will answer him: I *will be* with him in trouble; I will deliver him, and honour him**" (Ps.91:15).

(2) Listen to what God's Word says about public worship.

"**And he came to Nazareth, where he had been brought up: and, as his custom was, he went into the synagogue on the sabbath day, and stood up for to read**" (Lu.4:16).

"**Not forsaking the assembling of ourselves together, as the manner of some *is*; but exhorting *one another:* and so much the more, as ye see the day approaching**" (He.10:25).

"**Give unto the LORD the glory *due* unto his name: bring an offering, and come before him: worship the LORD in the beauty of holiness**" (1 Chr.16:29).

"**Surely goodness and mercy shall follow me all the days of my life: and I will dwell in the house of the LORD for ever**" (Ps.23:6).

"**LORD, I have loved the habitation of thy house, and the place where thine honour dwelleth**" (Ps.26:8).

"**One *thing* have I desired of the LORD, that will I seek after; that I may dwell in the house of the LORD all the days of my life, to behold the beauty of the LORD, and to enquire in his temple**" (Ps.27:4).

"O worship the LORD in the beauty of holiness: fear before him, all the earth" (Ps.96:9).
"I was glad when they said unto me, Let us go into the house of the LORD" (Ps.122:1).

3 (3:7-13) **Foundation, Essential, for Life—Life, Foundation of, Essential, Example—Temple, Second, Building of—Dedication Services, Second Temple—Foundation, of Second Temple, Celebrated**: the third task of the returned exiles was to build the temple, God's house of worship. There was no argument about the need to build the temple. It was one of the major purposes for which the exiles had returned. For years their hearts had longed to return to their homeland so they could rebuild their homes, nation, and the temple of the LORD.

OUTLINE	SCRIPTURE	SCRIPTURE	OUTLINE

3. Task 3: To begin building God's house of worship, laying a solid foundation
a. The preparations
  1) Hired skilled laborers: Masons & carpenters
  2) Made a trade agreement with Sidon & Tyre: To secure the best cedar logs
 	
b. The construction date: Second month of the second year, which was April–May (c.536 B.C.)
c. The project supervisors
  1) The two appointed superintendents: The governor Zerubbabel & the High Priest Jeshua or Joshua
  2) The project foremen: Levites 20 years old & older
 	
  3) The three chief foremen: The family heads of three clans
    • Jeshua oversaw his sons & brothers
    • Kadmiel oversaw his sons
    • Henadad oversaw his descendants
	7 They gave money also unto the masons, and to the carpenters; and meat, and drink, and oil, unto them of Zidon, and to them of Tyre, to bring cedar trees from Lebanon to the sea of Joppa, according to the grant that they had of Cyrus king of Persia.
	8 Now in the second year of their coming unto the house of God at Jerusalem, in the second month, began Zerubbabel the son of Shealtiel, and Jeshua the son of Jozadak, and the remnant of their brethren the priests and the Levites, and all they that were come out of the captivity unto Jerusalem; and appointed the Levites, from twenty years old and upward, to set forward the work of the house of the LORD.
	9 Then stood Jeshua *with* his sons and his brethren, Kadmiel and his sons, the sons of Judah, together, to set forward the workmen in the house of God: the sons of Henadad, *with* their sons and their brethren the Levites.
	10 And when the builders
		laid the foundation of the temple of the LORD, they set the priests in their apparel with trumpets, and the Levites the sons of Asaph with cymbals, to praise the LORD, after the ordinance of David king of Israel.
		11 And they sang together by course in praising and giving thanks unto the LORD; because *he is* good, for his mercy *endureth* for ever toward Israel. And all the people shouted with a great shout, when they praised the LORD, because the foundation of the house of the LORD was laid.
		12 But many of the priests and Levites and chief of the fathers, *who were* ancient men, that had seen the first house, when the foundation of this house was laid before their eyes, wept with a loud voice; and many shouted aloud for joy:
		13 So that the people could not discern the noise of the shout of joy from the noise of the weeping of the people: for the people shouted with a loud shout, and the noise was heard afar off.
			d. The dedication service celebrating the completion of the foundation
			  1) The priests dressed in their priestly robes, secured their trumpets, & took their places
			  2) The Levites secured their instruments & took their places
			  3) The musicians played & sang songs about God's goodness & His covenant, 1 Chr.16:34; 2 Chr.5:13; 7:3; Ps.106:1; 136:1; Je.33:10-11
			  4) The people shouted out praises to the LORD
			
			  5) The deep emotions shown by the whole assembly
			    • The older folks who remembered Solomon's temple wept: Was not as magnificent, Hag.2:1-9
			    • The younger folks shouted for joy
			
			    • The commotion of the weeping & shouting was so loud that it could be heard far away

a. Before the returnees came back home from worship, they made the decision to begin preparations for the rebuilding of the temple (v.7). An offering was given for reconstruction, and the people gave sacrificially.
⇒ Money was given to hire skilled workers: masons and carpenters.
⇒ Food, drink, and oil were given so that a trade agreement could be made with Sidon and Tyre for the cedar logs needed.

b. Preparations took a full seven months before construction could actually begin (v.8). The date was the second month of the second year after the returned exiles arrived in Jerusalem (April–May). Interestingly, this was the same month Solomon had begun the construction on the first temple.
c. The management of the project included two project superintendents, Zerubbabel and the High Priest Jeshua. In addition, the family heads of three clans and a number of Levites were appointed as foremen (vv.8-9).
d. Once construction finally began, the foundation was quickly laid. To the returnees, the event was so significant that they assembled together to celebrate the event in a dedication service (vv.10-13). Dressing in their priestly robes, the priests secured their trumpets and took their places for the worship service (v.10). The Levites also secured their instruments and took their places. Together they gave thanks and praised the LORD, singing a song that stressed the goodness and mercy of God: "He is good; for His mercy to Israel endures forever" (v.11; see 1 Chr.16:34; 2 Chr.5:13; 7:3; Ps.106:1; 136:1; Je.33:10-11). In response, the people shouted out a great praise to the LORD.
Note the deep but different emotions of the people. The older folks, who remembered how magnificent Solomon's Temple had been, were flooded with a deep longing for the old days.

But the younger crowd were as excited as they could be, for the temple of the LORD was at last under construction. Joy flooded their hearts. Because of the loud weeping and contrasting shouts of joy, a great commotion could be heard far away (v.13).

Thought 1. The returnees rejoiced over the foundation that had been laid for the temple. We too should rejoice over the foundation that God has laid for our lives. The foundation God has given us is Jesus Christ. He is the basis of our peace, security, provision, fulfillment, assurance, and hope of being accepted by God and given eternal life. Listen to what God's Holy Word says about Jesus Christ being the foundation of our lives.

"Therefore whosoever heareth these sayings of mine, and doeth them, I will liken him unto a wise man, which built his house upon a rock: And the rain descended, and the floods came, and the winds blew, and beat upon that house; and it fell not: for it was founded upon a rock. And every one that heareth these sayings of mine, and doeth them not, shall be likened unto a foolish man, which built his house upon the sand: And the rain descended, and the floods came, and the winds blew, and beat upon that house; and it fell: and great was the fall of it" (Mt.7:24-27).

"Jesus saith unto them, Did ye never read in the scriptures, The stone which the builders rejected, the same is become the head of the corner: this is the Lord's doing, and it is marvellous in our eyes?" (Mt.21:42).

"This is the stone which was set at nought of you builders, which is become the head of the corner. Neither is there salvation in any other: for there is none other name under heaven given among men, whereby we must be saved" (Ac.4:11-12).

"According to the grace of God which is given unto me, as a wise masterbuilder, I have laid the foundation, and another buildeth thereon. But let every man take heed how he buildeth thereupon. For other foundation can no man lay than that is laid, which is Jesus Christ. Now if any man build upon this foundation gold, silver, precious stones, wood, hay, stubble; Every man's work shall be made manifest: for the day shall declare it, because it shall be revealed by fire; and the fire shall try every man's work of what sort it is. If any man's work abide which he hath built thereupon, he shall receive a reward. If any man's work shall be burned, he shall suffer loss: but he himself shall be saved; yet so as by fire" (1 Co.3:10-15).

"And are built upon the foundation of the apostles and prophets, Jesus Christ himself being the chief corner *stone;* In whom all the building fitly framed together groweth unto an holy temple in the Lord: In whom ye also are builded together for an habitation of God through the Spirit" (Ep.2:20-22).

"Nevertheless the foundation of God standeth sure, having this seal, The Lord knoweth them that are his. And, Let every one that nameth the name of Christ depart from iniquity" (2 Ti.2:19).

"To whom coming, *as unto* a living stone, disallowed indeed of men, but chosen of God, *and* precious, Ye also, as lively stones, are built up a spiritual house, an holy priesthood, to offer up spiritual sacrifices, acceptable to God by Jesus Christ. Wherefore also it is contained in the scripture, Behold, I lay in Sion a chief corner stone, elect, precious: and he that believeth on him shall not be confounded. Unto you therefore which believe *he is* precious: but unto them which be disobedient, the stone which the builders disallowed, the same is made the head of the corner, And a stone of stumbling, and a rock of offence, *even to them* which stumble at the word, being disobedient: whereunto also they were appointed" (1 Pe.2:4-8).

CHAPTER 4

C. The Continuing Opposition Faced by the Returned Exiles: Being Attacked, Persecuted for One's Faith, 4:1-24

1. Attack 1: Being urged to co-operate, compromise with unbelievers
 a. The enemies' devious appeal: The Samaritans heard about the rebuilding of the temple & offered to help
  1) They were subversive enemies seeking to infiltrate the work force & derail the project
  2) They claimed to worship the same God (but not Him alone—they also worshipped other gods), 2 K. 17:33; also see 17:24-41
 b. The Jewish leaders' response: They rejected the offer
  1) Because the local residents had nothing to do with the temple: Were not true worshippers of the LORD
  2) Because Cyrus had commissioned the Jews alone to build the temple
2. Attack 2: Being threatened, coerced, harassed, & frightened
 a. The enemies' purpose: To discourage, stop the project
 b. The enemies' scheme: Bribed Persian officials to harass & intimidate the exile returnees
 c. The enemies' persistence: Harassed the Jews continually from Cyrus' to Darius' reign
3. Attack 3: Being falsely accused, lied about, & slandered
 a. The false accusation during the reign of Xerxes: Only mentioned, not discussed
 b. The false accusation during the reign of Artaxerxes: Sent in a letter of complaint
  1) The enemy leaders who wrote the letter are actually named
  2) The letter was written in Aramaic
  3) The letter was officially sent from the two highest Persian officials: Rehum, most likely the Persian governor, & Shimshai, the secretary
   • They claimed that the letter of complaint was not from a small, isolated

Now when the adversaries of Judah and Benjamin heard that the children of the captivity builded the temple unto the LORD God of Israel;
2 Then they came to Zerubbabel and to the chief of the fathers and said unto them, Let us build with you: for we seek your God, as ye *do;* and we do sacrifice unto him since the days of Esar-haddon king of Assur, which brought us up hither.
3 But Zerubbabel, and Jesua, and the rest of the chief of the fathers of Israel, said unto them, Ye have nothing to do with us to build an house unto our God; but we ourselves together will build unto the LORD God of Israel, as king Cyrus the king of Persia hath commanded us.
4 Then the people of the land weakened the hands of the people of Judah, and troubled them in building,
5 And hired counsellors against them, to frustrate their purpose, all the days of Cyrus king of Persia, even until the reign of Darius king of Persia.
6 And in the reign of Ahasuerus, in the beginning of his reign, wrote they *unto him* an accusation against the inhabitants of Judah and Jerusalem.
7 And in the days of Artaxerxes wrote Bishlam, Mithredath, Tabeel, and the rest of their companions, unto Artaxerxes king of Persia; and the writing of the letter *was* written in the Syrian tongue, and interpreted in the Syrian tongue.
8 Rehum the chancellor and Shimshai the scribe wrote a letter against Jerusalem to Artaxerxes the king in this sort:
9 Then *wrote* Rehum the chancellor, and Shimshai the scribe, and the rest of their companions; the Dinaites, the

Apharsathchites, the Tarpelites, the Apharsites, the Archevites, the Babylonians, the Susanchites, the Dehavites, *and* the Elamites,
10 And the rest of the nations whom the great and noble Asnapper brought over, and set in the cities of Samaria, and the rest *that are* on this side the river, and at such a time.
11 This *is* the copy of the letter that they sent unto him, *even* unto Artaxerxes the king; Thy servants the men on this side the river, and at such a time.
12 Be it known unto the king, that the Jews which came up from thee to us are come unto Jerusalem, building the rebellious and the bad city, and have set up the walls *thereof,* and joined the foundations.
13 Be it known now unto the king, that, if this city be builded, and the walls set up *again, then* will they not pay toll, tribute, and custom, and *so* thou shalt endamage the revenue of the kings.
14 Now because we have maintenance from *the king's* palace, and it was not meet for us to see the king's dishonour, therefore have we sent and certified the king;
15 That search may be made in the book of the records of thy fathers: so shalt thou find in the book of the records, and know that this city *is* a rebellious city, and hurtful unto kings and provinces, and that they have moved sedition within the same of old time: for which cause was this city destroyed.
16 We certify the king that, if this city be builded *again,* and the walls thereof set up, by this means thou shalt have no portion on this side the river.
17 *Then* sent the king an answer unto Rehum the chancellor, and *to* Shimshai the scribe, and *to* the rest of their companions that dwell in Samaria, and *unto* the rest beyond the river, Peace, and at such a time.
18 The letter which ye sent unto us hath been plainly read before me.

group but from leaders & officials throughout the Persian empire

 • They claimed that the complaint was from the local residents: The people who had been relocated by the Assyrian king Ashurbanipal (Asnapper) 200 years earlier
 4) The letter's complaint & warning

 • That the Jews were rebuilding the rebellious city of Jerusalem: Restoring the walls & repairing the foundations

 • That the Jews would disregard or refuse to pay their taxes if the city was rebuilt

 • That the honor of the king was at stake: They (the Samaritans) were therefore informing him about the danger created by the Jews

 • That a search of the royal records would reveal that the Jews were a rebellious people, which was why Jerusalem had been destroyed earlier

 • That the rebellious Jews might lead a revolt & the king might lose land west of the Euphrates

 c. The response & reply of King Artaxerxes
  1) His greeting to all the officials of the complaint

  2) His receipt of the letter: Had been translated & read to him

| 3) His immediate response: Had ordered the royal records searched
• Had found that Jerusalem had indeed been a source of rebellion down through history
• Had discovered that Jerusalem's kings had been powerful, ruling over the entire land west of the Euphrates

4) His demand, royal order
• The governor was to immediately stop the Jews from rebuilding Jerusalem | 19 And I commanded, and search hath been made, and it is found that this city of old time hath made insurrection against kings, and *that* rebellion and sedition have been made therein.
20 There have been mighty kings also over Jerusalem, which have ruled over all *countries* beyond the river; and toll, tribute, and custom, was paid unto them.
21 Give ye now commandment to cause these men to cease, and that this city be not builded, until *another* commandment shall be given | from me.
22 Take heed now that ye fail not to do this: why should damage grow to the hurt of the kings?
23 Now when the copy of king Artaxerxes' letter *was* read before Rehum, and Shimshai the scribe, and their companions, they went up in haste to Jerusalem unto the Jews, and made them to cease by force and power.
24 Then ceased the work of the house of God which *is* at Jerusalem. So it ceased unto the second year of the reign of Darius king of Persia. | • The governor was to act quickly, not delay: Lest the threat grow & royal interests be damaged
d. The immediate result of the opposition's efforts
1) The returned exiles were forced to stop rebuilding Jerusalem: Stopped by armed military force, Ne.1:1-3

2) The rebuilding of the temple was halted—at a standstill— for about 20 years (c.530–522 B.C.): Until the second year of Darius' reign |

DIVISION I

THE FIRST RETURN OF EXILES FROM CAPTIVITY AND THEIR RESETTLEMENT—LED BY ZERUBBABEL, 1:1–6:22

C. The Continuing Opposition Faced by the Returned Exiles: Being Attacked, Persecuted for One's Faith, 4:1-24

(4:1-24) **Introduction**: persecution is a terrible evil; yet all across the world people are persecuted on a regular basis. Even *ethnic cleansing* is taking place, that is, the extermination of people because they are of a different race, religion, nationality or culture. However, persecution also takes on many other forms, such as:

⇒ ridicule
⇒ embarrassment
⇒ shame
⇒ mockery
⇒ profanity
⇒ insults

⇒ physical, mental, and emotional abuse
⇒ discrimination
⇒ harassment
⇒ hatred
⇒ violent and deadly assaults
⇒ sexual mistreatment and exploitation

The list could go on and on. And tragically whether aimed at a group of people, animals, organizations, beliefs, or principles, persecution always harms our fellow human beings, people who are of equal value and worth as any of us. Every human being is loved by God. No matter the color of another person's skin, his religion, culture, or any other difference, God longs for all of us to respond to His love by loving Him and loving one another. Godly and brotherly love are to fill the heart of every human being. No brother or sister is to be persecuted by anyone. Nevertheless, it is a sad reality of life. Being attacked and persecuted is the subject of the present Scripture.

Remember, the foundation of the temple had just been completed and the Jewish returnees had held a dedication service to celebrate the wonderful event. But just when things seemed to be going so well, opposition reared its ugly head and halted the project. This is, *The Continuing Opposition Faced by the Returned Exiles: Being Attacked, Persecuted for One's Faith*, 4:1-24.

1. Attack 1: being urged to cooperate, compromise with unbelievers (vv.1-3).
2. Attack 2: being threatened, coerced, harassed, and frightened (vv.4-5).
3. Attack 3: being falsely accused, lied about, and slandered (vv.6-24).

1 (4:1-3) **Compromise, Temptation to, Rejected—Temptation, to Compromise, Rejected—Unbelievers, Influence of, Rejected—Separation, Duty, Not to Compromise—Worship, Compromise of, Rejected—False Profession, Example—Temptation, to Compromise, Example of—Syncretism, of Worship, Rejected—Religion, Mixed, Rejected—Exiles, Returned, Opposition to—Jews, Returned Exiles, Opposition**: the first attack against the Jews was a friendly, enticing suggestion to cooperate and compromise with their neighbors. But this was a subtle, deceptive, and very dangerous scheme for Scripture says that these neighbors were "enemies" of the Jews. They stood opposed to the Jews' return to the promised land and their rebuilding the temple. Two factors would have stirred opposition from the people or neighbors nearby:

⇒ A settlement of 50,000 Jews would have been a threat to the power, control, and authority of the surrounding communities. For that reason, the political and business leaders as well as large landowners would have strongly opposed their unexpected arrival.
⇒ The setting into which the Jews were returning was volatile, as the neighboring people were obviously anti-Semitic, deeply prejudiced against the Jews.

As soon as the Jews arrived back in the promised land, strong opposition began to form against them. This opposition was determined to make the Jews' fail in their efforts to rebuild their cities and temple. When the surrounding people heard about the Jews rebuilding their temple, they saw an opportunity to launch an insidious, deceptive scheme against the building project. Pretending to be friendly and cooperative neighbors, they offered to help the Jews build their temple. From all appearances their offer seemed reasonable, for they claimed to worship the same God as the Jews. By worshipping the same God, the temple could serve as their worship center as well as the worship center for the Jews. But appearances are not always what they seem. These people were enemies of the Jews, subversives who were seeking to infiltrate the workforce in order to derail the building project.

Who were these enemies of the Jews? They were the people who had lived in the land since the fall of Samaria, the capital of the Northern Kingdom of Israel (722 B.C.). When the Northern Kingdom fell, the Assyrians exiled most of the Israelites and brought in people from other lands to repopulate Israel. Through succeeding generations, the Jews who had been left behind intermarried with the new inhabitants. Thus, the Samaritans became a mixed race, and down through the years their religion became mixed as well. Although they claimed to worship the same God as the Jews, in truth they worshipped many so-called gods, all false. They did not worship the only living and true God, the LORD God Himself (Jehovah, Yahweh) (see 2 K.17:29, 32-34, 41, esp.v.33; also 2 K.17:24-41; Jn.4:22).

If the Samaritans had been allowed to help the Jews, they would have become close friends through socializing and mingling together. Eventually, the wicked lifestyle and false worship of the Samaritans would have influenced the Jews. As a result, the Jews too would have turned away from the LORD. They would have become corrupt and disobedient before Him, worshipping other gods and disobeying the commandments of God's Holy Word. Through intermarriage, they would have eventually lost their distinctiveness as the people of God.

Note this fact: if the deceptive scheme of the enemy had worked, then the distinctiveness of the Jewish race would have been lost. But as Scripture says, "salvation is of the Jews" (Jn.4:22). The gift of the Bible, God's Holy Word, and the coming of the Savior of the world, the Lord Jesus Christ, was to come through the Jewish race. Therefore, the Jewish returnees rejected the offer of the Samaritans and the remnant was preserved as Isaiah had prophesied (Is.10:20-21; 10:33–11:1). Obviously, they saw through the enemy's devious offer to help them rebuild the temple (v.3). The Jews gave two reasons for rejecting the offer:

⇒ The Samaritans had nothing to do with the temple, had no part in it. They were not true worshippers of the LORD, for true worshippers worshipped the LORD and Him alone. The Samaritans did not acknowledge that there is only one true and living God, only one true and living Savior of the world.

⇒ King Cyrus of Persia had commissioned the Jews alone to build the temple.

OUTLINE	SCRIPTURE	SCRIPTURE	OUTLINE
1. Attack 1: Being urged to co-operate, compromise with unbelievers a. The enemies' devious appeal: The Samaritans heard about the rebuilding of the temple & offered to help 1) They were subversive enemies seeking to infiltrate the work force & derail the project 2) They claimed to worship	Now when the adversaries of Judah and Benjamin heard that the children of the captivity builded the temple unto the LORD God of Israel; 2 Then they came to Zerubbabel, and to the chief of the fathers, and said unto them, Let us build with you: for we seek your God, as ye *do;* and we do sacrifice unto him since the	days of Esar-haddon king of Assur, which brought us up hither. 3 But Zerubbabel, and Jeshua, and the rest of the chief of the fathers of Israel, said unto them, Ye have nothing to do with us to build an house unto our God; but we ourselves together will build unto the LORD God of Israel, as king Cyrus the king of Persia hath commanded us.	the same God (but not Him alone—they also worshipped other gods), 2 K. 17:33; also see 17:24-41 b. The Jewish leaders' response: They rejected the offer 1) Because the local residents had nothing to do with the temple: Were not true worshippers of the LORD 2) Because Cyrus had commissioned the Jews alone

Thought 1. There is a strong lesson for us in this point. We must not give in to worldly compromise with unbelievers. Mingling, socializing, fellowshipping, and forming partnerships with unbelievers will undermine our lives as Christians. Sin looks good, tastes good, and feels good, so when unbelievers invite us to participate in some sinful behavior, we will be enticed to join in with them. And the more we mingle and socialize with unbelievers, the stronger the temptation will be. Resistance will become increasingly more difficult, at times almost impossible. We will find ourselves lusting after the object of temptation, whether a person or an article or something intangible. Then when lust conceives, it becomes sin. We must be ever watchful: if we compromise with the world and its wickedness, we will fall and doom ourselves to face the judgment of God. Listen to what God's Holy Word says about compromising with worldliness and sin:

"**And take heed to yourselves, lest at any time your hearts be overcharged with surfeiting, and drunkenness, and cares of this life, and so that day come upon you unawares**" (Lu.21:34).

"**And be not conformed to this world: but be ye transformed by the renewing of your mind, that ye may prove what *is* that good, and acceptable, and perfect, will of God**" (Ro.12:2).

"**And they that use this world, as not abusing *it:* for the fashion of this world passeth away**" (1 Co.7:31).

"**But God forbid that I should glory, save in the cross of our Lord Jesus Christ, by whom the world is crucified unto me, and I unto the world**" (Ga.6:14).

"**And you *hath he quickened,* who were dead in trespasses and sins; Wherein in time past ye walked according to the course of this world, according to the prince of the power of the air, the spirit that now worketh in the children of disobedience: Among whom also we all had our conversation in times past in the lusts of our flesh, fulfilling the desires of the flesh and of the mind; and were by nature the children of wrath, even as others**" (Ep.2:1-3).

"No man that warreth entangleth himself with the affairs of *this* life; that he may please him who hath chosen him to be a soldier" (2 Ti.2:4).

"Nevertheless the foundation of God standeth sure, having this seal, The Lord knoweth them that are his. And, Let every one that nameth the name of Christ depart from iniquity" (2 Ti.2:19).

"By faith Moses, when he was come to years, refused to be called the son of Pharaoh's daughter; Choosing rather to suffer affliction with the people of God, than to enjoy the pleasures of sin for a season" (He.11:24-25).

"Ye adulterers and adulteresses, know ye not that the friendship of the world is enmity with God? whosoever therefore will be a friend of the world is the enemy of God" (Js.4:4).

"Love not the world, neither the things *that are* in the world. If any man love the world, the love of the Father is not in him. For all that *is* in the world, the lust of the flesh, and the lust of the eyes, and the pride of life, is not of the Father, but is of the world" (1 Jn.2:15-16).

"Thou shalt not follow a multitude to *do* evil; neither shalt thou speak in a cause to decline after many to wrest *judgment*" (Ex.23:2).

"Take heed to thyself that thou be not snared by following them, after that they be destroyed from before thee; and that thou enquire not after their gods, saying, How did these nations serve their gods? even so will I do likewise" (De.12:30).

"And they rejected his statutes, and his covenant that he made with their fathers, and his testimonies which he testified against them; and they followed vanity, and became vain, and went after the heathen that *were* round about them, *concerning* whom the LORD had charged them, that they should not do like them" (2 K.17:15).

2 (4:4-5) **Enemy, Spiritual, Attack of—Fear, Cause, Spiritual Enemies—Harassment, Cause, Spiritual Enemies— Coercion, Cause, Spiritual Enemies—Jews, Returned Exiles, Opposition Faced by—Returnees, Jewish, Opposition Faced by—Threats, Cause, Spiritual Enemies**: the second attack by the Samaritans was to use intimidation, coercion, and harassment to strike fear in the hearts of the Jews. If enough fear could be aroused in the hearts of the returnees, perhaps they would stop the projects of rebuilding the temple and the city of Jerusalem. In day-to-day contacts, the Samaritans apparently threatened and hassled the Jewish workers. Naturally, any Jew who was spiritually weak and lacked commitment to the project would tend to quit the job and return home, seeking other employment. In addition to personal threats, the Samaritans actually bribed Persian officials to agitate and intimidate the exile returnees (v.5). Just how they intimidated and worked against the Jews is not stated. Most likely they sought to persuade the officials of Tyre and Sidon to refuse the requests of the Jews for building materials and supplies for the temple. In addition, they clearly sought to influence the Persian court against the Jewish returnees. Note that the enemies' opposition was not temporary, not just one or two attacks. It was a persistent opposition, a harassment that began during the reign of King Cyrus (559– 530 B.C.) and continue through the reign of King Darius (521–486 B.C.). The conflict would become so fierce that construction would stop in 530 B.C. and not resume again until 520 B.C., which was the second year of Darius reign (v.24). Thus the opposition by the Samaritan enemies was successful, at least for a period of time. This will be seen in the third attack covered in the next point.

OUTLINE	SCRIPTURE	SCRIPTURE	OUTLINE
2. Attack 2: Being threatened, coerced, harassed, & frightened a. The enemies' purpose: To discourage, stop the project b. The enemies' scheme: Bribed	4 Then the people of the land weakened the hands of the people of Judah, and troubled them in building, 5 And hired counsellors	against them, to frustrate their purpose, all the days of Cyrus king of Persia, even until the reign of Darius king of Persia.	Persian officials to harass & intimidate the exile returnees c. The enemies' persistence: Harassed the Jews continually from Cyrus' to Darius' reign

Thought 1. We must not be overcome by fear, nor by the harassment or threats of enemies. Whether the enemy is a man or a spiritual foe, we must not allow fear to dominate our lives, to defeat us, to discourage us, or to make us feel helpless. This is the clear teaching of God's Holy Word. God loves us and cares for us. He promises to uphold us if we will only call upon Him. then He promises to give us the strength to stand up against any attack and to be victorious in the face of harassment and fear. Listen to what God's Holy Word says:

"But the very hairs of your head are all numbered. Fear ye not therefore, ye are of more value than many sparrows" (Mt.10:30-31).

"For God hath not given us the spirit of fear; but of power, and of love, and of a sound mind" (2 Ti.1:7).

"And when I saw him [Jesus Christ], I fell at his feet as dead. And he laid his right hand upon me, saying unto me, Fear not; I am the first and the last: I *am* he that liveth, and was dead; and, behold, I am alive for evermore, Amen; and have the keys of hell and of death" (Re.1:17-18).

"And he answered, Fear not: for they that *be* with us *are* more than they that *be* with them" (2 K.6:16).

"I will not be afraid of ten thousands of people, that have set *themselves* against me round about" (Ps.3:6).

"The LORD *is* my light and my salvation; whom shall I fear? the LORD *is* the strength of my life; of whom shall I be afraid? When the wicked, *even* mine enemies and my foes, came upon me to eat up my flesh, they stumbled and fell. Though an host should encamp against me, my heart shall not fear: though war should rise against me, in this *will* I *be* confident" (Ps.27:1-3).

"I will say of the LORD, *He is* my refuge and my fortress: my God; in him will I trust. Surely he shall deliver thee from the snare of the fowler, *and* from the noisome pestilence. He shall cover thee with his feathers, and under his wings shalt thou trust: his truth *shall be thy* shield and buckler. Thou shalt not be afraid for the terror by night; *nor* for the arrow *that* flieth by day; Nor for the pestilence *that* walketh in darkness; *nor* for the destruction *that* wasteth at noonday" (Ps.91:2-6).

"The LORD *is* on my side; I will not fear: what can man do unto me?" (Ps.118:6).

"When thou liest down, thou shalt not be afraid: yea, thou shalt lie down, and thy sleep shall be sweet" (Pr.3:24).

"Behold, God *is* my salvation; I will trust, and not be afraid: for the LORD JEHOVAH *is* my strength and *my* song; he also is become my salvation" (Is.12:2).

"Fear thou not; for I *am* with thee: be not dismayed; for I *am* thy God: I will strengthen thee; yea, I will help thee; yea, I will uphold thee with the right hand of my righteousness" (Is.41:10).

"For I the LORD thy God will hold thy right hand, saying unto thee, Fear not; I will help thee" (Is.41:13).

"Fear not: for I have redeemed thee, I have called *thee* by thy name; thou *art* mine. When thou passest through the waters, I *will be* with thee; and through the rivers, they shall not overflow thee: when thou walkest through the fire, thou shalt not be burned; neither shall the flame kindle upon thee" (Is.43:1-2).

3 **(4:6-24) Accusation, False, Example of—Lies, Against the Jews, Example—Slander, Against the Jews, Example—Persecution, of the Jews, Example**: the third attack against the Jews was that of being falsely accused, lied about, and slandered. Even after the temple had been completed, the opposition toward the Jewish returnees continued for many years and through the reigns of several Persian kings:

⇒ Darius, the king who ruled Persia from 522 to 486 B.C. (vv.5, 24).
⇒ Xerxes or Ahasuerus, the king who married Esther and ruled from 486 to 465 B.C.
⇒ Artaxerxes I, the king who ruled from 465 to 424 B.C. (vv.7-23).

The opposition by the Samaritans was launched not only against rebuilding the temple but also against rebuilding Jerusalem and its wall. As long as the Jews were attempting to resettle in the promised land, rebuilding their cities, nation, and temple, the enemy was going to continue attacking them. Scripture shows just how determined and persistent the opposition was:

OUTLINE	SCRIPTURE	SCRIPTURE	OUTLINE
3. Attack 3: Being falsely accused, lied about, & slandered a. The false accusation during the reign of Xerxes: Only mentioned, not discussed b. The false accusation during the reign of Artaxerxes: Sent in a letter of complaint 1) The enemy leaders who wrote the letter are actually named 2) The letter was written in Aramaic 3) The letter was officially sent from the two highest Persian officials: Rehum, most likely the Persian governor, & Shimshai, the secretary • They claimed that the letter of complaint was not from a small, isolated group but from leaders & officials throughout the Persian empire • They claimed that the complaint was from the local residents: The people who had been relocated by the Assyrian king	6 And in the reign of Ahasuerus, in the beginning of his reign, wrote they *unto him* an accusation against the inhabitants of Judah and Jerusalem. 7 And in the days of Artaxerxes wrote Bishlam, Mithredath, Tabeel, and the rest of their companions, unto Artaxerxes king of Persia; and the writing of the letter *was* written in the Syrian tongue, and interpreted in the Syrian tongue. 8 Rehum the chancellor and Shimshai the scribe wrote a letter against Jerusalem to Artaxerxes the king in this sort: 9 Then *wrote* Rehum the chancellor, and Shimshai the scribe, and the rest of their companions; the Dinaites, the Apharsathchites, the Tarpelites, the Apharsites, the Archevites, the Babylonians, the Susanchites, the Dehavites, *and* the Elamites, 10 And the rest of the nations whom the great and noble Asnapper brought over, and set in the cities of Samaria, and the rest *that are* on	this side the river, and at such a time. 11 This *is* the copy of the letter that they sent unto him, *even* unto Artaxerxes the king; Thy servants the men on this side the river, and at such a time. 12 Be it known unto the king, that the Jews which came up from thee to us are come unto Jerusalem, building the rebellious and the bad city, and have set up the walls *thereof,* and joined the foundations. 13 Be it known now unto the king, that, if this city be builded, and the walls set up *again,* then will they not pay toll, tribute, and custom, and *so* thou shalt endamage the revenue of the kings. 14 Now because we have maintenance from *the king's* palace, and it was not meet for us to see the king's dishonour, therefore have we sent and certified the king; 15 That search may be made in the book of the records of thy fathers: so shalt thou find in the book of the records, and know that this city *is* a	Ashurbanipal (Asnapper) 200 years earlier 4) The letter's complaint & warning • That the Jews were rebuilding the rebellious city of Jerusalem: Restoring the walls & repairing the foundations • That the Jews would disregard or refuse to pay their taxes if the city was rebuilt • That the honor of the king was at stake: They (the Samaritans) were therefore informing him about the danger created by the Jews • That a search of the royal records would reveal that the Jews were a rebellious people, which was why Jerusa-

OUTLINE	SCRIPTURE	SCRIPTURE	OUTLINE
lem had been destroyed earlier	rebellious city, and hurtful unto kings and provinces, and that they have moved sedition within the same of old time: for which cause was this city destroyed.	20 There have been mighty kings also over Jerusalem, which have ruled over all *countries* beyond the river; and toll, tribute, and custom, was paid unto them.	• Had discovered that Jerusalem's kings had been powerful, ruling over the entire land west of the Euphrates
• That the rebellious Jews might lead a revolt & the king might lose land west of the Euphrates	16 We certify the king that, if this city be builded *again*, and the walls thereof set up, by this means thou shalt have no portion on this side the river.	21 Give ye now commandment to cause these men to cease, and that this city be not builded, until *another* commandment shall be given from me.	4) His demand, royal order • The governor was to immediately stop the Jews from rebuilding Jerusalem
c. The response & reply of King Artaxerxes 1) His greeting to all the officials of the complaint	17 *Then* sent the king an answer unto Rehum the chancellor, and *to* Shimshai the scribe, and *to* the rest of their companions that dwell in Samaria, and *unto* the rest beyond the river, Peace, and at such a time.	22 Take heed now that ye fail not to do this: why should damage grow to the hurt of the kings?	• The governor was to act quickly, not delay: Lest the threat grow & royal interests be damaged
2) His receipt of the letter: Had been translated & read to him	18 The letter which ye sent unto us hath been plainly read before me.	23 Now when the copy of king Artaxerxes' letter *was* read before Rehum, and Shimshai the scribe, and their companions, they went up in haste to Jerusalem unto the Jews, and made them to cease by force and power.	d. The immediate result of the opposition's efforts 1) The returned exiles were forced to stop rebuilding Jerusalem: Stopped by armed military force, Ne.1:1-3
3) His immediate response: Had ordered the royal records searched • Had found that Jerusalem had indeed been a source of rebellion down through history	19 And I commanded, and search hath been made, and it is found that this city of old time hath made insurrection against kings, and *that* rebellion and sedition have been made therein.	24 Then ceased the work of the house of God which *is* at Jerusalem. So it ceased unto the second year of the reign of Darius king of Persia.	2) The rebuilding of the temple was halted—at a standstill— for about 20 years (c.530–522 B.C.): Until the second year of Darius' reign

a. Some years later, right after King Xerxes or Ahasuerus took the throne, the Samaritan enemies wrote a letter to the king falsely accusing the Jews of an unlawful act. Just what the false accusation was is not discussed, nor is Xerxes' response to the letter given. But whatever the charge, it apparently stopped the work on the building projects. Thus, in this case, the attack by the opposition was successful.

b. During the reign of King Artaxerxes, another letter making a false accusation about the Jews was sent (vv.7-16). Three local Samaritan leaders took the initiative in launching this serious complaint. But they apparently had the support of all the local leadership. The three leaders named were Bishlam, Mithredath, and Tabeel.

Seeking even more support, these three men convinced the two highest ranking Persian officials of the local province to write the letter. Hence the letter, written in the Aramaic language, was sent from the Persian governor Rehum and the secretary Shimshai (v.8). By doing this, the letter of complaint against the Jews had the highest authority possible from the local province of which Judah was a part. The letter no doubt carried great weight with the king.

In beginning the letter, the governor and secretary stated that the grievance was not from just a small, isolated group. On the contrary, it was from leaders and officials from all over the Persian Empire (v.9). In addition, the complaint was coming from the local residents, the very people who had been relocated in the city of Samaria and throughout the Province of Trans-Euphrates. These people had been relocated to populate the area some 200 years earlier by the Assyrian King Ashurbanipal (v.10; see 2 Chr.33:11).

Suggesting that they were concerned only with the welfare of the king and the empire, the governor and secretary declared they were servants of the king. They then made five accusations against the Jews (vv.11-16):
⇒ The Jews were rebuilding the rebellious city of Jerusalem, restoring the walls and repairing the foundations (v.12).
⇒ If the city and its walls were rebuilt, the Jews would rebel and refuse to pay their taxes (v.13).
⇒ The honor of the king was at stake; therefore they were informing him of danger on the horizon if the Jews continued to rebuild their nation. (v.14).
⇒ A search of the royal records would reveal that the Jews were a rebellious people, which was the very reason that Jerusalem had been earlier destroyed (v.15).
⇒ The rebellious Jews might lead a revolt and the king might lose all the land west of the Euphrates River (v.16).

c. After receiving the letter, King Artaxerxes responded by greeting all the officials of the complaint and informing them that the letter had been translated and read to him (vv.17-22). He also followed their advice by ordering the royal records searched and found that Jerusalem had indeed been a hotbed of rebellion down through history (vv.19-20). Not surprisingly, the search also revealed that Jerusalem's kings had been powerful rulers, dominating the entire land west of the Euphrates. In light of all he had read and heard, the king agreed with the complaint. The governor was to issue an immediate order to stop the rebuilding of Jerusalem. And the order was to remain in effect until the king himself reversed it. Moreover, the governor must act quickly, not delaying lest the threat grow and royal interest be damaged (vv.21-22).

d. As soon as King Xerxes' response reached the local governor and secretary, they took immediate action. Sadly the returning exiles were compelled to stop rebuilding Jerusalem (vv.23-24). Note that military force was used to stop the work. Apparently, this included destroying the sections of wall that had already been rebuilt (v.23; also see Ne.1:1-3; 2:12-16). But remember this fact: long before the work order was given to stop the rebuilding of Jerusalem and its walls, the rebuilding of the temple had been brought to a halt (v.24). For a period of about 10 years, no work whatsoever took place on the temple (c.530-520 B.C.). It had been stopped at the end of King Cyrus' reign (c.530 B.C.) and did not resume until King Darius became king (c.520 B.C.). Note that verses 6–23 discuss the opposition to the Jews' rebuilding Jerusalem and its walls, whereas verse 24 returns to the discussion about rebuilding the temple.

Thought 1. The Jewish returnees were falsely accused and slandered. Just as they suffered opposition and persecution, so will the believer. No matter who we are, if we are true followers of the LORD, we will suffer some degree of persecution. Some will...
- falsely accuse, lie about, and slander us
- ridicule and mock us
- spread rumors and gossip about us
- oppose, argue with, and take a stand against us
- seek to embarrass and shame us
- attempt to turn our friends and others away from us

Persecution may also involve physical violence, assaults, or perhaps even call upon us to pay the ultimate sacrifice with our lives. We must bear in mind that when we seek to keep the commandments of God, living righteous and holy lives, those who live in sin and wickedness are bound to oppose us. Righteousness always stands opposed to sinful behavior, and the commandments of God condemn wicked behavior. God warns us against sin, death, and judgment to come. No person living a sinful, wicked life wants to hear God's message of righteousness or His warning of the coming day of wrath against all wicked behavior. As a result, the wicked of this earth oppose any of us who live and proclaim the righteousness and judgment of God. As genuine believers, we must be prepared for persecution.

"Behold, I send you forth as sheep in the midst of wolves: be ye therefore wise as serpents, and harmless as doves. But beware of men: for they will deliver you up to the councils, and they will scourge you in their synagogues; And ye shall be brought before governors and kings for my sake, for a testimony against them and the Gentiles. But when they deliver you up, take no thought how or what ye shall speak: for it shall be given you in that same hour what ye shall speak. For it is not ye that speak, but the Spirit of your Father which speaketh in you. And the brother shall deliver up the brother to death, and the father the child: and the children shall rise up against *their* parents, and cause them to be put to death. And ye shall be hated of all *men* for my name's sake: but he that endureth to the end shall be saved" (Mt.10:16-22).

"Then shall they deliver you up to be afflicted, and shall kill you: and ye shall be hated of all nations for my name's sake" (Mt.24:9).

"Blessed are ye, when men shall hate you, and when they shall separate you *from their company,* and shall reproach *you,* and cast out your name as evil, for the Son of man's sake" (Lu.6:22).

"But before all these, they shall lay their hands on you, and persecute *you,* delivering *you* up to the synagogues, and into prisons, being brought before kings and rulers for my name's sake" (Lu.21:12).

"Remember the word that I said unto you, The servant is not greater than his lord. If they have persecuted me, they will also persecute you; if they have kept my saying, they will keep yours also" (Jn.15:20).

"They shall put you out of the synagogues: yea, the time cometh, that whosoever killeth you will think that he doeth God service" (Jn.16:2).

"The Spirit itself beareth witness with our spirit, that we are the children of God: And if children, then heirs; heirs of God, and joint-heirs with Christ; if so be that we suffer with *him,* that we may be also glorified together" (Ro.8:16-17).

"For unto you it is given in the behalf of Christ, not only to believe on him, but also to suffer for his sake" (Ph.1:29).

"For therefore we both labour and suffer reproach, because we trust in the living God, who is the Saviour of all men, specially of those that believe" (1 Ti.4:10).

"Yea, and all that will live godly in Christ Jesus shall suffer persecution" (2 Ti.3:12).

"By faith Moses, when he was come to years, refused to be called the son of Pharaoh's daughter; Choosing rather to suffer affliction with the people of God, than to enjoy the pleasures of sin for a season; Esteeming the reproach of Christ greater riches than the treasures in Egypt: for he had respect unto the recompence of the reward" (He.11:24-26).

"Take, my brethren, the prophets, who have spoken in the name of the Lord, for an example of suffering affliction, and of patience" (Js.5:10).

"For what glory *is it,* if, when ye be buffeted for your faults, ye shall take it patiently? but if, when ye do well, and suffer *for it,* ye take it patiently, this *is* acceptable with God" (1 Pe.2:20).

"But and if ye suffer for righteousness' sake, happy *are ye:* and be not afraid of their terror, neither be troubled; But sanctify the Lord God in your hearts: and *be* ready always to *give* an answer to every man that asketh you a reason of the hope that is in you with meekness and fear: Having a good conscience; that, whereas they speak evil of you, as of evildoers, they may be ashamed that falsely accuse your good conversation in Christ" (1 Pe.3:14-16).

"Beloved, think it not strange concerning the fiery trial which is to try you, as though some strange thing happened unto you: But rejoice, inasmuch as ye are partakers of Christ's sufferings; that, when his glory shall be revealed, ye may be glad also with exceeding joy. If ye be reproached for the name of Christ, happy *are ye;* for the spirit of glory and of God resteth upon you: on their part he is evil spoken of, but on your part he is glorified. But let none of you suffer as a murderer, or *as* a thief, or *as* an evildoer, or as a busybody in other men's matters. Yet if *any man suffer* as a Christian, let him not be ashamed; but let him glorify God on this behalf" (1 Pe.4:12-16).

"But the God of all grace, who hath called us unto his eternal glory by Christ Jesus, after that ye have suffered a while, make you perfect, stablish, strengthen, settle *you*" (1 Pe.5:10).

"Fear none of those things which thou shalt suffer: behold, the devil shall cast *some* of you into prison, that ye may be tried; and ye shall have tribulation ten days: be thou faithful unto death, and I will give thee a crown of life" (Re.2:10).

"I *am* small and despised: *yet* do not I forget thy precepts" (Ps.119:141).

CHAPTER 5

D. The Completion of the Temple by the Returned Exiles: Four Pictures Demonstrating God's Faithfulness, 5:1–6:22

1. **The building of the temple begun anew, spurred on by God's prophets: A picture of a new beginning**
   a. The prophets Haggai & Zechariah & their arousing message, Hag.1:3-11; Zec.1:1-6, 16
   b. The prophets' stirring message to the leaders Zerubbabel & Jeshua, Hag.2:4; Zec.4:9
      1) The two leaders restarted construction
      2) The prophets helped
2. **The building of the temple officially investigated: A picture of God's eyes watching over & protecting the church & His people**
   a. The investigation by the state governor Tattenai
      1) He asked who had authorized the project
      2) He asked for a complete list of the men working on the project
      3) He was moved by the LORD to allow the construction to continue until he could check with King Darius: Moved by the LORD's watchful eye & His protection of His people
   b. The report of the governor & his officials to King Darius
      1) He greeted the king

      2) He informed the king: The temple of the great God—in the district of Judah—was being rebuilt

      • Large stones & timbers were being used

      • Rapid progress was being made
      3) He related his two demands
      • To know who authorized the project

Then the prophets, Haggai the prophet, and Zechariah the son of Iddo, prophesied unto the Jews that *were* in Judah and Jerusalem in the name of the God of Israel, *even* unto them.
2 Then rose up Zerubbabel the son of Shealtiel, and Jeshua the son of Jozadak, and began to build the house of God which *is* at Jerusalem: and with them *were* the prophets of God helping them.
3 At the same time came to them Tatnai, governor on this side the river, and Shethar-boznai, and their companions, and said thus unto them, Who hath commanded you to build this house, and to make up this wall?
4 Then said we unto them after this manner, What are the names of the men that make this building?
5 But the eye of their God was upon the elders of the Jews, that they could not cause them to cease, till the matter came to Darius: and then they returned answer by letter concerning this *matter*.
6 The copy of the letter that Tatnai, governor on this side the river, and Shethar-boznai, and his companions the Apharsachites, which *were* on this side the river, sent unto Darius the king:
7 They sent a letter unto him, wherein was written thus; Unto Darius the king, all peace.
8 Be it known unto the king, that we went into the province of Judea, to the house of the great God, which is builded with great stones, and timber is laid in the walls, and this work goeth fast on, and prospereth in their hands.
9 Then asked we those elders, *and* said unto them thus, Who commanded you to build this house, and to make up these walls?
10 We asked their names also, to certify thee, that we might write the names of the men that *were* the chief of them.
11 And thus they returned us answer, saying, We are the servants of the God of heaven and earth, and build the house that was builded these many years ago, which a great king of Israel builded and set up.
12 But after that our fathers had provoked the God of heaven unto wrath, he gave them into the hand of Nebuchadnezzar the king of Babylon, the Chaldean, who destroyed this house, and carried the people away into Babylon.
13 But in the first year of Cyrus the king of Babylon *the same* king Cyrus made a decree to build this house of God.
14 And the vessels also of gold and silver of the house of God, which Nebuchadnezzar took out of the temple that *was* in Jerusalem, and brought them into the temple of Babylon, those did Cyrus the king take out of the temple of Babylon, and they were delivered unto *one,* whose name *was* Sheshbazzar, whom he had made governor;
15 And said unto him, Take these vessels, go, carry them into the temple that *is* in Jerusalem, and let the house of God be builded in his place.
16 Then came the same Sheshbazzar, *and* laid the foundation of the house of God which *is* in Jerusalem: and since that time even until now hath it been in building, and *yet* it is not finished.
17 Now therefore, if *it seem* good to the king, let there be search made in the king's treasure house, which *is* there at Babylon, whether it be *so,* that a decree was made of Cyrus the king to build this house of God at Jerusalem, and let the king send his pleasure to us concerning this matter.

• To secure a list of the leaders to pass on to the king

4) He reported the rights claimed by the Jews
• They claimed the *religious right* to rebuild: They were servants of the God of heaven & earth
• They claimed a *citizen's right* to rebuild their ancient temple
• They claimed a *historical right*: God had aroused Nebuchadnezzar to destroy their temple & exile their ancestors—all because of their sins

• They claimed the *legal right* to rebuild: King Cyrus had issued a decree for the temple to be rebuilt
5) He reported the detailed explanation of the legal claim given by the Jews
• They claimed that King Cyrus returned all the gold & silver furnishings of the temple that Nebuchadnezzar had plundered

• They said that King Cyrus appointed a man named Sheshbazzar as governor: The king had charged him to return the furnishings & to rebuild the temple
• They claimed that Sheshbazzar laid the foundation of the temple & that they had been working on it ever since, though it was not yet finished
6) He made two requests of King Darius
• That the king search the royal archives to verify the story
• That the king reply, sending his decision concerning the matter

3. The building of the temple approved by King Darius: A picture of God's sovereignty

a. The search of the archives: A record of King Cyrus' decree was found in the fortress of Achmetha or Ecbatana

1) Cyrus had ordered that the temple be rebuilt: As a place of worship, a place to present sacrifices

• Its dimensions

• Its materials

2) Cyrus had ordered that the costs be paid by the royal treasury

3) Cyrus had also ordered that the gold & silver furnishings be returned & placed in the temple

b. The orders by King Darius
1) He ordered Tattenai & his officials to stay away from Jerusalem, not to interfere with the construction

2) He ordered that the temple be rebuilt on its former site
3) He even decreed that the governor Tattenai help finance the project
• By using tax money from his (the governor's) district of West Euphrates

• By daily providing whatever animals were needed for sacrifice, along with the required food items (wheat, salt, wine, & oil)

CHAPTER 6

Then Darius the king made a decree, and search was made in the house of the rolls, where the treasures were laid up in Babylon.
2 And there was found at Achmetha, in the palace that *is* in the province of the Medes, a roll, and therein *was* a record thus written:
3 In the first year of Cyrus the king *the same* Cyrus the king made a decree *concerning* the house of God at Jerusalem, Let the house be builded, the place where they offered sacrifices, and let the foundations thereof be strongly laid; the height thereof threescore cubits, *and* the breadth thereof threescore cubits;
4 *With* three rows of great stones, and a row of new timber: and let the expenses be given out of the king's house:
5 And also let the golden and silver vessels of the house of God, which Nebuchadnezzar took forth out of the temple which *is* at Jerusalem, and brought unto Babylon, be restored, and brought again unto the temple which *is* at Jerusalem, *every one* to his place, and place *them* in the house of God.
6 Now *therefore,* Tatnai, governor beyond the river, Shethar-boznai, and your companions the Apharsachites, which *are* beyond the river, be ye far from thence:
7 Let the work of this house of God alone; let the governor of the Jews and the elders of the Jews build this house of God in his place.
8 Moreover I make a decree what ye shall do to the elders of these Jews for the building of this house of God: that of the king's goods, *even* of the tribute beyond the river, forthwith expenses be given unto these men, that they be not hindered.
9 And that which they have need of, both young bullocks, and rams, and lambs, for the burnt offerings of the God of heaven, wheat, salt, wine, and oil, according to the appointment of the priests which *are* at Jerusalem, let it

be given them day by day without fail:
10 That they may offer sacrifices of sweet savours unto the God of heaven, and pray for the life of the king, and of his sons.
11 Also I have made a decree, that whosoever shall alter this word, let timber be pulled down from his house, and being set up, let him be hanged thereon; and let his house be made a dunghill for this.
12 And the God that hath caused his name to dwell there destroy all kings and people, that shall put to their hand to alter *and* to destroy this house of God which *is* at Jerusalem. I Darius have made a decree; let it be done with speed.
13 Then Tatnai, governor on this side the river, Shethar-boznai, and their companions, according to that which Darius the king had sent, so they did speedily.
14 And the elders of the Jews builded, and they prospered through the prophesying of Haggai the prophet and Zechariah the son of Iddo. And they builded, and finished *it,* according to the commandment of the God of Israel, and according to the commandment of Cyrus, and Darius, and Artaxerxes king of Persia.
15 And this house was finished on the third day of the month Adar, which was in the sixth year of the reign of Darius the king.
16 And the children of Israel, the priests, and the Levites, and the rest of the children of the captivity, kept the dedication of this house of God with joy,
17 And offered at the dedication of this house of God an hundred bullocks, two hundred rams, four hundred lambs; and for a sin offering for all Israel, twelve he goats, according to the number of the tribes of Israel.
18 And they set the priests in their divisions, and the Levites in their courses, for the service of God, which *is* at Jerusalem; as it is written in the book of Moses.
19 And the children of the

4) He stated his purpose: So the Jews could please their God of heaven & offer up prayers for the king & his family
5) He decreed a severe penalty to anyone who violated his orders & opposed the rebuilding of the temple
• The violators were to be executed & their houses destroyed

• The violators—king or people—were also to suffer God's curse

4. The completion of the temple: A picture of great joy & celebration
a. The completion
1) The Persian officials assisted as ordered by Darius
2) The returned exiles continued to build
3) The prophets of God—Haggai & Zechariah—encouraged the people
4) The leaders of the nation finished the construction
• As commanded by God

• As decreed by the kings of Persia

5) The Jews completed the temple on the 3rd day of Adar (March 12) during the sixth year of Darius' reign
b. The dedication service
1) The whole community of returned exiles celebrated: The priests, the Levites, & all the freed captives

2) The worship included a large number of sacrificial offerings
• 100 bulls, 200 rams, & 400 lambs
• A sin offering of 12 male goats: Represented the 12 tribes of Israel
c. The installation of the priests & Levites: Were organized into their various divisions & assigned their duties, Ex.29; Le.8; Nu.3; 8:5-26; 18:1-32

d. The reinstitution of the

Passover & the Feast of Un-leavened Bread 1) The priests & Levites pu-rified themselves: By the ritual of washing with wa-ter, Ex.29:4; Nu.8:7 2) The Levites slaughtered the Passover lamb for all the exiles 3) The Passover meal was eaten by both the returned exiles & the Jews of the land who had spiritually	captivity kept the passover upon the fourteenth *day* of the first month. 20 For the priests and the Levites were purified togeth-er, all of them *were* pure, and killed the passover for all the children of the captiv-ity, and for their brethren the priests, and for themselves. 21 And the children of Isra-el, which were come again out of captivity, and all such as had separated themselves	unto them from the filthiness of the heathen of the land, to seek the LORD God of Israel, did eat, 22 And kept the feast of un-leavened bread seven days with joy: for the LORD had made them joy-ful, and turned the heart of the king of Assyria unto them, to strengthen their hands in the work of the house of God, the God of Is-rael.	separated themselves—who had turned away from the sins of their neighbors in order to seek the LORD 4) The Feast of Unleavened Bread was celebrated with great joy because the LORD had worked in the heart of Assyria's king (the Persian Darius) to as-sist them: The exile was now ended; fellowship with God was at last re-stored

THE FIRST RETURN OF EXILES FROM CAPTIVITY AND THEIR RESETTLEMENT—LED BY ZERUBBABEL, 1:1–6:22

D. The Completion of the Temple by the Returned Exiles: Four Pictures Demonstrating God's Faithfulness, 5:1–6:22

(5:1–6:22) **Introduction**: finding dependable people is often difficult. Think of the individuals who miss work without justifiable reason. Think of the unfinished projects, the absences in schools, the promises broken, the marriage commit-ments shattered, the personal decisions or resolutions made but soon ignored or forgotten. Dependable people—people who follow through, who are trustworthy and faithful, truthful and honest—are a rarity among us.

But not God. God is faithful and truthful. He keeps His Word, every promise He has ever made. God is perfectly de-pendable and reliable. He can be trusted to do exactly what He says. This is the practical subject of the present Scripture. Four pictures of God's faithfulness—His steadfastness and reliability—are painted for the reader.

For well over a decade the construction work on the temple had been stopped and the project untouched. A sense of failure and disappointment was bound to strike the hearts of true believers as they walked past the temple site. The unfin-ished project was a constant reminder that they had failed to carry out the command of the LORD to rebuild the temple. But once again the LORD Himself stepped forward and proved to be faithful. True to His promises, God provided exactly what was needed to arouse the people. He stirred them to once again undertake the construction of the temple. This is, *The Completion of the Temple by the Returned Exiles: Four Pictures, Demonstrating God's Faithfulness*, 5:1–6:22.

1. The building of the temple begun anew, spurred on by God's prophets: a picture of a new beginning (5:1-2).
2. The building of the temple officially investigated: a picture of God's eyes watching over and protecting the church and His people (5:3-17).
3. The building of the temple approved by King Darius: a picture of God's sovereignty (6:1-12).
4. The completion of the temple: a picture of great joy and celebration (6:13-22).

1 (5:1-2) **New Beginning, Example of—Starting Over, Example of—Renewal, Example of—Temple, Second, Du-ty, to Rebuild—Haggai, the Prophet, Message of—Zechariah, the Prophet, Message of**: finally the building of the temple was begun anew, but only after God's prophets spurred the people on. For a decade or more the returnees had stopped their work on the temple because of persecution by their neighbors. The neighbors' harassment had led the king to issue a *work-stop order* on the temple (4:21-24). But now it was time to start building again. However, a serious prob-lem existed: the Jewish returnees were discouraged, disheartened that they had walked away from the building project. To meet the need of the hour, the LORD raised up two prophets to arouse the people. These prophets, Haggai and Zechariah, stirred the Jews to make a renewed commitment to rebuilding of the temple. Haggai delivered his messages between Au-gust and December 520 B.C., and Zechariah between October and February 519 B.C. (Hag.1:1; Zec.1:1). Through the years the returned exiles had slipped away from the LORD, forgetting God's commandments and His charge to rebuild the temple. Instead, they were focused upon the provisions of this world, that is, upon housing, food, clothing, productivity, the harvesting of crops, and earning large wages (Hag.1:3-6). The people desperately needed to repent, to turn back to the LORD. Zechariah declared that if the people would repent and return to the LORD, the LORD would turn to them (Zec.1:3).

As a result of the prophets' preaching, the local governor Zerubbabel and the High Priest Jeshua or Joshua mobilized the people to restart the construction project. While the people worked, the two prophets exhorted and encouraged them in their renewed commitment to the LORD.

OUTLINE	SCRIPTURE	SCRIPTURE	OUTLINE
1. The building of the temple begun anew, spurred on by God's prophets: A picture of a new beginning a. The prophets Haggai & Zecha-riah & their arousing message, Hag.1:3-11; Zec.1:1-6, 16	Then the prophets, Haggai the prophet, and Zechariah the son of Iddo, prophesied unto the Jews that *were* in Judah and Jerusalem in the name of the God of Israel, *even* unto them.	2 Then rose up Zerubbabel the son of Shealtiel, and Je-shua the son of Jozadak, and began to build the house of God which *is* at Jerusalem: and with them *were* the prophets of God helping them.	b. The prophets' stirring mes-sage to the leaders Zerubba-bel & Jeshua, Hag.2:4; Zec.4:9 1) The two leaders restarted construction 2) The prophets helped

Thought 1. There is a need for renewed commitments in life. When we feel discouraged, disappointed, defeated, depressed, or crushed by life's problems and setbacks, there is a need for our hearts to be aroused and renewed. When we become tired, stressed, pressured, or even disgusted, we sometimes turn away from our responsibilities, and fail to fulfill our tasks. For those of us who are overwhelmed by a major problem, who have failed, sinned, slipped back, turned away, or have a sense that we are coming up short—there is wonderful news. We can have a new beginning, a fresh start. If we will turn to the Lord, He will turn to us and rekindle our hearts. We can make a brand new commitment and begin all over again. Listen to what God's Holy Word says:

"I beseech you therefore, brethren, by the mercies of God, that ye present your bodies a living sacrifice, holy, acceptable unto God, *which is* your reasonable service. And be not conformed to this world: but be ye transformed by the renewing of your mind, that ye may prove what is that good, and acceptable, and perfect, will of God" (Ro.12:1-2).

"For which cause we faint not; but though our outward man perish, yet the inward *man* is renewed day by day. For our light affliction, which is but for a moment, worketh for us a far more exceeding *and* eternal weight of glory; While we look not at the things which are seen, but at the things which are not seen: for the things which are seen *are* temporal; but the things which are not seen *are* eternal" (2 Co.4:16-18).

"Therefore if any man *be* in Christ, *he is* a new creature: old things are passed away; behold, all things are become new" (2 Co.5:17).

"That ye put off concerning the former conversation [conduct, behavior] the old man, which is corrupt according to the deceitful lusts; And be renewed in the spirit of your mind; And that ye put on the new man, which after God is created in righteousness and true holiness" (Ep.4:22-24).

"For it is God which worketh in you both to will and to do of *his* good pleasure" (Ph.2:13).

"And have put on the new *man*, which is renewed in knowledge after the image of him that created him" (Col.3:10).

"O that there were such an heart in them, that they would fear me, and keep all my commandments always, that it might be well with them, and with their children for ever!" (De.5:29).

"Create in me a clean heart, O God; and renew a right spirit within me" (Ps.51:10).

"My heart is fixed, O God, my heart is fixed: I will sing and give praise" (Ps.57:7).

"But they that wait upon the LORD shall renew *their* strength; they shall mount up with wings as eagles; they shall run, and not be weary; *and* they shall walk, and not faint" (Is.40:31).

"And I will give them an heart to know me, that I *am* the LORD: and they shall be my people, and I will be their God: for they shall return unto me with their whole heart" (Je.24:7).

"And I will give them one heart, and I will put a new spirit within you; and I will take the stony heart out of their flesh, and will give them an heart of flesh" (Eze.11:19).

"A new heart also will I give you, and a new spirit will I put within you: and I will take away the stony heart out of your flesh, and I will give you an heart of flesh" (Eze.36:26).

2 (5:3-17) **Protection, God's, Example—God, Eyes of, Sees and Protects—Church, Protection of—Protection, of Believers, Example—Temple, Second, Rebuilding of**: as soon as construction on the temple resumed, an official investigation was initiated by the regional governor himself to find out what was going on. Most likely this was not a threatening investigation but a normal procedure followed to protect the welfare of the Persian Empire. Throughout the entire Persian Empire there were only 20 regional governors, which meant that they were powerful men holding high royal positions in the empire. This particular royal governor named Tattenai ruled over the large province of Trans-Euphrates, which included Syria, Palestine, and all other territory west of the Euphrates River. Scripture gives a detailed account of the investigation.

OUTLINE	SCRIPTURE	SCRIPTURE	OUTLINE
2. The building of the temple officially investigated: A picture of God's eyes watching over & protecting the church & His people a. The investigation by the state governor Tattenai 1) He asked who had authorized the project 2) He asked for a complete list of the men working on the project 3) He was moved by the LORD to allow the construction to continue until he could check with King	3 At the same time came to them Tatnai, governor on this side the river, and Shethar-boznai, and their companions, and said thus unto them, Who hath commanded you to build this house, and to make up this wall? 4 Then said we unto them after this manner, What are the names of the men that make this building? 5 But the eye of their God was upon the elders of the Jews, that they could not cause them to cease, till the	matter came to Darius: and then they returned answer by letter concerning this *matter*. 6 The copy of the letter that Tatnai, governor on this side the river, and Shethar-boznai, and his companions the Apharsachites, which *were* on this side the river, sent unto Darius the king: 7 They sent a letter unto him, wherein was written thus; Unto Darius the king, all peace. 8 Be it known unto the king, that we went into the province of Judea, to the	Darius: Moved by the LORD's watchful eye & His protection of His people b. The report of the governor & his officials to King Darius 1) He greeted the king 2) He informed the king: The temple of the great God—in the district of Judah—was being rebuilt

OUTLINE	SCRIPTURE	SCRIPTURE	OUTLINE
• Large stones & timbers were being used • Rapid progress was being made 3) He related his two demands • To know who authorized the project • To secure a list of the leaders to pass on to the king 4) He reported the rights claimed by the Jews • They claimed the *religious right* to rebuild: They were servants of the God of heaven & earth • They claimed a *citizen's right* to rebuild their ancient temple • They claimed a *historical right*: God had aroused Nebuchadnezar to destroy their temple & exile their ancestors—all because of their sins • They claimed the *legal right* to rebuild: King Cyrus had issued a decree for the temple to	house of the great God, which is builded with great stones, and timber is laid in the walls, and this work goeth fast on, and prospereth in their hands. 9 Then asked we those elders, *and* said unto them thus, Who commanded you to build this house, and to make up these walls? 10 We asked their names also, to certify thee, that we might write the names of the men that *were* the chief of them. 11 And thus they returned us answer, saying, We are the servants of the God of heaven and earth, and build the house that was builded these many years ago, which a great king of Israel builded and set up. 12 But after that our fathers had provoked the God of heaven unto wrath, he gave them into the hand of Nebuchadnezzar the king of Babylon, the Chaldean, who destroyed this house, and carried the people away into Babylon. 13 But in the first year of Cyrus the king of Babylon *the same* king Cyrus made a decree to build this house of	God. 14 And the vessels also of gold and silver of the house of God, which Nebuchadnezzar took out of the temple that *was* in Jerusalem, and brought them into the temple of Babylon, those did Cyrus the king take out of the temple of Babylon, and they were delivered unto *one,* whose name *was* Sheshbazzar, whom he had made governor; 15 And said unto him, Take these vessels, go, carry them into the temple that *is* in Jerusalem, and let the house of God be builded in his place. 16 Then came the same Sheshbazzar, *and* laid the foundation of the house of God which *is* in Jerusalem: and since that time even until now hath it been in building, and *yet* it is not finished. 17 Now therefore, if *it seem* good to the king, let there be search made in the king's treasure house, which *is* there at Babylon, whether it be *so,* that a decree was made of Cyrus the king to build this house of God at Jerusalem, and let the king send his pleasure to us concerning this matter.	be rebuilt 5) He reported the detailed explanation of the legal claim given by the Jews • They claimed that King Cyrus returned all the gold & silver furnishings of the temple that Nebuchadnezzar had plundered • They said that King Cyrus appointed a man named Sheshbazzar as governor: The king had charged him to return the furnishings & to rebuild the temple • They claimed that Sheshbazzar laid the foundation of the temple & that they had been working on it ever since, though it was not yet finished 6) He made two requests of King Darius • That the king search the royal archives to verify the story • That the king reply, sending his decision concerning the matter

a. Apparently the Persian governor Tattenai launched his investigation right after hearing about the Jewish activity in rebuilding their temple (vv.3-5). Accompanying the governor on his investigation were several associates and a man named Shethar-Bozenai, who was probably Tattenai's secretary. On arriving in Jerusalem, the governor made two reasonable requests of the Jewish leaders. He asked for the name of the person who had authorized the rebuilding of the temple and for a complete list of the men who were working on the project.

Note a wonderful fact pointed out by the author of *Ezra*. Behind the scenes, the LORD was moving the heart of the governor to allow the construction to continue until he could check with King Darius (v.5). The eye of God was watching over His people, protecting both them and their service for the LORD. The people had made a renewed commitment to the LORD and to the rebuilding of the temple. In response, the LORD had accepted their recommitment and was now moving world events so that they could continue their renewed service to Him.

b. The actual report sent by the governor to King Darius is recorded in the remaining verses of this chapter (vv.6-17). To add weight to the report, the governor included the names of the other officials as being part of the investigative committee. The report can be more easily grasped by being divided into six parts.

1) First, the governor greeted the king (v.6). Greetings were coming from him and from all the other regional officials.
2) Second, the governor informed the king that the temple of the great God was being rebuilt in the district of Judah (v.8). Large stones and timbers were being used in the construction of the walls. By mentioning this fact, the governor seems to have had some concern that the temple might be used as a fortress. He also mentioned that rapid progress was being made in the construction.
3) Third, the governor mentioned that he had made two demands of the Jewish returnees (vv.9-10). To begin with, they needed to provide the name of the person(s) who authorized the project. Next, they needed to provide a list of the leaders so the information could be passed on to the king.
4) Fourth, the governor shared the answer that the Jews had given to his inquiries (vv.11-13). Note that the returnees made four claims that gave them the right to continue rebuilding their temple:
⇒ They claimed the *religious right* to rebuild (v.11). Courageously, they gave a strong testimony for the LORD by claiming that they were servants of the God of heaven and earth. This title means that God created the

heavens and that He rules over the universe from heaven (see outline and note 1:1-4, pt.3a for more discussion).

⇒ They also claimed *citizens' rights* to rebuild their ancient temple. As citizens of the empire, they had the right to build a temple for worship. In their case they were simply rebuilding a temple that had been constructed many years before by one of their great kings. Of course, this was a reference to Solomon who had built the first temple some 500 years earlier (c.966 B.C.).

⇒ They claimed a *historical right* to rebuild the temple (v.12). Years before, their God had aroused Nebuchadnezzar to destroy their temple and exile their ancestors—all because of their sins. Implied in this statement is the strong testimony that they had now repented of their sins. Therefore, they had the right at this time to rebuild the temple so they could once again worship and serve the God of heaven and earth.

⇒ They claimed the *legal right* to rebuild the temple (v.13). The Jews informed the governor that King Cyrus had some years before issued a decree for the temple to be rebuilt. Naturally, this was the strongest claim the Jews had, for once a decree had been issued, it could not be changed or revoked.

5) Fifth, the governor reported the detailed explanation of the legal claim given by the Jews (vv.14-16). The Jews had claimed that King Cyrus had even returned all the furnishings of the temple that Nebuchadnezzar had plundered (v.14). In addition, King Cyrus had appointed a man named Sheshbazzar as governor, charging him with the duty of returning the furnishings to Jerusalem and rebuilding the temple (vv.14-15). Furthermore, the Jews claimed that Sheshbazzar had laid the foundation of the temple and that they had been working on it ever since. However, the temple had not yet been finished.

6) Sixth, in closing his report the governor made two requests of King Darius (v.17). The governor asked that the king search the royal archives to verify the Jews' story and then send a reply to him with the king's decision concerning the matter.

Thought 1. God's eyes were watching over His people, protecting them and allowing them to continue their service for the LORD. Likewise, God's eyes watch over us as true believers, protecting us as we walk about day by day. No matter who we are or what our daily tasks may be, if we are truly following and trusting the LORD, keeping His commandments, the LORD is right there with us. He is taking care of us, protecting us from the enemies of this life. We are not necessarily delivered *from* trials, but we are delivered *through* trials. As we walk through hardships and suffering, we learn to draw closer and closer to the LORD. And as we draw closer to Him, He infuses peace within our hearts, giving us the strength to conquer the trial. When His peace and strength are demonstrated within our lives, the world sees a strong testimony for the LORD. They too can turn to Him for peace and strength through the trials of this life.

Through all the hardships and trials of life, God protects His people, never failing us. He always provides whatever is needed for the moment: either His power to deliver us *from* the hardship or *through* the hardship. Listen to what God's Holy Word says about the watchful eyes of the LORD, His protective power:

> "But there shall not an hair of your head perish" (Lu.21:18).
> "The eternal God *is thy* refuge, and underneath *are* the everlasting arms: and he shall thrust out the enemy from before thee; and shall say, Destroy *them*" (De.33:27).
> "For the eyes of the LORD run to and fro throughout the whole earth, to show himself strong in the behalf of *them* whose heart *is* perfect toward him. Herein thou hast done foolishly: therefore from henceforth thou shalt have wars" (2 Chr.16:9).
> "Keep me as the apple of the eye, hide me under the shadow of thy wings" (Ps.17:8).
> "For in the time of trouble he shall hide me in his pavilion: in the secret of his tabernacle shall he hide me; he shall set me up upon a rock" (Ps.27:5).
> "Thou shalt hide them in the secret of thy presence from the pride of man: thou shalt keep them secretly in a pavilion from the strife of tongues" (Ps.31:20).
> "Thou *art* my hiding place; thou shalt preserve me from trouble; thou shalt compass me about with songs of deliverance. Selah" (Ps.32:7).
> "The eyes of the LORD *are* upon the righteous, and his ears *are open* unto their cry" (Ps.34:15).
> "God *is* our refuge and strength, a very present help in trouble" (Ps.46:1).
> "He shall cover thee with his feathers, and under his wings shalt thou trust: his truth *shall be thy* shield and buckler" (Ps.91:4).
> "Thou *art* my hiding place and my shield: I hope in thy word" (Ps.119:114).

3 (6:1-12) **Sovereignty, of God, Example—Temple, Second, Building of, Approved—Darius, King of Persia, Approved the Jewish Temple**: when King Darius received the investigative report, he did just as the governor Tattenai requested. He searched the archives to confirm the Jewish claims, and discovered that the claims were accurate. He immediately decreed that construction on the temple be allowed to continue. Scripture gives a detailed account of the steps King Darius took:

OUTLINE	SCRIPTURE	SCRIPTURE	OUTLINE
3. The building of the temple approved by King Darius: A picture of God's sovereignty a. The search of the archives: A record of King Cyrus' decree was found in the fortress of Achmetha or Ecbatana 1) Cyrus had ordered that the temple be rebuilt: As a place of worship, a place to present sacrifices • Its dimensions • Its materials 2) Cyrus had ordered that the costs be paid by the royal treasury 3) Cyrus had also ordered that the gold & silver furnishings be returned & placed in the temple b. The orders by King Darius 1) He ordered Tattenai & his officials to stay away from Jerusalem, not to interfere with the construction 2) He ordered that the temple	Then Darius the king made a decree, and search was made in the house of the rolls, where the treasures were laid up in Babylon. 2 And there was found at Achmetha, in the palace that *is* in the province of the Medes, a roll, and therein *was* a record thus written: 3 In the first year of Cyrus the king *the same* Cyrus the king made a decree *concerning* the house of God at Jerusalem, Let the house be builded, the place where they offered sacrifices, and let the foundations thereof be strongly laid; the height thereof threescore cubits, *and* the breadth thereof threescore cubits; 4 *With* three rows of great stones, and a row of new timber: and let the expenses be given out of the king's house: 5 And also let the golden and silver vessels of the house of God, which Nebuchadnezzar took forth out of the temple which *is* at Jerusalem, and brought unto Babylon, be restored, and brought again unto the temple which *is* at Jerusalem, *every one* to his place, and place *them* in the house of God. 6 Now *therefore,* Tatnai, governor beyond the river, Shethar-boznai, and your companions the Apharsachites, which *are* beyond the river, be ye far from thence:	7 Let the work of this house of God alone; let the governor of the Jews and the elders of the Jews build this house of God in his place. 8 Moreover I make a decree what ye shall do to the elders of these Jews for the building of this house of God: that of the king's goods, *even* of the tribute beyond the river, forthwith expenses be given unto these men, that they be not hindered. 9 And that which they have need of, both young bullocks, and rams, and lambs, for the burnt offerings of the God of heaven, wheat, salt, wine, and oil, according to the appointment of the priests which *are* at Jerusalem, let it be given them day by day without fail: 10 That they may offer sacrifices of sweet savours unto the God of heaven, and pray for the life of the king, and of his sons. 11 Also I have made a decree, that whosoever shall alter this word, let timber be pulled down from his house, and being set up, let him be hanged thereon; and let his house be made a dunghill for this. 12 And the God that hath caused his name to dwell there destroy all kings and people, that shall put to their hand to alter *and* to destroy this house of God which *is* at Jerusalem. I Darius have made a decree; let it be done	be rebuilt on its former site 3) He even decreed that the governor Tattenai help finance the project • By using tax money from his (the governor's) district of West Euphrates • By daily providing whatever animals were needed for sacrifice, along with the required food items (wheat, salt, wine, & oil) 4) He stated his purpose: So the Jews could please their God of heaven & offer up prayers for the king & his family 5) He decreed a severe penalty to anyone who violated his orders & opposed the rebuilding of the temple • The violators were to be executed & their houses destroyed • The violators—king or people—were also to suffer God's curse

a. Following the suggestion of the governor, King Darius issued an order that the archives at Babylon be searched to see if the Jewish claims were accurate (vv.1-5). Finding no such decree in Babylon, he ordered that a search be made in the summer palace at Achmetha or Ecbatana. The decree was found in the archives at the summer palace. Interestingly, King Darius discovered that the decree was given in great detail. Not only had King Cyrus ordered the temple to be rebuilt as a place of worship where sacrifices could be made by the Jews, but the very dimensions and materials to be used in the construction were spelled out (vv.3-4). Cyrus had even ordered the cost to be paid by the royal treasury (v.4). Moreover, as the Jews had claimed, Cyrus had ordered the gold and silver furnishings to be returned and placed in the temple (v.5).

b. Having learned that the Jewish claims were accurate, King Darius made his decision in favor of the Jews and issued immediate orders to the governor and the other regional officials (vv.6-12). His decree fully supported the Jewish claims and the decree of King Cyrus. He spelled out his orders in five straightforward commands that could not be misunderstood by the local officials.

1) He ordered the governor Tattenai and his officials to stay away from Jerusalem, not to interfere with the construction (vv.6-7).
2) He even ordered that the temple be rebuilt on its former site, the very place it had originally been located. The commentator Mervin Breneman points out that there was one significant difference between this temple and the first temple built by Solomon:

There would be no ark of the covenant in the Most Holy Place symbolizing the Presence of God. It would be awaiting, in a sense, the LORD of the temple, the Messianic "Messenger of the covenant" to make His Presence known there (Mal.3:1; cf. Mt.21:12-17; Jn.7:14).[1]

3) Just as King Cyrus had decreed, King Darius ordered the governor Tattenai to help finance the project (vv.8-9). Tax money from the governor's province or region was to be used to finance the construction. In addition, the governor was to provide whatever animals were needed to sacrifice, along with the required food items (wheat, salt, wine, and oil).

4) King Darius then stated his purpose: he wanted the Jews to be able to please their God and to offer up prayers for the king and his family (v.10).

5) The king also decreed a severe penalty to anyone who violated his orders and opposed the rebuilding of the temple (vv.11-12). The violators were to suffer the most severe penalty, that of being executed. Likewise, the house of any person who opposed this edict of the king was to be destroyed. Note that the king even summoned a divine curse upon any person who violated his orders (v.12). Mervin Breneman again gives a statement that is worth quoting:

Darius was in fact speaking almost prophetically. As Daniel prophesied, God would do this very thing, destroying the king and kingdom that would oppose him and his people and then would establish an everlasting kingdom of righteousness (Da.7:23-27).[2]

Thought 1. The decree of King Darius granting permission to rebuild the temple is a clear picture of the sovereignty of God. God had raised up the prophets Haggai and Zechariah to stir the people to begin rebuilding. And the LORD had moved upon the hearts of the returnees, arousing them to a recommitment to resume construction. Moreover the LORD had moved upon the heart of the governor to allow the returnees to continue building until he could check with King Darius. Through the years since King Cyrus had freed the Jewish exiles, the LORD had protected the records of the king's decree. As a result, King Darius was able to find the decree in the archives at the summer palace. Through event after event the hand of God's sovereignty can be seen. So it is with us. God loves us and promises to look after us. Whatever we need—physically, emotionally, mentally, or spiritually—God promises to provide. He will move heaven and earth to fulfill His promises to us. If needed, world events as well as daily activities will be shifted, maneauvered, twisted, and even stopped in order to fulfill His promises. God is sovereign, controlling all events and all things in order to fulfill His Word, His promises, and His will. It is through His sovereign, omnipotent power that all our needs are met. Listen to what God's Holy Word says:

"And lead us not into temptation, but deliver us from evil: For thine is the kingdom, and the power, and the glory, for ever. Amen" (Mt.6:13).

"And we know that all things work together for good to them that love God, to them who are the called according to *his* purpose. For whom he did foreknow, he also did predestinate *to be* conformed to the image of his Son, that he might be the firstborn among many brethren" (Ro.8:28-29).

"Thou wilt say then unto me, Why doth he yet find fault? For who hath resisted his will? Nay but, O man, who art thou that repliest against God? Shall the thing formed say to him that formed *it*, Why hast thou made me thus? Hath not the potter power over the clay, of the same lump to make one vessel unto honour, and another unto dishonour?" (Ro.9:19-21).

"For he must reign, till he hath put all enemies under his feet" (1 Co.15:25).

"Wherefore God also hath highly exalted him, and given him a name which is above every name: That at the name of Jesus every knee should bow, of *things* in heaven, and *things* in earth, and *things* under the earth; And *that* every tongue should confess that Jesus Christ *is* Lord, to the glory of God the Father" (Ph.2:9-11).

"Now unto the King eternal, immortal, invisible, the only wise God, *be* honour and glory for ever and ever. Amen" (1 Ti.1:17).

"And they sing the song of Moses the servant of God, and the song of the Lamb, saying, Great and marvellous *are* thy works, Lord God Almighty; just and true *are* thy ways, thou King of saints" (Re.15:3).

"The LORD shall reign for ever and ever" (Ex.15:18).

"Know therefore this day, and consider *it* in thine heart, that the LORD he *is* God in heaven above, and upon the earth beneath: *there is* none else" (De.4:39).

"Both riches and honour *come* of thee, and thou reignest over all; and in thine hand *is* power and might; and in thine hand *it is* to make great, and to give strength unto all" (1 Chr.29:12).

"And said, O LORD God of our fathers, *art* not thou God in heaven? and rulest *not* thou over all the kingdoms of the heathen? and in thine hand *is there not* power and might, so that none is able to withstand thee?" (2 Chr.20:6).

"Thy throne, O God, *is* for ever and ever: the sceptre of thy kingdom *is* a right sceptre" (Ps.45:6).

"That *men* may know that thou, whose name alone *is* JEHOVAH, *art* the most high over all the earth" (Ps.83:18).

"The LORD hath prepared his throne in the heavens; and his kingdom ruleth over all" (Ps.103:19).

---

1 Mervin Breneman. *Ezra, Nehemiah, Esther.* "The New American Commentary," Vol.10. (Nashville, TN: Broadman & Holman Publishers, 1993), p.116.
2 Ibid., p.118.

"Whatsoever the LORD pleased, *that* did he in heaven, and in earth, in the seas, and all deep places" (Ps.135:6).

"The king's heart *is* in the hand of the LORD, *as* the rivers of water: he turneth it whithersoever he will" (Pr.21:1).

"Of the increase of *his* government and peace *there shall be* no end, upon the throne of David, and upon his kingdom, to order it, and to establish it with judgment and with justice from henceforth even for ever. The zeal of the LORD of hosts will perform this" (Is.9:7).

"Thus saith the LORD, thy redeemer, and he that formed thee from the womb, I *am* the LORD that maketh all *things;* that stretcheth forth the heavens alone; that spreadeth abroad the earth by myself; That frustrateth the tokens of the liars, and maketh diviners mad; that turneth wise *men* backward, and maketh their knowledge foolish" (Is.44:24-25).

"Behold, the days come, saith the LORD, that I will raise unto David a righteous Branch, and a King shall reign and prosper, and shall execute judgment and justice in the earth" (Je.23:5).

"Daniel answered and said, Blessed be the name of God for ever and ever: for wisdom and might are his" (Da.2:20).

"And all the inhabitants of the earth *are* reputed as nothing: and he doeth according to his will in the army of heaven, and *among* the inhabitants of the earth: and none can stay his hand, or say unto him, What doest thou?" (Da.4:35).

"And there was given him dominion, and glory, and a kingdom, that all people, nations, and languages, should serve him: his dominion *is* an everlasting dominion, which shall not pass away, and his kingdom *that* which shall not be destroyed" (Da.7:14).

---

4 (6:13-22) **Joy, Example of—Hope, Fulfilled, Example—Temple, Second, Completion of—Returnees, Jewish, Built the Temple**: at last, the temple was completed, and the returned exiles celebrated with great joy. Their hope of worshipping the LORD in the new temple could now be fulfilled. A description of the wonderful event is given by Scripture:

OUTLINE	SCRIPTURE	SCRIPTURE	OUTLINE
4. The completion of the temple: A picture of great joy & celebration a. The completion 　1) The Persian officials assisted as ordered by Darius 　2) The returned exiles continued to build 　3) The prophets of God—Haggai & Zechariah—encouraged the people 　4) The leaders of the nation finished the construction 　• As commanded by God 　• As decreed by the kings of Persia 　5) The Jews completed the temple on the 3rd day of Adar (March 12) during the sixth year of Darius' reign b. The dedication service 　1) The whole community of returned exiles celebrated: The priests, the Levites, & all the freed captives 　2) The worship included a large number of sacrificial offerings 　• 100 bulls, 200 rams, & 400 lambs 　• A sin offering of 12 male goats: Represented the	13 Then Tatnai, governor on this side the river, Shethar-boznai, and their companions, according to that which Darius the king had sent, so they did speedily. 14 And the elders of the Jews builded, and they prospered through the prophesying of Haggai the prophet and Zechariah the son of Iddo. And they builded, and finished *it,* according to the commandment of the God of Israel, and according to the commandment of Cyrus, and Darius, and Artaxerxes king of Persia. 15 And this house was finished on the third day of the month Adar, which was in the sixth year of the reign of Darius the king. 16 And the children of Israel, the priests, and the Levites, and the rest of the children of the captivity, kept the dedication of this house of God with joy, 17 And offered at the dedication of this house of God an hundred bullocks, two hundred rams, four hundred lambs; and for a sin offering for all Israel, twelve he goats, according to the number of	the tribes of Israel. 18 And they set the priests in their divisions, and the Levites in their courses, for the service of God, which *is* at Jerusalem; as it is written in the book of Moses. 19 And the children of the captivity kept the passover upon the fourteenth *day* of the first month. 20 For the priests and the Levites were purified together, all of them *were* pure, and killed the passover for all the children of the captivity, and for their brethren the priests, and for themselves. 21 And the children of Israel, which were come again out of captivity, and all such as had separated themselves unto them from the filthiness of the heathen of the land, to seek the LORD God of Israel, did eat, 22 And kept the feast of unleavened bread seven days with joy: for the LORD had made them joyful, and turned the heart of the king of Assyria unto them, to strengthen their hands in the work of the house of God, the God of Israel.	12 tribes of Israel c. The installation of the priests & Levites: Were organized into their various divisions & assigned their duties, Ex.29; Le.8; Nu.3; 8:5-26; 18:1-32 d. The reinstitution of the Passover & the Feast of Unleavened Bread 　1) The priests & Levites purified themselves: By the ritual of washing with water, Ex.29:4; Nu.8:7 　2) The Levites slaughtered the Passover lamb for all the exiles 　3) The Passover meal was eaten by both the returned exiles & the Jews of the land who had spiritually separated themselves—who had turned away from the sins of their neighbors in order to seek the LORD 　4) The Feast of Unleavened Bread was celebrated with great joy because the LORD had worked in the heart of Assyria's king (the Persian Darius) to assist them: The exile was now ended; fellowship with God was at last restored

a. Just as Darius had ordered, Governor Tattenai and the other Persian officials worked diligently to carry out the commands of the king (v.13). No doubt, a renewed vigor flooded the hearts of the returned exiles, strengthening them to work harder than ever before to complete the temple (v.14). Note that God's prophets Haggai and Zechariah continued to encourage the people, obviously assuring them of the LORD's presence and the fulfillment of His promises.

Then, at last, the day for which they had all longed finally came. The temple was completed. Construction was just finished as commanded by God and decreed by the kings of Persia: Cyrus, Darius, and Artaxerxes (v.14). Although Artaxerxes had not issued a decree that involved the building of the temple, he had contributed timber for the building of the walls of Jerusalem (Ne.2:1, 8). In addition he had ordered that sacrifices be provided for the worship services at the temple (7:12-17).

The temple was completed on the third day of the month Adar, in the sixth year of King Darius' reign. Based on the modern calendar, this was March 12, 515 B.C.

b. After the temple had been completed, a special dedication service was held to commemorate the event (vv.16-17). All the returned exiles celebrated, including the priests, Levites, and people. In giving their thanks to the LORD, they offered up the sacrifice of 100 bulls, 200 rams, and 400 lambs. They also presented a sin offering of 12 male goats, which represented the 12 tribes of Israel. To get some idea of the contrast between the first and second temples, when King Solomon dedicated the first temple, so many sacrifices were offered that they could not be counted (I K.8:5). Over and above Solomon's personal sacrifices, 22,000 cattle and 120,000 sheep and goats were offered in behalf of the people (1 K.8:63). This shows the poverty of the returned exiles, their need to depend utterly upon the LORD for their day-by-day survival.

c. During the dedication celebration, an installation service was held for the priests and Levites (v.18). They were organized in the various divisions and assigned their various duties. Hereafter, they would be functioning in their day-to-day activities, worshipping the LORD and ministering to various people (Ex.29; Le.8; Nu.3; 8:5-26; 18:1-32).

d. About three weeks after the dedication service, the Passover was celebrated. The Feast of Unleavened Bread also was instituted as one of the annual feasts that was to be faithfully observed by the people (vv.19-22). As instructed by the LORD in His Holy Word, the priests and Levites purified themselves through the ritual washing with water (Ex.29:4; Nu.8:7). After cleansing themselves, the Levites slaughtered the Passover lamb for all the exiles as well as for the priests and Levites themselves (v.20).

The Passover meal was then eaten by both the returned exiles and the Jews of the land who had spiritually separated themselves (v.21). This is a wonderful indication that many of the Jews who had escaped exile by the Assyrians and Babylonians were now repenting. They were turning away from the sins of their neighbors in order to seek the LORD and join in the fellowship with their fellow believers, the returned exiles.

The celebration of the *Feast of Unleavened Bread* was to begin the day after Passover. For seven days the people celebrated with great joy because the LORD had changed the heart of the king toward them. He had helped them rebuild the temple of God (v.22). Note that the Persian king Darius is said to be the king of Assyria. This is because Persia now ruled over Assyria; consequently, Darius could be called the king of Assyria as well as the king of Persia. Joy flooded the hearts of the returnees, for the exile was now ended and fellowship with God was at last restored.

The Bible Knowledge Commentary concludes this section of Ezra with a statement that is well worth quoting in its entirety:

> Perhaps this title was a grim reminder that Assyria's harsh tactics were now ended. She was the first to deport Israelites from their land; but now a contingent of Jews was settled back in their land.
> This eight-day celebration...900 years after the first Passover, signaled the end of the exile, for a remnant of the nation was once again back in fellowship with Yahweh. Since the temple worship was restored, it was important for people who wanted to be in fellowship with God and live according to the covenantal obligation to be in the place where the sacrificial system was being practiced. The people had seen first hand that God works through history, for He had caused pagan kings to issue decrees which let them return to the land of promise (much as he had caused Egypt's Pharaoh to release Israel). The original readers of Ezra's book would rejoice in that fact and would be encouraged to participate in the temple worship, which had been reestablished at such great cost.[3]

Thought 1. Just as the returned exiles joyed and rejoiced in the LORD, so we are to joy and rejoice in Him who has loved us and given Himself for us, even the Lord Jesus Christ. Listen to what God's Holy Word says about joy:
(1) Joy is found in the presence of the LORD Himself.

"And now come I to thee; and these things I speak in the world, that they might have my joy fulfilled in themselves" (Jn.17:13).
"Thou wilt show me the path of life: in thy presence *is* fulness of joy; at thy right hand *there are* pleasures for evermore" (Ps.16:11).

(2) If we trust the LORD, our weeping will endure only for a night and joy will come forth in the morning.

"For his anger *endureth but* a moment; in his favour is life: weeping may endure for a night, but joy *cometh* in the morning" (Ps.30:5).

(3) If we bear strong witness, shedding tears over the lost of the world, we will reap great joy.

"And when he hath found *it* [the lost sheep], he layeth *it* on his shoulders, rejoicing" (Lu.15:5).
"They that sow in tears shall reap in joy" (Ps.126:5).

---

3 John F. Walvoord and Ray B. Zuck, Editors. *The Bible Knowledge Commentary*, pp.664-665.

(4) Great joy can be drawn from the depth of the riches of salvation.

"Therefore with joy shall ye draw water out of the wells of salvation" (Is.12:3).
"I will greatly rejoice in the LORD, my soul shall be joyful in my God; for he hath clothed me with the garments of salvation, he hath covered me with the robe of righteousness, as a bridegroom decketh *himself* with ornaments, and as a bride adorneth *herself* with her jewels" (Is.61:10).
"Yet I will rejoice in the LORD, I will joy in the God of my salvation" (Hab.3:18).

(5) The ransomed will march to Zion (heaven) with songs and everlasting joy flooding their hearts.

"And the ransomed of the LORD shall return, and come to Zion with songs and everlasting joy upon their heads: they shall obtain joy and gladness, and sorrow and sighing shall flee away" (Is.35:10).
"And the angel said unto them, Fear not: for, behold, I bring you good tidings of great joy, which shall be to all people" (Lu.2:10).

(6) Joy is found in the Word of God.

"These things have I spoken unto you, that my joy might remain in you, and *that* your joy might be full" (Jn.15:11).
"That I should be the minister of Jesus Christ to the Gentiles, ministering the gospel of God, that the offering up of the Gentiles might be acceptable, being sanctified by the Holy Ghost" (Ro.15:16).

(7) Joy is found in prayer and in receiving the answer to our prayers.

"Hitherto have ye asked nothing in my name: ask, and ye shall receive, that your joy may be full" (Jn.16:24).

(8) The kingdom of God floods our hearts with joy in the Holy Spirit.

"For the kingdom of God is not meat and drink; but righteousness, and peace, and joy in the Holy Ghost" (Ro.14:17).

(9) We are to rejoice and joy in the Lord Jesus, whom we love.

"Whom having not seen, ye love; in whom, though now ye see *him* not, yet believing, ye rejoice with joy unspeakable and full of glory" (1 Pe.1:8).

(10) We are to joy and rejoice through all the trials and temptations of this life.

"And they departed from the presence of the council, rejoicing that they were counted worthy to suffer shame for his name" (Ac.5:41).
"And when they had laid many stripes upon them, they cast *them* into prison, charging the jailer to keep them safely: Who, having received such a charge, thrust them into the inner prison, and made their feet fast in the stocks. And at midnight Paul and Silas prayed, and sang praises unto God: and the prisoners heard them" (Ac.16:23-25).
"As sorrowful, yet alway rejoicing; as poor, yet making many rich; as having nothing, and *yet* possessing all things" (2 Co.6:10).
"For ye had compassion of me in my bonds, and took joyfully the spoiling of your goods, knowing in yourselves that ye have in heaven a better and an enduring substance" (He.10:34).
"Looking unto Jesus the author and finisher of *our* faith; who for the joy that was set before him endured the cross, despising the shame, and is set down at the right hand of the throne of God" (He.12:2).
"[Christ] Whom having not seen, ye love; in whom, though now ye see *him* not, yet believing, ye rejoice with joy unspeakable and full of glory" (1 Pe.1:8).

DIVISION II — EZRA

THE SECOND RETURN OF EXILES FROM CAPTIVITY AND THEIR REFORM—LED BY EZRA, 7:1–10:44

(7:1–10:44) **DIVISION OVERVIEW**: almost sixty years after Zerubbabel led the first Jewish exiles back to the promised land, Ezra came on the scene. After receiving permission from King Artaxerxes, Ezra led the second group back to their homeland. While this second caravan was not as large in number, it was just as important. In the intervening years since the first return, the Jews in Jerusalem had slipped away from the LORD. Thus, Ezra's commission was to take another group of exiles back to Jerusalem. He was to:

⇒ investigate the situation
⇒ stir the people to make a renewed commitment to rebuild the nation
⇒ restore true worship in the temple

Ezra was a priest and a man of strong character. Therefore, he was the right person for God to use to stir genuine revival among the people. Furthermore, he was a godly leader who could arouse the backslidden priests and Levites to return to their duties in the temple.

Remember that Ezra was writing primarily to the exiles who had returned from Babylonian captivity and to the succeeding generations of Jews. As leader of the second group to return, Ezra had to exhort them to continue in their devotion to the LORD. Above all else, they had to remain faithful to the LORD. If they and the generations to come were faithful, genuinely trusting in the LORD and living righteously, He would continue to guide and protect them. He would also continue to bless them with the richness of the promised land. As a newly resettled nation, the Jews must never again risk captivity by giving in to the wicked and faithless idolatry of the nations around them. Most of their ancestors had lived wickedly; all future generations must live righteously. They had to remain strong in their commitment, unwavering in their devotion and worship of the LORD.

As the reader studies the return of the Jews from captivity under Ezra's direction, this fact should be kept in mind: the LORD watches over His people to make sure they remain totally devoted to Him. Total dedication is essential if God's people are to continue to flourish.

> **"For we were bondmen; yet our God hath not forsaken us in our bondage, but hath extended mercy unto us in the sight of the kings of Persia, to give us a reviving, to set up the house of our God, and to repair the desolations thereof, and to give us a wall in Judah and Jerusalem" (Ezra 9:9).**

THE SECOND RETURN OF EXILES FROM CAPTIVITY AND THEIR REFORM—LED BY EZRA, 7:1–10:44

A. Ezra's Royal Commission to Return to the Promised Land: The Picture of a Strong and Dedicated Leader, 7:1-28

B. Ezra's Preparations and Return to the Promised Land (Almost 60 Years After the Completion of the Temple): A Picture of Preparing for the Promised Land (a Type of Heaven), 8:1-36

C. Ezra's Confrontation with the People Over Their Evil Associations: A Picture of Genuine Revival, 9:1–10:44

CHAPTER 7

II. THE SECOND RETURN OF EXILES FROM CAPTIVITY & THEIR REFORM—LED BY EZRA, 7:1–10:44

A. Ezra's Royal Commission to Return to the Promised Land: The Picture of a Strong & Dedicated Leader, 7:1-28

1. The introduction of Ezra: A man wholly committed to the LORD & His Word
   a. Ezra's godly roots
      1) He was a priest from a long line of godly ancestors
         • Hilkiah, 2 K.22:1-20
         • Zadok, 2 S.15:24-37; 17:15; 1 K.1:8, 26

         • Phinehas, Nu.25:1-25; Ps.106:30
      2) He was a descendant of Aaron the High Priest, the brother of Moses
   b. Ezra's profession: A scribe or teacher who was well versed in the Law, God's Word
   c. Ezra's skilled leadership: Led the second group of exiles from captivity
      1) A gift of persuasion
         • Secured the king's help
         • Convinced people to leave their homes & security to make the long, hard, dangerous return to an uncertain future

      2) A strong will, iron determination
         • Completed the awesome task in the 7th year of King Artaxerxes
         • Took 4 months to achieve
      3) A total commitment to service: The hand of God was on his life, empowering & blessing him

   d. Ezra's wholehearted devotion to the LORD & His Word
      1) He studied God's Law
      2) He obeyed God's Law
      3) He taught God's laws
2. The royal commission to return given to Ezra by King Artaxerxes: A man sent on a mission
   a. The commission of Ezra

Now after these things, in the reign of Artaxerxes king of Persia, Ezra the son of Seraiah, the son of Azariah, the son of Hilkiah,

2 The son of Shallum, the son of Zadok, the son of Ahitub,

3 The son of Amariah, the son of Azariah, the son of Meraioth,

4 The son of Zerahiah, the son of Uzzi, the son of Bukki,

5 The son of Abishua, the son of Phinehas, the son of Eleazar, the son of Aaron the chief priest:

6 This Ezra went up from Babylon; and he *was* a ready scribe in the law of Moses, which the LORD God of Israel had given: and the king granted him all his request, according to the hand of the LORD his God upon him.

7 And there went up *some* of the children of Israel, and of the priests, and the Levites, and the singers, and the porters, and the Nethinims, unto Jerusalem, in the seventh year of Artaxerxes the king.

8 And he came to Jerusalem in the fifth month, which *was* in the seventh year of the king.

9 For upon the first *day* of the first month began he to go up from Babylon, and on the first *day* of the fifth month came he to Jerusalem, according to the good hand of his God upon him.

10 For Ezra had prepared his heart to seek the law of the LORD, and to do *it,* and to teach in Israel statutes and judgments.

11 Now this *is* the copy of the letter that the king Artaxerxes gave unto Ezra the priest, the scribe, *even* a scribe of the words of the commandments of the LORD, and of his statutes to Israel.

12 Artaxerxes, king of kings, unto Ezra the priest, a scribe of the law of the God of heaven, perfect *peace,* and at such a time.

13 I make a decree, that all they of the people of Israel, and *of* his priests and Levites, in my realm, which are minded of their own freewill to go up to Jerusalem, go with thee.

14 Forasmuch as thou art sent of the king, and of his seven counsellors, to enquire concerning Judah and Jerusalem, according to the law of thy God which *is* in thine hand;

15 And to carry the silver and gold, which the king and his counsellors have freely offered unto the God of Israel, whose habitation *is* in Jerusalem,

16 And all the silver and gold that thou canst find in all the province of Babylon, with the freewill offering of the people, and of the priests, offering willingly for the house of their God which *is* in Jerusalem:

17 That thou mayest buy speedily with this money bullocks, rams, lambs, with their meat offerings and their drink offerings, and offer them upon the altar of the house of your God which *is* in Jerusalem.

18 And whatsoever shall seem good to thee, and to thy brethren, to do with the rest of the silver and the gold, that do after the will of your God.

19 The vessels also that are given thee for the service of the house of thy God, *those* deliver thou before the God of Jerusalem.

20 And whatsoever more shall be needful for the house of thy God, which thou shalt have occasion to bestow, bestow *it* out of the king's treasure house.

21 And I, *even* I Artaxerxes the king, do make a decree to all the treasurers which *are* beyond the river, that whatsoever Ezra the priest, the scribe of the law of the God of heaven, shall require of you, it be done speedily,

22 Unto an hundred talents

confirmed in a royal letter: Made Ezra a representative of the king himself
   b. The qualifications of Ezra: A priest, teacher, & scholar in the Law

   c. The permission granted to Ezra: To encourage all Israelites who wished to return to Jerusalem to do so

   d. The clearly stated purpose given to Ezra: To investigate & make sure the people were obeying the Law, God's Word

   e. The oversight of finances assigned to Ezra: To oversee gifts for the temple
      1) The source of the money
         • The king & his officials gave silver & gold
         • The officials in the province (district) of Babylon gave silver & gold
         • The Jewish people & priests were to give offerings

      2) The use of the donated money
         • To buy animals & food items to be sacrificed & offered at the worship services of the temple

         • To use any money left over as felt needed, but for God's service not for selfish desires

      3) The responsibility for the gifts & temple furnishings: To return all to the temple

      4) The right to requisition the royal treasury: If the temple faced a shortage of funds

   f. The right given to Ezra to request help from political officials
      1) The king's command to all Persian officials beyond the Euphrates River: To help Ezra as needed
      2) The abundant supply

promised Ezra • Silver: 7,500 pounds; wheat: 500 bushels • Wine & olive oil: 500 gallons; salt: no limit 3) The warning to the Persian officials • They were to provide quickly for the temple of God: To secure His protection, prevent His wrath • They were not to tax any religious worker serving at the temple g. The royal authority given to Ezra 1) To appoint magistrates & judges to govern all the people in the province (district) west of the	of silver, and to an hundred measures of wheat, and to an hundred baths of wine, and to an hundred baths of oil, and salt without prescribing *how much*. 23 Whatsoever is commanded by the God of heaven, let it be diligently done for the house of the God of heaven: for why should there be wrath against the realm of the king and his sons? 24 Also we certify you, that touching any of the priests and Levites, singers, porters, Nethinims, or ministers of this house of God, it shall not be lawful to impose toll, tribute, or custom, upon them. 25 And thou, Ezra, after the wisdom of thy God, that *is* in thine hand, set magistrates and judges, which may judge all the people that *are* beyond the river, all such as know	the laws of thy God; and teach ye them that know *them* not. 26 And whosoever will not do the law of thy God, and the law of the king, let judgment be executed speedily upon him, whether *it be* unto death, or to banishment, or to confiscation of goods, or to imprisonment. 27 Blessed *be* the LORD God of our fathers, which hath put *such a thing* as this in the king's heart, to beautify the house of the LORD which *is* in Jerusalem: 28 And hath extended mercy unto me before the king, and his counsellors, and before all the king's mighty princes. And I was strengthened as the hand of the LORD my God *was* upon me, and I gathered together out of Israel chief men to go up with me.	Euphrates River 2) To teach the Law of God 3) To execute justice: Carried out either by Ezra or the Persian governor & officials h. The response of Ezra 1) He praised the LORD • Because God moved the heart of the king to honor the LORD's house • Because God showed mercy: Stirred the king & his officials to appoint him for this great mission • Because God's hand was upon him 2) He was encouraged & began to recruit people to return to the promised land with him

DIVISION II

THE SECOND RETURN OF EXILES FROM CAPTIVITY AND THEIR REFORM—LED BY EZRA, 7:1–10:44

A. Ezra's Royal Commission to Return to the Promised Land: The Picture of a Strong and Dedicated Leader, 7:1-28

(7:1-28) **Introduction**: if there has ever been a day when strong men and women and strong leaders are needed, it is today. There are few people of integrity, few who are upright and honest, moral and pure, decisive and steadfast, enduring and persevering. Far too many of us are weak, lacking the strength to follow through with decisions and commitments. How many of us make a commitment to marriage and then break the commitment? How many work hard at our jobs, giving our employers a full days' work for a full days' wage? How many employers are fair and just with their employees? How many are filled with greed and covetousness, craving more and more instead of giving to meet the needs of the world? How many of us are genuinely gripped with a spirit of compassion and mercy, forgiving those who wrong us? Where are men and women of integrity who turn away from lying and deception, speaking the truth in love? Where are the men and women of morality who will uphold the bond of marriage and other commitments? Who will develop strong but tender hearts that are decisive yet compassionate and merciful? Where are the men and women who will build up society, strengthening others instead of tearing them down through selfishness, gossip, rumors, and a negative spirit?

In the present Scripture, a man of enormous strength and leadership skills steps forth to introduce himself. This man is Ezra, the man for whom this great book of Holy Scripture is named. It had been about 57 years since the end of chapter six and the beginning of chapter seven, 57 years since the temple had been completed and dedicated by the first returnees to Jerusalem (vv.7-9; 8:31). Now the LORD raised up a man to lead a second group of exiles back to the promised land of God. This is, *Ezra's Royal Commission to Return to the Promised Land: the Picture of a Strong and Dedicated Leader*, 7:1-28.

1. The introduction of Ezra: a man wholly committed to the LORD and His Word (vv.1-10).
2. The royal commission to return given to Ezra by King Artaxerxes: a man sent on a mission (vv.11-28).

1 (7:1-10) **Word of God, Commitment to—God, Commitment to—Bible, Study of—Devotion, to the Word of God—Commitment, Duty—Ezra, Genealogy of—Ezra, Leadership of—Ezra, Commitment of—Exile Returnees, Under Ezra's Leadership—Jewish Exiles, Returned, Under Ezra's Leadership**: the man for whom this book is named finally steps on the scene. Ezra is now introduced to the reader. Four significant areas of Ezra's life are covered by Scripture: his godly roots, his profession, his skilled leadership, and his devotion to the LORD and His Holy Word.

OUTLINE	SCRIPTURE	SCRIPTURE	OUTLINE

1. The introduction of Ezra: A man wholly committed to the LORD & His Word
a. Ezra's godly roots
  1) He was a priest from a long line of godly ancestors
    • Hilkiah, 2 K.22:1-20
    • Zadok, 2 S.15:24-37; 17:15; 1 K.1:8, 26
 	
    • Phinehas, Nu.25:1-25; Ps.106:30
  2) He was a descendant of Aaron the High Priest, the brother of Moses
b. Ezra's profession: A scribe or teacher who was well versed in the Law, God's Word
c. Ezra's skilled leadership: Led the second group of exiles from captivity
  1) A gift of persuasion
	Now after these things, in the reign of Artaxerxes king of Persia, Ezra the son of Seraiah, the son of Azariah, the son of Hilkiah,
	2 The son of Shallum, the son of Zadok, the son of Ahitub,
	3 The son of Amariah, the son of Azariah, the son of Meraioth,
	4 The son of Zerahiah, the son of Uzzi, the son of Bukki,
	5 The son of Abishua, the son of Phinehas, the son of Eleazar, the son of Aaron the chief priest:
	6 This Ezra went up from Babylon; and he *was* a ready scribe in the law of Moses, which the LORD God of Israel had given: and the king granted him all his request, according to the hand of the LORD his God upon
		him.
		7 And there went up *some* of the children of Israel, and of the priests, and the Levites, and the singers, and the porters, and the Nethinims, unto Jerusalem, in the seventh year of Artaxerxes the king.
		8 And he came to Jerusalem in the fifth month, which *was* in the seventh year of the king.
		9 For upon the first *day* of the first month began he to go up from Babylon, and on the first *day* of the fifth month came he to Jerusalem, according to the good hand of his God upon him.
		10 For Ezra had prepared his heart to seek the law of the LORD, and to do *it,* and to teach in Israel statutes and judgments.
			• Secured the king's help
			• Convinced people to leave their homes & security to make the long, hard, dangerous return to an uncertain future
			
			  2) A strong will, iron determination
			    • Completed the awesome task in the 7th year of King Artaxerxes
			    • Took 4 months to achieve
			  3) A total commitment to service: The hand of God was on his life, empowering & blessing him
			d. A wholehearted devotion to the LORD & His Word
			  1) To study God's Law
			  2) To obey God's Law
			  3) To teach God's laws

a. Ezra had a strong, godly heritage (vv.1-5). He was a priest from a long line of spiritual leaders. These leaders had served as priests to the nation of Israel down through the centuries. A few of these leaders were...

- Hilkiah, who had discovered the Law of God while the temple was being repaired during the days of King Josiah (2 K.22:1-20).
- Zadok, who served as High Priest during the days of David and who proved loyal to David during some of the most difficult trials confronted by the king (2 S.15:24-37; 17:15; 1 K.1:8, 26).
- Phinehas, who proved his zeal and loyalty for the LORD during the wilderness journeys. He helped purge the land of apostasy and immorality (Nu.25:1-25; Ps.106:30).

Ezra could also trace his ancestry all the way back to the very first High Priest, Aaron, who was the brother of Moses himself (v.5). In Ezra is seen the fulfillment of God's wonderful promise to bless the descendants of the godly (De.4:40; Ps.128:1-6).

b. Ezra was a scribe or teacher by profession, well versed in the Law, God's Holy Word (v.6). Note the statement that the Law is God's Holy Word. The LORD Himself had given the Law to Moses. How much of the Law did Ezra have? Probably most of the writings that had been completed up to that time, which would have included the Pentateuch, some of the historical writings, and some of the prophets' messages. Whatever the case, the fact that Ezra was well versed in the Law of God shows that the exiles at least had access to many of the writings of Holy Scripture.

c. Ezra was a man of exceptional leadership skills. He was also a man wholly devoted to the LORD and His Holy Word (vv.6-10). He was the man appointed by the LORD and King Artaxerxes to lead the second group of exiles from captivity back to the promised land of God. His exceptional skills are seen in four facts:

1) Ezra was very skilled in the art of persuasion (vv.6-7). Everything he asked of the king, the king granted. Nothing was withheld, and no request was left unanswered, for the hand of the LORD was upon him. Note that this statement is used six times concerning Ezra (7:6, 9, 28; 8:18, 22, 31). God had definitely chosen Ezra to be the man to free the second group of exiles from captivity, and the LORD was proving His call by giving exceptional skills of persuasion to Ezra. Using his skill to the fullest degree possible, Ezra was able to convince people to leave their homes and security to make the long, hard, dangerous return to an uncertain future in Jerusalem (v.7).

2) Ezra also had an exceptionally strong will and an iron determination (vv.8-9). Lying out before Ezra was a long, treacherous journey of about 900 miles. The roadway was infested with bandits and led through the territory of enemies who bitterly despised the Jews (8:22, 31). Despite these difficulties, the major problem did not lie with Ezra himself making the journey. The problem was that he personally had to lead a caravan of 5,000 exiles through the dangerous territory. Nevertheless, with fierce determination, Ezra completed the awesome task in just four months. In the seventh year of King Artaxerxes's reign, he was able to complete the task (v.9; 8:31).

3) Ezra was a man who was totally committed to service, serving both the LORD and His people. The LORD had charged him with the incredible mission of delivering His people from captivity and returning them to the promised land. To this task, Ezra was totally committed. Thus, "the good [gracious] hand of God was upon him," guiding and meeting his every need.

d. Ezra was a man wholeheartedly devoted to the LORD and the LORD's Word (v.10). Three facts are stated about his devotion to the Word of God:

1) Ezra studied God's Word, His Holy commandments. The implication is that Ezra walked throughout the day meditating upon the Word of God.

2) Ezra obeyed God's Word and made a deliberate effort to keep His holy commandments. He sought daily to live out God's Word in his life.

3) Ezra taught God's Holy Word to others. Remember that the people of that day had no other way to learn God's Word. There were not many scrolls available and few people had enough money to purchase what copies might be available. Ezra was a man who dedicated himself to teaching God's Word so that people could have the fullness of life promised in its holy pages.

Thought 1. One of the great needs in the world today is for men and women to be totally committed to the LORD and to His Holy Word. Most of the world is ignorant of the LORD and His Word. To prove the point, think how little time most of us spend in daily prayer and study of the Bible. We each need to ask ourselves, How much time do I spend in daily prayer? Daily Bible study? In serving the LORD by meeting the needs of others?

A person who is totally committed to the LORD and His Holy Word will draw near God through prayer. The committed person will also study God's Holy Word and minister to other people. In fact, a committed person will set aside a certain amount of time every day to draw near the LORD through prayer and Bible study. In addition, the person will pray continually as he or she walks throughout the activities of the day, ministering to the needs of fellow workers, neighbors, and even strangers. Being totally committed means that we study, live, and bear witness to the LORD, doing exactly what He instructs in His Holy Word. We keep God's commandments, live them out, practice them, living holy and righteous lives. Keeping in mind that Ezra was a man totally devoted to God's Word, listen to what the LORD says about His Holy Word:

(1) We are to love, joy, and rejoice in God's Holy Word.

> "Ye have not chosen me, but I have chosen you, and ordained you, that ye should go and bring forth fruit, and *that* your fruit should remain: that whatsoever ye shall ask of the Father in my name, he may give it you" (Jn.15:16).
> "And I will delight myself in thy commandments, which I have loved" (Ps.119:47).
> "The law of thy mouth *is* better unto me than thousands of gold and silver" (Ps.119:72).
> "Mine eyes fail for thy word, saying, When wilt thou comfort me?" (Ps.119:82).
> "O how love I thy law! it *is* my meditation all the day" (Ps.119:97).
> "Thy word *is* very pure: therefore thy servant loveth it" (Ps.119:140).
> "Thy words were found, and I did eat them; and thy word was unto me the joy and rejoicing of mine heart: for I am called by thy name, O LORD God of hosts" (Je.15:16).

(2) God's Holy Word feeds the hunger and thirst of a human heart.

> "As newborn babes, desire the sincere milk of the word, that ye may grow thereby: If so be ye have tasted that the Lord *is* gracious" (1 Pe.2:2-3).
> "He that hath an ear, let him hear what the Spirit saith unto the churches; To him that overcometh will I give to eat of the hidden manna [Word of God], and will give him a white stone, and in the stone a new name written, which no man knoweth saving he that receiveth *it*" (Re.2:17).
> "And he humbled thee, and suffered thee to hunger, and fed thee with manna, which thou knewest not, neither did thy fathers know; that he might make thee know that man doth not live by bread only, but by every *word* that proceedeth out of the mouth of the LORD doth man live" (De.8:3).
> "Neither have I gone back from the commandment of his lips; I have esteemed the words of his mouth more than my necessary *food*" (Jb.23:12).
> "How sweet are thy words unto my taste! *yea, sweeter* than honey to my mouth!" (Ps.119:103).
> "Wherefore do ye spend money for *that which is* not bread? and your labour for *that which* satisfieth not? hearken diligently unto me, and eat ye *that which is* good, and let your soul delight itself in fatness" (Is.55:2).
> "And I will give you pastors according to mine heart, which shall feed you with knowledge and understanding" (Je.3:15).
> "Thy words were found, and I did eat them; and thy word was unto me the joy and rejoicing of mine heart: for I am called by thy name, O LORD God of hosts" (Je.15:16).

(3) The Word of God is inspired, "God-breathed."

> "Men *and* brethren, this scripture must needs have been fulfilled, which the Holy Ghost by the mouth of David spake before concerning Judas, which was guide to them that took Jesus" (Ac.1:16).
> "All scripture *is* given by inspiration of God, and *is* profitable for doctrine, for reproof, for correction, for instruction in righteousness" (2 Ti.3:16).
> "Searching what, or what manner of time the Spirit of Christ which was in them did signify, when it testified beforehand the sufferings of Christ, and the glory that should follow" (1 Pe.1:11).
> "We have also a more sure word of prophecy; whereunto ye do well that ye take heed, as unto a light that shineth in a dark place, until the day dawn, and the day star arise in your hearts: Knowing this first, that no prophecy of the scripture is of any private interpretation. For the prophecy came not in old time by the will of man: but holy men of God spake *as they were* moved by the Holy Ghost" (2 Pe.1:19-21).

"And I heard a voice from heaven saying unto me, Write, Blessed *are* the dead which die in the Lord from henceforth: Yea, saith the Spirit, that they may rest from their labours; and their works do follow them" (Re.14:13).

"Take thee a roll of a book, and write therein all the words that I have spoken unto thee against Israel, and against Judah, and against all the nations, from the day I spake unto thee, from the days of Josiah, even into this day" (Je.36:2).

"The word of the LORD came expressly unto Ezekiel the priest, the son of Buzi, in the land of the Chaldeans by the river Chebar; and the hand of the LORD was there upon him" (Eze.1:3).

(4) The Word of God is to be held tightly in our hearts.

"But what saith it? The word is nigh thee, *even* in thy mouth, and in thy heart: that is, the word of faith, which we preach" (Ro.10:8).

"Let the word of Christ dwell in you richly in all wisdom; teaching and admonishing one another in psalms and hymns and spiritual songs, singing with grace in your hearts to the Lord" (Co.3:16).

"And these words, which I command thee this day, shall be in thine heart" (De.6:6).

"Therefore shall ye lay up these my words in your heart and in your soul, and bind them for a sign upon your hand, that they may be as frontlets between your eyes" (De.11:18).

"Thy word have I hid in mine heart, that I might not sin against thee" (Ps.119:11).

(5) The Word of God is to be a light and a guide to our lives.

"The statutes of the LORD *are* right, rejoicing the heart: the commandment of the LORD *is* pure, enlightening the eyes" (Ps.19:8).

"Thy word *is* a lamp unto my feet, and a light unto my path" (Ps.119:105).

"The entrance of thy words giveth light; it giveth understanding unto the simple" (Ps.119:130).

"For the commandment *is* a lamp; and the law *is* light; and reproofs of instruction *are* the way of life" (Pr.6:23).

"But he that lacketh these things [God's instructions] is blind, and cannot see afar off, and hath forgotten that he was purged from his old sins" (2 Pe.1:9).

(6) The Word of God cleanses and purifies us.

"Now ye are clean through the word which I have spoken unto you" (Jn.15:3).

"Sanctify them through thy truth: thy word is truth" (Jn.17:17).

"Seeing ye have purified your souls in obeying the truth [God's Word] through the Spirit unto unfeigned love of the brethren, *see that ye* love one another with a pure heart fervently" (1 Pe.1:22).

"Wherewithal shall a young man cleanse his way? by taking heed *thereto* according to thy word" (Ps.119:9).

(7) The Word of God is to be reverenced, for it is sacred to the LORD.

"And if any man shall take away from the words of the book of this prophecy, God shall take away his part out of the book of life, and out of the holy city, and *from* the things which are written in this book" (Re.22:19).

"Ye shall not add unto the word which I command you, neither shall ye diminish *ought* from it, that ye may keep the commandments of the LORD your God which I command you" (De.4:2).

"What thing soever I command you, observe to do it: thou shalt not add thereto, nor diminish from it" (De.12:32).

"Add thou not unto his words, lest he reprove thee, and thou be found a liar" (Pr.30:6).

(8) The Word of God is to be studied.

"Search the scriptures; for in them ye think ye have eternal life: and they are they which testify of me" (Jn.5:39).

"These were more noble than those in Thessalonica, in that they received the word with all readiness of mind, and searched the scriptures daily, whether those things were so" (Ac.17:11).

"For whatsoever things were written aforetime were written for our learning, that we through patience and comfort of the scriptures might have hope" (Ro.15:4).

"Study to shew thyself approved unto God, a workman that needeth not to be ashamed, rightly dividing the word of truth" (2 Ti.2:15).

"And it shall be with him, and he shall read therein all the days of his life: that he may learn to fear the LORD his God, to keep all the words of this law and these statutes, to do them" (De.17:19).

"Seek ye out of the book of the LORD, and read: no one of these shall fail, none shall want her mate: for my mouth it hath commanded, and his spirit it hath gathered them" (Is.34:16).

(9) The Word of God is absolutely trustworthy, and its promises will always be fulfilled.

"But while he thought on these things, behold, the angel of the Lord appeared unto him in a dream, saying, Joseph, thou son of David, fear not to take unto thee Mary thy wife: for that which is conceived in her is of the Holy Ghost. And she shall bring forth a son, and thou shalt call his name JESUS: for he shall save his people from their sins. Now all this was done, that it might be fulfilled which was spoken of the Lord by the prophet, saying, Behold, a virgin shall be with child, and shall bring forth a son, and they shall call his name Emmanuel, which being interpreted is, God with us" (Mt.1:20-23).

"For verily I say unto you, Till heaven and earth pass, one jot or one tittle shall in no wise pass from the law, till all be fulfilled" (Mt.5:18).

"Heaven and earth shall pass away: but my words shall not pass away" (Lu.21:33).

"And he said unto them, These *are* the words which I spake unto you, while I was yet with you, that all things must be fulfilled, which were written in the law of Moses, and *in* the prophets, and *in* the psalms, concerning me" (Lu.24:44).

"But those things, which God before had shewed by the mouth of all his prophets, that Christ should suffer, he hath so fulfilled" (Ac.3:18).

"And when they had fulfilled all that was written of him, they took *him* down from the tree, and laid *him* in a sepulchre" (Ac.13:29).

"Blessed *be* the LORD, that hath given rest unto his people Israel, according to all that he promised: there hath not failed one word of all his good promise, which he promised by the hand of Moses his servant" (1 K.8:56).

"The works of his hands *are* verity and judgment; all his commandments *are* sure" (Ps.111:7).

"For I *am* the LORD: I will speak, and the word that I shall speak shall come to pass; it shall be no more prolonged: for in your days, O rebellious house, will I say the word, and will perform it, saith the Lord GOD" (Eze.12:25).

(10) The Word of God must be obeyed, the commandments kept.

"Not every one that saith unto me, Lord, Lord, shall enter into the kingdom of heaven; but he that doeth the will of my Father which is in heaven. Many will say to me in that day, Lord, Lord, have we not prophesied in thy name? and in thy name have cast out devils? and in thy name done many wonderful works? And then will I profess unto them, I never knew you: depart from me, ye that work iniquity. Therefore whosoever heareth these sayings of mine, and doeth them, I will liken him unto a wise man, which built his house upon a rock: And the rain descended, and the floods came, and the winds blew, and beat upon that house; and it fell not: for it was founded upon a rock. And every one that heareth these sayings of mine, and doeth them not, shall be likened unto a foolish man, which built his house upon the sand: And the rain descended, and the floods came, and the winds blew, and beat upon that house; and it fell: and great was the fall of it. And it came to pass, when Jesus had ended these sayings, the people were astonished at his doctrine: For he taught them as *one* having authority, and not as the scribes" (Mt.7:21-29).

"Jesus answered and said unto him, If a man love me, he will keep my words: and my Father will love him, and we will come unto him, and make our abode with him" (Jn.14:23).

"If ye keep my commandments, ye shall abide in my love; even as I have kept my Father's commandments, and abide in his love" (Jn.15:10).

"Blessed *are* they that do his commandments, that they may have right to the tree of life, and may enter in through the gates into the city" (Re.22:14).

"Now therefore, if ye will obey my voice indeed, and keep my covenant, then ye shall be a peculiar treasure unto me above all people: for all the earth *is* mine" (Ex.19:5).

"This day the LORD thy God hath commanded thee to do these statutes and judgments: thou shalt therefore keep and do them with all thine heart, and with all thy soul" (De.26:16).

"This book of the law shall not depart out of thy mouth; but thou shalt meditate therein day and night, that thou mayest observe to do according to all that is written therein: for then thou shalt make thy way prosperous, and then thou shalt have good success" (Jos.1:8).

"Be ye therefore very courageous to keep and to do all that is written in the book of the law of Moses, that ye turn not aside therefrom *to* the right hand or *to* the left" (Jos.23:6).

"Whoso keepeth the law *is* a wise son: but he that is a companion of riotous *men* shameth his father" (Pr.28:7).

[2] **(7:11-28) Mission, Fulfillment of, Example—Ezra, Commission of—Artaxerxes, King of Persia, Commission to Ezra**: the royal commission for Ezra to return to Jerusalem was given by King Artaxerxes of Persia. What now follows is actually a copy of the letter that the king presented to Ezra. Scripture spells out exactly what Ezra was being commissioned to do:

OUTLINE	SCRIPTURE	SCRIPTURE	OUTLINE
2. The royal commission to return given to Ezra by King Artaxerxes: A man sent on a mission a. The commission of Ezra confirmed in a royal letter: Made Ezra a representative of the king himself b. The qualifications of Ezra: A priest, teacher, & scholar in the Law c. The permission granted to Ezra: To encourage all Israelites who wished to return to Jerusalem to do so d. The clearly stated purpose given to Ezra: To investigate & make sure the people were obeying the Law, God's Word e. The oversight of finances assigned to Ezra: To oversee gifts for the temple 1) The source of the money • The king & his officials gave silver & gold • The officials in the province (district) of Babylon gave silver & gold • The Jewish people & priests were to give offerings 2) The use of the donated money • To buy animals & food items to be sacrificed & offered at the worship services of the temple • To use any money left over as felt needed, but for God's service not for selfish desires 3) The responsibility for the gifts & temple furnishings: To return all to the temple 4) The right to requisition the royal treasury: If the temple faced a shortage of funds	11 Now this *is* the copy of the letter that the king Artaxerxes gave unto Ezra the priest, the scribe, *even* a scribe of the words of the commandments of the LORD, and of his statutes to Israel. 12 Artaxerxes, king of kings, unto Ezra the priest, a scribe of the law of the God of heaven, perfect *peace,* and at such a time. 13 I make a decree, that all they of the people of Israel, and *of* his priests and Levites, in my realm, which are minded of their own freewill to go up to Jerusalem, go with thee. 14 Forasmuch as thou art sent of the king, and of his seven counsellors, to enquire concerning Judah and Jerusalem, according to the law of thy God which *is* in thine hand; 15 And to carry the silver and gold, which the king and his counsellors have freely offered unto the God of Israel, whose habitation *is* in Jerusalem, 16 And all the silver and gold that thou canst find in all the province of Babylon, with the freewill offering of the people, and of the priests, offering willingly for the house of their God which *is* in Jerusalem: 17 That thou mayest buy speedily with this money bullocks, rams, lambs, with their meat offerings and their drink offerings, and offer them upon the altar of the house of your God which *is* in Jerusalem. 18 And whatsoever shall seem good to thee, and to thy brethren, to do with the rest of the silver and the gold, that do after the will of your God. 19 The vessels also that are given thee for the service of the house of thy God, *those* deliver thou before the God of Jerusalem. 20 And whatsoever more shall be needful for the house of thy God, which thou shalt have occasion to bestow, bestow *it* out of the king's	treasure house. 21 And I, *even* I Artaxerxes the king, do make a decree to all the treasurers which *are* beyond the river, that whatsoever Ezra the priest, the scribe of the law of the God of heaven, shall require of you, it be done speedily, 22 Unto an hundred talents of silver, and to an hundred measures of wheat, and to an hundred baths of wine, and to an hundred baths of oil, and salt without prescribing *how much.* 23 Whatsoever is commanded by the God of heaven, let it be diligently done for the house of the God of heaven: for why should there be wrath against the realm of the king and his sons? 24 Also we certify you, that touching any of the priests and Levites, singers, porters, Nethinims, or ministers of this house of God, it shall not be lawful to impose toll, tribute, or custom, upon them. 25 And thou, Ezra, after the wisdom of thy God, that *is* in thine hand, set magistrates and judges, which may judge all the people that *are* beyond the river, all such as know the laws of thy God; and teach ye them that know *them* not. 26 And whosoever will not do the law of thy God, and the law of the king, let judgment be executed speedily upon him, whether *it be* unto death, or to banishment, or to confiscation of goods, or to imprisonment. 27 Blessed *be* the LORD God of our fathers, which hath put *such a thing* as this in the king's heart, to beautify the house of the LORD which *is* in Jerusalem: 28 And hath extended mercy unto me before the king, and his counsellors, and before all the king's mighty princes. And I was strengthened as the hand of the LORD my God *was* upon me, and I gathered together out of Israel chief men to go up with me.	f. The right given to Ezra to request help from political officials 1) The king's command to all Persian officials beyond the Euphrates River: To help Ezra as needed 2) The abundant supply promised Ezra • Silver: 7,500 pounds; wheat: 500 bushels • Wine & olive oil: 500 gallons; salt: no limit 3) The warning to the Persian officials • They were to provide quickly for the temple of God: To secure His protection, prevent His wrath • They were not to tax any religious worker serving at the temple g. The royal authority given to Ezra 1) To appoint magistrates & judges to govern all the people in the province (district) west of the Euphrates River 2) To teach the Law of God 3) To execute justice: Carried out either by Ezra or the Persian governor & officials h. The response of Ezra 1) He praised the LORD • Because God moved the heart of the king to honor the LORD's house • Because God showed mercy: Stirred the king & his officials to appoint him for this great mission • Because God's hand was upon him 2) He was encouraged & began to recruit people to return to the promised land

a. The commission appointed Ezra as a personal representative of the king himself (v.11). As a representative of the king, Ezra was assured of receiving the rights and the help spelled out by the king.

b. The letter listed the qualifications of Ezra by addressing him as a priest, teacher, and scholar in the Law of the "God of heaven" (v.12).

c. Artaxerxes decreed the right for any Israelite who wished to return to Jerusalem with Ezra to do so (v.13). Any Israelite anywhere in the great empire of Persia could be freed from captivity and returned to his homeland.

d. The letter clearly stated the purpose for which Ezra was being sent to Jerusalem and Judah (v.14). His purpose was to investigate and to make sure his people were obeying the Law, God's Word. If not, then Ezra was to teach the Law of God and enforce obedience to the LORD's commandments (vv.25-26). Remember that the earlier exiles who had returned under Zerubbabel had been commissioned to rebuild the temple and the cities of Judah. But in the intervening 57 years, the earlier returnees had slipped away from the LORD and were no longer committed to completing the task. Thus, Ezra's commission was to return to Jerusalem, investigate the situation, and stir the people to make a renewed commitment to rebuild their nation and to restore true worship in the temple.

e. The letter also assigned the oversight of the finances to Ezra. He was to oversee all the gifts that had been given for the temple, as well as all the money and gifts he was yet to obtain from the province of Babylon after he arrived in Jerusalem. Note four facts spelled out by the letter:

⇒ Ezra was given and placed in charge of a large treasure. The large sum of money was given to help Ezra achieve his purpose and was contributed to by...
- the king and his officials, who had obviously given a large amount of silver and gold.
- the government officials and the province of Babylon, who were instructed by King Artaxerxes to give whatever silver or gold Ezra felt was needed.
- the Jewish people and priests in Jerusalem who were also expected to give freewill offerings.

⇒ All this money and wealth was to be overseen by Ezra. He was to use everything that was donated to help the people get settled in their homeland and to help with whatever repairs might be needed on the temple. But he was also to use the money to buy animals and food items to be sacrificed and offered at the worship services of the temple (vv.17-18). Any money left over was to be used as he felt needed. But he was to make sure that it was used for God's service, not for selfish desires.

⇒ In addition to the money and wealth, some temple furnishings and articles were placed into Ezra's care. He was to return all these to the temple (v.19).

⇒ Interestingly, the king gave Ezra the right to requisition the royal treasury for whatever he needed (v.20). If he ran short of any supply or faced a lack of funds for anything, he could call upon the royal treasury of the local province to provide it.

f. Artaxerxes also gave Ezra the right to request help from the political officials who governed the empire west of the Euphrates (vv.21-24). This was a large territory, which meant that the taxes collected by the government amounted to huge sums of money for the royal treasury. Hence, Ezra's needs were assured of being met. Note that a limit was placed upon the request he could make, though the limit was generous...
- 100 talents of silver (7,500 pounds)
- 500 measures or bushels of wheat
- 100 baths of wine (500 gallons)
- 100 baths of olive oil (500 gallons)
- an unlimited supply of salt

To make sure the officials supplied whatever Ezra needed, Artaxerxes issued a warning to the officials (vv.23-24). They were to provide quickly for the temple of God in order to secure the protection of the Jewish God and to prevent His wrath from falling upon them. Why would Artaxerxes fear the God of the Jews when the Jews had been so easily conquered under the Babylonians and the Persians? No doubt, in his mind, the God of Israel had not been able to protect the Jews. Why, then, would he now be thinking that the God of the Jews could protect them or cast His wrath upon the Persian Empire? Scripture says nothing about the matter. Perhaps Artaxerxes had heard of God's astounding, miraculous deliverance of the Jews from the Assyrians during Hezekiah's reign in Israel. The backbone of the Assyrian army had been broken. In one night, 185,000 soldiers were killed by the angel of the LORD (Is.37:36). Whatever the case, it seems evident that God was at work in the heart of Artaxerxes, moving him to show favor to the returning exiles. The king further instructed the officials not to tax any religious worker serving at the temple (v.24).

g. In closing his letter of commission, the king gave Ezra a threefold royal authority (vv.25-26). First, he gave Ezra the authority to appoint magistrates and judges. They were to govern all the Jews in the province west of the Euphrates River.

Second, he was given the royal authority to teach the Law of God to the Jewish people. He was to make sure that all the Jews knew and obeyed the Law.

Third, he was to execute justice upon any who did not obey the commandments as spelled out in the Law of God and in the law of the king (v.26). Justice was to be carried out either by Ezra personally or by the Persian governor and his officials. These sentences included the verdict of death as well as banishment, confiscation of property, and imprisonment. All civil and religious laws were to be obeyed by the Jews.

h. Ezra's response to the commission given him was that of praise (vv.27-28). But note who it is that he praised: not the king, but rather the LORD. He praised the LORD...
- because God had moved the heart of the king to honor the LORD's house
- because God had shown mercy by stirring the king and his officials to appoint him (Ezra) for this great mission
- because the hand of the LORD was upon him

After receiving the king's commission, Ezra immediately initiated a recruitment program. He began to encourage people to return to the promised land with him.

Thought 1. Every believer has been commissioned by the LORD, commissioned to lead people to the promised land of heaven. Sadly, many people are not going to heaven because they are alienated from God, cut off from Him. They are neglecting and ignoring the LORD, even denying Him. Tragically, they have nothing to do with the LORD in this life; consequently, they will have nothing to do with Him in the next life. If they live apart or separated from God now, they will live apart and be separated from God through all eternity. For this reason, the LORD commissions us as believers to go forth to proclaim the truth to the world. What is the truth? The gospel of the Lord Jesus Christ, that He alone is the Savior and Messiah of the world. Through Him alone can a person become acceptable to God. If a person wishes to approach God, he must approach through the Lord Jesus Christ. Jesus Christ is *The Way* to God. He is *The Truth* we are to live by. He is *The Life* we are to receive and live. As Christ Himself declared, "I am the way, the truth, and the life: no man comes to the Father but by me" (Jn.14:6).

We must proclaim the gospel of Christ, for no person will live in heaven who approaches God any other way. We are commissioned, sent forth as the ambassadors and witnesses to a world reeling in sin, lost and alienated from God. Listen to what God's Holy Word says about the Great Commission given us:

> "**Go ye therefore, and teach all nations, baptizing them in the name of the Father, and of the Son, and of the Holy Ghost**" (Mt.28:19).
>
> "**And the gospel must first be published among all nations**" (Mk.13:10).
>
> "**And he said unto them, Go ye into all the world, and preach the gospel to every creature**" (Mk.16:15).
>
> "**And beginning at Moses and all the prophets, he expounded unto them in all the scriptures the things concerning himself**" (Lu.24:27).
>
> "**Then said Jesus to them again, Peace** be **unto you: as** *my* **Father hath sent me, even so send I you**" (Jn.20:21).
>
> "**But ye shall receive power, after that the Holy Ghost is come upon you: and ye shall be witnesses unto me both in Jerusalem, and in all Judaea, and in Samaria, and unto the uttermost part of the earth**" (Ac.1:8).
>
> "**To wit, that God was in Christ, reconciling the world unto himself, not imputing their trespasses unto them; and hath committed unto us the word of reconciliation. Now then we are ambassadors for Christ, as though God did beseech** *you* **by us: we pray** *you* **in Christ's stead, be ye reconciled to God. For he hath made him** *to be* **sin for us, who knew no sin; that we might be made the righteousness of God in him**" (2 Co.5:19-21).

CHAPTER 8

B. Ezra's Preparations & Return to the Promised Land (Almost 60 Years After the Completion of the Temple): A Picture of Preparing for the Promised Land (a Type of Heaven), 8:1-36

1. Preparation through recruiting people to return: Shows the great need for laborers

a. The recruitment of *special* family leaders

  1) The two priests' families: From Phinehas, Gershom returned; from Ithamar, Daniel

  2) The royal line of David: Hattush returned, of the family of Shecaniah

b. The recruitment of people from 12 major families

  1) Parosh: Zechariah returned with 150 men

  2) Pahath-Moab: Eliehoenai returned with 200 men

  3) Zattu: Shecaniah returned with 300 men

  4) Adin: Ebed returned with 50 men

  5) Elam: Jeshaiah returned with 70 men

  6) Shephatiah: Zebadiah returned with 80 men

  7) Joab: Obadiah returned with 218 men

  8) Bani: Shelomith returned with 160 men

  9) Bebai: Zechariah returned with 28 men

  10) Azgad: Johanan returned with 110 men

  11) Adonikam, the last family to remain in Babylon: Eliphelet, Jeuel, & Shemaiah returned with 60 men

  12) Bigvai: Uthai & Zaccur returned with 70 men

These *are* now the chief of their fathers, and *this is* the genealogy of them that went up with me from Babylon, in the reign of Artaxerxes the king.

2 Of the sons of Phinehas; Gershom: of the sons of Ithamar; Daniel: of the sons of David; Hattush.

3 Of the sons of Shechaniah, of the sons of Pharosh; Zechariah: and with him were reckoned by genealogy of the males an hundred and fifty.

4 Of the sons of Pahath-moab; Elihoenai the son of Zerahiah, and with him two hundred males.

5 Of the sons of Shechaniah; the son of Jahaziel, and with him three hundred males.

6 Of the sons also of Adin; Ebed the son of Jonathan, and with him fifty males.

7 And of the sons of Elam; Jeshaiah the son of Athaliah, and with him seventy males.

8 And of the sons of Shephatiah; Zebadiah the son of Michael, and with him fourscore males.

9 Of the sons of Joab; Obadiah the son of Jehiel, and with him two hundred and eighteen males.

10 And of the sons of Shelomith; the son of Josiphiah, and with him an hundred and threescore males.

11 And of the sons of Bebai; Zechariah the son of Bebai, and with him twenty and eight males.

12 And of the sons of Azgad; Johanan the son of Hakkatan, and with him an hundred and ten males.

13 And of the last sons of Adonikam, whose names *are* these, Eliphelet, Jeiel, and Shemaiah, and with them threescore males.

14 Of the sons also of Bigvai; Uthai, and Zabbud, and with them seventy males.

15 And I gathered them together to the river that runneth to Ahava; and there abode we in tents three days: and I viewed the people, and the priests, and found there none of the sons of Levi.

16 Then sent I for Eliezer, for Ariel, for Shemaiah, and for Elnathan, and for Jarib, and for Elnathan, and for Nathan, and for Zechariah, and for Meshullam, chief men; also for Joiarib, and for Elnathan, men of understanding.

17 And I sent them with commandment unto Iddo the chief at the place Casiphia, and I told them what they should say unto Iddo, *and* to his brethren the Nethinims, at the place Casiphia, that they should bring unto us ministers for the house of our God.

18 And by the good hand of our God upon us they brought us a man of understanding, of the sons of Mahli, the son of Levi, the son of Israel; and Sherebiah, with his sons and his brethren, eighteen;

19 And Hashabiah, and with him Jeshaiah of the sons of Merari, his brethren and their sons, twenty;

20 Also of the Nethinims, whom David and the princes had appointed for the service of the Levites, two hundred and twenty Nethinims: all of them were expressed by name.

21 Then I proclaimed a fast there, at the river of Ahava, that we might afflict ourselves before our God, to seek of him a right way for us, and for our little ones, and for all our substance.

22 For I was ashamed to require of the king a band of soldiers and horsemen to help us against the enemy in the way: because we had spoken unto the king, saying, The hand of our God *is* upon all them for good that seek him; but his power and his wrath *is* against all them that forsake him.

23 So we fasted and besought our God for this: and he was intreated of us.

24 Then I separated twelve of the chief of the priests, Sherebiah, Hashabiah, and ten of their brethren with them,

c. The recruitment of Levites

  1) The three-day assembly of the returnees at the Ahava River or canal

  2) The sad discovery: No Levites had made a commitment to return

  3) The appointment of a special delegation to recruit Levites: Nine leaders & two scholars

  4) The delegation sent to Iddo, the leader of a band of Levites
    • Sent to Casiphia: The place where a worship center or school of Levites was located
    • Instructed what to say

  5) The success of the delegation in recruiting Levites
    • Due to the LORD's hand of blessing
    • Due to a very capable Levite leader named Sherebiah: Recruited 18 Levites
    • Due to two other leading Levites named Hashabiah & Jeshaiah: Recruited 20 Levites

  6) The success in recruiting 220 temple servants
    • Were assistants to the Levites
    • Were first instituted by David

2. Preparation through seeking God: Reveals the importance of prayer & fasting

a. The reasons for the prayer

  1) Because they needed a safe journey, God's guidance & protection

  2) Because the trip was lengthy & perilous

  3) Because Ezra was ashamed to ask the king for a military escort: In securing permission to return, he had stressed the LORD's blessing on all who seek Him & His wrath toward all who oppose Him

b. The fasting & prayer of the returning exiles: Were answered by God

3. Preparation through organizing leaders to guard the treasure: Conveys the necessity for faithful stewardship

a. The twelve leaders placed in charge of the treasures
b. The donated treasure weighed & recorded

1) Silver: 24 tons
2) Silver items: 7,500 pounds
3) Gold: 7,500 pounds

4) Twenty gold bowls: Equal to 1,000 gold coins
5) Two bronze items: As precious as gold

c. The charge given to the guards
1) The facts
 • They & the treasure were holy, set apart to God
 • The treasure had been given to the LORD
2) The charge: Must guard the treasure carefully, for it was to be reweighed at the temple before being turned over to the religious & civil leaders of Jerusalem
d. The responsibility for the treasure turned over to the guards by Ezra

4. Preparation through trusting the LORD to fulfill His promise (of the promised land): Stresses our dependence upon

25 And weighed unto them the silver, and the gold, and the vessels, *even* the offering of the house of our God, which the king, and his counsellors, and his lords, and all Israel *there* present, had offered:
26 I even weighed unto their hand six hundred and fifty talents of silver, and silver vessels an hundred talents, *and* of gold an hundred talents;
27 Also twenty basons of gold, of a thousand drams; and two vessels of fine copper, precious as gold.
28 And I said unto them, Ye *are* holy unto the LORD; the vessels *are* holy also; and the silver and the gold *are* a freewill offering unto the LORD God of your fathers.
29 Watch ye, and keep *them,* until ye weigh *them* before the chief of the priests and the Levites, and chief of the fathers of Israel, at Jerusalem, in the chambers of the house of the LORD.
30 So took the priests and the Levites the weight of the silver, and the gold, and the vessels, to bring *them* to Jerusalem unto the house of our God.
31 Then we departed from the river of Ahava on the twelfth *day* of the first month, to go unto Jerusalem:

and the hand of our God was upon us, and he delivered us from the hand of the enemy, and of such as lay in wait by the way.
32 And we came to Jerusalem, and abode there three days.
33 Now on the fourth day was the silver and the gold and the vessels weighed in the house of our God by the hand of Meremoth the son of Uriah the priest; and with him *was* Eleazar the son of Phinehas; and with them *was* Jozabad the son of Jeshua, and Noadiah the son of Binnui, Levites;
34 By number *and* by weight of every one: and all the weight was written at that time.
35 *Also* the children of those that had been carried away, which were come out of the captivity, offered burnt offerings unto the God of Israel, twelve bullocks for all Israel, ninety and six rams, seventy and seven lambs, twelve he goats *for* a sin offering: all *this was* a burnt offering unto the LORD.
36 And they delivered the king's commissions unto the king's lieutenants, and to the governors on this side the river: and they furthered the people, and the house of God.

God's protection & security

a. The departure date: Day 12, first month, Nisan (c. April 19)
b. The protection of God
c. The safe arrival & utter exhaustion of the returnees: Rested three days
d. The accounting of the treasure: Was deposited in the temple
1) Each item was inventoried by two priests, Meremoth & Eleazar, & two Levites, Jozabad & Noadiah

2) Each item was recorded by number & weight

e. The first action of the returning captives: They worshipped God
1) Approached God through the substitute sacrifice
2) Sacrificed 12 bulls & 12 male goats: Represented the 12 tribes of Israel
3) Worshipped God in the promised land for the first time in their lives
f. The king's letter & orders taken to the Syrian officials
1) The orders: They were to assist Ezra, 7:21-24
2) The response: They assisted as needed

DIVISION II

THE SECOND RETURN OF EXILES FROM CAPTIVITY AND THEIR REFORM—LED BY EZRA, 7:1–10:44

B. Ezra's Preparations and Return to the Promised Land (Almost 60 Years After the Completion of the Temple): A Picture of Preparing for the Promised Land (a Type of Heaven), 8:1-36

(8:1-36) **Introduction**: the human heart longs for a perfect world...
 • a world in which there is no pain or suffering, no hatred or bitterness, no lawlessness or violence, no murder or war, no unkindness or harsh speech, no strife or divorce, no assaults or abuse, no depression or loneliness, no emptiness or lack of purpose, no hunger or starvation, no poverty or homelessness
 • a world that is filled with perfect love, joy, peace, security, purpose, fulfillment, and economic prosperity
 • a life that is victorious, conquering all the evils of this world

Underlying all our cravings is the struggle for life itself—the struggle to conquer death and to live forever in a perfect body.

The wonderful news of God's Holy Word is that such a life is possible. God has provided eternal life for us, that is, for genuine believers, a life of perfection that is free not only from all suffering and pain but also from all trials and temptations. This place is what Christ and the Holy Scriptures identify as *heaven*. Heaven is the eternal world, the spiritual dimension of being that is to replace the present heavens and earth. Some day in the future, the power of God will melt the present universe with fervent heat and create a new universe, a new heavens and earth (2 Pe.3:10-11).

Preparing for the promised land of heaven is the practical message of the present Scripture. Ezra had just been granted permission by King Artaxerxes to lead a group of returnees back to Jerusalem, the promised land of God. But before he could lead the people from their captivity, certain preparations had to be made. This is, *Ezra's Preparations and Return to*

the Promised Land (Almost 60 Years After the Completion of the Temple): A Picture of Preparing for the Promised Land (a Type of Heaven), 8:1-36.
1. Preparation through recruiting people to return: shows the great need for laborers (vv.1-20).
2. Preparation through seeking God: reveals the importance of prayer and fasting (vv.21-23).
3. Preparation through organizing leaders to guard the treasure: conveys the necessity for faithful stewardship (vv.24-30).
4. Preparation through trusting the LORD to fulfill His promise (of the promised land): Stresses our dependence upon God's protection and security (vv.31-36).

1 (8:1-20) **Laborers, Need for, Example—Recruitment, of Laborers, Example—Enlistment, of Laborers, Example—Returnees from Exile, Led by Ezra, List of—Jews, Exiles Returned, List of:** after receiving his commission from the Persian king to return to Jerusalem, Ezra launched a recruitment program to enlist people to return with him. Ezra needed all the laborers he could find. He had been commissioned to arouse the people to rebuild their nation and to restore true worship in the temple (1:1-5; 4:12; 6:1-12). The first returnees under Zerubbabel had slipped away from the LORD and were disobeying His commandments. They were neglecting the temple and their worship of the LORD. In addition, they had failed to finish rebuilding Jerusalem and its walls. Thus a renewed commitment was desperately needed. It was Ezra's purpose to stir a genuine revival among the people, a revival that would motivate them to turn back to the LORD and their God-given task of rebuilding their nation. The people needed to serve God faithfully. They needed to worship and witness to the only living and true God. In the present Scripture, a list of family heads who returned is given as well as the number of males who returned with each of the families.

OUTLINE	SCRIPTURE	SCRIPTURE	OUTLINE

1. Preparation through recruiting people to return: Shows the great need for laborers
a. The recruitment of *special* family leaders
  1) The two priests' families: From Phinehas, Gershom returned; from Ithamar, Daniel
  2) The royal line of David: Hattush returned, of the family of Shecaniah
b. The recruitment of people from 12 major families
  1) Parosh: Zechariah returned with 150 men
  2) Pahath-Moab: Eliehoenai returned with 200 men
 	
  3) Zattu: Shecaniah returned with 300 men
 	
  4) Adin: Ebed returned with 50 men
  5) Elam: Jeshaiah returned with 70 men
  6) Shephatiah: Zebadiah returned with 80 men
  7) Joab: Obadiah returned with 218 men
 	
  8) Bani: Shelomith returned with 160 men
 	
  9) Bebai: Zechariah returned with 28 men
	These *are* now the chief of their fathers, and *this is* the genealogy of them that went up with me from Babylon, in the reign of Artaxerxes the king.
	2 Of the sons of Phinehas; Gershom: of the sons of Ithamar; Daniel: of the sons of David; Hattush.
	3 Of the sons of Shechaniah, of the sons of Pharosh; Zechariah: and with him were reckoned by genealogy of the males an hundred and fifty.
	4 Of the sons of Pahath-moab; Elihoenai the son of Zerahiah, and with him two hundred males.
	5 Of the sons of Shechaniah; the son of Jahaziel, and with him three hundred males.
	6 Of the sons also of Adin; Ebed the son of Jonathan, and with him fifty males.
	7 And of the sons of Elam; Jeshaiah the son of Athaliah, and with him seventy males.
	8 And of the sons of Shephatiah; Zebadiah the son of Michael, and with him fourscore males.
	9 Of the sons of Joab; Obadiah the son of Jehiel, and with him two hundred and eighteen males.
	10 And of the sons of Shelomith; the son of Josiphiah, and with him an hundred and threescore males.
	11 And of the sons of Bebai; Zechariah the son of Bebai, and with him twenty and
		eight males.
		12 And of the sons of Azgad; Johanan the son of Hakkatan, and with him an hundred and ten males.
		13 And of the last sons of Adonikam, whose names *are* these, Eliphelet, Jeiel, and Shemaiah, and with them threescore males.
		14 Of the sons also of Bigvai; Uthai, and Zabbud, and with them seventy males.
		15 And I gathered them together to the river that runneth to Ahava; and there abode we in tents three days: and I viewed the people, and the priests, and found there none of the sons of Levi.
		16 Then sent I for Eliezer, for Ariel, for Shemaiah, and for Elnathan, and for Jarib, and for Elnathan, and for Nathan, and for Zechariah, and for Meshullam, chief men; also for Joiarib, and for Elnathan, men of understanding.
		17 And I sent them with commandment unto Iddo the chief at the place Casiphia, and I told them what they should say unto Iddo, *and* to his brethren the Nethinims, at the place Casiphia, that they should bring unto us ministers for the house of our God.
		18 And by the good hand of our God upon us they brought us a man of understanding, of the sons of Mahli, the son of Levi, the son of
			10) Azgad: Johanan returned with 110 men
			
			11) Adonikam, the last family to remain in Babylon: Eliphelet, Jeuel, & Shemaiah returned with 60 men
			12) Bigvai: Uthai & Zaccur returned with 70 men
			
			c. The recruitment of Levites
			  1) The three-day assembly of the returnees at the Ahava River or canal
			  2) The sad discovery: No Levites had made a commitment to return
			  3) The appointment of a special delegation to recruit Levites: Nine leaders & two scholars
			
			  4) The delegation sent to Iddo, the leader of a band of Levites
			    • Sent to Casiphia: The place where a worship center or school of Levites was located
			    • Instructed what to say
			
			  5) The success of the delegation in recruiting Levites
			    • Due to the LORD's hand of blessing
			    • Due to a very capable

OUTLINE	SCRIPTURE	SCRIPTURE	OUTLINE
Levite leader named Sherebiah: Recruited 18 Levites • Due to two other leading Levites named Hashabiah & Jeshaiah: Recruited 20 Levites	Israel; and Sherebiah, with his sons and his brethren, eighteen; 19 And Hashabiah, and with him Jeshaiah of the sons of Merari, his brethren and their sons, twenty;	20 Also of the Nethinims, whom David and the princes had appointed for the service of the Levites, two hundred and twenty Nethinims: all of them were expressed by name.	6) The success in recruiting 220 temple servants • Were assistants to the Levites • Were first instituted by David

a. Knowing that he needed help in the recruitment process, Ezra wisely enlisted three family heads or leaders to help him (vv.1-2). Because of their influence he chose two priests, one leader from each of the two priestly families. From the priestly family of Phinehas, he recruited a descendant named Gershom; and from the priestly family of Ithamar, he chose a descendant named Daniel. Both Gershom and Daniel would have had tremendous influence in helping Ezra recruit others for the task that lay ahead of them in Jerusalem. Along with these two priests, Ezra reached out to recruit someone from the royal line of David, a man named Hattush, a descendant of the family of Shechaniah.

b. Ezra and the three special family heads were able to recruit a large number of people from 12 major families (vv.3-14). In all there were 1,511 men who made the commitment to return to Jerusalem. Adding in Ezra and the three special family heads brought the total number of men recruited to 1,515. When the women and children were added to the list, there were probably about 5,000 exiles returning with Ezra. This was a much smaller number than the 50,000 who had returned about 80 years earlier under Zerubbabel's leadership.

c. Apparently Ezra had instructed those recruited to assemble at the Ahava Canal. There they spent three days making preparations for the journey and checking the list of returnees to make sure everyone was present. But when Ezra checked the list of recruits, he made a sad discovery. Not a single Levite had made a commitment to return to the promised land. There were some priests present, but no Levites. And Levites were needed, for they were the assistants to the priests. They were obviously not willing to leave the comfortable, prosperous, and successful lives they had achieved in Babylon. Also keep in mind that this was a new generation that had never before seen Jerusalem, never had a glimpse of the promised land.

To solve the problem, Ezra appointed a special delegation to recruit Levites. The delegation included nine leaders and two scholars (v.16). After their appointment Ezra sent the delegation to a prominent leader among the Levites, a man named Iddo. This Levite leader lived in the city of Casiphia where there was evidently a worship center or school of Levites located (v.17). The delegation was successful in recruiting Levites, and three reasons are given as to why (vv.18-19). They were successful...

- due to the LORD's hand guiding and blessing them
- due to a very capable Levite leader named Sherebiah who personally recruited 18 Levites
- due to two other leading Levites named Hashabiah and Jeshaiah who were able to recruit 10 more Levites (v.19)

In addition to the Levites, the delegation also recruited 220 temple servants (v.20). These servants, a group of temple workers who had first been instituted by David, were assistants to the Levites. After their recruitment, their names were added to the register of returnees who had made the commitment to return to the promised land with Ezra.

Thought 1. Ezra needed laborers, people who would make a solid commitment to the awesome task of rebuilding the Jewish nation and restoring true worship in the temple. We too need laborers who will make a commitment to the LORD and to the awesome task of the church. No greater mission exists than the one assigned to the church, that of taking the gospel of salvation to the world and of meeting the needs of people. People are lost and without hope, for they are separated from God. They do not know that salvation comes only through the Lord Jesus Christ, that no person can approach and become acceptable to God except through His Son (Jn.14:6). In addition to those who are lost, there are many people who are hurting and in desperate need, suffering all kinds of trials, hardships, and temptations.

Laborers are needed, desperately needed. Some among us right now need to make a commitment to the Lord, surrendering our lives to become laborers for Christ. As never before, we need to bear strong witness to the saving power of Jesus Christ and to reach out in compassion to those who are in desperate need. Listen to what God's Holy Word says about the need for laborers:

"And he saith unto them, Follow me, and I will make you fishers of men" (Mt.4:19).

"Then saith he unto his disciples, The harvest truly *is* plenteous, but the labourers *are* few; Pray ye therefore the Lord of the harvest, that he will send forth labourers into his harvest" (Mt.9:37-38).

"And they come unto him, bringing one sick of the palsy, which was borne of four" (Mk.2:3).

"Philip findeth Nathanael, and saith unto him, We have found him, of whom Moses in the law, and the prophets, did write, Jesus of Nazareth, the son of Joseph" (Jn.1:45).

"Say not ye, There are yet four months, and *then* cometh harvest? behold, I say unto you, Lift up your eyes, and look on the fields; for they are white already to harvest. And he that reapeth receiveth wages, and gathereth fruit unto life eternal: that both he that soweth and he that reapeth may rejoice together" (Jn.4:35-36).

"Therefore said he unto them, The harvest truly *is* great, but the labourers *are* few: pray ye therefore the Lord of the harvest, that he would send forth labourers into his harvest" (Lu.10:2).

"Then departed Barnabas to Tarsus, for to seek Saul: And when he had found him, he brought him unto Antioch. And it came to pass, that a whole year they assembled themselves with the church, and taught much people. And the disciples were called Christians first in Antioch" (Ac.11:25-26).

"For though I be free from all *men,* yet have I made myself servant unto all, that I might gain the more. And unto the Jews I became as a Jew, that I might gain the Jews; to them that are under the law, as under the law, that I might gain them that are under the law" (1 Co.9:19-20).

"Therefore, my beloved brethren, be ye stedfast, unmovable, always abounding in the work of the Lord, forasmuch as ye know that your labour is not in vain in the Lord" (1 Co.15:58).

"Brethren, if a man be overtaken in a fault, ye which are spiritual, restore such an one in the spirit of meekness; considering thyself, lest thou also be tempted. Bear ye one another's burdens, and so fulfil the law of Christ" (Ga.6:1-2).

"And let us not be weary in well doing: for in due season we shall reap, if we faint not. As we have therefore opportunity, let us do good unto all *men,* especially unto them who are of the household of faith" (Ga.6:9-10).

"And others save with fear, pulling *them* out of the fire; hating even the garment spotted by the flesh" (Jude 1:23).

"The fruit of the righteous *is* a tree of life; and he that winneth souls *is* wise" (Pr.11:30).

"And they that be wise shall shine as the brightness of the firmament; and they that turn many to righteousness as the stars for ever and ever" (Da.12:3).

2 (8:21-23) **Prayer, Example—Fasting, Example—Preparation, Spiritual, Example—Spiritual Preparation, Example—Ezra, Prayer Life—Exile Returnees, Preparation by—Jews, Returned Exiles, Preparation of**: before beginning the long 900 mile trip, Ezra encouraged the people to prepare themselves spiritually. He challenged them to seek the LORD through prayer and fasting (vv.21-23). Prayer was urgently needed for three reasons:

⇒ The people needed to seek the LORD for a safe journey, for God's guidance and protection.
⇒ The people needed to seek the LORD because the trip was lengthy, demanding, and perilous, especially with children present. The roads of that day were infested with bandits and gangs of marauders. Furthermore, they would be passing through territory that was held by various anti-Semitic groups.
⇒ The people needed to seek the LORD because Ezra felt uneasy about asking the king for a military escort (v.22). In securing permission to return to the promised land, Ezra had stressed the LORD's blessing on all who seek Him and His wrath on all who oppose Him. If he now requested a military escort, the king might misunderstand, for Ezra had publicly announced to the king that God would take care of the exiles as they returned to Jerusalem. Such a request would contradict his testimony of faith in God's protection. Therefore even though Ezra was now sensing the need for a military escort, he felt a greater need to present a consistent testimony to the king. For this reason, he made a deliberate decision not to ask for an escort.

A question naturally arises about the wisdom of Ezra, especially since other believers down through the years have requested armed escorts from civil officials. Nehemiah would later request a military escort when he returned to Jerusalem (Ne.2:9). And Paul the Apostle requested the Romans to protect him on his journey from Jerusalem to Caesarea (Ac.23:12-35).

Does this mean that Ezra trusted the LORD more than Nehemiah and Paul and others who have been helped by civil authorities? In thinking about the question, we must keep in mind God's purpose for us all. His purpose is to teach us to draw closer to Him, to fellowship and commune with Him. Nothing causes us to draw nearer the LORD than trials and hardships. Thus God puts us in situations where we have to cast ourselves totally upon Him, trusting Him to protect and provide for us. Because some of us are more difficult to teach than others, the LORD occasionally has to put us totally on our own without any help from anyone else. There are occasions when we have to be prepared for greater missions. Evidently this was the case with Ezra. The LORD knew that during this season of his life, Ezra needed to cast himself totally upon the LORD, needed to draw near the LORD in fellowship and communion. This dear servant needed to trust the LORD as never before. Thus the LORD worked out the circumstances so it would be unwise for Ezra to request a military escort. His only hope for protection was the LORD Himself.

In response to Ezra's request, the people fasted and prayed. And their prayer was answered. As will be seen, the LORD protected and returned the exiles safely to the promised land.

OUTLINE	SCRIPTURE	SCRIPTURE	OUTLINE
2. Preparation through seeking God: Reveals the importance of prayer & fasting a. The reasons for the prayer 　1) Because they needed a safe journey, God's guidance & protection 　2) Because the trip was lengthy & perilous 　3) Because Ezra was ashamed to ask the king	21 Then I proclaimed a fast there, at the river of Ahava, that we might afflict ourselves before our God, to seek of him a right way for us, and for our little ones, and for all our substance. 22 For I was ashamed to require of the king a band of soldiers and horsemen to help us against the	enemy in the way: because we had spoken unto the king, saying, The hand of our God *is* upon all them for good that seek him; but his power and his wrath *is* against all them that forsake him. 23 So we fasted and besought our God for this: and he was intreated of us.	for a military escort: In securing permission to return, he had stressed the LORD's blessing on all who seek Him & His wrath toward all who oppose Him b. The prayer & fasting of the returning exiles: Were an-

Thought 1. A genuine believer should undertake every task with prayer. Indeed, prayer should be the very first step taken. And if the task is large or significant, both prayer and fasting should precede the endeavor. If we are concerned enough to pray and fast, God will hear and answer. No matter what our need is, if we turn to the LORD, He

will protect and provide for us, granting exactly what we need. God will never leave us alone to face the hardships and sufferings of this life on our own.

(1) Listen to what God says about prayer:

"Ask, and it shall be given you; seek, and ye shall find; knock, and it shall be opened unto you" (Mt.7:7).

"Watch and pray, that ye enter not into temptation: the spirit indeed *is* willing, but the flesh *is* weak" (Mt.26:41).

"Therefore I say unto you, What things soever ye desire, when ye pray, believe that ye receive *them*, and ye shall have *them*" (Mk.11:24).

"And whatsoever ye shall ask in my name, that will I do, that the Father may be glorified in the Son. If ye shall ask any thing in my name, I will do *it*" (Jn.14:13-14).

"If ye abide in me, and my words abide in you, ye shall ask what ye will, and it shall be done unto you" (Jn.15:7).

"Hitherto have ye asked nothing in my name: ask, and ye shall receive, that your joy may be full" (Jn.16:24).

"And whatsoever we ask, we receive of him, because we keep his commandments, and do those things that are pleasing in his sight. And this is his commandment, That we should believe on the name of his Son Jesus Christ, and love one another, as he gave us commandment" (1 Jn.3:22-23).

"But if from thence thou shalt seek the LORD thy God, thou shalt find *him*, if thou seek him with all thy heart and with all thy soul" (De.4:29).

"If my people, which are called by my name, shall humble themselves, and pray, and seek my face, and turn from their wicked ways; then will I hear from heaven, and will forgive their sin, and will heal their land" (2 Chr.7:14).

"He shall call upon me, and I will answer him: I *will be* with him in trouble; I will deliver him, and honour him" (Ps.91:15).

"*When* the poor and needy seek water, and *there is* none, *and* their tongue faileth for thirst, I the LORD will hear them, *I* the God of Israel will not forsake them" (Is.41:17).

"Then shalt thou call, and the LORD shall answer; thou shalt cry, and he shall say, Here I *am*. If thou take away from the midst of thee the yoke, the putting forth of the finger, and speaking vanity" (Is.58:9).

"And it shall come to pass, that before they call, I will answer; and while they are yet speaking, I will hear" (Is.65:24).

"Call unto me, and I will answer thee, and show thee great and mighty things, which thou knowest not" (Je.33:3).

(2) Listen to what God's Holy Word says about fasting:

"But thou, when thou fastest, anoint thine head, and wash thy face; That thou appear not unto men to fast, but unto thy Father which is in secret: and thy Father, which seeth in secret, shall reward thee openly" (Mt.6:17-18).

"And Jesus rebuked the devil; and he departed out of him: and the child was cured from that very hour. Then came the disciples to Jesus apart, and said, Why could not we cast him out? And Jesus said unto them, Because of your unbelief: for verily I say unto you, If ye have faith as a grain of mustard seed, ye shall say unto this mountain, Remove hence to yonder place; and it shall remove; and nothing shall be impossible unto you. Howbeit this kind goeth not out but by prayer and fasting" (Mt.17:18-21).

"And Jesus being full of the Holy Ghost returned from Jordan, and was led by the Spirit into the wilderness, Being forty days tempted of the devil. And in those days he did eat nothing: and when they were ended, he afterward hungered" (Lu.4:1-2).

"And he was three days without sight, and neither did eat nor drink" (Ac.9:9).

"As they ministered to the Lord, and fasted, the Holy Ghost said, Separate me Barnabas and Saul for the work whereunto I have called them. And when they had fasted and prayed, and laid *their* hands on them, they sent *them* away" (Ac.13:2-3).

"And when they had ordained them elders in every church, and had prayed with fasting, they commended them to the Lord, on whom they believed" (Ac.14:23).

"And he was there with the LORD forty days and forty nights; he did neither eat bread, nor drink water. And he wrote upon the tables the words of the covenant, the ten commandments" (Ex.34:28).

"Sanctify ye a fast, call a solemn assembly, gather the elders *and* all the inhabitants of the land *into* the house of the LORD your God, and cry unto the LORD" (Joel 1:14).

"Therefore also now, saith the LORD, turn ye *even* to me with all your heart, and with fasting, and with weeping, and with mourning" (Joel 2:12).

---

3 (8:24-30) **Stewardship, Example—Giving, Example—Benevolence, Example—Treasurers, Duty, Example—Money-Handlers, Duty—Church, Duty, to Safely Handle Money**: Ezra also saw in his preparations the need to guard the treasure that had been entrusted into his care by the Persian government (v.24). He delegated the responsibility for the treasure to two leading priests, Sherbiah and Hashabiah. These two priests appointed ten other priests to serve with them. After their appointment, Ezra weighed, counted, and recorded the donated treasure (vv.25-27). There was a large quantity of wealth being taken to the temple in Jerusalem:

⇒ 650 talents of silver that amounted to 24 tons
⇒ various silver items that weighed 100 talents or 7,500 pounds
⇒ gold that weighed 100 talents or 7,500 pounds
⇒ 20 gold bowls that were equal to 1,000 drachmas or 1,000 gold coins
⇒ two bronze items that were as precious as gold

After weighing all these items and wealth, Ezra reminded the guards that both they and the treasure were holy, set apart to God (vv.28-29). The treasure had been given as a freewill offering to the LORD. For this reason, they must carefully guard the treasure until it was delivered to Jerusalem and placed in the house of the LORD. The treasure would then be reweighed and counted in Jerusalem before being turned over to the religious and civil leaders at the temple. Briefly stated, Ezra was charging the guards to take special care of the treasure, making sure that nothing was stolen or lost along the way. After giving his charge, Ezra turned the treasure over to the guards.

OUTLINE	SCRIPTURE	SCRIPTURE	OUTLINE
3. Preparation through organizing leaders to guard the treasure: Conveys the example of faithful stewardship a. The twelve leaders placed in charge of the treasures b. The donated treasure weighed & recorded 1) Silver: 24 tons 2) Silver items: 7,500 pounds 3) Gold: 7,500 pounds 4) Twenty gold bowls: Equal to 1,000 gold coins	24 Then I separated twelve of the chief of the priests, Sherebiah, Hashabiah, and ten of their brethren with them, 25 And weighed unto them the silver, and the gold, and the vessels, *even* the offering of the house of our God, which the king, and his counsellors, and his lords, and all Israel *there* present, had offered: 26 I even weighed unto their hand six hundred and fifty talents of silver, and silver vessels an hundred talents, *and* of gold an hundred talents; 27 Also twenty basons of gold, of a thousand drams;	and two vessels of fine copper, precious as gold. 28 And I said unto them, Ye *are* holy unto the LORD; the vessels *are* holy also; and the silver and the gold *are* a freewill offering unto the LORD God of your fathers. 29 Watch ye, and keep *them,* until ye weigh *them* before the chief of the priests and the Levites, and chief of the fathers of Israel, at Jerusalem, in the chambers of the house of the LORD. 30 So took the priests and the Levites the weight of the silver, and the gold, and the vessels, to bring *them* to Jerusalem unto the house of our God.	5) Two bronze items: As precious as gold c. The charge given to the guards 1) The facts • They & the treasure were holy, set apart to God • The treasure had been given to the LORD 2) The charge: Must guard the treasure carefully, for it was to be reweighed at the temple before being turned over to the religious & civil leaders of Jerusalem d. The responsibility for the treasure turned over to the guards by Ezra

Thought 1. Ezra has left us with a strong example of faithful stewardship. We too must be faithful stewards of all that God has given us, whether money, abilities, or responsibility. We are to carefully protect and increase what God has given. Nothing is to go unused, be left undeveloped. Rather, we are to use our skills and abilities as a strong witness to further the kingdom of God, to bring Him more glory. So it is with the responsibilities and duties assigned us. We are not to neglect nor fail to carry out any task entrusted to us, whether at work, home, school, or anywhere else. When a responsibility is set before us, we are to tackle and complete the work, giving a strong witness of diligence in serving the LORD.

When it comes to the stewardship of money, we are to guard all that is entrusted in our care. We are not to carelessly handle money, losing it, allowing it to be stolen, or spending it foolishly. Money is a trust from God. In fact, Scripture teaches that we are to invest and increase our money. We are to work hard and make wise investments in order to have enough to give to the needy of this world. Note His commandment:

"Let him that stole steal no more: but rather let him labour, working with *his* hands the thing which is good, that he may have to give to him that needeth" (Ep.4:28).

Listen to what God's Holy Word says about faithful stewardship:

"Give to him that asketh thee, and from him that would borrow of thee turn not thou away" (Mt.5:42).
"But lay up for yourselves treasures in heaven, where neither moth nor rust doth corrupt, and where thieves do not break through nor steal" (Mt.6:20).
"Therefore is the kingdom of heaven likened unto a certain king, which would take account of his servants" (Mt.18:23).
"Jesus said unto him, If thou wilt be perfect, go *and* sell that thou hast, and give to the poor, and thou shalt have treasure in heaven: and come *and* follow me" (Mt.19:21).
"For *the kingdom of heaven is* as a man travelling into a far country, *who* called his own servants, and delivered unto them his goods. And unto one he gave five talents, to another two, and to another one; to every man according to his several ability; and straightway took his journey. Then he that had received the five talents went and traded with the same, and made *them* other five talents. And likewise he that *had received* two, he also gained other two. But he that had received one went and digged in the

earth, and hid his lord's money. After a long time the lord of those servants cometh, and reckoneth with them" (Mt.25:14-19).

"And went to *him,* and bound up his wounds, pouring in oil and wine, and set him on his own beast, and brought him to an inn, and took care of him. And on the morrow when he departed, he took out two pence, and gave *them* to the host, and said unto him, Take care of him; and whatsoever thou spendest more, when I come again, I will repay thee" (Lu.10:34-35).

"Sell that ye have, and give alms; provide yourselves bags which wax not old, a treasure in the heavens that faileth not, where no thief approacheth, neither moth corrupteth" (Lu.12:33).

"For unto whomsoever much is given, of him shall be much required: and to whom men have committed much, of him they will ask the more" (Lu.12:48).

"And he called his ten servants, and delivered them ten pounds, and said unto them, Occupy till I come" (Lu.19:13).

"And it came to pass, that when he was returned, having received the kingdom, then he commanded these servants to be called unto him, to whom he had given the money, that he might know how much every man had gained by trading" (Lu.19:15).

"Moreover it is required in stewards, that a man be found faithful" (1 Co.4:2).

---

4 (8:31-36) **Protection, of God, Example—Security, of God, Example—Returned Exiles, Safe Arrival—Exiles, Arrival in Jerusalem—Return, of Exiles, to Jerusalem**: after completing their preparations, Ezra and the other Jewish returnees launched out on their long 900 mile journey. Four months later they safely arrived in Jerusalem, the land that had been promised them by God centuries before. Down through the years, God had always protected a remnant of Jewish believers, men and women who truly trusted and continued to follow the LORD. This present Jewish remnant left the land of their captivity on the twelfth day of the first month, which was the month of Nissan (c.April 19). They traveled about 900 miles and arrived in Jerusalem on the first day of the fifth month, as mentioned about four months later (7:9). Interestingly, nothing is said about the journey itself except the fact that God protected them from enemies and bandits along the way. God had clearly answered their prayers (vv.21-22). But the people were utterly exhausted from the prolonged voyage, desperately needing to stop. For the first three days after arriving, they did nothing but relax, sleep, and secure the break they so yearned for (v.22). On the fourth day, Ezra and the leadership took the treasure into the temple (vv.33-34). Each item was inventoried by two priests and two Levites. The two priests were Meremoth and Eleazar, and the two Levites were Jozabad and Noadiah. Each item was also recorded by number and weighed to make sure that nothing had been stolen or lost along the way (v.34).

Note the first thing the returning exiles did: they worshipped God, praising and thanking Him for protecting them and bringing them safely to the promised land (vv.35-36). For the first time in their lives, this new generation of Jewish believers was worshiping at the temple in the land that had been promised to them by God. Joy beyond measure was bound to be swelling up in the hearts of Ezra and countless others. Approaching God through the substitute sacrifice, the returned exiles sacrificed 12 bulls and 12 male goats. No doubt the number 12 was to represent the 12 tribes of Israel, which indicates that there were most likely returnees from all 12 tribes.

After the worship service, Ezra and the leaders delivered a decree from King Artaxerxes to the local officials (v.36). Remember that the decree instructed the local officials to give assistance to the Jewish returnees and to the temple as requested by Ezra (7:21-24). Being careful to follow the orders of the king, the local officials cooperated by supporting both the people and the temple as needed.

OUTLINE	SCRIPTURE	SCRIPTURE	OUTLINE
4. Preparation through trusting the LORD to fulfill His promise (of the promised land): Stresses our dependence upon God's protection & security	31 Then we departed from the river of Ahava on the twelfth *day* of the first month, to go unto Jerusalem: and the	nui, Levites;	
a. The departure date: Day 12, first month, Nisan (c. April 19)	hand of our God was upon us, and he delivered us from	34 By number *and* by weight of every one: and all the weight was written at that time.	2) Each item was recorded by number & weight
b. The protection of God	the hand of the enemy, and of	35 *Also* the children of those	e. The first action of the return-
c. The safe arrival & utter exhaustion of the returnees: Rested three days	such as lay in wait by the way.	that had been carried away, which were come out of the captivity, offered burnt offer-	ing captives: They worshipped God
d. The accounting of the treasure: Was deposited in the temple	32 And we came to Jerusalem, and abode there three days.	ings unto the God of Israel, twelve bullocks for all Israel,	1) Approached God through the substitute sacrifice
1) Each item was inventoried by two priests, Meremoth & Eleazar, & two Levites, Jozabad & Noadiah	33 Now on the fourth day was the silver and the gold and the vessels weighed in the house of our God by the hand of Meremoth the son of Uriah the priest; and with him *was* Eleazar the son of Phinehas; and with them *was* Jozabad the son of Jeshua, and Noadiah the son of Bin-	ninety and six rams, seventy and seven lambs, twelve he goats *for* a sin offering: all *this was* a burnt offering unto the LORD.	2) Sacrificed 12 bulls & 12 male goats: Represented the 12 tribes of Israel
		36 And they delivered the king's commissions unto the king's lieutenants, and to the governors on this side the river: and they furthered the people, and the house of God.	3) Worshipped God in the promised land for the first time in their lives
			f. The king's letter & orders taken to the Syrian officials
			1) The orders: They were to assist Ezra, 7:21-24
			2) The response: They assisted as needed

Thought 1. God protected and brought the returnees safely to Jerusalem. And just as the LORD looked after the returning exiles, so He will take care of us. As we walk and travel about day by day, we have the wonderful promise

of God's protection. If we trust the Lord, look to Him as our Protector and Savior, He will look after us. When temptations lure us, or hardships face us or enemies attack us—whatever the trial or suffering—the Lord will protect us and provide whatever strength we need to conquer or walk through the hardship or suffering victoriously. Listen to what God's Holy Word says about His protective care:

"Who shall separate us from the love of Christ? *shall* tribulation, or distress, or persecution, or famine, or nakedness, or peril, or sword?...Nay, in all these things we are more than conquerors through him that loved us. For I am persuaded, that neither death, nor life, nor angels, nor principalities, nor powers, nor things present, nor things to come, Nor height, nor depth, nor any other creature, shall be able to separate us from the love of God, which is in Christ Jesus our Lord" (Ro.8:35, 37-39).

"But there shall not an hair of your head perish" (Lu.21:18).

"For though we walk in the flesh, we do not war after the flesh: (For the weapons of our warfare *are* not carnal, but mighty through God to the pulling down of strong holds;) Casting down imaginations, and every high thing that exalteth itself against the knowledge of God, and bringing into captivity every thought to the obedience of Christ" (2 Co.10:3-5).

"And the Lord shall deliver me from every evil work, and will preserve *me* unto his heavenly kingdom: to whom *be* glory for ever and ever. Amen" (2 Ti.4:18).

"Casting all your care upon him; for he careth for you" (1 Pe.5:7).

"And, behold, I *am* with thee, and will keep thee in all *places* whither thou goest, and will bring thee again into this land; for I will not leave thee, until I have done *that* which I have spoken to thee of" (Ge.28:15).

"The LORD shall fight for you, and ye shall hold your peace" (Ex.14:14).

"The eternal God *is thy* refuge, and underneath *are* the everlasting arms: and he shall thrust out the enemy from before thee; and shall say, Destroy *them*" (De.33:27).

"For the eyes of the LORD run to and fro throughout the whole earth, to show himself strong in the behalf of *them* whose heart *is* perfect toward him. Herein thou hast done foolishly: therefore from henceforth thou shalt have wars" (2 Chr.16:9).

"With him *is* an arm of flesh; but with us *is* the LORD our God to help us, and to fight our battles." (2 Chr.32:8).

"Thou hast also given me the shield of thy salvation: and thy right hand hath holden me up, and thy gentleness hath made me great" (Ps.18:35).

"The angel of the LORD encampeth round about them that fear him, and delivereth them" (Ps.34:7).

"Through thee will we push down our enemies: through thy name will we tread them under that rise up against us" (Ps.44:5).

"He shall cover thee with his feathers, and under his wings shalt thou trust: his truth *shall be thy* shield and buckler" (Ps.91:4).

"Behold, he that keepeth Israel shall neither slumber nor sleep" (Ps.121:4).

"*As* the mountains *are* round about Jerusalem, so the LORD *is* round about his people from henceforth even for ever" (Ps.125:2).

"Fear thou not; for I *am* with thee: be not dismayed; for I *am* thy God: I will strengthen thee; yea, I will help thee; yea, I will uphold thee with the right hand of my righteousness" (Is.41:10).

"And *even* to *your* old age I *am* he; and *even* to hoar [gray] hairs will I carry *you*: I have made, and I will bear; even I will carry, and will deliver *you*" (Is.46:4).

CHAPTER 9

C. Ezra's Confrontation with the People Over Their Evil Associations: A Picture of Genuine Revival, 9:1–10:44

1. The need for revival: The people were participating in the worldly, sinful behavior of unbelievers—even marrying unbelievers

a. The fact reported to Ezra by a group of leaders: Less than five months after arriving in the promised land, 7:9; 10:9

b. The worldly, sinful behavior

  1) Not living lives of *spiritual separation*

  2) Divorcing (Mal.2:16) & intermarrying with unbelievers, Ex.34:14-16; De.7:1-6; 20:10-18

c. The tragedy: Some leaders—both civil & religious—were the worst offenders, the most unfaithful, sinful, & worldly

2. The deep concern & prayer of Ezra for revival: The people desperately needed to confess

a. Ezra's heavy spirit of mourning

  1) He was soon joined by other faithful believers

  2) He sat mourning, expressing his grief until the evening sacrifice

b. Ezra's prayer of confession: He stood & then fell to his knees, lifting up his hands to the LORD

  1) He confessed their shame & their past sins
- Had been piled up higher than their heads, drowning them
- Had reached higher than the heavens
- Had tragically continued in sin through the generations—bringing God's judgment down upon the kings, priests, & people, which brought death, captivity, loss of wealth, & humiliation

Now when these things were done, the princes came to me, saying, The people of Israel, and the priests, and the Levites, have not separated themselves from the people of the lands, *doing* according to their abominations, *even* of the Canaanites, the Hittites, the Perizzites, the Jebusites, the Ammonites, the Moabites, the Egyptians, and the Amorites.

2 For they have taken of their daughters for themselves, and for their sons: so that the holy seed have mingled themselves with the people of *those* lands: yea, the hand of the princes and rulers hath been chief in this trespass.

3 And when I heard this thing, I rent my garment and my mantle, and plucked off the hair of my head and of my beard, and sat down astonied.

4 Then were assembled unto me every one that trembled at the words of the God of Israel, because of the transgression of those that had been carried away; and I sat astonied until the evening sacrifice.

5 And at the evening sacrifice I arose up from my heaviness; and having rent my garment and my mantle, I fell upon my knees, and spread out my hands unto the LORD my God.

6 And said, O my God, I am ashamed and blush to lift up my face to thee, my God: for our iniquities are increased over *our* head, and our trespass is grown up unto the heavens.

7 Since the days of our fathers *have* we *been* in a great trespass unto this day; and for our iniquities have we, our kings, and our priests, been delivered into the hand of the kings of the lands, to the sword, to captivity, and to a spoil, and to confusion of face, as *it is* this day.

8 And now for a little space grace hath been *showed* from the LORD our God, to leave us a remnant to escape, and to give us a nail in his holy place, that our God may lighten our eyes, and give us a little reviving in our bondage.

9 For we *were* bondmen; yet our God hath not forsaken us in our bondage, but hath extended mercy unto us in the sight of the kings of Persia, to give us a reviving, to set up the house of our God, and to repair the desolations thereof, and to give us a wall in Judah and in Jerusalem.

10 And now, O our God, what shall we say after this? for we have forsaken thy commandments,

11 Which thou hast commanded by thy servants the prophets, saying, The land, unto which ye go to possess it, is an unclean land with the filthiness of the people of the lands, with their abominations, which have filled it from one end to another with their uncleanness.

12 Now therefore give not your daughters unto their sons, neither take their daughters unto your sons, nor seek their peace or their wealth for ever: that ye may be strong, and eat the good of the land, and leave *it* for an inheritance to your children for ever.

13 And after all that is come upon us for our evil deeds, and for our great trespass, seeing that thou our God hast punished us less than our iniquities *deserve,* and hast given us *such* deliverance as this;

14 Should we again break thy commandments, and join in affinity with the people of these abominations? wouldest not thou be angry with us till thou hadst consumed *us,* so that *there should be* no remnant nor escaping?

15 O LORD God of Israel, thou *art* righteous: for we remain yet escaped, as *it is* this day: behold, we *are* before thee in our trespasses: for we cannot stand before thee because of this.

  2) He confessed God's goodness to them
- Had left them a remnant
- Had given them a place in the promised land
- Had given them light
- Had given them relief from captivity
- Had not deserted them even in their bondage
- Had revived them & given them new life: So they could rebuild the temple
- Had given them a wall of protection (His power) in the promised land

  3) He confessed their present sins (which had placed them back in bondage)
- Had forsaken God's commandments: Engaged in the corrupt, detestable, & impure behavior of their unbelieving neighbors

- Had intermarried with unbelievers
- Had sought evil associations: The friendship, social life, & wealth of unbelievers
- Had jeopardized the future: Rejected the promise of God to make them strong, bless them, & give the land to their children

  4) He confessed their unworthiness
- Because of their terrible wickedness & guilt
- Because of God's goodness: Had punished them less than they deserved
- Because they were again breaking God's commandments: Mixing with unbelievers & their evil ways
- Because they deserved God's judgment

- Because of God's righteousness
- Because they were only a small remnant—once again guilty before God & not worthy to stand in His presence

3. The experience of revival: The people confessed & repented

a. The people's response to Ezra's brokenness & his fervent prayer: Were remorseful over their sin

1) A large crowd gathered & joined Ezra in seeking the LORD: They wept bitterly

2) A man named Shecaniah arose & stepped in as the leader of the people

• He confessed their sin & unfaithfulness

• He declared there was still hope in God

• He suggested they repent & make a covenant with God to divorce the unbelieving wives & to send them away with the children (De.7:3; 22:19, 29; 24:1-4; Is.50:1; Je.3:8)

• He encouraged Ezra to stand up & take charge: They would follow & support him

b. Ezra's response to Shecaniah's call to leadership

1) Ezra arose & took decisive action: Led the people to swear they would do as suggested

2) Ezra then withdrew & continued his fervent prayer

• Withdrew to the room of Jehohanan, grandson of Eliashib the High Priest, Ne.12:10-11, 23; 13:28

• Fasted, neither eating nor drinking

3) Ezra sent a proclamation throughout Judah calling all the returned exiles to assemble in Jerusalem

4) Ezra & the leaders made attendance compulsory: Failure to appear within three days had severe consequences

• Loss of all property

• Exiled from the nation

c. The people's response to the call for repentance & spiritual separation

CHAPTER 10

Now when Ezra had prayed, and when he had confessed, weeping and casting himself down before the house of God, there assembled unto him out of Israel a very great congregation of men and women and children: for the people wept very sore.

2 And Shechaniah the son of Jehiel, *one* of the sons of Elam, answered and said unto Ezra, We have trespassed against our God, and have taken strange wives of the people of the land: yet now there is hope in Israel concerning this thing.

3 Now therefore let us make a covenant with our God to put away all the wives, and such as are born of them, according to the counsel of my lord, and of those that tremble at the commandment of our God; and let it be done according to the law.

4 Arise; for *this* matter *belongeth* unto thee: we also *will be* with thee: be of good courage, and do *it*.

5 Then arose Ezra, and made the chief priests, the Levites, and all Israel, to swear that they should do according to this word. And they sware.

6 Then Ezra rose up from before the house of God, and went into the chamber of Johanan the son of Eliashib: and *when* he came thither, he did eat no bread, nor drink water: for he mourned because of the transgression of them that had been carried away.

7 And they made proclamation throughout Judah and Jerusalem unto all the children of the captivity, that they should gather themselves together unto Jerusalem;

8 And that whosoever would not come within three days, according to the counsel of the princes and the elders, all his substance should be forfeited, and himself separated from the congregation of those that had been carried away.

9 Then all the men of Judah and Benjamin gathered themselves together unto Jerusalem

within three days. It *was* the ninth month, on the twentieth *day* of the month; and all the people sat in the street of the house of God, trembling because of *this* matter, and for the great rain.

10 And Ezra the priest stood up, and said unto them, Ye have transgressed, and have taken strange wives, to increase the trespass of Israel.

11 Now therefore make confession unto the LORD God of your fathers, and do his pleasure: and separate yourselves from the people of the land, and from the strange wives.

12 Then all the congregation answered and said with a loud voice, As thou hast said, so must we do.

13 But the people *are* many, and *it is* a time of much rain, and we are not able to stand without, neither *is* this a work of one day or two: for we are many that have transgressed in this thing.

14 Let now our rulers of all the congregation stand, and let all them which have taken strange wives in our cities come at appointed times, and with them the elders of every city, and the judges thereof, until the fierce wrath of our God for this matter be turned from us.

15 Only Jonathan the son of Asahel and Jahaziah the son of Tikvah were employed about this *matter:* and Meshullam and Shabbethai the Levite helped them.

16 And the children of the captivity did so. And Ezra the priest, *with* certain chief of the fathers, after the house of their fathers, and all of them by *their* names, were separated, and sat down in the first day of the tenth month to examine the matter.

17 And they made an end with all the men that had taken strange wives by the first day of the first month.

18 And among the sons of the priests there were found that had taken strange wives: *namely,* of the sons of Jeshua the son of Jozadak, and his brethren; Maaseiah, and Eliezer, and Jarib, and Gedaliah.

1) The people assembled within three days

• Met on day 20 of the 9th month (Dec.) in the square before the temple

• Were trembling with concern over their sin & the heavy rainfall

2) Ezra preached a message to all the people

• The people had sinned by mixing with & even marrying unbelievers

• The people must confess their sin to the LORD & repent: Separate from the worldly unbelievers around them & divorce their unbelieving spouses

3) The people responded by giving a resounding promise to do exactly as Ezra commanded

d. The people's reasonable & practical suggestion: That the public meeting be dismissed & the guilty parties dealt with on a local basis

1) The reasons: The rain was heavy & so many people were involved

2) The suggestion: That the local officials of each town act on behalf of the nation

• To handle each case by appointment

• To investigate & identify the guilty persons

3) The suggestion was accepted: Only four men dissented & opposed the idea

e. The people's associations & marriages investigated

1) Ezra wisely appointed leaders of each family or clan to judge the cases of his own family

2) The family judges began their investigation on the 1st day of the tenth month & completed the task on the 1st day of the first month: A period of three months

f. The people's obedience: A record of the repentant sinners

1) The priests who were descendants of the High Priest

• They vowed to divorce their wives (not to mix with unbelievers)

• They offered sacrifices, seeking forgiveness	19 And they gave their hands that they would put away their wives; and *being* guilty, *they offered* a ram of the flock for their trespass.	Adaiah, Jashub, and Sheal, and Ramoth.
2) The other priests	20 And of the sons of Immer; Hanani, and Zebadiah.	30 And of the sons of Pahath-moab; Adna, and Chelal, Benaiah, Maaseiah, Mattaniah, Bezaleel, and Binnui, and Manasseh.
	21 And of the sons of Harim; Maaseiah, and Elijah, and Shemaiah, and Jehiel, and Uzziah.	31 And *of* the sons of Harim; Eliezer, Ishijah, Malchiah, Shemaiah, Shimeon,
	22 And of the sons of Pashur; Elioenai, Maaseiah, Ishmael, Nethaneel, Jozabad, and Elasah.	32 Benjamin, Malluch, *and* Shemariah.
3) The Levites	23 Also of the Levites; Jozabad, and Shimei, and Kelaiah, (the same *is* Kelita,) Pethahiah, Judah, and Eliezer.	33 Of the sons of Hashum; Mattenai, Mattathah, Zabad, Eliphelet, Jeremai, Manasseh, *and* Shimei.
		34 Of the sons of Bani; Maadai, Amram, and Uel,
4) The Levite singers & doorkeepers	24 Of the singers also; Eliashib: and of the porters; Shallum, and Telem, and Uri.	35 Benaiah, Bedeiah, Chelluh,
		36 Vaniah, Meremoth, Eliashib,
5) The other Israelites	25 Moreover of Israel: of the sons of Parosh; Ramiah, and Jeziah, and Malchiah, and Miamin, and Eleazar, and Malchijah, and Benaiah.	37 Mattaniah, Mattenai, and Jaasau,
		38 And Bani, and Binnui, Shimei,
		39 And Shelemiah, and Nathan, and Adaiah,
	26 And of the sons of Elam; Mattaniah, Zechariah, and Jehiel, and Abdi, and Jeremoth, and Eliah.	40 Machnadebai, Shashai, Sharai,
		41 Azareel, and Shelemiah, Shemariah,
	27 And of the sons of Zattu; Elioenai, Eliashib, Mattaniah, and Jeremoth, and Zabad, and Aziza.	42 Shallum, Amariah, *and* Joseph.
		43 Of the sons of Nebo; Jeiel, Mattithiah, Zabad, Zebina, Jadau, and Joel, Benaiah.
	28 Of the sons also of Bebai; Jehohanan, Hananiah, Zabbai, *and* Athlai.	44 All these had taken strange wives: and *some* of them had wives by whom they had children.
	29 And of the sons of Bani; Meshullam, Malluch, and	

DIVISION II

THE SECOND RETURN OF EXILES FROM CAPTIVITY AND THEIR REFORM—LED BY EZRA, 7:1–10:44

C. Ezra's Confrontation with the People Over Their Evil Associations: A Picture of Genuine Revival, 9:1–10:44

(9:1–10:44) **Introduction**: seldom in history has revival been needed as much as it is today. This is a day of terrible immorality and wickedness, lawlessness and violence, dishonesty and deceit. By the hundreds and thousands people are feeling restless, empty, purposeless, lonely, discouraged, and depressed. Others feel hopeless to escape the distress and anguish they feel within their souls. Millions desperately need to be revived, aroused to experience life in all its fullness—life that can be found only in Jesus Christ.

Even within the church many are found to be caught up in the possessions and pleasures of the world and in its corrupt, immoral, and wicked behavior. If the church has ever needed revival, it is today.

About five months after Ezra and the returnees arrived in Jerusalem (7:9; 10:9), Ezra was confronted with a crisis that threatened the very life of the small community of exiles who had returned. The crisis involved terrible sin that had seeped into the lives of the returned exiles. Many of them were engaging in the detestable, evil behavior of their unbelieving neighbors. This is, *Ezra's Confrontation with the People Over Their Evil Associations: A Picture of Genuine Revival*, 9:1–10:44.

1. The need for revival: the people were participating in the worldly, sinful behavior of unbelievers—even marrying unbelievers (9:1-2).
2. The deep concern and prayer of Ezra for revival: the people desperately needed to confess (9:3-15).
3. The experience of revival: the people confessed and repented (10:1-44).

65

1 (9:1-2) **Revival, Need for—Worldliness, Example of—Marriage, Duty—Associations, Evil, Example of—Spiritual Separation, Failure—Separation, Spiritual, Failure in—Walk, Sinful, Example of—Life, Sinful, Example of—Believers, Sins of**: after being in Jerusalem for about five months (7:9; 10:9), Ezra began to sense a deep need for revival among the people. He obviously had begun a teaching ministry among the people after they arrived, instructing them in the Word of the LORD. Apparently, a spirit of conviction struck the hearts of some, in particular the leaders. They came to Ezra confessing their sins. However, many of the people were not living lives of spiritual separation as commanded by God. They were engaging in the detestable, immoral, and wicked behavior of unbelievers, following the evil lifestyle and false worship of their neighbors. Note the neighbors listed: the Canaanites, Hittites, Perizzites, Jebusites, Ammonites, Moabites, Egyptians, and Amorites (v.1).

Not only were these Jews committing immorality and wickedness, but some were also intermarrying with unbelievers. This was in direct violation of God's Holy commandments:

> **"For thou shalt worship no other god: for the LORD, whose name *is* Jealous, *is* a jealous God: Lest thou make a covenant with the inhabitants of the land, and they go a whoring after their gods, and do sacrifice unto their gods, and *one* call thee, and thou eat of his sacrifice; And thou take of their daughters unto thy sons, and their daughters go a whoring after their gods, and make thy sons go a whoring after their gods" (Ex.34:14-16; also see De.7:1-6; 20:10-18).**

Even more tragic, some of the men had divorced their Jewish wives in order to marry unbelieving women. Although this is not mentioned by Ezra in the present Scripture, the prophet Malachi preached against this sin that seemed to be common among the returning exiles:

> **"Judah hath dealt treacherously, and an abomination is committed in Israel and in Jerusalem; for Judah hath profaned the holiness of the LORD which he loved, and hath married the daughter of a strange god. The LORD will cut off the man that doeth this, the master and the scholar, out of the tabernacles of Jacob, and him that offereth an offering unto the LORD of hosts. And this have ye done again, covering the altar of the LORD with tears, with weeping, and with crying out, insomuch that he regardeth not the offering any more, or receiveth *it* with good will at your hand. Yet ye say, Wherefore? Because the LORD hath been witness between thee and the wife of thy youth, against whom thou hast dealt treacherously: yet *is* she thy companion, and the wife of thy covenant. And did not he make one? Yet had he the residue of the spirit. And wherefore one? That he might seek a godly seed. Therefore take heed to your spirit, and let none deal treacherously against the wife of his youth. For the LORD, the God of Israel, saith that he hateth putting away: for *one* covereth violence with his garment, saith the LORD of hosts: therefore take heed to your spirit, that ye deal not treacherously" (Mal.2:11-16).**

God's law did allow Jews to marry foreigners if the foreigners turned away from their false worship and wicked lifestyles and turned to the LORD. The book of *Ruth* shows this. However, the Jews were never allowed to marry any of the native Canaanites because of the depth of sin to which they had fallen. Even before the Israelites had arrived in the promised land of Canaan, the Canaanites had become so steeped in sin that they were beyond repentance. They were doomed to eternal judgment (see DEEPER STUDY #1—Jos.11:20 for more discussion). In the present situation, leaders—both civil and religious—were the worst offenders. They were the most unfaithful, sinful, and worldly. By marrying unbelievers and engaging in the detestable practices of immorality and wickedness, God's people had polluted or corrupted themselves. Believers were mingling, associating with unbelievers and corrupting "the holy seed," the holy race being created by God. Note how verse two drives home this point.

OUTLINE	SCRIPTURE	SCRIPTURE	OUTLINE
1. **The need for revival: The people were participating in the worldly, sinful behavior of unbelievers—even marrying unbelievers**	Now when these things were done, the princes came to me, saying, The people of Israel, and the priests, and the Levites, have not separated themselves from the people	ites, the Egyptians, and the Amorites.	*itual separation*
a. The fact reported to Ezra by a group of leaders: Less than five months after arriving in the promised land, 7:9; 10:9	of the lands, *doing* according to their abominations, *even* of the Canaanites, the Hittites,	2 For they have taken of their daughters for themselves, and for their sons: so that the holy seed have mingled themselves with the people of *those* lands: yea, the hand of the princes and rulers hath been chief in this trespass.	2) Divorcing (Mal.2:16) & intermarrying with unbelievers, Ex.34:14-16; De.7:1-6; 20:10-18
b. The worldly, sinful behavior	the Perizzites, the Jebusites,		c. The tragedy: Some leaders—both civil & religious—were the worst offenders, the most unfaithful, sinful, & worldly
1) Not living lives of *spir-*	the Ammonites, the Moab-		

Thought 1. Believers are to be spiritually separated from the wicked and evil of this earth. We are not to participate in the sinful, worldly behavior of unbelievers. Immorality, gossip, hatred, greed, covetousness, lying, stealing, cheating, and all other sinful behaviors are not to be a part of our lifestyle. If neighbors, fellow workers, classmates or relatives engage in such wicked behavior, we must not follow in their steps. We are to take a strong stand for righteousness, morality, and peace. When dealing with immorality and unrighteousness, we are to live lives of spiritual separation, having nothing to do with wicked behavior. God does not expect us to become extremists, to isolate ourselves from fellow workers, classmates, and neighbors. In fact, He commands us to be witnesses to the lost of the world and to disciple them, which involves associating with them. But God's instructions are clear: we must not fellowship and socialize with the wicked of this earth. If we socialize with them, eventually they will seduce and influence us to participate in their wicked and immoral behavior. Note what Holy Scripture says:

"And take heed to yourselves, lest at any time your hearts be overcharged with surfeiting, and drunkenness, and cares of this life, and so that day come upon you unawares" (Lu.21:34).

"If ye were of the world, the world would love his own: but because ye are not of the world, but I have chosen you out of the world, therefore the world hateth you" (Jn.15:19).

"And with many other words did he testify and exhort, saying, Save yourselves from this untoward generation" (Ac.2:40).

"I beseech you therefore, brethren, by the mercies of God, that ye present your bodies a living sacrifice, holy, acceptable unto God, *which is* your reasonable service. And be not conformed to this world: but be ye transformed by the renewing of your mind, that ye may prove what is that good, and acceptable, and perfect, will of God" (Ro.12:1-2).

"I wrote unto you in an epistle not to company with fornicators: Yet not altogether with the fornicators of this world, or with the covetous, or extortioners, or with idolaters; for then must ye needs go out of the world. But now I have written unto you not to keep company, if any man that is called a brother be a fornicator, or covetous, or an idolater, or a railer, or a drunkard, or an extortioner; with such an one no not to eat" (1 Co.5:9-11).

"And they that use this world, as not abusing *it:* for the fashion of this world passeth away" (1 Co.7:31).

"Be ye not unequally yoked together with unbelievers: for what fellowship hath righteousness with unrighteousness? and what communion hath light with darkness? And what concord hath Christ with Belial? or what part hath he that believeth with an infidel? And what agreement hath the temple of God with idols? for ye are the temple of the living God; as God hath said, I will dwell in them, and walk in *them;* and I will be their God, and they shall be my people" (2 Co.6:14-16).

"Wherefore come out from among them, and be ye separate, saith the Lord, and touch not the unclean *thing;* and I will receive you, And will be a Father unto you, and ye shall be my sons and daughters, saith the Lord Almighty" (2 Co.6:17-18).

"But God forbid that I should glory, save in the cross of our Lord Jesus Christ, by whom the world is crucified unto me, and I unto the world" (Ga.6:14).

"And have no fellowship with the unfruitful works of darkness, but rather reprove *them*" (Ep.5:11).

"Set your affection on things above, not on things on the earth" (Col.3:2).

"Now we command you, brethren, in the name of our Lord Jesus Christ, that ye withdraw yourselves from every brother that walketh disorderly, and not after the tradition which he received of us" (2 Th.3:6).

"No man that warreth entangleth himself with the affairs of *this* life; that he may please him who hath chosen him to be a soldier" (2 Ti.2:4).

"Nevertheless the foundation of God standeth sure, having this seal, The Lord knoweth them that are his. And, Let every one that nameth the name of Christ depart from iniquity" (2 Ti.2:19).

"Teaching us that, denying ungodliness and worldly lusts, we should live soberly, righteously, and godly, in this present world; Looking for that blessed hope, and the glorious appearing of the great God and our Saviour Jesus Christ" (Tit.2:12-13).

"By faith Moses, when he was come to years, refused to be called the son of Pharaoh's daughter; Choosing rather to suffer affliction with the people of God, than to enjoy the pleasures of sin for a season" (He.11:24-25).

"Love not the world, neither the things *that are* in the world. If any man love the world, the love of the Father is not in him. For all that *is* in the world, the lust of the flesh, and the lust of the eyes, and the pride of life, is not of the Father, but is of the world" (1 Jn.2:15-16).

"Ye adulterers and adulteresses, know ye not that the friendship of the world is enmity with God? whosoever therefore will be a friend of the world is the enemy of God" (Js.4:4).

"Thou shalt not follow a multitude to *do* evil; neither shalt thou speak in a cause to decline after many to wrest *judgment*" (Ex.23:2).

"Blessed *is* the man that walketh not in the counsel of the ungodly, nor standeth in the way of sinners, nor sitteth in the seat of the scornful" (Ps.1:1).

"My son, if sinners entice thee, consent thou not....My son, walk not thou in the way with them; refrain thy foot from their path" (Pr.1:10, 15).

"Enter not into the path of the wicked, and go not in the way of evil *men*" (Pr.4:14).

"Make no friendship with an angry man; and with a furious man thou shalt not go: Lest thou learn his ways, and get a snare to thy soul" (Pr.22:24-25).

"Eat thou not the bread of *him that hath* an evil eye, neither desire thou his dainty meats: For as he thinketh in his heart, so *is* he: Eat and drink, saith he to thee; but his heart *is* not with thee" (Pr.23:6-7).

"Be not thou envious against evil men, neither desire to be with them" (Pr.24:1).

"Depart ye, depart ye, go ye out from thence, touch no unclean *thing;* go ye out of the midst of her; be ye clean, that bear the vessels of the LORD" (Is.52:11).

---

2 (9:3-15) **Confession, Prayer of, Example—Prayer, Example—Revival, Concern for, Example—Sin, Confession of, Example—Church, Revival**: Ezra's heart was immediately gripped by a deep concern for the people. Thus he did the only thing he could: he went to the LORD in prayer, confessing the people's sins and asking the LORD to send revival among them. In describing the scene, Scripture paints the picture of a man with a tender heart, a man who sincerely trusted the LORD and cared deeply for his people.

OUTLINE	SCRIPTURE	SCRIPTURE	OUTLINE
2. The deep concern & prayer of Ezra for revival: The people desperately needed to confess a. Ezra's heavy spirit of mourning 1) He was soon joined by other faithful believers 2) He sat mourning, expressing his grief until the evening sacrifice b. Ezra's prayer of confession: He stood & then fell to his knees, lifting up his hands to the LORD 1) He confessed their shame & their past sins • Had been piled up higher than their heads, drowning them • Had reached higher than the heavens • Had tragically continued in sin through the generations—bringing God's judgment down upon the kings, priests, & people, which brought death, captivity, loss of wealth, & humiliation 2) He confessed God's goodness to them • Had left them a remnant • Had given them a place in the promised land • Had given them light • Had given them relief from captivity • Had not deserted them even in their bondage • Had revived them & given them new life: So they could rebuild the temple	3 And when I heard this thing, I rent my garment and my mantle, and plucked off the hair of my head and of my beard, and sat down astonied. 4 Then were assembled unto me every one that trembled at the words of the God of Israel, because of the transgression of those that had been carried away; and I sat astonied until the evening sacrifice. 5 And at the evening sacrifice I arose up from my heaviness; and having rent my garment and my mantle, I fell upon my knees, and spread out my hands unto the LORD my God. 6 And said, O my God, I am ashamed and blush to lift up my face to thee, my God: for our iniquities are increased over *our* head, and our trespass is grown up unto the heavens. 7 Since the days of our fathers *have* we *been* in a great trespass unto this day; and for our iniquities have we, our kings, and *our* priests, been delivered into the hand of the kings of the lands, to the sword, to captivity, and to a spoil, and to confusion of face, as *it is* this day. 8 And now for a little space grace hath been *showed* from the LORD our God, to leave us a remnant to escape, and to give us a nail in his holy place, that our God may lighten our eyes, and give us a little reviving in our bondage. 9 For we *were* bondmen; yet our God hath not forsaken us in our bondage, but hath extended mercy unto us in the sight of the kings of Persia, to give us a reviving, to set up	the house of our God, and to repair the desolations thereof, and to give us a wall in Judah and in Jerusalem. 10 And now, O our God, what shall we say after this? for we have forsaken thy commandments, 11 Which thou hast commanded by thy servants the prophets, saying, The land, unto which ye go to possess it, is an unclean land with the filthiness of the people of the lands, with their abominations, which have filled it from one end to another with their uncleanness. 12 Now therefore give not your daughters unto their sons, neither take their daughters unto your sons, nor seek their peace or their wealth for ever: that ye may be strong, and eat the good of the land, and leave *it* for an inheritance to your children for ever. 13 And after all that is come upon us for our evil deeds, and for our great trespass, seeing that thou our God hast punished us less than our iniquities *deserve,* and hast given us *such* deliverance as this; 14 Should we again break thy commandments, and join in affinity with the people of these abominations? wouldest not thou be angry with us till thou hadst consumed *us,* so that *there should be* no remnant nor escaping? 15 O LORD God of Israel, thou *art* righteous: for we remain yet escaped, as *it is* this day: behold, we *are* before thee in our trespasses: for we cannot stand before thee because of this.	• Had given them a wall of protection (His power) in the promised land 3) He confessed their present sins (which had placed them back in bondage) • Had forsaken God's commandments: Engaged in the corrupt, detestable, & impure behavior of their unbelieving neighbors • Had intermarried with unbelievers • Had sought evil associations: The friendship, social life, & wealth of unbelievers • Had jeopardized the future: Rejected the promise of God to make them strong, bless them, & give the land to their children 4) He confessed their unworthiness • Because of their terrible wickedness & guilt • Because of God's goodness: Had punished them less than they deserved • Because they were again breaking God's commandments: Mixing with unbelievers & their evil ways • Because they deserved God's judgment • Because of God's righteousness • Because they were only a small remnant—once again guilty before God & not worthy to stand in His presence

a. When Ezra heard about the sins of the people, he was gripped by a heavy spirit of mourning (vv.3-4). Scripture actually says that he was utterly *appalled*, shocked, horrified at the terrible sins of the people. This was indicated by his tearing his clothing and pulling his hair and beard. It was the custom of that day to express one's grief in this way. Apparently Ezra had gone to the temple to express his grief and to seek the LORD. Naturally, the worshippers wanted to know what was troubling him so deeply. Soon all the faithful believers, those who feared God and trembled at His Word, joined Ezra in mourning over the sins of the people. In utter dismay, Ezra sat there in the temple until the evening sacrifice.

b. When it was time for the evening sacrifice, Ezra offered up his prayer of confession (vv.5-15). He rose from where he had been sitting, fell to his knees, then lifted up his hands to the LORD in prayer and intercession for the people. In his prayer, Ezra made four confessions:

1) Ezra confessed the shame of both his and the people's *past sins* (vv.6-7). He identified himself with the people, confessing that both he and the people were guilty before the LORD.
- ⇒ He confessed that their sins had been piled up higher than their heads, which meant that they were drowning in the deep waters of sin (v.6).
- ⇒ He confessed that their sins and guilt had reached higher than the heavens themselves, which meant that they were provoking God and threatening to arouse His judgment (v.6).
- ⇒ He confessed that the people had tragically continued in sin down through the generations, which had brought God's judgment upon the kings, priests, and people. God's judgment could be seen in the death, captivity, humiliation, and loss of wealth the people had suffered, even up until that very day.

2) Ezra then confessed God's goodness, which He had showered upon the present generation (vv.8-9). Scripture actually says that the present generation had been given a very special grace by God, at least for a little while, a brief moment (v.8). Ezra spelled out seven facts that proved God's goodness was being showered upon the returnees:
- ⇒ First, the LORD had left the Jews a remnant, a small body of believers who had escaped the enslavement of Babylon. But Ezra knew that the *remnant* must live obedient and righteous lives if God was going to fulfill His promises to them. If the remnant had not been faithful to the LORD, God's plan of redemption would have never been carried out through the Jews. Neither the Savior nor the Word of God would have come through them. His promises would not have been fulfilled. Thus the remnant must live righteous and obedient lives before the LORD.
- ⇒ Second, God had given them a *nail* in His holy place or sanctuary. The *nail* signifies a strong, binding, and secure place in the sanctuary of God's presence. As long as they followed the LORD, obeying His holy commandments, they had security in Him.
- ⇒ Third, God had given light to their eyes. That is, He had enlightened their eyes so they could see and have hope in the future. He had revived their spirits.
- ⇒ Fourth, He had delivered them from the bondage of captivity, giving them relief and freedom.
- ⇒ Fifth, He had not forsaken them, not deserted them in their bondage (v.9). Although they were still subject to the Persian Empire, they had been set free to return to their own homeland where they could worship God freely. The LORD had not deserted them, not completely nor permanently.
- ⇒ Sixth, the LORD had given them revival and the opportunity of a new life (v.9). They had been allowed to return in order to rebuild their nation and their temple.
- ⇒ Seventh, the LORD had given them a wall of protection in the promised land, the protection of His very own power.

3) Ezra confessed the sins of the people. Their sins had, in reality, placed them back in bondage to the world and its lifestyle of wickedness (vv.10-12). Ezra was so shaken by the depth and gravity of the evil that he was almost speechless. "What can we say after this?" he asked the LORD. The present generation was guilty of four sins in particular:
- ⇒ They had forsaken God's commandments (vv.10-11). They were engaging in the corrupt, detestable, and impure behavior of their unbelieving neighbors.
- ⇒ They had intermarried with unbelievers (v.12).
- ⇒ They had coveted evil associations, the friendship and social life of unbelievers.
- ⇒ They had jeopardized their and their children's future by rejecting the promises of God to make them strong and to give the promised land to their children as an eternal inheritance (v.12).

4) Ezra confessed their unworthiness, confessed that they were undeserving of any blessing of God (vv.13-15). He pointed out six facts:
- ⇒ They were guilty of terrible wickedness.
- ⇒ God in His goodness had punished them far less than they deserved.
- ⇒ They were breaking God's commandments, in particular by mixing with unbelievers and engaging in appallingly wicked behavior (v.14).
- ⇒ They deserved God's judgment because of their unworthiness.
- ⇒ They were clearly and totally short of God's righteousness (v.15).
- ⇒ They were only a small remnant, but once again the remnant was guilty before God. In fact, they were so sinful and guilty that they were not worthy to stand in God's presence (v.15).

Thought 1. Confession is an absolute essential to receive forgiveness of sin. Therefore, when we sin, we must confess before God. Failure to confess means that we bear the guilt of sin ourselves. Picture a person who breaks a law of the land. For his violation, he must pay the stated or agreed upon penalty for his violation or else be forgiven for his disobedience. Likewise, when we break the law of God, we must either seek His forgiveness or else bear the guilt and punishment ourselves. And God is unwavering about the punishment! Thus, confessing our sins is the key to escaping God's coming judgment. God's Holy Word declares this undeniable truth:

> **"For the wages of sin *is* death; but the gift of God [forgiveness] *is* eternal life through Jesus Christ our Lord" (Ro.6:23).**
> **"If we confess our sins, he is faithful and just to forgive us *our* sins, and to cleanse us from all unrighteousness" (1 Jn.1:9).**
> **"If my people, which are called by my name, shall humble themselves, and pray, and seek my face, and turn from their wicked ways; then will I hear from heaven, and will forgive their sin, and will heal their land" (2 Chr.7:14).**

"Now therefore make confession unto the LORD God of your fathers, and do his pleasure: and separate yourselves from the people of the land, and from the strange wives" (Ezr.10:11).

"Have mercy upon me, O God, according to thy lovingkindness: according unto the multitude of thy tender mercies blot out my transgressions. Wash me throughly from mine iniquity, and cleanse me from my sin. For I acknowledge my transgressions: and my sin *is* ever before me. Against thee, thee only, have I sinned, and done *this* evil in thy sight" (Ps.51:1-4).

"He that covereth his sins shall not prosper: but whoso confesseth and forsaketh *them* shall have mercy" (Pr.28:13).

"Only acknowledge thine iniquity, that thou hast transgressed against the LORD thy God, and hast scattered thy ways to the strangers under every green tree, and ye have not obeyed my voice, saith the LORD" (Je.3:13).

"Cast away from you all your transgressions, whereby ye have transgressed; and make you a new heart and a new spirit: for why will ye die, O house of Israel?" (Eze.18:31).

"Take with you words, and turn to the LORD: say unto him, Take away all iniquity, and receive *us* graciously: so will we render the calves of our lips" (Ho.14:2).

"Therefore also now, saith the LORD, turn ye *even* to me with all your heart, and with fasting, and with weeping, and with mourning" (Joel 2:12).

3 (10:1-44) **Confession, Example of—Repentance, Example of—Revival, Example of—Returned Exiles, Revival Experienced—Spiritual Separation, Example of—Evil Associations, Repentance of**: amazingly, revival broke out among the people, a genuine revival of confession and repentance of sin. All this was due to one man, to Ezra's broken heart and prayer. Scripture records the stunning, wonderful event:

OUTLINE	SCRIPTURE	SCRIPTURE	OUTLINE
3. The experience of revival: The people confessed & repented a. The people's response to Ezra's brokenness & his fervent prayer: Were remorseful over their sin 1) A large crowd gathered & joined Ezra in seeking the LORD: They wept bitterly 2) A man named Shecaniah arose & stepped in as the leader of the people • He confessed their sin & unfaithfulness • He declared there was still hope in God	Now when Ezra had prayed, and when he had confessed, weeping and casting himself down before the house of God, there assembled unto him out of Israel a very great congregation of men and women and children: for the people wept very sore. 2 And Shechaniah the son of Jehiel, *one* of the sons of Elam, answered and said unto Ezra, We have trespassed against our God, and have taken strange wives of the people of the land: yet now	there is hope in Israel concerning this thing. 3 Now therefore let us make a covenant with our God to put away all the wives, and such as are born of them, according to the counsel of my lord, and of those that tremble at the commandment of our God; and let it be done according to the law. 4 Arise; for *this* matter *belongeth* unto thee: we also *will be* with thee: be of good courage, and do *it*.	• He suggested they repent & make a covenant with God to divorce the unbelieving wives & to send them away with the children (De.7:3; 22:19, 29; 24:1-4; Is.50:1; Je.3:8) • He encouraged Ezra to stand up & take charge: They would follow & support him

a. On the very day of Ezra's mourning, the people responded (10:1-4). The scene of their godly leader and teacher prostrate upon the ground in front of the temple, confessing and weeping in deep agony, attracted attention. Other worshippers as well as all who passed nearby the temple soon gathered to join Ezra in seeking the LORD. Everyone wept loudly and bitterly. At some point, a man named Shecaniah got up and stepped in as the leader for the people. Note this fact: by taking the leadership, he was taking a stand against his own father. His father Jehiel was guilty of having married an unbeliever (v.26). As the people's spokesman, Shecaniah offered great hope to the people:

⇒ First, he confessed their sin and unfaithfulness, their guilt for marrying unbelievers and engaging in their wicked lifestyle (v.2).

⇒ Second, he declared there was still hope in God (v.2). Despite their sinfulness, God would have mercy upon them and renew their hope for rebuilding the nation and restoring true worship.

⇒ Third, he suggested they repent and make a covenant with God to divorce the unbelieving wives, sending them away with the children (v.3). As drastic as this action seemed, it was necessary for a crisis had been created. The Jews were only a remnant of the nation, quite small in number, which meant that their survival was shaky at best. The curse of sin and disobedience was threatening to destroy them. Without God, their nation and testimony to the only true God would be erased forever. Knowing this, Shecaniah felt deeply that the people needed to repent and make a renewed covenant, a renewed commitment to obey God's law. In Shecaniah's mind, this appeared to be the only way to handle the problem, for they must be careful to act only as the law dictated. Exactly what law he was referring to is not known, but perhaps it was the law against intermarriage (De.7:3; also see the laws dealing with divorce: De.24:1-4; 22:19, 29; Is.50:1; Je.3:8).

The act of divorcing unbelievers may seem drastic and harsh to people today, but the returnees were concerned with the sinfulness of intermarriage. They sensed a deep need that this and all other sin must be put out of their lives. Although believers today are not to be unequally yoked with unbelievers, the New Testament teaches that once people are married, they are to stay married if at all possible (1 Co.7:12-16).

⇒ Fourth, he encouraged Ezra to arise and take charge of the crisis (v.4). Being their leader and teacher, it was Ezra's responsibility. No doubt with firmness in his voice, Shecaniah assured Ezra that they would follow and support him (v.4).

b. Ezra immediately arose and took decisive action, and the people responded to his strong leadership (vv.5-8). He placed the people under oath, arousing them to swear they would do exactly as had been suggested (v.5). After kindling the fire under the people, Ezra left the front of the temple and sought privacy in the room of Jehohanan, the grandson of the High Priest Eliashib (Ne.12:10-11, 23; 13:28). Continuing to seek the face of the LORD over the sins of the people, Ezra fasted—neither eating nor drinking.

As quickly as possible, a proclamation was prepared and sent throughout Judah, calling all the returned exiles to assemble in Jerusalem (v.7). And note, attendance was compulsory (v.8). Failure to appear within three days had severe consequences: the person would lose all of his property and be exiled from the nation. The money from the sale of his property would go to the temple (Le.27:28-29). Note that even before the Jews returned to Judah, Artaxerxes had given Ezra the authority to take this action, if necessary (7:26).

OUTLINE	SCRIPTURE	SCRIPTURE	OUTLINE
b. Ezra's response to Shecaniah's call to leadership 1) Ezra arose & took decisive action: Led the people to swear they would do as suggested 2) Ezra then withdrew & continued his fervent prayer • Withdrew to the room of Jehohanan, grandson of Eliashib the High Priest, Ne.12:10-11, 23; 13:28 • Fasted, neither eating nor drinking	5 Then arose Ezra, and made the chief priests, the Levites, and all Israel, to swear that they should do according to this word. And they sware. 6 Then Ezra rose up from before the house of God, and went into the chamber of Johanan the son of Eliashib: and *when* he came thither, he did eat no bread, nor drink water: for he mourned because of the transgression of them that had been carried away.	7 And they made proclamation throughout Judah and Jerusalem unto all the children of the captivity, that they should gather themselves together unto Jerusalem; 8 And that whosoever would not come within three days, according to the counsel of the princes and the elders, all his substance should be forfeited, and himself separated from the congregation of those that had been carried away.	3) Ezra sent a proclamation throughout Judah calling all the returned exiles to assemble in Jerusalem 4) Ezra & the leaders made attendance compulsory: Failure to appear within three days had severe consequences • Loss of all property • Exiled from the nation

c. When the people arrived in Jerusalem, they responded to the call for repentance and spiritual separation (vv.9-12). So far as is known, all the people assembled within the three days allowed (v.9). The date was the 20th day of the ninth month, which was December according to modern-day calendars. Sitting in the square before the house of God, the people were trembling both because of conviction over their sins and because it was raining. Ezra was preaching, declaring that they had sinned by mixing with unbelievers and intermarrying with them (vv.10-11). He challenged the people to confess their sins to the LORD and repent, to separate from the worldly unbelievers around them and divorce their unbelieving spouses.

In response, the people gave a resounding promise to do exactly what Ezra commanded (v.12). With a loud voice they shouted out in unison that he was correct. They must do what he said.

OUTLINE	SCRIPTURE	SCRIPTURE	OUTLINE
c. The people's response to the call for repentance & spiritual separation 1) The people assembled within three days • Met on day 20 of the 9th month (Dec.) in the square before the temple • Were trembling with concern over their sin & the heavy rainfall 2) Ezra preached a message to all the people • The people had sinned	9 Then all the men of Judah and Benjamin gathered themselves together unto Jerusalem within three days. It *was* the ninth month, on the twentieth *day* of the month; and all the people sat in the street of the house of God, trembling because of *this* matter, and for the great rain. 10 And Ezra the priest stood up, and said unto them, Ye have transgressed, and	have taken strange wives, to increase the trespass of Israel. 11 Now therefore make confession unto the LORD God of your fathers, and do his pleasure: and separate yourselves from the people of the land, and from the strange wives. 12 Then all the congregation answered and said with a loud voice, As thou hast said, so must we do.	by mixing with & even marrying unbelievers • The people must confess their sin to the LORD & repent: Separate from the worldly unbelievers around them & divorce their unbelieving spouses 3) The people responded by giving a resounding promise to do exactly as Ezra commanded

d. A number of leaders representing the people soon made a reasonable and practical suggestion: that the public meeting be dismissed and the guilty parties be dealt with on a local basis (v.13). The reasons were obvious: the rains were heavy, and there were so many people involved in the sinful affair that the matter could not be taken care of in a day or two. For these reasons, it was suggested that local officials from each town act on behalf of the nation (v.14). By doing this, each case could be handled by appointment, investigated, and the guilty persons identified.

Realizing the wisdom of the suggestion, the majority immediately approved the idea. Only four men dissented and opposed it (v.15).

OUTLINE	SCRIPTURE	SCRIPTURE	OUTLINE
d. The people's reasonable & practical suggestion: That the public meeting be dismissed & the guilty parties dealt with on a local basis 1) The reasons: The rain was heavy & so many people were involved 2) The suggestion: That the local officials of each town act on behalf of the	13 But the people *are* many, and *it is* a time of much rain, and we are not able to stand without, neither *is this* a work of one day or two: for we are many that have transgressed in this thing. 14 Let now our rulers of all the congregation stand, and let all them which have taken strange wives in our	cities come at appointed times, and with them the elders of every city, and the judges thereof, until the fierce wrath of our God for this matter be turned from us. 15 Only Jonathan the son of Asahel and Jahaziah the son of Tikvah were employed about this *matter:* and Meshullam and Shabbethai the Levite helped them.	nation • To handle each case by appointment • To investigate & identify the guilty persons 3) The suggestion was accepted: Only four men dissented & opposed the idea

e. Following the proposal that had been laid out, the local officials began to counsel and investigate the cases of intermarriage among the Jews (vv.16-17). Wisely, Ezra appointed leaders of each family or clan to judge the cases of his own family. This meant there was a close bond between the judge and the guilty parties. In all likelihood, both counseling and encouraging unbelievers to become converts to the only true God were part of the investigation. Being a family affair also meant that each case would be handled with more compassion and understanding. More pressure would be placed upon the family head to do all he could to lead the unbelievers to the LORD and the guilty Jews to true repentance. The family judges began their investigations on the first day of the tenth month and completed the task on the first day of the first month. Altogether it took three months to complete the task.

OUTLINE	SCRIPTURE	SCRIPTURE	OUTLINE
e. The people's associations & marriages investigated 1) Ezra wisely appointed leaders of each family or clan to judge the cases of his own family 2) The family judges began	16 And the children of the captivity did so. And Ezra the priest, *with* certain chief of the fathers, after the house of their fathers, and all of them by *their* names, were separated, and sat down	in the first day of the tenth month to examine the matter. 17 And they made an end with all the men that had taken strange wives by the first day of the first month.	their investigation on the 1st day of the tenth month & completed the task on the 1st day of the first month: A period of three months

f. The people kept their oath. They divorced their foreign, unbelieving wives who refused to accept the LORD. They then offered sacrifices to the LORD, seeking His forgiveness (10:18-44). This included the guilty priests and Levites (vv.18-24) as well as the Israelite laymen (vv.25-44). *The Bible Knowledge Commentary* says this:

> "Each case was judged individually so that justice would be done. By this action the community was not saying that divorce was good. It was a matter of following God's Law about the need for religious purity in the nation. (Ex.34:11-16; De.7:-14). **Ezra** wrote nothing about what happened to these **foreign women** or their children. Presumably they returned to their pagan countries."[1]

In *The New American Commentary*, Mervin Breneman discusses the crisis of intermarriage that the Jews were facing. His discussion is well worth quoting in its entirety:

> Ezra knew that marriage was instituted by God and considered a permanent and exclusive relationship (Gen 2:24, quoted in Matt 19:5; Eph 5:31). If Malachi preached about Ezra's time or just before, Ezra was surely familiar with his teaching on divorce in 2:16 (" 'I hate divorce,' says the Lord God of Israel"). Much of biblical ethics has to do with the sanctity of the marriage relationship. In fact, God even uses marriage to illustrate his own relationship to his people (Hos 1–3; Eph 5). Since the family is the basis of society, any offense against the family is an offense against God.
>
> The moral dilemma Ezra faced, however, was caused by the pagan influence these foreign women would have on the children of these mixed marriages and on the newly reestablished community of faith. Ezra knew the story of Solomon and his foreign wives and the devastating effect this had had on Israel (1 Kgs 11:1-11; cf. Neh 13:26-27). The family and the convictions of the whole religious community were at stake. Ezra's action was drastic, but he chose the path most likely to protect the covenant community from pagan syncretism [the combining of different forms of belief or practice] (cf. Gal 3:23; 1 Cor 5). There is wisdom in Homgren's statement: "Sometimes preservation of a way of life dictates a policy which disappoints the democratic, ecumenical spirit."[2]
>
> Nevertheless, if Ezra emphasized God's law, how could he support the decision to divorce these foreign wives? Deuteronomy 24:1-14 indicates that sometimes divorce was permitted in the Old Testament (also 22:19, 29; Isa 50:1; Jer 3:8). Also, the situation in Ezra was different from that envisioned elsewhere, for in Ezra pagan wives were involved. These marriages were wrong from the outset. Malachi's statement that God hates divorce, although true in an absolute sense, is given in response to Jews who had divorced their Jewish wives in order to take foreign women. In this historically unique case, Ezra and the Jewish leaders considered that the importance of maintaining the purity of the religious community superceded that of these marital relationships.
>
> In the New Testament, Jesus plainly teaches that divorce is not God's will: "What God has joined together, let no man separate" (Matt 19:6). Especially in our times when irresponsibility and selfishness are often renamed "individual

---

1 John F. Walvoord and Roy B. Zuck, Editors. *The Bible Knowledge Commentary*, Old Testament, p.671.
2 F.C. Homgren. *Ezra and Nehemiah*. (Grand Rapids, MI: Eerdmans Publishing Co., 1987), p.85.

freedom," the sanctity and permanence of marriage must be emphasized. Yet Matt 19:9 and 1 Cor 7:11,15 recognize that in certain cases divorce will occur. Churches have differed concerning the toleration of divorce and remarriage. The Catholic Church has consistently prohibited it, as have some Protestant groups. It has become an ever-increasing moral issue. The teaching of the Old and New Testaments has led many Christians to accept that in some circumstances divorce may be accepted as a tragic last resort when the marriage has completely broken down and no possibility of restoration exists. These chapters in Ezra, however, are descriptive, not prescriptive. They cannot be taken as authorization for divorcing an unbelieving spouse. In 1 Cor 7:12-16 Paul exhorts one who has an unbelieving partner not to divorce: but if the unbelieving partner leaves, the believer is "not bound in such circumstances." Most Christian leaders agree that each case must be studied carefully in light of Scripture and in light of its own particular situation.

This episode shows the danger of moral and spiritual apathy and the importance of maintaining the identity of the believing community in a pagan world. The commission of Artaxerxes to Ezra was to develop Judaism as a religious community. According to Malachi, some men already had divorced their Jewish wives to take foreign women, and the process of assimilation had already begun (Mal 2:10-17; 3:13-15). So the threat to the community was real. It also shows the seriousness with which the Bible treats marriage between believers and unbelievers (2 Cor 6:14-18). Furthermore, this episode also shows the wisdom of Ezra's leadership. As vital as his leadership was, he did not force his decision on the people. Rather, he influenced the leaders and people, relying on the power of God's Word and Spirit; and the decision was made by the community of believers. We can learn from his teaching, his patience, and his example. This shows how strong convictions, held deeply by one leader or a minority, can influence the future of the whole community's life and thought. Just as in Ezra's time, the believing community today often faces crises that demand strong leadership and decisive, united community action.[3]

OUTLINE	SCRIPTURE	SCRIPTURE	OUTLINE
f. The people's obedience: A record of the repentant sinners 1) The priests who were descendants of the High Priest • They vowed to divorce their wives (not to mix with unbelievers) • They offered sacrifices, seeking forgiveness	18 And among the sons of the priests there were found that had taken strange wives: *namely,* of the sons of Jeshua the son of Jozadak, and his brethren; Maaseiah, and Eliezer, and Jarib, and Gedaliah. 19 And they gave their hands that they would put away their wives; and *being* guilty, *they offered* a ram of the flock for their trespass.	Jehohanan, Hananiah, Zabbai, *and* Athlai. 29 And of the sons of Bani; Meshullam, Malluch, and Adaiah, Jashub, and Sheal, and Ramoth. 30 And of the sons of Pahath-moab; Adna, and Chelal, Benaiah, Maaseiah, Mattaniah, Bezaleel, and Binnui, and Manasseh.	
2) The other priests	20 And of the sons of Immer; Hanani, and Zebadiah. 21 And of the sons of Harim; Maaseiah, and Elijah, and Shemaiah, and Jehiel, and Uzziah. 22 And of the sons of Pashur; Elioenai, Maaseiah, Ishmael, Nethaneel, Jozabad, and Elasah.	31 And *of* the sons of Harim; Eliezer, Ishijah, Malchiah, Shemaiah, Shimeon, 32 Benjamin, Malluch, *and* Shemariah. 33 Of the sons of Hashum; Mattenai, Mattathah, Zabad, Eliphelet, Jeremai, Manasseh, *and* Shimei. 34 Of the sons of Bani; Maadai, Amram, and Uel,	
3) The Levites	23 Also of the Levites; Jozabad, and Shimei, and Kelaiah, (the same *is* Kelita,) Pethahiah, Judah, and Eliezer.	35 Benaiah, Bedeiah, Chelluh, 36 Vaniah, Meremoth, Eliashib, 37 Mattaniah, Mattenai, and Jaasau,	
4) The Levite singers & doorkeepers	24 Of the singers also; Eliashib: and of the porters; Shallum, and Telem, and Uri.	38 And Bani, and Binnui, Shimei,	
5) The other Israelites	25 Moreover of Israel: of the sons of Parosh; Ramiah, and Jeziah, and Malchiah, and Miamin, and Eleazar, and Malchijah, and Benaiah. 26 And of the sons of Elam; Mattaniah, Zechariah, and Jehiel, and Abdi, and Jeremoth, and Eliah. 27 And of the sons of Zattu; Elioenai, Eliashib, Mattaniah, and Jeremoth, and Zabad, and Aziza. 28 Of the sons also of Bebai;	39 And Shelemiah, and Nathan, and Adaiah, 40 Machnadebai, Shashai, Sharai, 41 Azareel, and Shelemiah, Shemariah, 42 Shallum, Amariah, *and* Joseph. 43 Of the sons of Nebo; Jeiel, Mattithiah, Zabad, Zebina, Jadau, and Joel, Benaiah. 44 All these had taken strange wives: and *some* of them had wives by whom they had children.	

---

3 Mervin Breneman. *Ezra, Nehemiah, Esther*, pp.163-165.

Thought 1. Revival can come only through *confession* and *repentance* of sin. A person who continues in his sin will not experience revival. Why? Because the heart cannot be truly revived, put at peace and made restful, if it is alienated from God. And sin alienates, separates the human heart from God. The heart is restless—dissatisfied, unfulfilled, and somewhat insecure—until it finds its rest in God. True revival of the human heart can only come if we confess and repent of our sins.

So it is with the church. The church will be truly revived, awakened to righteousness, only when its members confess and repent of their sins. But when they do confess and repent, the most wonderful experience of revival will flood the church. Revival brings a sense of peace, rest, and fulfillment to the heart of the church. In addition, the church is aroused with a renewed spirit of purpose and mission, bearing a far stronger testimony for the LORD. But this fact must be kept in mind: to experience revival we must confess and repent of our sins.

(1) Listen to what God's Holy Word says about repentance and confession:

"Blessed *are* they that mourn: for they shall be comforted" (Mt.5:4).

"I say unto you, that likewise joy shall be in heaven over one sinner that repenteth, more than over ninety and nine just persons, which need no repentance" (Lu.15:7).

"Then Peter said unto them, Repent, and be baptized every one of you in the name of Jesus Christ for the remission of sins, and ye shall receive the gift of the Holy Ghost" (Ac.2:38).

"Repent ye therefore, and be converted, that your sins may be blotted out, when the times of refreshing shall come from the presence of the Lord" (Ac.3:19).

"If we confess our sins, he is faithful and just to forgive us *our* sins, and to cleanse us from all unrighteousness" (1 Jn.1:9).

"If my people, which are called by my name, shall humble themselves, and pray, and seek my face, and turn from their wicked ways; then will I hear from heaven, and will forgive their sin, and will heal their land" (2 Chr.7:14).

"The LORD *is* nigh unto them that are of a broken heart; and saveth such as be of a contrite spirit" (Ps.34:18).

"Let the wicked forsake his way, and the unrighteous man his thoughts: and let him return unto the LORD, and he will have mercy upon him; and to our God, for he will abundantly pardon" (Is.55:7).

(2) Listen to what God's Holy Word says about revival and renewal of the human heart:

"I beseech you therefore, brethren, by the mercies of God, that ye present your bodies a living sacrifice, holy, acceptable unto God, *which is* your reasonable service. And be not conformed to this world: but be ye transformed by the renewing of your mind, that ye may prove what is that good, and acceptable, and perfect, will of God" (Ro.12:1-2).

"For which cause we faint not; but though our outward man perish, yet the inward *man* is renewed day by day. For our light affliction, which is but for a moment, worketh for us a far more exceeding *and* eternal weight of glory; While we look not at the things which are seen, but at the things which are not seen: for the things which are seen *are* temporal; but the things which are not seen *are* eternal" (2 Co.4:16-18).

"That ye put off concerning the former conversation [behavior, conduct] the old man, which is corrupt according to the deceitful lusts; And be renewed in the spirit of your mind; And that ye put on the new man, which after God is created in righteousness and true holiness" (Ep.4:22-24).

"And have put on the new *man,* which is renewed in knowledge after the image of him that created him" (Col.3:10).

"Not by works of righteousness which we have done, but according to his mercy he saved us, by the washing of regeneration, and renewing of the Holy Ghost" (Tit.3:5).

"Create in me a clean heart, O God; and renew a right spirit within me" (Ps.51:10).

"Restore unto me the joy of thy salvation; and uphold me *with thy* free spirit. *Then* will I teach transgressors thy ways; and sinners shall be converted unto thee" (Ps.51:12-13).

"Turn us again, O God of hosts, and cause thy face to shine; and we shall be saved" (Ps.80:7).

"Wilt thou not revive us again: that thy people may rejoice in thee?" (Ps.85:6).

"Until the spirit be poured upon us from on high, and the wilderness be a fruitful field, and the fruitful field be counted for a forest. Then judgment shall dwell in the wilderness, and righteousness remain in the fruitful field. And the work of righteousness shall be peace; and the effect of righteousness quietness and assurance for ever" (Is.32:15-17).

"But they that wait upon the LORD shall renew *their* strength; they shall mount up with wings as eagles; they shall run, and not be weary; *and* they shall walk, and not faint" (Is.40:31).

"And I will give them an heart to know me, that I *am* the LORD: and they shall be my people, and I will be their God: for they shall return unto me with their whole heart" (Je.24:7).

"O LORD, I have heard thy speech, *and* was afraid: O LORD, revive thy work in the midst of the years, in the midst of the years make known; in wrath remember mercy" (Hab.3:2).

RESOURCES

EZRA

TYPES, SYMBOLS, AND PICTURES
THE BOOK OF EZRA

ALPHABETICAL OUTLINE

What is a biblical type or symbol? Simply put, a *biblical type* is a *foreshadowing* of what was to come at a later time in history. Through a person, place, or thing, a biblical type points toward a New Testament fulfillment.

In addition to biblical types, there are what we may call *biblical pictures*. A biblical picture is a lesson that we can see in the Scriptures *without distorting the truth*. The study of biblical types and pictures is a valuable tool in that it helps us apply the truth of the Scriptures in our lives. Scripture itself tells us this:

"Now all these things happened unto them for examples: and they are written for our admonition, upon whom the ends of the world are come" (1 Co.10:11).
"For whatsoever things were written aforetime were written for our learning, that we through patience and comfort of the scriptures might have hope" (Ro.15:4).

PERSON/PLACE/THING	SCRIPTURE, OUTLINE AND DISCUSSION
PREPARATION. *By Ezra*. To return to the promised land. A picture of preparing oneself for heaven.	Ezra 8:1-36
By the returning exiles. With Zerubbabel. A striking picture of believers preparing to serve the LORD.	Ezra 1:5-11
PROMISED LAND. *A type of heaven.*	Ezra 1:5; 2:1-70; 8:31-36
SACRIFICE. *Animal*. A symbol of the sacrificial death of Jesus Christ for our sins.	Ezra 3:1-6
TEMPLE. A symbol of God's presence.	Ezra 6:5-8
Rebuilding of. *Approved by King Darius*. A picture of God's sovereignty in the life and work of the believer.	Ezra 6:1-12
Begun anew. A picture of a new beginning.	Ezra 5:1-2
Completion of. A picture of the church's great joy and celebration in worship.	Ezra 6:13-22
Investigation of. A picture of God's eyes watching over and protecting the church and His people.	Ezra 5:3-17

TYPES, SYMBOLS, AND PICTURES
THE BOOK OF EZRA

CHRONOLOGICAL OUTLINE

What is a *biblical type* or *symbol*? Simply put, a biblical type is a *foreshadowing* of what was to come at a later time in history. Through a person, place, or thing, a biblical type or symbol points toward a New Testament fulfillment.

In addition to biblical types, there are what we may call *biblical pictures*. A biblical picture is a lesson that we can see in the Scriptures *without distorting the truth*. The study of biblical types and pictures is a valuable tool in that it helps us apply the truth of Scripture to our lives. Scripture itself tells us this:

> "Now all these things happened unto them for examples: and they are written for our admonition, upon whom the ends of the world are come" (1 Co.10:11).

> "For whatsoever things were written aforetime were written for our learning, that we through patience and comfort of the scriptures might have hope" (Ro.15:4).

PERSON/PLACE/THING	SCRIPTURE, OUTLINE AND DISCUSSION
PROMISED LAND. *A type of heaven.*	Ezra 1:5; 2:1-70; 8:31-36
PREPARATION. *By the returning exiles. With Zerubbabel. A striking picture of believers preparing to serve the LORD.*	Ezra 1:5-11
SACRIFICE. *Animal. A symbol of the sacrificial death of Jesus Christ for our sins.*	Ezra 3:1-6
TEMPLE. *Rebuilding of.* *Begun anew. A picture of a new beginning.*	Ezra 5:1-2
Investigation of. A picture of God's eyes watching over and protecting the church and His people.	Ezra 5:3-17
Approved by King Darius. A picture of God's sovereignty in the life and work of the believer.	Ezra 6:1-12
TEMPLE. *A symbol of God's presence.*	Ezra 6:5-8
TEMPLE. *Rebuilding of. Completion of. A picture of the church's great joy and celebration in worship.*	Ezra 6:13-22
PREPARATION. *By Ezra. To return to the promised land. A picture of preparing oneself for heaven.*	Ezra 8:1-36

REMEMBER: When you look up a subject and turn to the Scripture reference, you have not just the Scripture but also an outline and a discussion (commentary) of the Scripture and subject.

This is one of the GREAT FEATURES of *The Preacher's Outline & Sermon Bible*®. Once you have all the volumes, you will have not only what all other Bible indexes give you, that is, a list of all the subjects and their Scripture references, but in addition you will have...

- an outline of every Scripture and subject in the Bible
- a discussion (commentary) on every Scripture and subject
- every subject supported by other Scripture, already written out or cross referenced

DISCOVER THE UNIQUE VALUE for yourself. Quickly glance below to the first subject of the Index. It is:

> **ACCUSATION**
> Against the Jews.
> Listed and explained. 4:11-16

Turn to the first reference. Glance at the Scripture and the outline, then read the commentary. You will immediately see the TREMENDOUS BENEFIT of the INDEX of *The Preacher's Outline & Sermon Bible*®.

OUTLINE AND SUBJECT INDEX

ACCUSATION (See **PERSECU-TION**)
Against the Jews.
  Listed and explained. 4:11-16
  Result. The rebuilding of Jerusa-lem was stopped. 4:23-24
False. Example. By the enemies of the returned exiles. 4:7-16

AHASUERUS
Decrees by. That the temple work be stopped. 4:21-22
King. Of Persia. 4:6-24
Letters.
  From. Declaring that the work on the temple be stopped. 4:17-22
  To. By the enemies of the Jews. To stop the work on the tem-ple. 4:6-16

ALLIANCE
Close. With unbelievers.
  Forbidden by God. 4:1-3, Thgt.1
  Result. Will undermine our lives. 4:1-3, Thgt.1

ANIMAL SACRIFICE (See **SACRI-FICE**, Animal)

ANTI-SEMITISM
Example. By the Samaritans. Lied and slandered the Jews. 4:4-5; 5:9-10

ARMOR
Of God. Need for. To be able to serve God. 1:5-11, Thgt.1

ARTAXERXES
Commission. To Ezra. To lead the Jews back to the Promised Land. 7:11-28

Decrees by.
  All Jews disobedient to the Law of Moses would be disciplined as Ezra saw fit. 7:26
  Ezra and all willing Jews could return to the Promised Land. 7:13
  Ezra would teach the Law of Mo-ses to all the Jews. 7:25
  Persia would finance the return under Ezra's leadership. 7:14-23
  Priests and Levites must not be taxed. 7:24
Favor of. Toward the Jews. To allow them to return to the Promised Land. 7:13
King. Of Persia. 7:1-10:44
Letter by. Of Ezra's commission. 7:11-26
Policy of. Toward the Jews.
  To enforce obedience to the Law of Moses. 7:25-26
  To help them in every way possi-ble in the worship of the One True God. 7:14-24

ASNAPPAR
Deeds. Deported many of the Jews. 4:10
Identity. Ashurbanipal. 4:10
King. Of Assyria. 4:10

ASSOCIATIONS
Evil.
  Example. The Jews had made evil **a**. by marrying unbelieving wives. 9:1-2
  Forbidden. By Scripture. 9:1-2, Thgt.1
With the world. Purpose. So we can be witnesses. 9:1-2, Thgt.1

ASSYRIA
Kingdom of. Conquered by the Bab-ylonians. 1:1-4

Kings.
  Asnapper. 4:10
  Esarhaddon. 4:2

ATONEMENT (See **SALVATION**)

ATTACK (See **PERSECUTION**)
Example. The Samaritans **a**. the re-turned exiles with lies and har-assment. 4:4-24

BABYLON
Captivity by. Of the Jews.
  Allowed by God because of Ju-dah's idolatry. 1:1-2:70, Intro.
  Length of. Seventy years. 1:1-2:70, Intro.
Kingdom of. Conquered by the Medo-Persians. 1:1-4
Wars of. Against Judah. Described. 1:1-2:70, Intro.

BEGINNING
New. Example. Rebuilding of the temple. Begun anew. A picture of a new **b**. 5:1-2

BELIEVER
Attitude of. Toward sin. Humility, prayer, mourning and repentance. 9:5; 10:1
Blessings to.
  God watches over the **b**. 5:3-17, Thgt.1
  Peace. 5:3-17, Thgt.1
  Protection by God. 8:31-36
  Security. 8:31-36
  Strength to overcome trials. 5:3-17, Thgt.1
Commission. Of every **b**. To lead people to heaven. 7:11-28, Thgt.1

Duty.
To God.
Not to be overcome by fear. 4:4-5, Thgt.1
Not to compromise with unbelievers. 4:1-3, Thgt.1
To be good stewards of our possessions. 8:24-30, Thgt.1
To follow His leadership. 1:5-11, Thgt.1
To have a clean heart. 1:5-11, Thgt.1
To have a right spirit. 1:5-11, Thgt.1
To obey God and His Word. 1:5-11, Thgt.1; 5:3-17, Thgt.1; 7:1-10, Thgt.1
To offer our bodies in service. 1:5-11, Thgt.1
To pray continually. 1:5-11, Thgt.1
To prepare spiritually for service. 1:5-11, Thgt.1
To put off the old man. 1:5-11, Thgt.1
To put on the new man. 1:5-11, Thgt.1
To put on the whole armor of God. 1:5-11, Thgt.1
To reverence His Word. 7:1-10, Thgt.1
To seek heavenly things. 1:5-11, Thgt.1
To seek the LORD for strength. 1:5-11, Thgt.1
To study His Word. 7:1-10, Thgt.1
To support the work of the church. 1:5-11, Thgt.1
To trust God. 1:5-11, Thgt.1
To witness to the lost. 7:11-28, Thgt.1; 9:1-2, Thgt.1
To others.
To care for one's family. 3:1, Thgt.1
To evangelize. 7:11-28, Thgt.1; 9:1-2, Thgt.1
To the church.
To be a good steward. 8:24-30
To continue the work of God. 4:4-5, Thgt.1
To take good care of the church treasury. 8:24-30, Thgt.1
Needs of.
Fasting. 8:21-23, Thgt.1
Prayer. 8:21-23, Thgt.1
Seeking God. 8:21-23, Thgt.1
Persecution of. Preparation for. Is necessary because persecution is to be expected. 4:6-24, Thgt.1
Temptations of. Materialism and corruption of the world. 9:3-15, Thgt.1; 10:1-44, Thgt.1
Testimony of. To the world. Is strong when the **b**. has peace through trials. 5:3-17, Thgt.1

Trials of. Result. Draws us closer to the Lord. 5:3-17, Thgt.1

BENEVOLENCE (See **GIVING**)

BIBLE (See **WORD OF GOD**)

BISHLAM
Enemy. Of the Jews. 4:7-16
Leader. Of the Persians. 4:7
Service of. Under King Ahasuerus. 4:7

CAPTIVITY (See **EXILE**)
Freedom from. For the Jews.
By proclamation of Cyrus. 1:1-4
Date of. 538 B.C.
Prophesied. 1:1-4
Of exiles.
End of. By decree of Cyrus. 1:1-4
Length. Seventy years. 1:1-2:70, Intro.
Result. Discussed. 1:1-2:70, Intro.
Return from.
Difficulty of. Discussed. 1:5-11
With Ezra. 7:1-8:36
With Zerubbabel. 1:1-2:70
Source. Sin. 1:1-2:70, Intro.

CELEBRATION
At the completion of the temple. 6:16-22
Of the Feast of Unleavened Bread. 6:22
Of the Passover. 6:19-21

CHARACTER
Dependability. Fact. Is rare. 5:1-6:22, Intro.

CHARGES (See **ACCUSATION; PERSECUTION**)

CHILDREN
Duty of. To obey their parents. 3:1, Thgt.1

CHRIST (See **JESUS CHRIST**)

CHURCH
Protection of. By God. Discussed. 5:3-17, Thgt.1
Revival of. Pictured by Ezra and the leaders mourning and confessing the sins of the nation. 9:5-10:2
Treasury of.
Duty toward. To be good stewards. 8:24-30, Thgt.1
Purpose. To care for the needs of the church and of the needy in the world. 8:24-30, Thgt.1

CLEANSING
Source. The Word of God. 7:1-10, Thgt.1

COERCION (See **HARASSMENT**)

COMMISSION
Example.
Cyrus **c**. the Jews to rebuild the temple. 3:7; 4:3
Artaxerxes **c**. Ezra to lead the Jews back to the Promised Land. 7:11-28

COMMITMENT
Duty toward. For the believer. To be **c**. to God and to His Word. 7:1-10
Evidence of.
Bible study. 7:1-10, Thgt.1
Prayer. 7:1-10, Thgt.1
Example.
Exile returnees. 2:1-70
Ezra. Was **c**. to leading the Jews back to the Promised Land. 7:1-28
Lack of. Result. Quitting the work of God. 5:1-2, Thgt.1
Need for.
To avoid the destruction of sin. 2:1-70, Thgt.1
To overcome discouragement so we can fulfill our tasks. 5:1-2, Thgt.1
Response to. By God. He moves to help believers who renew their **c**. 5:5
Result. The help of the LORD. 5:5
To the Word of God.
Example. Ezra. 7:1-10
Need for. 7:1-10, Thgt.1

COMPASSION (See **SALVATION**)

COMPROMISE
Forms of. Listed and discussed. 4:1-3, Thgt.1
Temptation to. Rejected. By the returned exiles. 4:3
With unbelievers.
Duty concerning. Of believers. To avoid **c**. 4:1-3, Thgt.1
Problem of. Tempts us to sin. 4:1-24, Intro.
Result.
Failure. 4:1-3, Thgt.1
Will undermine our lives. 4:1-3, Thgt.1
Warning against. Is clear in Scripture. 4:1-24, Intro.

CONFESSION
Of Sin.
Example. Ezra. 9:5-15;
Need for.
Discussed. 9:1-10:44, Intro.
For forgiveness of sins. 9:3-15, Thgt.1
Prayer of. Example. Ezra. 9:5-15

CONFRONTATION
Example. By Ezra. Over evil associations. 9:1-10:44

CONQUERING (See **OVERCOM-ING**)

CONVICTION
Example. The Jewish leaders were c. about their illegal marriages. 9:1-2

CORRUPTION
Temptation of. To believers. Fact. Is the trap of many. 9:1-10:44, Intro.

CRITICISM (See **ACCUSATION; PERSECUTION**)

CYRUS
Commissions by. For the Jews to rebuild the temple. 3:7; 4:3
King. Of Persia. When the Jews were freed from captivity. 1:1-4:5
Proclamation of.
　Explanations for. Various. Listed and discussed. 1:1-4
　Points of. Listed and explained. 1:2-4
　Reason for. The LORD stirred the heart of C. 1:2
　To free the Jews from captivity. 1:1-4
Reign of. Summary. 1:1

DARIUS
Decrees by.
　That the temple be rebuilt.
　　To assist in the rebuilding of the temple. A picture of God's sovereignty. 6:1-10
　　Carried out. By Tattenai and his staff. 6:13-15
　　To execute anyone who interfered with the temple work. 6:11-12
King of Persia. 5:1-6:22
Letters of.
　From Tattenai. Investigating the temple project. 5:3-17
　To Tattenai. Approving the temple project and protecting it. 6:1-12

DECEPTION
Example. The Samaritans tried to d. the Jews, pretending to be true worshipers. 4:1-2

DEDICATION
Of the heart. (See **COMMIT-MENT; DEVOTION**)
Of the second temple. 6:16-17

DEPENDABILITY
In people. Fact. Is rare. 5:1-6:22, Intro.
Lack of. Results. Listed and discussed. 5:1-6:22, Intro.

DEPRAVITY (See **EVIL; SIN; WICKEDNESS**)

DETERMINATION (See **FAITH-FULNESS**)

DEVOTION
Of Ezra. Studied and practiced the Law of God. 7:10
Of the Jews. Reinstituted the new moon or month sacrifice even before there was a temple. 3:6

DILIGENCE (See **FAITHFUL-NESS**)

DISOBEDIENCE (See **EVIL; OBE-DIENCE; SIN; WICKED-NESS**)
Example. Some of the Jews d. the Law of Moses by divorcing their wives. 9:1-2
Warnings against. To children. 3:1, Thgt.1

DIVORCE
Avoidance of. Example. Those Jews who could convince their wives to follow the LORD. 10:11, 17
Evil of. Is often rooted in wicked desires. 9:1-2
Example. Some of the Jews d. their wives in order to marry foreign unbelieving wives. 9:1-2
List of. Jews needing a d. of their unbelieving wives. 10:20-44
Need for. Example. Ezra ordered that those wives who refused to serve the Lord be d. from their Jewish husbands. 10:10-12

DUTY
Of the believer. (See **BELIEVER**, Duty)
To family. Discussed. 3:1-13, Intro.

END TIMES
Certainty of. Discussed. 8:1-36, Intro.
Events of.
　Creation of new heaven and earth. 8:1-36, Intro.
　Destruction of current heaven and earth. 8:1-36, Intro.
　Judgment of every person. 8:1-36, Intro.

ENDURANCE (See **FAITHFUL-NESS**)

ENEMY
Physical. Example. The Samaritans were e. to the returned exiles. 4:1-3
Spiritual.
　Attack of. Duty toward. Must stand against. 4:4-5, Thgt.1
　Opposition by. Fact. Is persistent. 4:4-5, Thgt.1

ENLISTMENT (See **LABORERS**, Recruitment of)

EQUALITY
Of humanity. Fact of. 4:1-24, Intro.

ESARHADDON
Deeds of. Deported some of the Jews. 4:2
King. Of Assyria. In the days before the exile. 1:1-4

EVANGELISM (See **WITNESSING**)

EVIL (See **SIN; WICKEDNESS**)
Associations.
　Example. Some of the Jews had married foreign unbelieving wives. 9:2; 10:2
Conquering of. Is craved by the human heart. 8:1-36, Intro.
Example. Many of the people were engaging in the detestable, e. behavior of their unbelieving neighbors. 9:2; 10;2
How to avoid. Discipline. 3:1-13, Intro.
Kinds of.
　Listed. 3:1-13, Intro.
　Persecution. 4:1-24, Intro.
Protection from. By God. During trials. 5:3-17, Thgt.1
Separation from. Is a necessity for the believer. 9:1-2, Thgt.1

EXILES (Jewish, See **JEWS**)
Fact. Were from every tribe. 1:5
Prophecies about. Listed. 1:1-4
Resettlement.
　By Zerubbabel. 1:1-6:22
　In Judah. After seventy years of captivity. 1:1-2:70
　Support for.
　　From Cyrus. Gave back all the articles for the temple. 1:6
　　From those remaining. Was generous. 1:6
Returned. From captivity.
　Leaders of.
　　With Ezra. Listed. 8:16-19
　　With Zerubbabel. 2:2
　　Zerubbabel and Ezra. 1:2; 8:2
　Preparation by.
　　A striking picture of serving the LORD. 1:5-11, Thgt.1
　　Before returning with Ezra. 8:21-23
　Protection of. By God. 8:24-36
　With Ezra.
　　Account of. 7:1-8:32
　　Commissioned. By Artaxerxes. 7:1-8:32
　　List of. 8:2-14
　　Number of. About 5000. 8:3-14
　　Problem. No Levites volunteered to return. 8:15
　　Time of. About sixty years after the temple was completed. 7:1-28, Intro.

With Zerubbabel.
    Accomplishments. Rebuilt the
        temple. 4:1-6:15
    Commitment of. Was strong.
        2:1-70
    Difficulty of. Discussed. 1:5-11
    Establishing of. Was a mam-
        moth task. 3:1-13, Intro.
    Facts about. Listed and dis-
        cussed. 2:1-70
    Faith of. Was strong and un-
        wavering. 1:5
    Identity.
        Account of. 1:1-2:70
        From the main tribe of
            Judah. Now known as
            the Jews. 4:12, 23; 5:1,
            5; 6:7-8, 14
        List of. 1:2-67
        Number of. About 50,000.
            2:2-67
    Opposition to. By enemies try-
        ing to stop their work. 4:1-24
    Reason for. The LORD moved
        on their hearts. 1:5
    Tasks of. Listed and dis-
        cussed. 3:1-13
    Unity among. Was strong. 3:1
Worship of.
    Description of. 3:1-6
    Reestablishing of.
        By celebrating the Feast of
            Tabernacles. 3:4
        By celebrating the feasts re-
            quired by the Law. 3:5
        By giving freewill offerings.
            3:6
        By rebuilding the altar. 3:1
        By sacrificing to the LORD.
            3:6
    Was reestablished in Jerusalem.
        3:1-6

EZRA
Commission of. (See also **AR-
    TAXERXES**, Decrees by.)
    Given by King Artaxerxes. 7:13-26
    To lead Jews back to the Prom-
        ised Land. 7:11-13
    To reestablish proper worship of
        the One True God. 7:14-20
Commitment of. E. was wholly
    committed to the LORD and to
    His Word. 7:6-10
Confrontation by. Over evil asso-
    ciations. 9:1-10:44
Devotion of. To the LORD and to
    His Word. Demonstrated by.
    Obeyed. 7:10
    Studied. 7:10
    Taught. 7:10
Duties.
    To care for the temple treasury.
        7:15-24; 8:24-30
    To enforce the Law of Moses.
        7:25-26
    To lead the Jews back to the
        Promised land. 7:11-14

Genealogy. Priestly line. 7:1-5
Heritage. E. had a strong, godly
    heritage. 7:1-5
Leadership of.
    Skills in. Demonstrated by.
        Art of persuasion. 7:6-7
        Good steward. 7:15-24; 8:24-30
        Strong will and determination.
            7:8-9
        Total commitment to service.
            7:9
        Wholehearted devotion to the
            LORD and to His Word.
            7:10
        Was strong. 7:6, 28; 10:1
Mission of. To establish proper
    worship in Jerusalem. 7:11-28
Prayers of.
    For protection and guidance.
        8:21-23
    Of repentance. 9:5-15
Preparations by. To return to the
    Promised Land. A striking pic-
    ture of believers preparing to
    serve the LORD. 8:1-36
Profession of. Priest, scribe and
    teacher of the Law of Moses.
    7:6-10
Reaction of. To sin. Prayed and
    mourned. 9:5; 10:1
Return by. To Jerusalem. Time of.
    About sixty years after the tem-
    ple was completed. 8:1-36, Intro.
Trust of. In God. For the long and
    dangerous trip back to the Prom-
    ised Land. 8:31-36
Worship by. Reasons.
    Favor from the king. 7:27-28
    Hand of the LORD upon him.
        7:28
    Mercy for the mission. 7:28

FAITHFULNESS
Example. Ezra. As a leader and
    good steward. 8:1-36
In people. Fact. Is rare. 5:1-6:22,
    Intro.
Of God. (See **GOD**, Faithfulness of)

FALSE WORSHIP (See **WORSHIP**,
False)

FAMILY
Care for. Duty to. A person must
    labor diligently. 3:1-13, Intro.
Duty toward. To care for. Is the re-
    sponsibility of every member of
    the **f**. 3:1
Responsibility. Discussed. 3:1

FASTING
Example. Ezra and the leaders be-
    fore going to the Promised Land.
    8:21-23
Need for. In seeking God. To show
    God our earnest desire. 8:21-23,
    Thgt.1
Scriptures about. 8:21-23, Thgt.1

FAVOR
Example. Artaxerxes showed **f**. to
    the Jews, allowing them to return
    to the Promised Land. 7:13
Of God. Was upon the Jews who
    wished to establish true worship.
    7:9; 8:18

FEAR
Answer to. To stand in the strength
    of the Lord. 4:4-5, Thgt.1
Cause. Spiritual enemies. 4:4-5
Fact. Will defeat us if we allow **f**.
    to dominate. 4:4-5, Thgt.1
Result. The stopping of God's
    work. 4:4-5

FEASTS
Celebration of. By the returned ex-
    iles. Described. 3:1-6
Passover. 6:19-21
Unleavened Bread. 6:22

FELLOWSHIP
Close. With unbelievers. Forbidden
    by God. 4:1-3, Thgt.1
With God. Restored. Example. Af-
    ter the second temple was com-
    pleted. 6:22

FESTIVAL (See **FEASTS**)

FORGIVENESS (See **SALVATION**)

FOUNDATION
Firm.
    Lack of. Result. Failure. 3:1-13,
        Intro.
    Need for. In life. Discussed. 3:1-
        13, Intro.
    Rewards for. Discussed. 3:1-13,
        Intro.

FREEDOM
Decree of. Issued. By Cyrus. 1:1-4
Example. The Jews were **f**. from
    captivity. 1:1-4
Of the Jews. Prophesied. By Isaiah
    and Jeremiah. 1:1-2:70, Intro.
Way to. By committing our lives to
    God. 2:1-70, Thgt.1

FUTURE (See **END TIMES**)

GIVING
Example. The Persian government
    g. liberally to the temple project.
    7:19-22; 8:24-27
Need for. To be able to serve God.
    1:5-11, Thgt.1

GOD
Commitment to. Example. Ezra.
    7:1-10
Eyes of. Watching the church and
    His people. Pictured by the in-
    vestigation of the temple by
    Governor Tattenai. 5:3-17

Faithfulness of.
Demonstrated. By the completion of the temple. 5:1-6:22, Intro.
Is dependable. 5:1-6:22, Intro.
Keeps His Word. 5:1-6:22, Intro.
Fellowship with. Restoration of. Example. After the second temple was completed. 6:22
Love of. Of every human. Is a fact. 4:1-24, Intro.
Obedience to. Need for. To serve Him. 1:5-11, Thgt.1
Power of.
To see and protect. 5:3-17, Thgt.1
To stir lives. Seen in the returned exiles. 1:5-11
Presence of.
Fact. Is a source of joy. 6:13-22, Thgt.1
Symbolized. By the temple. 6:5-8
Promises of.
Fact. Are always kept. 5:1-6:22, Intro.
Faith in. Example. By the returned exiles. 1:5-11
Surety of. Will always come to pass. 1:1-4, Thgt.1
To the believer.
His presence. 8:21-23, Thgt.1
To give strength to stand. 4:4-5, Thgt.1
To protect. 8:21-23, Thgt.1; 8:24-30, Thgt.1
To provide what is needed for the work of the kingdom. 6;1-12, Thgt.1; 8:21-23, Thgt.1
To uphold in any circumstance. 4:4-5, Thgt.1
Protection by. Of believers.
Example. The Jews led by Ezra were protected as they traveled to the Promised Land. 8:31-36
Pictured by the investigation and approval of the rebuilding of the temple. 5:3-6:12
Promise of. Discussed. 8:21-23, Thgt.1
Provision of. For His work. Example. God worked in the circumstances so that the temple could be finished. 5:1-6:15
Seeking of. Need for. With prayer and fasting. 8:21-23
Sovereignty of.
Example. Moved on the hearts of leaders so the temple would be completed. 5:1-6:22; 6:1-12, Thgt.1
Fact of. Is able to accomplish His will. 5:1-6:22, Intro.
Pictured. By the approval of King Darius for the rebuilding of the temple. 6:1-12
Stirring by. For service. Example. Of the returned exiles. 1:5-11

Trust in. Example. Ezra. For the long and dangerous trip back to the Promised Land. 8:31-36
Warnings by. To children. That they must obey their parents. 3:1, Thgt.1

GODS, False (See **WORSHIP**, False)
Of the world. Influence by.
Example. Marriage of Jews to unbelievers. 9:2; 10:2
Led to the exile. 1:1-2:70, Intro.
Worship of. Example. By the Samaritans. 4:1-3

GOSPEL (See **WITNESSING**)

GOVERNMENT
Of Persia.
Help from.
For Ezra and the returning Jews. 6:3-12; 7:11-26
Structure of. Described. 5:3-17
Of the Jews. By tribes. 1:5; 8:1

HAGGAI
Message. Exhorted the Jews to complete the temple. 5:1; 6:14
Prophet. To the Jews after the exile. 5:1-2

HALFHEARTEDNESS (See **COMMITMENT**)

HARASSMENT
Cause. Spiritual enemies. 4:4-5
Conquering. How to. By standing in the strength of the Lord. 4:4-5, Thgt.1
Example. By the enemies of the returned exiles. 4:4-5

HARDSHIP (See **TRIALS**)

HEART
Clean. Need for. To be able to serve God. 1:5-11, Thgt.1
Conviction of. Example. Of the Jewish leaders and of Ezra. 9:1-2; 10:1
Fear within. Must be overcome by the love of God. 4:4-5, Thgt.1
Influence of. By God. Example.
Upon King Aratxerxes. To allow the Jews to return with Ezra and to give generously to the temple. 7:12-13 (See also **ARTAXERXES**, Decrees by)
Upon King Cyrus. To allow the Jews to return with Zerubbabel. 1:1 (See also **CYRUS**, Decrees by)
Upon King Darius. To allow the Jews to build the temple and to protect them. 6:3-12 (See also **DARIUS**, Decrees by)
Upon Governor Tattenai. To allow the building of the temple

until he investigated the matter. 5:5
Motive of. Should be moved by love. 4:1-24, Intro.
Of Ezra. Was deeply devoted to the Word of God. 7:10
Of the believer. Fact. Has the Holy Spirit within. 3:1-6, Thgt.1
Peace within. Cause. Drawing close to God. 5:3-17, Thgt.1
Tender. Need for. 7:1-28, Intro.

HEAVEN
Desire for. By every person. 8:1-36, Intro.
Entering. Way to. By repenting and turning to Jesus Christ. 2:1-70, Thgt.1
Leading others to. Fact. Is the commission of every believer. 7:11-28, Thgt.1
Preparation for. Fact. Is an absolute necessity. 8:1-36, Intro.
Type of. The Promised Land. 1:5; 2:1-70, Thgt.1; 8:1-36, Intro.

HOLY SPIRIT
Assurance of. Fact. Is within the life of the believer. 3:1-6, Thgt.1

HOPE (See **TRUST**)
Example. The Jewish leaders saw h. when they repented of sin. 10:1-2
Fulfilled. Example.
The Jews completed the second temple. 6:13-22
The Jews returned to the Promised Land. 1:5-2:39
To worship the Lord. In the temple. Was fulfilled when the second temple was completed. 6:13-22

HUMANITY (See **SOCIETY**; **WORLD**)
Dependability of. Fact. Is rare. 5:1-6:22, Intro.
Desires of. A perfect world. 8:1-36, Intro.
Equality of. Fact of. 4:1-24, Intro.
Needs of. Discussed. 8:1-36, Intro.

IDDO (Not the prophet)
Home. Casiphia. 8:17
Leader. Of the Levites. 8:17
Recruited. By Ezra. To go back to the Promised Land. 8:17

INFLUENCE
Of the world. (See **WICKEDNESS**, Dangers of.)

INTEGRITY
Definition. A person of truth, morality and commitment. 7:1-28, Intro.
Lack of. Results. Tears down a society. 7:1-28, Intro.

LYING (See **ACCUSATION**)
Example. By the Samaritans.
Against the Jews. 4:11-16

MARRIAGE
Duty. Of believers. To marry another believer. 9:1-2
With unbelievers.
Conditions for. Only if they turn
to the Lord, forsaking their
life of sin. 9:1-2
Example. Many of the Jews who
had returned with Ezra. 9:1-2

MATERIALISM
Temptation of. To believers. Fact.
Is the trap of many. 9:1-10:44,
Intro.

MERCY (See **SALVATION**)

MINISTERS
Fellowship among. Example. Hag-
gai and Zechariah. 5:1-2; 6:14
Support. Example. Haggai and
Zechariah gave spiritual support
to the Jews. 6:14

MISSION (See **COMMISSION**)
Fulfillment of. Example. Ezra.
Took the Jews back to the Prom-
ised Land. 7:11-28

MITHREDATH
Enemy. Of the Jews. 4:7-16
Head. Over the treasury. Under
King Cyrus. 1:8
Leader. Of the Persians. 4:7
Persian. 1:8

MONEY-HANDLERS (See
TREASURY)

NEEDS
Of servants. Of the LORD. Listed
and explained. 1:5-11, Thgt.1

NEW BEGINNING (See **BEGIN-
NING**, New)

OBEDIENCE (See **COMMIT-
MENT**; **DEVOTION**)
To God.
Enforced. By Ezra. 7:25-26
Need for. To be able to serve
Him. 1:5-11, Thgt.1
To leadership. Example. The peo-
ple o. the decision of the leaders
to put away all unbelievers.
10:18-19

OFFERING (See **GIVING**; **SACRI-
FICE**)

OPPOSITION (See **PERSECU-
TION**)
Example. Faced by the returned ex-
iles. 4:1-24

ORGANIZATION
Of leaders.
Example. By Ezra. 8:24-30
Need for. 8:24-30, Thgt.1

OVERCOMING (See **VICTORY**)
Example. The Jews o. their discouragement and completed the
temple. 5:1-6:15
Trials. Fact. Is possible for the believer by the strength the Lord
gives. 5:3-17, Thgt.1

PARTNERSHIP (See **ALLIANCE**)

PASSOVER
Celebrated. By the Jews after the
completed of the temple. 6:19-21

PEACE
Cause. Drawing closer to the Lord.
5:3-17, Thgt.1
Fact. Is a blessing to the believer.
5:3-17, Thgt.1

PEOPLE (See **HUMANITY**)

PERFECTION
Desire for. By humanity. Because
of the problems in the world.
8:1-36, Intro.

PERSECUTION (See **ACCUSA-
TION**)
Answer to. To love everyone
equally. 4:1-24, Intro.
Attitude toward. By the believer. Is
to be expected. 4:6-24, Thgt.1
Certainty of. Of the righteous by
sinners. 4:6-24, Thgt.1
Example. The Samaritans p. the
Jews with lies and harassment.
4:4-24
Forms of. Listed. 4:1-24, Intro.;
4:6-24, Thgt.1
Preparation for. Is necessary for the
believer. 4:6-24, Thgt.1
Problem of. Discussed. 4:1-24, In-
tro.
Reason for. Because righteousness
stands opposed to sinful behav-
ior. 4:6-24, Thgt.1

PERSIA
Government.
Help from. For Ezra and the re-
turning Jews. 7:11-26
Structure of. Described. 5:3-17
Governor. Rehum. 4:8-23
Kings of.
Ahasuerus. 4:6-24
Artaxerxes. 7:1-10:44
Cyrus. 1:1-4:5
Darius. 5:1-6:22
Leaders.
Investigating the temple project.
Tattenai. 5:3-6:13
Opposing the Jews. Bishlam,
Mithredath, Tabeel. 4:7

Secretary. Shimshai. 4:8-23
Treasury of. Head of. Mithredath.
1:8

POWER (See **STRENGTH**)
Of God. (See **GOD**, Power of)

PRAISE (See **WORSHIP**)

PRAYER
Continual. Need for. To be able to
serve God. 1:5-11, Thgt.1
Example. Ezra.
For protection and guidance. With
the Jewish leaders. 8:21-23
Of confession. For the nation.
9:5-15
Fact.
Is a source of joy. 6:13-22,
Thgt.1
Is an absolute necessity. 8:21-23,
Thgt.1
Fasting during.
Example. Ezra. 8:21-23
Purpose. To show God we are
humble and serious. 8:21-23
Need for.
In seeking God. 8:21-23
Reasons. Listed and discussed.
8:21-23
Scriptures about. 8:21-23, Thgt.1

PREJUDICE
Anti-Semitism. Example. By the
Samaritans. 4:4-5; 5:9-10

PREPARATION
By Ezra. To return to the Promised
Land. A picture of preparing
oneself for heaven. 8:1-36
By the returning exiles. With
Zerubbabel. A striking picture of
believers preparing to serve the
LORD. 1:5-11
Example. The exiles p. to serve
God before they returned to the
Promised Land. 1:5-11
Spiritual.
By the Jewish leaders with Ezra.
8:21-23
For service. Seven ways to.
Listed and explained. 1:5-11,
Thgt.1
To see God. Requirements for.
Listed and discussed. 1:5-11,
Thgt.1

PRESENCE OF GOD (See **GOD**,
Presence of.)

PRIESTS
Excluded. The sons of Habaiah.
Because there was no record of
their lineage. 2:61
Exempt. From taxes. 7:24
For the second temple. Reorganized
and installed. 6:18
Head of. Jeshua. 3:2
Jeshua. High priest. 3:2

Purification of. For Passover. 6:20
Sons. Of Jedaiah. 2:36
Taxes on. Prohibited. 7:24

PROBLEMS
Of believers. Persecution. 4:6-24,
Thgt.1
Of society.
Answer to. Revival. 9:3-15
Discussed. 8:1-36, Intro.
Listed. 9:1-10:44, Intro.
Of the world.
Answer to. Revival. 9:3-15
Discussed. 8:1-36, Intro.
Listed. 9:1-10:44, Intro.

PROFESSION
False. Example. By the enemies of
the Jews. 4:2

PROMISED LAND
Commitment to. Example. The
Jews returning from captivity
were committed to rebuild the
P.L. 2:1-70
Picture. Of heaven. 2:1-70, Thgt.1
Return to. By the Jewish exiles.
With Ezra. Preparations for.
Listed and explained. 8:1-36
With Zerubbabel. Difficulty of.
Discussed. 1:5-11
Type. Of heaven. 1:5; 2:1-70,
Thgt.1; 8:1-36, Intro.

PROMISES, Of God (See **GOD**,
Promises of)

PROPHECY
Example. Haggai and Zechariah
preached to exhort the people to
finish the temple. 5:1-2; 6:14
Fulfillment of.
Example.
Jews freed. From captivity
just as Isaiah and Jeremiah
had **p**. 1:1-4.
Proclamation of Cyrus. **P.**
several years before his
birth. 1:1
Of the Word of God. Is sure. 1:1-4,
Thgt.1

PROPHETS
Haggai. 5:1; 6:14
Zechariah 5:1; 6:14

PROTECTION
By God.
Example. God **p.** the Jews by in-
fluencing government offi-
cials. 5:3-17
(See also, **GOD**, Protection by)
Of believers. By God. Discussed.
5:3-17, Thgt.1

PURIFICATION (See **CLEAN-
SING**)

QUICKENING (See **STIRRING**)

QUITTING
Of God's work. Causes.
Fear. 4:4-5
Lack of commitment. 4:4-5

RECRUITMENT (See **LABORERS**,
Recruitment of)

REFORM
Spiritual. Example. Ezra led the
Jews to put away the false relig-
ions. 9:1-10:44

REHUM
Governor. Of Persia. 4:8-23
Service of. Under King Ahasuerus.
4:8-23

REJOICING (See **JOY**)

RELIGION
Mixed. Rejected. By the Jews. 4:3

RENEWAL
Example. The Jews made a **r.**
commitment to rebuild the temple. 5:1-2
Need for. To overcome discouragement and to complete our
tasks. 5:1-2, Thgt.1

REPENTANCE
Call to. By the prophets Haggai and
Zechariah. 5:1-2
Example. By the Jews.
Celebrated the Passover, indicat-
ing their **r.** 5:21
Confessed the sins of their ances-
tors. 5:12
Need for.
To have victory. 2:1-70, Thgt.1
To overcome the world. 9:1-
10:44, Intro.
Result. The favor of the Lord. 5:1-2

RESETTLEMENT
Of exiles. Was a mammoth task.
3:1-13, Intro.

RESTORATION
Of fellowship. With God. Example.
After the second temple was
completed. 6:22

RETURN (See **EXILES**, Returned)
By the exiles.
From captivity. 1:5-2:39
Preparation for. The exiles were
prepared to serve God upon
their **r.** 1:5-11
With Ezra. 7:1-8:32
With Zerubbabel. 1:1-2:70
From captivity. To the Promised
Land.
With Ezra. 8:1-36
With Zerubbabel. 1:1-2:70

RETURNEES (See **EXILES**, Returned)

REVIVAL
Discussed. 10:1-44, Thgt.1
Example. Led by Ezra. 9:3-10:2
Need for. In order to be spiritually
separated from the world. 9:1-2
Requirement for. Confession and
repentance of sin. 10:1-44,
Thgt.1
Result. Peace, rest and fulfillment.
10:1-44, Thgt.1

SACRIFICE
Animal.
Example. After returning from
captivity. 8:35
Provision for.
By Artaxerxes. 7:17
By Cyrus. 1:4
By Darius. 6:9-10
Symbol. Of the sacrifice of Jesus
Christ for our sins. 3:3
Worship through. 3:2-3
Of lifestyle. Example. The Jews s.
their known lifestyle in captivity
to return to the Promised Land.
2:1
Of ourselves. Need for. To be able
to serve God. 1:5-11, Thgt.1
Of the new moon or month. Rein-
stituted. Even before there was a
temple. 3:6

SADNESS (See **SORROW**)

SALVATION
Fact. Is a source of joy. 6:13-22,
Thgt.1
Message of. Must be taken to the
world. 7:11-28, Thgt.1; 8:1-20,
Thgt.1
Need for. To be able to serve God.
1:5-11, Thgt.1
Source. Fact. Only through Jesus
Christ. 8:1-20, Thgt.1

SAMARITANS
Enemy. To the Jews. 4:1-3
Identity. Jews who intermarried with
foreigners during the exile. 4:1-3
Persecution by. Of the Jews who
were rebuilding the temple. 4:1-24
Religion of. Worshiped many gods.
4:1-3

SCRIPTURE (See **WORD OF GOD**)

SECURITY
In God. Example. The Jews led by
Ezra. 8:31-36

SEDUCTION
Of the world. (See **WICKED-
NESS**, Dangers of.)

SEEKING
God. (See **GOD**, Seeking of)
Of heavenly things. Need for. To
be able to serve God. 1:5-11,
Thgt.1

SEPARATION
Duty. Of believers. Not to compromise. 4:1-3, Thgt.1
Spiritual.
Failure. Example. The Jews returning with Ezra had married
unbelievers. 9:1-2
Need for. Believers must be s.
from the wickedness of the
world. 9:1-2, Thgt.1

SERVICE
Preparation for.
By the returned exiles. A striking
picture of believers preparing
to s. the LORD. 1:5-11, Thgt.1
How to. Seven ways. Listed and
explained. 1:5-11, Thgt.1
To God. Preparation for.
Example. The exiles. 1:5-11
Need for. Discussed. 1:5-11,
Thgt.1

**SHESHBAZZAR (See ZERUBBA-
BEL)**

SHETHAR-BOZENAI
Assistant. To Tattenai, Persian governor. 5:3, 6; 6:6, 13
Official. In the Persian government.
5:3, 6; 6:6, 13

SHIMSHAI
Secretary. Of Persia. 4:8-23
Service of. Under King Ahasuerus.
4:8-23

SIEGE
Example. Of Jerusalem. By Babylon. 1:1-2:70, Intro.

SIN (See EVIL; WICKEDNESS)
Confession. Example. Ezra. For the
nation. 9:5-15
Effects of. Destruction and captiv-
ity. 2:1-70, Thgt.1
Fact. Is attractive. 4:1-3, Thgt.1
Reaction to. Proper. Humility,
prayer, mourning and repen-
tance. 9:5; 10:1
Repentance of.
Example. Ezra and the Jewish
leaders. 10:1-2
Result. Hope. For the future.
10:2
Temptation by. Is increased when
we compromise. 4:1-3, Thgt.1

SLANDER
Example. By the enemies of the returned exiles. 4:11-16

SLAVERY (See CAPTIVITY)

**SOCIETY (See HUMANITY;
WORLD)**
Needs of.
Integrity. 7:1-28, Intro.
Leadership. 7:1-28, Intro.

Problems of.
Answer to. Revival. 9:3-15
Discussed. 8:1-36, Intro.
For believers. Persecution. 4:1-
24, Intro.
Listed. 9:1-10:44, Intro.

SORROW
Cause. Sin. 9:5; 10:1
Example. Those remembering the
glory of Solomon's temple, at the
laying of the foundation for the
second temple. 3:12-13

**SOVEREIGNTY (See GOD, Sover-
eignty of)**

SPIRIT
Of God. (See HOLY SPIRIT)
Right. Need for. To be able to
serve God. 1:5-11, Thgt.1

**SPIRITUAL REFORM (See RE-
FORM, Spiritual)**

**SPIRITUAL SEPARATION (See
SEPARATION, Spiritual)**

**STARTING OVER (See BEGIN-
NING, New)**

STEWARDSHIP
Duty.
In the church. Of the treas-
ury.8:24-30, Thgt.1
Of every believer. Of his posses-
sions. 8:24-30, Thgt.1
Example. Ezra showed excellent s.
with the temple treasury. 8:24-30

STIRRING
For service. By God. Example. Of
the returned exiles. 1:5-11

STOPPING (See QUITTING)

STRENGTH
Seeking. Need for. To be able to
serve God. 1:5-11, Thgt.1

SUCCESS
In recruiting. Example. The enlist-
ment of the Levite to go with Ezra
to the Promised Land. 8:16-20
Keys to.
Able leadership. 8:19
Guiding hand of the Lord. 8:19
Workers who will recruit others.
8:19

**SUFFERING (See PERSECUTION,
TEMPTATION, TRIALS)**
Deliverance from. Will not always
happen, but God will always help
us through s. 5:3-17, Thgt.1
Results. Draws us closer to the
Lord. 5:3-17, Thgt.1

**SYNCRETISM (See WORSHIP,
False)**
Example. The Jews mixed their
worship because they had married foreign unbelieving wives.
9:2
Of worship. Rejected. By the Jews.
4:3

TABEEL
Enemy. Of the Jews. 4:7-16
Leader. Of the Persians. 4:7
Service of. Under King Ahasuerus.
4:7

TATTENAI
Governor. In the Persian government. Of the Trans-Euphrates.
5:3, 6; 6:6, 13
Investigation by. Of the temple
project.
Details of. 5:3-6:13
Resulted in the construction
beginning again by order of
Darius the king. 5:6-6:13
Letter. To Darius. Asked for information concerning the temple
project. 5:6-17
Report. To Darius. Concerning the
temple project. Summary. 5:6-16

TAXES
Example. By the Jews. 7:24
Exemption. For the priests. 7:24

TEACHERS
Ezra. Of the Law of Moses. 7:10,
25-26
Need for. So the people will know
God's Word. 7:1-10, Thgt.1
Of Ezra's time. Joiarib and
Elthanan. 8:16

TEMPLE (Second)
Celebration for. When the founda-
tion was had been laid. 3:10-13
Completion of. 6:13-22
Dedication of.
After the building was complete.
6:16-17
After the foundation was laid.
3:10-13
Foundation of. Laid.
By the returned exiles. 3:11
Reaction to. Both rejoicing and
weeping. 3:10-13
Priests for. Reorganized and in-
stalled. 6:18
Rebuilding of.
Approved. By King Darius of
Persia. A picture of God's
sovereignty in the life and
work of the believer. 6:1-12
Begun anew. A picture of a new
beginning. 5:1-2
By the returned exiles. 3:7-6:15
Completion of. A picture of
great joy and celebration in
worship by the church. 6:13-22

Duty to. By the returned Jews.
Spurred on by the preaching
of Haggai and Zecariah. 5:1-2
Help with. By Darius, the Per-
sian king. As a result of Tat-
tenai's investigation. 6:1-12
Investigation of. By Tattenai, the
Persian governor.
Picture of God's eyes
watching over and pro-
tecting the church. 5:3-17
Result. The Jews were al-
lowed to finish. 6:14-15
New beginning of. 6:14-15
Opposition to. By the Samari-
tans. Was fierce. 4:3-24
Stopping of.
Cause. The persistent opposi-
tion by the Samaritans. 4:4-5
Results.
Disappointment and failure
filled the hearts of the
Jews. 5:1-6:22, Intro.
God began to intervene to
get the project going
again. 5:1-6:22, Intro.
Report concerning.
By Tattenai. To see whether the
project were legal. 5:6-17
Response. King Darius approved
the project and protected the
workers. 6:1-12
Symbol. Of God's presence. 6:5-8
Treasury of.
Account of. 8:24-27
Source. The Persian government.
7:19-22; 8:24-30
Stewardship of. Entrusted by
Ezra into the hands of twelve
priests. 8:24-25

TEMPTATION (See **WICKED-
NESS**, Danger of.)
Source. Compromise. 4:1-3, Thgt.1
To compromise.
Example. The Jews were t. to
compromise with the Samari-
tans. 4:1-3
Rejected. By the returned exiles.
4:3

TESTIMONY
Of the believer (See **BELIEVER**,
Testimony of)

THANKSGIVING (See **WORSHIP**)

THREAT
Cause. Spiritual enemies. 4:4-5,
Thgt.1
Example. By the enemies of the re-
turned exiles. 4:4-5

TRAVEL
Safety during. By trusting in God.
Example. Ezra. 8:21-23, 31-36

TREASURY
Duty toward. Example. Ezra en-
trusted the t. to twelve of the
priests. 8:24-27
Of the church.
Duty toward. To be good stew-
ards. 8:24-30, Thgt.1
Purpose. To care for the needs of
the church and of the needy in
the world. 8:24-30, Thgt.1
Of the temple.
Account of. 8:24-27
Source. The Persian government.
7:19-22; 8:25

TRIALS (See **PERSECUTION,
SUFFERING, TEMPTATION**)
Deliverance from. Of the believer.
Fact. Will happen, or else God
will help the believer through the
t. 5:3-17, Thgt.1
Joy during. Is possible for the be-
liever. 6:13-22, Thgt.1
Overcoming. Fact. Is possible with
the strength of the Lord. 5:3-17,
Thgt.1
Peace during. Is a privilege of the
believer. 5:3-17, Thgt.1
Protection during. Fact. Is the
promise of God. 8:31-36, Thgt.1
Reason for. So we will rely totally
upon God. 8:21-23

TRUST (See **HOPE**)
In God.
Example. Ezra. For the long and
dangerous trip back to the
Promised Land. 8:31-36
Need for. To be able to serve
God. 1:5-11, Thgt.1
In leaders. Example. The leaders of
the Jews t. Ezra to lead them.
8:15, 24, 31, 36

UNBELIEVERS
Compromise with.
Example. The Jews who married
foreign unbelieving wives. 9:2
Problem of. Tempts us to sin.
4:1-24, Intro.
Warning Against. Is clear in
Scripture. 4:1-24, Intro.
Influence of. Rejected. By the re-
turned exiles. 4:3

UNITY
Example. The u. of the returned ex-
iles was strong. 3:1
Need for. In the church. 3:1-6

VICTORY (See **OVERCOMING**)
How to have. By repenting and re-
newing our commitment to the
LORD. 2:1-70, Thgt.1

WARNINGS
Of Artaxerxes. Against any who
tried to prevent Ezra from ad-
ministering the Law of Moses.
7:25-26
Of Darius. Against any who tried to
stop the Jews from their work on
the temple or their worship. 6:3-12
Of God.
To believers. Against compromise. 4:1-24, Intro.
To children. Against disobedience. 3:1, Thgt.1
Of the prophets. To be strong and
committed to the work of the
Lord. 5:1-2

WEEPING (See **SORROW**)

WICKEDNESS (See **EVIL; SIN**)
Danger of. When associating to
closely with the world. Dis-
cussed. 9:1-2, Thgt.1
Example.
Some of the Jews divorced in or-
der to marry foreign unbeliev-
ing wives. 9:1-2
Of the world. Discussed. 9:1-2,
Thgt.1
Separation from. Fact. Is the duty
of the believer. 9:1-2, Thgt.1

WITNESSING
Definition of. Proclaiming the gos-
pel of Jesus Christ. 7:11-28,
Thgt.1
Fact. Is the duty of every believer.
7:11-28, Thgt.1
Means of. Must associate with the
world to a point. 9:1-2, Thgt.1
Motives for.
Compassion. 8:1-20, Thgt.1
Obedience. 8:1-20, Thgt.1
Need for. So the needs of people
can be met. 8:1-20, Thgt.1

WORD OF GOD
Benefits of. Listed. 7:1-10, Thgt.1
Commitment to. Example. Ezra.
7:1-10
Devotion to. Fact. Is a great need
of the world. 7:1-10, Thgt.1
Fact.
Is a source of joy. 6:13-22,
Thgt.1
Is dependable. 5:1-6:22, Intro.
Fulfillment of. Is sure. 1:1-4,
Thgt.1
Inspiration of. Fact. Is God-
breathed. 7:1-10, Thgt.1
Prophecies of. Major. Listed and
discussed. 1:1-4, Thgt.1
Study of. Example. Ezra knew the
Law of Moses thoroughly. 7:1-10

WORKERS (See **LABORERS**)

WORLD (See **HUMANITY**; **SOCIETY**)

Future of. Judgment. 8:1-36, Intro.

Needs of.
  Integrity. 7:1-28, Intro.
  Leadership. 7:1-28, Intro.

Persecution by. Of believers. Is to be expected. 4:6-24, Thgt.1

Problems in.
  Answer to. Revival. 9:3-15
  Discussed. 8:1-36, Intro.
  For believers. Persecution. 4:1-24, Intro.
  Listed. 9:1-10:44, Intro.

WORLDLINESS

Compromise with. Fact. Will destroy a person. 4:1-3, Thgt.1

Example. Many of the Jews had married unbelievers. 9:1-2

Result. Destruction. 3:1-13, Intro.

WORSHIP (See **SACRIFICE**)

Benefits of. Listed. 3:1-6, Thgt.1

Compromise of. Rejected. By the returned exiles. 4:3

Discussed. 3:1-6, Thgt.1

Establishing of. Example. The returning exiles.
  With Ezra. 8:1-20
  With Zerubbabel. 3:1-6

False.
  Cause. Of captivity. 1:1-2:70, Intro.
  Example.
    By the Jews who married foreign unbelievers. 9:1-2
    By the Samaritans. 4:1-3
  Rejected. By the returned exiles. 4:3
  Warnings against. Judah was warned repeatedly by the prophets. 1:1-2:70, Intro.

Joy in. At the completion of the temple. A picture of the great joy and celebration in **w.** by the church. 6:13-22

Reasons for.
  Favor from authority. 7:27-28
  Hand of the LORD upon us. 7:28
  Mercy to complete our assigned tasks. 7:28
  To keep our relationship with God close and alive. 3:1-6, Thgt.1

Renewal of. By the returned exiles. In Jerusalem. 3:1-6

True. Need for. To have God's blessing. 8:1-36

XERXES (See **AHASUERUS**)

ZECHARIAH

Message.
  Exhorted the Jews to complete the temple. 5:1; 6:14
  That if the Jews would repent, the LORD would help them. 5:1-2

Prophet. To the Jews after the exile. 5:1-2

Son. Of Iddo. 5:1; 6:14

ZERUBBABEL

Commitment of. Refused to compromise the work of the LORD. 4:3

Leadership of. Of the exiles. Led a group back from captivity to Judah. 1:1-6:22

Names of. Persian. Sheshbazzar. 1:8, 11; 5:13, 16

THE BOOK OF

NEHEMIAH

THE BOOK OF
NEHEMIAH

AUTHOR: more than one theory has been proposed over the years concerning the authorship of *Nehemiah*. But the following evidence suggests that Nehemiah, the leader of the third group of Jewish exiles to return to Jerusalem, wrote the book of *Nehemiah*.

1. The first verse clearly states, "The words of Nehemiah the son of Hachaliah." Verse one onward records his personal record of the events of the third return.

2. There is no direct evidence to indicate that the first verse is speaking of a different Nehemiah.

3. The book of *Nehemiah* was written from the perspective of a leader. *Nehemiah* is an inspiring account of the Jews' great determination to rebuild the wall of Jerusalem, to reestablish worship of the one true God, and to rebuild their nation. The author has three distinct purposes in mind:
   ⇒ to show the steadfast faithfulness of the returned exiles in the face of severe opposition
   ⇒ to show the right path to purity of worship, the worship of the one true God
   ⇒ to encourage God's people of every generation to be faithful in their commitment and service to the LORD as they face difficult tasks that confront them

These facts point toward a powerful leader's having written the great book of *Nehemiah*. Much of *Nehemiah* seems to be from the author's personal diary.

4. The book of *Nehemiah* was apparently written no later than 430 B.C., but after the return from captivity, since the rebuilding of the temple is discussed. The sources available to the author were: official letters given to Nehemiah by King Artaxerxes of Persia (1:7-9), the family records of the different tribes (Ezr.2:1-70; Ne.7:5-73), the records of Nehemiah's own experiences (1:1-7:5; 12:27-43; 13:4-31), and the author's personal contact with Ezra (Ne.8:9; 12:26). Of course, all these sources point to Nehemiah himself being the author.

5. The facts were known to Nehemiah personally, from his own experience and contact with other Jews (1:2-3; 2:17-18).

6. There is no early tradition challenging the authorship of *Nehemiah*.

7. The book of *Nehemiah* was written in a form of Hebrew typical of writings after the exile.

Although the human author cannot be known for certain, the Divine Author is clearly known. The Holy Spirit of God *breathed* or *inspired* the great book of *Nehemiah*. Through His inspiration, the Holy Spirit has given to the world an inspiring account of the very events God wanted recorded about the restoration of the Jews, their return from captivity, their steadfast determination to rebuild the wall of Jerusalem, and their successful restoration of true worship and renewed identity as a nation. A study of these events show our constant need for devotion to the LORD, for a lasting and close relationship with the LORD …

- Who is worthy of all worship
- Who always fulfills His promises
- Who gives us favor and authority
- Who has His hand upon all believers who trust in Him
- Who gives us mercy and protection to complete our assigned tasks

The inspiring account of the book of *Nehemiah* was written as both a warning and a promise to every reader.

DATE: Just after 425 B.C., shortly after the events described in the book and during the time of the great Persian empire. There were three groups of Jews who left Babylonian captivity to return to Jerusalem. The final of these three groups was led by Nehemiah. All three groups of returnees were from the southern kingdom of Judah. No group returned separately to the *promised land* from the northern kingdom of Israel. Thereafter, the exile returnees for which *First* and *Second Chronicles, Ezra,* and *Nehemiah* were written were known simply as the Jews.

There were three groups of Jews who returned to Jerusalem from exile. However, this fact is important to note: all three groups of original exile returnees were from the Southern Kingdom of Judah. As far as is known, no organized group from the Northern Kingdom of Israel—the Israelites who had been exiled by Assyria—ever returned to the promised land. Thus the exile returnees, for whom *First* and *Second Chronicles, Ezra,* and *Nehemiah* were written, were the Jews from Judah.

THE FIRST GROUP RETURNED UNDER ZERUBBABEL'S LEADERSHIP

In 539 B.C., the Persians and Medes under King Cyrus defeated the Babylonians in a fierce battle for world domination. Just as the prophet Daniel had predicted, the Babylonians were so soundly defeated that the capital Babylon opened its city gates to the Persians without a fight (Da.5:1-31).

Like the Babylonians, the Persians adopted a wise policy of incorporating captured exiles into the society of the nation to which they were deported. These captives were given the right to rebuild their lives despite being exiled to a strange, foreign land. They had the right to secure personal employment, hold property, build homes, and start businesses. Of course, this policy strengthened the nations of Babylon and Persia both economically and militarily. But the Persian king Cyrus went a step further.

One year after his conquest of Babylon (538 B.C.), King Cyrus proclaimed himself as the *Liberator of the People*. He allowed any exile who wished to return to his or her homeland to do so. Among those released were the Jews who had been taken captive at the fall of Jerusalem in 586 B.C. At this first release, Cyrus appointed Zerubbabel governor over Judah and the returning exiles. Almost 50,000 exiles were released to return to their homeland in Judah. When they arrived, the very first work undertaken by Zerubbabel was the building of an altar to offer sacrifices to the LORD. Soon thereafter, he and the returning exiles undertook the construction of the temple. However, opposition soon arose from the enemies of the Israelites, those of surrounding tribes and peoples who did not want to see Jerusalem and the temple rebuilt. The opposition was successful in stopping the work for a number of years. But in 520 B.C., the building of the temple was resumed. It was completed four years later (516 B.C.) (Ezra 4:1-6:22; Zec.6:16-22).

But, tragically, these first returnees under Zerubbabel soon drifted back into apostasy. Just as their fathers had done, they too turned away from the LORD, committing sin after sin, such as:

⇒ intermarriage with unbelieving neighbors (Mal.2:11; Ezr.9:1-2)
⇒ neglecting the worship of the LORD (Mal.1:6-14)
⇒ failing to offer sacrifices to the LORD as commanded by Him
⇒ participating in witchcraft and sorcery (Mal.3:5)
⇒ committing adultery (Mal.3:5)
⇒ bearing false witness and using profanity (Mal.3:5)
⇒ oppressing and stealing from people, even the wages due widows and orphans (Mal.3:5)
⇒ mistreating people (Mal.3:5)
⇒ failing to fear and show reverence for the LORD (Mal.3:5)
⇒ disobeying the commandments of the LORD (Mal.3:7)
⇒ stealing the tithe that belonged to God (Mal.3:8-9)

THE SECOND GROUP RETURNED UNDER EZRA'S LEADERSHIP

About 80 years after the first exiles returned to Judah, Ezra secured permission from the Persian king Artaxerxes to lead a second and smaller band of exiles back to Jerusalem. It was the year 458 B.C., and Ezra's purpose for returning to Jerusalem was to carry out spiritual and religious reforms, to stir a revival among the new nation of Israel. Revival and reformation were desperately needed because of the people's wickedness. They had slipped and turned away from the LORD. In stating his purpose for returning, Ezra clearly says that he had prepared his heart, that he was determined to study and obey the law of the LORD and to teach the law and commandments of God to the people (Ezr.7:10). Only about 1,800 Jewish exiles chose to return with Ezra. Leading the small band of exiles, he and they struck out and traveled over 900 miles, reaching Jerusalem some four months later (458 B.C.).

THE THIRD GROUP RETURNED UNDER NEHEMIAH'S LEADERSHIP

In 445 B.C., Nehemiah was visited by one of his brothers and a number of other men who had just returned from Judah. Interested in how the exile returnees were doing, Nehemiah asked about them. When they reported that things were not going well, that the returned exiles were suffering severe affliction and reproach from the surrounding people and nations and that the wall and gates of the city had been destroyed, Nehemiah was heartbroken. Scripture actually says that he wept and mourned for days, fasting and praying before the LORD.

Nehemiah held an official position in the royal court of the Persian king. He was the *cupbearer* to King Artaxerxes (Ne.1:11; 2:1). The cupbearer was a royal official who personally served wine to the king and who was sometimes required to taste the wine before serving it in the event an assassination attempt was being made upon the king. The *cupbearer* was a man who was greatly trusted by the king, a man in whom the king put a great deal of confidence. Thus, a close relationship was sometimes formed between a ruler and his cupbearer, which was obviously the case with Nehemiah and Artaxerxes.

The heartbreaking news about the returnees had a devastating effect upon Nehemiah. Grief and sorrow gripped him for days. In fact, the next time Nehemiah served wine to the king, he still exposed a sad countenance or appearance—so much so that the ruler asked him why he was so sad. Using the opportunity to share the affliction and distress of his people back in their homeland, he requested permission to personally return to Jerusalem. He expressed the desire to rebuild the wall and to make other improvements to the capital city. Having been granted permission, Nehemiah returned to his homeland.

After spending three days in Jerusalem, he privately surveyed the wall of the city at night in order to study the situation and determine what needed to be done. The next day, he called a meeting with the rulers of Jerusalem and shared with them how God had moved upon his heart when He heard about their distress. After sharing the decree of the king with the local rulers, he organized them to rebuild the wall of the city. Under his capable and courageous leadership, the construction project was, surprisingly, completed in 52 days (Neh.6:15). Throughout his stay in Jerusalem, Nehemiah supported the efforts of Ezra to stir revival among the people and to reform temple worship. In particular, Nehemiah supported Ezra's efforts to teach the law and commandments of the LORD to the people (Neh.8:1-18).

A quick glance at the chart on page 96 will help the reader grasp the returns of the three different groups of Jewish exiles.

TO WHOM WRITTEN: the Jews who had returned from captivity in particular, and the human race in general. The exile returnees who were allowed to return to the promised land had now rebuilt the temple, reestablished proper worship, and become a legitimate nation again. Under Nehemiah's strong leadership, they had also rebuilt the wall of Jerusalem. This generation and all who followed had to remain zealous for the work of the LORD. Would their spiritual fervor continue? Would they remain spiritually strong enough to overcome all opposition? They would if they listened to the message of the book of *Nehemiah*. It was to the three groups of exile returnees that the great book of *Nehemiah* was written. The returnees needed to know that the sovereign hand of God would always guide and protect them. And they needed to remain faithful, consistent in their testimony for the LORD. Consistency is an absolute essential for every generation of true believers if they are to be able to withstand the opposition that confronts them.

INTRODUCTION TO NEHEMIAH

PURPOSE:

1. The *Historical* Purpose:
   a. To document the return of the Jews from captivity led by Nehemiah and the rebuilding of the wall of Jerusalem.
   b. To document the restoration of the Jewish nation under Nehemiah's leadership.
   c. To show how the Northern and Southern Kingdoms merged into one nation during the captivity.
   d. To trace the genealogy of the returned exiles.
   e. To show that God had preserved the lineage of the Messiah.

2. The *Doctrinal* or *Spiritual* Purpose:
   a. To point out that God's plan for Israel was not void. In His sovereign power, God moved on the hearts of kings to allow His people to be released and to rebuild the temple. God would still allow His Name to be in Jerusalem. He would still honor the covenant He made with Abraham and King David. God's presence would still dwell in the midst of His people.
   b. To teach that believers must be united in their efforts to serve the LORD. Those who do the LORD's work must be willing to work diligently and to overcome all opposition by the enemy. They must be faithful in performing even undesirable jobs, fighting through exhaustion and remaining totally committed to the task at hand.
   c. To teach that God is a God of restoration.
   d. To teach that God's guiding hand is with the believer in all situations, good and bad.
   e. To teach that repentance and obedience always bring God's blessing. Peace, provision, protection, hope, victory, safety, the fullness of God's presence and more are available to the genuine believer who follows the LORD.
   f. To inspire all readers to stay fully committed to the LORD, allowing His blessings to continue to flow.
   g. To teach that there is spiritual rest and assurance for all who trust in the LORD. Just as God's blessings to the Jews include dwelling safely in the promised land, the eternal rest and reward of heaven awaits a life of faithful service.

3. The *Christological* or *Christ-Centered* Purpose: Jesus Christ, the Savior of the world, did come through David's family line. The genealogies contained in *Nehemiah* show the survival of the Jews and, therefore, the preservation of the family line through which the Messiah came. All true worship in Old Testament times celebrated forgiveness of sins. Thus, all true worship pointed forward to the sacrifice Christ so willing made on the cross. There He shed His life's blood to free us from sin. Everything is restored in the book of *Nehemiah* except the king on the throne. But the kingly line is very much alive, pointing forward to Jesus Christ, the King of kings and LORD of lords. The faithful service of the Jews and their commitment to the LORD and the rebuilding of the wall point to one very significant conclusion—Jesus Christ is worthy of all worship. We are to worship God and God alone, the Eternally Existent One, existing in three Persons—Father, Son, and Holy Spirit.

SPECIAL FEATURES:

1. *Nehemiah* is "The Great Book That Records the Return of the Third Group of Jews Out of Captivity and Back to the Promised Land" (1:1–2:20; 7:4-73).
2. *Nehemiah* is "The Great Book That Tells the Account of Rebuilding the Wall of Jerusalem with All of Its Gates" (3:1-32).
3. *Nehemiah* is "The Great Book That Teaches That All True Believers Will Have Opposition in the World" (4:1-23; 6:1-14).
4. *Nehemiah* is "The Great Book That Warns Against Oppressing Those Less Fortunate" (5:1-11).
5. *Nehemiah* is "The Great Book That Shows the Need of Repentance for Sin" (5:12-19; 9:1-37; 13:1-31).
6. *Nehemiah* is "The Great Book That Shows God's Sovereign Ability to Guide, Protect, and Provide for His Children, That They Might Overcome the World and Accomplish Their Assigned Tasks" (6:15-7:3).
7. *Nehemiah* is "The Great Book That Teaches Us of Our Need to Hear the Word of God" (8:1-12).
8. *Nehemiah* is "The Great Book That Teaches Us of Our Need to Obey the Word of God" (8:13-18).
9. *Nehemiah* is "The Great Book That Teaches Us of Our Need to Live in a Covenant Relationship with God, Worshipping the LORD with Commitment and Sincerity" (10:1-39).
10. *Nehemiah* is "The Great Book That Records the Occupation of Jerusalem by the Returned Exiles" (11:1-34).
11. *Nehemiah* is "The Great Book That Records the History of the Priests and Levites After the Return from Captivity" (12:1-26).
12. *Nehemiah* is "The Great Book That Records the Great Celebration as the Wall of Jerusalem was Dedicated to the LORD" (12:27-43).
13. *Nehemiah* is "The Great Book That Teaches Us the Responsibility to Support Our Ministers" (12:44-47).

400 SILENT YEARS

	FIRST RETURN UNDER ZERUBBABEL	SECOND RETURN UNDER EZRA	THIRD RETURN UNDER NEHEMIAH	
BIBLE REFERENCE	Ezra 1-6	Ezra 7-10	Nehemiah 1-13	
DATE	537 B.C.	458 B.C.	445 B.C.	
PERSIAN KING	Cyrus	Artaxerxes	Artaxerxes	
EXILES RETURNING	46,697 (Ezr.2:64-65)	1496 Men 38 Levites 220 Servants 1754 plus women and children (Ezr.8:21)	Unknown	
PURPOSE	To resettle in the land and rebuild the nation and temple: Under Persian rule	To teach God's law, stir revival and reformation, and renew temple worship	To rebuild the wall of Jerusalem and support Ezra's efforts of reformation	
RESULTS	Oppression by neighbors; rebuilt the temple, but slipped away from the LORD (Ezr.9:1-2; Mal.1:6-14; 2:11; 3:5)	Reformed temple worship and stirred revival, teaching God's Word to the people (Ezr.9:1-10:44; Neh.8:1-10:39)	Rebuilt the wall and worked with Ezra in his reformation and teaching ministry (Ne.8:1-10:39)	

GAP 57 YEARS

GAP 12 YEARS

NEHEMIAH'S SECOND RETURN (About 430—433 B.C.)

538 B.C. 515 B.C. 458 B.C. 456 B.C. 444 B.C. 432 B.C.

➤ Haggai (520 B.C.)
➤ Zechariah (520–518 B.C.)

➤ Malachi (450–430 B.C.)(?)

CAPTIVITY 70 YEARS
(605 – 536 B.C.)

OUTLINE OF NEHEMIAH

THE PREACHER'S OUTLINE AND SERMON BIBLE® is *unique*. It differs from all other Study Bibles and Sermon Resource Materials in that every Passage and Subject is outlined right beside the Scripture. When you choose any *Subject* below and turn to the reference, you have not only the Scripture but also an outline of the Scripture and Subject *already prepared for you—verse by verse*.

For a quick example, choose one of the subjects below and turn over to the Scripture; you will find this to be a marvelous help for more organized and streamlined study.

In addition, every point of the Scripture and Subject is *fully developed in a Commentary with supporting Scripture* at the end of each point. Again, this arrangement makes sermon preparation much simpler and more efficient.

Note something else: the Subjects of *Nehemiah* have titles that are both Biblical and *practical*. The practical titles are often more appealing to people. This *benefit* is clearly seen for use on billboards, bulletins, church newsletters, etc.

A suggestion: for the *quickest* overview of *Nehemiah*, first read *all the Division titles* (I, II, III, etc.), then come back and read the individual outline titles.

OUTLINE OF NEHEMIAH

I. THE REBUILDING OF THE WALLS OF JERUSALEM, 1:1–7:73

A. The Broken Heart of Nehemiah Over Jerusalem: A Man of Deep Concern and Prayer, 1:1-11
B. Nehemiah's Royal Commission and His Preparations to Rebuild Jerusalem: A Man of Boldness, Filled with a Spirit of Exhortation, 2:1-20
C. Nehemiah's Rebuilding of the Wall of Jerusalem: Three Pictures of Diligent and Zealous Laborers, 3:1-32
D. Nehemiah's Struggle with External Opposition: Four Strategies Used by the Enemies of Believers, 4:1-23
E. Nehemiah's Struggle with Internal Strife: A Lesson on the Desperate Need to Love Our Neighbors As Ourselves, 5:1-19
F. Nehemiah's Struggle with Plots Against Him Personally: An Urgent Need for Discernment and Wisdom, 6:1-14
G. The Triumphant Completion of the Wall and the Restoration of Jerusalem: A Lesson on Diligence, 6:15-7:73

II. THE REBUILDING OF THE NATION AND THE PEOPLE 8:1–13:31

A. Step 1—Rebuilding Through God's Word: Stressing the Importance of the Holy Bible, 8:1-18
B. Step 2—Rebuilding Through a Revived Spirit: Stressing the Importance of Seeking God, His Goodness and Mercy, 9:1-37
C. Step 3—Rebuilding Through Making a Covenant of Commitment: Stressing the Importance of Total Devotion, 9:38–10:39
D. Step 4—Rebuilding Through Strengthening Both Jerusalem and the Spirit of the People: Three Essentials for a Strong Nation and People, 11:1-12:47
E. Step 5—Building Through Discipline, Correcting People's Violation of the Law: Stressing the Need for Continued Reformation, Revival, 13:1-31

DIVISION I — NEHEMIAH

THE REBUILDING OF THE WALLS OF JERUSALEM, 1:1–7:73

(1:1–7:73) **DIVISION OVERVIEW**: about thirteen years after Ezra led the second group of Jews back to the promised land, Nehemiah, the cupbearer to the Persian king, heard about the terrible oppression and defeated spirits of the Jews in Jerusalem. Nehemiah's heart was stricken with deep grief, a burden so distressing that he spent days in prayer. The great book of *Nehemiah* begins with the desperate situation of the Jews, Nehemiah's deep distress, and his commission from King Artaxerxes to go to Jerusalem. His commission was to encourage his people and to rebuild the wall of Jerusalem for their protection (2:4-8).

Once Nehemiah arrived in Jerusalem, he inspected what was left of the walls of Jerusalem and formed a plan to rebuild. Summoning the Jews to a meeting, Nehemiah laid out the reality of the task at hand and stirred the people to commit themselves to the project. The Jews were stricken in conscience and strongly motivated in their spirit to take up the task at hand. However, as soon as the work was started on the wall, opposition reared its ugly head (2:19-20). Foreigners had moved into Judah when the Jews were deported to Babylon. These foreigners now became enemies to the Jewish return-ees and did all they could to stop the progress on the wall. Yet no matter how much the opposition attacked, the LORD gave Nehemiah wisdom to counter the attack and enabled him to continue in the critical work of rebuilding the wall. But opposition from foreign enemies was not the only problem Nehemiah faced. Internal problems arose as well. Rich Jews were oppressing the poorer countrymen among them (5:1-5). Nehemiah confronted this problem head-on. Those Jews wrongly oppressing the poor repented, and unity was restored. When the wall was finally completed (7:1), Nehemiah made a public record of the genealogies of those living in Jerusalem. At last, the nation was reestablished and the Jews were able to rest in peace and safety.

Remember that Nehemiah was writing primarily to those who had faithfully worked alongside him. Together, they had completed the wall. Future generations would reap the benefits of their hard work. Above all else, the Jews had to be faithful to the LORD. Jerusalem had been rebuilt with great sacrifice. Now that the city of God was built, the Jews needed God's guiding hand upon them more than ever before. Nehemiah knew that constant devotion and continued revival were desperately needed for the people and the nation to remain strong. The Jews must not risk the wrath of God by giving in to compromise and evil associations as their ancestors had done.

As the reader studies this return of Jews from captivity under Nehemiah's direction and the rebuilding of the wall of Je-rusalem, this fact should be kept in mind: opposition will come into the life of every true believer. But God is faithful; He will guide, protect, and provide whatever is needed in any circumstance for the believer to overcome and complete his as-signed tasks.

"The God of heaven, he will prosper us; therefore we his servants will arise and build" (Ne.2:20).

THE REBUILDING OF THE WALLS OF JERUSALEM, 1:1–7:73

A. The Broken Heart of Nehemiah Over Jerusalem: A Man of Deep Con-cern and Prayer, 1:1-11

B. Nehemiah's Royal Commission and His Preparations to Rebuild Jerusa-lem: A Man of Boldness, Filled with a Spirit of Exhortation, 2:1-20

C. Nehemiah's Rebuilding of the Wall of Jerusalem: Three Pictures of Dil-igent and Zealous Laborers, 3:1-32

D. Nehemiah's Struggle with External Opposition: Four Strategies Used by the Enemies of Believers, 4:1-23

E. Nehemiah's Struggle with Internal Strife: A Lesson on the Desperate Need to Love Our Neighbors As Ourselves, 5:1-19

F. Nehemiah's Struggle with Plots Against Him Personally: An Urgent Need for Discernment and Wisdom, 6:1-14

G. The Triumphant Completion of the Wall and the Restoration of Jerusa-lem: A Lesson on Diligence, 6:15–7:73

THE BOOK OF
NEHEMIAH

CHAPTER 1

I. THE REBUILDING OF THE WALLS OF JERUSALEM, 1:1–7:73

A. The Broken Heart of Nehemiah Over Jerusalem: A Man of Deep Concern & Prayer, 1:1-11

1. **Nehemiah's distress at hearing the news from Jerusalem: A man of tender heart & genuine concern**
   a. The place: The Fortress of Susa, year 20 of Artaxerxes I
   b. The visit by Nehemiah's brother & others from Judah: Dark, dismal news from their homeland
      1) Concerned the returned exiles & those Jews who had survived the captivity & been left behind:
         • Were in distress & trouble
         • Were reproached & disgraced
      2) Concerned Jerusalem: Was in shambles with its wall torn down
   c. The effect on Nehemiah: A broken heart, concern, & care
      1) Wept & mourned
      2) Fasted & prayed—*for days*
2. **Nehemiah's prayer: A man who illustrated Christ's intercession**
   a. His acknowledgement of God
      1) God's supremacy
      2) God's power & majesty
      3) God's faithfulness
   b. His confession of sin

The words of Nehemiah the son of Hachaliah. And it came to pass in the month Chisleu, in the twentieth year, as I was in Shushan the palace,

2 That Hanani, one of my brethren, came, he and *certain* men of Judah; and I asked them concerning the Jews that had escaped, which were left of the captivity, and concerning Jerusalem.

3 And they said unto me, The remnant that are left of the captivity there in the province *are* in great affliction and reproach: the wall of Jerusalem also *is* broken down, and the gates thereof are burned with fire.

4 And it came to pass, when I heard these words, that I sat down and wept, and mourned *certain* days, and fasted, and prayed before the God of heaven,

5 And said, I beseech thee, O LORD God of heaven, the great and terrible God, that keepeth covenant and mercy for them that love him and observe his commandments:

6 Let thine ear now be attentive, and thine eyes open, that thou mayest hear the prayer of thy servant, which I pray before thee now, day and night, for the children of Israel thy servants, and confess the sins of the children of Israel, which we have sinned against thee: both I and my father's house have sinned.

7 We have dealt very corruptly against thee, and have not kept the commandments, nor the statutes, nor the judgments, which thou commandedst thy servant Moses.

8 Remember, I beseech thee, the word that thou commandedst thy servant Moses, saying, *If* ye transgress, I will scatter you abroad among the nations:

9 But *if* ye turn unto me, and keep my commandments, and do them; though there were of you cast out unto the uttermost part of the heaven, *yet* will I gather them from thence, and will bring them unto the place that I have chosen to set my name there.

10 Now these *are* thy servants and thy people, whom thou hast redeemed by thy great power, and by thy strong hand.

11 O Lord, I beseech thee, let now thine ear be attentive to the prayer of thy servant, and to the prayer of thy servants, who desire to fear thy name: and prosper, I pray thee, thy servant this day, and grant him mercy in the sight of this man. For I was the king's cupbearer.

1) He was an intercessor: Asked God to forgive the sins of Israel & those of his own family
2) He was a repentant sinner himself, identifying with the people: Asked God to forgive him

3) He spelled out all of their sins
   • Had lived corrupt, depraved, & appalling lives
   • Had disobeyed God's Word
c. His plea for God's help
1) He asked God to remember His Word—(covenant)
   • Concerning sin & judgment, De.4:25-31

   • Concerning repentance & obedience: If they returned to the LORD, they would be returned to the promised land

2) He asked God to remember their relationship: They were God's servants, the very people He had redeemed
3) He asked God to hear his prayer & the prayers of other servants who feared or revered His name
4) He asked God for success when he made his special request to King Artaxerxes

d. His position: Cupbearer to the king

DIVISION I

THE REBUILDING OF THE WALLS OF JERUSALEM, 1:1–7:73

A. The Broken Heart of Nehemiah Over Jerusalem: A Man of Deep Concern and Prayer, 1:1-11

(1:1-11) **Introduction**: people with needs are all around us, people with desperate needs. Now think of the great diversity of these needy people around the world, even within our very own communities, neighborhoods, and churches:
   ⇒ the single mothers who are destitute
   ⇒ the children who are physically, mentally, or sexually abused
   ⇒ the poverty-stricken who are hungry, thirsty, or homeless
   ⇒ the unemployed who have lost their jobs and cannot find adequate employment to support their families
   ⇒ the widows, widowers, and divorced who must face a new life on their own
   ⇒ the masses who are lonely, empty, and without purpose
   ⇒ the masses who are diseased, injured, or dying

NEHEMIAH 1:1-11

Men and women of compassion must step forward, men and women who have a genuine and deep concern about meeting the needs of others. Nehemiah was such a man. In fact, he was so gripped with concern for others that it is the first fact he mentions about himself in his great book. The entire first chapter focuses upon his tender heart and his concern for those in desperate need. This first chapter is, *The Broken Heart of Nehemiah Over Jerusalem: A Man of Deep Concern and Prayer*, 1:1-11.

    1. Nehemiah's distress at hearing the news from Jerusalem: a man of tender heart and genuine concern (vv.1-4).
    2. Nehemiah's prayer: a man who illustrated Christ's intercession (vv.5-11).

1 (1:1-4) **Heart, Tender, Example of—Concern, Example of—Care, Example of—Compassion, Example of—Nehemiah, Heart of—Jerusalem, Concern for—Returnees, Jewish, Condition and State of—Jerusalem, Condition of, at the Return of the Exiles**: while serving in the palace of the Persian king, Nehemiah received some alarming, distressful news from Jerusalem. From Nehemiah's reaction, we immediately see that he was a man with a tender heart and deep concern for his people, the Jews. What happened is briefly described by Scripture:

OUTLINE	SCRIPTURE	SCRIPTURE	OUTLINE
1. Nehemiah's distress at hearing the news from Jerusalem: A man of tender heart & genuine concern a. The place: The Fortress of Susa, year 20 of Artaxerxes I b. The visit by Nehemiah's brother & others from Judah: Dark, dismal news from their homeland 1) Concerned the returned exiles & those Jews who had survived the captivity & been left behind:	The words of Nehemiah the son of Hachaliah. And it came to pass in the month Chisleu, in the twentieth year, as I was in Shushan the palace, 2 That Hanani, one of my brethren, came, he and *certain* men of Judah; and I asked them concerning the Jews that had escaped, which were left of the captivity, and concerning Jerusalem.	3 And they said unto me, The remnant that are left of the captivity there in the province *are* in great affliction and reproach: the wall of Jerusalem also *is* broken down, and the gates thereof are burned with fire. 4 And it came to pass, when I heard these words, that I sat down and wept, and mourned *certain* days, and fasted, and prayed before the God of heaven,	• Were in distress & trouble • Were reproached & disgraced 2) Concerned Jerusalem: Was in shambles with its wall torn down c. The effect on Nehemiah: A broken heart, concern, & care 1) Wept & mourned 2) Fasted & prayed—*for days*

a. Nehemiah was in the palace fortress at Susa, the capital of the great Persian Empire. Because of the warmer climate there, the kings of Persia spent their winter months at Susa. They spent their summer months at Ecbatana. Nehemiah was the cupbearer to the Persian king Artaxerxes I. As the cupbearer, his primary responsibility was to always taste the wine being served to the king in order to protect the king from an assassination attempt by means of poison (v.11). The cupbearer was a very prominent, honored, responsible, and influential position within the kingdom. Furthermore, the cupbearer had to be an honest and trusted man, a man in whom the king could put his complete confidence. A king placed his very life in the hands of his cupbearer. Because of this, the cupbearer sometimes became a trusted advisor to the king, which was apparently true with Nehemiah (2:1-8).

The present event took place in the month of Kislev (November–December), the twentieth year of the reign of Artaxerxes I. Artaxerxes I ruled from c.465–423 B.C., which means that this event occurred in 445 B.C.

b. While serving in the palace at Susa, Nehemiah was visited by his brother and a number of other men who had just made a trip to Judah (vv.2-3). With keen interest, Nehemiah questioned them about the Jewish captives who had returned to Jerusalem from their exile. In response to Nehemiah's question, the men painted a dark, dismal picture of the returned exiles. They were in deep trouble and severe distress and were bearing terrible afflictions. They were being reproached and disgraced by the surrounding people and nations. In addition, the wall of Jerusalem had been torn down and the gates had been burned. Other Scriptures reveal the dreadful hardships the returned exiles were suffering:

⇒ They were suffering an economic depression due to famine (5:1-3). Famine naturally causes hunger, disease, and eventually starvation, unless relief comes. It also brings loss of income and jobs, decreased sales for businesses, and in some cases bankruptcy.

⇒ A large number of people were suffering oppression due to the greed of certain wealthy farmers and businessmen (5:4-5). In order to buy food, some of the people had to mortgage their homes and fields. Others had to borrow money in order to pay their taxes. The wealthy loaned money to the people, but they acted greedily in their own self-interest. They were forcing the adults and their children into some form of servitude or slavery in order to pay off their debts. In essence, the wealthy were not only amassing all the property of the less fortunate, but they were also enslaving them unjustly.

⇒ The people were suffering persecution in the form of anti-Semitism, ridicule, and harassment from their neighbors and other nationalities who surrounded them (Ezr.4:1-24).

⇒ Above and beyond all their personal suffering, the people were defenseless against enemy attacks since the wall of Jerusalem had been torn down and its gates burned with fire (v.3).

c. Hearing this bleak and discouraging news about his homeland broke Nehemiah's heart (v.4). Grave concern gripped the inner recesses of his soul. He began to weep and mourn over the severe distress of his people. Utterly broken, Nehemiah began to fast and pray for *many days* on their behalf. Just how many days is not stated by Scripture. But *day after day* he sought the LORD, begging the LORD to help his people through these dire circumstances.

Thought 1. Nehemiah's tender heart and deep concern for others were evident in his life by his actions. When others suffered, he was gripped by compassion for their welfare. So it must be with us. When we see or hear about people in need, we must feel empathy, identifying with their need. But even more important than just feeling for

101

others, we must act. We must be benevolent in meeting the needs of others both at home and abroad. On a larger scale, think of these very real and very desperate needs around the world...

- people are literally starving to death on a daily basis, whether due to famine, war, or the greed of their leaders
- the nations whose people have known nothing but war, death, and destruction, whose citizens both young and old live in a constant state of fear
- the nations whose people have been enslaved, oppressed, and dominated by ignorant and cruel individuals or governments
- the nations whose people have contracted and spread dangerous, even deadly, diseases, whose governments lack the knowledge or funding or compassion to seek a solution

The list could go on and on. Countless numbers are hurting in countless ways. Like Nehemiah, we must arouse ourselves to show tender concern for the hurting and suffering of this world. We must reach out in compassion to help all we can. Listen to what God's Holy Word says:

"For I was an hungred, and ye gave me meat: I was thirsty, and ye gave me drink: I was a stranger, and ye took me in: Naked, and ye clothed me: I was sick, and ye visited me: I was in prison, and ye came unto me. Then shall the righteous answer him, saying, Lord, when saw we thee an hungred, and fed *thee?* or thirsty, and gave *thee* drink? When saw we thee a stranger, and took *thee* in? or naked, and clothed *thee?* Or when saw we thee sick, or in prison, and came unto thee? And the King shall answer and say unto them, Verily I say unto you, Inasmuch as ye have done *it* unto one of the least of these my brethren, ye have done *it* unto me" (Mt.25:35-40).

"But a certain Samaritan, as he journeyed, came where he was: and when he saw him, he had compassion *on him,* And went to *him,* and bound up his wounds, pouring in oil and wine, and set him on his own beast, and brought him to an inn, and took care of him" (Lu.10:33-34).

"I have showed you all things, how that so labouring ye ought to support the weak, and to remember the words of the Lord Jesus, how he said, It is more blessed to give than to receive" (Ac.20:35).

"Therefore if thine enemy hunger, feed him; if he thirst, give him drink: for in so doing thou shalt heap coals of fire on his head" (Ro.12:20).

"We then that are strong ought to bear the infirmities of the weak, and not to please ourselves" (Ro.15:1).

"Bear ye one another's burdens, and so fulfil the law of Christ" (Ga.6:2).

"As we have therefore opportunity, let us do good unto all *men,* especially unto them who are of the household of faith" (Ga.6:10).

"Put on therefore, as the elect of God, holy and beloved, bowels of mercies, kindness, humbleness of mind, meekness, longsuffering" (Co.3:12).

"Remember them that are in bonds, as bound with them; *and* them which suffer adversity, as being yourselves also in the body" (He.13:3).

"Pure religion and undefiled before God and the Father is this, To visit the fatherless and widows in their affliction, *and* to keep himself unspotted from the world" (Js.1:27).

"But whoso hath this world's good, and seeth his brother have need, and shutteth up his bowels *of compassion* from him, how dwelleth the love of God in him? My little children, let us not love in word, neither in tongue; but in deed and in truth" (1 Jn.3:17-18).

"*Is* not this the fast that I have chosen? to loose the bands of wickedness, to undo the heavy burdens, and to let the oppressed go free, and that ye break every yoke? *Is it* not to deal thy bread to the hungry, and that thou bring the poor that are cast out to thy house? when thou seest the naked, that thou cover him; and that thou hide not thyself from thine own flesh?" (Is.58:6-7).

2 (1:5-11) **Prayer, Example of—Humility, Example of—Nehemiah, Prayer of**: day after day Nehemiah knocked at the door of heaven, seeking the face of the LORD on behalf of the Jews who had returned to Judah. According to the model that Jesus Christ later taught His followers, Nehemiah asked, sought, and knocked at the door of heaven. Scripture will reveal that he received what he asked for, found what he sought, and the door was opened to him by the LORD (Mt.7:8). Nehemiah became an intercessor, seeking the LORD on behalf of his people. Twelve prayers are recorded in his book, nine of which were offered up by Nehemiah himself (1:5-11; 2:4; 4:4-5, 9; 5:19; 6:9, 14; 9:5-37; 13:14, 22, 29, 31). In the present Scripture, his prayer is spelled out point by point:

OUTLINE	SCRIPTURE	SCRIPTURE	OUTLINE
2. Nehemiah's prayer: A man who illustrated Christ's intercession a. His acknowledgement of God 　1) God's supremacy 　2) God's power & majesty 　3) God's faithfulness b. His confession of sin 　1) He was an intercessor:	5 And said, I beseech thee, O LORD God of heaven, the great and terrible God, that keepeth covenant and mercy for them that love him and observe his commandments: 6 Let thine ear now be attentive, and thine eyes open,	that thou mayest hear the prayer of thy servant, which I pray before thee now, day and night, for the children of Israel thy servants, and confess the sins of the children of Israel, which we have sinned against thee: both I and my father's house have sinned.	Asked God to forgive the sins of Israel & those of his own family 2) He was a repentant sinner himself, identifying with the people: Asked God to forgive him

OUTLINE	SCRIPTURE	SCRIPTURE	OUTLINE
3) He spelled out all of their sins • Had lived corrupt, depraved, & appalling lives • Had disobeyed God's Word c. His plea for God's help 1) He asked God to remember His Word—(covenant) • Concerning sin & judgment, De.4:25-31 • Concerning repentance & obedience: If they returned to the LORD, they would be returned to the promised land	7 We have dealt very corruptly against thee, and have not kept the commandments, nor the statutes, nor the judgments, which thou commandedst thy servant Moses. 8 Remember, I beseech thee, the word that thou commandedst thy servant Moses, saying, If ye transgress, I will scatter you abroad among the nations: 9 But if ye turn unto me, and keep my commandments, and do them; though there were of you cast out unto the uttermost part of the heaven, yet will I gather them	from thence, and will bring them unto the place that I have chosen to set my name there. 10 Now these are thy servants and thy people, whom thou hast redeemed by thy great power, and by thy strong hand. 11 O Lord, I beseech thee, let now thine ear be attentive to the prayer of thy servant, and to the prayer of thy servants, who desire to fear thy name: and prosper, I pray thee, thy servant this day, and grant him mercy in the sight of this man. For I was the king's cupbearer.	2) He asked God to remember their relationship: They were God's servants, the very people He had redeemed 3) He asked God to hear his prayer & the prayers of other servants who feared or revered His name 4) He asked God for success when he made his special request to King Artaxerxes d. His position: Cupbearer to the king

a. First, Nehemiah began his prayer by acknowledging God, praising Him for who He is and what He has done (v.5).
⇒ Nehemiah acknowledged God's supremacy over all by addressing Him as the "LORD God of Heaven." As the God of heaven, He is supreme, sovereign over all the universe, all that is in heaven and earth. He rules and reigns over all, controlling all events, including the affairs of men.
⇒ Nehemiah addressed God as the "great and terrible [or awesome] God." This refers to the power and majesty of God. As the great God, He possesses all power and might. As the awesome God, He is the Supreme Being who possesses all the glory and majesty of perfection and holiness. He is totally set apart from all other beings.
⇒ Nehemiah also addressed the LORD as the "One who keeps His covenant with all who love Him and obey His commandments." God always keeps His Word, His promises to those who choose to love and obey Him. Nehemiah praised the LORD for His faithfulness.

Emphasizing God's love for those who seek after Him, Nehemiah indicated that he was going to be crying out for the mercy of God upon his people. The only question remaining was whether or not the people would turn to the LORD and obey Him. Would they truly repent of their sins and keep His commandments?
b. Second, Nehemiah identified with the people by confessing both their sins and his own before the LORD (vv.6-7). He became an intercessor for the people before God, asking God to forgive the sins of Israel and of his own family. Note that Nehemiah did not make this request only once. He sought God's forgiveness day and night (v.6).
Yet Nehemiah did not ask God to forgive his and Israel's sins in general. Rather, he spelled out their sins (v.7). They had lived extremely wicked and corrupt lives, defiantly disobeying God's Word, His Holy Commandments, His statutes and laws.
c. Third, Nehemiah pleaded for God's mercy and help (vv.8-11). He asked God to remember His Holy Word, the covenant He had made with His people (vv.8-9; see De.4:25-31; 28:15-68, esp.58-68; 30:1-10). The covenant concerned sin and judgment. If the people sinned, they would suffer the hand of God's judgment by being scattered among the nations, which is exactly what had happened. But the covenant also concerned repentance and obedience and the wonderful experience of God's mercy. If the people returned to the LORD, they would be returned to the promised land. This was the eternal promise of God. Accordingly, if the people of Nehemiah's day would return to the LORD, the blessings of God would fall upon them. They would be delivered from their deep distress and trouble.
Nehemiah then asked God to remember their relationship: they were God's servants, the very people He had redeemed by His great power and mighty hand (v.10). Thus he begged God to hear his prayer and the prayers of other servants who feared and revered his name (v.11).
Lastly, Nehemiah made a very practical request of the LORD. He asked the LORD to make an opportunity for him to approach the king because he wanted to request the king's help (v.11). This was a prayer Nehemiah had apparently been offering up for several months (1:1; 2:1). Now, at last, the door was opened for him to approach the king. This was the day. Thus, Nehemiah asked the LORD to give him success in this critically important matter. King Artaxerxes needed to be aroused or stirred by God to grant the special request Nehemiah was going to make. The actual details of Nehemiah's appeal to the king will be covered in the next chapter. For now, the point to observe is that Nehemiah closed his prayer by asking God for specific help in dealing with the king. Bear in mind Nehemiah's prominent and influential position in the royal court. He was the cupbearer to the king (v.11).

Thought 1. In his prayer, Nehemiah illustrated the coming intercession of Jesus Christ. That is, Nehemiah stood in the gap between his people and the LORD. Nehemiah became the intercessor, the representative of the Jewish exiles who wished to plead their case before the LORD. This is exactly what Jesus Christ has done for us. Jesus Christ is our Intercessor, our Representative, our Advocate who presents our case before God. When we turn to the Lord Jesus Christ with any distress or trouble, Christ presents our need to the Father. And the Father hears the plea of Christ on our behalf. Through Jesus Christ we can receive forgiveness of sins and be given a victorious, triumphant life. The power to conquer all the trials, hardships, and distressing circumstances of life can be obtained only through Jesus Christ. As stated, He is our Intercessor, Advocate, and Representative before God. Listen to what the Holy Word of God says:

"But I have prayed for thee, that thy faith fail not: and when thou art converted, strengthen thy brethren" (Lu.22:32).

"Then said Jesus, Father, forgive them; for they know not what they do. And they parted his raiment, and cast lots" (Lu.23:34).

"And I will pray the Father, and he shall give you another Comforter, that he may abide with you for ever" (Jn.14:16).

"Who *is* he that condemneth? *It is* Christ that died, yea rather, that is risen again, who is even at the right hand of God, who also maketh intercession for us" (Ro.8:34).

"Wherefore in all things it behoved him to be made like unto *his* brethren, that he might be a merciful and faithful high priest in things *pertaining* to God, to make reconciliation for the sins of the people" (He.2:17).

"Seeing then that we have a great high priest, that is passed into the heavens, Jesus the Son of God, let us hold fast *our* profession. For we have not an high priest which cannot be touched with the feeling of our infirmities; but was in all points tempted like as *we are, yet* without sin. Let us therefore come boldly unto the throne of grace, that we may obtain mercy, and find grace to help in time of need" (He.4:14-16).

"For every high priest taken from among men is ordained for men in things *pertaining* to God, that he may offer both gifts and sacrifices for sins: Who can have compassion on the ignorant, and on them that are out of the way; for that he himself also is compassed with infirmity. And by reason hereof he ought, as for the people, so also for himself, to offer for sins. And no man taketh this honour unto himself, but he that is called of God, as *was* Aaron. So also Christ glorified not himself to be made an high priest; but he that said unto him, Thou art my Son, to day have I begotten thee" (He.5:1-5).

"Which *hope* we have as an anchor of the soul, both sure and stedfast, and which entereth into that within the veil; Whither the forerunner is for us entered, *even* Jesus, made an high priest for ever after the order of Melchisedec" (He.6:19-20).

"Wherefore he is able also to save them to the uttermost that come unto God by him, seeing he ever liveth to make intercession for them. For such an high priest became us, *who is* holy, harmless, undefiled, separate from sinners, and made higher than the heavens; Who needeth not daily, as those high priests, to offer up sacrifice, first for his own sins, and then for the people's: for this he did once, when he offered up himself" (He.7:25-27).

"Now of the things which we have spoken *this is* the sum: We have such an high priest, who is set on the right hand of the throne of the Majesty in the heavens" (He.8:1).

"But Christ being come an high priest of good things to come, by a greater and more perfect tabernacle, not made with hands, that is to say, not of this building; Neither by the blood of goats and calves, but by his own blood he entered in once into the holy place, having obtained eternal redemption *for us.* For if the blood of bulls and of goats, and the ashes of an heifer sprinkling the unclean, sanctifieth to the purifying of the flesh: How much more shall the blood of Christ, who through the eternal Spirit offered himself without spot to God, purge your conscience from dead works to serve the living God?" (He.9:11-14).

"And *having* an high priest over the house of God; Let us draw near with a true heart in full assurance of faith, having our hearts sprinkled from an evil conscience, and our bodies washed with pure water" (He.10:21-22).

"Therefore will I divide him *a portion* with the great, and he shall divide the spoil with the strong; because he hath poured out his soul unto death: and he was numbered with the transgressors; and he bare the sin of many, and made intercession for the transgressors" (Is.53:12).

Thought 2. Nehemiah was a man who believed in prayer and who prayed often and much. This is clearly seen in the present Scripture. His prayer life stands as a strong example for us: we should pray, pray often, and pray much. Listen to what God's Holy Word says about prayer:

"Ask, and it shall be given you; seek, and ye shall find; knock, and it shall be opened unto you: For every one that asketh receiveth; and he that seeketh findeth; and to him that knocketh it shall be opened" (Mt.7:7-8).

"Watch and pray, that ye enter not into temptation: the spirit indeed *is* willing, but the flesh *is* weak" (Mt.26:41).

"And he spake a parable unto them *to this end,* that men ought always to pray, and not to faint" (Lu.18:1).

"And whatsoever ye shall ask in my name, that will I do, that the Father may be glorified in the Son. If ye shall ask any thing in my name, I will do *it*" (Jn.14:13-14).

"If ye abide in me, and my words abide in you, ye shall ask what ye will, and it shall be done unto you" (Jn.15:7).

"Hitherto have ye asked nothing in my name: ask, and ye shall receive, that your joy may be full" (Jn.16:24).

"Praying always with all prayer and supplication in the Spirit, and watching thereunto with all perseverance and supplication for all saints" (Ep.6:18).

"Be careful for nothing; but in every thing by prayer and supplication with thanksgiving let your requests be made known unto God. And the peace of God, which passeth all understanding, shall keep your hearts and minds through Christ Jesus" (Ph.4:6-7).

"Continue in prayer, and watch in the same with thanksgiving; Withal praying also for us, that God would open unto us a door of utterance, to speak the mystery of Christ, for which I am also in bonds" (Col.4:2-3).

"Pray without ceasing" (1 Th.5:17).

"Is any among you afflicted? let him pray. Is any merry? let him sing psalms. Is any sick among you? let him call for the elders of the church; and let them pray over him, anointing him with oil in the name of the Lord" (Ja.5:13-14).

"And whatsoever we ask, we receive of him, because we keep his commandments, and do those things that are pleasing in his sight. And this is his commandment, That we should believe on the name of his Son Jesus Christ, and love one another, as he gave us commandment" (1 Jn.3:22-23).

"Seek the LORD and his strength, seek his face continually" (1 Chr.16:11).

"If my people, which are called by my name, shall humble themselves, and pray, and seek my face, and turn from their wicked ways; then will I hear from heaven, and will forgive their sin, and will heal their land" (2 Chr.7:14).

"He shall call upon me, and I will answer him: I *will be* with him in trouble; I will deliver him, and honour him" (Ps.91:15).

"*When* the poor and needy seek water, and *there is* none, *and* their tongue faileth for thirst, I the LORD will hear them, *I* the God of Israel will not forsake them" (Is.41:17).

"Then shalt thou call, and the LORD shall answer; thou shalt cry, and he shall say, Here I *am*. If thou take away from the midst of thee the yoke, the putting forth of the finger, and speaking vanity" (Is.58:9).

"And it shall come to pass, that before they call, I will answer; and while they are yet speaking, I will hear" (Is.65:24).

"And ye shall seek me, and find *me,* when ye shall search for me with all your heart" (Je.29:13).

"And I will bring the third part through the fire, and will refine them as silver is refined, and will try them as gold is tried: they shall call on my name, and I will hear them: I will say, It *is* my people: and they shall say, The LORD *is* my God" (Zec.13:9).

CHAPTER 2

B. Nehemiah's Royal Commission & His Preparations to Rebuild Jerusalem: A Man of Boldness, Filled with a Spirit of Exhortation, 2:1-20

1. Nehemiah's royal commission to rebuild Jerusalem: A man who spoke openly & boldly

a. Nehemiah's sad appearance while serving the king
  1) The king noticed his sadness & questioned him

  2) The king struck fear in his heart: Because royal officials were never to show negative emotions—due to the king's wrath

b. Nehemiah's respectful but bold reply
  1) He showed proper respect in addressing the king
  2) He explained his sadness: His home city lay in ruins

  3) He stirred the king to ask what he wanted
  4) He quickly, silently prayed

  5) He requested a royal commission to travel to Judah to rebuild his home city, the city where his family ancestors were buried: Ended up staying 12 years, 5:14

c. Nehemiah's request granted
  1) He was questioned about the time frame by the king with the queen sitting beside him
  2) He set the time & the request was granted
  3) He requested letters for safe passage & provisions for the journey: Was necessary to present to the governors of West Euphrates because of the large military escort with him, 9
  4) He asked also for an official letter to secure building materials from the king's forest

d. Nehemiah's strong testimony: His bold request was granted because of God's goodness

And it came to pass in the month Nisan, in the twentieth year of Artaxerxes the king, *that* wine *was* before him: and I took up the wine, and gave *it* unto the king. Now I had not been *beforetime* sad in his presence.
2 Wherefore the king said unto me, Why *is* thy countenance sad, seeing thou *art* not sick? this *is* nothing *else* but sorrow of heart. Then I was very sore afraid,
3 And said unto the king, Let the king live for ever: why should not my countenance be sad, when the city, the place of my fathers' sepulchres, *lieth* waste, and the gates thereof are consumed with fire?
4 Then the king said unto me, For what dost thou make request? So I prayed to the God of heaven.
5 And I said unto the king, If it please the king, and if thy servant have found favour in thy sight, that thou wouldest send me unto Judah, unto the city of my fathers' sepulchres, that I may build it.
6 And the king said unto me, (the queen also sitting by him,) For how long shall thy journey be? and when wilt thou return? So it pleased the king to send me; and I set him a time.
7 Moreover I said unto the king, If it please the king, let letters be given me to the governors beyond the river, that they may convey me over till I come into Judah;
8 And a letter unto Asaph the keeper of the king's forest, that he may give me timber to make beams for the gates of the palace which *appertained* to the house, and for the wall of the city, and for the house that I shall enter into. And the king granted me, according to the good hand of my God upon me.

9 Then I came to the governors beyond the river, and gave them the king's letters. Now the king had sent captains of the army and horsemen with me.
10 When Sanballat the Horonite, and Tobiah the servant, the Ammonite, heard *of it,* it grieved them exceedingly that there was come a man to seek the welfare of the children of Israel.
11 So I came to Jerusalem, and was there three days.
12 And I arose in the night, I and some few men with me; neither told I *any* man what my God had put in my heart to do at Jerusalem: neither *was there any* beast with me, save the beast that I rode upon.
13 And I went out by night by the gate of the valley, even before the dragon well, and to the dung port, and viewed the walls of Jerusalem, which were broken down, and the gates thereof were consumed with fire.
14 Then I went on to the gate of the fountain, and to the king's pool: but *there was* no place for the beast *that was* under me to pass.
15 Then went I up in the night by the brook, and viewed the wall, and turned back, and entered by the gate of the valley, and *so* returned.
16 And the rulers knew not whither I went, or what I did; neither had I as yet told *it* to the Jews, nor to the priests, nor to the nobles, nor to the rulers, nor to the rest that did the work.
17 Then said I unto them, Ye see the distress that we *are* in, how Jerusalem *lieth* waste, and the gates thereof are burned with fire: come, and let us build up the wall of Jerusalem, that we be no more a reproach.
18 Then I told them of the hand of my God which was good upon me; as also the king's words that he had spoken unto me. And they said, Let us rise up and build. So they strengthened their hands for *this* good *work.*
19 But when Sanballat the Horonite, and Tobiah the servant, the Ammonite, and Geshem the Arabian, heard *it,* they laughed us to scorn, and

2. Nehemiah's journey to Jerusalem & his preparations to rebuild the city walls: A man who exhorted & challenged others

a. Nehemiah's armed escort & his visit to the governor
b. Nehemiah's first hint of coming opposition: Two officials were very angry that a new governor (5:14) had been sent to rebuild Jerusalem
  1) Sanballat the Horonite
  2) Tobiah the Ammonite
c. Nehemiah's arrival in Jerusalem: He rested 3 days
d. Nehemiah's secret inspection of the walls at night: He needed to examine the situation & lay plans for rebuilding
  1) He took only a few trusted men with him & one horse
  2) He went out through the Valley Gate, past the Serpent well & Dung Gate

  3) He went on to the Fountain Gate & to the King's Pool, where he had to stop following so close to the wall because of the rubble
  4) He turned & rode through the Kidron Valley looking at the wall from a distance

  5) He kept his purpose to himself & conducted his investigation in secret: Was necessary until he could formulate his plans
e. Nehemiah's assembly & motivation of the people to action
  1) He presented the problem facing them: The city & walls were in ruins
  2) He challenged them to action: He appealed for them to join him in rebuilding the walls

  3) He gave his personal testimony: He assured them of God's presence & guidance
  4) He achieved the desired result: The people made a commitment to rebuild

f. Nehemiah's pattern of boldly standing against opponents
  1) The opposition sought to dishearten the people: Mocked & ridiculed the

project as foolish & ac-cused the Jews of rebellion 2) Nehemiah gave a forceful, threefold answer: • The Lord would help	despised us, and said, What *is* this thing that ye do? will ye rebel against the king? 20 Then answered I them, and said unto them, The God	of heaven, he will prosper us; therefore we his servants will arise and build: but ye have no portion, nor right, nor memorial, in Jerusalem.	• They would start rebuild-ing—no matter what • The opponents had no claim in Jerusalem, God's Holy City

DIVISION I

THE REBUILDING OF THE WALLS OF JERUSALEM, 1:1–7:73

B. Nehemiah's Royal Commission and His Preparations to Rebuild Jerusalem: A Man of Boldness, Filled with a Spirit of Exhortation, 2:1-20

(2:1-20) **Introduction**: bold and righteous leaders are needed today. Being just bold is not enough, because uncontrolled boldness can violate the rights of people, dominating and trampling them under foot. And being just righteous is not enough, because without initiative and the courage to follow through with ideas and projects, nothing is accomplished. So, while boldness is needed by leaders, their boldness must be controlled by righteousness. A leader must know right from wrong, and know what is right and know the right thing to do. He must then act decisively, and boldly carry out the righteous act.

In addition to boldness and righteousness, there is a crying need for visionary leaders, leaders who will challenge us with great visions of the future. Most people want an ideal to follow, a cause to which they can commit themselves, a purpose for living, a goal to strive for, a task that is fulfilling, and work that is satisfying. But first comes the vision. Someone somewhere has an idea, sees a need, solves a problem—and thus begins the process. Visionary leaders are desperately needed, leaders who can drive us to better ourselves and our society. The ministry of exhortation, of challenging people to a higher cause than themselves, is one of the greatest needs for which the human heart cries. We all want to be encouraged, pushed to be better and to do better and to achieve more. If the cause is great enough, most of us will sacrifice much, if not all that we have, to achieve the cause. In fact, this is the very demand of Jesus Christ, the challenge He presents to us:

"If any man will come after me, let him deny himself, and take up his cross daily, and follow me. For whosoever will save his life shall lose it: but whosoever will lose his life for my sake, the same shall save it. For what is a man advantaged, if he gained the whole world, and lose himself, or be cast away?" (Lu.9:23-25).

Nehemiah was such a man. He was a true leader, a visionary who was both bold and righteous. He was a leader who exhorted and challenged others to action. Remember that Nehemiah was the cupbearer to King Artaxerxes of Persia. While in the palace at the capital Susa, he had received alarming news from Jerusalem. The exiles who had returned to Jerusalem were facing terrible trouble and suffering, being reproached and disgraced by people all around them. In addition, the city of Jerusalem was in shambles with its walls torn down. Hearing this news had broken Nehemiah's heart, arousing deep concern within him. For many days he had fasted and prayed about the matter. And during these days he had sought the LORD for an opportunity to bring up the subject with the king, to seek his help for the distressed Jews back in Jerusalem. He personally wanted to return to help the people himself, but first, he had to secure permission from the king. However, seeking a long leave of absence from the king could be dangerous. If the request displeased the king, he could imprison Nehemiah and even have him executed. Because of the seriousness of his request, Nehemiah took four months to carefully plan his strategy for approaching Artaxerxes (1:1; 2:1). The suspenseful drama is graphically depicted in this chapter. This is, *Nehemiah's Royal Commission and His Preparations to Rebuild Jerusalem: A Man of Boldness, Filled with a Spirit of Exhortation*, 2:1-20.

1. Nehemiah's royal commission to rebuild Jerusalem: a man who spoke openly and boldly (vv.1-8).
2. Nehemiah's journey to Jerusalem and his preparations to rebuild the city walls: a man who exhorted and challenged others (vv.9-20).

1 (2:1-8) **Boldness, Example of—Trust, in God, Example of—Confidence, in God, Example of—Nehemiah, Trust in God—Nehemiah, Commission, to Rebuild Jerusalem—Jerusalem, Rebuilt, Commissioned by Nehemiah—Artaxerxes, Commission to Nehemiah, to Rebuild Jerusalem**: Nehemiah requested and secured a royal commission from the king to rebuild Jerusalem and its walls. It was now the month of Nisan (March–April), four months since he had received news about the dark, dismal circumstances of the Jews who had returned to Jerusalem (1:1-4). During these four long months Nehemiah was heavy hearted, gripped with concern over their desperate plight. Day by day he had been seeking the LORD for an opportunity to approach the king about helping his people. Nehemiah felt compelled to do all he could to relieve their terrible distress and suffering. At last, he sensed from the LORD that the time had come to safely approach the king. Scripture paints an intriguing picture of Nehemiah's apprehension as he shared his broken heart and request with the king. Yet, despite Nehemiah's fear in approaching the king, note how courageous he was and how well he had prepared to grasp the opportunity:

OUTLINE	SCRIPTURE	SCRIPTURE	OUTLINE
1. Nehemiah's royal commission to rebuild Jerusalem: A man who spoke openly & boldly	And it came to pass in the month Nisan, in the twentieth year of Artaxerxes the king, *that* wine *was* before him:	and I took up the wine, and gave *it* unto the king. Now I had not been *beforetime* sad in his presence.	a. Nehemiah's sad appearance while serving the king 1) The king noticed his sadness & questioned him

OUTLINE	SCRIPTURE	SCRIPTURE	OUTLINE
2) The king struck fear in his heart: Because royal officials were never to show negative emotions—due to the king's wrath b. Nehemiah's respectful but bold reply 1) He showed proper respect in addressing the king 2) He explained his sadness: His home city lay in ruins 3) He stirred the king to ask what he wanted 4) He quickly, silently prayed 5) He requested a royal commission to travel to Judah to rebuild his home city, the city where his family ancestors were buried: Ended up staying 12 years, 5:14	2 Wherefore the king said unto me, Why *is* thy countenance sad, seeing thou *art* not sick? this *is* nothing *else* but sorrow of heart. Then I was very sore afraid, 3 And said unto the king, Let the king live for ever: why should not my countenance be sad, when the city, the place of my fathers' sepulchres, *lieth* waste, and the gates thereof are consumed with fire? 4 Then the king said unto me, For what dost thou make request? So I prayed to the God of heaven. 5 And I said unto the king, If it please the king, and if thy servant have found favour in thy sight, that thou wouldest send me unto Judah, unto the city of my fathers' sepulchres, that I may build it.	6 And the king said unto me, (the queen also sitting by him,) For how long shall thy journey be? and when wilt thou return? So it pleased the king to send me; and I set him a time. 7 Moreover I said unto the king, If it please the king, let letters be given me to the governors beyond the river, that they may convey me over till I come into Judah; 8 And a letter unto Asaph the keeper of the king's forest, that he may give me timber to make beams for the gates of the palace which *appertained* to the house, and for the wall of the city, and for the house that I shall enter into. And the king granted me, according to the good hand of my God upon me.	c. Nehemiah's request granted 1) He was questioned about the time frame by the king with the queen sitting beside him 2) He set the time & the request was granted 3) He requested letters for safe passage & provisions for the journey: Was necessary to present to the governors of West Euphrates because of the large military escort with him, 9 4) He asked also for an official letter to secure building materials from the king's forest d. Nehemiah's strong testimony: His bold request was granted because of God's goodness

a. While serving the king, Nehemiah did a courageous but dangerous thing: he showed a sad countenance, acted downcast and distressed. His behavior was dangerous because the king could have become suspicious of a plot to assassinate him. In most cases a king was sheltered from all the sorrowful experiences and suffering of human life (Est.4:1-2). To appear in the presence of a monarch with any attitude other than a positive, uplifting one was extremely hazardous. Thus in light of this, Nehemiah was risking his life by appearing unhappy and distraught before the king.

However, on this particular day, the LORD had obviously prepared the way for Nehemiah. When the king noticed his cupbearer's distressed countenance, his thoughts did not turn suspicious. Rather, a sympathetic spirit arose, for the king asked Nehemiah why he was so sad when he was not ill.

Just as Nehemiah hoped, the door was wide open for him to make his request of the king. But as Scripture says, intense fear gripped Nehemiah's heart. He knew the king had stopped the building of Jerusalem years before. The king had feared a Jewish rebellion if they were allowed to rebuild their city and nation (Ezr.4:6-24, esp.vv.18-24). Now, here was Nehemiah risking his life, ready to ask the king to reverse his decision—a very dangerous thing to do. Nevertheless, during Nehemiah's four months of intense prayer and planning, he had thought through the most wise approach he could make to the king.

b. With his heart pounding rapidly, Nehemiah respectfully but anxiously approached the king with the common form of address: "May the king live forever!" He then wisely explained his sadness with a question that would hopefully arouse compassion within the king: How could he keep from being sad when his home city lay in ruins and its gates burned with fire, the very city where his ancestors were buried? Note how Nehemiah showed a deep respect for his ancestors and a broken heart over the plight of his home city. Mentioning these two facts was intended to arouse the king's sympathy for his cupbearer, for ancestral grave sights held great meaning for Eastern cultures.

As hoped, the king's interest and concern for Nehemiah was stirred, and he asked how he could help (v.4). Before answering, Nehemiah offered up a quick prayer. He asked the LORD to give wisdom and to move the king's heart to grant his request.

Wording his petition in the most humble way he could, Nehemiah acknowledged that it could be granted only by the king himself. Additionally, the request should be granted only if it pleased the king and only if Nehemiah, the king's servant, had found favor in his sight. Then, after acknowledging the supreme authority of the king, Nehemiah boldly made his petition. And it was bold! He asked for a royal commission to travel to Judah to rebuild his home city. This meant that the king would lose the services of his trusted official. No doubt, the appeal shocked the king, for the thought that he would be losing his trusted servant was bound to cross the king's mind. A suspenseful silence hung in the air for a few seconds, perhaps for a minute. Then the king gave his answer.

c. Nehemiah's petition was granted (vv.6-8). With the queen sitting by his side, the king questioned Nehemiah about how long he would be gone and when he would return. Undoubtedly after some discussion, a time was agreed upon and the request was granted (v.6). The time frame is not spelled out by Scripture; however, Nehemiah ended up staying in Jerusalem for 12 years (5:14).

Having planned carefully, Nehemiah knew exactly what he needed for the building project. Thus he made several additional appeals to the king (vv.7-8). He asked for letters for safe passage and provisions for his journey. The letters were necessary to present to the governors who ruled over the Persian territory west of the Euphrates River. Nehemiah needed the cooperation of these governors in order to be given safe passage through their territory. Also, he would have a large military escort accompanying him, an escort that could be interpreted as a threat to the local governors. Nehemiah even asked for an official letter to secure building materials from the king's forest (v.8). He needed timber for three projects: the building of the gates, the city walls, and his own personal residence.

d. Special attention should be paid to Nehemiah's strong testimony (v.8). His bold request was granted by the king because of God Himself. The LORD's gracious hand was upon Nehemiah, so the LORD stirred the heart of the king to grant Nehemiah's request.

Thought 1. Nehemiah was a man with a fearless spirit and a strong trust in the LORD. He *boldly* went before the king because he trusted the LORD to guide and help him. And because of his trust, the LORD gave him this spirit of strong determination. So it is with us. When we trust the LORD, He gives us a spirit of courage and stamina to carry out our tasks. Scripture teaches us two wonderful facts about boldness.

(1) We can boldly approach God for help in times of need. However, we can approach Him only through Christ. It is Christ alone who gives us access into God's presence. But when we come to Christ and approach God through Him, Christ gives us the right to be bold before God. We can then boldly request that God meet our needs. And He wonderfully promises to hear us.

> "In whom we have boldness and access with confidence by the faith of him" (Ep.3:12).
> "For we have not an high priest which cannot be touched with the feeling of our infirmities; but was in all points tempted like as *we are, yet* without sin. Let us therefore come boldly unto the throne of grace, that we may obtain mercy, and find grace to help in time of need" (He.4:15-16).
> "Having therefore, brethren, boldness to enter into the holiest by the blood of Jesus, By a new and living way, which he hath consecrated for us, through the veil, that is to say, his flesh; And *having* an high priest over the house of God; Let us draw near with a true heart in full assurance of faith, having our hearts sprinkled from an evil conscience, and our bodies washed with pure water" (He.10:19-22).
> "Herein is our love made perfect, that we may have boldness in the day of judgment: because as he is, so are we in this world" (1 Jn.4:17).

(2) If we will be bold in our work for the LORD, He will guide, deliver, and protect us. Through Him we will have the power to be strong, courageous, and fearless in the face of difficult or trying situations.

> "Only let your conversation [conduct, behavior] be as it becometh the gospel of Christ: that whether I come and see you, or else be absent, I may hear of your affairs, that ye stand fast in one spirit, with one mind striving together for the faith of the gospel; And in nothing terrified by your adversaries: which is to them an evident token of perdition, but to you of salvation, and that of God" (Ph.1:27-28).
> "Be strong and of a good courage, fear not, nor be afraid of them: for the LORD thy God, he *it is* that doth go with thee; he will not fail thee, nor forsake thee" (De.31:6).
> "The LORD *is* my light and my salvation; whom shall I fear? the LORD *is* the strength of my life; of whom shall I be afraid? When the wicked, *even* mine enemies and my foes, came upon me to eat up my flesh, they stumbled and fell. Though an host should encamp against me, my heart shall not fear: though war should rise against me, in this *will I be* confident" (Ps.27:1-3).
> "I will say of the LORD, *He is* my refuge and my fortress: my God; in him will I trust. Surely he shall deliver thee from the snare of the fowler, *and* from the noisome pestilence. He shall cover thee with his feathers, and under his wings shalt thou trust: his truth *shall be thy* shield and buckler. Thou shalt not be afraid for the terror by night; *nor* for the arrow *that* flieth by day; *Nor* for the pestilence *that* walketh in darkness; *nor* for the destruction *that* wasteth at noonday" (Ps.91:2-6).
> "Only be thou strong and very courageous, that thou mayest observe to do according to all the law, which Moses my servant commanded thee: turn not from it *to* the right hand or *to* the left, that thou mayest prosper whithersoever thou goest" (Jos.1:7).
> "Behold, God *is* my salvation; I will trust, and not be afraid: for the LORD JEHOVAH *is* my strength and *my* song; he also is become my salvation" (Is.12:2).

2 (2:9-20) **Exhortation, Duty—Challenge, Duty—Stirring, Duty—Arousal, Duty—Courage, Duty—Admonish, Duty—Persuade, Duty—Motivate, Duty—Inspire, Duty—Spur, Duty—Stimulate, Duty—Nehemiah, Preparations to Rebuild Jerusalem—Jerusalem, Rebuilding of, Preparations of**: Nehemiah's journey to Jerusalem and all his preparations were for the purpose of rebuilding the city and its walls. The journey from the capital Susa to Jerusalem would have taken about two to three months. Nothing whatsoever about the journey is recorded by Scripture. However, after Nehemiah arrived in Jerusalem, events began to happen rather quickly, events that suggested the unfolding of a suspenseful drama about to happen. Scripture describes the gripping events:

OUTLINE	SCRIPTURE	SCRIPTURE	OUTLINE
2. Nehemiah's journey to Jerusalem & his preparations to rebuild the city walls: A man who exhorted & challenged others a. Nehemiah's armed escort & his visit to the governor b. Nehemiah's first hint of coming opposition: Two of-	9 Then I came to the governors beyond the river, and gave them the king's letters. Now the king had sent captains of the army and horsemen with me. 10 When Sanballat the Horonite, and Tobiah the ser-	vant, the Ammonite, heard *of it,* it grieved them exceedingly that there was come a man to seek the welfare of the children of Israel. 11 So I came to Jerusalem, and was there three days. 12 And I arose in the night, I	ficials were very angry that a new governor (5:14) had been sent to rebuild Jerusalem 1) Sanballat the Horonite 2) Tobiah the Ammonite c. Nehemiah's arrival in Jerusalem: He rested 3 days d. Nehemiah's secret inspection

OUTLINE	SCRIPTURE	SCRIPTURE	OUTLINE
of the walls at night: He needed to examine the situation & lay plans for re-building 1) He took only a few trust-ed men with him & one horse 2) He went out through the Valley Gate, past the Serpent well & Dung Gate 3) He went on to the Foun-tain Gate & to the King's Pool, where he had to stop following so close to the wall because of the rubble 4) He turned & rode through the Kidron Valley look-ing at the wall from a dis-tance 5) He kept his purpose to himself & conducted his investigation in secret: Was necessary until he could formulate his plans e. Nehemiah's assembly & mo-tivation of the people to action	and some few men with me; neither told I *any* man what my God had put in my heart to do at Jerusalem: neither *was there any* beast with me, save the beast that I rode up-on. 13 And I went out by night by the gate of the valley, even before the dragon well, and to the dung port, and viewed the walls of Jerusalem, which were broken down, and the gates thereof were consumed with fire. 14 Then I went on to the gate of the fountain, and to the king's pool: but *there was* no place for the beast *that was* under me to pass. 15 Then went I up in the night by the brook, and viewed the wall, and turned back, and entered by the gate of the valley, and *so* returned. 16 And the rulers knew not whither I went, or what I did; neither had I as yet told *it* to the Jews, nor to the priests, nor to the nobles, nor to the rulers, nor to the rest that did the work.	17 Then said I unto them, Ye see the distress that we *are* in, how Jerusalem *lieth* waste, and the gates thereof are burned with fire: come, and let us build up the wall of Je-rusalem, that we be no more a reproach. 18 Then I told them of the hand of my God which was good upon me; as also the king's words that he had spo-ken unto me. And they said, Let us rise up and build. So they strengthened their hands for *this* good *work*. 19 But when Sanballat the Horonite, and Tobiah the servant, the Ammonite, and Geshem the Arabian, heard *it,* they laughed us to scorn, and despised us, and said, What *is* this thing that ye do? will ye rebel against the king? 20 Then answered I them, and said unto them, The God of heaven, he will pros-per us; therefore we his ser-vants will arise and build: but ye have no portion, nor right, nor memorial, in Jeru-salem.	1) He presented the problem facing them: The city & walls were in ruins 2) He challenged them to ac-tion: He appealed for them to join him in re-building the walls 3) He gave his personal tes-timony: He assured them of God's presence & guidance 4) He achieved the desired result: The people made a commitment to rebuild f. Nehemiah's pattern of boldly standing against opponents 1) The opposition sought to dishearten the people: Mocked & ridiculed the project as foolish & ac-cused the Jews of rebel-lion 2) The threefold answer of Nehemiah was forceful: • The LORD would help • They would start rebuild-ing—no matter what • The opponents had no claim in Jerusalem, God's Holy City

a. After crossing the Euphrates River, Nehemiah went at once to the governor of the province to present his letter of authority from the king. This was necessary to gain safe passage through the territory, in particular since Nehemiah had a large armed escort of cavalry accompanying him (v.9). Without the king's authority, the armed regiment could have aroused suspicion of a revolt. But with the king's authority and cavalry regiment, the governor and officials clearly knew that Nehemiah had the king's support behind him and his building efforts. Yet not everyone was willing to offer their support.

b. Almost immediately Nehemiah got his first hint of coming opposition (v.10). Another Scripture tells us that Nehemiah had actually been appointed as the new governor of Jerusalem (5:14). Two officials in particular, Sanballat and Tobiah, were very angry that a new governor had been sent to rebuild Jerusalem. Sanballat was a Horonite, which means that he was from Beth Horan, a town about 12 to 18 miles from Jerusalem. Although Scripture does not say that he was the governor of Samaria, archeology has discovered an ancient letter that actually refers to him as the governor of that district (The Elephantine Papryus or letter). [1]

Apparently Tobiah the Ammonite was either the governor of Ammon or else a high official who served under San-ballat. Tobiah was married to the daughter of Shecaniah, one of Nehemiah's key workers (3:29; 6:18). And his son Jeho-hanan married the daughter of Meshullam, one of the supervisors of the building project (3:4, 30; 6:18). Thus through marriage, Tobiah had both family and friends working in the crews employed by Nehemiah to rebuild the city. In addi-tion to this fact, Tobiah was closely related to the High Priest Eliashib (13:4-7). Of course, both of these officials, San-ballat and Tobiah, served under the authority of King Artaxerxes. In view of this, they had to be very careful in opposing or plotting against Nehemiah, for their very livelihood or political positions were dependent upon the favor of the king. But for now, the point to note is their disturbance over Nehemiah's mission to rebuild Jerusalem and its walls. Obviously, they feared Nehemiah politically, feared they would lose some of their power and authority and influence over the peo-ple. Thus Nehemiah was a threat to them.

c. On arriving in Jerusalem, Nehemiah rested for three days. The trip had been exhausting, so he did just what many of us would do: he took care of his body and gave it the necessary rest (Mk.6:31). In all probability, Nehemiah used this time for prayer, planning, and getting acquainted with some of the people in the city.

d. At the end of the three days' rest, Nehemiah secretly inspected the walls at night (vv.12-16). As a wise planner and builder, he knew the need for surveying, inspecting, and evaluating the awesome task that lay before him. This he needed to do before he revealed his plans and attempted to motivate the people to join him in the awesome task ahead. Taking only a few trusted men and one horse, he crept out through the Valley Gate, past the Serpent or Jackal Well and the Dung Gate (vv.12-13). Nehemiah then went on to the Fountain Gate and to the King's Pool, where he had to stop following the wall because of the huge mound of rubble from Jerusalem's earlier destruction (v.14). He then turned and rode through the Kidron Valley where he could look up at the wall from a distance (v.15). At some point, he was either unable to

---

1 Mervin Breneman. *Ezra, Nehemiah, Esther*, p.178.

continue his inspection due to so much rubble or, feeling that he had seen enough, made the decision to return. Note the emphasis upon the secrecy of Nehemiah's inspection: he conducted his investigation without the knowledge of any of the leadership. This was necessary until he could formulate the details of his plans (v.16).

e. Once Nehemiah completed his plans, he assembled and motivated the people to action (v.17). The assembled group included all the Jews of Jerusalem and the surrounding territory, which would have included the common people, the landowners or farmers, the business owners, the religious and political leaders—all who would be contributing to the work of rebuilding the city and its walls.

In addressing the people, Nehemiah first presented the problem they faced. Jerusalem and its walls lay in ruins (v.17). Although he had been with them for just a few days, note how he identified with them. It was not the trouble the people were in, but rather the trouble *"We are in."* As long as the walls remained unbuilt, the people were in serious trouble, being fully exposed and left without any protection from marauders or enemies.

Second, Nehemiah challenged the people to action, to join him in rebuilding the walls in the great city of God (v.17). This was not a new vision for the people. The very first exiles had also returned with the great hope of rebuilding their temple and homeland. But due to opposition through the years, they had backed off the project and become lethargic and complacent. They had resigned themselves to the dark, dismal circumstances of their lives and to the hardships they were to suffering. But at last, here was a *man of God,* Nehemiah, who challenged the people to arise and recommit themselves anew to rebuilding the city.

Third, Nehemiah closed the challenge by giving his personal testimony (v.18). He shared how God's gracious hand had been upon him and guided him in securing the very authority of the king himself. Through his personal testimony, the people could rest assured that God would be present with them in the awesome task of rebuilding the walls and city (v.18).

Obviously, the Spirit of God was working in the hearts of the people, for they responded to Nehemiah's challenge. They made a strong commitment to start rebuilding immediately (v.18). And they began the "good work."

f. But immediately after launching the work, Nehemiah was forced to take a bold stand against those who opposed the project (vv.19-20). The opposition had quickly reared its ugly head up, seeking to dishearten the people. Sanballat, Tobiah, and a third opponent known as Geshem the Arab began to mock the project as foolish. Moreover, they actually accused the Jews of rebelling against the king. Their opposition will be discussed in more detail later (Chs.4–7), but in the present passage they begin their destructive path through ridicule, mockery, and false accusations. Because the walls and city had been so completely destroyed, any attempt to rebuild must have seemed foolish. Making the most of this fact, these three key adversaries aroused their followers to mockingly laugh and scorn the workers as they tackled such an unrealistic project. They called the Jews fools for attempting to rebuild. Also, by planting the charge of rebellion against the workers, these opponents hoped to instill fear of the king's retaliation within the Jews.

Just how Nehemiah responded to this enemy's first attack was very important. If he miscued, the workers could have easily become discouraged. Thankfully, Nehemiah was walking faithfully with the LORD. Thus the LORD clearly strengthened him and gave him just the right answer for these enemies. He withstood their attack and dealt forcefully with them. His response was threefold:

⇒ The LORD would help the builders, give them success and prosper their efforts.

⇒ The workers were totally committed to the project: they would rebuild the walls and the city—no matter what.

⇒ The opponents had no claim—no share, no authority, no rights—in Jerusalem (God's Holy City, the promised land of God). Up until this time, while the city was devastated and lay in ruins, they may have exercised some authority over the city and the unprotected exiles who had returned. But no longer. Their authority was now ended. Legally, they had no claim to any part of Jerusalem, and they had no authority over its citizens. Politically, Nehemiah had been appointed governor by King Artaxerxes himself. Spiritually and historically, the city had been given by God to the Jews who followed and obeyed the LORD.

Thought 1. Nehemiah was a man of exhortation, a man who challenged others to follow the LORD and to complete their tasks. Likewise, as true believers in the LORD, we must exhort and challenge others to follow the LORD, to keep His commandments and live righteous lives, fulfilling their God-given tasks.

These are days of complacency, days when many are lethargic, self-satisfied, and unconcerned. Far too many of us have become spiritually lazy, apathetic, disinterested, and passive. Some of us have even become drowsy and sluggish, paying little attention to the Word of God, prayer, and worship. We are living self-centered lives, doing what we want when we want. We disobey God's commandments, never giving a second thought to the righteousness He demands. We are living sinful, wicked, and shameful lives, breaking one commandment after another. The fact that we must live for Jesus Christ, faithfully worshipping Him and bearing strong testimony for Him, seldom if ever crosses our minds.

If there has ever been a day when the ministry of exhortation and challenging people to follow Christ is needed, it is today. Listen to what God's Holy Word says about the need for us to exhort others:

"Go ye therefore, and teach all nations, baptizing them in the name of the Father, and of the Son, and of the Holy Ghost: Teaching them to observe all things whatsoever I have commanded you: and, lo, I am with you alway, *even* unto the end of the world. Amen" (Mt.28:19-20).

"And he said unto them, Go ye into all the world, and preach the gospel to every creature" (Mk.16:15).

"Till I come, give attendance to reading, to exhortation, to doctrine" (1 Ti.4:13).

"And the things that thou hast heard of me among many witnesses, the same commit thou to faithful men, who shall be able to teach others also" (2 Ti.2:2).

"Preach the word; be instant in season, out of season; reprove, rebuke, exhort with all longsuffering and doctrine" (2 Ti.4:2).

"For a bishop [minister] must be blameless, as the steward of God; not selfwilled, not soon angry, not given to wine, no striker, not given to filthy lucre; But a lover of hospitality, a lover of good men, sober, just, holy, temperate; Holding fast the faithful word as he hath been taught, that he may be able by sound doctrine both to exhort and to convince the gainsayers" (Tit.1:7-9).

"These things speak, and exhort, and rebuke with all authority. Let no man despise thee" (Tit.2:15).

"Take heed, brethren, lest there be in any of you an evil heart of unbelief, in departing from the living God. But exhort one another daily, while it is called To day; lest any of you be hardened through the deceitfulness of sin" (He.3:12-13).

"Let us hold fast the profession of *our* faith without wavering; (for he is faithful that promised;) And let us consider one another to provoke unto love and to good works: Not forsaking the assembling of ourselves together, as the manner of some *is;* but exhorting *one another:* and so much the more, as ye see the day approaching. For if we sin wilfully after that we have received the knowledge of the truth, there remaineth no more sacrifice for sins, But a certain fearful looking for of judgment and fiery indignation, which shall devour the adversaries" (He.10:23-27).

CHAPTER 3

C. Nehemiah's Rebuilding of the Wall of Jerusalem: Three Pictures of Diligent & Zealous Laborers, 3:1-32

1. The workers on the north wall & its gates: Some laborers worked together in a spirit of unity, but others refused to work
a. The Sheep Gate
   1) The priests themselves worked: Built & dedicated this gate & a section of the wall
   2) The men of Jericho built the adjoining section & Zaccur next to them: Pictured cooperation, unity
b. The Fish Gate
   1) The family of Hassenaah built this gate, one of the main entrances, 2 Chr.33:14
   2) Several families who labored cooperatively built the adjoining three sections
      • Meremoth built two sections, 4, 21
      • Meshullam built two sections, 4, 30
      • Zadok built one section
   3) The leaders or nobles (aristocrats) of Tekoa refused to work, but others cooperated & built two sections, 5, 27
c. The Old City (Jeshanah) Gate
   1) This gate was built by the families of two men

   2) The next section was built by men from Gibeon & Mizpah, cities under the authority of the governor of the Trans-Euphrates district, see 19
   3) The next two sections were rebuilt by two business leaders: They restored the wall as far as the Broad Wall
      • Uzziel, a goldsmith
      • Hananiah, a manufacturer of perfume
   4) The next section was built by one of the two rulers of Jerusalem, Rephaiah
   5) The adjoining two sections were built by men whose

Then Eliashib the high priest rose up with his brethren the priests, and they builded the sheep gate; they sanctified it, and set up the doors of it; even unto the tower of Meah they sanctified it, unto the tower of Hananeel.
2 And next unto him builded the men of Jericho. And next to them builded Zaccur the son of Imri.
3 But the fish gate did the sons of Hassenaah build, who *also* laid the beams thereof, and set up the doors thereof, the locks thereof, and the bars thereof.
4 And next unto them repaired Meremoth the son of Urijah, the son of Koz. And next unto them repaired Meshullam the son of Berechiah, the son of Meshezabeel. And next unto them repaired Zadok the son of Baana.
5 And next unto them the Tekoites repaired; but their nobles put not their necks to the work of their Lord.
6 Moreover the old gate repaired Jehoiada the son of Paseah, and Meshullam the son of Besodeiah; they laid the beams thereof, and set up the doors thereof, and the locks thereof, and the bars thereof.
7 And next unto them repaired Melatiah the Gibeonite, and Jadon the Meronothite, the men of Gibeon, and of Mizpah, unto the throne of the governor on this side the river.
8 Next unto him repaired Uzziel the son of Harhaiah, of the goldsmiths. Next unto him also repaired Hananiah the son of *one of* the apothecaries, and they fortified Jerusalem unto the broad wall.
9 And next unto them repaired Rephaiah the son of Hur, the ruler of the half part of Jerusalem.
10 And next unto them repaired Jedaiah the son of Ha-

rumaph, even over against his house. And next unto him repaired Hattush the son of Hashabniah.
11 Malchijah the son of Harim, and Hashub the son of Pahath-moab, repaired the other piece, and the tower of the furnaces.
12 And next unto him repaired Shallum the son of Halohesh, the ruler of the half part of Jerusalem, he and his daughters.
13 The valley gate repaired Hanun, and the inhabitants of Zanoah; they built it, and set up the doors thereof, the locks thereof, and the bars thereof, and a thousand cubits on the wall unto the dung gate.
14 But the dung gate repaired Malchiah the son of Rechab, the ruler of part of Beth-haccerem; he build it, and set up the doors thereof, the locks thereof, and the bars thereof.
15 But the gate of the fountain repaired Shallun the son of Col-hozeh, the ruler of part of Mizpah; he built it, and covered it, and set up the doors thereof, the locks thereof, and the bars thereof, and the wall of the pool of Siloah by the king's garden, and unto the stairs that go down from the city of David.
16 After him repaired Nehemiah the son of Azbuk, the ruler of the half part of Bethzur, unto *the place* over against the sepulchres of David, and to the pool that was made, and unto the house of the mighty.
17 After him repaired the Levites, Rehum the son of Bani. Next unto him repaired Hashabiah, the ruler of the half part of Keilah, in his part.
18 After him repaired their brethren, Bavai the son of Henadad, the ruler of the half part of Keilah.
19 And next to him repaired Ezer the son of Jeshua, the ruler of Mizpah, another piece over against the going up to the armoury at the turning *of the wall.*
20 After him Baruch the son of Zabbai earnestly repaired the other piece, from the turning *of the wall* unto the door of the house of Eliashib

houses sat next to the wall: Jedaiah & Hattush, 23, 28-30

   6) The next section & a tower—the Tower of the Ovens—were built by two men: Malkijah & Hasshub

   7) The other ruler of Jerusalem, Shallum—with the help of his daughters—built the next section

2. The workers on the west wall: Some humbled themselves & took on the undesirable jobs
a. The Valley Gate: This gate & 500 yards of the wall were rebuilt by Hanun & the residents of Zanoah

b. The Dung or Refuse Gate: This undesirable building task was humbly taken by a leader, the district ruler Recab

3. The workers on the east wall: Some were hard & diligent workers filled with zeal
a. The Fountain Gate
   1) The gate & a section of the wall of the Pool of Siloam was built by Shallun

   2) The next section was built by a ruler also named Nehemiah: Ran to a point opposite the royal cemetery, as far as the water reservoir & the House of the Heroes
   3) The next section was built by the Levites
   4) The next two sections were built by the two district rulers of Keilah
      • Hashabiah
      • Bavai or Binnui
   5) The next section was built by the ruler of Mizpah: Began opposite the Armory & ran to the corner, the angle or turning point of the wall

   6) The next section was rebuilt by Baruch, who was known for his zeal & diligence: Ran up to the door of the High Priest's house

7) The section that ran from the High Priest's door to the end of his house was rebuilt by Meremoth, who built two sections, see v.4

8) The next section was built by the priests from the surrounding region, see v.1

9) The next three sections were repaired by three men whose houses sat next to the wall: Benjamin, Hasshub, & Azariah

10) The section from Azariah's house to the turning point or corner was built by Binnui

11) The next section was built by Uzai: Was opposite the corner & the tower that projected out from the king's palace (near the court of the guard)

b. The Water Gate
1) The temple servants under the supervision of Parosh repaired the wall opposite the Water Gate

the high priest.

21 After him repaired Meremoth the son of Urijah the son of Koz another piece, from the door of the house of Eliashib even to the end of the house of Eliashib.

22 And after him repaired the priests, the men of the plain.

23 After him repaired Benjamin and Hashub over against their house. After him repaired Azariah the son of Maaseiah the son of Ananiah by his house.

24 After him repaired Binnui the son of Henadad another piece, from the house of Azariah unto the turning *of the wall,* even unto the corner.

25 Palal the son of Uzai, over against the turning *of the wall,* and the tower which lieth out from the king's high house, that *was* by the court of the prison. After him Pedaiah the son of Parosh.

26 Moreover the Nethinims dwelt in Ophel, unto *the place* over against the water gate toward the east, and the tower that lieth out.

27 After them the Tekoites repaired another piece, over against the great tower that lieth out, even unto the wall of Ophel.

28 From above the horse gate repaired the priests, every one over against his house.

29 After them repaired Zadok the son of Immer over against his house. After him repaired also Shemaiah the son of Shechaniah, the keeper of the east gate.

30 After him repaired Hananiah the son of Shelemiah, and Hanun the sixth son of Zalaph, another piece. After him repaired Meshullam the son of Berechiah over against his chamber.

31 After him repaired Malchiah the goldsmith's son unto the place of the Nethinims, and of the merchants, over against the gate Miphkad, and to the going up of the corner.

32 And between the going up of the corner unto the sheep gate repaired the goldsmiths and the merchants.

2) The residents of Jekoa rebuilt their second section: From the Great Projecting Tower to the Wall of Ophel, see v.5

c. The Horse Gate
1) The priests made repairs opposite their own houses
2) Zadok repaired the adjoining section opposite his house

d. The East Gate
1) The guard of this gate repaired the next section
2) Three other diligent workers built the next three sections
 • Hananiah
 • Hanun
 • Meshullam

e. The Inspection Gate
1) The section opposite this gate was rebuilt by a goldsmith: Ran from the housing for the temple servants & merchants to the Upper Room above the corner
2) The last section of the wall from the corner to the Sheep Gate was rebuilt by the other goldsmiths & merchants, see v.1

DIVISION I

THE REBUILDING OF THE WALLS OF JERUSALEM, 1:1–7:73

C. Nehemiah's Rebuilding of the Wall of Jerusalem: Three Pictures of Workers, Laborers, 3:1-32

(3:1-32) **Introduction**: one of the most honorable endeavors in all the world is that of work, the privilege of using our God given abilities, talents, and resources for a worthwhile cause or project. In fact, our very nature craves meaning, significance, and purpose in life. Thus if we are not actively involved in a meaningful task, project, or employment, we sense a lack of purpose and fulfillment. If we sit around doing nothing, working halfheartedly, or engaging in meaningless or selfish activity most of the time, there is always a sense of emptiness and purposelessness.

On the other hand, if we work hard at our jobs and are diligent in all the tasks we undertake, we are filled with a sense of purpose and fulfillment. This is our very nature, the way God has made us. Therefore, to experience purpose and fulfillment in life, we must strive to work hard and be diligent in everything that we do, seeking to fill our lives with meaningful activities and tasks.

When Nehemiah undertook the task of rebuilding the wall of Jerusalem, he needed above all else workers who would be diligent and zealously committed to the building project. A description of these workers is given in the present Scripture. They stand before us as dynamic examples of how we should work. This is, *Nehemiah's Rebuilding of the Wall of Jerusalem: Three Pictures of Diligent and Zealous Laborers*, 3:1-32.

1. The workers on the north wall and its gates: some laborers worked together in a spirit of unity, but others refused to work (vv.1-12).
2. The workers on the west wall: some humbled themselves and took on the undesirable jobs (vv.13-14).
3. The workers on the east wall: some were hard and diligent workers filled with zeal (vv.15-32).

DEEPER STUDY # 1

(3:1-32) **Protection, Picture of—Security, Picture of**: due to the length of this Deeper Study, it is being placed at the end of this commentary discussion after major point three.

DEEPER STUDY # 2

(3:1-32) **Gates, of Jerusalem**: due to the length of this Deeper Study, it is being placed after DEEPER STUDY #1 at the end of this commentary.

1 (3:1-12) **Workers, Duty—Employees, Duty—Laborers, Duty—Cooperation, Duty—Unity, Duty—Pride, Example of—Sin, Listed, Refusing to Work and Cooperate—Laborers, Sins of, Refusing to Work**: first, the workers on the north wall and its gates are discussed. Some of these laborers are dynamic examples of working together in a spirit of unity. But, sadly, others were uncooperative, refusing to work. Note how both the cooperative and uncooperative spirits are emphasized in this point:

OUTLINE	SCRIPTURE	SCRIPTURE	OUTLINE
1. The workers on the north wall & its gates: Some laborers worked together in a spirit of unity, but others refused to work	Then Eliashib the high priest rose up with his brethren the priests, and they builded the sheep gate; they sanctified it, and set up the doors of it; even unto the tower of Meah they sanctified it, unto the tower of Hananeel.	the doors thereof, and the locks thereof, and the bars thereof.	
a. The Sheep Gate		7 And next unto them repaired Melatiah the Gibeonite, and Jadon the Meronothite, the men of Gibeon, and of Mizpah, unto the throne of the governor on this side the river.	2) The next section was built by men from Gibeon & Mizpah, cities under the authority of the governor of the Trans-Euphrates district, see 19
1) The priests themselves worked: Built & dedicated this gate & a section of the wall			
2) The men of Jericho built the adjoining section & Zaccur next to them: Pictured cooperation, unity	2 And next unto him builded the men of Jericho. And next to them builded Zaccur the son of Imri.	8 Next unto him repaired Uzziel the son of Harhaiah, of the goldsmiths. Next unto him also repaired Hananiah the son of *one of* the apothecaries, and they fortified Jerusalem unto the broad wall.	3) The next two sections were rebuilt by two business leaders: They restored the wall as far as the Broad Wall
b. The Fish Gate			• Uzziel, a goldsmith
1) The family of Hassenaah built this gate, one of the main entrances, 2 Chr.33:14	3 But the fish gate did the sons of Hassenaah build, who *also* laid the beams thereof, and set up the doors thereof, the locks thereof, and the bars thereof.	9 And next unto them repaired Rephaiah the son of Hur, the ruler of the half part of Jerusalem.	• Hananiah, a manufacturer of perfume
2) Several families who labored cooperatively built the adjoining three sections	4 And next unto them repaired Meremoth the son of Urijah, the son of Koz. And next unto them repaired Meshullam the son of Berechiah, the son of Meshezabeel. And next unto them repaired Zadok the son of Baana.	10 And next unto them repaired Jedaiah the son of Harumaph, even over against his house. And next unto him repaired Hattush the son of Hashabniah.	4) The next section was built by one of the two rulers of Jerusalem, Rephaiah, see 12
• Meremoth built two sections, 4, 21			5) The adjoining two sections were built by men whose houses sat next to the wall: Jedaiah & Hattush, 23, 28-30
• Meshullam built two sections, 4, 30			
• Zadok built one section		11 Malchijah the son of Harim, and Hashub the son of Pahath-moab, repaired the other piece, and the tower of the furnaces.	6) The next section & a tower—the Tower of the Ovens—were built by two men: Malkijah & Hasshub
3) The leaders or nobles (aristocrats) of Tekoa refused to work, but others cooperated & built two sections, 5, 27	5 And next unto them the Tekoites repaired; but their nobles put not their necks to the work of their Lord.		
c. The Old City (Jeshanah) Gate	6 Moreover the old gate repaired Jehoiada the son of Paseah, and Meshullam the son of Besodeiah; they laid the beams thereof, and set up	12 And next unto him repaired Shallum the son of Halohesh, the ruler of the half part of Jerusalem, he and his daughters.	7) The other ruler of Jerusalem, Shallum—with the help of his daughters—built the next section
1) This gate was built by the families of two men			

a. Significantly, the Sheep Gate as well as a section of the wall were built by the priests (vv.1-2). The priests worked on the construction project just as much as the lay workers. Even the High Priest himself put his hands to work instead of merely supervising the other priests. The adjoining section of wall was built by men from Jericho and the section next to them by a man named Zaccur. The picture is that of cooperation, a unified effort by both clergy and laymen. Everyone, regardless of position or authority, was working together to rebuild the city and its wall.

The Sheep Gate was on the north wall, the only section that had no natural barrier for defense such as a hill. As a result, two lookout or defensive towers were built along the north wall, the Tower of the Hundred and the Tower of Hananel.

The Sheep Gate was close to the temple; thus it was the gate through which animals were brought to be sacrificed at the temple. No doubt it was named the Sheep Gate because of the continual flow of animals that were herded through its entrance.

b. The Fish Gate, one of the main entrances, was built by the family of Hassenaah (vv.3-5; 2 Chr.33:14). Three adjoining sections were built by several families, all cooperating together to accomplish the enormous project. Note that two of the three families actually built two sections each, the families of Meremoth (vv.4, 21) and Meshullam (vv.4, 30). Perhaps these families were larger and able to provide more workers. Or possibly the sections of wall assigned to them were shorter, easier to reconstruct or did not involve removing as much debris. Whatever the case, these families were so committed to the building project that they each undertook two sections of the wall. The family of Zadok built one section of the wall.

Note the word "repaired" (chazaq or hazaq). It means to be strengthened, made strong and firm to withstand attacks. The workers were not laboring halfheartedly, building a flimsy wall. Rather, they were totally committed to doing their best, to building the strongest wall they could.

Unfortunately, not everyone was committed to the project. Some did not cooperate, even refused to take part in the rebuilding project. This is seen in the next section that was built by the people of Tekoa. Their leaders and nobles refused to help. They would not put their shoulders to the work. Tekoa was a small town about 11 miles just south of Jerusalem, and was the hometown of Amos (Am.1:1). The city was close to territory controlled by the Arab Geshem, an opponent of Nehemiah's and the Jewish returnees. Apparently the leaders of Tekoa either feared Nehemiah or felt like they would lose some of their authority if he became successful in rebuilding the Jewish settlements. Or perhaps the Tekoa leaders and nobles were just too proud to do the work of a common laborer. Whatever the case, the common people and citizens of Tekoa cooperated fully, committing themselves totally to the building project. Note that they built two sections of the wall (vv.5, 27).

The Fish Gate was also protected by the two towers that were strategically placed to defend the north wall. It was probably named the Fish Gate because it was the site where the commercial marketing of fish took place or else because the city's major fish market was nearby.

c. In building the Old Gate and the sections of wall adjoining it, two great truths are seen: first, how God uses all kinds of people to get a task done and, second, how important a unified, cooperative spirit is. Note these facts:

    1) The Old Gate was built by the families of two men: Joiada and Meshullam (v.6). The gate was also known as the Jeshanah Gate, which referred to the city to which the road led, the city that lay on the border between Judah and Samaria (2 Chr.13:19). It was also known as the Mishneh Gate, which referred to the second district of Jerusalem lying on the western hill (2 K.22:14; Zep.1:10).[1]

    2) People from Gibeon and Mizpah also helped in the project, building the next section (v.7). Their cooperation and commitment to the project is significant, for these two cities were under the authority of the governor of Trans-Euphrates. This means that the governor himself supported the project.

    3) Business leaders and tradesmen also supported the project, building the next section (v.8). One of the business leaders was a goldsmith named Uzziel, and the other was a perfume maker named Hananiah. These two business leaders undertook the construction as far as the Broad Wall.

    4) Even the political leaders became involved in the building project. The chief ruler of a half-district of Jerusalem repaired the section adjoining the work of the two businessmen (v.12).

    5) People who had houses sitting next to the wall also joined in the project (vv.10, 23, 28-30). This suggests the importance of neighbors cooperating together in looking out for and taking care of their neighborhood.

    6) The next section and a tower—the Tower of the Ovens—were built by two men, Malkijah and Hasshub (v.11).

    7) The other ruler of the half-district of Jerusalem, Shallum, built the next section of wall. Significantly, his daughters jumped in and helped him in the construction, which indicates that both sexes were involved in the project.

The facts to note are that everyone was assigned very specific tasks and that everyone cooperated together in a unified effort. Each person kept his or her eyes on a specific task and worked to accomplish the project. Each used the specific gift God had given. Throughout this chapter, 38 workers and 42 different groups are named, all cooperating and working together to build their city and its walls. Practically everyone was taking part in the project:

    ⇒ political leaders (vv.9, 12, 14, 16, 19)
    ⇒ priests (vv.1, 22)
    ⇒ common people, both men and women (vv.2-4, 12)
    ⇒ business leaders (vv.8, 32) and craftsmen

Thought 1. Cooperation is an absolute essential in achieving any task that requires more than one person. Oneness of spirit is a must. Unless there is unity, people are moving in different directions, pulling against each other and accomplishing little. The result of pulling against each other is dissension and divisiveness. Think how often dissension and divisiveness rip apart families, friends, workers, classmates, athletes, businesses, social organizations, churches, communities, political parties, nations, and a host of other relationships.

For these reasons and so many more, success in maintaining order and achieving goals is largely dependent upon the harmony of the participants. Listen to what God's Holy Word says:

    "Again I say unto you, That if two of you shall agree on earth as touching any thing that they shall ask, it shall be done for them of my Father which is in heaven" (Mt.18:19).

    "And the second _is_ like unto it, Thou shalt love thy neighbour as thyself" (Mt.22:39).

    "A new commandment I give unto you, That ye love one another; as I have loved you, that ye also love one another. By this shall all _men_ know that ye are my disciples, if ye have love one to another" (Jn.13:34-35).

    "That they all may be one; as thou, Father, _art_ in me, and I in thee, that they also may be one in us: that the world may believe that thou hast sent me" (Jn.17:21).

    "So we, _being_ many, are one body in Christ, and every one members one of another" (Ro.12:5).

    "Now I beseech you, brethren, by the name of our Lord Jesus Christ, that ye all speak the same thing, and _that_ there be no divisions among you; but _that_ ye be perfectly joined together in the same mind and in the same judgment" (1 Co.1:10).

    "For we _being_ many are one bread, _and_ one body: for we are all partakers of that one bread" (1 Co.10:17).

    "Finally, brethren, farewell. Be perfect, be of good comfort, be of one mind, live in peace; and the God of love and peace shall be with you" (2 Co.13:11).

    "There is neither Jew nor Greek, there is neither bond nor free, there is neither male nor female: for ye are all one in Christ Jesus" (Ga.3:28).

---

[1] Mervin Breneman. _Ezra, Nehemiah, Esther_, p.187.

"For he is our peace, who hath made both one, and hath broken down the middle wall of partition *between us*" (Ep.2:14).

"Endeavouring to keep the unity of the Spirit in the bond of peace" (Ep.4:3).

"Till we all come in the unity of the faith, and of the knowledge of the Son of God, unto a perfect man, unto the measure of the stature of the fulness of Christ" (Ep.4:13).

"Only let your conversation [conduct, behavior] be as it becometh the gospel of Christ: that whether I come and see you, or else be absent, I may hear of your affairs, that ye stand fast in one spirit, with one mind striving together for the faith of the gospel" (Ph.1:27).

"I beseech Euodias, and beseech Syntyche, that they be of the same mind in the Lord. And I intreat thee also, true yokefellow, help those women which laboured with me in the gospel, with Clement also, and *with* other my fellowlabourers, whose names *are* in the book of life" (Ph.4:2-3).

"That their hearts might be comforted, being knit together in love, and unto all riches of the full assurance of understanding, to the acknowledgement of the mystery of God, and of the Father, and of Christ" (Col.2:2).

"And the Lord make you to increase and abound in love one toward another, and toward all *men*, even as we *do* toward you" (1 Th.3:12).

"Seeing ye have purified your souls in obeying the truth through the Spirit unto unfeigned love of the brethren, *see that ye* love one another with a pure heart fervently" (1 Pe.1:22).

"Finally, *be ye* all of one mind, having compassion one of another, love as brethren, *be* pitiful, *be* courteous" (1 Pe.3:8).

"I *am* a companion of all *them* that fear thee, and of them that keep thy precepts" (Ps.119:63).

---

2 **(3:13-14) Humility, Duty—Labor, Duty—Work, Duty—Jerusalem, Rebuilding, Spirit Needed—Wall, of Jerusalem, Rebuilt, Spirit Needed**: the construction of the west wall was an enormous project that included two gates and over 500 yards of wall ("a thousand cubits" or about 1720 feet). Both the Valley Gate and the 500 yards plus of wall were rebuilt by a man named Hanun and the residents of Zanoah (v.13). Undertaking such a long section of the wall suggests a total commitment to the project by these workers. It is also possible that this section of wall was in better condition than most of the other sections.

The Dung or Refuse Gate was located at the southern point of the city and set above the Valley of Hinnom, which was where the rubbish or garbage dump was located. The stench from the constant burning of garbage must have been almost unbearable. This fact made this particular building project most undesirable, suggesting that these workers humbled themselves to take on the undesirable job.

OUTLINE	SCRIPTURE	SCRIPTURE	OUTLINE
2. The workers on the west wall: Some humbled themselves & took on the undesirable jobs a. The Valley Gate: This gate & 500 yards of the wall were rebuilt by Hanun & the residents of Zanoah	13 The valley gate repaired Hanun, and the inhabitants of Zanoah; they built it, and set up the doors thereof, the locks thereof, and the bars thereof, and a thousand cubits on the wall unto the dung gate.	14 But the dung gate repaired Malchiah the son of Rechab, the ruler of part of Beth-haccerem; he build it, and set up the doors thereof, the locks thereof, and the bars thereof.	b. The Dung or Refuse Gate: This undesirable building task was humbly taken by a leader, the district ruler Recab

Thought 1. At times in life we all come face-to-face with unpleasant or undesirable tasks that must be done. How we approach these distasteful or lowly tasks reveals much about our character and attitude. Some people are too prideful to touch lowly tasks, feeling they are too important or too intelligent. Other people would never dirty their hands with common labor, feeling that such work is for common and uneducated laborers.

Far too many of us exalt ourselves above others. We think too highly of ourselves, feeling that we are better, superior, or of more value than others. But this is not what God teaches us. Listen to what God's Holy Word says:

"Whosoever therefore shall humble himself as this little child, the same is greatest in the kingdom of heaven" (Mt.18:4).

"But when thou art bidden, go and sit down in the lowest room; that when he that bade thee cometh, he may say unto thee, Friend, go up higher: then shalt thou have worship in the presence of them that sit at meat with thee" (Lu.14:10).

"And he said unto them, The kings of the Gentiles exercise lordship over them; and they that exercise authority upon them are called benefactors. But ye *shall* not *be* so: but he that is greatest among you, let him be as the younger; and he that is chief, as he that doth serve" (Lu.22:25-26).

"For I say, through the grace given unto me, to every man that is among you, not to think *of himself* more highly than he ought to think; but to think soberly, according as God hath dealt to every man the measure of faith" (Ro.12:3).

"*Let* nothing *be done* through strife or vainglory; but in lowliness of mind let each esteem other better than themselves. Look not every man on his own things, but every man also on the things of others. Let this mind be in you, which was also in Christ Jesus" (Ph.2:3-5).

"And being found in fashion as a man, he humbled himself, and became obedient unto death, even the death of the cross" (Ph.2:8).

"Humble yourselves in the sight of the Lord, and he shall lift you up" (Js.4:10).

"Likewise, ye younger, submit yourselves unto the elder. Yea, all *of you* be subject one to another, and be clothed with humility: for God resisteth the proud, and giveth grace to the humble. Humble yourselves therefore under the mighty hand of God, that he may exalt you in due time" (1 Pe.5:5-6).

"Love not the world, neither the things *that are* in the world. If any man love the world, the love of the Father is not in him. For all that *is* in the world, the lust of the flesh, and the lust of the eyes, and the pride of life, is not of the Father, but is of the world" (1 Jn.2:15-16).

"*When* pride cometh, then cometh shame: but with the lowly *is* wisdom" (Pr.11:2).

"Pride *goeth* before destruction, and an haughty spirit before a fall" (Pr.16:18).

"Better *it is to be* of an humble spirit with the lowly, than to divide the spoil with the proud" (Pr.16:19).

"An high look, and a proud heart, *and* the plowing of the wicked, *is* sin" (Pr.21:4).

"By humility *and* the fear of the LORD *are* riches, and honour, and life" (Pr.22:4).

"A man's pride shall bring him low: but honour shall uphold the humble in spirit" (Pr.29:23).

"For thus saith the high and lofty One that inhabiteth eternity, whose name *is* Holy; I dwell in the high and holy *place*, with him also *that is* of a contrite and humble spirit, to revive the spirit of the humble, and to revive the heart of the contrite ones" (Is.57:15).

"He hath showed thee, O man, what *is* good; and what doth the LORD require of thee, but to do justly, and to love mercy, and to walk humbly with thy God?" (Mi.6:8).

3 (3:15-32) **Diligence, Duty—Work, Duty—Labor, Duty—Zeal, Duty**: work on the east wall included the construction of five gates, named in the Scripture and outline below. However, the important thing to note is the hard, diligent labor of the workers. They were filled with a very special zeal for the task assigned them. One worker in particular, Baruch, was known for his zeal and diligence (v.20). Several other workers are said to have built two sections of the wall, suggesting that they also had a very special zeal for the work (21, 27). The Scripture and outline are sufficient in helping the reader grasp these verses:

OUTLINE	SCRIPTURE	SCRIPTURE	OUTLINE

3. The workers on the east wall: Some were hard & diligent workers filled with zeal
a. The Fountain Gate
  1) The gate & a section of the wall of the Pool of Siloam was built by Shallun
	15 But the gate of the fountain repaired Shallun the son of Col-hozeh, the ruler of part of Mizpah; he built it, and covered it, and set up the doors thereof, the locks thereof, and the bars thereof, and the wall of the pool of Siloah by the king's garden, and unto the stairs that go down from the city of David.	ing *of the wall* unto the door of the house of Eliashib the high priest.
		21 After him repaired Meremoth the son of Urijah the son of Koz another piece, from the door of the house of Eliashib even to the end of the house of Eliashib.
			igence: Ran up to the door of the High Priest's house
			  7) The section that ran from the High Priest's door to the end of his house was rebuilt by Meremoth, who built two sections, see v.4

2) The next section was built by a ruler also named Nehemiah: Ran to a point opposite the royal cemetery, as far as the water reservoir & the House of the Heroes	16 After him repaired Nehemiah the son of Azbuk, the ruler of the half part of Beth-zur, unto *the place* over against the sepulchres of David, and to the pool that was made, and unto the house of the mighty.	22 And after him repaired the priests, the men of the plain. 23 After him repaired Benjamin and Hashub over against their house. After him repaired Azariah the son of Maaseiah the son of Ananiah by his house.	8) The next section was built by the priests from the surrounding region, see v.1 9) The next three sections were repaired by three men whose houses sat next to the wall: Benjamin, Hasshub, & Azariah

3) The next section was built by the Levites
  4) The next two sections were built by the two district rulers of Keilah
    • Hashabiah
    • Bavai or Binnui
  5) The next section was built by the ruler of Mizpah: Began opposite the Armory & ran to the corner, the angle or turning point of the wall
	17 After him repaired the Levites, Rehum the son of Bani. Next unto him repaired Hashabiah, the ruler of the half part of Keilah, in his part.
	18 After him repaired their brethren, Bavai the son of Henadad, the ruler of the half part of Keilah.
	19 And next to him repaired Ezer the son of Jeshua, the ruler of Mizpah, another piece over against the going up to the armoury at the turning *of the wall.*
		24 After him repaired Binnui the son of Henadad another piece, from the house of Azariah unto the turning *of the wall,* even unto the corner.
		25 Palal the son of Uzai, over against the turning *of the wall,* and the tower which lieth out from the king's high house, that *was* by the court of the prison. After him Pedaiah the son of Parosh.
			10) The section from Azariah's house to the turning point or corner was built by Binnui
			  11) The next section was built by Uzai: Was opposite the corner & the tower that projected out from the king's palace (near the court of the guard)

6) The next section was rebuilt by Baruch, who was known for his zeal & dil-	20 After him Baruch the son of Zabbai earnestly repaired the other piece, from the turn-	26 Moreover the Nethinims dwelt in Ophel, unto *the place* over against the water gate toward the east, and the tower that lieth out.
		27 After them the Tekoites repaired another piece, over against the great tower that
			b. The Water Gate
			  1) The temple servants under the supervision of Parosh repaired the wall opposite the Water Gate
			  2) The residents of Jekoa rebuilt their second section:

OUTLINE	SCRIPTURE	SCRIPTURE	OUTLINE

From the Great Projecting Tower to the Wall of Ophel, see v.5
c. The Horse Gate
  1) The priests made repairs opposite their own houses
 	
  2) Zadok repaired the adjoining section opposite his house
d. The East Gate
  1) The guard of this gate repaired the next section
  2) Three other diligent workers built the next
	lieth out, even unto the wall of Ophel.
	28 From above the horse gate repaired the priests, every one over against his house.
	29 After them repaired Zadok the son of Immer over against his house. After him repaired also Shemaiah the son of Shechaniah, the keeper of the east gate.
	30 After him repaired Hananiah the son of Shelemiah, and Hanun the sixth son of
		Zalaph, another piece. After him repaired Meshullam the son of Berechiah over against his chamber.
		31 After him repaired Malchiah the goldsmith's son unto the place of the Nethinims, and of the merchants, over against the gate Miphkad, and to the going up of the corner.
		32 And between the going up of the corner unto the sheep gate repaired the goldsmiths and the merchants.
			three sections
			  • Hananiah
			  • Hanun
			  • Meshullam
			
			e. The Inspection Gate
			  1) The section opposite this gate was rebuilt by a goldsmith: Ran from the housing for the temple servants & merchants to the Upper Room above the corner
			  2) The last section of the wall from the corner to

Thought 1. The hard, diligent labor of these workers is a dynamic example for us. In undertaking any task we must be filled with a zeal to do our best.

⇒ Before the Lord, only our best effort is acceptable.

⇒ Think how much could be achieved throughout the world if laziness and inexcusable absences were eliminated from the workplace.

⇒ Think how much cleaner and more beautiful our communities and highways would be if we all joined hands to restore the unappealing sights and then committed ourselves to keeping them clean.

⇒ Think how much longer possessions—homes, vehicles, furnishings, clothes, toys, etc.—would last if we protected them, treasured them, and took care of them.

⇒ Think what students could accomplish if they applied themselves diligently in their classes and studies, striving to put to good use all they had learned.

On and on the list could go. How much more could be accomplished and achieved in every area of life if we worked hard in the areas for which we are responsible. Hard, diligent work—a heart filled with zeal for simply being responsible and for doing all things well—is the duty of every human being. Listen to what God's Holy Word says:

"Not slothful in business; fervent in spirit; serving the Lord" (Ro.12:11).

"Therefore, my beloved brethren, be ye stedfast, unmovable, always abounding in the work of the Lord, forasmuch as ye know that your labour is not in vain in the Lord" (1 Co.15:58).

"Let him that stole steal no more: but rather let him labour, working with *his* hands the thing which is good, that he may have to give to him that needeth" (Ep.4:28).

"And whatsoever ye do in word or deed, *do* all in the name of the Lord Jesus, giving thanks to God and the Father by him" (Col.3:17).

"And whatsoever ye do, do *it* heartily, as to the Lord, and not unto men" (Col.3:23).

"And that ye study to be quiet, and to do your own business, and to work with your own hands, as we commanded you; That ye may walk honestly toward them that are without, and *that* ye may have lack of nothing" (1 Th.4:11-12).

"For even when we were with you, this we commanded you, that if any would not work, neither should he eat. For we hear that there are some which walk among you disorderly, working not at all, but are busybodies. Now them that are such we command and exhort by our Lord Jesus Christ, that with quietness they work, and eat their own bread" (2 Th.3:10-12).

"Nevertheless we, according to his promise, look for new heavens and a new earth, wherein dwelleth righteousness. Wherefore, beloved, seeing that ye look for such things, be diligent that ye may be found of him in peace, without spot, and blameless" (2 Pe.3:13-14).

"And the LORD God took the man, and put him into the garden of Eden to dress it and to keep it" (Ge.2:15).

"In the sweat of thy face shalt thou eat bread, till thou return unto the ground; for out of it wast thou taken: for dust thou *art,* and unto dust shalt thou return" (Ge.3:19).

"Go to the ant, thou sluggard; consider her ways, and be wise" (Pr.6:6).

"He becometh poor that dealeth *with* a slack hand: but the hand of the diligent maketh rich" (Pr.10:4).

"He that gathereth in summer *is* a wise son: *but* he that sleepeth in harvest *is* a son that causeth shame" (Pr.10:5).

"He that tilleth his land shall be satisfied with bread: but he that followeth vain *persons is* void of understanding" (Pr.12:11).

"The soul of the sluggard desireth, and *hath* nothing: but the soul of the diligent shall be made fat" (Pr.13:4).

"In all labour there is profit: but the talk of the lips *tendeth* only to penury" (Pr.14:23).

"Love not sleep, lest thou come to poverty; open thine eyes, *and* thou shalt be satisfied with bread" (Pr.20:13).

"Whatsoever thy hand findeth to do, do *it* with thy might; for *there is* no work, nor device, nor knowledge, nor wisdom, in the grave, whither thou goest" (Ec.9:10).

DEEPER STUDY # 1

(3:1-32) **Protection, Picture of—Security, Picture of**: to many readers, *Nehemiah* chapter 3 seems unimportant, and there is a temptation to skip over the endless list of workers who took part in rebuilding Jerusalem and its walls. But this is a mistake. God has included the account of the construction project in His Holy Word for a reason. There are a number of very important truths gleaned from the passage, truths that speak forcefully to our hearts. The outline of the Scripture gives three of these significant truths. In addition, when we give careful thought to the rebuilt walls, we see at least five practical results.

1. The rebuilt walls of Jerusalem—the Holy City of God—represented security, protection from enemies. So it is with believers. Once we enter the gates of God's Holy City of salvation and deliverance, we are protected from our enemies. And as long as we stay within the city, rejecting the seductions and temptations to return to the world, we remain secure. We are continually delivered *through* all temptations and trials, living victorious lives and being filled with the perfect assurance of God's presence, guidance, and the hope of eternal life.

> "For the which cause I also suffer these things: nevertheless I am not ashamed: for I know whom I have believed, and am persuaded that he is able to keep that which I have committed unto him against that day" (2 Ti.1:12).
> "And the Lord shall deliver me from every evil work, and will preserve *me* unto his heavenly kingdom: to whom *be* glory for ever and ever. Amen" (2 Ti.4:18).
> "Who are kept by the power of God through faith unto salvation ready to be revealed in the last time" (1 Pe.1:5).
> "Now unto him that is able to keep you from falling, and to present *you* faultless before the presence of his glory with exceeding joy" (Jude 1:24).
> "The eternal God *is thy* refuge, and underneath *are* the everlasting arms: and he shall thrust out the enemy from before thee; and shall say, Destroy *them*" (De.33:27).

2. The rebuilt walls of Jerusalem represented spiritual separation. When a person settled down in the walls of the Holy City, the person was declaring that he was turning away from the unbelievers of the world and setting himself apart to God and to the worship of Him alone. This is a clear picture of spiritual separation for the believer. When a believer turns to the LORD for salvation, he separates himself from the wicked lifestyle and false worship of unbelievers.

> "I wrote unto you in an epistle not to company with fornicators: Yet not altogether with the fornicators of this world, or with the covetous, or extortioners, or with idolaters; for then must ye needs go out of the world. But now I have written unto you not to keep company, if any man that is called a brother be a fornicator, or covetous, or an idolater, or a railer, or a drunkard, or an extortioner; with such an one no not to eat" (1 Co.5:9-11).
> "Be ye not unequally yoked together with unbelievers: for what fellowship hath righteousness with unrighteousness? and what communion hath light with darkness? And what concord hath Christ with Belial? or what part hath he that believeth with an infidel? And what agreement hath the temple of God with idols? for ye are the temple of the living God; as God hath said, I will dwell in them, and walk in *them;* and I will be their God, and they shall be my people" (2 Co.6:14-16).
> "Wherefore come out from among them, and be ye separate, saith the Lord, and touch not the unclean *thing;* and I will receive you, And will be a Father unto you, and ye shall be my sons and daughters, saith the Lord Almighty" (2 Co.6:17-18).
> "And have no fellowship with the unfruitful works of darkness, but rather reprove *them*" (Ep.5:11).

3. The rebuilt walls of Jerusalem represented deliverance and salvation. The person living in the security of God's Holy City had been rescued from the captivity of enemies, and he was being allowed to live within the promised land of God. So it is with any person who turns to the LORD, seeking the right to live in the Holy City of God. The LORD saves the genuine seeker, delivers him from the captivity of sin, death, and judgment to come. The LORD then gives the seeker the right to live in the promised land of God, which is a striking picture of heaven itself.

> "For God so loved the world, that he gave his only begotten Son, that whosoever believeth in him should not perish, but have everlasting life. For God sent not his Son into the world to condemn the world; but that the world through him might be saved. He that believeth on him is not condemned: but he that believeth not is condemned already, because he hath not believed in the name of the only begotten Son of God" (Jn.3:16-18).
> "Verily, verily, I say unto you, He that heareth my word, and believeth on him that sent me, hath everlasting life, and shall not come into condemnation; but is passed from death unto life" (Jn.5:24).
> "And it shall come to pass, *that* whosoever shall call on the name of the Lord shall be saved" (Ac.2:21).
> "For the wages of sin *is* death; but the gift of God *is* eternal life through Jesus Christ our Lord" (Ro.6:23).
> "For whosoever shall call upon the name of the Lord shall be saved" (Ro.10:13).

"For the grace of God that bringeth salvation hath appeared to all men, Teaching us that, denying ungodliness and worldly lusts, we should live soberly, righteously, and godly, in this present world" (Tit.2:11-12).

"The Lord is not slack concerning his promise, as some men count slackness; but is longsuffering to us-ward, not willing that any should perish, but that all should come to repentance. But the day of the Lord will come as a thief in the night; in the which the heavens shall pass away with a great noise, and the elements shall melt with fervent heat, the earth also and the works that are therein shall be burned up. *Seeing* then *that* all these things shall be dissolved, what manner *of persons* ought ye to be in *all* holy conversation and godliness, Looking for and hasting unto the coming of the day of God, wherein the heavens being on fire shall be dissolved, and the elements shall melt with fervent heat? Nevertheless we, according to his promise, look for new heavens and a new earth, wherein dwelleth righteousness" (2 Pe.3:9-13).

4. The rebuilt walls of Jerusalem represented the need for watchfulness and diligence. They needed a constant guard to stand watch against any attacks by the enemy. Spiritually, the believer must be vigilant in guarding himself. He must guard against leaving the safety of God's protective walls. If a person turns away from the LORD and returns to the wicked behavior of the world, he loses the sense of God's presence and day-to-day guidance. He is also sure to face the discipline or chastisement of God's Holy hand.

"Watch therefore, for ye know neither the day nor the hour wherein the Son of man cometh" (Mt.25:13).

"Blessed *are* those servants, whom the lord when he cometh shall find watching: verily I say unto you, that he shall gird himself, and make them to sit down to meat, and will come forth and serve them" (Lu.12:37).

"Wherefore let him that thinketh he standeth take heed lest he fall" (1 Co.10:12).

"Watch ye, stand fast in the faith, quit you like men, be strong" (1 Co.16:13).

"Continue in prayer, and watch in the same with thanksgiving" (Col.4:2).

"Ye are all the children of light, and the children of the day: we are not of the night, nor of darkness. Therefore let us not sleep, as *do* others; but let us watch and be sober" (1 Th.5:5-6).

"Be sober, be vigilant; because your adversary the devil, as a roaring lion, walketh about, seeking whom he may devour: Whom resist stedfast in the faith, knowing that the same afflictions are accomplished in your brethren that are in the world" (1 Pe.5:8-9).

"Behold, I come quickly: hold that fast which thou hast, that no man take thy crown" (Re.3:11).

"Behold, I come as a thief. Blessed *is* he that watcheth, and keepeth his garments, lest he walk naked, and they see his shame" (Re.16:15).

5. The rebuilt walls represented God's presence, righteousness, provision, guidance, and blessings. To the returned Jews, Jerusalem was the *Holy City of God.* Thus, living within the Holy City, worshipping the LORD, and keeping His commandments meant that the LORD would grant His presence. He would grant all the wonderful blessings He had promised through the prophets and servants of God down through the centuries. When a person today turns to the LORD and keeps His commandments, seeking to live in the eternal city of God, the LORD promises to be present with the person. The LORD will pour out His richest blessings upon him.

"But seek ye first the kingdom of God, and his righteousness; and all these things shall be added unto you" (Mt.6:33).

"In my Father's house are many mansions: if *it were* not so, I would have told you. I go to prepare a place for you. And if I go and prepare a place for you, I will come again, and receive you unto myself; that where I am, *there* ye may be also" (Jn.14:2-3).

"But my God shall supply all your need according to his riches in glory by Christ Jesus" (Ph.4:19).

"*Let your* conversation *be* without covetousness; *and be* content with such things as ye have: for he hath said, I will never leave thee, nor forsake thee. So that we may boldly say, The Lord *is* my helper, and I will not fear what man shall do unto me" (He.13:5-6).

"And ye shall serve the LORD your God, and he shall bless thy bread, and thy water; and I will take sickness away from the midst of thee" (Ex.23:25).

"The LORD *is* my shepherd; I shall not want. He maketh me to lie down in green pastures: he leadeth me beside the still waters. He restoreth my soul: he leadeth me in the paths of righteousness for his name's sake. Yea, though I walk through the valley of the shadow of death, I will fear no evil: for thou *art* with me; thy rod and thy staff they comfort me. Thou preparest a table before me in the presence of mine enemies: thou anointest my head with oil; my cup runneth over. Surely goodness and mercy shall follow me all the days of my life: and I will dwell in the house of the LORD for ever" (Ps.23:1-6).

"*Oh* how great *is* thy goodness, which thou hast laid up for them that fear thee; *which* thou hast wrought for them that trust in thee before the sons of men!" (Ps.31:19).

"Fear thou not; for I *am* with thee: be not dismayed; for I *am* thy God: I will strengthen thee; yea, I will help thee; yea, I will uphold thee with the right hand of my righteousness" (Is.41:10).

DEEPER STUDY # 2
(3:1-32) **Gates, of Jerusalem, Discussed—Jerusalem, Gates of, Spiritual Truths Pictured**: the author of *Nehemiah* actually organized the rebuilding of Jerusalem's walls around the ten gates. The ten gates tell the story of the rebuilding project.

As the reader scans this chapter, he or she immediately notices that the material is arranged around the ten gates. For the sake of future history, the author recorded the list of people who rebuilt the walls of Jerusalem. But he presented this *honor roll of builders* by showing how Nehemiah used the ten gates to organize and divide up the building project. When the names of the gates and facts about them are closely studied, some important lessons can be gleaned.

1. **The Sheep Gate** (3:1): this gate was on the north wall close to the temple. It was the gate through which animals were brought to be sacrificed at the temple. It was probably named so because of the continual flow of animals that were herded through its entrance.

The *Sheep Gate* reminds us of the sacrificial death of Jesus Christ, the Lamb of God.

> "The next day John seeth Jesus coming unto him, and saith, Behold the Lamb of God, which taketh away the sin of the world" (Jn.1:29).
> "Who gave himself for our sins, that he might deliver us from this present evil world, according to the will of God and our Father" (Ga.1:4).
> "And walk in love, as Christ also hath loved us, and hath given himself for us an offering and a sacrifice to God for a sweetsmelling savour" (Ep.5:2).
> "Who gave himself for us, that he might redeem us from all iniquity, and purify unto himself a peculiar people, zealous of good works" (Tit.2:14).
> "Unto him that loved us, and washed us from our sins in his own blood" (Re.1:5).

2. **The Fish Gate** (3:3): this gate was also on the north wall and was protected by two towers strategically placed to defend the north wall. These towers were necessary because there was no natural barrier or defense on the north side—such as a hill.

The Fish Gate was probably so named because it was the site where the commercial marketing of fish took place or either the city's major fish market was nearby.

Whatever the case, the Fish Gate is a reminder of Christ's challenge to us:

> "Follow me, and I will make you fishers of men" (Mt.4:19).
> "Now when he had left speaking, he said unto Simon, Launch out into the deep, and let down your nets for a draught. And Simon answering said unto him, Master, we have toiled all the night, and have taken nothing: nevertheless at thy word I will let down the net. And when they had this done, they inclosed a great multitude of fishes: and their net brake. And they beckoned unto *their* partners, which were in the other ship, that they should come and help them. And they came, and filled both the ships, so that they began to sink. When Simon Peter saw *it*, he fell down at Jesus' knees, saying, Depart from me; for I am a sinful man, O Lord. For he was astonished, and all that were with him, at the draught of the fishes which they had taken: And so *was* also James, and John, the sons of Zebedee, which were partners with Simon. And Jesus said unto Simon, Fear not; from henceforth thou shalt catch men. And when they had brought their ships to land, they forsook all, and followed him" (Lu.5:4-11).
> "The fruit of the righteous *is* a tree of life; and he that winneth souls *is* wise" (Pr.11:30).
> "And they that be wise shall shine as the brightness of the firmament; and they that turn many to righteousness as the stars for ever and ever" (Da.12:3).

3. **The Old Gate** (3:6): this gate was located at the northwest corner of the wall, near the present-day site of the Holy Sepulcher (12:39). It was also known as...
- The Jeshannah Gate, which referred to the fact that the road led to the city of Jeshanah (2 Chr.13:19).
- The Mishneh Gate, meaning *New Quarter* or *New Neighborhood* which referred to the northwest section of the city (Zep.1:10).
- The Corner Gate (2 K.14:13; Je.31:38).

In gleaning for our lives the message from the Old Gate, both Jeremiah and Christ tell us that we have a great treasure in old things as well as in new things.
a. By standing in the old gates or in the old ways, Jeremiah says that we will find rest for our souls.

> "Thus saith the LORD, Stand ye in the ways, and see, and ask for the old paths, where is the good way, and walk therein, and ye shall find rest for your souls. But they said, We will not walk *therein*" (Je.6:16).

b. Jesus Christ says that a Christian believer or teacher is like the owner of a house who brings forth new treasures as well as old.

> "Then said he unto them, Therefore every scribe *which is* instructed unto the kingdom of heaven is like unto a man *that is* an householder, which bringeth forth out of his treasure *things* new and old." (Mt.13:52).

c. The believer possesses an enormous treasure that includes both old and new wealth.
1) The treasure of the Old and New Testament.

"For whatsoever things were written aforetime were written for our learning, that we through patience and comfort of the scriptures might have hope" (Ro.15:4).

"Now all these things happened unto them for ensamples: and they are written for our admonition, upon whom the ends of the world are come" (1 Co.10:11).

2) The treasure of the old and new revelation.

"For the law was given by Moses, *but* grace and truth came by Jesus Christ. No man hath seen God at any time; the only begotten Son, which is in the bosom of the Father, he hath declared *him*" (Jn.1:17-18).

3) The treasure of the old and new truth.

"For the law was given by Moses, *but* grace and truth came by Jesus Christ" (Jn.1:17). "Jesus saith unto him, I am the way, the truth, and the life: no man cometh unto the Father, but by me" (Jn.14:6; also see Ps.119:142).

4) The treasure of the old and new message.

"Think not that I am come to destroy the law, or the prophets: I am not come to destroy, but to fulfil" (Mt.5:17).

"For what the law could not do, in that it was weak through the flesh, God sending his own Son in the likeness of sinful flesh, and for sin, condemned sin in the flesh" (Ro.8:3).

5) The treasure of the old and new covenants.

"But now hath he obtained a more excellent ministry, by how much also he is the mediator of a better covenant, which was established upon better promises" (He.8:6).

"How much more shall the blood of Christ, who through the eternal Spirit offered himself without spot to God, purge your conscience from dead works to serve the living God? And for this cause he is the mediator of the new testament, that by means of death, for the redemption of the transgressions *that were* under the first testament, they which are called might receive the promise of eternal inheritance" (He.9:14-15).

4. **The Valley Gate** (3:13): this gate was in the southwest corner of the wall and most likely led down into the Tyropaeon Valley, which lay between the Hinnom and Kidron Valleys. It is mentioned four times by Nehemiah (2:13; 3:13; 12:31, 39). In the present passage the Valley Gate is said to have been 1000 cubits—over 500 yards—from the Dung Gate. A valley setting in the midst of towering mountains or hills reminds us of humility. Thus the Valley Gate can teach us two lessons:

a. We are to walk humbly before others, following the pattern of humility Christ set for us.

"*Let* nothing *be done* through strife or vainglory; but in lowliness of mind let each esteem other better than themselves. Look not every man on his own things, but every man also on the things of others. Let this mind be in you, which was also in Christ Jesus: Who, being in the form of God, thought it not robbery to be equal with God: But made himself of no reputation, and took upon him the form of a servant, and was made in the likeness of men" (Ph.2:3-7).

"Put on therefore, as the elect of God, holy and beloved, bowels of mercies, kindness, humbleness of mind, meekness, longsuffering" (Col.3:12).

"Likewise, ye younger, submit yourselves unto the elder. Yea, all *of you* be subject one to another, and be clothed with humility: for God resisteth the proud, and giveth grace to the humble. Humble yourselves therefore under the mighty hand of God, that he may exalt you in due time" (1 Pe.5:5-6).

b. We will "walk through the valley of the shadow of death," but the LORD will be with us. He will personally comfort us as we walk through the final valley on earth. And we will "dwell in the house of the LORD [heaven itself] forever."

"Yea, though I walk through the valley of the shadow of death, I will fear no evil: for thou *art* with me; thy rod and thy staff they comfort me.... Surely goodness and mercy shall follow me all the days of my life: and I will dwell in the house of the LORD for ever" (Ps.23:4,6).

5. **The Dung Gate** (3:14): this gate was located near the southeast corner of the city wall, on the hill Ophel. It was obviously named this because it sat above the Valley of Hinnon, the garbage dump of the city. It was the main gate used by the people in disposing of their rubbish, garbage, and dung.

Tragically, the Valley of Hinnom had originally been the site where the false religionists' practice of sacrificing children took place (2 Ch.33:6). For this reason, the godly king Josiah desecrated the valley by turning it into the city garbage dump (2 K.23:10). The Dung Gate reminds us of two facts:

123

a. We must walk through this gate spiritually. We must cleanse our lives and homes of all garbage and filth.

> "Having therefore these promises, dearly beloved, let us cleanse ourselves from all filthiness of the flesh and spirit, perfecting holiness in the fear of God" (2 Co.7:1).
> "If a man therefore purge himself from these, he shall be a vessel unto honour, sanctified, and meet for the master's use, *and* prepared unto every good work" (2 Ti.2:21).
> "Draw nigh to God, and he will draw nigh to you. Cleanse *your* hands, *ye* sinners; and purify *your* hearts, *ye* double minded" (Js.4:8).
> "Beloved, now are we the sons of God, and it doth not yet appear what we shall be: but we know that, when he shall appear, we shall be like him; for we shall see him as he is. And every man that hath this hope in him purifieth himself, even as he is pure" (1 Jn.3:2-3).
> "Wash you, make you clean; put away the evil of your doings from before mine eyes; cease to do evil" (Is.1:16).
> "Wash thine heart from wickedness, that thou mayest be saved. How long shall thy vain thoughts lodge within thee?" (Je.4:14).

b. Jesus Christ referred to the garbage dump as *gehenna*, which means the Valley of Hinnom. Through the centuries the dump had become a perpetual fire, the site of slow burning and smelly garbage. Thus Christ pointed to the site as a picture of what hell is like, a picture where all who reject Him and live wicked lives will spend eternity.

> "But I say unto you, That whosoever is angry with his brother without a cause shall be in danger of the judgment: and whosoever shall say to his brother, Raca, shall be in danger of the council: but whosoever shall say, Thou fool, shall be in danger of hell fire" (Mt.5:22).
> "Ye have heard that it was said by them of old time, Thou shalt not commit adultery: But I say unto you, That whosoever looketh on a woman to lust after her hath committed adultery with her already in his heart. And if thy right eye offend thee, pluck it out, and cast *it* from thee: for it is profitable for thee that one of thy members should perish, and not *that* thy whole body should be cast into hell. And if thy right hand offend thee, cut if off, and cast it from thee: for it is profitable for thee that one of thy members should perish, and not *that* thy whole body should be cast into hell" (Mt.5:27-30).

6. The Fountain Gate (3:15): this gate was on the east wall near the pool. which was most likely the Pool of Siloam. The Fountain Gate was also "the gate between the two walls" (2 K.25:4), which was near the king's garden, the old city of David, and the water tunnel that had been built by King Hezekiah (2 K.20:20; 2 Chr.32:30). The gate was located near the Fountain Head, the main water service for the city.

The Fountain Gate reminds us of a wonderful truth about Jesus Christ. He is the Head of the Fountain of life, the Spring of Water provided by God Himself. Jesus Christ is the *Living Water of Life*.

> "Jesus answered and said unto her, If thou knewest the gift of God, and who it is that saith to thee, Give me to drink; thou wouldest have asked of him, and he would have given thee living water" (Jn.4:10).
> "But whosoever drinketh of the water that I shall give him shall never thirst; but the water that I shall give him shall be in him a well of water springing up into everlasting life" (Jn.4:14).
> "In the last day, that great *day* of the feast, Jesus stood and cried, saying, If any man thirst, let him come unto me, and drink. He that believeth on me, as the scripture hath said, out of his belly shall flow rivers of living water" (Jn.7:37-38).
> "For the Lamb which is in the midst of the throne shall feed them, and shall lead them unto living fountains of waters: and God shall wipe away all tears from their eyes" (Re.7:17).
> "And the Spirit and the bride say, Come. And let him that heareth say, Come. And let him that is athirst come. And whosoever will, let him take the water of life freely" (Re.22:17).

7. The Water Gate (3:26): this gate was also located on the east wall. It was close to the Gihon Spring, which was one of the main sources of water for Jerusalem citizens. Unlike most major cities, Jerusalem was not built on a major river. Consequently, its citizens had to depend upon transporting (carrying) water into the city from surrounding springs and reservoirs that captured rainwater. For this reason Hezekiah had built the water tunnel mentioned above. But even after its construction, the people were still dependent upon the springs and reservoirs.

Note this fact: there was a large public square at the entrance of the Water Gate. It was there that Nehemiah and Ezra assembled all the people together to read the law—God's Word—to them (8:1, 3, 16; 12:37).

Thus the Water Gate reminds us of the Word of God.

> "Now ye are clean through the word which I have spoken unto you" (Jn.15:3).
> "Sanctify them through thy truth: thy word is truth" (Jn.17:17).
> "That he might sanctify and cleanse it [the church] with the washing of water by the word" (Ep.5:26).
> "Seeing ye have purified your souls in obeying the truth through the Spirit unto unfeigned love of the brethren, *see that ye* love one another with a pure heart fervently" (1 Pe.1:22).
> "Wherewithal shall a young man cleanse his way? by taking heed *thereto* according to thy word" (Ps.119:9).

8. **The Horse Gate** (3:28): this gate was located on the eastern wall close to the palace grounds (2 Chr.23:15) and the temple area. It was the site where the wicked Queen Athaliah was executed (2 Chr.23:15). Being close to the palace and leading into the Kidron Valley, the Horse Gate was probably one of the major gates used for access to the palace.

The Horse Gate stirs thoughts of warfare. As believers we are in a constant warfare against the corruption of this world and against the wickedness launched by the forces of Satan himself. We must prepare ourselves to stand against the evil forces of this world:

> "For though we walk in the flesh, we do not war after the flesh: (For the weapons of our warfare *are* not carnal, but mighty through God to the pulling down of strong holds;) Casting down imaginations, and every high thing that exalteth itself against the knowledge of God, and bringing into captivity every thought to the obedience of Christ" (2 Co.10:3-5).

> "Finally, my brethren, be strong in the Lord, and in the power of his might. Put on the whole armour of God, that ye may be able to stand against the wiles of the devil. For we wrestle not against flesh and blood, but against principalities, against powers, against the rulers of the darkness of this world, against spiritual wickedness in high *places*. Wherefore take unto you the whole armour of God, that ye may be able to withstand in the evil day, and having done all, to stand. Stand therefore, having your loins girt about with truth, and having on the breastplate of righteousness; And your feet shod with the preparation of the gospel of peace; Above all, taking the shield of faith, wherewith ye shall be able to quench all the fiery darts of the wicked. And take the helmet of salvation, and the sword of the Spirit, which is the word of God: Praying always with all prayer and supplication in the Spirit, and watching thereunto with all perseverance and supplication for all saints" (Ep.6:10-18).

> "This charge I commit unto thee, son Timothy, according to the prophecies which went before on thee, that thou by them mightest war a good warfare; Holding faith, and a good conscience; which some having put away concerning faith have made shipwreck" (1 Ti.1:18-19).

> "But thou, O man of God, flee these things; and follow after righteousness, godliness, faith, love, patience, meekness. Fight the good fight of faith, lay hold on eternal life, whereunto thou art also called, and hast professed a good profession before many witnesses" (1 Ti.6:11-12).

> "Thou therefore endure hardness, as a good soldier of Jesus Christ. No man that warreth entangleth himself with the affairs of *this* life; that he may please him who hath chosen him to be a soldier" (2 Ti.2:3-4).

9. **The East Gate** (3:29): this gate was naturally located on the east wall and led directly to the temple. Warren Wiersbe points out that the Turks sealed up the gate in the sixteenth century, but it is probably what is known today as the Golden Gate. The Golden Gate is connected to the Messiah's coming in both Jewish and Christian worship and to future judgment among the Muslims.[2]

In one of his visions, Ezekiel saw the glory of the LORD leave the temple and depart through the East Gate (Eze.10:18-22; 11:22-25). Sometime later Ezekiel was given another vision showing God's glory returning to the temple through the East Gate (43:1-3). These facts plus the natural fact that the East Gate faces the rising sun suggests the coming again of Jesus Christ. As Scripture declares:

> "For the Son of man shall come in the glory of his Father with his angels; and then he shall reward every man according to his works" (Mt.16:27).

> "When the Son of man shall come in his glory, and all the holy angels with him, then shall he sit upon the throne of his glory: And before him shall be gathered all nations: and he shall separate them one from another, as a shepherd divideth *his* sheep from the goats" (Mt.25:31-32).

> "And there shall be signs in the sun, and in the moon, and in the stars; and upon the earth distress of nations, with perplexity; the sea and the waves roaring; Men's hearts failing them for fear, and for looking after those things which are coming on the earth: for the powers of heaven shall be shaken. And then shall they see the Son of man coming in a cloud with power and great glory. And when these things begin to come to pass, then look up, and lift up your heads; for your redemption draweth nigh" (Lu.21:25-28).

> "Which also said, Ye men of Galilee, why stand ye gazing up into heaven? this same Jesus, which is taken up from you into heaven, shall so come in like manner as ye have seen him go into heaven" (Ac.1:11).

> "For our conversation [conduct, behavior] is in heaven; from whence also we look for the Saviour, the Lord Jesus Christ: Who shall change our vile body, that it may be fashioned like unto his glorious body, according to the working whereby he is able even to subdue all things unto himself" (Ph.3:20-21).

> "For the Lord himself shall descend from heaven with a shout, with the voice of the archangel, and with the trump of God: and the dead in Christ shall rise first: Then we which are alive *and* remain shall be caught up together with them in the clouds, to meet the Lord in the air: and so shall we ever be with the Lord. Wherefore comfort one another with these words" (1 Th.4:16-18).

> "Teaching us that, denying ungodliness and worldly lusts, we should live soberly, righteously, and godly, in this present world; Looking for that blessed hope, and the glorious appearing of the great God and our Saviour Jesus Christ" (Tit.2:12-13).

> "And now, little children, abide in him; that, when he shall appear, we may have confidence, and not be ashamed before him at his coming" (1 Jn.2:28).

---

2 Warren W. Wiersbe. *Be Determined.* (Wheaton, IL: Victor Books, 1992), p.46.

10. **The Miphkad** or **Inspection Gate** (3:31): this gate was located on the east wall, close to the northeast corner. Its name Miphkad means review, numbering, counting, registering, inspecting. It is even called the Inspection Gate by some Bible translators. When a foreigner entered the city, he was to enter this gate and be registered. This was also the gate where the army was mobilized, registered, and marched in review.

The Inspection Gate reminds us that we too—both believers and unbelievers—will face the inspection and judgment of God.

a. Believers will have their works, their service for the LORD, inspected and judged.

> "According to the grace of God which is given unto me, as a wise masterbuilder, I have laid the foundation, and another buildeth thereon. But let every man take heed how he buildeth thereupon. For other foundation can no man lay than that is laid, which is Jesus Christ. Now if any man build upon this foundation gold, silver, precious stones, wood, hay, stubble; Every man's work shall be made manifest: for the day shall declare it, because it shall be revealed by fire; and the fire shall try every man's work of what sort it is. If any man's work abide which he hath built thereupon, he shall receive a reward. If any man's work shall be burned, he shall suffer loss: but he himself shall be saved; yet so as by fire" (1 Co.3:10-15).

> "For we must all appear before the judgment seat of Christ; that every one may receive the things *done* in *his* body, according to that he hath done, whether *it be* good or bad" (2 Co.5:10).

b. Unbelievers will be judged because they have not accepted Jesus Christ as their Savior and Lord.

> "When the Son of man shall come in his glory, and all the holy angels with him, then shall he sit upon the throne of his glory: And before him shall be gathered all nations: and he shall separate them one from another, as a shepherd divideth *his* sheep from the goats: And he shall set the sheep on his right hand, but the goats on the left.…Then shall he say also unto them on the left hand, Depart from me, ye cursed, into everlasting fire, prepared for the devil and his angels" (Mt.25:31-33, 41).

> "For God so loved the world, that he gave his only begotten Son, that whosoever believeth in him should not perish, but have everlasting life. For God sent not his Son into the world to condemn the world; but that the world through him might be saved. He that believeth on him is not condemned: but he that believeth not is condemned already, because he hath not believed in the name of the only begotten Son of God" (Jn.3:16-18).

> "He that believeth on the Son hath everlasting life: and he that believeth not the Son shall not see life; but the wrath of God abideth on him" (Jn.3:36).

> "I said therefore unto you, that ye shall die in your sins: for if ye believe not that I am *he,* ye shall die in your sins" (Jn.8:24).

> "The Lord knoweth how to deliver the godly out of temptations, and to reserve the unjust unto the day of judgment to be punished" (2 Pe.2:9).

> "And Enoch also, the seventh from Adam, prophesied of these, saying, Behold, the Lord cometh with ten thousands of his saints, To execute judgment upon all, and to convince all that are ungodly among them of all their ungodly deeds which they have ungodly committed, and of all their hard *speeches* which ungodly sinners have spoken against him" (Jude 1:14-15).

1. Strategy 1—Ridicule, mockery: Overcome by prayer & perseverance

a. The anger of Sanballat, the Samaritan governor: Ridiculed the Jews before the officials & army
  1) Ridiculed the workers: The "feeble Jews"
  2) Ridiculed their hope to protect themselves
  3) Ridiculed their religion: Would take more than God to rebuild the wall
  4) Ridiculed the materials: Using burned, cracked stones

b. The ridicule by Tobiah the Ammonite: Mocked the weakness of the wall, suggesting it would collapse under the weight of a fox

c. The answer to ridicule: Prayer & perseverance
  1) Nehemiah prayed to God
    • Shared the insults
    • Requested that the enemy reap what they had sown
    • Requested that true justice be executed

  2) Nehemiah & the people persevered, continued the work: The wall was completed to half its original height

2. Strategy 2—Conspiracy, devious plots: Overcome by standing watch & praying

a. The response of the surrounding enemies to the building of the wall: A growing anger, fury
  1) The enemies listed

  2) The plot: They formed an alliance & laid plans to attack Jerusalem

b. The answer to preventing or frustrating an attack by the enemy: Watching & praying

3. Strategy 3—Discouragement & fatigue: Overcome by drawing on the LORD's strength

a. The people's complaint: Weary
b. The answer: A strong commitment despite hardship, 13-23

CHAPTER 4

D. Nehemiah's Struggle with External Opposition: Four Strategies Used by the Enemies of Believers, 4:1-23

But it came to pass, that when Sanballat heard that we builded the wall, he was wroth, and took great indignation, and mocked the Jews.
2 And he spake before his brethren and the army of Samaria, and said, What do these feeble Jews? will they fortify themselves? will they sacrifice? will they make an end in a day? will they revive the stones out of the heaps of the rubbish which are burned?
3 Now Tobiah the Ammonite *was* by him, and he said, Even that which they build, if a fox go up, he shall even break down their stone wall.
4 Hear, O our God; for we are despised: and turn their reproach upon their own head, and give them for a prey in the land of captivity:
5 And cover not their iniquity, and let not their sin be blotted out from before thee: for they have provoked *thee* to anger before the builders.
6 So built we the wall; and all the wall was joined together unto the half thereof: for the people had a mind to work.
7 But it came to pass, *that* when Sanballat, and Tobiah, and the Arabians, and the Ammonites, and the Ashdodites, heard that the walls of Jerusalem were made up, *and* that the breaches began to be stopped, then they were very wroth,
8 And conspired all of them together to come *and* to fight against Jerusalem, and to hinder it.
9 Nevertheless we made our prayer unto our God, and set a watch against them day and night, because of them.
10 And Judah said, The strength of the bearers of burdens is decayed, and *there is* much rubbish; so that we are not able to build the wall.

---

11 And our adversaries said, They shall not know, neither see, till we come in the midst among them, and slay them, and cause the work to cease.
12 And it came to pass, that when the Jews which dwelt by them came, they said unto us ten times, From all places whence ye shall return unto us *they will be upon you.*
13 Therefore set I in the lower places behind the wall, *and* on the higher places, I even set the people after their families with their swords, their spears, and their bows.
14 And I looked, and rose up, and said unto the nobles, and to the rulers, and to the rest of the people, Be not ye afraid of them: remember the Lord, *which is* great and terrible, and fight for your brethren, your sons, and your daughters, your wives, and your houses.
15 And it came to pass, when our enemies heard that it was known unto us, and God had brought their counsel to nought, that we returned all of us to the wall, every one unto his work.
16 And it came to pass from that time forth, *that* the half of my servants wrought in the work, and the other half of them held both the spears, the shields, and the bows, and the habergeons; and the rulers *were* behind all the house of Judah.
17 They which builded on the wall, and they that bare burdens, with those that laded, *every one* with one of his hands wrought in the work, and with the other *hand* held a weapon.
18 For the builders, every one had his sword girded by his side, and *so* builded. And he that sounded the trumpet *was* by me.
19 And I said unto the nobles, and to the rulers, and to the rest of the people, The work *is* great and large, and we are separated upon the wall, one far from another.
20 In what place *therefore* ye hear the sound of the trumpet, resort ye thither unto us: our God shall fight for us.
21 So we laboured in the work: and half of them held

---

4. Strategy 4—Fear, threats, intimidation: Overcome by being armed & trusting God's power

a. The whispering campaign of the enemy
  1) They spread the rumor of a secret attack throughout the countryside
  2) Their purpose: To strike fear in the hearts of the Jewish builders

b. The answer to fear
  1) Nehemiah armed the people
    • Stationed them at the weak & exposed areas of the wall
    • Posted them by families
  2) Nehemiah assured & challenged the people
    • Assured them of the LORD's presence & power
    • Challenged them to not fear but remember the LORD, to pray & to be ready to fight

  3) Nehemiah led the people back to work: God frustrated the enemies' plans by helping to prepare His people

  4) Nehemiah organized the people for both work & battle
    • The people were divided into two groups: One-half stood guard while the others worked

    • The officers stood guard behind the workers
    • The people—all of them—bore weapons while working on the wall

    • The trumpet was to sound, warning of an attack

    • The people were to rest assured: God would fight for them; therefore, they were to immediately gather for battle at the sound of the trumpet

    • The people were assigned to work long hours,

from first light to pitch dark, & half the men were always on guard • The workers who lived outside the city camped in Jerusalem where guards were posted all night long	the spears from the rising of the morning till the stars appeared. 22 Likewise at the same time said I unto the people, Let every one with his servant lodge within Jerusalem, that in the night they may be a guard	to us, and labour on the day. 23 So neither I, nor my brethren, nor my servants, nor the men of the guard which followed me, none of us put off our clothes, *saving that* every one put them off for washing.	• The people stood ready for battle every moment of every day & night

DIVISION I

THE REBUILDING OF THE WALLS OF JERUSALEM, 1:1–7:73

D. Nehemiah's Struggle with External Opposition: Four Strategies Used by the Enemies of Believers, 4:1-23

(4:1-23) **Introduction**: persecution is a fact of life for true followers of Christ. If a person truly believes in Jesus Christ, he will live a righteous and holy life, keeping the commandments of God. But most people want little to do with God's commandments, with holy and righteous living. God's commandments demand that we live lives of unselfishness and service, but most people want to do what they want when they want. Few of us are willing to serve others wholeheartedly, giving sacrificially to meet the desperate needs of the world. Few of us are willing to love sacrificially, upholding others to the point of hurting ourselves. Few of us are willing to lay aside our prejudices, embracing those who are different, those who are poorer, less educated, less attractive or those of a different social class. How many of us are willing to truly love those who hate and despise us? What is our response when people curse and verbally abuse us or slander and spread rumors about us? What is our response when others ridicule or mock us, assault or attack us, or even murder a loved one? Do we love only those who love us? Or do we love everyone in the name of Jesus Christ?

The strategies used by the devil and his followers is the practical subject of this present Scripture. Satan will use every strategy possible to attack genuine believers, any person who truly follows Christ and seeks to keep the commandments of God.

In the former Scripture Nehemiah and the Jewish returnees had begun to rebuild the walls of the city. News of rebuilding the wall quickly traveled to the Jews' enemies. A strong Jerusalem was a threat to Sanballat and the officials of the other surrounding nations. And if the Jews became strong enough, Sanballat and his associates would lose power and influence. They would lose their position, recognition, and honor as local leaders of the area. In addition, they would lose the wealth and other payoffs they received from local businesses and commodities produced throughout Judah. In view of these things, they despised the Jews. Apparently, a spirit of anti-Semitism flowed heavily throughout the area. The neighbors bitterly hated and opposed the Jews, wanting to keep them weak and subservient, under the thumb of their influence and power. For all these reasons, the surrounding opposition sought to stop the rebuilding of Jerusalem and its walls. Four strategies were immediately devised to attack the Jews and stop the work. This is, *Nehemiah's Struggle with External Opposition: Four Strategies Used By the Enemies of Believers*, 4:1-23.

1. Strategy 1—ridicule, mockery: overcome by prayer and perseverance (vv.1-6).
2. Strategy 2—conspiring, plotting to attack: overcome by standing watch and praying (vv.7-9).
3. Strategy 3—discouragement and fatigue: overcome by drawing the LORD's strength (v.10).
4. Strategy 4—fear, threats, intimidation: overcome by being armed and trusting God's power (v.11-23).

1 (4:1-6) **Ridicule, Example of—Mockery, Strategy of the Devil—Scorn, Example of—Insult, Example of—Making Fun of, Example—Taunting, Example of—Ridicule, How to Conquer, Prayer—Perseverance, Answer to, Ridicule**: the first strategy used by the enemy was that of ridicule, insults, mockery. From the very first the opposition had determined to dishearten the Jews from rebuilding. Earlier, when they had first heard about the plans of Nehemiah to rebuild, the opposition had reared its ugly head and mocked the project as foolish. Furthermore, the opposition had actually accused the Jews of plotting to rebel against the Persians (2:19). But now, since the construction had actually begun, the opposition formulated a concrete strategy of taunting and scoffing to discourage the workers from rebuilding the walls of Jerusalem. Scripture describes exactly what happened:

OUTLINE	SCRIPTURE	SCRIPTURE	OUTLINE

1. **Strategy 1—Ridicule, mockery: Overcome by prayer & perseverance**
a. The anger of Sanballat, the Samaritan governor: Ridiculed the Jews before the officials & army
  1) Ridiculed the workers: The "feeble Jews"
  2) Ridiculed their hope to
	But it came to pass, that when Sanballat heard that we builded the wall, he was wroth, and took great indignation, and mocked the Jews.
	2 And he spake before his brethren and the army of Samaria, and said, What do these feeble Jews? will they
		fortify themselves? will they sacrifice? will they make an end in a day? will they revive the stones out of the heaps of the rubbish which are burned?
		3 Now Tobiah the Ammonite *was* by him, and he said, Even that which they build, if a fox go up, he shall even
			protect themselves
			  3) Ridiculed their religion: Would take more than God to rebuild the wall
			  4) Ridiculed the materials: Using burned, cracked stones
			b. The ridicule by Tobiah the Ammonite: Mocked the weakness of the wall, sug-

OUTLINE	SCRIPTURE	SCRIPTURE	OUTLINE
gesting it would collapse under the weight of a fox c. The answer to ridicule: Prayer & perseverance 1) Nehemiah prayed to God • Shared the insults • Requested that the enemy reap what they had sown • Requested that true jus-	break down their stone wall. 4 Hear, O our God; for we are despised: and turn their reproach upon their own head, and give them for a prey in the land of captivity: 5 And cover not their iniquity, and let not their sin	be blotted out from before thee: for they have provoked *thee* to anger before the builders. 6 So built we the wall; and all the wall was joined together unto the half thereof: for the people had a mind to work.	tice be executed 2) Nehemiah & the people persevered, continued the work: The wall was completed to half its original height

a. As soon as the construction began, news of the rebuilding quickly reached Sanballat, the Samaritan governor. He bitterly opposed the appointment of Nehemiah as governor of Jerusalem and, naturally, opposed the rebuilding of Jerusalem and its walls. The rebuilding project would strengthen the Jews, which in turn would cause Sanballat to lose his power and influence over the local area. Thus, hearing about the project made him very angry, so much so that he burned with rage against the Jews. Apparently he called a meeting of all his associates who opposed the Jews, and during the meeting he mobilized the Samarian army in an attempt to frighten the Jews. After the opposition had gathered, he publicly ridiculed the Jews before the officials and his army (v.2). In a series of rhetorical questions Sanballat sought to start a campaign of scorn and insults against Nehemiah and the Jews.

1) First, Sanballat ridiculed the workers by asking what the "feeble Jews" thought they were doing? The word *feeble* (amelal) means frail, miserable, powerless, withered, weak. From all outward appearance the Jews were a powerless people. They were poverty-stricken with no economic wealth whatsoever and no military to defend themselves. Being so feeble and undertaking such an enormous project made the Jews look foolish, laughable. Thus Sanballat aroused his followers to mockingly laugh, scorn, and ridicule the workers as they attempted this seemingly impossible job. There was simply too much destruction and debris, thousands of tons of stone and rubble to clean up as well as thousands of stones to be laid in building the wall. The Jews were fools and deserved to be mocked for undertaking such an unachievable task.

2) Second, Sanballat ridiculed the Jews' hope of protecting themselves by building the wall. He mockingly asked if they sought to strengthen themselves by hiding behind a restored, fortified wall. How could such a feeble people build a wall strong enough to protect themselves and their city from the attack of any army? In the minds of Sanballat and the opposition, the walls of Jerusalem had been so ruined that they could never be rebuilt to withstand any significant force. Hence the Jews' hope for protection was foolish and deserved to be mocked.

3) Third, Sanballat ridiculed the Jews' religion. He asked if they were going to offer sacrifices to seek their God's help in rebuilding the walls. He was suggesting that it would take more than God to rebuild such a devastated city and wall. No matter how much they prayed and sacrificed, their God was not powerful enough to use such a feeble people to complete such an impossible project.

4) Last of all, Sanballat even ridiculed the materials the Jews were using to rebuild the wall, that is, the stones taken out of the rubble. In fact, many of the stones were cracked and damaged as a result of the intense heat created when the city was burned by the Babylonians decades earlier.

b. Standing by Sanballat's side was Tobiah. Tobiah was an Ammonite official and also a fierce opponent of Nehemiah and the Jews (v.3). He joined in the ridicule by echoing Sanballat's mockery of the wall. Sneering at the Jews, he mockingly claimed that the wall was flimsy, so flimsy it would collapse if a fox climbed up and walked on it.

c. What was Nehemiah's answer to the ridicule and the threat of the Samaritan army? He prayed and persevered in the work (vv.4-6). When Nehemiah heard about the ridicule by the opposition and the mobilization of the Samaritan army, he immediately turned to the LORD in prayer. He shared the insults with the LORD and requested that the enemy reap exactly what they had sown. He asked the LORD to turn their scorn and mockery back upon their own heads and to give them over as captives in a foreign land. Furthermore Nehemiah requested that true justice be executed upon the opposition, that their sins and guilt not be ignored by the LORD nor their sins forgiven. Why would Nehemiah make what seems to be such harsh requests? Because the enemy had committed blasphemy against the LORD Himself, provoking the LORD to anger by opposing God's work. By opposing the Jews they were actually opposing God Himself and His Work through His people.

Note how Nehemiah's prayer is similar to the *imprecatory prayers* found in the Psalms and Jeremiah (Ps.5:10; 28:4-5; 31:17-18; 35:4-8; 58:6-11; 59:5, 11-13; 69:22-28; 79:6-7, 12; 83:9-18; 109:6-15; 137:7-9; 139:19-22; 140:9-11; Je.11:18-20; 15:15; 17:18; 18:19-23). When looking at imprecatory prayers such as these, two facts must always be kept in mind: the prayer is a request that *wicked people* reap exactly what they sow and that *true justice* always be executed. A personal, emotional vengeance is not the purpose of the prayer but rather to honor God and to deliver God's people. This justice is achieved when the wicked reap what they have sown and when true justice is executed.

Nehemiah had a second answer to those who were mocking and ridiculing the work: the answer of perseverance, of continuing on with the work (v.6). Thankfully, Nehemiah did not allow the insults to stop the work. He and the people stopped to pray. But once their prayer was finished, they immediately got back to work! Despite facing constant scorn and ridicule, they continued to work diligently toward the goal of completing the project. As a result, they soon completed the wall to half its original height.

Thought 1. Too many of us give up, back off, and get defeated when we are ridiculed, mocked, or scorned. When the world makes fun of or insults our testimony for Christ, far too many of us turn away from the LORD and turn back to the world. Some of us no longer witness for Christ or seek to win the lost to Him because of the ridicule. The fear of being scorned or embarrassed causes us to keep silent about the salvation that is in Christ. Others of us are committing sin and wickedness because we have given in to the taunting and pressure of friends. When they first invited us to join them in some forbidden behavior, we let them know that we did not engage in such conduct. But when they mocked and continued to offer the enticing seduction, some of us gave in. And we participated in the sin instead of taking a stand for righteousness. We simply could not stand up to their hurtful teasing and bullying.

The answer to this and all other mistreatment is prayer, trusting God for help. If we call upon the LORD, He will strengthen us to stand against every abuse and ill-treatment, against every trial and temptation that confronts us. Through prayer and perseverance we can conquer all who oppose us in the world:

(1) Through prayer we can be conquerors over all trials and temptations.

> "Ask, and it shall be given you; seek, and ye shall find; knock, and it shall be opened unto you: For every one that asketh receiveth; and he that seeketh findeth; and to him that knocketh it shall be opened" (Mt.7:7-8).
>
> "Watch and pray, that ye enter not into temptation: the spirit indeed *is* willing, but the flesh *is* weak" (Mt.26:41).
>
> "Therefore I say unto you, What things soever ye desire, when ye pray, believe that ye receive *them,* and ye shall have *them*" (Mk.11:24).
>
> "And he spake a parable unto them *to this end,* that men ought always to pray, and not to faint" (Lu.18:1).
>
> "And whatsoever ye shall ask in my name, that will I do, that the Father may be glorified in the Son. If ye shall ask any thing in my name, I will do *it*" (Jn.14:13-14).
>
> "If ye abide in me, and my words abide in you, ye shall ask what ye will, and it shall be done unto you" (Jn.15:7).
>
> "Hitherto have ye asked nothing in my name: ask, and ye shall receive, that your joy may be full" (Jn.16:24).
>
> "Praying always with all prayer and supplication in the Spirit, and watching thereunto with all perseverance and supplication for all saints" (Ep.6:18).
>
> "Is any among you afflicted? let him pray. Is any merry? let him sing psalms. Is any sick among you? let him call for the elders of the church; and let them pray over him, anointing him with oil in the name of the Lord" (Js.5:13-14).
>
> "And the prayer of faith shall save the sick, and the Lord shall raise him up; and if he have committed sins, they shall be forgiven him. Confess *your* faults one to another, and pray one for another, that ye may be healed. The effectual fervent prayer of a righteous man availeth much. Elias was a man subject to like passions as we are, and he prayed earnestly that it might not rain: and it rained not on the earth by the space of three years and six months. And he prayed again, and the heaven gave rain, and the earth brought forth her fruit" (Js.5:15-18).
>
> "But if from thence thou shalt seek the LORD thy God, thou shalt find *him,* if thou seek him with all thy heart and with all thy soul" (De.4:29).
>
> "He shall call upon me, and I will answer him: I *will be* with him in trouble; I will deliver him, and honour him" (Ps.91:15).
>
> "*When* the poor and needy seek water, and *there is* none, *and* their tongue faileth for thirst, I the LORD will hear them, *I* the God of Israel will not forsake them" (Is.41:17).

(2) We can conquer whatever the world throws at us by being steadfast and persevering to the end.

> "And ye shall be hated of all *men* for my name's sake: but he that endureth to the end shall be saved" (Mt.10:22).
>
> "As the Father hath loved me, so have I loved you: continue ye in my love" (Jn.15:9).
>
> "Therefore, my beloved brethren, be ye stedfast, unmovable, always abounding in the work of the Lord, forasmuch as ye know that your labour is not in vain in the Lord" (1 Co.15:58).
>
> "Stand fast therefore in the liberty wherewith Christ hath made us free, and be not entangled again with the yoke of bondage" (Ga.5:1).
>
> "And let us not be weary in well doing: for in due season we shall reap, if we faint not" (Ga.6:9).
>
> "Only let your conversation [behavior, conduct] be as it becometh the gospel of Christ: that whether I come and see you, or else be absent, I may hear of your affairs, that ye stand fast in one spirit, with one mind striving together for the faith of the gospel" (Ph.1:27).
>
> "Wherefore seeing we also are compassed about with so great a cloud of witnesses, let us lay aside every weight, and the sin which doth so easily beset *us,* and let us run with patience the race that is set before us, Looking unto Jesus the author and finisher of *our* faith; who for the joy that was set before him endured the cross, despising the shame, and is set down at the right hand of the throne of God. For consider him that endured such contradiction of sinners against himself, lest ye be wearied and faint in your minds. Ye have not yet resisted unto blood, striving against sin" (He.12:1-4).
>
> "Blessed *is* the man that endureth temptation: for when he is tried, he shall receive the crown of life, which the Lord hath promised to them that love him" (Js.1:12).
>
> "Wherefore gird up the loins of your mind, be sober, and hope to the end for the grace that is to be brought unto you at the revelation of Jesus Christ" (1 Pe.1:13).

"For this *is* thankworthy, if a man for conscience toward God endure grief, suffering wrongfully" (1 Pe.2:19).

"Be sober, be vigilant; because your adversary the devil, as a roaring lion, walketh about, seeking whom he may devour: Whom resist stedfast in the faith, knowing that the same afflictions are accomplished in your brethren that are in the world" (1 Pe.5:8-9).

"Ye therefore, beloved, seeing ye know *these things* before, beware lest ye also, being led away with the error of the wicked, fall from your own stedfastness. But grow in grace, and *in* the knowledge of our Lord and Saviour Jesus Christ. To him *be* glory both now and for ever. Amen" (2 Pe.3:17-18).

"Behold, I come quickly: hold that fast which thou hast, that no man take thy crown" (Re.3:11).

"The righteous also shall hold on his way, and he that hath clean hands shall be stronger and stronger" (Jb.17:9).

2 (4:7-9) **Standing Watch, Example—Prayer, Watching in, Example—Watchfulness, Example**: the second strategy of the opposition was to conspire against the Jews, plotting to attack them. When the opponents heard that half the wall had already been built, they knew that their strategy of ridicule and scorn had failed to stop the work. Scripture says that people in the surrounding areas were very *angry*, about the ongoing project. For this reason, the opponents formed an alliance and laid plans to attack the Jews who were rebuilding Jerusalem. No doubt they could have easily defeated the Jews, killing them and justifying their action by falsely accusing them of revolting against Persia. King Artaxerxes would most likely have accepted their false accusation since it involved a revolt against his throne. The same kind of situation had already been faced once before. Years earlier some opponents had accused the Jews of threatening to revolt and Artaxerxes had forced the Jewish exiles to stop rebuilding (Ezr.4:19-22). Note that the Jews were now completely surrounded by enemies:

⇒ in the north were Sanballat and the Samaritans
⇒ in the east were Tobiah and the Ammonites
⇒ in the south were Geshem (2:19) and the Arabs
⇒ in the west were the Ashdodites, who were the Philistines

What was Nehemiah's response when he heard about the plot of a secret attack against him and the Jews? He took the only action he could. He called the people to prayer and set guards all about the city to watch for the enemy's attack.

OUTLINE	SCRIPTURE	SCRIPTURE	OUTLINE
2. **Strategy 2—Conspiracy, devious plots: Overcome by standing watch & praying** a. The response of the surrounding enemies to the building of the wall: A growing anger, fury 1) The enemies listed	7 But it came to pass, *that* when Sanballat, and Tobiah, and the Arabians, and the Ammonites, and the Ashdodites, heard that the walls of Jerusalem were made up, *and* that the breaches began to be stopped, then they were very wroth,	8 And conspired all of them together to come *and* to fight against Jerusalem, and to hinder it. 9 Nevertheless we made our prayer unto our God, and set a watch against them day and night, because of them.	2) The plot: They formed an alliance & laid plans to attack Jerusalem b. The answer to preventing or frustrating an attack by the enemy: Watching & praying

Thought 1. Standing guard and praying are the very first steps to take against the enemy's attack. We must be spiritually alert, watching out for the seductive temptations and terrifying trials that Satan launches against us. He deposits evil thoughts in our minds, immoral and lawless and violent thoughts. But if we are watching and praying as we walk throughout the day, we can cast down evil imaginations and reject immoral and violent thoughts. We can capture every thought and subject it to Christ (2 Co.10:5). By watching and praying we can focus our minds only upon things that are true, honest, just, pure, lovely, and of good report (Ph.4:8). By controlling our thoughts we will naturally control our behavior, conquering the attacks of the enemy.

Even when unbelievers are aroused to persecute us because of our Christian testimony, we can overcome their attacks through watching and praying. God will strengthen us to walk through the attack, strengthen us to endure whatever insults or pain the enemy may inflict upon us. And if it is time for us to die and be carried home to heaven, even while the enemy is attacking us, quicker than the eye can blink, the LORD will transfer us into His very presence. And we will then be filled with joy and rejoicing beyond human measure.

However, the only way to conquer the attacks of Satan, whether spiritual, mental, or physical, is through a continuous walk of prayer and watching. We must guard ourselves against the evil attacks. Listen to what God's Holy Word says about watching and praying:

"Watch and pray, that ye enter not into temptation: the spirit indeed *is* willing, but the flesh *is* weak" (Mt.26:41).

"And he spake a parable unto them *to this end,* that men ought always to pray, and not to faint" (Lu.18:1).

"For I know this, that after my departing shall grievous wolves enter in among you, not sparing the flock. Also of your own selves shall men arise, speaking perverse things, to draw away disciples after them. Therefore watch, and remember, that by the space of three years I ceased not to warn every one night and day with tears. And now, brethren, I commend you to God, and to the word of his grace, which is able to build you up, and to give you an inheritance among all them which are sanctified." (Ac.20:29-32).

"Wherefore let him that thinketh he standeth take heed lest he fall" (1 Co.10:12).

"Watch ye, stand fast in the faith, quit you like men, be strong" (1 Co.16:13).

"Praying always with all prayer and supplication in the Spirit, and watching thereunto with all perseverance and supplication for all saints" (Ep.6:18).

"Continue in prayer, and watch in the same with thanksgiving" (Col.4:2).

"Be sober, be vigilant; because your adversary the devil, as a roaring lion, walketh about, seeking whom he may devour: Whom resist stedfast in the faith, knowing that the same afflictions are accomplished in your brethren that are in the world" (1 Pe.5:8-9).

"Be watchful, and strengthen the things which remain, that are ready to die: for I have not found thy works perfect before God. Remember therefore how thou hast received and heard, and hold fast, and repent. If therefore thou shalt not watch, I will come on thee as a thief, and thou shalt not know what hour I will come upon thee" (Re.3:2-3).

"Only take heed to thyself, and keep thy soul diligently, lest thou forget the things which thine eyes have seen, and lest they depart from thy heart all the days of thy life: but teach them thy sons, and thy sons' sons" (De.4:9).

"I said, I will take heed to my ways, that I sin not with my tongue: I will keep my mouth with a bridle, while the wicked is before me" (Ps.39:1).

3 **(4:10) Discouragement, Example of—Fatigue, Example of—Tired, Example of**: the third strategy of the opposition was to discourage the Jewish workers, to stir up complaints of weakness and fatigue. Physically, the workers were bound to be utterly exhausted. With so much rubbish to remove and so much heavy weight to lift, the people's energy no doubt often gave out. As a result, some of the people began to complain of stumbling under the weight of the heavy rubbish being removed and the heavy stones being lifted up for the masons. Long, hard hours had weakened the workers, so the complaint was that some were about to be crushed not only physically but also mentally and emotionally. Staggering under the enormous weights and the long exhausting hours, a number of people were on the verge of collapse.

It was an ideal time for the opponents to begin complaining and discouraging the people. The leaders of the opposition aroused some Judean workers to begin murmuring and grumbling against the heavy work load and long hours. Their purpose was to stir a revolt against such exhausting work. Why? Because these Judean workers were secretly cooperating with the opposition. They were related by marriage to some of the enemies and had apparently struck a deal to subvert the building project (6:17-19; 15-22). Instead of being wholly committed to the LORD, they sought to increase their influence and wealth by compromising with the unbelievers of the world. Coveting some payoff—a political or economic gain—they agreed to launch a campaign of complaints against such lengthy and strenuous hours of work. Thus they sought to stop the work of God through discouraging the other workers.

Nehemiah's specific answers to the people's complaints and discouragement are found in the next point. But first he needed to lead the people to make a stronger commitment to the LORD. Despite the hardship, they needed to work even harder, enduring the long hours and backbreaking work.

OUTLINE	SCRIPTURE
3. Strategy 3—Discouragement & fatigue: Overcome by drawing on the LORD's strength a. The people's complaint: Weary b. The answer: A strong commitment despite hardship, 13-23	10 And Judah said, The strength of the bearers of burdens is decayed, and *there is* much rubbish; so that we are not able to build the wall.

Thought 1. The answer to discouragement is to draw on the LORD's strength. Endurance, perseverance, and steadfastness in the task at hand come only through a strong commitment to the LORD and through His power. When discouragement strikes our hearts, we must press on, not giving in to feelings of despondency, depression, or disappointment. Giving in to discouragement will lead only to defeat, to an unfinished task, an incomplete project. Instead, we need to turn to the LORD more than ever and draw on *His* strength, asking Him to sustain and deliver us from a spirit of darkness and despair. Then we need to arise and get back to work. Seeing progress take place always encourages the human heart. Being fruitful and productive always stirs us to do more and more. Hence, the basic answer to discouragement is to get back to the work at hand, work harder, more diligently. Listen to what God's Holy Word says about endurance, being steadfast:

"Therefore, my beloved brethren, be ye stedfast, unmovable, always abounding in the work of the Lord, forasmuch as ye know that your labour is not in vain in the Lord" (1 Co.15:58).

"And let us not be weary in well doing: for in due season we shall reap, if we faint not" (Ga.6:9).

"Wherefore seeing we also are compassed about with so great a cloud of witnesses, let us lay aside every weight, and the sin which doth so easily beset us, and let us run with patience the race that is set before us, Looking unto Jesus the author and finisher of *our* faith; who for the joy that was set before him endured the cross, despising the shame, and is set down at the right hand of the throne of God. For consider him that endured such contradiction of sinners against himself, lest ye be wearied and faint in your minds. Ye have not yet resisted unto blood, striving against sin" (He.12:1-4).

"Blessed *is* the man that endureth temptation: for when he is tried, he shall receive the crown of life, which the Lord hath promised to them that love him" (Ja.1:12).

"Behold, we count them happy which endure. Ye have heard of the patience of Job, and have seen the end of the Lord; that the Lord is very pitiful, and of tender mercy" (Ja.5:11).

"For this *is* thankworthy, if a man for conscience toward God endure grief, suffering wrongfully" (1 Pe.2:19).

"Ye therefore, beloved, seeing ye know *these things* before, beware lest ye also, being led away with the error of the wicked, fall from your own stedfastness. But grow in grace, and *in* the knowledge of our Lord and Saviour Jesus Christ. To him *be* glory both now and for ever. Amen" (2 Pe.3:17-18).

4 (4:11-23) **Fear, Cause, Intimidation by Enemies—Threats, Results of, Fear—Intimidation, Answer to, Prayer and Arming Oneself—Fear, Answer to—Overcoming, Source of Strength**: the fourth strategy of the opposition was to strike fear in the hearts of the Jews by threatening and intimidating them. If an overwhelming fear gripped the Jews, they would be too troubled to continue their work in rebuilding the wall and city:

OUTLINE	SCRIPTURE	SCRIPTURE	OUTLINE
4. Strategy 4—Fear, threats, intimidation: Overcome by being armed & trusting God's power	11 And our adversaries said, They shall not know, neither see, till we come in the midst among them, and slay them, and cause the work to cease.	*were* behind all the house of Judah. 17 They which builded on the wall, and they that bare burdens, with those that laded, *every one* with one of his	
a. The whispering campaign of the enemy		hands wrought in the work, and with the other *hand* held a weapon.	• The officers stood guard behind the workers • The people—all of them—bore weapons while working on the wall
1) They spread the rumor of a secret attack throughout the countryside	12 And it came to pass, that when the Jews which dwelt by them came, they said unto		
2) Their purpose: To strike fear in the hearts of the Jewish builders	us ten times, From all places whence ye shall return unto us *they will be upon you.*	18 For the builders, every one had his sword girded by his side, and *so* builded. And he that sounded the trumpet	• The trumpet was to sound warning of an attack
b. The answer to fear	13 Therefore set I in the lower places behind the wall,	*was* by me.	
1) Nehemiah armed the people		19 And I said unto the nobles, and to the rulers, and to	
• Stationed them at the weak & exposed areas of the wall	*and* on the higher places, I even set the people after their families with their	the rest of the people, The work *is* great and large, and we are separated upon the wall, one far from another.	• The people were to rest assured: God would fight for them; therefore, they were to immediately gather for battle at the sound of the trumpet
• Posted them by families	swords, their spears, and their bows.	20 In what place *therefore* ye hear the sound of the trumpet,	
2) Nehemiah assured & challenged the people	14 And I looked, and rose up, and said unto the nobles, and to the rulers, and to the	resort ye thither unto us: our God shall fight for us.	
• Assured them of the LORD's presence & power	rest of the people, Be not ye afraid of them: remember the	21 So we laboured in the work: and half of them held	
• Challenged them to not fear but remember the LORD, to pray & to be ready to fight	Lord, *which is* great and terrible, and fight for your brethren, your sons, and your daughters, your wives, and your houses.	the spears from the rising of the morning till the stars appeared.	• The people were assigned to work long hours, from first light to pitch dark, & half the men were always on guard
3) Nehemiah led the people back to work: God frustrated the enemies' plans by helping to prepare His people	15 And it came to pass, when our enemies heard that it was known unto us, and God had brought their counsel to nought, that we returned all of us to the wall, every one unto his work.	22 Likewise at the same time said I unto the people, Let every one with his servant lodge within Jerusalem, that in the night they may be a guard to us, and labour on the day.	• The workers who lived outside the city camped in Jerusalem where guards were posted all night long
4) Nehemiah organized the people for both work & battle	16 And it came to pass from that time forth, *that* the half of my servants wrought in the work, and the other half of them held both the spears, the	23 So neither I, nor my brethren, nor my servants, nor the men of the guard which followed me, none of us put off our clothes, *saving*	• The people stood ready for battle every moment of every day & night
• The people were divided into two groups: One-half stood guard while the others worked	shields, and the bows, and the habergeons; and the rulers	*that* every one put them off for washing.	

a. The enemy's alliance initiated a whispering campaign that threatened an impending attack against the Jews. Rumors of the secret attack were planted within the villages and spread throughout the entire countryside of Judah (vv.11-12). Just as the enemy had anticipated, the report of an impending attack was repeated to Nehemiah and the Jews "ten times over," which means repeatedly—many, many times. It was rumored that the attack would come from all directions as well as unexpectedly, secretly. The opposition was continually advancing and expanding upon the rumor in order to keep the threat of attack alive in the minds of the Jewish workers, hoping to strike a numbing fear in their hearts.

b. When Nehemiah first heard of the threat, he immediately prepared to combat any possible conflict (vv.13-23). He took four steps to prepare the Jewish people for any secret attack that might be launched.

1) First, Nehemiah armed the people and stationed them at the weak and exposed areas of the wall (v.13). He posted the people by families, knowing that they would more readily fight and defend their own children, wives, relatives, and property (also see v.14). He then made sure that every family had swords, spears, and bows.

2) After reviewing the situation, Nehemiah assembled all the people together and challenged them (v.14). Assuring them of the LORD's presence and power, he challenged them to not fear, but to remember the LORD who is great and awesome. He assured them that the LORD would help and deliver them if they would just fight for their families and homes.

3) Nehemiah then led the people back to work, which demonstrated both their trust in the LORD and their endurance. Soon thereafter the enemy heard about the indomitable spirit of the Jewish workers. They knew that their plots had been frustrated. It was the LORD Himself who had frustrated their plots and brought their attacks against the Jews to nothing (Ps.33:10-11).

4) Knowing that the defense of the city was necessary while the workers continued the project, Nehemiah organized the people for both work and battle (vv.16-23). The steps taken were somewhat detailed:
⇒ The people were divided into two groups, one half standing guard while the other half worked (v.16).
⇒ The officers themselves stood guard behind the workers where they could protect and warn them of any impending attack (v.17).
⇒ All the people bore weapons while working on the wall (v.17). Those who carried materials carried their weapons with them, and those who were involved in actually building the wall had swords girded to their sides (v.18).
⇒ The warning of attack was to be sounded by a trumpeter who accompanied Nehemiah. Obviously, there were several other trumpeters stationed at strategic points who would also sound the warning to the workers up and down the wall.
⇒ The people were to rest assured that God would fight for them. Therefore, they were to immediately gather for battle at the sound of the trumpet (vv.19-20).
⇒ The people were assigned long hours, from first light to pitch dark. Half of the men were always on guard against an impending attack by the enemy (v.21).
⇒ The workers who lived outside the city were instructed to encamp in Jerusalem where guards were posted all night long (v.22).
⇒ The people stood ready for battle every moment of every day and night. They never took off their clothes nor set their weapons aside (v.23). Even when going for water, the worker took his weapon with him.

Thought 1. The way to overcome fear, threats, or intimidation is to do just what Nehemiah did: arm ourselves and trust God's power to deliver us. As we walk throughout life, enemy after enemy will attack us:
⇒ Some people may be irritated or offended by our personalities, may dislike and avoid us, may not want anything to do with us.
⇒ Other people may spread rumors about us or falsely accuse us, seeking to damage our reputations or images.
⇒ Others may seek some position, honor, or recognition that is due us, and do us harm in order to secure the benefit for themselves.
⇒ Still others may oppose us, curse or verbally assault us.
⇒ Others may even hate or despise us, assault, attack, or perhaps even murder us.

As believers in the Lord Jesus Christ, we take a stand for Christ and His righteousness. We bear witness to His saving grace and proclaim to the world the way of righteousness, that men and women must obey the commandments of God. As a result, many unbelievers in the world oppose us. And in some cases they even persecute us through ridicule, scorn, plots and schemes. In addition, they attempt to strike fear in our hearts through threats and intimidation. The answer to such attacks by unbelievers is twofold: we must arm ourselves and we must trust God's power to deliver us through the attacks.

(1) Listen to what God's Word says about being spiritually armed to stand against the attacks of the devil and his followers.

"**And that, knowing the time, that now *it is* high time to awake out of sleep: for now *is* our salvation nearer than when we believed. The night is far spent, the day is at hand: let us therefore cast off the works of darkness, and let us put on the armour of light**" (Ro.13:11-12).

"**By the word of truth, by the power of God, by the armour of righteousness on the right hand and on the left**" (2 Co.6:7).

"**For though we walk in the flesh, we do not war after the flesh: (For the weapons of our warfare *are* not carnal, but mighty through God to the pulling down of strong holds;) Casting down imaginations, and every high thing that exalteth itself against the knowledge of God, and bringing into captivity every thought to the obedience of Christ**" (2 Co.10:3-5).

"**Finally, my brethren, be strong in the Lord, and in the power of his might. Put on the whole armour of God, that ye may be able to stand against the wiles of the devil. For we wrestle not against flesh and blood, but against principalities, against powers, against the rulers of the darkness of this world, against spiritual wickedness in high *places*. Wherefore take unto you the whole armour of God, that ye may be able to withstand in the evil day, and having done all, to stand. Stand therefore, having your loins girt about with truth, and having on the breastplate of righteousness; And your feet shod with the preparation of the gospel of peace; Above all, taking the shield of faith,** wherewith ye shall be able to quench all the fiery darts of the wicked. And take the helmet of salvation, and the sword of the Spirit, which is the word of God: Praying always with all prayer and supplication in the Spirit, and watching thereunto with all perseverance and supplication for all saints" (Ep.6:10-18).

"But let us, who are of the day, be sober, putting on the breastplate of faith and love; and for an helmet, the hope of salvation. For God hath not appointed us to wrath, but to obtain salvation by our Lord Jesus Christ" (1 Th.5:8-9).

"But thou, O man of God, flee these things; and follow after righteousness, godliness, faith, love, patience, meekness. Fight the good fight of faith, lay hold on eternal life, whereunto thou art also called, and hast professed a good profession before many witnesses" (1 Ti.6:11-12).

"Thou therefore endure hardness, as a good soldier of Jesus Christ. No man that warreth entangleth himself with the affairs of *this* life; that he may please him who hath chosen him to be a soldier" (2 Ti.2:3-4).

"For the word of God *is* quick, and powerful, and sharper than any twoedged sword, piercing even to the dividing asunder of soul and spirit, and of the joints and marrow, and *is* a discerner of the thoughts and intents of the heart" (He.4:12).

"Be sober, be vigilant; because your adversary the devil, as a roaring lion, walketh about, seeking whom he may devour: Whom resist stedfast in the faith, knowing that the same afflictions are accomplished in your brethren that are in the world. But the God of all grace, who hath called us unto his eternal glory by Christ Jesus, after that ye have suffered a while, make you perfect, stablish, strengthen, settle *you*" (1 Pe.5:8-10).

"And they overcame him by the blood of the Lamb, and by the word of their testimony; and they loved not their lives unto the death" (Re.12:11).

(2) Listen to what God's Word says about trusting the power of God for deliverance:

"And Jesus came and spake unto them, saying, All power is given unto me in heaven and in earth" (Mt.28:18).

"But ye shall receive power, after that the Holy Ghost is come upon you: and ye shall be witnesses unto me both in Jerusalem, and in all Judaea, and in Samaria, and unto the uttermost part of the earth" (Ac.1:8).

"And with great power gave the apostles witness of the resurrection of the Lord Jesus: and great grace was upon them all" (Ac.4:33).

"And he said unto me, My grace is sufficient for thee: for my strength is made perfect in weakness. Most gladly therefore will I rather glory in my infirmities, that the power of Christ may rest upon me. Therefore I take pleasure in infirmities, in reproaches, in necessities, in persecutions, in distresses for Christ's sake: for when I am weak, then am I strong" (2 Co.12:9-10).

"Now unto him that is able to do exceeding abundantly above all that we ask or think, according to the power that worketh in us" (Ep.3:20).

"Who through faith subdued kingdoms, wrought righteousness, obtained promises, stopped the mouths of lions, Quenched the violence of fire, escaped the edge of the sword, out of weakness were made strong, waxed valiant in fight, turned to flight the armies of the aliens" (He.11:33-34).

"But they that wait upon the LORD shall renew *their* strength; they shall mount up with wings as eagles; they shall run, and not be weary; *and* they shall walk, and not faint" (Is.40:31).

"Fear thou not; for I *am* with thee: be not dismayed; for I *am* thy God: I will strengthen thee; yea, I will help thee; yea, I will uphold thee with the right hand of my righteousness" (Is.41:10).

"Fear not: for I have redeemed thee, I have called *thee* by thy name; thou *art* mine. When thou passest through the waters, I *will be* with thee; and through the rivers, they shall not overflow thee: when thou walkest through the fire, thou shalt not be burned; neither shall the flame kindle upon thee" (Is.43:1-2).

CHAPTER 5

E. Nehemiah's Struggle with Internal Strife: A Lesson on the Desperate Need to Love Our Neighbors As Ourselves, 5:1-19

1. The loud cry of protest against the rich Jews' selfishness: A picture of greed, covetousness, & insensitivity

a. Three groups were being oppressed during a famine, 3
1) The poor who did not have enough food to survive
2) Property owners who had to mortgage their fields & homes to buy food

3) Others who had to borrow money to pay their taxes

b. The complaint
1) During the famine, the wealthy were loaning money & charging too much interest, even demanding property & working-age children as collateral on their loans
2) The result: The peoples' property was being lost & their children enslaved

2. The godly anger of Nehemiah & his rebuke of the creditors: A need for the rich to repent

a. Nehemiah personally pondered the situation
b. Nehemiah called a public meeting to confront the guilty
1) He pointed out their inconsistent, contradictory behavior
• They had actually been buying back Jewish relatives who had been enslaved to Gentiles
• They themselves were now enslaving their fellow countrymen

2) He warned them: They must fear God
3) He challenged them to be witnesses for God: To avoid being reproached, mocked by the world
4) He gave his personal testimony: He, his family, & his officials were lending money to the needy but were not robbing them

And there was a great cry of the people and of their wives against their brethren the Jews.
2 For there were that said, We, our sons, and our daughters, *are* many: therefore we take up corn *for them,* that we may eat, and live.
3 *Some* also there were that said, We have mortgaged our lands, vineyards, and houses, that we might buy corn, because of the dearth.
4 There were also that said, We have borrowed money for the king's tribute, *and that upon* our lands and vineyards.
5 Yet now our flesh *is* as the flesh of our brethren, our children as their children: and, lo, we bring into bondage our sons and our daughters to be servants, and *some* of our daughters are brought unto bondage *already:* neither *is it* in our power *to redeem them;* for other men have our lands and vineyards.
6 And I was very angry when I heard their cry and these words.
7 Then I consulted with myself, and I rebuked the nobles, and the rulers, and said unto them, Ye exact usury, every one of his brother. And I set a great assembly against them.
8 And I said unto them, We after our ability have redeemed our brethren the Jews, which were sold unto the heathen; and will ye even sell your brethren? or shall they be sold unto us? Then held they their peace, and found nothing *to answer.*
9 Also I said, It *is* not good that ye do: ought ye not to walk in the fear of our God because of the reproach of the heathen our enemies?
10 I likewise, *and* my brethren, and my servants, might exact of them money and corn: I pray you, let us leave off this usury.

11 Restore, I pray you, to them, even this day, their lands, their vineyards, their oliveyards, and their houses, also the hundredth *part* of the money, and of the corn, the wine, and the oil, that ye exact of them.
12 Then said they, We will restore *them,* and will require nothing of them; so will we do as thou sayest. Then I called the priests, and took an oath of them, that they should do according to this promise.
13 Also I shook my lap, and said, So God shake out every man from his house, and from his labour, that performeth not this promise, even thus be he shaken out, and emptied. And all the congregation said, Amen, and praised the LORD. And the people did according to this promise.
14 Moreover from the time that I was appointed to be their governor in the land of Judah, from the twentieth year even unto the two and thirtieth year of Artaxerxes the king, *that is,* twelve years, I and my brethren have not eaten the bread of the governor.
15 But the former governors that *had been* before me were chargeable unto the people, and had taken of them bread and wine, beside forty shekels of silver; yea, even their servants bare rule over the people: but so did not I, because of the fear of God.
16 Yea, also I continued in the work of this wall, neither bought we any land: and all my servants *were* gathered thither unto the work.
17 Moreover *there were* at my table an hundred and fifty of the Jews and rulers, beside those that came unto us from among the heathen that *are* about us.
18 Now *that* which was prepared *for me* daily *was* one ox *and* six choice sheep; also fowls were prepared for me, and once in ten days store of all sorts of wine: yet for all this required not I the bread of the governor, because the bondage was heavy upon this people.
19 Think upon me, my God, for good, *according* to all that I have done for this people.

5) He called upon them to repent
• To return all property
• To return all interest charged

c. Nehemiah's rebuke bore fruit: The wealthy repented & promised to return the property & interest
1) Nehemiah quickly summoned the priests & placed the wealthy under oath
2) Nehemiah then symbolically & verbally warned the wealthy
• Symbolically, he shook out the folds in his robe
• Verbally, he asked God to shake out the possessions & house of any person who failed to keep his promise

3. The unselfish example of Nehemiah: A need for compassion & service

a. Nehemiah did not use the governor's expense account for his personal use, nor did he collect taxes from the people: He & his officials paid their own expenses

1) His contrast to the former governors
• They had placed a heavy tax burden on the people
• Their assistants had oppressed the people
2) His reason for compassion: He feared God
b. Nehemiah devoted himself to building the wall & serving the people, not to personal gain or acquiring land through tax default
c. Nehemiah shared his wealth with others
1) He supported 150 government officials & employees as well as returning exiles
2) He provided one ox, six sheep, & a large amount of poultry to be served every day & a large supply of wine every ten days—at his own expense
3) He never demanded provisions from the people: He had compassion on them

d. Nehemiah sought only to please the LORD: Asked God to remember him & his sacrificial service to the people

DIVISION I

THE REBUILDING OF THE WALLS OF JERUSALEM, 1:1–7:73

E. Nehemiah's Struggle with Internal Strife: A Lesson on the Desperate Need to Love Our Neighbors As Ourselves, 5:1-19

(5:1-19) **Introduction**: love is desperately needed in the world today. By the multiplied thousands, people are crying out for someone to love them, genuinely love and care for them. Just think of the fatherless children in the world, how desperately they need the love and guidance of a father. And the motherless children, how desperately they need the tender care and love of a mother. Think of the orphans in the world who have neither parent nor close relative to love and rear them. Think of the single mother struggling to rear her children with no help from the father, in many cases living in poverty. Think of the slow learner or shy or unpopular classmate who seems to have no friends. Think about the host of people who need someone to reach out to them in friendship and care: family members, relatives, fellow workers, or neighbors. No matter where we look, there is a desperate need for love. God Himself commands us to love one another, to love our neighbors as ourselves. This is the practical message of this Scripture.

In chapter four, Nehemiah faced stiff, external opposition to rebuilding the walls. In chapter six, he will again struggle with external opposition. But here in chapter five, Nehemiah faces the most serious threat of all, that of internal strife. The strife was so divisive that it threatened to destroy the unifying spirit and purpose of the people. If the strife was allowed to continue, the rebuilding of Jerusalem and the nation could cease. The Jewish people could cease to exist as a distinct nationality. If this was allowed to happen, the promises of God that were to come through the Jewish people would never be fulfilled. The world would never have the Holy Bible, God's Holy Word. Nor would we have the promised seed, the Messiah and Savior of the world, the Lord Jesus Christ. The world would be without both the Word of God and the Savior of the world. The heavy burden of solving the strife rested upon the shoulders of Nehemiah. How God used him to restore unity among the people and to guarantee the fulfillment of God's promises through the Jewish people is the historical subject of the present Scripture. This is, *Nehemiah's Struggle with Internal Strife: A Lesson on the Desperate Need to Love Our Neighbors As Ourselves,* 5:1-19.

1. The loud cry of protest against the rich Jews' selfishness: a picture of greed, covetousness, and insensitivity (vv.1-5).
2. The godly anger of Nehemiah and his rebuke of the creditors: a need for the rich to repent (vv.6-13).
3. The unselfish example of Nehemiah: a need for compassion and service (vv.14-19).

1 (5:1-5) **Selfishness—Greed—Covetousness—Insensitivity—Hard Heart—Wealthy, Sins of—Rich, the—Returnees, Jewish, Wealthy—Oppression, by the Wealthy, Three Examples**: there was a loud cry of protest against the wealthy Jews, for they were creating a serious economic crisis for the returnees. Right in the middle of rebuilding the walls of Jerusalem, the rich were oppressing the workers through exploitation and extortion in order to gain more for themselves. In desperation both husbands and wives approached Nehemiah with a loud cry of protest against the wealthy.

OUTLINE	SCRIPTURE	SCRIPTURE	OUTLINE
1. The loud cry of protest against the rich Jews' selfishness: A picture of greed, covetousness, & insensitivity	And there was a great cry of the people and of their wives against their brethren the Jews.	We have borrowed money for the king's tribute, *and that upon* our lands and vineyards.	row money to pay their taxes
a. Three groups were being oppressed during a famine, 3	2 For there were that said, We, our sons, and our daughters, *are* many: therefore we take up corn *for them,* that we may eat, and live.	5 Yet now our flesh *is* as the flesh of our brethren, our children as their children: and, lo, we bring into bondage our sons and our daughters to be servants, and *some* of our daughters are brought unto bondage *already:* neither *is it* in our power *to redeem them;* for other men have our lands and	b. The complaint
1) The poor who did not have enough food to survive			1) During the famine, the wealthy were loaning money & charging too much interest, even demanding property & working-age children as collateral on their loans
2) Property owners who had to mortgage their fields & homes to buy food	3 *Some* also there were that said, We have mortgaged our lands, vineyards, and houses, that we might buy corn, because of the dearth.		2) The result: The peoples' property was being lost & their children enslaved
3) Others who had to bor-	4 There were also that said,		

a. Three groups were being oppressed by the rich, who were taking advantage of the workers. First, there was a famine in the land (vv.1-4). Second, the workers had been laboring a long time on the wall, which was bound to cause a shortage of workers for their harvest. As a result, many families were evidently facing a crisis in gathering in the harvest. Also, remember that the workers from outlying villages had been forced to stay in Jerusalem for their safety because of the threat from surrounding nations (4:7-23, esp. 22-23). All these factors contributed to a serious economic and financial crisis for most of the workers: they were having to borrow money from the wealthy. Three groups in particular were being oppressed by the rich Jews:

⇒ the poor Jews who did not have enough food to survive (v.2)
⇒ the property owners who had to mortgage their fields and homes in order to buy food (v.3)
⇒ others who had to borrow money to pay their taxes to the Persian government (v.4)

b. The complaint was a loud outcry against the wealthy. They were helping by loaning money, but they were charging too much interest and were demanding property as collateral. In some cases, they were even demanding children as collateral, using them to work as slaves in their fields and businesses. The result was tragic, for the committed workers were losing what little money and property they had as well as their children.

The wealthy were exposing the true core of their hearts. They were basically selfish, insensitive, and hard-hearted toward others. Greed and covetousness gripped their hearts. Sadly, they were disobeying the LORD's commandments, for it was unlawful for Jews—true brothers in the LORD—to charge interest on money they loaned to one another (De.23:19-20). It was also wrong for fellow Jews to enslave one another. They could hire themselves out for labor, but they were never to be enslaved (Le.25:35-46). Brotherly love was to be the basic rule between the Jews, a love that was selfless and always sensitive to the needs of others (Ex.22:25-27; De.24:10-13). No one was to allow greed or covetousness to grip his or her heart.

Thought 1. Hard and selfish hearts cause all kinds of problems within society. Think what happens when the hearts of family members are hard and insensitive toward one another: adultery, incest, abuse, and many other forms of mistreatment take place. Think what happens in businesses when employers, employees, and fellow workers are hard-hearted and insensitive toward one another: lying, stealing, cheating, slander, unjust wages, prejudice, and a lack of recognition and appreciation take place. In truth, a selfish, hard, and insensitive heart is the cause of most wicked behavior in the world.

(1) Listen to what God's Holy Word says about hard, insensitive hearts:

"Then Judas, which had betrayeth him, when he saw that he was condemned, repented himself, and brought again the thirty pieces of silver to the chief priests and elders, Saying, I have sinned in that I have betrayed the innocent blood. And they said, What *is that* to us? see thou *to that*" (Mt.27:3-4).

"For the heart of this people is waxed gross, and their ears are dull of hearing, and their eyes have they closed; lest they should see with *their* eyes, and hear with *their* ears, and understand with *their* heart, and should be converted, and I should heal them" (Ac.28:27).

"But after thy hardness and impenitent heart treasurest up unto thyself wrath against the day of wrath and revelation of the righteous judgment of God; Who will render to every man according to his deeds: To them who by patient continuance in well doing seek for glory and honour and immortality, eternal life: But unto them that are contentious, and do not obey the truth, but obey unrighteousness, indignation and wrath, Tribulation and anguish, upon every soul of man that doeth evil, of the Jew first, and also of the Gentile" (Ro.2:5-9).

"This I say therefore, and testify in the Lord, that ye henceforth walk not as other Gentiles walk, in the vanity of their mind, Having the understanding darkened, being alienated from the life of God through the ignorance that is in them, because of the blindness of their heart: Who being past feeling have given themselves over unto lasciviousness, to work all uncleanness with greediness" (Ep.4:17-19).

"Now the Spirit speaketh expressly, that in the latter times some shall depart from the faith, giving heed to seducing spirits, and doctrines of devils; Speaking lies in hypocrisy; having their conscience seared with a hot iron" (1 Ti.4:1-2).

"Take heed, brethren, lest there be in any of you an evil heart of unbelief, in departing from the living God. But exhort one another daily, while it is called To day; lest any of you be hardened through the deceitfulness of sin" (He.3:12-13).

"Harden not your heart, as in the provocation, *and as in* the day of temptation in the wilderness: When your fathers tempted me, proved me, and saw my work. Forty years long was I grieved with *this* generation, and said, It *is* a people that do err in their heart, and they have not known my ways: Unto whom I sware in my wrath that they should not enter into my rest" (Ps.95:8-11).

"Happy *is* the man that feareth alway: but he that hardeneth his heart shall fall into mischief" (Pr.28:14).

"He, that being often reproved hardeneth *his* neck, shall suddenly be destroyed, and that without remedy" (Pr.29:1).

(2) Listen to what God says about selfishness, greed, and covetousness:

"I was a stranger, and ye took me not in: naked, and ye clothed me not: sick, and in prison, and ye visited me not. Then shall they also answer him, saying, Lord, when saw we thee an hungred, or athirst, or a stranger, or naked, or sick, or in prison, and did not minister unto thee? Then shall he answer them, saying, Verily I say unto you, Inasmuch as ye did *it* not to one of the least of these, ye did *it* not to me. And these shall go away into everlasting punishment: but the righteous into life eternal" (Mt.25:43-46).

"And he said unto them, Take heed, and beware of covetousness: for a man's life consisteth not in the abundance of the things which he possesseth. And he spake a parable unto them, saying, The ground of a certain rich man brought forth plentifully: And he thought within himself, saying, What shall I do, because I have no room where to bestow my fruits? And he said, This will I do: I will pull down my barns, and build greater; and there will I bestow all my fruits and my goods. And I will say to my soul, Soul, thou hast much goods laid up for many years; take thine ease, eat, drink, *and* be merry. But God said unto him, *Thou* fool, this night thy soul shall be required of thee: then whose shall those things be, which thou hast provided? So *is* he that layeth up treasure for himself, and is not rich toward God" (Lu.12:15-21).

"Mortify therefore your members which are upon the earth; fornication, uncleanness, inordinate affection, evil concupiscence, and covetousness, which is idolatry: For which things' sake the wrath of God cometh on the children of disobedience" (Col.3:5-6).

"For the love of money is the root of all evil: which while some coveted after, they have erred from the faith, and pierced themselves through with many sorrows" (1 Ti.6:10).

"This know also, that in the last days perilous times shall come. For men shall be lovers of their own selves, covetous, boasters, proud, blasphemers, disobedient to parents, unthankful, unholy, Without natural affection, trucebreakers, false accusers, incontinent, fierce, despisers of those that are good, Traitors, heady, highminded, lovers of pleasures more than lovers of God; Having a form of godliness, but denying the power thereof: from such turn away" (2 Ti.3:1-5).

"*Let your* conversation [behavior, conduct] *be* without covetousness; *and be* content with such things as ye have: for he hath said, I will never leave thee, nor forsake thee" (He.13:5).

"Hereby perceive we the love *of God*, because he laid down his life for us: and we ought to lay down *our* lives for the brethren. But whoso hath this world's good, and seeth his brother have need, and shutteth up his bowels *of compassion* from him, how dwelleth the love of God in him? My little children, let us not love in word, neither in tongue; but in deed and in truth" (1 Jn.3:16-18).

"Thou shalt not covet thy neighbour's house, thou shalt not covet thy neighbour's wife, nor his manservant, nor his maidservant, nor his ox, nor his ass, nor any thing that *is* thy neighbour's" (Ex.20:17).

"He that withholdeth corn, the people shall curse him: but blessing *shall be* upon the head of him that selleth *it*" (Pr.11:26).

"The desire of the slothful killeth him; for his hands refuse to labour. He coveteth greedily all the day long: but the righteous giveth and spareth not" (Pr.21:25-26).

"He that loveth silver shall not be satisfied with silver; nor he that loveth abundance with increase: this *is* also vanity" (Ec.5:10).

"Woe unto them that join house to house, *that* lay field to field, till *there be* no place, that they may be placed alone in the midst of the earth!" (Is.5:8).

"For from the least of them even unto the greatest of them every one *is* given to covetousness; and from the prophet even unto the priest every one dealeth falsely" (Je.6:13).

"As the partridge sitteth *on eggs,* and hatcheth *them* not; *so* he that getteth riches, and not by right, shall leave them in the midst of his days, and at his end shall be a fool" (Je.17:11).

"And they come unto thee as the people cometh, and they sit before thee *as* my people, and they hear thy words, but they will not do them: for with their mouth they show much love, *but* their heart goeth after their covetousness" (Eze.33:31).

"*Seemeth it* a small thing unto you to have eaten up the good pasture, but ye must tread down with your feet the residue of your pastures? and to have drunk of the deep waters, but ye must foul the residue with your feet?" (Eze.34:18).

"And they covet fields, and take *them* by violence; and houses, and take *them* away: so they oppress a man and his house, even a man and his heritage" (Mi.2:2).

"Woe to him that coveteth an evil covetousness to his house, that he may set his nest on high, that he may be delivered from the power of evil!" (Hab.2:9).

2 (5:6-13) **Repentance, Example of, the Rich—Wealthy, Repentance of, Example—Anger, Against Oppression, Example of—Rebuke, Example of, the Rich—Wealthy, Rebuke of, by Nehemiah**: Nehemiah became very angry at the wealthy and strongly rebuked them. Scripture records exactly what Nehemiah did:

OUTLINE	SCRIPTURE	SCRIPTURE	OUTLINE
2. The godly anger of Nehemiah & his rebuke of the creditors: A need for the rich to repent	6 And I was very angry when I heard their cry and these words.	they be sold unto us? Then held they their peace, and found nothing *to answer*.	low countrymen
a. Nehemiah personally pondered the situation	7 Then I consulted with myself, and I rebuked the nobles, and the rulers, and said unto them, Ye exact usury, every one of his brother. And I set a great assembly against them.	9 Also I said, It *is* not good that ye do: ought ye not to walk in the fear of our God because of the reproach of the heathen our enemies?	2) He warned them: They must fear God
b. Nehemiah then called a public meeting to confront them			3) He challenged them to be a witness for God: To avoid being reproached, mocked by the world
1) He pointed out their inconsistent, contradictory behavior	8 And I said unto them, We after our ability have redeemed our brethren the Jews, which were sold unto the heathen; and will ye even sell your brethren? or shall	10 I likewise, *and* my brethren, and my servants, might exact of them money and corn: I pray you, let us leave off this usury.	4) He gave his personal testimony: He, his family, & his officials were lending money to the needy, but were not robbing them
• They had actually been buying back Jewish relatives who had been enslaved to Gentiles		11 Restore, I pray you, to them, even this day, their lands, their vineyards, their	5) He called upon them to repent
• They themselves were now enslaving their fel-			

OUTLINE	SCRIPTURE	SCRIPTURE	OUTLINE
• To return all property • To return all interest charged c. Nehemiah's rebuke bore fruit: The wealthy repented & promised to return the property & interest 1) Nehemiah quickly summoned the priests & placed the wealthy under	oliveyards, and their houses, also the hundredth *part* of the money, and of the corn, the wine, and the oil, that ye exact of them. 12 Then said they, We will restore *them,* and will require nothing of them; so will we do as thou sayest. Then I called the priests, and took an oath of them, that they should do according to	this promise. 13 Also I shook my lap, and said, So God shake out every man from his house, and from his labour, that performeth not this promise, even thus be he shaken out, and emptied. And all the congregation said, Amen, and praised the LORD. And the people did according to this promise.	oath 2) Nehemiah then symbolically & verbally warned the wealthy • Symbolically, he shook out the folds in his robe • Verbally, he asked God to shake out the possessions & house of any person who failed to keep his promise

a. Although Nehemiah was angry—very angry—he controlled himself. A terrible *social injustice* was being committed, and the very economy of the new Jewish community and nation was being threatened. A few of the rich were accumulating the wealth of the nation, leaving the rest of the people to suffer under their oppression and exploitation. After all, it was the rich who had the resources to help those who were suffering due to the famine. The rich should have been compassionate, reaching out to meet the needs of those who were hurting and who had so little. Thus, Nehemiah's anger was justified, and his righteous indignation flared up against oppression and exploitation.

Yet, Nehemiah controlled his anger. He exercised restraint by getting alone and pondering the situation. He wisely and carefully spent time thinking through the action that needed to be taken. And action was definitely needed, for the rebuilding of Jerusalem and its walls was at risk. In fact, the very future of the nation was being threatened.

b. Having thought through the problem, Nehemiah called a public meeting to confront the wealthy nobles and officials of the land (vv.7-11). Standing face-to-face with them, he laid out a five point rebuke of their sinful, oppressive behavior.

1) He pointed out their inconsistent, contradictory behavior (vv.7-8). Since returning from exile, Nehemiah and the people had been buying back Jewish relatives who had been enslaved to various Gentiles throughout the Persian Empire. But, now, in the present situation, the wealthy were enslaving their fellow countrymen, which meant that the previously enslaved (to Babylon) had been freed only to be enslaved once again. However, this time they were being enslaved by their own Jewish brothers. In some cases, the wealthy were even selling their fellow countrymen into slavery in order to increase their own financial wealth and cash flow (Eze.27:13; Joel 3:3-8; Am.1:9).

2) Nehemiah warned the wealthy of the land: they must *fear God*. Fearing God means both to reverence God and to fear His coming judgment. A person who fears God is a person who bows before Him, acknowledging that He is the Creator who deserves the worship and service of all people. To reverence God means to praise and give thanks to Him for all the blessings and gifts of life. But a person must also fear the holiness and righteousness of God, bear the fact that He will execute justice on the earth. All people will face the hand of God's judgment for their evil and wickedness. For this reason, Nehemiah was compelled to warn the wealthy among the Jews that they must fear God. They must show reverence by worshipping Him, and they must fear the hand of His judgment if they continued in their exploitation and oppression of the poor.

3) Nehemiah then challenged the wealthy to be witnesses for God (v.9). Presently, they were anything but witnesses. Instead of being a testimony of brotherly love to the unbelievers of the world, they were causing the unbelievers to mock the Name of God. The Jews professed to be followers of the LORD, but here they were dishonoring and disobeying Him. Their disobedience became a scandal throughout the surrounding nations. Because of this wicked behavior, the Gentile unbelievers were mocking both the Name of God and the Jews themselves.

4) Nehemiah gave his own personal testimony to the wealthy (v.10). He, his family, and his associates were lending money and grain to the needy as well, but they were not charging interest. They were not robbing them. Thus Nehemiah forcefully demanded that the rich stop charging interest for the loans to their brothers.

5) Finally, Nehemiah called upon the wealthy to repent of their sinful, wicked exploitation and oppression (v.11). He demanded that they return all property they had confiscated, including fields, vineyards, olive groves, and houses. He also demanded that they return all interest they had been charging for their loans. This apparently amounted to 12 percent a year, for the "hundredth part" would most likely refer to one percent per month. All the property and the interest charged were to be returned at once.

c. Nehemiah's rebuke made an immediate impact on the wealthy. They promised to repent and to return the property and interest they had accumulated (vv.12-13). In order to seal their commitment, Nehemiah quickly summoned the priests and placed the wealthy under oath. Knowing that promises were often not carried out, Nehemiah symbolically warned the wealthy (v.13). He shook out the folds in his robe, which was a picture of exactly what God would do with the wealthy if they failed to fulfill their promise. Verbally, Nehemiah asked God to shake out the possessions and house of any of the wealthy who failed to keep their promise. In response, the whole assembly responded with a resounding, "Amen." They were expressing their strong agreement with the action that had been taken by Nehemiah and the repentance of the wealthy.

Thought 1. The wealthy of the land were guilty of oppression and exploitation, of stealing from others in order to increase their own wealth. Therefore, they needed to repent. So it is with any of us: when we commit sin, we too need to repent. We need to turn from whatever wickedness we are committing and turn back to God. Wickedness will result in the hand of God's judgment falling upon us. And the only way to escape the judgment of God is to repent, turn back to Him. Whether rich or poor, if we are committing sin, we must repent or else face the terrifying judgment of God. Listen to what God's Word says about repentance:

"I tell you, Nay: but, except ye repent, ye shall all likewise perish" (Lu.13:3).

"Then Peter said unto them, Repent, and be baptized every one of you in the name of Jesus Christ for the remission of sins, and ye shall receive the gift of the Holy Ghost" (Ac.2:38).

"Repent ye therefore, and be converted, that your sins may be blotted out, when the times of refreshing shall come from the presence of the Lord" (Ac.3:19).

"Repent therefore of this thy wickedness, and pray God, if perhaps the thought of thine heart may be forgiven thee" (Ac.8:22).

"If my people, which are called by my name, shall humble themselves, and pray, and seek my face, and turn from their wicked ways; then will I hear from heaven, and will forgive their sin, and will heal their land" (2 Chr.7:14).

"The LORD is nigh unto them that are of a broken heart; and saveth such as be of a contrite spirit" (Ps.34:18).

"The sacrifices of God are a broken spirit: a broken and a contrite heart, O God, thou wilt not despise" (Ps.51:17).

"Let the wicked forsake his way, and the unrighteous man his thoughts: and let him return unto the LORD, and he will have mercy upon him; and to our God, for he will abundantly pardon" (Is.55:7).

---

3 (5:14-19) **Compassion, Example of—Service, Example of—Example, of Unselfish Service—Nehemiah, Compassion and Service of—Leadership, of Nehemiah, a Strong Example—Leadership, Duty, to Be Unselfish; to Be Compassionate; to Serve**: Nehemiah was a sterling role model for leaders of all succeeding generations. Although he was governor for 12 years during the reign of King Artaxerxes, he did not use his position to build a kingdom for himself. Rather, he used his authority to serve the people. As a national leader, Nehemiah's unselfish service sets a dynamic example for leaders of all generations.

OUTLINE	SCRIPTURE	SCRIPTURE	OUTLINE
3. The unselfish example of Nehemiah: A need for compassion & service a. Nehemiah did not use the governor's expense account for his personal use, nor did he collect taxes from the people: He & his officials paid their own expenses 1) His contrast to the former governors • They had placed a heavy tax burden on the people • Their assistants had oppressed the people 2) His reason for compassion: He feared God b. Nehemiah devoted himself to building the wall & serving the people, not to personal	14 Moreover from the time that I was appointed to be their governor in the land of Judah, from the twentieth year even unto the two and thirtieth year of Artaxerxes the king, that is, twelve years, I and my brethren have not eaten the bread of the governor. 15 But the former governors that had been before me were chargeable unto the people, and had taken of them bread and wine, beside forty shekels of silver; yea, even their servants bare rule over the people: but so did not I, because of the fear of God. 16 Yea, also I continued in the work of this wall, neither bought we any land: and all	my servants were gathered thither unto the work. 17 Moreover there were at my table an hundred and fifty of the Jews and rulers, beside those that came unto us from among the heathen that are about us. 18 Now that which was prepared for me daily was one ox and six choice sheep; also fowls were prepared for me, and once in ten days store of all sorts of wine: yet for all this required not I the bread of the governor, because the bondage was heavy upon this people. 19 Think upon me, my God, for good, according to all that I have done for this people.	gain or acquiring land through tax default c. Nehemiah shared his wealth with others 1) He supported 150 government officials & employees as well as returning exiles 2) He provided one ox, six sheep, & a large amount of poultry to be served every day & a large supply of wine every ten days—at his own expense 3) He never demanded provisions from the people: He had compassion on them d. Nehemiah sought only to please the LORD: Asked God to remember him & his sacrificial service to the people

a. First, Nehemiah did not use the governor's expense account for his own personal use nor did he collect taxes from the people (vv.14-15). Instead, he and his officials paid their own expenses. This was in contrast to the former governors and officials. Like so many in positions of authority, the former politicians had placed a heavy tax burden on the people. Their assistants had also sought to increase their own wealth by making excessive demands and taking advantage of the people. But not Nehemiah and his officials. They feared and reverenced God and His judgment if they proved to be disobedient and selfish, seeking their own gain.

b. Second, Nehemiah devoted himself to the task assigned him, that of rebuilding the walls of Jerusalem. He and his officials had a definite task to achieve, and they were totally committed to completing their task. Gaining personal wealth and acquiring property was not their purpose. Unlike some of the wealthy, Nehemiah and his officials did not confiscate any property due to the people's failure to pay taxes or debts.

c. Thirdly, rather than building the wealth of his own estate, Nehemiah shared his wealth with others (vv.17-18). In fact, he supported 150 officials and employees who served in his government, as well as many of the exiles who had returned from the Babylonian captivity. Each day he provided an ox, six sheep, and a large amount of poultry. In addition he served a large supply of wine every ten days. All this was at his own expense, which indicates that he was very wealthy. Of course, he was responsible to entertain all guests and visitors who came to Judah on official business. Underwriting such a large government expense from his own personal savings was bound to be very costly. He did this throughout the entire 12 years of his governorship, never demanding provisions from the people. Obviously, he felt the people had enough pressure on them in rebuilding their homes, city, and its walls. They also bore the weight of excessive taxation demanded by the Persians. Although Nehemiah had the right to demand some taxation to support the local government, he had compassion on the people, never demanding the taxes allowed the governor. He longed for them to complete their task of rebuilding their city and its walls, as well as their own personal homes.

d. During the entirety of Nehemiah's 12 years as leader, he sought only to please the LORD. God had given him a task to do, and he was totally devoted to completing his task. In obedience to the LORD's call, Nehemiah served the people with an unselfish, compassionate heart. He served the LORD faithfully. Thus at the end of his governorship, he asked God to remember him with favor. He had sacrificially served the people, just as the LORD had appointed him to do.

Thought 1. All over the world there is a desperate need for compassion and service. People are in pain, hurting and suffering. Every community is filled with those who are suffering emotional, physical, or mental pain. Still more are financially burdened or in need materially. Think about...

- the orphans, widows and widowers
- the brokenhearted, backslidden and prisoner
- the diseased, injured, handicapped
- the hungry, thirsty, poverty-stricken
- the empty, lonely, depressed
- the hospitalized, shut-ins, dying

A staggering number of people are suffering every day, people within our communities, villages, and cities. In many cases the needs of these people will never be met unless we help them. Their only hope is for us to reach out in service to them and have compassion.

(1) Listen to what God's Holy Word says about compassion:

"Jesus said unto him, If thou wilt be perfect, go *and* sell that thou hast, and give to the poor, and thou shalt have treasure in heaven: and come *and* follow me" (Mt.19:21).

"And the second *is* like unto it, Thou shalt love thy neighbour as thyself" (Mt.22:39).

"For I was an hungred, and ye gave me meat: I was thirsty, and ye gave me drink: I was a stranger, and ye took me in: Naked, and ye clothed me: I was sick, and ye visited me: I was in prison, and ye came unto me. Then shall the righteous answer him, saying, Lord, when saw we thee an hungred, and fed *thee?* or thirsty, and gave *thee* drink? When saw we thee a stranger, and took *thee* in? or naked, and clothed *thee?* Or when saw we thee sick, or in prison, and came unto thee? And the King shall answer and say unto them, Verily I say unto you, Inasmuch as ye have done *it* unto one of the least of these my brethren, ye have done *it* unto me" (Mt.25:35-40).

"But a certain Samaritan, as he journeyed, came where he was: and when he saw him, he had compassion *on him,* And went to *him,* and bound up his wounds, pouring in oil and wine, and set him on his own beast, and brought him to an inn, and took care of him" (Lu.10:33-34).

"I have showed you all things, how that so labouring ye ought to support the weak, and to remember the words of the Lord Jesus, how he said, It is more blessed to give than to receive" (Ac.20:35).

"Therefore if thine enemy hunger, feed him; if he thirst, give him drink: for in so doing thou shalt heap coals of fire on his head" (Ro.12:20).

"We then that are strong ought to bear the infirmities of the weak, and not to please ourselves" (Ro.15:1).

"Let no man seek his own, but every man another's *wealth*" (1 Co.10:24).

"Even as I please all *men* in all *things*, not seeking mine own profit, but the *profit* of many, that they may be saved" (1 Co.10:33).

"For ye know the grace of our Lord Jesus Christ, that, though he was rich, yet for your sakes he became poor, that ye through his poverty might be rich" (2 Co.8:9).

"Bear ye one another's burdens, and so fulfil the law of Christ" (Ga.6:2).

"Put on therefore, as the elect of God, holy and beloved, bowels of mercies, kindness, humbleness of mind, meekness, longsuffering" (Col.3:12).

"Remember them that are in bonds, as bound with them; *and* them which suffer adversity, as being yourselves also in the body" (He.13:3).

"Pure religion and undefiled before God and the Father is this, To visit the fatherless and widows in their affliction, *and* to keep himself unspotted from the world" (Js.1:27).

"But whoso hath this world's good, and seeth his brother have need, and shutteth up his bowels *of compassion* from him, how dwelleth the love of God in him? My little children, let us not love in word, neither in tongue; but in deed and in truth" (1 Jn.3:17-18).

"Love ye therefore the stranger: for ye were strangers in the land of Egypt" (De.10:19).

"I was eyes to the blind, and feet *was* I to the lame. I *was* a father to the poor: and the cause *which* I knew not I searched out" (Jb.29:15-16).

"She stretcheth out her hand to the poor; yea, she reacheth forth her hands to the needy" (Pr.31:20).

"The Lord GOD hath given me the tongue of the learned, that I should know how to speak a word in season to *him that is* weary: he wakeneth morning by morning, he wakeneth mine ear to hear as the learned" (Is.50:4).

"*Is* not this the fast that I have chosen? to loose the bands of wickedness, to undo the heavy burdens, and to let the oppressed go free, and that ye break every yoke? *Is it* not to deal thy bread to the hungry, and that thou bring the poor that are cast out to thy house? when thou seest the naked, that thou cover him; and that thou hide not thyself from thine own flesh?" (Is.58:6-7).

(2) Listen to what God's Word says about service:

"And whosoever shall give to drink unto one of these little ones a cup of cold *water* only in the name of a disciple, verily I say unto you, he shall in no wise lose his reward" (Mt.10:42).

"But so shall it not be among you: but whosoever will be great among you, shall be your minister: And whosoever of you will be the chiefest, shall be servant of all. For even the Son of man came not to be ministered unto, but to minister, and to give his life a ransom for many" (Mk.10:43-45).

"And Jesus answering said, A certain *man* went down from Jerusalem to Jericho, and fell among thieves, which stripped him of his raiment, and wounded *him*, and departed, leaving *him* half dead. And by chance there came down a certain priest that way: and when he saw him, he passed by on the other side. And likewise a Levite, when he was at the place, came and looked *on him*, and passed by on the other side. But a certain Samaritan, as he journeyed, came where he was: and when he saw him, he had compassion *on him*, And went to *him*, and bound up his wounds, pouring in oil and wine, and set him on his own beast, and brought him to an inn, and took care of him. And on the morrow when he departed, he took out two pence, and gave *them* to the host, and said unto him, Take care of him; and whatsoever thou spendest more, when I come again, I will repay thee. Which now of these three, thinkest thou, was neighbour unto him that fell among the thieves?" (Lu.10:30-36).

"If I then, *your* Lord and Master, have washed your feet; ye also ought to wash one another's feet" (Jn.13:14).

"He saith to him again the second time, Simon, *son* of Jonas, lovest thou me? He saith unto him, Yea, Lord; thou knowest that I love thee. He saith unto him, Feed my sheep" (Jn.21:16).

"How God anointed Jesus of Nazareth with the Holy Ghost and with power: who went about doing good, and healing all that were oppressed of the devil; for God was with him" (Ac.10:38).

"Bear ye one another's burdens, and so fulfil the law of Christ" (Ga.6:2).

"As we have therefore opportunity, let us do good unto all *men*, especially unto them who are of the household of faith" (Ga.6:10).

"Charge them that are rich in this world, that they be not highminded, nor trust in uncertain riches, but in the living God, who giveth us richly all things to enjoy; That they do good, that they be rich in good works, ready to distribute, willing to communicate [give, show benevolence]; Laying up in store for themselves a good foundation against the time to come, that they may lay hold on eternal life" (1 Ti.6:17-19).

"They that sow in tears shall reap in joy. He that goeth forth and weepeth, bearing precious seed, shall doubtless come again with rejoicing, bringing his sheaves *with him*" (Ps.126:5-6).

CHAPTER 6

F. Nehemiah's Struggle with Plots Against Him Personally: An Urgent Need for Discernment & Wisdom, 6:1-14

1. Scheme 1: Compromise, co-operation with worldly unbelievers
a. The enemies' scheme
   1) They heard that the wall had been almost completed: Only the gates remained to be hung
   2) They sent a message to Nehemiah pretending to desire compromise & co-operation: Tried to lure, seduce him to a meeting so they could kill him
b. Nehemiah's wise reply
   1) He could not leave the work unsupervised
   2) He suspected foul play, but left the door open for them to suggest meeting in Jerusalem—if they were sincere
c. The enemies' insincerity: Rather than suggesting a meeting in Jerusalem, they sent the same message *four* times

2. Scheme 2: Slander, rumor, lies
a. The enemies' scheme: They sent an *unsealed letter* to Nehemiah so people would read it & spread its lies
   1) Sanballat charged Nehemiah with plotting a rebellion to set himself up as king
      • Alleged that this was the real reason he was building the wall
      • Alleged that certain prophets were already proclaiming him king

Now it came to pass, when Sanballat, and Tobiah, and Geshem the Arabian, and the rest of our enemies, heard that I had builded the wall, and *that* there was no breach left therein; (though at that time I had not set up the doors upon the gates;)
2 That Sanballat and Geshem sent unto me, saying, Come, let us meet together in *some one of* the villages in the plain of Ono. But they thought to do me mischief.
3 And I sent messengers unto them, saying, I *am* doing a great work, so that I cannot come down: why should the work cease, whilst I leave it, and come down to you?
4 Yet they sent unto me four times after this sort; and I answered them after the same manner.
5 Then sent Sanballat his servant unto me in like manner the fifth time with an open letter in his hand;
6 Wherein *was* written, It is reported among the heathen, and Gashmu saith *it, that* thou and the Jews think to rebel: for which cause thou buildest the wall, that thou mayest be their king, according to these words.
7 And thou hast also appointed prophets to preach of thee at Jerusalem, saying, *There is* a king in Judah: and

now shall it be reported to the king according to these words. Come now therefore, and let us take counsel together.
8 Then I sent unto him, saying, There are no such things done as thou sayest, but thou feignest them out of thine own heart.
9 For they all made us afraid, saying, Their hands shall be weakened from the work, that it be not done. Now therefore, *O God,* strengthen my hands.
10 Afterward I came unto the house of Shemaiah the son of Delaiah the son of Mehetabeel, who *was* shut up; and he said, Let us meet together in the house of God, within the temple, and let us shut the doors of the temple: for they will come to slay thee; yea, in the night will they come to slay thee.
11 And I said, Should such a man as I flee? and who *is there,* that, *being as I am,* would go into the temple to save his life? I will not go in.
12 And, lo, I perceived that God had not sent him; but that he pronounced this prophecy against me: for Tobiah and Sanballat had hired him.
13 Therefore *was* he hired, that I should be afraid, and do so, and sin, and *that* they might have *matter* for an evil report, that they might reproach me.
14 My God, think thou upon Tobiah and Sanballat according to these their works, and on the prophetess Noadiah, and the rest of the prophets, that would have put me in fear.

   2) Sanballat warned Nehemiah that this report would be taken to the king of Persia—unless he met with them
b. Nehemiah's immediate response
   1) He denied the slander
   2) He boldly charged the enemy with lying & deception
   3) He prayed for strength: Because he knew the enemy was using intimidation to stop the work

3. Scheme 3: Acting cowardly & disobeying God
a. The enemies' scheme: They hired the priest Shemaiah to deceive Nehemiah & lead him into a trap
   1) He warned Nehemiah of an assassination plot to happen that very night
   2) He suggested they hide in the temple (Holy Place)
b. Nehemiah's refusal
   1) He must not be cowardly
   2) He would not disobey God: Only priests could enter the Holy Place, Nu.18:7
   3) He knew that his enemies Tobiah & Sanballat had hired the priest

   • To strike fear in Nehemiah
   • To seduce Nehemiah to sin & discredit himself

c. Nehemiah's prayer: That God would execute true justice against Tobiah & Sanballat, against the prophetess Noadiah, & against some other unnamed prophets who opposed God's work

DIVISION I

THE REBUILDING OF THE WALLS OF JERUSALEM, 1:1–7:73

F. Nehemiah's Struggle with Plots Against Him Personally: An Urgent Need for Discernment and Wisdom, 6:1-14

(6:1-14) **Introduction**: two of the greatest traits a person can have are those of discernment and wisdom. If a person can discern between good and evil and then make wise decisions based upon that knowledge, he can exercise control over his life, doing good and reaping good. He can live a fruitful, productive, and victorious life. But having the ability to discern and make wise decisions does not free us from the problems and difficulties of life. While we live in this corruptible world, there will always be both spiritual and human forces who will oppose us. No matter how gracious or kind we may be, some people will dislike us, shun us, and want no contact with us. Some may even become bitter toward us, hating and despising us. Others may abuse, assault, or seek to do us bodily harm. There will also be a barrage of temptations and trials that confront us from day-to-day.

When we are opposed by others or attacked spiritually through enticing temptations or difficult trials, we need the ability to discern between what is true and false, what is good and bad. Then we need the wisdom and courage to know how to respond to and conquer the situation. The constant need for discernment and wisdom is the practical subject of the present Scripture.

Nehemiah's opponents had failed miserably in their attempt to derail his rebuilding of Jerusalem and it's wall. Therefore, they changed their strategy. Instead of launching disruptive strikes against the construction project itself, they sought to attack Nehemiah personally. They were now desperate, for the wall was near completion. If it was ever finished, they would lose all hope of continuing to control the people of Judah and to profit off of them commercially. Their authority over the area would be greatly diminished. Furthermore, they would never be able to attack Jerusalem militarily because the Persian king himself had appointed Nehemiah to rebuild the city and its wall. Thus once completed, the wall would allow the Jewish returnees to become more settled and grow stronger year by year. In coming decades, there was even the possibility that the Jews could become more powerful than the surrounding nations and begin to exert control over them. In desperation, the officials of the surrounding nations plotted to assassinate Nehemiah and to discredit him among the people. Three different schemes were launched against God's lay servant, schemes that are still used by the enemies of God's people today. This is, *Nehemiah's Struggle with Plots Against Him Personally: An Urgent Need for Discernment and Wisdom*, 6:1-14.

1. Scheme 1: compromise, cooperation with worldly unbelievers (vv.1-4).
2. Scheme 2: slander, rumor, lies (vv.5-9).
3. Scheme 3: acting cowardly and disobeying God (vv.10-14).

1 (6:1-4) **Compromise, Sinful and Evil, Example—Cooperation, with Unbelievers, Example—Plots and Schemes, Example—Nehemiah, Plot Against—Sanballat, Opponent of Nehemiah, Sought to Kill—Tobiah, Opponent of Nehemiah, Sought to Kill—Geshem or Gashmu, Opponent of Nehemiah, Sought to Kill**: the first scheme used against Nehemiah was the temptation to compromise, to lead him to cooperate with unbelievers. This is a scheme often used by Satan and the enemies of believers. If a believer can be led to compromise and to cooperate with the worldly of this earth, the believer's testimony is soon discredited. Despite all the opposition, Nehemiah and the returned Jews had accomplished an impossible feat: they had completely finished the wall. Only the gates remained to be hung. But as soon as the wall was completed, news was immediately carried by some spies to the leaders of the surrounding nations who had stood so opposed to the resettlement and rebuilding project. These leaders were Sanballat, Tobiah, Geshem the Arab, and the remaining enemies who had formed an alliance against Nehemiah and the Jews (v.1). Disappointed that their early attempts to stop the rebuilding project had miserably failed, these enemies now reversed their tactics. Instead of standing opposed to the rebuilding project, they sought to lead Nehemiah into thinking they wanted to compromise. Therefore they began to discuss the differences with him supposedly to work out some kind of mutual agreement. To initiate this scheme they sent an invitation for Nehemiah to meet them on neutral ground, a site in one of the villages in the plain of Ono. Ono was about 20 miles from Jerusalem, in the upper northwest part of Judah. It was very near the border of Samaria, but it had been settled by the Jews who had returned from Babylonian and Persian exile (7:37; 11:35; Ezr.2:33). From all appearances, it seemed that these opponents finally wanted to make peace and establish economic trade with the Jews.

But Nehemiah saw through their scheme, sensing that they were seeking to get him alone in order to kill him (vv.2-3). To protect himself, Nehemiah devised a reply that would either prove their sincerity or else expose their deception. He simply stated that he could not leave the work unsupervised because the project was at a critical state. It was just too important for him to leave at that time. Of course, Nehemiah suspected foul play. Nevertheless he was leaving the door open for the opponents to suggest meeting in Jerusalem—just in case they were sincere or had a change of heart. As he suspected, the enemies' insincerity was exposed. Rather than suggesting a meeting in Jerusalem, they sent the same message to him repeatedly. Four successive times they sent the *very same* message (v.4).

OUTLINE	SCRIPTURE	SCRIPTURE	OUTLINE

1. Scheme 1: Compromise, cooperation with worldly unbelievers
a. The enemies' scheme
  1) They heard that the wall had been almost completed: Only the gates remained to be hung
 	
  2) They sent a message to Nehemiah pretending to desire compromise & cooperation: Tried to lure,
	Now it came to pass, when Sanballat, and Tobiah, and Geshem the Arabian, and the rest of our enemies, heard that I had builded the wall, and *that* there was no breach left therein; (though at that time I had not set up the doors upon the gates;)
	2 That Sanballat and Geshem sent unto me, saying, Come, let us meet together in *some one of* the villages in
		the plain of Ono. But they thought to do me mischief.
		3 And I sent messengers unto them, saying, I *am* doing a great work, so that I cannot come down: why should the work cease, whilst I leave it, and come down to you?
		4 Yet they sent unto me four times after this sort; and I answered them after the same manner.
			seduce him to a meeting so they could kill him
			b. Nehemiah's wise reply
			  1) He could not leave the work unsupervised
			  2) He suspected foul play, but left the door open for them to suggest meeting in Jerusalem—if they were sincere
			c. The enemies' insincerity: Rather than suggesting a meeting in Jerusalem, they sent the same message *four* times

Thought 1. One of the major tactics of attack used by Satan and his followers is that of compromise. If a believer can be led to compromise, his or her testimony is ruined. The believer becomes discredited and the name of Christ dishonored. Compromise can be good when it is based upon moral and spiritual truth, obeying the laws of a nation or of God. But when compromise is immoral, illegal, or disobedient to society's or God's laws, then it becomes sinful and evil. For example, how many of us have been lured or seduced to compromise...

- by engaging in immoral or illicit sexual acts or adultery
- by stealing, cheating or deceiving others
- by joining the crowd in smoking, drinking alcoholic beverages, or taking drugs—all of which damage the human body
- by joining the crowd in immodest behavior or dress that can lead to unwanted advances and assaults
- by engaging in unlawful or violent behavior

Compromising with those who walk in sin and wickedness will destroy our testimony for Christ and sometimes even destroy our lives. Listen to what God's Holy Word says about compromising with the sinful and wicked of this earth:

"For what is a man profited, if he shall gain the whole world, and lose his own soul? or what shall a man give in exchange for his soul?" (Mt.16:26).

"And take heed to yourselves, lest at any time your hearts be overcharged with surfeiting, and drunkenness, and cares of this life, and so that day come upon you unawares" (Lu.21:34).

"And be not conformed to this world: but be ye transformed by the renewing of your mind, that ye may prove what is that good, and acceptable, and perfect, will of God" (Ro.12:2).

"And they that use this world, as not abusing *it:* for the fashion of this world passeth away" (1 Co.7:31).

"And you *hath he quickened,* who were dead in trespasses and sins; Wherein in time past ye walked according to the course of this world, according to the prince of the power of the air, the spirit that now worketh in the children of disobedience: Among whom also we all had our conversation in times past in the lusts of our flesh, fulfilling the desires of the flesh and of the mind; and were by nature the children of wrath, even as others" (Ep.2:1-3).

"And have no fellowship with the unfruitful works of darkness, but rather reprove *them*" (Ep.5:11).

"Set your affection on things above, not on things on the earth" (Col.3:2).

"Now we command you, brethren, in the name of our Lord Jesus Christ, that ye withdraw yourselves from every brother that walketh disorderly, and not after the tradition which he received of us" (2 Th.3:6).

"For Demas hath forsaken me, having loved this present world, and is departed unto Thessalonica; Crescens to Galatia, Titus unto Dalmatia" (2 Ti.4:10).

"Teaching us that, denying ungodliness and worldly lusts, we should live soberly, righteously, and godly, in this present world; Looking for that blessed hope, and the glorious appearing of the great God and our Saviour Jesus Christ" (Tit.2:12-13).

"Ye adulterers and adulteresses, know ye not that the friendship of the world is enmity with God? whosoever therefore will be a friend of the world is the enemy of God" (Js.4:4).

"Love not the world, neither the things *that are* in the world. If any man love the world, the love of the Father is not in him. For all that *is* in the world, the lust of the flesh, and the lust of the eyes, and the pride of life, is not of the Father, but is of the world" (1 Jn.2:15-16).

"Thou shalt not follow a multitude to *do* evil; neither shalt thou speak in a cause to decline after many to wrest *judgment*" (Ex.23:2).

"Take heed to thyself that thou be not snared by following them, after that they be destroyed from before thee; and that thou enquire not after their gods, saying, How did these nations serve their gods? even so will I do likewise" (De.12:30).

"Depart from me, ye evildoers: for I will keep the commandments of my God" (Ps.119:115).

"Depart ye, depart ye, go ye out from thence, touch no unclean *thing;* go ye out of the midst of her; be ye clean, that bear the vessels of the LORD" (Is.52:11).

2 **(6:5-9) Slander, Example—Rumor, Example—Lies, Example—Enemy, Spiritual, Strategies of, Example—Strategies, of the Devil and His Followers—Nehemiah, Plots Against:** the second scheme used against Nehemiah and the Jews was that of slandering Nehemiah's name and spreading rumors and lies about him. The opponents were not going to give up, for they were desperate to maintain their authority and economic control over the territory of Judah. Somehow, some way they had to keep the Jews from hanging all the gates, which was all that was needed to finish the walls, and from rebuilding the city of Jerusalem. When Sanballat and the other opponents realized that Nehemiah was not going to leave Jerusalem to meet with them alone, they again switched their line of attack.

a. For the fifth time, they sent a letter to Nehemiah. But this time they changed the contents of the letter, and they sent it unsealed. Sending a letter unsealed in that day and time was most unusual. In ancient days when an official letter was sent it was always rolled up, tied, and sealed so it would only be opened and read by the person to whom it was being sent. But in this case Sanballat sent an *unsealed letter* to Nehemiah. Obviously, his purpose was to have the letter read by the messenger and many others along the route. They would naturally spread the lies contained in the letter. The letter listed two major charges against Nehemiah:

1) Sanballat charged Nehemiah with plotting a rebellion against Persia for the purpose of setting himself up as king of Judah (vv.6-7). He even accused the godly governor of appointing certain prophets to move among the people throughout Jerusalem, proclaiming him to be the appointed king. *The Bible Knowledge Commentary* says there could be some truth to this particular charge. Some of the returned Jews could have been unwisely excited over the rebuilding of their nation. They could have felt that Nehemiah was the fulfillment of the Old Testament

prophesies of the coming king. For example, the earlier prophet Zechariah had predicted that the future king of Jerusalem was coming and that he would bring deliverance to the Jewish people (Zec.9:9).

Of course, the charge that Nehemiah was revolting against Persia to establish himself as king was a false and vicious lie. Sanballat's plot was to spread the rumor so that the returned Jews would become discouraged and stop the rebuilding project.

2) Sanballat's letter also warned Nehemiah that this report would be taken to the king of Persia; therefore, it was essential to meet with him and his associates (v.7). Knowing that the slander and lies about him were being spread throughout Judah, Nehemiah could have easily buckled under the pressure and met with the opponents. He could have easily faced the enemy to defend himself against the false charges. He knew that they were determined to kill him. Nevertheless, he was forced to answer the false accusations. If the slander and rumors were left unchecked, his reputation would be ruined, discredited among the people. The Persian king would then quickly have him arrested and most likely executed. Subsequently the rebuilding of Jerusalem would be stopped in its tracks.

b. To prevent the catastrophic events from taking place, Nehemiah carefully thought through the best way to respond to the malicious lies and rumors. One fact stood out above all others: the slander was totally false. There was no truth whatsoever to the charges. Thus Nehemiah concluded that the best response was threefold:

⇒ to forcefully deny the slander and lies
⇒ to boldly charge the enemy with lying and deception
⇒ to pray for strength (v.9)

Nehemiah knew that the opponents were using intimidation to weaken his and his workers' hands in order to stop the construction project. Nehemiah simply turned to the LORD and asked Him to *strengthen* their hands, for the answer to men's intimidation is to be *strengthened by God*.

OUTLINE	SCRIPTURE	SCRIPTURE	OUTLINE
2. Scheme 2: Slander, rumor, lies	5 Then sent Sanballat his servant unto me in like manner the fifth time with an open letter in his hand;	now shall it be reported to the king according to these words. Come now therefore, and let us take counsel together.	miah that this report would be taken to the king of Persia—unless he met with them
a. The enemies' scheme: They sent an *unsealed letter* to Nehemiah so people would read it & spread its lies	6 Wherein *was* written, It is reported among the heathen, and Gashmu saith *it, that* thou and the Jews think to rebel: for which cause thou buildest the wall, that thou mayest be their king, according to these words.	8 Then I sent unto him, saying, There are no such things done as thou sayest, but thou feignest them out of thine own heart.	b. Nehemiah's immediate response
1) Sanballat charged Nehemiah with plotting a rebellion to set himself up as king			1) He denied the slander
• Alleged that this was the real reason he was building the wall		9 For they all made us afraid, saying, Their hands shall be weakened from the work, that it be not done. Now therefore, *O God,* strengthen my hands.	2) He boldly charged the enemy with lying & deception
• Alleged that certain prophets were already proclaiming him king	7 And thou hast also appointed prophets to preach of thee at Jerusalem, saying, *There is* a king in Judah: and		3) He prayed for strength: Because he knew the enemy was using intimidation to stop the work
2) Sanballat warned Nehe-			

Thought 1. Spreading slander and lies is a vicious behavior. It causes intense pain and often destroys a person's reputation and character. Slander and lies can cause all kinds of terrible consequences such as...

- separation and divorce
- broken friendships
- loss of employment
- removal from office
- financial difficulty or bankruptcy

- failed diplomacy
- broken agreements
- failed treaties or war among nations
- unbearable friction at home, school, work, or even church

Slander and lies are two of the most terrible evils that people can commit. Their results are always harmful and often devastating. And just as harmful as slander and lies is *gossip,* for it is gossip that spreads the rumors, slander, and lies.

The best answer to false accusations is to have a strong *character,* to be a person *of integrity*. Most people will not accept malicious slander against us if we are people of integrity. People will tend to believe in us if we have a reputation of strong character and integrity. Thus, when lies and slander are used to attack us, we need to follow in the footsteps of Nehemiah:

⇒ deny the slander
⇒ charge the enemy with lying and deception
⇒ cry out to the LORD for strength

But underlying these three steps must be a strong character of integrity. We must walk in the truth of God's Holy Word, obeying His commandments and living righteously before the public. We must be a strong testimony to the righteousness of the LORD. This is the best defense against slander and lies. Listen to what God's Holy Word says about those who commit such behavior:

"Let all bitterness, and wrath, and anger, and clamour, and evil speaking, be put away from you, with all malice" (Ep.4:31).

"Lie not one to another, seeing that ye have put off the old man with his deeds" (Col.3:9).

"Put them in mind to be subject to principalities and powers, to obey magistrates, to be ready to every good work, To speak evil of no man, to be no brawlers, *but* gentle, shewing all meekness unto all men" (Tit.3:1-2).

"But the fearful, and unbelieving, and the abominable, and murderers, and whoremongers, and sorcerers, and idolaters, and all liars, shall have their part in the lake which burneth with fire and brimstone: which is the second death" (Re.21:8).

"Thou shalt destroy them that speak leasing [lying]: the LORD will abhor the bloody and deceitful man" (Ps.5:6).

"But the king shall rejoice in God; every one that sweareth by him shall glory: but the mouth of them that speak lies shall be stopped" (Ps.63:11).

"Whoso privily slandereth his neighbour, him will I cut off: him that hath an high look and a proud heart will not I suffer" (Ps.101:5).

"He that worketh deceit shall not dwell within my house: he that telleth lies shall not tarry in my sight" (Ps.101:7).

"He that hideth hatred *with* lying lips, and he that uttereth a slander, *is* a fool" (Pr.10:18).

"Lying lips *are* abomination to the LORD: but they that deal truly *are* his delight" (Pr.12:22).

"A false witness shall not be unpunished, and *he that* speaketh lies shall not escape" (Pr.19:5).

"The getting of treasures by a lying tongue *is* a vanity tossed to and fro of them that seek death" (Pr.21:6).

---

3 (6:10-14) **Disobedience, Duty—Coward, Acts of, Duty—Nehemiah, Plots Against—Shemaiah, Plot Against Nehemiah—Nodaiah, the Prophetess, Plotted Against Nehemiah**: the third scheme of the enemies was to lead Nehemiah to act cowardly and to disobey God. It was a clever scheme to discredit and perhaps even assassinate him. The enemy hired the priest Shemaiah to deceive Nehemiah and to lead him into a trap within the temple. Note that Shemaiah was home locked behind closed doors and that Nehemiah went to Shemaiah's home to see him. Apparently Shemaiah had sent word for Nehemiah to come because there was a threat against the governor's life. When Nehemiah arrived, Shemaiah warned Nehemiah of the assassination plot that was planned for that very night. He next suggested that they hide in the temple, within the Holy Place itself. While Nehemiah had initially trusted Shemaiah as one of the priestly leaders, he immediately detected a hoax or plot when Shemaiah suggested they hide in the Holy Place. Thus he refused to flee and hide in the temple as suggested. He forcefully responded that he could not disobey God by entering the Holy Place. Only priests could enter the Holy Place of the temple. To hide in the place assigned for priests alone would have been a grievous sin against the LORD (Ex.29:31-33; 33:20; Nu.18:7). Moreover, he could not act cowardly, fleeing the task that God had given him.

OUTLINE	SCRIPTURE	SCRIPTURE	OUTLINE
3. Scheme 3: Acting cowardly & disobeying God	10 Afterward I came unto the house of Shemaiah the son of Delaiah the son of Mehetabeel, who *was* shut up; and he said, Let us meet together in the house of God, within the temple, and let us shut the doors of the temple: for they will come to slay thee; yea, in the night will they come to slay thee.	God had not sent him; but that he pronounced this prophecy against me: for Tobiah and Sanballat had hired him.	Tobiah & Sanballat had hired the priest
a. The enemies' scheme: They hired the priest Shemaiah to deceive Nehemiah & lead him into a trap			
1) He warned Nehemiah of an assassination plot to happen that very night		13 Therefore *was* he hired, that I should be afraid, and do so, and sin, and *that* they might have *matter* for an evil report, that they might reproach me.	• To strike fear in Nehemiah
2) He suggested they hide in the temple (Holy Place)			• To seduce Nehemiah to sin & discredit himself
b. Nehemiah's refusal	11 And I said, Should such a man as I flee? and who *is there*, that, *being* as I *am*, would go into the temple to save his life? I will not go in.	14 My God, think thou upon Tobiah and Sanballat according to these their works, and on the prophetess Noadiah, and the rest of the prophets, that would have put me in fear.	c. Nehemiah's prayer: That God would execute true justice against Tobiah & Sanballat, against the prophetess Noadiah, & against some other unnamed prophets who opposed God's work
1) He must not be cowardly			
2) He would not disobey God: Only priests could enter the Holy Place, Nu.18:7			
3) He knew that his enemies	12 And, lo, I perceived that		

Because of Shemaiah's suggestion, Nehemiah knew that his enemies Tobiah and Sanballat had hired this priest to entrap him. By exposing the plot of assassination, they had hoped to strike so much fear in him that he would hide out in the Holy Place. They would thereby be able to discredit Nehemiah's name because he had committed this terrible sin and desecrated the temple of God.

Sometime later, when all alone, Nehemiah sought the LORD in prayer. He asked the LORD to execute true justice against Tobiah and Sanballat as well as against some prophets who had not been mentioned until now but who had opposed God's work. Note that the prophetess Noadiah is named. Just who she and the other prophets were is not known. But the fact that they and the priest Shemaiah opposed Nehemiah shows just how strong the opposition to him was. This godly layman was apparently opposed by a body of *political, business,* and *religious leaders.* Nevertheless, Nehemiah stood fast and persevered until the end, completing the great task God had assigned him.

Thought 1. The lesson for us is clear: we must not act cowardly nor disobey God. A coward is a person who runs away from trouble, who avoids the difficulties that arise, who fails to undertake the task or assignment he or she is given or is responsible for. A coward has weak character that is clearly exposed when he backs off or flees a difficult situation. When a believer acts cowardly, he damages his testimony and dishonors the Name of the LORD. When any of us fail to stand up for righteousness, people know that our profession of faith is weak and that we lack genuineness within our hearts. Our testimony for Christ suffers, and some individuals even look upon us as being hypocritical. If we profess Christ and the importance of living righteously yet accept wicked behavior and seldom speak up for righteousness, we are acting cowardly. We are fleeing opportunities to bear strong testimony to God, to His commandments, and to righteous behavior.

Our testimony is truly discredited when we disobey God. Being caught or seen committing sin always bring shame upon our profession of Christ. And sin always dishonors the Name of the Lord.

(1) Listen to what the Word of God says about fearing the unbelievers of the world and acting cowardly:

> **"Ye shall not respect persons in judgment; *but* ye shall hear the small as well as the great; ye shall not be afraid of the face of man; for the judgment *is* God's: and the cause that is too hard for you, bring *it* unto me, and I will hear it" (De.1:17).**

> **"The fear of man bringeth a snare: but whoso putteth his trust in the LORD shall be safe" (Pr.29:25).**

> **"I, *even* I, *am* he that comforteth you: who *art* thou, that thou shouldest be afraid of a man *that* shall die, and of the son of man *which* shall be made as grass" (Is.51:12).**

(2) Note several major examples of cowardly behavior found in Scripture:
  ⇒   The cowardly behavior of the ten spies sent into the land of Canaan

> **"And there we saw the giants, the sons of Anak, *which come* of the giants: and we were in our own sight as grasshoppers, and so we were in their sight. And all the congregation lifted up their voice, and cried; and the people wept that night. And all the children of Israel murmured against Moses and against Aaron: and the whole congregation said unto them, Would God that we had died in the land of Egypt! or would God we had died in this wilderness! And wherefore hath the LORD brought us unto this land, to fall by the sword, that our wives and our children should be a prey? were it not better for us to return into Egypt? And they said one to another, Let us make a captain, and let us return into Egypt. Then Moses and Aaron fell on their faces before all the assembly of the congregation of the children of Israel" (Nu.13:33–14:5).**

  ⇒   The cowardly behavior of most of Gideon's army

> **"Now therefore go to, proclaim in the ears of the people, saying, Whosoever *is* fearful and afraid, let him return and depart early from mount Gilead. And there returned of the people twenty and two thousand; and there remained ten thousand" (Jud.7:3).**

  ⇒   The cowardly behavior of Israel's army as it faced the giant Goliath

> **"And all the men of Israel, when they saw the man, fled from him, and were sore afraid" (1 S.17:24).**

  ⇒   The cowardly behavior of the Lord's disciples when He was being arrested

> **"In that same hour said Jesus to the multitudes, Are ye come out as against a thief with swords and staves for to take me? I sat daily with you teaching in the temple, and ye laid no hold on me. But all this was done, that the scriptures of the prophets might be fulfilled. Then all the disciples forsook him, and fled" (Mt.26:55-56).**

  ⇒   The cowardly behavior of most people during the ministry of Christ when He was so fiercely opposed

> **"And there was much murmuring among the people concerning him: for some said, He is a good man: others said, Nay; but he deceiveth the people. Howbeit no man spake openly of him for fear of the Jews" (Jn.7:12-13).**

  ⇒   The cowardly behavior of many religious leaders who claimed to believe in Christ but refused to confess Him because of their fear of other religious leaders

> **"Nevertheless among the chief rulers also many believed on him; but because of the Pharisees they did not confess *him,* lest they should be put out of the synagogue" (Jn.12:42).**

⇒ The cowardly behavior of Peter when confronted by a number of religious leaders

"For before that certain came from James, he did eat with the Gentiles: but when they were come, he withdrew and separated himself, fearing them which were of the circumcision" (Ga.2:12).

(3) Listen to what God's Holy Word says about disobedience:

"When the Son of man shall come in his glory, and all the holy angels with him, then shall he sit upon the throne of his glory: And before him shall be gathered all nations: and he shall separate them one from another, as a shepherd divideth *his* sheep from the goats: And he shall set the sheep on his right hand, but the goats on the left....Then shall he say also unto them on the left hand, Depart from me, ye cursed, into everlasting fire, prepared for the devil and his angels: For I was an hungred, and ye gave me no meat: I was thirsty, and ye gave me no drink: I was a stranger, and ye took me not in: naked, and ye clothed me not: sick, and in prison, and ye visited me not. Then shall they also answer him, saying, Lord, when saw we thee an hungred, or athirst, or a stranger, or naked, or sick, or in prison, and did not minister unto thee? Then shall he answer them, saying, Verily I say unto you, Inasmuch as ye did *it* not to one of the least of these, ye did *it* not to me. And these shall go away into everlasting punishment: but the righteous into life eternal" (Mt.25:31-33, 41-46).

"But fornication, and all uncleanness, or covetousness, let it not be once named among you, as becometh saints; Neither filthiness, nor foolish talking, nor jesting, which are not convenient: but rather giving of thanks. For this ye know, that no whoremonger, nor unclean person, nor covetous man, who is an idolater, hath any inheritance in the kingdom of Christ and of God. Let no man deceive you with vain words: for because of these things cometh the wrath of God upon the children of disobedience" (Ep.5:3-6).

"And to you who are troubled rest with us, when the Lord Jesus shall be revealed from heaven with his mighty angels, In flaming fire taking vengeance on them that know not God, and that obey not the gospel of our Lord Jesus Christ: Who shall be punished with everlasting destruction from the presence of the Lord, and from the glory of his power" (2 Th.1:7-9).

"For if the word spoken by angels was stedfast, and every transgression and disobedience received a just recompence of reward; How shall we escape, if we neglect so great salvation; which at the first began to be spoken by the Lord, and was confirmed unto us by them that heard *him*" (He.2:2-3).

"And a curse, if ye will not obey the commandments of the LORD your God, but turn aside out of the way which I command you this day, to go after other gods, which ye have not known" (De.11:28).

"But if ye will not obey the voice of the LORD, but rebel against the commandment of the LORD, then shall the hand of the LORD be against you, as *it was* against your fathers" (1 S.12:15).

1. The triumphant completion of the wall: Being diligent to persevere

a. The amazing time for completion: 52 days

b. The impact upon the enemies
  1) They were disheartened: They had failed to stop the project
  2) They were frightened: Jerusalem was now stronger & God was helping them

c. The wall completed despite continued opposition: Letters of complaint had flowed constantly between Tobiah & some influential opponents
  1) Many Jewish leaders were loyal to Tobiah: Coveted political & economic gain
    • Through sworn allegiance: Probably refers to business contracts or dealings
    • Through marriage
  2) Many had become traitors & sought to promote Tobiah's reputation: To gain a greater reward when Nehemiah was removed

2. The security of the city put in place: Being diligent to secure protection

a. The appointment of religious workers as gatekeepers

b. The appointment of Nehemiah's military leaders
  1) Hanani, his brother, & Hananiah, the military commander: Were given charge of all Jerusalem
  2) The strong charge to the two assistants: Must immediately set security measures in place
    • To open the gates only after sunrise
    • To organize a neighborhood watch: To post citizens on the wall

c. The striking need of the city: More people & housing

G. The Triumphant Completion of the Wall & the Restoration of Jerusalem: A Lesson on Diligence, 6:15–7:73

15 So the wall was finished in the twenty and fifth *day* of *the month* Elul, in fifty and two days.
16 And it came to pass, that when all our enemies heard *thereof,* and all the heathen that *were* about us saw *these things,* they were much cast down in their own eyes: for they perceived that this work was wrought of our God.
17 Moreover in those days the nobles of Judah sent many letters unto Tobiah, and *the letters* of Tobiah came unto them.
18 For *there were* many in Judah sworn unto him, because he *was* the son in law of Shechaniah the son of Arah; and his son Johanan had taken the daughter of Meshullam the son of Berechiah.
19 Also they reported his good deeds before me, and uttered my words to him. *And* Tobiah sent letters to put me in fear.

CHAPTER 7

Now it came to pass, when the wall was built, and I had set up the doors, and the porters and the singers and the Levites were appointed,
2 That I gave my brother Hanani, and Hananiah the ruler of the palace, charge over Jerusalem: for he *was* a faithful man, and feared God above many.
3 And I said unto them, Let not the gates of Jerusalem be opened until the sun be hot; and while they stand by, let them shut the doors, and bar *them:* and appoint watches of the inhabitants of Jerusalem, every one in his watch, and every one *to be* over against his house.
4 Now the city *was* large and great: but the people *were* few therein, and the houses *were* not builded.

5 And my God put into mine heart to gather together the nobles, and the rulers, and the people, that they might be reckoned by genealogy. And I found a register of the genealogy of them which came up at the first, and found written therein,
6 These *are* the children of the province, that went up out of the captivity, of those that had been carried away, whom Nebuchadnezzar the king of Babylon had carried away, and came again to Jerusalem and to Judah, every one unto his city;
7 Who came with Zerubbabel, Jeshua, Nehemiah, Azariah, Raamiah, Nahamani, Mordecai, Bilshan, Mispereth, Bigvai, Nehum, Baanah. The number, *I say,* of the men of the people of Israel *was this;*
8 The children of Parosh, two thousand an hundred seventy and two.
9 The children of Shephatiah, three hundred seventy and two.
10 The children of Arah, six hundred fifty and two.
11 The children of Pahath-moab, of the children of Jeshua and Joab, two thousand and eight hundred *and* eighteen.
12 The children of Elam, a thousand two hundred fifty and four.
13 The children of Zattu, eight hundred forty and five.
14 The children of Zaccai, seven hundred and threescore.
15 The children of Binnui, six hundred forty and eight.
16 The children of Bebai, six hundred twenty and eight.
17 The children of Azgad, two thousand three hundred twenty and two.
18 The children of Adonikam, six hundred threescore and seven.
19 The children of Bigvai, two thousand threescore and seven.
20 The children of Adin, six hundred fifty and five.
21 The children of Ater of Hezekiah, ninety and eight.
22 The children of Hashum, three hundred twenty and eight.

d. The idea of a census aroused by God: To choose additional people to move into Jerusalem

3. The census or list of captives who had returned from exile: Being diligent to follow the example of the true *pioneers* & *ancestors of faith*

a. The original leaders
  1) Zerubbabel: The governor
  2) Jeshua: The High Priest, 5:2; Zec.3:1
  3) Ten others

b. The various families or clans

c. The people from various cities & towns

23 The children of Bezai, three hundred twenty and four.
24 The children of Hariph, an hundred and twelve.
25 The children of Gibeon, ninety and five.
26 The men of Bethlehem and Netophah, an hundred fourscore and eight.
27 The men of Anathoth, an hundred twenty and eight.
28 The men of Beth-azmaveth, forty and two.
29 The men of Kirjath-jearim, Chephirah, and Beeroth, seven hundred forty and three.
30 The men of Ramah and Gaba, six hundred twenty and one.
31 The men of Michmas, an hundred and twenty and two.
32 The men of Bethel and Ai, an hundred twenty and three.
33 The men of the other Nebo, fifty and two.
34 The children of the other Elam, a thousand two hundred fifty and four.
35 The children of Harim, three hundred and twenty.
36 The children of Jericho, three hundred forty and five.
37 The children of Lod, Hadid, and Ono, seven hundred twenty and one.
38 The children of Senaah, three thousand nine hundred and thirty.

d. The priests

39 The priests: the children of Jedaiah, of the house of Jeshua, nine hundred seventy and three.
40 The children of Immer, a thousand fifty and two.
41 The children of Pashur, a thousand two hundred forty and seven.
42 The children of Harim, a thousand and seventeen.

e. The Levites, including the Levite singers & gatekeepers
1) The Levites

43 The Levites: the children of Jeshua, of Kadmiel, and of the children of Hodevah, seventy and four.

2) The singers

44 The singers: the children of Asaph, an hundred forty and eight.

3) The gatekeepers

45 The porters: the children of Shallum, the children of Ater, the children of Talmon, the children of Akkub, the children of Hatita, the children of Shobai, an hundred thirty and eight.

f. The temple servants & the

46 The Nethinims: the children of Ziha, the children of Hashupha, the children of Tabbaoth,
47 The children of Keros, the children of Sia, the children of Padon,
48 The children of Lebana, the children of Hagaba, the children of Shalmai,
49 The children of Hanan, the children of Giddel, the children of Gahar,
50 The children of Reaiah, the children of Rezin, the children of Nekoda,
51 The children of Gazzam, the children of Uzza, the children of Phaseah,
52 The children of Besai, the children of Meunim, the children of Nephishesim,
53 The children of Bakbuk, the children of Hakupha, the children of Harhur,
54 The children of Bazlith, the children of Mehida, the children of Harsha,
55 The children of Barkos, the children of Sisera, the children of Tamah,
56 The children of Neziah, the children of Hatipha.
57 The children of Solomon's servants: the children of Sotai, the children of Sophereth, the children of Perida,
58 The children of Jaala, the children of Darkon, the children of Giddel,
59 The children of Shephatiah, the children of Hattil, the children of Pochereth of Zebaim, the children of Amon.
60 All the Nethinims, and the children of Solomon's servants, were three hundred ninety and two.
61 And these were they which went up also from Telmelah, Telharesha, Cherub, Addon, and Immer: but they could not show their father's house, nor their seed, whether they were of Israel.
62 The children of Delaiah, the children of Tobiah, the children of Nekoda, six hundred forty and two.
63 And of the priests: the children of Habaiah, the children of Koz, the children of Barzillai, which took one of the daughters of Barzillai the Gileadite to wife, and was called after their name.

servants of Solomon
1) Descendants of various clans

2) Descendants of several servants of Solomon

g. The people whose ancestry was questionable & could not be proven
1) The Babylonian town from which they came

2) The three families or clans from which they descended

3) The priests who had no record to prove they were true priests

• Were excluded from the priesthood	64 These sought their register *among* those that were reckoned by genealogy, but it was not found: therefore were they, as polluted, put from the priesthood.	sand seven hundred and twenty asses.
• Were not given the priests' share of sacred food until their priesthood was established—by a priest seeking the LORD through casting lots	65 And the Tirshatha said unto them, that they should not eat of the most holy things, till there stood *up* a priest with Urim and Thummim.	70 And some of the chief of the fathers gave unto the work. The Tirshatha gave to the treasure a thousand drams of gold, fifty basons, five hundred and thirty priests' garments.
h. The totals	66 The whole congregation together *was* forty and two thousand three hundred and threescore,	71 And *some* of the chief of the fathers gave to the treasure of the work twenty thousand drams of gold, and two thousand and two hundred pounds of silver.
1) The exiles or captives		
2) The servants 3) The singers	67 Beside their manservants and their maidservants, of whom *there were* seven thousand three hundred thirty and seven: and they had two hundred forty and five singing men and singing women.	72 And *that* which the rest of the people gave *was* twenty thousand drams of gold, and two thousand pounds of silver, and threescore and seven priests' garments.
4) The livestock	68 Their horses, seven hundred thirty and six: their mules, two hundred forty and five: 69 *Their* camels, four hundred thirty and five: six thou-	73 So the priests, and the Levites, and the porters, and the singers, and *some* of the people, and the Nethinims, and all Israel, dwelt in their cities; and when the seventh month came, the children of Israel *were* in their cities.

i. The contributions given to the work 1) The governor: 1,000 gold coins, 50 gold basins, & 530 robes for priests	
2) Other leaders: 20,000 gold coins & 2,200 pounds of silver	
3) Other people: 20,000 gold coins, 2,000 pounds of silver, & 67 robes for priests	
j. The settlement of the returning exiles: Settled in the towns from which their families had been taken captive & exiled to Babylon	

DIVISION I

THE REBUILDING OF THE WALLS OF JERUSALEM, 1:1–7:73

G. The Triumphant Completion of the Wall and the Restoration of Jerusalem: A Lesson on Diligence, 6:15–7:73

(6:15–7:73) **Introduction**: vigilance is an absolute essential in life. Vigilance means to keep watch, stay awake, in particular to avoid danger. A vigilant person walks carefully throughout life, keeping a watchful eye for the pitfalls and dangers that might lie ahead. As we walk throughout life we must be alert, attentive, cautiously on the lookout for any obstacles that might cause us to stumble, fall, or injure ourselves. To be vigilant means that we keep our eyes open, wide awake so that we can guard ourselves against all the temptations and trials that stand in our path. Vigilance is the major lesson of the present Scripture. Nehemiah and the returned exiles completed the protective wall of Jerusalem, but this was just the first step in rebuilding the city and nation. There was still much work to be done. The immediate work at hand for these Jews is the discussion of this chapter. Without delay, three things in particular had to be done. This is, *The Triumphant Completion of the Wall and the Restoration of Jerusalem: A Lesson on Diligence*, 6:15–7:73.

1. The triumphant completion of the wall: being diligent to persevere (6:15-19).
2. The security of the city put in place: being diligent to secure protection (7:1-5).
3. The census or list of captives who had returned from exile: being diligent to follow the example of the true *pioneers* and *ancestors of faith* (7:6-73).

---

1 (6:15-19) **Perseverance, Duty in Completing One's Task—Endurance, Example of—Steadfastness, Duty—Nehemiah, Perseverance of—Jerusalem, Rebuilding the Wall, Completion—Nehemiah, Completion of the Wall—Wall, of Jerusalem, Rebuilt**: the wall of Jerusalem was completed. What a triumphant, victorious statement! Amazingly, the wall was completed in just 52 days. For nearly a century and a half the walls had laid in ruins. But once the people were mobilized by God's appointed servant, the walls were completed in less than two months. Despite the utter ruin of the city, the people worked hard, to the point of exhaustion, laboring day and night to finish the project. Despite all the vicious opposition from the leaders of surrounding provinces or districts, they triumphantly completed the wall. Through perseverance, endurance, and steadfastness, they completed the awesome task on the 25th day of the month of Elul, as stated, in the brief time span of just 52 days.

The impact upon the malicious enemies who had so viciously opposed the project was immediate. First, they were disheartened, crestfallen, crushed in spirit. They had failed to stop the project. Their spiteful opposition had actually aroused the returned exiles to complete the wall as quickly as possible in order to protect themselves.

Second, the leaders of the surrounding nations became frightened, for the Jews were now rebuilding Jerusalem. Moreover, it was evident that God was helping them. The project could never have been completed within two months unless the LORD was supporting and taking care of them. Completing the project in 52 days was clearly a miraculous feat. In addition, the surrounding nations knew that the Jews would be strengthening themselves throughout the coming decades. They would be growing stronger politically, economically, and militarily. Thus, in the future the Jews would become more of a threat to the political authority and economic influence of the surrounding nations.

From the very first of Nehemiah's arrival, the surrounding nations had maliciously opposed the rebuilding project (vv.17-19). If Jerusalem and its wall were rebuilt, they knew they would lose their power and influence over the Jews and Judah. Nehemiah was a threat to their political and economic influence throughout the area. A strong Jewish economy would become a strong competitor and put constraints on their own authority, weakening their position and power. The hostility of the opposition has been seen in earlier chapters (4:1–6:14). One of their major tactics was an insidious letter writing campaign that sought to tear down Nehemiah's reputation and sabotage the project. Throughout the entire two months of construction, letters of complaint flowed between the opponent Tobiah and some influential Jews who strongly opposed Nehemiah's nationalistic policies. They wanted to maintain strong relations with the surrounding nations, coveting trade and economic dealings with them. For this reason, they were loyal to Tobiah and his opposition. Obviously, these influential Jewish leaders had entered business contracts with Tobiah and, no doubt, with some of the other surrounding nations. In some cases these influential Jewish opponents of Nehemiah were related to Tobiah through marriage. For example, Tobiah had personally married into the distinguished family of Shecaniah, having married his daughter (v.18). And Tobiah's son had actually married the daughter of one of the major workers on the wall, Meshullam, an influential leader who had built two sections of the wall (3:4, 30). In addition, Tobiah had a close, influential relationship with the High Priest Eliashib, most likely due to a marriage relationship (13:4).

These Jewish opponents campaign to undermine Nehemiah's creditability and ruin the building project put undue pressure on Nehemiah. They promoted Tobiah's reputation and did all they could to constrain Nehemiah to cooperate with their relative. In turn, they reported Nehemiah's response and actions to Tobiah. Tobiah himself kept constant pressure on Nehemiah by sending letters of complaint, seeking to intimidate him.

The point to see is the relentless pressure being put upon Nehemiah by the conspiracy of certain influential leaders. Yet Nehemiah persevered through all the attacks. He endured, stood fast, and triumphantly completed the task God had given him.

OUTLINE	SCRIPTURE	SCRIPTURE	OUTLINE

1. **The triumphant completion of the wall: Being diligent to persevere**
a. The amazing time for completion: 52 days
b. The impact upon the enemies
  1) They were disheartened: They had failed to stop the project
  2) They were frightened: Jerusalem was now stronger & God was helping them
c. The wall completed despite continued opposition: Letters of complaint had flowed
	15 So the wall was finished in the twenty and fifth *day of the month* Elul, in fifty and two days.
	16 And it came to pass, that when all our enemies heard *thereof,* and all the heathen that *were* about us saw *these things,* they were much cast down in their own eyes: for they perceived that this work was wrought of our God.
	17 Moreover in those days the nobles of Judah sent many letters unto Tobiah, and
		the letters of Tobiah came unto them.
		18 For *there were* many in Judah sworn unto him, because he *was* the son in law of Shechaniah the son of Arah; and his son Johanan had taken the daughter of Meshullam the son of Berechiah.
		19 Also they reported his good deeds before me, and uttered my words to him. *And* Tobiah sent letters to put me in fear.
			constantly between Tobiah & some influential opponents
			1) Many Jewish leaders were loyal to Tobiah: Coveted political & economic gain
			  • Through sworn allegiance: Probably refers to business contracts or dealings
			  • Through marriage
			2) Many had become traitors & sought to promote Tobiah's reputation: To gain a greater reward when Nehemiah was removed

Thought 1. Perseverance is essential to complete any task. No matter what the task may be, we should work until the job is finished. Often, this is especially true when opposition arises. When people defy or disagree with us, there is a tendency to withdraw, to flee from whatever we are doing. Even if our project or task is essential or the timing is crucial, far too many of us stop the work. We turn and run away, failing to persevere and complete our task. Think of just a few scenarios that require perseverance in life: important or critical.

⇒ husbands and wives should persevere in their marriage
⇒ children should persevere in their studies
⇒ workers should persevere, laboring diligently and being thankful for their jobs
⇒ leaders should persevere in fulfilling their promises and in carrying out the duties given them
⇒ pastors and ministers should persevere in their God-given call and duties
⇒ church workers should persevere in their teaching and other responsibilities
⇒ professing believers should persevere for Christ, turning away from wicked behavior and living righteous lives, bearing strong witness to the saving power of Christ

Every day of our lives we undertake one task after another. To finish any of these jobs or chores perseverance is demanded. We must endure, stand fast and persevere to accomplish anything worthwhile in life. Listen to what God's Holy Word says about perseverance, endurance, and standing fast.

"And ye shall be hated of all *men* for my name's sake: but he that endureth to the end shall be saved" (Mt.10:22).

"Therefore, my beloved brethren, be ye stedfast, unmovable, always abounding in the work of the Lord, forasmuch as ye know that your labour is not in vain in the Lord" (1 Co.15:58).

"Stand fast therefore in the liberty wherewith Christ hath made us free, and be not entangled again with the yoke of bondage" (Ga.5:1).

"And let us not be weary in well doing: for in due season we shall reap, if we faint not" (Ga.6:9).

"Only let your conversation [conduct, behavior] be as it becometh the gospel of Christ: that whether I come and see you, or else be absent, I may hear of your affairs, that ye stand fast in one spirit, with one mind striving together for the faith of the gospel" (Ph.1:27).

"Wherefore seeing we also are compassed about with so great a cloud of witnesses, let us lay aside every weight, and the sin which doth so easily beset us, and let us run with patience the race that is set before us, Looking unto Jesus the author and finisher of *our* faith; who for the joy that was set before him endured the cross, despising the shame, and is set down at the right hand of the throne of God. For consider him that endured such contradiction of sinners against himself, lest ye be wearied and faint in your minds. Ye have not yet resisted unto blood, striving against sin" (He.12:1-4).

"Blessed *is* the man that endureth temptation: for when he is tried, he shall receive the crown of life, which the Lord hath promised to them that love him" (Js.1:12).

"Behold, we count them happy which endure. Ye have heard of the patience of Job, and have seen the end of the Lord; that the Lord is very pitiful, and of tender mercy" (Js.5:11).

"Wherefore gird up the loins of your mind, be sober, and hope to the end for the grace that is to be brought unto you at the revelation of Jesus Christ" (1 Pe.1:13).

"For this *is* thankworthy, if a man for conscience toward God endure grief, suffering wrongfully. For what glory *is it*, if, when ye be buffeted for your faults, ye shall take it patiently? but if, when ye do well, and suffer *for it*, ye take it patiently, this *is* acceptable with God. For even hereunto were ye called: because Christ also suffered for us, leaving us an example, that ye should follow his steps" (1 Pe.2:19-21).

"Be sober, be vigilant; because your adversary the devil, as a roaring lion, walketh about, seeking whom he may devour: Whom resist stedfast in the faith, knowing that the same afflictions are accomplished in your brethren that are in the world" (1 Pe.5:8-9).

"Ye therefore, beloved, seeing ye know *these things* before, beware lest ye also, being led away with the error of the wicked, fall from your own stedfastness. But grow in grace, and *in* the knowledge of our Lord and Saviour Jesus Christ. To him *be* glory both now and for ever. Amen" (2 Pe.3:17-18).

"Behold, I come quickly: hold that fast which thou hast, that no man take thy crown" (Re.3:11).

"The righteous also shall hold on his way, and he that hath clean hands shall be stronger and stronger" (Jb.17:9).

---

2 **(7:1-5) Protection, Organization for, Example—Security, Organization for, Example—Jerusalem, Security of, Organization—Protection, of Jerusalem, Organization for—Nehemiah, Works of, Organized the Security for Jerusalem—Leadership, of Jerusalem, Organized by Nehemiah**: immediately after completing the rebuilding of the wall, Nehemiah appointed leaders to secure and protect the city. Then after setting the gates in place, he appointed the gatekeepers. The gatekeepers usually guarded the doors of the temple, but because of the continuing threat by the surrounding nations, Nehemiah appointed them to stand guard at the gates of the city. In addition, Nehemiah assigned to the singers and Levites, assistants to the priests, the additional duty of helping the gatekeepers guard the city. Of course, the additional religious workers at the gates meant a much greater number of guards to protect against any enemy's infiltrating the population to carry out terrorist actions.

Next, Nehemiah appointed two military leaders, each one being assigned the responsibility for half of the city (3:9-12). One of these military officers was Hanani, Nehemiah's brother. This was the brother who had originally brought the dark, dismal report back to Nehemiah when Nehemiah was the cupbearer to the king (1:2). The other military officer was Hananiah, who had earlier been appointed commander of the citadel or palace (3:8). He was now being given this important responsibility because he was a man of integrity who feared God more than most people did. In assigning their duties Nehemiah gave them a strong charge: they must immediately set security measures in place (v.3). Rumor after rumor of an impending attack had been spreading throughout the countryside, almost from the very day of Nehemiah's arrival and the launch of the building project (4:11-12). Thus security measures had to be set in place at once. Furthermore, Nehemiah instructed the two military officers to make sure the gates were open only after sunrise. Waiting until the sun had fully risen would make sure the citizens had risen from their night of sleep. Thereby they could not be caught off guard while sleeping. The two officers were also to organize a neighborhood watch, posting citizens on the wall either next to or near their own houses. Every adult citizen was to be involved in protecting the city and securing his or her own property. If an attack came, these citizens would fight harder and more fiercely to protect their own families, homes, and property.

Although the walls had been rebuilt and guards were now posted for security, there were still two vital needs: more people and more housing. There was simply not enough population to protect the city, and there was not enough housing for a large population to live within the city walls. As a result, Jerusalem was facing a critical situation.

At some point, the LORD aroused within Nehemiah the idea for a census. Accordingly, he assembled all the leadership together to present to them the need for additional population within Jerusalem (v.5). However, he wanted to make sure that the citizens within the city were of pure Jewish blood or descent. Through a census, pure-blooded Jews could be identified (11:1-24). A census would additionally show the distribution of the population throughout the nation, exactly how many citizens were living within each of the cities, towns, villages, and countryside. Knowing the population's distribution would help them prevent too many people from moving to Jerusalem from any one area. If too many residents moved from a particular area, that area would be weakened.

Having received the leadership's approval, Nehemiah launched a search of the genealogical records of those who had first returned from Babylonian captivity.

OUTLINE	SCRIPTURE	SCRIPTURE	OUTLINE

2. The security of the city put in place: Being diligent to secure protection
a. The appointment of religious workers as gatekeepers
b. The appointment of Nehemiah's military leaders
  1) Hanani, his brother, & Hananiah, the military commander: Were given charge of all Jerusalem
  2) The strong charge to the two assistants: Must immediately set security measures in place
    • To open the gates only after sunrise
	Now it came to pass, when the wall was built, and I had set up the doors, and the porters and the singers and the Levites were appointed,
	2 That I gave my brother Hanani, and Hananiah the ruler of the palace, charge over Jerusalem: for he *was* a faithful man, and feared God above many.
	3 And I said unto them, Let not the gates of Jerusalem be opened until the sun be hot; and while they stand by, let them shut the doors, and bar *them:* and appoint watches of
		the inhabitants of Jerusalem, every one in his watch, and every one *to be* over against his house.
		4 Now the city *was* large and great: but the people *were* few therein, and the houses *were* not builded.
		5 And my God put into mine heart to gather together the nobles, and the rulers, and the people, that they might be reckoned by genealogy. And I found a register of the genealogy of them which came up at the first, and found written therein,
			• To organize a neighborhood watch: To post citizens on the wall
			
			c. The striking need of the city: More people & housing
			
			d. The idea of a census aroused by God: To choose additional people to move into Jerusalem

Thought 1. As believers, it is not enough to know that we are citizens of the holy city of God, the promised land of heaven. Although we may be saved, the battle is not over. Once we have trusted Christ and become citizens of heaven, we still remain citizens of this earth. Our citizenship is in both heaven and earth. Heaven is our future residence, already bought and paid for. And we are guaranteed the privilege of living in heaven once we leave this earth. But until that day our citizenship on earth continues to expose us to the corruption of the world. In truth, as long as we live in this corruptible world, we will be attacked by enemy forces. Temptation will confront us, seducing us into immoral, lawless, and violent behavior. Furthermore, all kinds of trials, hardships, and sufferings will face us.

To stand against the barrage of temptations and trials, we must have the protection and security of God Himself. This is the wonderful promise of God. No matter the temptation or trial, He will protect us. He will hold us securely in His hand, allowing no person or entity or thing to remove us. Even if we are assaulted and our lives suddenly snatched away, the LORD will transfer us immediately into His presence. Quicker than the eye can blink, His hand of protection will rescue us from the terrifying hands of death and deliver us into His very own presence. No believer ever tastes or experiences death or hell. God protects and secures us. Listen to what God's Holy Word says about His protection and security:

"**But there shall not an hair of your head perish**" (Lu.21:18).

"**Who shall separate us from the love of Christ?** *shall* **tribulation, or distress, or persecution, or famine, or nakedness, or peril, or sword? As it is written, For thy sake we are killed all the day long; we are accounted as sheep for the slaughter. Nay, in all these things we are more than conquerors through him that loved us. For I am persuaded, that neither death, nor life, nor angels, nor principalities, nor powers, nor things present, nor things to come, Nor height, nor depth, nor any other creature, shall be able to separate us from the love of God, which is in Christ Jesus our Lord**" (Ro.8:35-39).

"**Now thanks** *be* **unto God, which always causeth us to triumph in Christ, and maketh manifest the savour of his knowledge by us in every place**" (2 Co.2:14).

"**For though we walk in the flesh, we do not war after the flesh: (For the weapons of our warfare** *are* **not carnal, but mighty through God to the pulling down of strong holds;) Casting down imaginations, and every high thing that exalteth itself against the knowledge of God, and bringing into captivity every thought to the obedience of Christ**" (2 Co.10:3-5).

"**And the Lord shall deliver me from every evil work, and will preserve** *me* **unto his heavenly kingdom: to whom** *be* **glory for ever and ever. Amen**" (2 Ti.4:18).

"*Let your* **conversation [conduct, behavior]** *be* **without covetousness;** *and be* **content with such things as ye have: for he hath said, I will never leave thee, nor forsake thee. So that we may boldly say, The Lord** *is* **my helper, and I will not fear what man shall do unto me**" (He.13:5-6).

"**For whatsoever is born of God overcometh the world: and this is the victory that overcometh the world,** *even* **our faith. Who is he that overcometh the world, but he that believeth that Jesus is the Son of God?**" (1 Jn.5:4-5).

"**The LORD shall fight for you, and ye shall hold your peace**" (Ex.14:14).

"**And the LORD commanded us to do all these statutes, to fear the LORD our God, for our good always, that he might preserve us alive, as** *it is* **at this day**" (De.6:24).

"**For the LORD our God, he** *it is* **that brought us up and our fathers out of the land of Egypt, from the house of bondage, and which did those great signs in our sight, and preserved us in all the way wherein we went, and among all the people through whom we passed**" (Jos.24:17).

"For the eyes of the LORD run to and fro throughout the whole earth, to show himself strong in the behalf of *them* whose heart *is* perfect toward him. Herein thou hast done foolishly: therefore from henceforth thou shalt have wars" (2 Chr.16:9).

"With him *is* an arm of flesh; but with us *is* the LORD our God to help us, and to fight our battles. And the people rested themselves upon the words of Hezekiah king of Judah" (2 Chr.32:8).

"O love the LORD, all ye his saints: *for* the LORD preserveth the faithful, and plentifully rewardeth the proud doer" (Ps.31:23).

"The angel of the LORD encampeth round about them that fear him, and delivereth them" (Ps.34:7).

"For the LORD loveth judgment, and forsaketh not his saints; they are preserved for ever: but the seed of the wicked shall be cut off" (Ps.37:28).

"Through thee will we push down our enemies: through thy name will we tread them under that rise up against us" (Ps.44:5).

"He shall cover thee with his feathers, and under his wings shalt thou trust: his truth *shall be thy* shield and buckler" (Ps.91:4).

"He shall not be afraid of evil tidings: his heart is fixed, trusting in the LORD" (Ps.112:7).

"*As* the mountains *are* round about Jerusalem, so the LORD *is* round about his people from henceforth even for ever" (Ps.125:2).

"The LORD openeth *the eyes of* the blind: the LORD raiseth them that are bowed down: the LORD loveth the righteous: The LORD preserveth the strangers; he relieveth the fatherless and widow: but the way of the wicked he turneth upside down. The LORD shall reign for ever, *even* thy God, O Zion, unto all generations. Praise ye the LORD" (Ps.146:8-10).

"He keepeth the paths of judgment, and preserveth the way of his saints" (Pr.2:8).

"When thou liest down, thou shalt not be afraid: yea, thou shalt lie down, and thy sleep shall be sweet" (Pr.3:24).

"For thou hast been a strength to the poor, a strength to the needy in his distress, a refuge from the storm, a shadow from the heat, when the blast of the terrible ones *is* as a storm *against* the wall" (Is.25:4).

"Fear thou not; for I *am* with thee: be not dismayed; for I *am* thy God: I will strengthen thee; yea, I will help thee; yea, I will uphold thee with the right hand of my righteousness" (Is.41:10).

"And *even* to *your* old age I *am* he; and *even* to hoar [gray] hairs will I carry *you:* I have made, and I will bear; even I will carry, and will deliver *you*" (Is.46:4).

---

3 (7:6-73) **Faith, Pioneers of, Exile Returnees—New Beginning, Sought, by Exile Returnees—New Life, Sought, by Exile Returnees—Fresh Start, Sought, by Exile Returnees—Commitment, Example of, Exile Returnees— Promised Land, Commitment to, by Exile Returnees—Jerusalem, Returned to, by Exile Returnees—List, Exile Returnees—Returnees, Exiles, List of—Census, of Exile Returnees**: what follows is a list of the exiles who returned from captivity in Babylon and Persia. These were true *pioneers of faith*, people who sought a new beginning and a new life in the promised land of God. Frankly, however, many people just skip over this passage instead of reading the long list of names. But it should always be remembered that the people listed here were true *ancestors of the faith*. They genuinely believed God and His promises. With all their hearts they trusted God, believing that He would fulfill His promise to send the future King and Savior—the Lord Jesus Christ—into the world.

They believed God would preserve His Holy Word and His promise to restore the promised land (a symbol of heaven) to them. It was just such people that Nehemiah wanted as citizens of Jerusalem, people of strong faith and commitment in the promises of God. This was the very reason he insisted that the city be populated with people of pure Jewish blood or descent (11:1-24).

This census or genealogy is essentially the same as the one found in Ezra (Ezr.2:1-70). However, a few of the names and numbers differ. This does not mean that the Holy Scripture is not inspired, that God's Word has errors or contradictions. Most of the errors and discrepancies can be explained by copyist errors. When scribes were copying the original manuscripts, they easily could have missed a simple stroke, which would have changed a particular number or total count. Also, when lists or numbers differ by either the addition or elimination of a name, it could be due simply to the dying out of a family or the addition of a family between Ezra's and Nehemiah's time. No doubt some of the families who made the trip with Ezra did die out, and obviously some Jewish exiles had returned to Jerusalem during the decades since Ezra's pilgrimage. Whatever the case, we must always remember that the Word of God is authoritative, accurate, and absolutely trustworthy for both faith and doctrine. Down through the centuries God has protected His Holy Word and given us an accurate account of the original manuscripts.

The genealogy is broken down into ten points by the outline of the Scripture. The outline points and in some cases brief comments are sufficient to understand the Scripture.

OUTLINE	SCRIPTURE	SCRIPTURE	OUTLINE
3. The census or list of captives who had returned from exile: Being diligent to follow the example of the true *pioneers & ancestors of faith*	6 These *are* the children of the province, that went up out of the captivity, of those that had been carried away, whom Nebuchadnezzar the king of Babylon had carried away,	and came again to Jerusalem and to Judah, every one unto his city; 7 Who came with Zerubbabel, Jeshua, Nehemiah, Azariah, Raamiah, Nahamani,	a. The original leaders 1) Zerubbabel: The governor 2) Jeshua: The High Priest,

157

OUTLINE	SCRIPTURE	SCRIPTURE	OUTLINE
5:2; Zec.3:1 3) Ten others	Mordecai, Bilshan, Misper-eth, Bigvai, Nehum, Baanah. The number, *I say,* of the men of the people of Israel *was this;*	30 The men of Ramah and Gaba, six hundred twenty and one.	
	8 The children of Parosh, two thousand an hundred seventy and two.	31 The men of Michmas, an hundred and twenty and two.	
b. The various families or clans	9 The children of Shephatiah, three hundred seventy and two.	32 The men of Bethel and Ai, an hundred twenty and three.	
	10 The children of Arah, six hundred fifty and two.	33 The men of the other Ne-bo, fifty and two.	
	11 The children of Pahath-moab, of the children of Jeshua and Joab, two thou-sand and eight hundred *and* eighteen.	34 The children of the other Elam, a thousand two hun-dred fifty and four.	
	12 The children of Elam, a thousand two hundred fifty and four.	35 The children of Harim, three hundred and twenty.	
	13 The children of Zattu, eight hundred forty and five.	36 The children of Jericho, three hundred forty and five.	
	14 The children of Zaccai, seven hundred and three-score.	37 The children of Lod, Hadid, and Ono, seven hun-dred twenty and one.	
	15 The children of Binnui, six hundred forty and eight.	38 The children of Senaah, three thousand nine hundred and thirty.	
	16 The children of Bebai, six hundred twenty and eight.	39 The priests: the children of Jedaiah, of the house of Jeshua, nine hundred seventy and three.	d. The priests
	17 The children of Azgad, two thousand three hundred twenty and two.	40 The children of Immer, a thousand fifty and two.	
	18 The children of Adoni-kam, six hundred threescore and seven.	41 The children of Pashur, a thousand two hundred forty and seven.	
	19 The children of Bigvai, two thousand threescore and seven.	42 The children of Harim, a thousand and seventeen.	
	20 The children of Adin, six hundred fifty and five.	43 The Levites: the children of Jeshua, of Kadmiel, *and* of the children of Hodevah, sev-enty and four.	e. The Levites, including the Levite singers & gatekeepers 1) The Levites
	21 The children of Ater of Hezekiah, ninety and eight.	44 The singers: the children of Asaph, an hundred forty and eight.	2) The singers
	22 The children of Hashum, three hundred twenty and eight.	45 The porters: the children of Shallum, the children of Ater, the children of Talmon, the children of Akkub, the children of Hatita, the chil-dren of Shobai, an hundred thirty and eight.	3) The gatekeepers
	23 The children of Bezai, three hundred twenty and four.		
	24 The children of Hariph, an hundred and twelve.	46 The Nethinims: the chil-dren of Ziha, the children of Hashupha, the children of Tabbaoth,	f. The temple servants & the servants of Solomon 1) Descendants of various clans
	25 The children of Gibeon, ninety and five.	47 The children of Keros, the children of Sia, the children of Padon,	
c. The people from various cit-ies & towns	26 The men of Bethlehem and Netophah, an hundred fourscore and eight.	48 The children of Lebana, the children of Hagaba, the children of Shalmai,	
	27 The men of Anathoth, an hundred twenty and eight.	49 The children of Hanan, the children of Giddel, the children of Gahar,	
	28 The men of Beth-azmaveth, forty and two.	50 The children of Reaiah, the children of Rezin, the children of Nekoda,	
	29 The men of Kirjath-jearim, Chephirah, and Beeroth, seven hundred forty and three.		

OUTLINE	SCRIPTURE	SCRIPTURE	OUTLINE
	51 The children of Gazzam, the children of Uzza, the children of Phaseah, 52 The children of Besai, the children of Meunim, the children of Nephishesim, 53 The children of Bakbuk, the children of Hakupha, the children of Harhur, 54 The children of Bazlith, the children of Mehida, the children of Harsha, 55 The children of Barkos, the children of Sisera, the children of Tamah, 56 The children of Neziah, the children of Hatipha.	was not found: therefore were they, as polluted, put from the priesthood. 65 And the Tirshatha said unto them, that they should not eat of the most holy things, till there stood *up* a priest with Urim and Thummim.	• Were not given the priests' share of sacred food until their priesthood was established—by a priest seeking the LORD through casting lots
2) Descendants of several servants of Solomon	57 The children of Solomon's servants: the children of Sotai, the children of Sophereth, the children of Perida, 58 The children of Jaala, the children of Darkon, the children of Giddel, 59 The children of Shephatiah, the children of Hattil, the children of Pochereth of Zebaim, the children of Amon. 60 All the Nethinims, and the children of Solomon's servants, *were* three hundred ninety and two.	66 The whole congregation together *was* forty and two thousand three hundred and threescore, 67 Beside their manservants and their maidservants, of whom *there were* seven thousand three hundred thirty and seven: and they had two hundred forty and five singing men and singing women. 68 Their horses, seven hundred thirty and six: their mules, two hundred forty and five: 69 *Their* camels, four hundred thirty and five: six thousand seven hundred and twenty asses.	h. The totals 1) The exiles or captives 2) The servants 3) The singers 4) The livestock
g. The people whose ancestry was questionable & could not be proven 1) The Babylonian town from which they came	61 And these *were* they which went up *also* from Telmelah, Telharesha, Cherub, Addon, and Immer: but they could not show their father's house, nor their seed, whether they *were* of Israel.	70 And some of the chief of the fathers gave unto the work. The Tirshatha gave to the treasure a thousand drams of gold, fifty basons, five hundred and thirty priests' garments.	i. The contributions given to the work 1) The governor: 1,000 gold coins, 50 gold basins, & 530 robes for priests
2) The three families or clans from which they descended	62 The children of Delaiah, the children of Tobiah, the children of Nekoda, six hundred forty and two.	71 And *some* of the chief of the fathers gave to the treasure of the work twenty thousand drams of gold, and two thousand and two hundred pounds of silver.	2) Other leaders: 20,000 gold coins & 2,200 pounds of silver
3) The priests who had no record to prove they were true priests	63 And of the priests: the children of Habaiah, the children of Koz, the children of Barzillai, which took *one* of the daughters of Barzillai the Gileadite to wife, and was called after their name.	72 And *that* which the rest of the people gave *was* twenty thousand drams of gold, and two thousand pounds of silver, and threescore and seven priests' garments.	3) Other people: 20,000 gold coins, 2,000 pounds of silver, & 67 robes for priests
• Were excluded from the priesthood	64 These sought their register *among* those that were reckoned by genealogy, but it	73 So the priests, and the Levites, and the porters, and the singers, and *some* of the people, and the Nethinims, and all Israel, dwelt in their cities; and when the seventh month came, the children of Israel *were* in their cities.	j. The settlement of the returning exiles: Settled in the towns from which their families had been taken captive & exiled to Babylon

Thought 1. These *pioneers* and *ancestors of faith* set a dynamic example for us. Just as they believed and acted in faith, we too must believe in the LORD and trust Him to fulfill His promises. Only those who believe are accepted by God. Listen to what God's Holy Word says:

(1) If we wish to be saved from sin, death, and hell, we must believe in the LORD.

> **"That whosoever believeth in him should not perish, but have eternal life. For God so loved the world, that he gave his only begotten Son, that whosoever believeth in him should not perish, but have everlasting life" (Jn.3:15-16).**

> **"Verily, verily, I say unto you, He that heareth my word, and believeth on him that sent me, hath everlasting life, and shall not come into condemnation; but is passed from death unto life" (Jn.5:24).**

> **"Jesus said unto her, I am the resurrection, and the life: he that believeth in me, though he were dead, yet shall he live" (Jn.11:25).**

"I am come a light into the world, that whosoever believeth on me should not abide in darkness" (Jn.12:46).

"But these are written, that ye might believe that Jesus is the Christ, the Son of God; and that believing ye might have life through his name" (Jn.20:31).

"Therefore being justified by faith, we have peace with God through our Lord Jesus Christ" (Ro.5:1).

"That if thou shalt confess with thy mouth the Lord Jesus, and shalt believe in thine heart that God hath raised him from the dead, thou shalt be saved. For with the heart man believeth unto righteousness; and with the mouth confession is made unto salvation" (Ro.10:9-10).

"In whom we have redemption through his blood, the forgiveness of sins, according to the riches of his grace" (Ep.1:7).

(2) If we wish to be blessed by God and to receive the promises of God, we must believe and trust Him.

"Jesus said unto him, If thou canst believe, all things *are* possible to him that believeth" (Mk.9:23).

"Therefore I say unto you, What things soever ye desire, when ye pray, believe that ye receive *them,* and ye shall have *them*" (Mk.11:24).

"But as many as received him, to them gave he power to become the sons of God, *even* to them that believe on his name" (Jn.1:12).

"Then said they unto him, What shall we do, that we might work the works of God? Jesus answered and said unto them, This is the work of God, that ye believe on him whom he hath sent" (Jn.6:28-29).

"And Jesus said unto them, I am the bread of life: he that cometh to me shall never hunger; and he that believeth on me shall never thirst" (Jn.6:35).

"I am come a light into the world, that whosoever believeth on me should not abide in darkness" (Jn.12:46).

"Let not your heart be troubled: ye believe in God, believe also in me. In my Father's house are many mansions: if *it were* not so, I would have told you. I go to prepare a place for you" (Jn.14:1-2).

"Verily, verily, I say unto you, He that believeth on me, the works that I do shall he do also; and greater *works* than these shall he do; because I go unto my Father" (Jn.14:12).

"For I am not ashamed of the gospel of Christ: for it is the power of God unto salvation to every one that believeth; to the Jew first, and also to the Greek" (Ro.1:16).

"And we know that all things work together for good to them that love God, to them who are the called according to *his* purpose" (Ro.8:28).

"Above all, taking the shield of faith, wherewith ye shall be able to quench all the fiery darts of the wicked" (Ep.6:16).

"But without faith *it is* impossible to please *him:* for he that cometh to God must believe that he is, and *that* he is a rewarder of them that diligently seek him" (He.11:6).

"If any of you lack wisdom, let him ask of God, that giveth to all *men* liberally, and upbraideth not; and it shall be given him. But let him ask in faith, nothing wavering. For he that wavereth is like a wave of the sea driven with the wind and tossed" (Js.1:5-6).

"And this is his commandment, That we should believe on the name of his Son Jesus Christ, and love one another, as he gave us commandment" (1 Jn.3:23).

"And they rose early in the morning, and went forth into the wilderness of Tekoa: and as they went forth, Jehoshaphat stood and said, Hear me, O Judah, and ye inhabitants of Jerusalem; Believe in the LORD your God, so shall ye be established; believe his prophets, so shall ye prosper" (2 Chr.20:20).

"*Oh* how great *is* thy goodness, which thou hast laid up for them that fear thee; *which* thou hast wrought for them that trust in thee before the sons of men! Thou shalt hide them in the secret of thy presence from the pride of man: thou shalt keep them secretly in a pavilion from the strife of tongues" (Ps.31:19-20).

"Many sorrows *shall be* to the wicked: but he that trusteth in the LORD, mercy shall compass him about" (Ps.32:10).

"The LORD redeemeth the soul of his servants: and none of them that trust in him shall be desolate" (Ps.34:22).

"Trust in the LORD, and do good; *so* shalt thou dwell in the land, and verily thou shalt be fed" (Ps.37:3).

"Commit thy way unto the LORD; trust also in him; and he shall bring *it* to pass" (Ps.37:5).

"They that trust in the LORD *shall be* as mount Zion, *which* cannot be removed, *but* abideth for ever" (Ps.125:1).

"Trust in the LORD with all thine heart; and lean not unto thine own understanding. In all thy ways acknowledge him, and he shall direct thy paths" (Pr.3:5-6).

"The fear of man bringeth a snare: but whoso putteth his trust in the LORD shall be safe" (Pr.29:25).

"Thou wilt keep *him* in perfect peace, *whose* mind *is* stayed *on thee:* because he trusteth in thee. Trust ye in the LORD for ever: for in the LORD JEHOVAH *is* everlasting strength" (Is.26:3-4).

DIVISION II — NEHEMIAH

THE REBUILDING OF THE NATION
AND THE PEOPLE 8:1–13:31

(8:1–13:31) **DIVISION OVERVIEW**: once the wall of Jerusalem was completed and the people were officially registered in the public records by genealogy, it was time to build a strong spiritual foundation, one that would last for generations to come. Nehemiah understood well that rebuilding a nation meant rebuilding the people. He knew that the Jews would have to seek God with all their hearts, obey His holy Word, and be totally devoted to the LORD.

Nehemiah summoned all the people to a great "Celebration and Dedication Service." At the meeting, Ezra the scribe read and taught the Law of Moses to the people (8:1-8). No doubt it was a powerful and moving sermon, for the people were immediately struck in their hearts to obey God's Word, praying and confessing their sins to the LORD. The people made a firm covenant to obey the LORD wholeheartedly (9:3). Whatever was read from God's Word, they immediately put into practice. It was a complete revival of the entire nation.

Remember that Nehemiah was writing both to the Jews who had faithfully worked with him to complete the wall and to future generations who also needed to remain faithful. Above all else, the Jews had to be faithful to the LORD. Jerusalem had been rebuilt with great sacrifice. Now that the city of God was built, the Jews needed God's guiding hand upon them more than ever before. Nehemiah knew that constant devotion and continued revival were desperately needed for the people and the nation to remain strong. The Jews must not risk the wrath of God by giving in to compromise and evil associations as their ancestors had done.

As the reader studies how God used Nehemiah to rebuild the Jewish nation and to lead the people in revival, this fact should be kept in mind: spiritual renewal is constantly needed among God's people. However, a spirit of revival can be maintained only through the purifying effect of the Word of God. People must live in God's Word—reading, studying, and applying God Word to their lives. Every person, civic and social group, community, society, nation, and church should be founded upon the unchanging Word of God, the Holy Bible.

> "Thou, *even* thou, *art* LORD alone; thou hast made heaven, the heaven of heavens, with all their host, the earth, and all *things* that *are* therein, the seas, and all that *is* therein, and thou preservest them all; and the host of heaven worshippeth thee" (Ne.9:6).

THE REBUILDING OF THE NATION AND THE
PEOPLE 8:1–13:31

A. Step 1—Rebuilding Through God's Word: Stressing the Importance of the Holy Bible, 8:1-18

B. Step 2—Rebuilding Through a Revived Spirit: Stressing the Importance of Seeking God, His Goodness and Mercy, 9:1-37

C. Step 3—Rebuilding Through Making a Covenant of Commitment: Stressing the Importance of Total Devotion, 9:38–10:39

D. Step 4—Rebuilding Through Strengthening Both Jerusalem and the Spirit of the People: Three Essentials for a Strong Nation and People, 11:1-12:47

E. Step 5—Building Through Discipline, Correcting People's Violation of the Law: Stressing the Need for Continued Reformation, Revival, 13:1-31

1. The reading of God's Law by Ezra: A lesson on the dire need to study God's Word

a. The assembly of the people
   1) They met in the large public square at the Water Gate
   2) They hungered for God's Word: Asked Ezra to read the Law of God to them

b. The reading of God's Word by Ezra: On the first day of the seventh month (Oct.8)

   1) Ezra read God's Word from early morning until noon, about six hours
   2) Ezra read to all the people old enough to understand: All listened attentively

   3) Ezra read from a high wooden platform
      • On his right stood six assistants
      • On his left stood seven other assistants

   4) Ezra opened the book & all the people immediately stood up: Arose in honor of God's Word

   5) Ezra praised the LORD, the great God, before teaching the Word of God: The people responded
      • By raising their hands
      • By answering, "Amen!"
      • By bowing down & worshipping the LORD

   6) Ezra instructed thirteen Levites to help explain God's Word to the people: Because of language differences & the need for

---

CHAPTER 8

II. THE REBUILDING OF THE NATION & THE PEOPLE: 8:1–13:31

A. Step 1—Rebuilding Through God's Word: Stressing the Importance of the Holy Bible, 8:1-18

And all the people gathered themselves together as one man into the street that *was* before the water gate; and they spake unto Ezra the scribe to bring the book of the law of Moses, which the LORD had commanded to Israel.

2 And Ezra the priest brought the law before the congregation both of men and women, and all that could hear with understanding, upon the first day of the seventh month.

3 And he read therein before the street that *was* before the water gate from the morning until midday, before the men and the women, and those that could understand; and the ears of all the people *were attentive* unto the book of the law.

4 And Ezra the scribe stood upon a pulpit of wood, which they had made for the purpose; and beside him stood Mattithiah, and Shema, and Anaiah, and Urijah, and Hilkiah, and Maaseiah, on his right hand; and on his left hand, Pedaiah, and Mishael, and Malchiah, and Hashum, and Hashbadana, Zechariah, *and* Meshullam.

5 And Ezra opened the book in the sight of all the people; (for he was above all the people;) and when he opened it, all the people stood up:

6 And Ezra blessed the LORD, the great God. And all the people answered, Amen, Amen, with lifting up their hands: and they bowed their heads, and worshipped the LORD with *their* faces to the ground.

7 Also Jeshua, and Bani, and Sherebiah, Jamin, Akkub, Shabbethai, Hodijah, Maaseiah, Kelita, Azariah, Jozabad, Hanan, Pelaiah, and

---

the Levites, caused the people to understand the law: and the people *stood* in their place.

8 So they read in the book in the law of God distinctly, and gave the sense, and caused *them* to understand the reading.

9 And Nehemiah, which *is* the Tirshatha, and Ezra the priest the scribe, and the Levites that taught the people, said unto all the people, This day *is* holy unto the LORD your God; mourn not, nor weep. For all the people wept, when they heard the words of the law.

10 Then he said unto them, Go your way, eat the fat, and drink the sweet, and send portions unto them for whom nothing is prepared: for *this* day *is* holy unto our Lord: neither be ye sorry; for the joy of the LORD is your strength.

11 So the Levites stilled all the people, saying, Hold your peace, for the day *is* holy; neither be ye grieved.

12 And all the people went their way to eat, and to drink, and to send portions, and to make great mirth, because they had understood the words that were declared unto them.

13 And on the second day were gathered together the chief of the fathers of all the people, the priests, and the Levites, unto Ezra the scribe, even to understand the words of the law.

14 And they found written in the law which the LORD had commanded by Moses, that the children of Israel should dwell in booths in the feast of the seventh month:

15 And that they should publish and proclaim in all their cities, and in Jerusalem, saying, Go forth unto the mount, and fetch olive branches, and pine branches, and myrtle branches, and palm branches, and branches of thick trees, to make booths, as *it is* written.

16 So the people went forth, and brought *them,* and made themselves booths, every one upon the roof of his house,

---

translation

   • They read from the book
   • They explained the meaning of the Scripture

c. The study of God's Word
   1) The study produced two results
      • Conviction of sin: The people mourned & wept
      • Rejoicing of heart
   2) The leaders instructed the people
      • To stop their mourning & to consider the day as holy, sacred
      • To celebrate by feasting & by sharing with those in need
      • To stop grieving, for the joy of the LORD was their strength

   3) The Levites helped to quiet & calm the people
   4) The people did as instructed
      • They went home to celebrate a festive meal
      • They now understood the words read from God's Law

2. The obeying of God's law: A lesson on the dire need to obey God's Word

a. The leadership's continued hunger for God's Word
   1) They met with Ezra the very next day for more study
   2) They discovered God's command to celebrate the Festival of Tabernacles during the seventh month, Le.23:33-44
      • To live in shelters during the Festival
      • To celebrate the wilderness journeys when the people lived in tents, a symbol of God's provision in this temporary, fleeting world

b. The people's obedience to God's Word
   1) They built shelters
      • On their roofs

• In their courtyards • In the temple courts • In the public squares of the Water Gate & the Ephraim Gate 2) They celebrated the festival with great joy: It had not been celebrated with so much joy since the days of Joshua	and in their courts, and in the courts of the house of God, and in the street of the water gate, and in the street of the gate of Ephraim. 17 And all the congregation of them that were come again out of the captivity made booths, and sat under the booths: for since the days of Jeshua the son of Nun unto	that day had not the children of Israel done so. And there was very great gladness. 18 Also day by day, from the first day unto the last day, he read in the book of the law of God. And they kept the feast seven days; and on the eighth day *was* a solemn assembly, according unto the manner.	3) They studied God's Word daily 4) They celebrated for seven days, as God's Word instructed

DIVISION II

THE REBUILDING OF THE NATION AND THE PEOPLE 8:1–13:31

A.   Step 1—Rebuilding Through God's Word: Stressing the Importance of the Holy Bible, 8:1-18

(8:1-18) **Introduction**: the importance of God's Word cannot be overstressed, because it is God's Holy Word that tells us how to build strong, stable lives, lives filled with love, joy, and peace; that are useful and productive; that are victorious and that rise above life's trials and temptations. When we build our lives upon God's Holy Word, we become strong, more than conquerors in this life (Ro.8:37). When we as a nation obey the commandments of God we establish...

- a nation of brotherly love that conquers prejudice and discrimination
- a nation of righteousness that controls lawlessness and violence
- a nation of justice that protects property, life, and the rights of individuals

The significance of God's every Word cannot be overstated. The Holy Bible should be the foundation of every individual's life as well as every society and every nation on this earth. God's Holy Word will firmly establish and build up any person or people who will follow God's commandments.

The returned exiles of Nehemiah's day were facing the rebuilding of their society and their nation. There was only one hope for carrying out this mammoth undertaking: God's Holy Word. If they obeyed God's commandments, God would help them establish a society of righteousness, justice, and brotherly love. They would be basing their society upon the golden rule, a society in which everyone would treat his neighbor as he himself wished to be treated (Mt.7:12). Rebuilding through God's Word was the very first step the Jewish returnees took in rebuilding their nation and society. This is, *Step 1—Rebuilding Through God's Word: Stressing the Importance of the Holy Bible*, 8:1-18.

1. The reading of God's Law by Ezra: a lesson on the dire need to study God's Word (vv.1-12).
2. The obeying of God's Law: a lesson on the dire need to obey God's Word (vv.13-18).

1 (8:1-12) **Word of God, Hunger for; Duty, to Study—Scripture, Duty, to Study—Bible, Duty, to Teach—Ezra, Taught God's Word; Stirred Revival—Nehemiah, Stirred Revival—Returnees, Jewish, Experienced Revival**: the reading of God's Law by Ezra is an extremely significant event. To celebrate all that God had done, Nehemiah summoned all the people to a celebration and dedication service. The service was held in the town square in the seventh month after the returned exiles had settled down in their hometowns (7:73). The LORD had freed them from captivity under the Babylonians, enabled them to rebuild the wall of Jerusalem in just 52 days, and helped them to rebuild their homes. Under the leadership of Nehemiah, the LORD had blessed them richly. Once again the LORD had proven to be worthy of worship and praise, and the people owed Him their very lives and freedom, their worship and service. The Scripture and outline show how the service focused upon the reading of God's Law, His Holy Word:

OUTLINE	SCRIPTURE	SCRIPTURE	OUTLINE

1. The reading of God's Law by Ezra: A lesson on the dire need to study God's Word
a. The assembly of the people
  1) They met in the large public square at the Water Gate
  2) They hungered for God's Word: Asked Ezra to read the Law of God to them
b. The reading of God's Word by Ezra: On the first day of the seventh month (Oct.8)
	And all the people gathered themselves together as one man into the street that *was* before the water gate; and they spake unto Ezra the scribe to bring the book of the law of Moses, which the LORD had commanded to Israel.
	2 And Ezra the priest brought the law before the congregation both of men and women, and all that could hear with understanding, up-
		on the first day of the seventh month.
		3 And he read therein before the street that *was* before the water gate from the morning until midday, before the men and the women, and those that could understand; and the ears of all the people *were attentive* unto the book of the law.
		4 And Ezra the scribe stood upon a pulpit of wood, which they had made for the
			1) Ezra read God's Word from early morning until noon, about six hours
			2) Ezra read to all the people old enough to understand: All listened attentively
			
			3) Ezra read from a high wooden platform
			  • On his right stood six

OUTLINE	SCRIPTURE	SCRIPTURE	OUTLINE
assistants • On his left stood seven other assistants	purpose; and beside him stood Mattithiah, and Shema, and Anaiah, and Urijah, and Hilkiah, and Maaseiah, on his right hand; and on his left hand, Pedaiah, and Mishael, and Malchiah, and Hashum, and Hashbadana, Zechariah, *and* Meshullam.	and gave the sense, and caused *them* to understand the reading. 9 And Nehemiah, which *is* the Tirshatha, and Ezra the priest the scribe, and the Levites that taught the people, said unto all the people, This day *is* holy unto the LORD your God;	• They explained the meaning of the Scripture c. The study of God's Word 1) The study produced two results • Conviction of sin: The people mourned & wept • Rejoicing of heart
4) Ezra opened the book & all the people immediately stood up: Arose in honor of God's Word	5 And Ezra opened the book in the sight of all the people; (for he was above all the people;) and when he opened it, all the people stood up:	mourn not, nor weep. For all the people wept, when they heard the words of the law.	2) The leaders instructed the people • To stop their mourning & to consider the day as holy, sacred
5) Ezra praised the LORD, the great God, before teaching the Word of God: The people responded • By raising their hands • By answering, "Amen!" • By bowing down & worshipping the LORD	6 And Ezra blessed the LORD, the great God. And all the people answered, Amen, Amen, with lifting up their hands: and they bowed their heads, and worshipped the LORD with *their* faces to the ground.	10 Then he said unto them, Go your way, eat the fat, and drink the sweet, and send portions unto them for whom nothing is prepared: for *this* day *is* holy unto our Lord: neither be ye sorry; for the joy of the LORD is your strength.	• To celebrate by feasting & by sharing with those in need • To stop grieving, for the joy of the LORD was their strength
6) Ezra instructed thirteen Levites to help explain God's Word to the people: Because of language differences & the need for translation	7 Also Jeshua, and Bani, and Sherebiah, Jamin, Akkub, Shabbethai, Hodijah, Maaseiah, Kelita, Azariah, Jozabad, Hanan, Pelaiah, and the Levites, caused the people to understand the law: and the people *stood* in their place.	11 So the Levites stilled all the people, saying, Hold your peace, for the day *is* holy; neither be ye grieved. 12 And all the people went their way to eat, and to drink, and to send portions, and to make great mirth, because they had understood the	3) The Levites helped to quiet & calm the people 4) The people did as instructed • They went home to celebrate a festive meal • They now understood the words read from God's Law
• They read from the book	8 So they read in the book in the law of God distinctly,	words that were declared unto them.	

a. The people assembled in the large public square at the Water Gate. Interestingly Ezra, not Nehemiah, led the worship service. Ezra was a priest and a scribe, a man who studied and taught the Word of God. God's Holy Word at that time included the Law of Moses (the first five books of the Bible) and probably the other historical records that had been preserved and are included in our Bibles today. Although this is the first mention of Ezra in Nehemiah, remember that he had been sent to Jerusalem by King Artaxerxes some 15 years earlier (458 B.C.). His primary purpose for returning was to help rebuild the nation. Specifically, he was to establish true worship among the people and teach the Law of God so people would live righteous lives and build a law-abiding society. When Ezra had first arrived in Jerusalem, he found the people engaging in the detestable, immoral, and wicked behavior of unbelievers. They were following the evil lifestyle and false worship of their neighbors, a most discouraging scene. But Ezra was faithful to his call and commission: he began to teach the Word of God among the people, instructing them in the commandments of the LORD. As a result, the people were convicted and repented of their sins, and a spirit of genuine revival broke out throughout the nation (Ezr.9:1–10:44). Apparently, the people continued to study the Law of God under Ezra's teaching ministry. When Nehemiah arrived, the people readily responded to his leadership in rebuilding Jerusalem and its wall. There was no hesitation whatsoever in accepting this challenge. Their response was immediate, obviously because their hearts had been prepared by Ezra's strong teaching of God's Word. Ezra's teaching ministry had been most effective in preparing the people for Nehemiah's mission.

No doubt during the building project, the people were so busy they were unable to attend their Bible study sessions under Ezra. As a result, a great hunger for God's Word had been gripping their hearts. Obviously, Nehemiah had sensed this deep hunger for God's Word among the people, as had Ezra. This plus the fact that God's Word had stirred the earlier revival under Ezra aroused Nehemiah to focus the celebration service on the Word of God. God's Law was to be the very foundation upon which their nation was to be rebuilt. Thus Nehemiah turned the service over to Ezra, asking him to read the Law of God to the people.

b. Taking charge of the service, Ezra read God's Word as requested by the governor (vv.2-3). This great *Bible conference* was held on the first day of the seventh month, a very special month in the life of Israel. Three significant events took place during the seventh month...

- the Feast of Trumpets was celebrated on the first day, a day that was later celebrated as the New Year on the Jewish calendar
- the Day of Atonement was celebrated on the tenth day
- the Feast of Tabernacles was celebrated on the fifteenth day (Le.23:23-44)

Throughout these verses the focus is on *the people* understanding the Word of God. The *people* are referred to 15 times (vv.1-12) and the word *understanding* is used 6 times (vv.2-3, 7-8, 12-13). From the very beginning of Ezra's ministry, Scripture gives a wonderful testimony about his dedication and commitment to God's Word:

> **"For Ezra had prepared [determined, devoted] his heart to seek the law of the LORD, and to do *it*, and to teach in Israel statutes and judgments" (Ezr.7:10).**

Unquestionably, Ezra was wholly devoted to teaching God's Word. God's Word burned in his heart just as it had Jeremiah's (Je.20:9). As is seen below, the LORD blessed Ezra's teaching of His Word and brought about another revival among the people (vv.9-12). Six facts should be noted about Ezra's teaching.

1) Ezra read God's Word from early morning to noon, about six hours (v.3). What did he read? Since it is impossible to read all five books of Moses within six hours, he obviously read and explained only certain portions of the Law (the Torah, the books of the Law written by Moses). Imagine the hunger for God's Word that gripped their hearts, a hunger so intense that they actually stood or sat for six hours under Ezra's teaching.

2) Ezra read God's Word to all the people who were old enough to understand (v.3). This included all the men, women and children old enough to grasp the meaning of God's Word. Note the emphasis of Scripture: they were attentive. They focused and gave close attention, listening carefully to the reading and explanation of God's Word. They hungered so much for His Holy Word that they consumed all they could. What an indictment against so many of our attitudes toward the Word of God!

3) Ezra read from a high wooden platform that had been built for this special occasion (v.4). Surrounding him were 13 assistants, six standing on his right and seven on his left (v.4). Most likely these were influential lay leaders among the Jews.

4) When Ezra opened the book or scroll, all the people immediately arose (v.5). They stood in reverence of the LORD and in honor of His Holy Law, the Word of God. The multitude knew they would not be listening to the words of a man, but they would be hearing the very Word of God itself. Having given them His Law, the LORD deserved to be reverenced. And His Word deserved to be honored by being read and obeyed. It was their full intention to obey, as well as to listen to it being read. They understood a fact that so many down through the centuries have never grasped. God's purpose for giving His Law, His Word to the world is to reveal the truth to people, providing guidance and showing them how to live. Therefore, they must study and obey God's Word.

5) Before Ezra began to read and teach God's Word, he took a moment to praise the LORD, the great God (v.6). In response the people raised their hands and answered, "Amen! Amen!" These two acts indicated that the people affirmed, agreed with Ezra's prayer of praise. They then bowed down to worship the LORD.

6) Ezra had instructed 13 Levites to help him explain God's Word to the people (vv.7-8). This was necessary because of language differences and the need for translation in some cases. Remember, most of these people had lived in captivity to the Babylonians all their lives. As a result, some of them would not have understood Hebrew, the language in which the Old Testament was written. Obviously the 13 Levites were stationed throughout the crowd. As the need arose, they would explain the Scripture being read and answer any questions the people might have. *The Bible Knowledge Commentary* suggests there may have been between 30,000 to 50,000 people present for the study of God's Word (7:66-67).[1] Based on the census figures of chapter 7, the crowd was massive. Thus it was necessary to have teachers scattered throughout the crowd to explain the meaning of the Scripture as it was read.

c. Throughout the day as the Word of God was being studied, a phenomenal event took place. The people were being convicted of sin. Eventually, so many people came under conviction that their mourning and weeping began to disrupt the service. As a result, the leaders were forced to instruct the people to stop their mourning. This service was to be a time of celebration, a day that was holy, sacred to the LORD. Instead of mourning and weeping, they were to celebrate by feasting and sharing with those who were in need. The people needed to understand a wonderful truth: once they confessed and repented of their sins, the LORD forgave them. There was no longer reason for mourning and crying. Once forgiven, they were to stop grieving and give thanks and praise to the LORD for His forgiveness. But they needed to believe God, trust His Holy Word that He had forgiven them. And if they truly believed, they now needed to joy and rejoice.

With the Levites' help, Ezra and Nehemiah conveyed this message to the mass of people. The people eventually quieted and calmed down, and they did as Ezra had instructed. They went home to celebrate a joyful meal, sharing some of the food with the poor who had nothing to prepare (v.12; also see v.10). Note the very important statement of Scripture, that the people now understood the words that had been taught from God's Law, His Holy Word (v.12).

Thought 1. There is a dire need within society for Christian believers to study God's Holy Word. It is His commandments that build up society, teaching people how to live righteous and law-abiding lives. And the wonderful truth of God's Word is that it not only teaches God's commandments but it also teaches *how* to keep His commandments. There is actually a power within God's Word—a *living power*—that arouses us to obey His commandments. This *living power* stirs us to live righteous lives, loving one another and treating others as we want to be treated. It is the Word of God that arouses us to show mercy and compassion as well as justice in all of our dealings. God Himself—the Creator of the universe—has ordained that His Holy Word be the very foundation of human life and of society. But contrary to God's purpose, we have turned away from God's Word and corrupted this earth. Instead of living in love and righteousness, obeying God's commandments and executing justice, we have become haters of others, abusing, assaulting, even killing our fellowmen. Filled with worldly irreverence and indifference, we have become foul-mouthed, swearing, cursing, and even taking the Name of God Himself in vain. We have become an immoral society without conscience, a society that divorces hastily and easily, without regard for the consequences.

---

[1] F. Walvoord and Roy B. Zuck, Editors. *The Bible Knowledge Commentary*, p.689.

Divorce severely damages not only the spouses but also the extended family and society as a whole. We have become a society of thieves, stealing multiplied millions of dollars from one another, from businesses, and from other nations. We have become a depraved society of adulterers, homosexuals, and savage abusers of children, all because we have rejected the Holy Bible as God's Word.

There has never been a more urgent need for the study of God's Holy Word than there is today. God's Word can change the human heart, transform a wicked heart to live righteously. And by changing human hearts, God's Word can change society. Any body of people—whether church or community or city or nation—can be radically changed for the good by turning to the Word of God, studying and living exactly as God dictates. Listen to what God says about studying His Holy Word:

"Go ye therefore, and teach all nations, baptizing them in the name of the Father, and of the Son, and of the Holy Ghost: Teaching them to observe all things whatsoever I have commanded you: and, lo, I am with you alway, *even* unto the end of the world. Amen" (Mt.28:19-20).

"And he said unto them, Go ye into all the world, and preach the gospel to every creature" (Mk.16:15).

"Search the scriptures; for in them ye think ye have eternal life: and they are they which testify of me" (Jn.5:39).

"These were more noble than those in Thessalonica, in that they received the word with all readiness of mind, and searched the scriptures daily, whether those things were so" (Ac.17:11).

"For whatsoever things were written aforetime were written for our learning, that we through patience and comfort of the scriptures might have hope" (Ro.15:4).

"Now these things were our examples, to the intent we should not lust after evil things, as they also lusted" (1 Co.10:6).

"Let the word of Christ dwell in you richly in all wisdom; teaching and admonishing one another in psalms and hymns and spiritual songs, singing with grace in your hearts to the Lord" (Co.3:16).

"And the things that thou hast heard of me among many witnesses, the same commit thou to faithful men, who shall be able to teach others also" (2 Ti.2:2).

"Study to shew thyself approved unto God, a workman that needeth not to be ashamed, rightly dividing the word of truth" (2 Ti.2:15).

"All scripture *is* given by inspiration of God, and *is* profitable for doctrine, for reproof, for correction, for instruction in righteousness" (2 Ti.3:16).

"As newborn babes, desire the sincere milk of the word, that ye may grow thereby: If so be ye have tasted that the Lord *is* gracious" (1 Pe.2:2-3).

"And thou shalt love the LORD thy God with all thine heart, and with all thy soul, and with all thy might. And these words, which I command thee this day, shall be in thine heart: And thou shalt teach them diligently unto thy children, and shalt talk of them when thou sittest in thine house, and when thou walkest by the way, and when thou liest down, and when thou risest up. And thou shalt bind them for a sign upon thine hand, and they shall be as frontlets between thine eyes. And thou shalt write them upon the posts of thy house, and on thy gates" (De.6:5-9).

"All the commandments which I command thee this day shall ye observe to do, that ye may live, and multiply, and go in and possess the land which the LORD sware unto your fathers. And thou shalt remember all the way which the LORD thy God led thee these forty years in the wilderness, to humble thee, *and* to prove thee, to know what *was* in thine heart, whether thou wouldest keep his commandments, or no. And he humbled thee, and suffered thee to hunger, and fed thee with manna, which thou knewest not, neither did thy fathers know; that he might make thee know that man doth not live by bread only, but by every *word* that proceedeth out of the mouth of the LORD doth man live" (De.8:1-3).

"Therefore shall ye lay up these my words in your heart and in your soul, and bind them for a sign upon your hand, that they may be as frontlets between your eyes. And ye shall teach them your children, speaking of them when thou sittest in thine house, and when thou walkest by the way, when thou liest down, and when thou risest up. And thou shalt write them upon the door posts of thine house, and upon thy gates" (De.11:18-20).

"Blessed *is* the nation whose God *is* the LORD: *and* the people *whom* he hath chosen for his own inheritance" (Ps.33:12).

"Wherewithal shall a young man cleanse his way? by taking heed *thereto* according to thy word" (Ps.119:9).

"Thy word have I hid in mine heart, that I might not sin against thee" (Ps.119:11).

"Thy testimonies have I taken as an heritage for ever: for they *are* the rejoicing of my heart" (Ps.119:111).

"By the blessing of the upright the city is exalted: but it is overthrown by the mouth of the wicked" (Pr.11:11).

"Righteousness exalteth a nation: but sin *is* a reproach to any people" (Pr.14:34).

"*It is* an abomination to kings to commit wickedness: for the throne is established by righteousness" (Pr.16:12).

"Thy words were found, and I did eat them; and thy word was unto me the joy and rejoicing of mine heart: for I am called by thy name, O LORD God of hosts" (Je.15:16).

Thought 2. In *The New American Commentary*, Mervin Breneman makes several excellent points on the Bible's importance that are well worth quoting:

> It is significant that this reading of the law and the worship service were not centered in the temple and not controlled by the priesthood. From this time on in Judaism, the Torah was more important than the temple. Likewise, for Christians, the living power of the Bible should be more important than any church building. Through Scripture the Holy Spirit brings people to abundant life.[2]

In another noteworthy statement Mr. Breneman says:

> The Jews became known as "the people of the book." The Old Testament emphasizes that God's Word is to be known and used by all the people, not only the priests and leaders. Early Christians adopted this same principle. This changed as time went on as fewer and fewer people had access to the Bible. The Protestant Reformation, with its emphasis on Sola Scriptura (on the Bible as the sole authority for faith and practice) returned to the biblical principle that every believer should read Scripture as God's Word for their lives.[3]

Mr. Breneman also gives an excellent application on the subject:

> The Word of God, when read, has the power to transform lives today just as it had in the time of both Josiah and Ezra (v.10; 2 K.22:11-13, 19). The Bible convicts, changes, and guides lives. In the time of Ezra the people realized that the Babylonian captivity was a result of disobedience. Only genuine repentance before God could bring about a real change in the community. The living power of the Word of God still liberates people from their own various forms of captivity.[4]

Thought 3. In dealing with translations of the Bible, Warren W. Wiersbe makes an excellent point:

> We need new translations of the Bible, not because the Bible changes, but because our language changes. Suppose you had to use John Wycliffe's Version of the Bible, the oldest version in English. How much of this passage would you understand if you did not already know it from another version?

> alle ye that traueilen & ben chargid come to me & I schal fulfille you. take ye my yok on you & lerne ye of me for I am mylde and meke in herte: and ye schulen finde rest to youre soulis/ for my yok is softe & my charge liyt.

> Wycliffe's translation goes back about 600 years (1382); but between Moses' writing of the Law and Ezra's reading of the Law, a thousand years had elapsed![5]

2 (8:13-18) **Word of God, Duty, to Obey—Obedience, Duty, to Obey God's Word—Law of God, Duty, to Obey—Leadership, of the Returned Jews, Hunger for God's Word—God's Word, Hunger for, by the Returned Jews—Jewish Feast, the Feast of Tabernacles**: the Jewish returnees were strictly obedient to God's Law. On the very next day after the great celebration service an extremely important event took place. Exactly what happened is dramatically described by the Scripture:

OUTLINE	SCRIPTURE	SCRIPTURE	OUTLINE
2. The obeying of God's Law: A lesson on the dire need to obey God's Word a. The leadership's continued hunger for God's Word 1) They met with Ezra the very next day for more study 2) They discovered God's command to celebrate the Festival of Tabernacles during the seventh month, Le.23:33-44 • To live in shelters during the Festival • To celebrate the wilderness journeys when the people lived in tents, a symbol of God's provision in this	13 And on the second day were gathered together the chief of the fathers of all the people, the priests, and the Levites, unto Ezra the scribe, even to understand the words of the law. 14 And they found written in the law which the LORD had commanded by Moses, that the children of Israel should dwell in booths in the feast of the seventh month: 15 And that they should publish and proclaim in all their cities, and in Jerusalem, saying, Go forth unto the mount, and fetch olive branches, and	pine branches, and myrtle branches, and palm branches, and branches of thick trees, to make booths, as *it is* written. 16 So the people went forth, and brought *them*, and made themselves booths, every one upon the roof of his house, and in their courts, and in the courts of the house of God, and in the street of the water gate, and in the street of the gate of Ephraim. 17 And all the congregation of them that were come again out of the captivity made booths, and sat under the booths: for since the days of Jeshua the son of Nun unto	temporary, fleeting world b. The people's obedience to God's Word 1) They built shelters • On their roofs • In their courtyards • In the temple courts • In the public squares of the Water Gate & the Ephraim Gate 2) They celebrated the festival with great joy: It had not been celebrated with so much joy since the days of Joshua

2 Mervin Breneman. *Ezra, Nehemiah, Esther*, p.224.
3 Ibid., p.224.
4 Ibid., p.227.
5 Warren W. Wiersbe. *Be Determined*, pp.99-100.

OUTLINE	SCRIPTURE	SCRIPTURE	OUTLINE
3) They studied God's Word daily	that day had not the children of Israel done so. And there was very great gladness. 18 Also day by day, from the first day unto the last day, he	read in the book of the law of God. And they kept the feast seven days; and on the eighth day *was* a solemn assembly, according unto the manner.	4) They celebrated for seven days, as God's Word instructed

a. With a craving hunger for God's Word still gnawing at their hearts, the family head, along with all the leaders, returned to Ezra for more study of God's Word (vv.13-15). Evidently their yearning for the Word was so strong that they could not stay away. As head of their families, they wanted to be the kind of fathers they should be, giving guidance and discipline when needed. They simply wanted to apply the teachings of God's Holy Word to their daily lives, learning how to build a loving and righteous family, living productive and fruitful lives in the midst of a corrupt world.

While studying God's Word, they discovered God's command to celebrate the Festival of Tabernacles during the seventh month (Le.23:33-44). The Day of Atonement was to be celebrated on the tenth day and the Feast of Tabernacles on the fifteenth day of the month. By making this discovery on the second day of the month, the timing was perfect, for this gave the people just enough time to prepare for the festival. In reading the Scripture they learned that they were to live in temporary booths or shelters during the seven days of the festival. These temporary shelters were to be made of branches from trees and plants. Living in these temporary shelters, the people would be reminded of the wilderness journeys of their forefathers, the time when their forefathers had to live in tents after their release from Egyptian slavery. God's people must always remember that they live in a temporary, fleeting world and that they are totally dependent upon the LORD's guidance, provision, and protection. This festival was a definite reminder to the returned exiles that they were living in an unsettled, threatening, fearful, and temporary world. For years they had been captives in the land of Babylon, and although they had been freed to return to Jerusalem, they were still under the thumb of Persian authority. They were forced to live under the laws of the Persians and to pay taxes to them. In addition, when they returned to their homeland, it lay in utter ruin. They faced the awesome task of rebuilding their homes, cities, government, and economy. If any people have ever known just how temporary and fleeting this world is, the Jewish returnees knew. For this reason, the Festival of Tabernacles had a very special meaning for them.

b. As soon as the returnees discovered that God commanded them to celebrate the festival, they immediately set about to obey His Word (vv.16-18). In fact, they left the meeting and went out to cut branches to build their temporary shelters. The families who lived in the city of Jerusalem built their shelters on their own roofs and in their courtyards. The priests built theirs in the courts of the temple; and the people from the countryside built theirs in the public squares of the Water Gate and the Ephraim Gate (v.16). Note that everyone who had returned from exile built booths and participated in the festival. For seven long days, they celebrated the festival with great joy. As Scripture says, the feast had not been celebrated this way since the days of Joshua. Through the years the people had apparently been faithful in celebrating the harvest season, yet they had been lax in making booths and living in them during the seven days. But not so during these days of Ezra and Nehemiah. Everyone participated and emphasized God's hand of provision and protection in this temporary, fleeting world. In obedience, they lived in the temporary shelters during the entire seven days of the festival.

But even more notably, they studied God's Word daily (v.18). Ezra read and explained God's Law, His Holy Word. For the entire seven days of the festival, they studied and celebrated the feast just as God's Word instructed.

Thought 1. The emphasis of this point is obedience to God's Word. The returned exiles obeyed God during the difficult days of Nehemiah and Ezra. Likewise, we must obey God's Word when circumstances are troubling and we are under heavy fire. Above all else, God expects obedience. As a parent expects obedience, so God expects obedience of His children. The very purpose for the existence of law is to protect human life and property. So it is with God's Law. He gives us commandments to protect us, our property, and our rights. Without laws and commandments, utter chaos takes over. There is little respect for life, property, and other people's rights. Without law, the selfishness of human nature runs wild, and the rampage of wickedness and evil takes over. People lie, steal, cheat, abuse, assault, and in some cases even kill others. Without law, the terrible evils of rape, sexual abuse of children, enslavement, brutality, and savagery—the most deplorably wicked behavior—take place within society.

This is the reason for God's Holy Word. And it is the reason for society and governments to establish laws. But just having the laws in written form is not enough. We must obey the law, do exactly what the law stipulates. Obedience is essential for us to have a righteous and just society. If we wish to have our lives protected, our rights honored, and our property respected, we must obey the law. Listen to what God's Holy Word says about obedience:

"Not every one that saith unto me, Lord, Lord, shall enter into the kingdom of heaven; but he that doeth the will of my Father which is in heaven." (Mt.7:22-23).

"Therefore whosoever heareth these sayings of mine, and doeth them, I will liken him unto a wise man, which built his house upon a rock: And the rain descended, and the floods came, and the winds blew, and beat upon that house; and it fell not: for it was founded upon a rock. And every one that heareth these sayings of mine, and doeth them not, shall be likened unto a foolish man, which built his house upon the sand: And the rain descended, and the floods came, and the winds blew, and beat upon that house; and it fell: and great was the fall of it" (Mt.7:24-27).

"Jesus answered and said unto him, If a man love me, he will keep my words: and my Father will love him, and we will come unto him, and make our abode with him" (Jn.14:23).

"If ye keep my commandments, ye shall abide in my love; even as I have kept my Father's commandments, and abide in his love....Ye are my friends, if ye do whatsoever I command you" (Jn.15:10, 14).

"But whoso looketh into the perfect law of liberty, and continueth *therein,* he being not a forgetful hearer, but a doer of the work, this man shall be blessed in his deed" (Js.1:25).

"For this is the love of God, that we keep his commandments: and his commandments are not grievous" (1 Jn.5:3).

"Here is the patience of the saints: here *are* they that keep the commandments of God, and the faith of Jesus" (Re.14:12).

"Blessed *are* they that do his commandments, that they may have right to the tree of life, and may enter in through the gates into the city" (Re.22:14).

"Now therefore, if ye will obey my voice indeed, and keep my covenant, then ye shall be a peculiar treasure unto me above all people: for all the earth *is* mine" (Ex.19:5).

"Thou shalt keep therefore his statutes, and his commandments, which I command thee this day, that it may go well with thee, and with thy children after thee, and that thou mayest prolong *thy* days upon the earth, which the LORD thy God giveth thee, for ever" (De.4:40).

"O that there were such an heart in them, that they would fear me, and keep all my commandments always, that it might be well with them, and with their children for ever!" (De.5:29).

"This day the LORD thy God hath commanded thee to do these statutes and judgments: thou shalt therefore keep and do them with all thine heart, and with all thy soul" (De.26:16).

"This book of the law shall not depart out of thy mouth; but thou shalt meditate therein day and night, that thou mayest observe to do according to all that is written therein: for then thou shalt make thy way prosperous, and then thou shalt have good success" (Jos.1:8).

"And Samuel said, Hath the LORD *as great* delight in burnt offerings and sacrifices, as in obeying the voice of the LORD? Behold, to obey *is* better than sacrifice, *and* to hearken than the fat of rams" (1 S.15:22).

"The statutes of the LORD *are* right, rejoicing the heart: the commandment of the LORD *is* pure, enlightening the eyes" (Ps.19:8).

"Then shall I not be ashamed, when I have respect unto all thy commandments" (Ps.119:6).

CHAPTER 9

B. Step 2—Rebuilding Through a Revived Spirit: Stressing the Importance of Seeking God, His Goodness & Mercy, 9:1-37

1. Seeking God through genuine confession

a. The people's assembly: Two days after the festival, 8:12-18
  1) They humbled themselves
  2) They separated themselves from all foreigners (unbelievers)

b. The people's worship service
  1) They confessed their sins
  2) They read God's Word for about three hours of daylight
  3) They spent another three hours of daylight in confession & worship

  4) They were led in worship, praise, & prayer by the Levites
    • They were divided into two groups
    • They called on the LORD

2. Seeking God through praise & thanksgiving

a. The people praised God for Himself, His supremacy
  1) That He is eternal
  2) That His name is glorious & to be exalted above all

  3) That He alone is God

b. The people praised God for creation
  1) He alone made the universe, heaven & earth, & all that is therein
  2) He alone preserves life
  3) He alone is worshipped in heaven

c. The people praised God for choosing Abraham & calling him to such a great purpose
  1) God called & renamed Abraham

  2) God found Abraham's heart faithful

  3) God gave Abraham & his descendants (all believers) the covenant of the promised land (a symbol of heaven), Ge.12:1-9; 15:1-21; 17:1-27

  4) God kept His promise:

Now in the twenty and fourth day of this month the children of Israel were assembled with fasting, and with sackclothes, and earth upon them. 2 And the seed of Israel separated themselves from all strangers, and stood and confessed their sins, and the iniquities of their fathers. 3 And they stood up in their place, and read in the book of the law of the LORD their God *one* fourth part of the day; and *another* fourth part they confessed, and worshipped the LORD their God. 4 Then stood up upon the stairs, of the Levites, Jeshua, and Bani, Kadmiel, Shebaniah, Bunni, Sherebiah, Bani, *and* Chenani, and cried with a loud voice unto the LORD their God. 5 Then the Levites, Jeshua, and Kadmiel, Bani, Hashabniah, Sherebiah, Hodijah, Shebaniah, *and* Pethahiah, said, Stand up *and* bless the LORD your God for ever and ever: and blessed be thy glorious name, which is exalted above all blessing and praise. 6 Thou, *even* thou, *art* LORD alone; thou hast made heaven, the heaven of heavens, with all their host, the earth, and all *things* that *are* therein, the seas, and all that *is* therein, and thou preservest them all; and the host of heaven worshippeth thee. 7 Thou *art* the LORD the God, who didst choose Abram, and broughtest him forth out of Ur of the Chaldees, and gavest him the name of Abraham; 8 And foundest his heart faithful before thee, and madest a covenant with him to give the land of the Canaanites, the Hittites, the Amorites, and the Perizzites, and the Jebusites, and the Girgashites, to give *it, I say,* to his seed, and hast performed thy words; for thou

art righteous:
9 And didst see the affliction of our fathers in Egypt, and heardest their cry by the Red sea; 10 And showedst signs and wonders upon Pharaoh, and on all his servants, and on all the people of his land: for thou knewest that they dealt proudly against them. So didst thou get thee a name, as *it is* this day. 11 And thou didst divide the sea before them, so that they went through the midst of the sea on the dry land; and their persecutors thou threwest into the deeps, as a stone into the mighty waters. 12 Moreover thou leddest them in the day by a cloudy pillar; and in the night by a pillar of fire, to give them light in the way wherein they should go. 13 Thou camest down also upon mount Sinai, and spakest with them from heaven, and gavest them right judgments, and true laws, good statutes and commandments: 14 And madest known unto them thy holy sabbath, and commandedst them precepts, statutes, and laws, by the hand of Moses thy servant: 15 And gavest them bread from heaven for their hunger, and broughtest forth water for them out of the rock for their thirst, and promisedst them that they should go in to possess the land which thou hadst sworn to give them. 16 But they and our fathers dealt proudly, and hardened their necks, and hearkened not to thy commandments, 17 And refused to obey, neither were mindful of thy wonders that thou didst among them; but hardened their necks, and in their rebellion appointed a captain to return to their bondage: but thou *art* a God ready to pardon, gracious and merciful, slow to anger, and of great kindness, and forsookest them not. 18 Yea, when they had made them a molten calf, and said, This *is* thy God that brought thee up out of Egypt, and had wrought great provocations;

Because He is righteous

d. The people praised God for delivering His people from Egypt (a symbol of being saved from the world's enslavement)
  1) God miraculously executed judgments upon the Egyptians: Because of their pride, arrogance
  2) God made a lasting name for Himself, Ex.13:17–14:31

    • By dividing the sea
    • By drowning the enemies (the Egyptians) in the sea

  3) God guided His people through the wilderness journeys: Symbolized by the pillar of cloud & the pillar of fire

e. The people praised God for giving the law & the Sabbath to His people, Ex.20:1-23
  1) Laws that are just, true, & good

  2) Laws that were given through Moses

f. The people praised God for His provision of food & water: He provided for His people as they made their way through the wilderness journeys, traveling to the promised land, Ex.16:4-8; 17:1-7

g. The people praised God for forgiving the sins of His people
  1) They were proud, stiffnecked, & disobedient
    • They failed to remember God's goodness
    • They rebelled & appointed a leader to replace Moses: To lead them back to Egypt, Nu.13:1–14:45
  2) They were not forsaken or abandoned by God: Because of His mercy & compassion, His readiness to forgive
  3) They were not forsaken by God even when they turned to false gods & false worship, Ex.32:1-35

170

h. The people praised God for sustaining His people as they walked toward the promised land (heaven)

1) He guided them day & night: By the pillar of cloud & the pillar of fire, Ex.13:21-22

2) He gave His Spirit to instruct them, Ps.51:11

3) He continued to meet their needs
- Providing food & water
- Sustaining them for 40 years
- Providing clothing
- Protecting their feet, their health

4) He gave them victory over those who opposed them—over all enemies

5) He blessed them with children, a large population, Ge.12:2; 15:5

6) He brought them to the promised land

i. The people praised God for the strength & power to conquer the enemies of the promised land

1) God empowered His people to subdue the Canaanites—all enemies who confronted them

2) God gave His people the wealth & fruitfulness of the promised land

j. The people praised God for His mercy & forgiveness despite continued, persistent backsliding

1) The people committed three serious offenses
- Rebelled & disobeyed
- Rejected the prophets
- Committed blasphemies

2) The LORD judged, chastised them: Allowed their enemies to oppress them

19 Yet thou in thy manifold mercies forsookest them not in the wilderness: the pillar of the cloud departed not from them by day, to lead them in the way; neither the pillar of fire by night, to show them light, and the way wherein they should go. 20 Thou gavest also thy good spirit to instruct them, and withheldest not thy manna from their mouth, and *gavest them water for* their thirst. 21 Yea, forty years didst thou sustain them in the wilderness, *so that* they lacked nothing; their clothes waxed not old, and their feet swelled not. 22 Moreover thou gavest them kingdoms and nations, and didst divide them into corners: so they possessed the land of Sihon, and the land of the king of Heshbon, and the land of Og king of Bashan. 23 Their children also multipliedst thou as the stars of heaven, and broughtest them into the land, concerning which thou hadst promised to their fathers, that they should go in to possess *it*. 24 So the children went in and possessed the land, and thou subduedst before them the inhabitants of the land, the Canaanites, and gavest them into their hands, with their kings, and the people of the land, that they might do with them as they would. 25 And they took strong cities, and a fat land, and possessed houses full of all goods, wells digged, vineyards, and oliveyards, and fruit trees in abundance: so they did eat, and were filled, and became fat, and delighted themselves in thy great goodness. 26 Nevertheless they were disobedient, and rebelled against thee, and cast thy law behind their backs, and slew thy prophets which testified against them to turn them to thee, and they wrought great provocations. 27 Therefore thou deliveredst them into the hand of their enemies, who vexed them: and in the time of their

trouble, when they cried unto thee, thou heardest *them* from heaven; and according to thy manifold mercies thou gavest them saviours, who saved them out of the hand of their enemies. 28 But after they had rest, they did evil again before thee: therefore leftest thou them in the hand of their enemies, so that they had the dominion over them: yet when they returned, and cried unto thee, thou heardest *them* from heaven; and many times didst thou deliver them according to thy mercies; 29 And testifiedst against them, that thou mightest bring them again unto thy law: yet they dealt proudly, and hearkened not unto thy commandments, but sinned against thy judgments, (which if a man do, he shall live in them;) and withdrew the shoulder, and hardened their neck, and would not hear. 30 Yet many years didst thou forbear them, and testifiedst against them by thy spirit in thy prophets: yet would they not give ear: therefore gavest thou them into the hand of the people of the lands. 31 Nevertheless for thy great mercies' sake thou didst not utterly consume them, nor forsake them; for thou *art* a gracious and merciful God. 32 Now therefore, our God, the great, the mighty, and the terrible God, who keepest covenant and mercy, let not all the trouble seem little before thee, that hath come upon us, on our kings, on our princes, and on our priests, and on our prophets, and on our fathers, and on all thy people, since the time of the kings of Assyria unto this day. 33 Howbeit thou *art* just in all that is brought upon us; for thou hast done right, but we have done wickedly: 34 Neither have our kings, our princes, our priests, nor our fathers, kept thy law, nor hearkened unto thy commandments and thy

3) The people repented, cried out to God

4) The LORD heard their cry & delivered them by raising up judges to lead them

5) The people backslid again, & the cycle of a compromising, inconsistent lifestyle repeated itself, Jud.2:1–3:6
- The LORD chastised His people another time
- The people repented & cried out once more
- The LORD had mercy & delivered His people yet again

k. The people praised God for His prophets & for their warning to repent

1) The LORD cautioned His people: Must return to His Word, His commandments

2) The people stubbornly continued to sin, rejecting God & His Word

3) The LORD continued to be patient: Admonished the people by speaking to them through the prophets

4) The people continued in their rejection

5) The LORD continued to chastise His people

6) The LORD continued to show mercy: Did not utterly destroy or abandon His people

3. **Pleading for mercy in the midst of present trouble & hardship**

a. The people pleaded with God because God is merciful & keeps His covenant

b. The people pleaded with God because of the difficulties & suffering being endured

1) Suffered by all, leaders & citizens alike

2) Suffered since the Assyrian captivity

3) Suffered because God is righteous & just

c. The people pleaded with God because no one had kept God's law or heeded His warnings: Not the leaders nor citizens of their day nor of

past history had obeyed	testimonies, wherewith thou didst testify against them.	that thou gavest unto our fathers to eat the fruit thereof	slaves in the land given by God
1) Did not obey even when they were in the promised land enjoying its fruitfulness & God's blessings 2) Did not serve God or turn from their wicked ways	35 For they have not served thee in their kingdom, and in thy great goodness that thou gavest them, and in the large and fat land which thou gavest before them, neither turned they from their wicked works.	and the good thereof, behold, we *are* servants in it: 37 And it yieldeth much increase unto the kings whom thou hast set over us because of our sins: also they have dominion over our bodies, and over our cattle, at their	1) Enslaved because of sin 2) Oppressed by others because of God's judgment
d. The people pleaded for mercy because they were all	36 Behold, we *are* servants this day, and *for* the land	pleasure, and we *are* in great distress.	

DIVISION II

THE REBUILDING OF THE NATION AND THE PEOPLE 8:1–13:31

B. Step 2—Rebuilding Through a Revived Spirit: Stressing the Importance of Seeking God, His Goodness and Mercy, 9:1-37

(9:1-37) **Introduction**: our world desperately needs an outpouring of God's goodness and mercy. We do not deserve it, but we urgently need it. However, the only way we can obtain these gifts is to seek God wholeheartedly. While a number of individuals in nearly every culture are genuine believers, the majority are not. If people all across the face of the earth would sincerely follow the LORD, looking to Him for guidance and strength, this would be a far different world. In seeking God, these people would demonstrate the desire to help build up their own societies and to better themselves. In finding and following God, the individuals would become more godly, modeling for others the excellent qualities of life. Our supreme model of all that is good and perfect is God: God the Father, God's Son, our Lord Jesus Christ, and God's Holy Spirit. Therefore, we must look at all that God is and all that He has done for us as we begin our quest to secure His goodness and mercy. While God's goodness is immeasurable, there are certain qualities that we can, through Him, attain. We can be...

- moral
- just
- kind
- loving
- caring
- honest
- honorable
- principled
- commendable
- praiseworthy
- responsible

- hard-working
- conscientious
- faithful
- loyal
- reliable
- trustworthy
- understanding
- sympathetic
- charitable
- generous
- considerate

- gracious
- kindhearted
- merciful
- compassionate
- tolerant
- true to our word
- well-behaved
- respectful
- courteous
- chaste
- untainted

Again, those who seek and receive God's goodness and mercy become better people, making significant contributions to society, building up the lives of others. Wherever *a good person* lives, those around him always benefit. A helping hand is ready to meet any need that arises. The person sets a dynamic example of man's best traits, a dynamic example of what God wants us to be and how He wants us to live. In the pursuit of God's *ideal, perfect goodness* and *mercy*, we will become more and more conformed to His image.

The returned exiles of Nehemiah's day were determined to seek after God, His goodness and mercy. They were faced with rebuilding their nation and society. To accomplish what was needed, they needed their spirits revived. They needed God to pour out the spirit of His goodness upon them, arousing all the people to work together to build a righteous, just, productive, and loving society. Thus, they determined to seek God, begging Him to give them a spirit of revival. With their spirits revitalized and renewed, they could be successful in rebuilding their nation. The promised land would once again be fruitful and economically productive, and the people would some day in the future be given the wonderful hope of living in permanent peace. They would be free from all the bondages and enslavements of this life. This is, *Step 2— Rebuilding Through a Revived Spirit: Stressing the Importance of Seeking God, His Goodness and Mercy*, 9:1-37.

1. Seeking God through genuine confession (vv.1-5).
2. Seeking God through praise and thanksgiving (vv.6-31).
3. Pleading for mercy in the midst of present trouble and hardship (vv.32-37).

1 (9:1-4) **Confession, of Sin, Essential, for Revival—Repentance, Essential, for Revival—Revival, Essentials, Confession and Repentance—Seeking, God, Essentials for—Returnees, Jewish, Sought Revival—Nehemiah, Stirred Revival—Ezra, Stirred Revival—Israel, Revivals of—Jews, Revivals of**: the first step in revival is to seek God through genuine confession and repentance. This was exactly what the Jewish returnees did under Ezra's and Nehemiah's leadership.

OUTLINE	SCRIPTURE	SCRIPTURE	OUTLINE

1. **Seeking God through genuine confession**
a. The people's assembly: Two days after the festival, 8:12-18
  1) They humbled themselves
  2) They separated themselves from all foreigners (unbelievers)
b. The people's worship service
  1) They confessed their sins
  2) They read God's Word for about three hours of
	Now in the twenty and fourth day of this month the children of Israel were assembled with fasting, and with sackclothes, and earth upon them.
	2 And the seed of Israel separated themselves from all strangers, and stood and confessed their sins, and the iniquities of their fathers.
	3 And they stood up in their place, and read in the book of
		the law of the LORD their God *one* fourth part of the day; and *another* fourth part they confessed, and worshipped the LORD their God.
		4 Then stood up upon the stairs, of the Levites, Jeshua, and Bani, Kadmiel, Shebaniah, Bunni, Sherebiah, Bani, *and* Chenani, and cried with a loud voice unto the LORD their God.
			daylight
			3) They spent another three hours of daylight in confession & worship
			
			4) They were led in worship, praise, & prayer by the Levites
			• They were divided into two groups
			• They called on the LORD

Just two days after celebrating the Festival of Tabernacles, the people assembled together again. Remember, the Festival of Tabernacles had lasted for seven days, and prior to that the people had met for two days in a special study of God's Word. So even before the present assembly began, the people had already been meeting for a total of nine days to study God's Holy Law and to worship Him. Now, after just one day's break, they gathered once more to study God's Word and to seek the LORD for a spirit of revival within their community. They made a deliberate decision to fast all day, wearing sackcloth and covering their heads with dust, which was an outward symbol of their hearts' being humbled before the LORD (v.1). They also made a deliberate decision to separate themselves from all foreigners, disallowing any foreigner to attend this particular worship service. Excluding the foreigners in this instance was understandable since their purpose was to confess the sins of their nation down through the centuries. They sought to reestablish the covenant or agreement between God and Israel. They wanted God to forgive their sins and to reestablish them as the nation of Israel within the promised land. They longed for God to fulfill all His promises to them and through them, the promises that had been given to Abraham and to David. These promises were basically threefold: they would receive the wonderful inheritance of the promised land of Canaan (a symbol of heaven); through them would come the promised seed, a king, who was to sit upon the throne of David eternally (fulfilled in the Lord Jesus Christ); and they would become a great nation of people who would be a blessing to the world. The Jews were to bless the world by being the channel through which the LORD sent the Messiah, the Lord Jesus Christ and His Holy Word, the Bible. The great nation promised to Abraham was fulfilled in the nation Israel and in all the leaders who walked in the faith of Abraham, who is the father of us all (true believers) (Ro.4:11-16). Thus, this worship service of the returned Jews had to do specifically with their relationship to the LORD and theirs alone. For this reason, they needed to meet privately with the LORD face-to-face without any foreigners being present.

The worship service itself included confession of their sins and the reading of God's Word. Keep in mind here that where Scripture refers to a quarter of the day, it most likely refers to the daylight hours. Reading God's Word lasted for about three hours (vv.2-3). Confessing their sins and worshipping the LORD took approximately another three hours, which meant that the worship service lasted a total of six hours. (Imagine a worship service today lasting six hours, three hours spent in reading and studying God's Word and another three hours in prayer!) Leading the worship service in praise and prayer were the Levites, who stood on the stairs of the platform that had been prepared just for these services (v.4; also see 8:4). The Levites were divided into two groups who lifted up their voices in prayer and praise to the LORD. Part of their prayer is given in the song that follows in the next point.

Thought 1. When God's children are seeking a spirit of revival, two acts are absolutely essential: genuine confession and genuine repentance of sin. Repentance means that we turn away from our sins. God cannot accept sin, for He is holy, righteous, and perfect in all His being. Sin is unacceptable to Him. In view of that, before we can ever approach God, our sins have to be removed. Sin can be removed only through the blood of the Lord Jesus Christ. Therefore when we approach God, we must come to God through the Name of the Lord Jesus Christ, confessing our faith in Him and asking God to forgive our sins. We must turn away from our sin and turn back to God, following Him and living righteous and moral lives. Once we have confessed and repented of our sin, God gives us a spirit of revival. Our spirits are stirred with praise and thanksgiving, aroused to live righteous, productive, and fruitful lives, lives that are triumphant and that overcome all the trials and temptations of this world. The privilege of living such victorious, successful lives comes only through Jesus Christ, confessing our sins and receiving His forgiveness. Listen to what God's Holy Word says about confession and repentance of sin:

"**And saying, Repent ye: for the kingdom of heaven is at hand**" (Mt.3:2).

"**Blessed *are* they that mourn: for they shall be comforted**" (Mt.5:4).

"**I say unto you, that likewise joy shall be in heaven over one sinner that repenteth, more than over ninety and nine just persons, which need no repentance**" (Lu.15:7).

"**Then Peter said unto them, Repent, and be baptized every one of you in the name of Jesus Christ for the remission of sins, and ye shall receive the gift of the Holy Ghost**" (Ac.2:38).

"**Repent ye therefore, and be converted, that your sins may be blotted out, when the times of refreshing shall come from the presence of the Lord**" (Ac.3:19).

"**If we confess our sins, he is faithful and just to forgive us *our* sins, and to cleanse us from all unrighteousness**" (1 Jn.1:9).

"If my people, which are called by my name, shall humble themselves, and pray, and seek my face, and turn from their wicked ways; then will I hear from heaven, and will forgive their sin, and will heal their land" (2 Chr.7:14).

"Now therefore make confession unto the LORD God of your fathers, and do his pleasure: and separate yourselves from the people of the land, and from the strange wives" (Ezr.10:11).

"He that covereth his sins shall not prosper: but whoso confesseth and forsaketh *them* shall have mercy" (Pr.28:13).

"Let the wicked forsake his way, and the unrighteous man his thoughts: and let him return unto the LORD, and he will have mercy upon him; and to our God, for he will abundantly pardon" (Is.55:7).

"Only acknowledge thine iniquity, that thou hast transgressed against the LORD thy God, and hast scattered thy ways to the strangers under every green tree, and ye have not obeyed my voice, saith the LORD" (Je.3:13).

"Cast away from you all your transgressions, whereby ye have transgressed; and make you a new heart and a new spirit: for why will ye die, O house of Israel?" (Eze.18:31).

"Take with you words, and turn to the LORD: say unto him, Take away all iniquity, and receive *us* graciously: so will we render the calves of our lips" (Ho.14:2).

"Therefore also now, saith the LORD, turn ye *even* to me with all your heart, and with fasting, and with weeping, and with mourning" (Joel 2:12).

2 (9:5-31) **Revival, Essentials, Praise and Thanksgiving—Praise, Essential, for Revival—Thanksgiving, Essential, for Revival—Worship, Essentials of, Praise and Thanksgiving—Worship, Service of, Praise and Thanksgiving—Services, Worship, Essentials—Returnees, Jewish, Sought Revival—Jewish Returnees, Worship of God, Eleven Praises—Israel, Songs of, Jewish Returnees—Songs, of Jewish Returnees—Praise, of God, Eleven Praises**: the second step in revival is to seek God through praise and thanksgiving. The song of praise in this passage is one of the most eloquent praises of God in all of Scripture. It is comparable to the other great songs of Holy Scripture such as…

- "Moses' Song of Praise for God's Great Deliverance" (Ex.15:1-21)
- "The Song of Moses that Stood as a Strong Warning and Witness to God's People" (De.32:1-52)
- "Deborah's Great Song of Victory" (Jud.5:1-31)
- "The Song of Hannah" (1 S.2:1-11)
- "David's Song of Grief," a funeral song composed for King Saul and his son Jonathan (2 S.1:17-27)

The Levites led the Jewish returnees in this prayerful song of praise and thanksgiving. The LORD was being praised for having led the nation of Israel down through the generations up through the present time. The praises to God begin with acknowledgment that the LORD God Himself exists eternally, prior even to creation, stretching on down through the ages to the prophets who were presently ministering among the people. The Levites sang from the depths of their hearts, mentioning eleven specific facts about God and His wonderful works.

OUTLINE	SCRIPTURE	SCRIPTURE	OUTLINE
2. Seeking God through praise & thanksgiving a. The people praised God for Himself, His supremacy 1) That He is eternal 2) That His name is glorious & to be exalted above all	5 Then the Levites, Jeshua, and Kadmiel, Bani, Hashabniah, Sherebiah, Hodijah, Shebaniah, *and* Pethahiah, said, Stand up *and* bless the LORD your God for ever and ever: and blessed be thy glorious name, which is exalted above all blessing and praise.	Girgashites, to give *it, I say,* to his seed, and hast performed thy words; for thou *art* righteous: 9 And didst see the affliction of our fathers in Egypt, and heardest their cry by the Red sea;	15:1-21; 17:1-27 4) God kept His promise: Because He is righteous d. The people praised God for delivering His people from Egypt (a symbol of being saved from the world's enslavement)
3) That He alone is God b. The people praised God for creation 1) He alone made the universe, heaven & earth, & all that is therein 2) He alone preserves life 3) He alone is worshipped in heaven	6 Thou, *even* thou, *art* LORD alone; thou hast made heaven, the heaven of heavens, with all their host, the earth, and all *things* that *are* therein, the seas, and all that *is* therein, and thou preservest them all; and the host of heaven worshippeth thee.	10 And showedst signs and wonders upon Pharaoh, and on all his servants, and on all the people of his land: for thou knewest that they dealt proudly against them. So didst thou get thee a name, as *it is* this day. 11 And thou didst divide the sea before them, so that they went through the midst of the sea on the dry land; and their persecutors thou threwest into the deeps, as a stone into the mighty waters.	1) God miraculously executed judgments upon the Egyptians: Because of their pride, arrogance 2) God made a lasting name for Himself, Ex.13:17–14:31 • By dividing the sea • By drowning the enemies (the Egyptians) in the sea
c. The people praised God for choosing Abraham & calling him to such a great purpose 1) God called & renamed Abraham 2) God found Abraham's heart faithful 3) God gave Abraham & his descendants (all believers) the covenant of the promised land (a symbol of heaven), Ge.12:1-9;	7 Thou *art* the LORD the God, who didst choose Abram, and broughtest him forth out of Ur of the Chaldees, and gavest him the name of Abraham; 8 And foundest his heart faithful before thee, and madest a covenant with him to give the land of the Canaanites, the Hittites, the Amorites, and the Perizzites, and the Jebusites, and the	12 Moreover thou leddest them in the day by a cloudy pillar; and in the night by a pillar of fire, to give them light in the way wherein they should go. 13 Thou camest down also upon mount Sinai, and	3) God guided His people through the wilderness wanderings: Symbolized by the pillar of cloud & the pillar of fire e. The people praised God for giving the law & the Sabbath

OUTLINE	SCRIPTURE	SCRIPTURE	OUTLINE
to His people, Ex.20:1-23 1) Laws that are just, true, & good 2) Laws that were given through Moses f. The people praised God for His provision of food & water: He provided for His people as they made their way through the wilderness wanderings, traveling to the promised land, Ex.16:4-8; 17:1-7 g. The people praised God for forgiving the sins of His people 1) They were proud, stiff-necked, & disobedient • They failed to remember God's goodness • They rebelled & appointed a leader to replace Moses: To lead them back to Egypt, Nu.13:1–14:45 2) They were not forsaken or abandoned by God: Because of His mercy & compassion, His readiness to forgive 3) They were not forsaken by God even when they turned to false gods & false worship, Ex.32:1-35 h. The people praised God for sustaining His people as they walked toward the promised land (heaven) 1) He guided them day & night: By the pillar of cloud & the pillar of fire, Ex.13:21-22 2) He gave His Spirit to instruct them, Ps.51:11 3) He continued to meet their needs • Providing food & water • Sustaining them for 40 years • Providing clothing • Protecting their feet, their health 4) He gave them victory over those who opposed them—over all enemies	spakest with them from heaven, and gavest them right judgments, and true laws, good statutes and commandments: 14 And madest known unto them thy holy sabbath, and commandedst them precepts, statutes, and laws, by the hand of Moses thy servant: 15 And gavest them bread from heaven for their hunger, and broughtest forth water for them out of the rock for their thirst, and promisedst them that they should go in to possess the land which thou hadst sworn to give them. 16 But they and our fathers dealt proudly, and hardened their necks, and hearkened not to thy commandments, 17 And refused to obey, neither were mindful of thy wonders that thou didst among them; but hardened their necks, and in their rebellion appointed a captain to return to their bondage: but thou *art* a God ready to pardon, gracious and merciful, slow to anger, and of great kindness, and forsookest them not. 18 Yea, when they had made them a molten calf, and said, This *is* thy God that brought thee up out of Egypt, and had wrought great provocations; 19 Yet thou in thy manifold mercies forsookest them not in the wilderness: the pillar of the cloud departed not from them by day, to lead them in the way; neither the pillar of fire by night, to show them light, and the way wherein they should go. 20 Thou gavest also thy good spirit to instruct them, and withheldest not thy manna from their mouth, and gavest them water for their thirst. 21 Yea, forty years didst thou sustain them in the wilderness, *so that* they lacked nothing; their clothes waxed not old, and their feet swelled not. 22 Moreover thou gavest them kingdoms and nations, and didst divide them into corners: so they possessed the land of Sihon, and the land of the king of Heshbon,	and the land of Og king of Bashan. 23 Their children also multipliedst thou as the stars of heaven, and broughtest them into the land, concerning which thou hadst promised to their fathers, that they should go in to possess *it.* 24 So the children went in and possessed the land, and thou subduedst before them the inhabitants of the land, the Canaanites, and gavest them into their hands, with their kings, and the people of the land, that they might do with them as they would. 25 And they took strong cities, and a fat land, and possessed houses full of all goods, wells digged, vineyards, and oliveyards, and fruit trees in abundance: so they did eat, and were filled, and became fat, and delighted themselves in thy great goodness. 26 Nevertheless they were disobedient, and rebelled against thee, and cast thy law behind their backs, and slew thy prophets which testified against them to turn them to thee, and they wrought great provocations. 27 Therefore thou deliveredst them into the hand of their enemies, who vexed them: and in the time of their trouble, when they cried unto thee, thou heardest *them* from heaven; and according to thy manifold mercies thou gavest them saviours, who saved them out of the hand of their enemies. 28 But after they had rest, they did evil again before thee: therefore leftest thou them in the hand of their enemies, so that they had the dominion over them: yet when they returned, and cried unto thee, thou heardest *them* from heaven; and many times didst thou deliver them according to thy mercies; 29 And testifiedst against them, that thou mightest bring them again unto thy law: yet they dealt proudly, and hearkened not unto thy commandments, but sinned	5) He blessed them with children, a large population, Ge.12:2; 15:5 6) He brought them to the promised land i. The people praised God for the strength & power to conquer the enemies of the promised land 1) God empowered His people to subdue the Canaanites—all enemies who confronted them 2) God gave His people the wealth & fruitfulness of the promised land j. The people praised God for His mercy & forgiveness despite continued, persistent backsliding 1) The people committed three serious offenses • Rebelled & disobeyed • Rejected the prophets • Committed blasphemies 2) The LORD judged, chastised them: Allowed their enemies to oppress them 3) The people repented, cried out to God 4) The LORD heard their cry & delivered them by raising up judges to lead them 5) The people backslid again, & the cycle of a compromising, inconsistent lifestyle repeated itself, Jud.2:1–3:6 • The LORD chastised His people another time • The people repented & cried out once more • The LORD had mercy & delivered His people yet again k. The people praised God for His prophets & for their warning to repent 1) The LORD cautioned His people: Must return to His Word, His command-

OUTLINE	SCRIPTURE	SCRIPTURE	OUTLINE
ments 2) The people stubbornly continued to sin, rejecting God & His Word 3) The LORD continued to be patient: Admonished the people by speaking to them through the prophets	against thy judgments, (which if a man do, he shall live in them;) and withdrew the shoulder, and hardened their neck, and would not hear. 30 Yet many years didst thou forbear them, and testifiedst against them by thy spirit in thy prophets: yet	would they not give ear: therefore gavest thou them into the hand of the people of the lands. 31 Nevertheless for thy great mercies' sake thou didst not utterly consume them, nor forsake them; for thou *art* a gracious and merciful God.	4) The people continued in their rejection 5) The LORD continued to chastise His people 6) The LORD continued to show mercy: Did not utterly destroy or abandon His people

a. The people praised God for His being, His supremacy (vv.5-6a). God is eternal, from everlasting to everlasting, and His Name is glorious. Therefore His name is to be exalted and praised. Nevertheless in praising the LORD, the worshipper must realize that God is so exalted and His Name so glorious that all human praise is inadequate. The glory of His Name far exceeds any and all praise that could be ever offered up to Him.

The LORD is also to be praised because He alone is God (v.6a). No other God exists, not a true and living God. All other gods are merely the creation of people's imaginations, gods invented by the human mind and hands. Accordingly, the Name of the LORD, and His Name alone, is to be praised. All praise and worship is due the LORD. Because of who He is, the one and only true God who exists from everlasting to everlasting.

> "For *there is* one God, and one mediator between God and men, the man Christ Jesus; Who gave himself a ransom for all, to be testified in due time" (1 Ti.2:5-6).
> "But, beloved, be not ignorant of this one thing, that one day *is* with the Lord as a thousand years, and a thousand years as one day" (2 Pe.3:8).
> "And God said unto Moses, I AM THAT I AM: and he said, Thus shalt thou say unto the children of Israel, I AM hath sent me unto you" (Ex.3:14).
> "Unto thee it was showed, that thou mightest know that the LORD he *is* God; *there is* none else beside him" (De.4:35).
> "Hear, O Israel: The LORD our God *is* one LORD: And thou shalt love the LORD thy God with all thine heart, and with all thy soul, and with all thy might" (De.6:4-5).
> "The eternal God *is thy* refuge, and underneath *are* the everlasting arms: and he shall thrust out the enemy from before thee; and shall say, Destroy *them*" (De.33:27).
> "For thou *art* great, and doest wondrous things: thou *art* God alone" (Ps.86:10).
> "Thy name, O LORD, *endureth* for ever; *and* thy memorial, O LORD, throughout all generations" (Ps.135:13).
> "Ye *are* my witnesses, saith the LORD, and my servant whom I have chosen: that ye may know and believe me, and understand that I *am* he: before me there was no God formed, neither shall there be after me" (Is.43:10).
> "Thus saith the LORD the King of Israel, and his redeemer the LORD of hosts; I *am* the first, and I *am* the last; and beside me *there is* no God....Fear ye not, neither be afraid: have not I told thee from that time, and have declared *it?* ye *are* even my witnesses. Is there a God beside me? yea, *there is* no God; I know not *any*" (Is.44:6, 8).
> "That they may know from the rising of the sun, and from the west, that *there is* none beside me. I *am* the LORD, and *there is* none else....Tell ye, and bring *them* near; yea, let them take counsel together: who hath declared this from ancient time? *who* hath told it from that time? *have* not I the LORD? and *there is* no God else beside me; a just God and a Saviour; *there is* none beside me. Look unto me, and be ye saved, all the ends of the earth: for I *am* God, and *there is* none else" (Is.45:6, 21-22).
> "Remember the former things of old: for I *am* God, and *there is* none else; *I am* God, and *there is* none like me" (Is.46:9).

b. The people praised God for creation (v.6). He alone made the universe, heaven and earth and all that is therein. The stars of the sky and the earth with all its vegetation, seas, and animal life were all made by the LORD. Furthermore, the LORD alone preserves life. As the great Creator of the universe, no person or being in heaven or earth can be compared to Him. Because of His creative power He is deserving of worship and praise.

> "And saying, Sirs, why do ye these things? We also are men of like passions with you, and preach unto you that ye should turn from these vanities unto the living God, which made heaven, and earth, and the sea, and all things that are therein" (Ac.14:15).
> "In the beginning God created the heaven and the earth" (Ge.1:1).
> "Behold, the heaven and the heaven of heavens *is* the LORD'S thy God, the earth *also,* with all that therein *is*" (De.10:14).
> "But will God indeed dwell on the earth? behold, the heaven and heaven of heavens cannot contain thee; how much less this house that I have builded?" (1 K.8:27).
> "And the heavens shall praise thy wonders, O LORD: thy faithfulness also in the congregation of the saints. For who in the heaven can be compared unto the LORD? *who* among the sons of the mighty can be likened unto the LORD? God is greatly to be feared in the assembly of the saints, and to be had in reverence of all *them that are* about him" (Ps.89:5-7).

"O give thanks unto the LORD; for *he is* good: for his mercy *endureth* for ever. O give thanks unto the God of gods: for his mercy *endureth* for ever. O give thanks to the Lord of lords: for his mercy *endureth* for ever. To him who alone doeth great wonders: for his mercy *endureth* for ever. To him that by wisdom made the heavens: for his mercy *endureth* for ever. To him that stretched out the earth above the waters: for his mercy *endureth* for ever. To him that made great lights: for his mercy *endureth* for ever: The sun to rule by day: for his mercy *endureth* for ever: The moon and stars to rule by night: for his mercy *endureth* for ever" (Ps.136:1-9).

"Praise ye the LORD. Praise ye the LORD from the heavens: praise him in the heights. Praise ye him, all his angels: praise ye him, all his hosts. Praise ye him, sun and moon: praise him, all ye stars of light. Praise him, ye heavens of heavens, and ye waters that *be* above the heavens. Let them praise the name of the LORD: for he commanded, and they were created" (Ps.148:1-5).

"For thus saith the LORD that created the heavens; God himself that formed the earth and made it; he hath established it, he created it not in vain, he formed it to be inhabited: I *am* the LORD; and *there is* none else" (Is.45:18).

c. The people praised God for choosing Abraham and for calling him to such a great purpose, giving his descendants (believers) the covenant of the promised land (vv.7-8). God had called Abraham to leave his home in Ur of the Chaldeas to go to an unnamed land that God would give him—if Abraham would commit his life to the LORD and follow Him. Abraham believed God, forsaking his *old life* and following God to the *new life* in the promised land (a symbol of heaven). Because of Abraham's faithfulness, God established a permanent covenant with him. The covenant included three wonderful gifts: the promise of the promised land, which was a symbol of heaven; the promise of the promised seed, which was fulfilled in Christ; and the promise of a great nation of descendants, which was fulfilled in all the descendants of faith who truly believed God.

Down through the centuries, the LORD had kept His promise—because He is righteous. The Jewish returnees were evidence of God's fulfilling His covenant, for they were the true believers of that day and time and they were in the promised land. Thus God's Name was to be praised for choosing Abraham and for giving his descendants (believers) the covenant of the promised land (Ge.12:1-9; Ge.15:1-21; Ge.17:1-27).

Thought 1. The promise of the promised land has been given to all believers, to all descendants of faith, all of us who walk in the steps of faith that Abraham demonstrated. In fact, Abraham is called the father of all believers, which means he was the first who walked in faith, believing God's promise concerning the promised land (the symbol of heaven and of spiritual rest and assurance).

"And he received the sign of circumcision, a seal of the righteousness of the faith which *he had yet* being uncircumcised: that he might be the father of all them that believe, though they be not circumcised; that righteousness might be imputed unto them also: And the father of circumcision to them who are not of the circumcision only, but who also walk in the steps of that faith of our father Abraham, which *he had* being *yet* uncircumcised. For the promise, that he should be the heir of the world, *was* not to Abraham, or to his seed, through the law, but through the righteousness of faith" (Ro.4:11-13).

"That I may know him, and the power of his resurrection, and the fellowship of his sufferings, being made conformable unto his death; If by any means I might attain unto the resurrection of the dead. Not as though I had already attained, either were already perfect: but I follow after, if that I may apprehend that for which also I am apprehended of Christ Jesus. Brethren, I count not myself to have apprehended: but *this* one thing *I do,* forgetting those things which are behind, and reaching forth unto those things which are before" (Ph.3:10-13).

"For our conversation [behavior, conduct]is in heaven; from whence also we look for the Saviour, the Lord Jesus Christ: Who shall change our vile body, that it may be fashioned like unto his glorious body, according to the working whereby he is able even to subdue all things unto himself" (Ph.3:20-21).

d. The people praised God for having delivered their forefathers from Egypt. God's wonderful deliverance was a symbol of His salvation, of His saving people down through the ages from the world's enslavement (see outline and notes—Ex.7:8–11:10 for more discussion). In order to free His people from Egyptian slavery, God had miraculously executed judgments upon the Egyptians. These judgments had fallen upon Pharaoh and his people because of their stubborn arrogance toward God and because of their brutal treatment of the Israelites.

Through God's mighty deliverance, He made a lasting Name for Himself. His wonderful deliverance of the Israelites from Egyptian slavery is still studied and talked about today just as it was in the days of the Jewish returnees. Yet God's mighty acts in behalf of Israel were not done. In Israel's escape from Egypt, God divided the Red Sea so that they could safely cross. He then drowned the pursuing Egyptians in the same sea. As the Israelites marched forth on their journey through the wilderness journeys, God continued to guide His people. And His guidance was symbolized in the spectacular pillar of cloud that led them by day and the pillar of fire that led them by night (v.12. also see Ex.13:17–14:31).

Thought 1. The LORD alone can deliver us from the enslavement of sin, death, and hell. He alone delivers us from the bondages of this life and from the fears that can so easily grip us.

"For God so loved the world, that he gave his only begotten Son, that whosoever believeth in him should not perish, but have everlasting life" (Jn.3:16).

"For we would not, brethren, have you ignorant of our trouble which came to us in Asia, that we were pressed out of measure, above strength, insomuch that we despaired even of life: But we had the sentence of death in ourselves, that we should not trust in ourselves, but in God which raiseth the dead: Who delivered us from so great a death, and doth deliver: in whom we trust that he will yet deliver *us*" (2 Co.1:8-10).

"Who gave himself for our sins, that he might deliver us from this present evil world, according to the will of God and our Father" (Ga.1:4).

"Giving thanks unto the Father, which hath made us meet to be partakers of the inheritance of the saints in light: Who hath delivered us from the power of darkness, and hath translated *us* into the kingdom of his dear Son: In whom we have redemption through his blood, *even* the forgiveness of sins" (Col.1:12-14).

"Forasmuch then as the children are partakers of flesh and blood, he also himself likewise took part of the same; that through death he might destroy him that had the power of death, that is, the devil; And deliver them who through fear of death were all their lifetime subject to bondage" (He.2:14-15).

e. The people praised God for giving the law and the Sabbath to His people (Ex.20:1-26; 21:1–24:18). Looking back through the history of their people, the Jewish returnees could see that the law and commandments given by God were *good*. God's law had established justice and righteousness throughout the land. And when the people obeyed the law, they experienced the blessings of God. A righteous and just society was established and peace was given to the nation. Moreover the people had productive and fruitful lives with a strong society, strong families, and a strong economy. When their ancestors obeyed the laws of God, they lived successful, victorious lives, lives that triumphed over all the temptations and trials of life.

In addition to the laws and commandments, God had given His people the Sabbath, a day for rest and worship. Six days were to be spent in diligent labor, but the seventh day was to be spent in worship and rest. Both the body and spirit were to be cared for. The body was to rest on the Sabbath, and the spirit was to be revived through worship.

Thought 1. God's law shows us just how short we come of God's perfection and glory, how desperately we need a Savior. God gave us the law for the purpose of showing us how to live righteous and just lives upon this earth, how to love and treat other people as we wish to be loved and treated. However when we attempt to keep or obey the law, we find ourselves failing and coming up ever so short. We break God's law over and over. For that reason we must pay the penalty and suffer the punishment for violating the law. The punishment for that violation, for disobeying God's law is death, both physical and eternal death. Eternal death means to be eternally separated from God, separated from His light, love, goodness, mercy, compassion, forgiveness and so much more. It also means an eternity without hope. Thus when we break the law of God, the first thing the law shows us is the fact that we desperately need a Savior. The law points us to Jesus Christ.

"Therefore by the deeds of the law there shall no flesh be justified in his sight: for by the law *is* the knowledge of sin" (Ro.3:20).

"What shall we say then? *Is* the law sin? God forbid. Nay, I had not known sin, but by the law: for I had not known lust, except the law had said, Thou shalt not covet" (Ro.7:7).

"For as many as are of the works of the law are under the curse: for it is written, Cursed *is* every one that continueth not in all things which are written in the book of the law to do them. But that no man is justified by the law in the sight of God, *it is* evident: for, The just shall live by faith. And the law is not of faith: but, The man that doeth them shall live in them. Christ hath redeemed us from the curse of the law, being made a curse for us: for it is written, Cursed *is* every one that hangeth on a tree" (Ga.3:10-13).

"Wherefore then *serveth* the law? It was added because of transgressions, till the seed [Christ] should come to whom the promise was made; *and it was* ordained by angels in the hand of a mediator....Wherefore the law was our schoolmaster *to bring us* unto Christ, that we might be justified by faith" (Ga.3:19, 24).

Thought 2. God gave us the Sabbath for both rest and worship. No matter what generation we live in, our bodies still need rest one day a week, and our spirits still need to join with others in one day of worship and praise to the LORD.

"And upon the first *day* of the week, when the disciples came together to break bread, Paul preached unto them, ready to depart on the morrow; and continued his speech until midnight" (Ac.20:7).

"And he came to Nazareth, where he had been brought up: and, as his custom was, he went into the synagogue on the sabbath day, and stood up for to read" (Lu.4:16).

"Not forsaking the assembling of ourselves together, as the manner of some *is*; but exhorting *one another*: and so much the more, as ye see the day approaching" (He.10:25).

"Remember the sabbath day, to keep it holy. Six days shalt thou labour, and do all thy work: But the seventh day *is* the sabbath of the LORD thy God: *in it* thou shalt not do any work, thou, nor thy son, nor thy daughter, thy manservant, nor thy maidservant, nor thy cattle, nor thy stranger that *is* within thy gates" (Ex.20:8-10).

f. The people praised God for His provision of food and water (v.15). As the Israelites had made their way through the wilderness wanderings, traveling to the promised land, the LORD miraculously provided for His people. The *Bread from Heaven*, known as manna, was graciously provided as needed on a daily basis. And when water was needed in the middle of the desert wanderings, the LORD again miraculously provided all that was needed (see outline and notes—Ex.16:4-8; 17:1-7 for more discussion).

Thought 1. God meets all the daily needs of those who truly follow Him, obeying His commandments and living righteously. When a person truly seeks the LORD first, He promises to provide food, clothing, shelter, or any other basic necessity of life that is lacking.

> "But seek ye first the kingdom of God, and his righteousness; and all these things shall be added unto you" (Mt.6:33).
> "Then Jesus said unto them, Verily, verily, I say unto you, Moses gave you not that bread from heaven; but my Father giveth you the true bread from heaven....I am the living bread which came down from heaven: if any man eat of this bread, he shall live for ever: and the bread that I will give is my flesh, which I will give for the life of the world....This is that bread which came down from heaven: not as your fathers did eat manna, and are dead: he that eateth of this bread shall live for ever" (Jn.6:32, 51, 58).
> "And God is able to make all grace abound toward you; that ye, always having all sufficiency in all things, may abound to every good work" (2 Co.9:8).
> "But my God shall supply all your need according to his riches in glory by Christ Jesus" (Ph.4:19).

g. The people praised God for having forgiven the sins of their ancestors or forefathers (vv.16-18). Throughout the wilderness journey, they had been proud, stiff-necked, and disobedient to God. Their forefathers had failed to keep God's commandments. They failed to remember God's goodness, instead rebelling against Him and even appointing a leader to replace Moses. They wanted this new leader to lead them back to Egypt, proclaiming that wandering about in the desert wilderness was too demanding, too difficult. They felt hope for the promised land was not worth all the suffering and hardship (see outline and notes—Nu.13:1–14:45 for more discussion). But despite the Israelites' disobedience and rebellion, the LORD had neither forgotten nor abandoned them. Because of His mercy and compassion, He was ready to forgive them when they confessed their sins, repented, and turned back to God. They were never forsaken, even when they turned to false gods and to false worship (see outline and notes—Ex.32:1-35 for more discussion).

Thought 1. We must always remember what God has done for us, the wonderful salvation and hope for heaven He has provided us through Jesus Christ. Forgetting what God has done always leads to disobedience. Even so, when we disobey and turn away from the LORD, we must always remember that God is merciful. If we confess and repent of our sins, He will forgive us our sins.

> "Repent therefore of this thy wickedness, and pray God, if perhaps the thought of thine heart may be forgiven thee" (Ac.8:22).
> "Be it known unto you therefore, men and brethren, that through this man is preached unto you the forgiveness of sins" (Ac.13:38).
> "In whom we have redemption through his blood, the forgiveness of sins, according to the riches of his grace" (Ep.1:7).
> "If we confess our sins, he is faithful and just to forgive us our sins, and to cleanse us from all unrighteousness" (1 Jn.1:9).
> "If my people, which are called by my name, shall humble themselves, and pray, and seek my face, and turn from their wicked ways; then will I hear from heaven, and will forgive their sin, and will heal their land" (2 Chr.7:14).

h. The people praised God for His sustaining power, for preserving His people as they walked toward the promised land (a symbol of heaven and of spiritual rest in the LORD) (vv.19-23). Out of compassion for His people, the LORD never abandoned them in the desert wilderness. On the contrary, He miraculously guided them day and night by the pillar of cloud and the pillar of fire (Ex.13:21-22). Even more significant, He gave them His Spirit to instruct them how to live righteously and how to survive in the desert wilderness. Day by day the LORD continued to meet their needs by providing food and water. For over 40 years He sustained them in the desert, and they lacked nothing. Amazingly, their clothes did not wear out nor did their feet swell. The LORD provided what clothing they needed and took care of their health. And when enemies confronted them, the LORD gave victory over all who would oppress them. It was also during their wilderness journeys that the Israelite population grew so astoundingly. In summary, during the entire 40 years of their desert journey, the LORD sustained them until He finally brought them to the promised land.

Thought 1. God's divine intervention and sustaining power look after us. Day by day God sustains us, taking care of all our needs. If we are genuine followers of the LORD and we need food or shelter or clothing, the LORD will provide these necessities of life. Even when we are attacked by the trials and temptations of life or persecuted by unbelievers, the LORD will walk with us through the crisis or give us victory over the attacks. Even in death—whether as a result of violence, disease, or natural cause—the LORD does not forsake us. As believers, we will never taste or experience death. Quicker than the eye can blink, the LORD will deliver us into His presence, and the horror of death and hell will never lay hold on us. The LORD's sustaining power will keep us as we walk toward the promised land of heaven, where we will live eternally with Him.

> "Henceforth there is laid up for me a crown of righteousness, which the Lord, the righteous judge, shall give me at that day: and not to me only, but unto all them also that love his appearing" (2 Ti.4:8).

"Ye have seen what I did unto the Egyptians, and *how* I bare you on eagles' wings, and brought you unto myself" (Ex.19:4).

"The eternal God *is thy* refuge, and underneath *are* the everlasting arms: and he shall thrust out the enemy from before thee; and shall say, Destroy *them*" (De.33:27).

"Fear thou not; for I *am* with thee: be not dismayed; for I *am* thy God: I will strengthen thee; yea, I will help thee; yea, I will uphold thee with the right hand of my righteousness" (Is.41:10).

i. The people praised God for the strength and power to conquer the enemies of the promised land (vv.24-25). When the Israelites reached the promised land of Canaan, the LORD gave them the power to conquer all the Canaanites, and any other enemy that confronted them (see outline and notes—Jos.6:1–12:24 for more discussion. Also see De.6:10-12; Jos.24:13.) Through His mighty power His people not only conquered all their enemies, but they also inherited the wealth and fruitfulness of the promised land.

Thought 1. The LORD promises to give power to believers, to all of us who truly trust Him. And supernatural power is essential, for believers wrestle against both physical and spiritual enemies. Physically, we face the normal trials and temptations of life that everyone faces. But in addition, genuine believers face the oppression and persecution of a hostile world of unbelievers. Unbelievers want little to do with the holy commandments of God, the commandments that demand righteousness and morality. Most unbelievers want to live with no constraints on their morals or lifestyle. Doing what they want—when they want—is the philosophy of their lives. Thus when we live righteous lives and proclaim the way of holiness, we are often persecuted through discrimination, ridicule, mockery, outright assault, and sometimes even martyrdom.

Spiritually, believers face the continuous attack of the devil and his followers, the attack of temptation to join in the carnal pleasures and passions of this world. Believers are also tempted often to compromise their morals and beliefs. To combat such attacks, whether physical or spiritual, the believer must rely upon the strength and power of God. Only the power of God can enable us to withstand the constant barrage of temptations, trials, and attacks that confront us as believers. Listen to the wonderful promise of God's Word:

"For with God nothing shall be impossible" (Lu.1:37).

"That he would grant you, according to the riches of his glory, to be strengthened with might by his Spirit in the inner man" (Ep.3:16).

"Now unto him that is able to do exceeding abundantly above all that we ask or think, according to the power that worketh in us" (Ep.3:20).

"Strengthened with all might, according to his glorious power, unto all patience and longsuffering with joyfulness" (Col.1:11).

"For God hath not given us the spirit of fear; but of power, and of love, and of a sound mind" (2 Ti.1:7).

j. The people praised God for His mercy and forgiveness despite their ancestors' persistent backsliding (vv.26-28). Israel's ancestors committed three serious offenses against the LORD:

⇒ They disobeyed and rebelled against the LORD, casting the Law of God behind their backs.
⇒ They rejected and killed the prophets who had encouraged the people to turn back to the LORD.
⇒ They had committed terrible blasphemies against the LORD.

As a result of these grave sins, the LORD chastised them by allowing their enemies to oppress them (v.27). Then when they were broken and under enemy control, the Israelites repented and cried out to the LORD for deliverance. In mercy the LORD had heard their cry and delivered them, raising judges to rescue them from the hand of the enemy.

But, sadly, time and again the Israelites' ancestors backslid, and the cycle of a compromising, inconsistent lifestyle repeated itself (see outline and notes—Jud.2:1–3:6 for more discussion; also see the entire book of *Judges* for more discussion). This cycle of inconsistency included the following steps:

⇒ the people's sin
⇒ the LORD's chastisement
⇒ the people's repentance and cry for deliverance
⇒ the LORD's rescue of them from the hands of their oppressors

Thought 1. Far too many of us backslide, turn away from the LORD in order to seek the pleasures and possessions of this world. We profess to know the LORD, but we do not keep His commandments. The LORD, however, sees and knows all that we do. Still, we must remember that God is merciful and forgiving. And as our loving heavenly Father, He chastens us. But note: He will forgive us only if we are sincere, if we truly repent of our sins. We must turn away from sin and turn back to Him.

"And as they were eating, Jesus took bread, and blessed *it,* and brake *it,* and gave *it* to the disciples, and said, Take, eat; this is my body. And he took the cup, and gave thanks, and gave *it* to them, saying, Drink ye all of it; For this is my blood of the new testament, which is shed for many for the remission of sins" (Mt.26:26-28).

"If we [continually] confess our sins, he is faithful and just to forgive us *our* sins, and to cleanse us from all unrighteousness" (1 Jn.1:9).

"My little children, these things write I unto you, that ye sin not. And if any man sin, we have an advocate with the Father, Jesus Christ the righteous: And he is the propitiation for our sins: and not for ours only, but also for *the sins of* the whole world" (1 Jn.2:1-2).

"Let the wicked forsake his way, and the unrighteous man his thoughts: and let him return unto the LORD, and he will have mercy upon him; and to our God, for he will abundantly pardon" (Is.55:7).

"Who *is* a God like unto thee, that pardoneth iniquity, and passeth by the transgression of the remnant of his heritage? he retaineth not his anger for ever, because he delighteth *in* mercy" (Mi.7:18).

k. The people praised God for His prophets and for their warning to repent (vv.29-31). Preaching with fervor in their souls, the prophets had warned the Israelites to return to God's Holy Word, His commandments. But the people were proud, stubborn, and obstinate. Refusing to listen, they continued in their sin, rejecting God and His Word (v.29). Nevertheless, the LORD continued to be patient, and His patience lasted many years (v.30). Despite the Israelites' repeated cycle of sin down through the centuries, God warned them through His prophets, speaking to them through His Holy Spirit. Still the Israelites continued to shut their ears against the prophets' warnings. As a result, the LORD was forced to continue chastising them by allowing their pagan neighbors to oppress and conquer them. But through all their shameful sin and rebellion, the LORD continued to show mercy. Although He had a perfect right to eradicate them from the face of the earth, He never allowed them to be totally destroyed. He never abandoned them (v.31).

Thought 1. We should praise and thank God for the prophets of our day, the ministers of the gospel who proclaim and teach the Word of God. They have been called to a difficult and often seemingly impossible mission. Basically, their call is to lead believers to meet the desperate needs of this earth and to arouse all of us to serve and worship the LORD, and Him alone. In addition, they are called to reach out to all the unbelievers of the world. In just these three fundamental tasks, imagine the heavy weight upon a true minister's shoulders. God is to be praised for giving us dedicated ministers who both stir us to be faithful in our service and witness for the LORD and to help us through the difficult times of life.

"And we beseech you, brethren, to know them which labour among you, and are over you in the Lord, and admonish you; And to esteem them very highly in love for their work's sake. *And* be at peace among yourselves" (1 Th.5:12-13).

"Let the elders that rule well be counted worthy of double honour, especially they who labour in the word and doctrine" (1 Ti.5:17).

"Remember them which have the rule over you, who have spoken unto you the word of God: whose faith follow, considering the end of *their* conversation" (He.13:7).

3 (9:32-37) **Mercy, of God, Pleading for—Prayer, What to Pray for, Mercy—Trouble, Deliverance from, Through Prayer—Hardship, Deliverance from, Through Prayer—Suffering, Deliverance from, Through Prayer—Disobedience, of Israel, Confessed—Jewish Exiles, Freed**: the third step in revival is pleading with God for mercy in the midst of trouble and hardship. Because of God's wonderful acts in behalf of His people down through the centuries, the Jewish returnees knew beyond question that God was merciful. Having just reviewed His acts of salvation, the people now pleaded with God for mercy in their own behalf. Four very specific pleas were made:

OUTLINE	SCRIPTURE	SCRIPTURE	OUTLINE
3. Pleading for mercy in the midst of present trouble & hardship	32 Now therefore, our God, the great, the mighty, and the terrible God, who keepest covenant and mercy, let not all the trouble seem little before thee, that hath come upon us, on our kings, on our princes, and on our priests, and on our prophets, and on our fathers, and on all thy people, since the time of the kings of Assyria unto this day.	testify against them. 35 For they have not served thee in their kingdom, and in thy great goodness that thou gavest them, and in the large and fat land which thou gavest before them, neither turned they from their wicked works.	obeyed 1) Did not obey even when they were in the promised land enjoying its fruitfulness & God's blessings 2) Did not serve God or turn from their wicked ways
a. The people pleaded with God because God is merciful & keeps His covenant			
b. The people pleaded with God because of the difficulties & suffering being endured		36 Behold, we *are* servants this day, and *for* the land that thou gavest unto our fathers to eat the fruit thereof and the good thereof, behold, we *are* servants in it:	d. The people pleaded for mercy because they were all slaves in the land given by God
1) Suffered by all, leaders & citizens alike			
2) Suffered since the Assyrian captivity	33 Howbeit thou *art* just in all that is brought upon us; for thou hast done right, but we have done wickedly:	37 And it yieldeth much increase unto the kings whom thou hast set over us because of our sins: also they have dominion over our bodies, and over our cattle, at their pleasure, and we *are* in great distress.	1) Enslaved because of sin 2) Oppressed by others because of God's judgment
3) Suffered because God is righteous & just			
c. The people pleaded with God because no one had kept God's law or heeded His warnings: Not the leaders nor citizens of their day nor of past history had	34 Neither have our kings, our princes, our priests, nor our fathers, kept thy law, nor hearkened unto thy commandments and thy testimonies, wherewith thou didst		

a. The returned exiles pleaded with God because God is merciful and keeps His covenant, never breaking His promises (v.32). Because He is faithful to His promises, they could call upon Him as "our God." They could look to Him as the great, mighty, and awesome God who could act in their behalf. Believers must always remember who God is. He is the believer's God, the only living and true God. He is the LORD of the universe, who has the might and the supreme power to act and to meet all the needs of the believer.

b. The returned exiles pleaded for mercy because of the trouble and hardship they were suffering (v.32). Ever since the Assyrian and Babylonian captivities, the people had suffered. No matter who the people were—kings, royal officials, priests, prophets, or citizens—they all had suffered as slaves in the captivity of foreign empires. And they were still suffering in the days of Nehemiah and Ezra. Keep in mind that their suffering was justified because they had sinned greatly, committing all kinds of wickedness. As a result, the LORD Himself had carried out His judgment upon them (v.33).

c. The returned exiles pleaded for mercy because none of the people had kept God's Law or headed His warnings. Neither the leaders nor the people of their day nor of past history had kept God's commandments. Even when they were in the promised land and enjoying the fruitfulness of God's blessings, they did not serve the LORD. They refused to turn from their wicked ways.

d. The Jewish returnees pleaded for mercy because they themselves were slaves in the promised land God had given them. Although they had been freed from Babylonian captivity, they were still under the control of Persian power. Because of their own sins, they were still being oppressed. God's judgment was still falling upon them. The harvest of the promised land was being paid in taxes to the Persians. Although they had been freed to return to the promised land, they were still in great distress because they were slaves within their own land. They longed to be totally free, subject only to the LORD. Therefore, they pleaded for the mercy of God and for His delivering power.

Thought 1. God is merciful beyond measure. Despite all the sin and wickedness of His people down through the ages, He still loved them and forgave them and heard their cries for mercy. This should be a great comfort to all believers. God still loves us and He will have mercy upon us. No matter the circumstances, if we cry out to God for mercy, He will hear our cry. He will come to our rescue and meet our needs. Think of any circumstance or need, such as:

⇒ marital problems   ⇒ a wayward child
⇒ financial difficulties   ⇒ overwhelming temptations
⇒ disease or illness   ⇒ crushed hopes
⇒ the death of a loved one   ⇒ broken hearts

The list could go on and on. But no matter what the circumstance or need, God will deliver us, giving us the power and strength to walk through and conquer the crisis or troubling situation.

In addition to being merciful, God keeps His covenant, His promises, that He has made with us. If we walk faithfully, trusting God and keeping His Holy commandments, the LORD will fulfill every promise He has ever made in our lives. He keeps His covenant, His promises if we follow Him sincerely and in truth.

(1) Listen to what God's Holy Word says about His mercy:

"**And his mercy *is* on them that fear him from generation to generation**" (Lu.1:50).

"**But God, who is rich in mercy, for his great love wherewith he loved us, Even when we were dead in sins, hath quickened us together with Christ, (by grace ye are saved;) And hath raised *us* up together, and made *us* sit together in heavenly *places* in Christ Jesus: That in the ages to come he might show the exceeding riches of his grace in *his* kindness toward us through Christ Jesus. For by grace are ye saved through faith; and that not of yourselves: *it is* the gift of God**" (Ep.2:4-8).

"**Not by works of righteousness which we have done, but according to his mercy he saved us, by the washing of regeneration, and renewing of the Holy Ghost; Which he shed on us abundantly through Jesus Christ our Saviour; That being justified by his grace, we should be made heirs according to the hope of eternal life**" (Tit.3:5-7).

"**Seeing then that we have a great high priest, that is passed into the heavens, Jesus the Son of God, let us hold fast *our* profession. For we have not an high priest which cannot be touched with the feeling of our infirmities; but was in all points tempted like as *we are*, *yet* without sin. Let us therefore come boldly unto the throne of grace, that we may obtain mercy, and find grace to help in time of need**" (He.4:14-16).

"**My mercy will I keep for him for evermore, and my covenant shall stand fast with him**" (Ps.89:28).

"**The LORD *is* merciful and gracious, slow to anger, and plenteous in mercy**" (Ps.103:8).

"**But the mercy of the LORD *is* from everlasting to everlasting upon them that fear him, and his righteousness unto children's children**" (Ps.103:17).

"**For thy mercy *is* great above the heavens: and thy truth *reacheth* unto the clouds**" (Ps.108:4).

"**Let the wicked forsake his way, and the unrighteous man his thoughts: and let him return unto the LORD, and he will have mercy upon him; and to our God, for he will abundantly pardon**" (Is.55:7).

"**Go and proclaim these words toward the north, and say, Return, thou backsliding Israel, saith the LORD; *and* I will not cause mine anger to fall upon you: for I *am* merciful, saith the LORD, *and* I will not keep *anger* for ever**" (Je.3:12).

"***It is of* the LORD'S mercies that we are not consumed, because his compassions fail not. *They are* new every morning**" (Lam.3:22-23).

"**And rend your heart, and not your garments, and turn unto the LORD your God: for he *is* gracious and merciful, slow to anger, and of great kindness, and repenteth him of the evil**" (Joel 2:13).

"Who *is* a God like unto thee, that pardoneth iniquity, and passeth by the transgression of the remnant of his heritage? he retaineth not his anger for ever, because he delighteth *in* mercy" (Mi.7:18).

(2) Listen to what God's Holy Word says about His faithfulness in keeping His covenant, His promises.

"He staggered not at the promise of God through unbelief; but was strong in faith, giving glory to God; And being fully persuaded that, what he had promised, he was able also to perform" (Ro.4:20-21).

"God *is* faithful, by whom ye were called unto the fellowship of his Son Jesus Christ our Lord" (1 Co.1:9).

"For all the promises of God in him *are* yea, and in him Amen, unto the glory of God by us" (2 Co.1:20).

"But the Lord is faithful, who shall stablish you, and keep *you* from evil" (2 Th.3:3).

"If we believe not, *yet* he abideth faithful: he cannot deny himself" (2 Ti.2:13).

"Wherefore in all things it behoved him to be made like unto *his* brethren, that he might be a merciful and faithful high priest in things *pertaining* to God, to make reconciliation for the sins of the people" (He.2:17).

"Wherein God, willing more abundantly to show unto the heirs of promise the immutability of his counsel, confirmed *it* by an oath: That by two immutable things, in which *it was* impossible for God to lie, we might have a strong consolation, who have fled for refuge to lay hold upon the hope set before us" (He.6:17-18).

"For this *is* the covenant that I will make with the house of Israel after those days, saith the Lord; I will put my laws into their mind, and write them in their hearts: and I will be to them a God, and they shall be to me a people" (He.8:10).

"Let us hold fast the profession of *our* faith without wavering; (for he is faithful that promised;)" (He.10:23).

"And to Jesus the mediator of the new covenant, and to the blood of sprinkling, that speaketh better things than *that of* Abel" (He.12:24).

"Now the God of peace, that brought again from the dead our Lord Jesus, that great shepherd of the sheep, through the blood of the everlasting covenant, Make you perfect in every good work to do his will, working in you that which is wellpleasing in his sight, through Jesus Christ; to whom *be* glory for ever and ever. Amen" (He.13:20-21).

"Wherefore let them that suffer according to the will of God commit the keeping of their souls *to him* in well doing, as unto a faithful Creator" (1 Pe.4:19).

"Whereby are given unto us exceeding great and precious promises: that by these ye might be partakers of the divine nature, having escaped the corruption that is in the world through lust" (2 Pe.1:4).

"And this is the promise that he hath promised us, *even* eternal life" (1 Jn.2:25).

"Know therefore that the LORD thy God, he *is* God, the faithful God, which keepeth covenant and mercy with them that love him and keep his commandments to a thousand generations" (De.7:9).

"Blessed *be* the LORD, that hath given rest unto his people Israel, according to all that he promised: there hath not failed one word of all his good promise, which he promised by the hand of Moses his servant" (1 K.8:56).

"Thy mercy, O LORD, *is* in the heavens; *and* thy faithfulness *reacheth* unto the clouds" (Ps.36:5).

"I will sing of the mercies of the LORD for ever: with my mouth will I make known thy faithfulness to all generations" (Ps.89:1).

"For the mountains shall depart, and the hills be removed; but my kindness shall not depart from thee, neither shall the covenant of my peace be removed, saith the LORD that hath mercy on thee" (Is.54:10).

"Incline your ear, and come unto me: hear, and your soul shall live; and I will make an everlasting covenant with you, *even* the sure mercies of David" (Is.55:3).

1. A binding commitment to follow God, to obey His Word totally, 10:28-29

a. The decision of the leaders: To write out their commitment in a binding document & sign it

b. The leaders who signed
1) The two civil leaders: Nehemiah & Zedekiah

2) The priestly leaders: 21 names (Ezra belonged to the family of Seraiah)

3) The Levite leaders: 17 names

4) The political leaders: 44 names

c. The rest of the people who

C. Step 3—Rebuilding Through Making a Covenant of Commitment: Stressing the Importance of Total Devotion, 9:38–10:39

38 And because of all this we make a sure *covenant,* and write *it;* and our princes, Levites, *and* priests, seal *unto it.*

CHAPTER 10

Now those that sealed *were,* Nehemiah, the Tirshatha, the son of Hachaliah, and Zidkijah,

2 Seraiah, Azariah, Jeremiah,

3 Pashur, Amariah, Malchijah,

4 Hattush, Shebaniah, Malluch,

5 Harim, Meremoth, Obadiah,

6 Daniel, Ginnethon, Baruch,

7 Meshullam, Abijah, Mijamin,

8 Maaziah, Bilgai, Shemaiah: these *were* the priests.

9 And the Levites: both Jeshua the son of Azaniah, Binnui of the sons of Henadad, Kadmiel;

10 And their brethren, Shebaniah, Hodijah, Kelita, Pelaiah, Hanan,

11 Micha, Rehob, Hashabiah,

12 Zaccur, Sherebiah, Shebaniah,

13 Hodijah, Bani, Beninu.

14 The chief of the people; Parosh, Pahath-moab, Elam, Zatthu, Bani,

15 Bunni, Azgad, Bebai,

16 Adonijah, Bigvai, Adin,

17 Ater, Hizkijah, Azzur,

18 Hodijah, Hashum, Bezai,

19 Hariph, Anathoth, Nebai,

20 Magpiash, Meshullam, Hezir,

21 Meshezabeel, Zadok, Jaddua,

22 Pelatiah, Hanan, Anaiah,

23 Hoshea, Hananiah, Hashub,

24 Hallohesh, Pileha, Shobek,

25 Rehum, Hashabnah, Maaseiah,

26 And Ahijah, Hanan, Anan,

27 Malluch, Harim, Baanah.

28 And the rest of the peo-

---

ple, the priests, the Levites, the porters, the singers, the Nethinims, and all they that had separated themselves from the people of the lands unto the law of God, their wives, their sons, and their daughters, every one having knowledge, and having understanding;

29 They clave to their brethren, their nobles, and entered into a curse, and into an oath, to walk in God's law, which was given by Moses the servant of God, and to observe and do all the commandments of the LORD our Lord, and his judgments and his statutes;

30 And that we would not give our daughters unto the people of the land, nor take their daughters for our sons:

31 And *if* the people of the land bring ware or any victuals on the sabbath day to sell, *that* we would not buy it of them on the sabbath, or on the holy day: and *that* we would leave the seventh year, and the exaction of every debt.

32 Also we made ordinances for us, to charge ourselves yearly with the third part of a shekel for the service of the house of our God;

33 For the showbread, and for the continual meat offering, and for the continual burnt offering, of the sabbaths, of the new moons, for the set feasts, and for the holy *things,* and for the sin offerings to make an atonement for Israel, and *for* all the work of the house of our God.

34 And we cast the lots among the priests, the Levites, and the people, for the wood offering, to bring *it* into the house of our God, after the houses of our fathers, at times appointed year by year, to burn upon the altar of the LORD our God, as *it is* written in the law:

35 And to bring the firstfruits of our ground, and the firstfruits of all fruit of all trees, year by year, unto the house of the LORD:

36 Also the firstborn of our sons, and of our cattle, as *it is* written in the law, and the

---

did not sign: They verbally agreed to follow God & His Word
1) They included the wives & the children who were old enough to understand
2) They also included converted foreigners

d. The stated purpose of the binding commitment: To have a written oath
1) The people swore they would obey God's law, His commandments
2) The people acknowledged God's curse if they disobeyed

2. A binding commitment to keep the family holy, set apart to God: Not to intermarry with unbelievers

3. A binding commitment to observe the Sabbath & all other holy days

a. To stop all buying & selling
b. To observe the sabbatical year
1) Let the land rest, Ex.23:10-11
2) Cancel all debts, De.15:1-2

4. A binding commitment to support the house of God

a. First, to support through the temple tax: Used to cover the expenses of the worship services & the other work of the temple

b. Second, to support through a wood offering: Used to keep the fire going on the brazen altar (Le.6:12-13)

c. Third, to support through the firstfruit offering: The people were to give the very first & best of their harvest, crops, & fruit, Ex.23:19; Nu.18:13; De.26:1-11; Eze.44:30

d. Fourth, to support through the dedication of the firstborn: They were to dedicate

their firstborn sons & firstborn animals to God, Ex.13:1-6	firstlings of our herds and of our flocks, to bring to the house of our God, unto the priests that minister in the house of our God:	Aaron shall be with the Levites, when the Levites take tithes: and the Levites shall bring up the tithe of the tithes unto the house of our God, to the chambers, into the treasure house.	the tithes being given to the Levites • The Levites were to tithe: Give one tenth to the house of God
e. Fifth, to support through a tithe 1) The people committed to give their tithe to support the priests 2) The people also gave a tithe to the Levites who ministered in their local towns	37 And *that* we should bring the firstfruits of our dough, and our offerings, and the fruit of all manner of trees, of wine and of oil, unto the priests, to the chambers of the house of our God; and the tithes of our ground unto the Levites, that the same Levites might have the tithes in all the cities of our tillage.	39 For the children of Israel and the children of Levi shall bring the offering of the corn, of the new wine, and the oil, unto the chambers, where *are* the vessels of the sanctuary, and the priests that minister, and the porters, and the singers: and we will not forsake	3) The Levites were to bring their tithes to the temple like everyone else
• A priest was to witness	38 And the priest the son of	the house of our God.	f. Sixth, never to neglect the House of God

DIVISION II

THE REBUILDING OF THE NATION AND THE PEOPLE, 8:1–13:31

C. Step 3—Rebuilding Through Making a Covenant of Commitment: Stressing the Importance of Total Devotion, 9:38–10:39

(9:38–10:39) **Introduction**: *devotion* means to be totally committed, completely loyal. A devoted person commits his energies and thoughts to whatever he is doing. Practically every person and every organization covet people of devotion. Businesses want devoted people, people who will commit their enthusiasm, loyalty, and ideas to their work. Husbands and wives want their spouses to be devoted, and children want devoted parents. Social organizations need dedicated, loyal people. And the church desperately needs people who are devoted, willing to commit their energies to the mission of the church. Teachers want devoted students, and students want teachers who are focused on teaching. Athletic teams need players, dedicated players who are committed to practice and to winning.

But superceding all the desires for devotion is the LORD's craving for loyalty and commitment. Above all the human need and desire for dedicated people, the LORD Himself craves, longs for people who will totally commit themselves to Him. The LORD craves the devotion of our hearts and our lives, our commitment and our loyalty. Total devotion is the subject of the present Scripture.

Remember, the returned exiles had gathered together for worship. They were fasting and praying, seeking God for revival. Not long before this gathering, they had completed the rebuilding of Jerusalem's wall and of their own homes (7:73). They were now somewhat settled on their own properties and were able to focus on rebuilding their society and nation. Above all else, they knew that the foundation of their lives and nation must be based upon God Himself and His Holy Word. They must be totally devoted to the LORD, totally committed and loyal to Him. For this reason, they had begun to meet together to seek the LORD and to study His law, His commandments. They were determined to rebuild their lives and nation by making five very basic commitments. The first two steps in the rebuilding process were as follows:

⇒ First, they sought to rebuild by making a commitment to God's Word (8:1-18).
⇒ Second, they sought to rebuild by making a commitment to seek revival (9:1-37).

The returnees sought to seal their commitment by making a written covenant with God. This is, *Step 3—Rebuilding Through Making a Covenant of Commitment: Stressing the Importance of Total Devotion,* 9:38–10:39.
  1. A binding commitment to follow God, to obey His Word totally, see 28-29 (9:38–10:29).
  2. A binding commitment to keep the family holy, set apart to God: not to intermarry with unbelievers (10:30).
  3. A binding commitment to observe the Sabbath, and all other days (10:31).
  4. A commitment to support the house of God (10:32-39).

1 (9:38–10:29) **Word of God, Duty, to Obey—Bible, Duty, to Obey—Obedience, Duty to Obey God's Word—Law, of God, Duty—Walk, Spiritual, Duty—Believers, Duty—Returnees, Jewish, Covenant or Agreement of, to Obey God's Word—Nehemiah, Work and Ministry, to Stir the People to Obey God's Word—Ezra, Ministry and Work—Covenant, of the Jewish Returnees, to Obey God's Word**: the covenant drawn up by the returnees was a binding commitment to follow God totally, to commit their lives to obeying the Law of God, His Holy Word. To be successful in rebuilding their lives and nation, it was necessary for the whole community to be involved. Everyone needed to do his or her share of the work and to do it diligently. Thus every family in the community needed to adopt this document, make a personal commitment to follow God and to make the Word of God the basic authority of their lives. If God's Word was to become the law of their nation, everyone had to make a commitment to obey the laws of God. Scripture explains how the Law of God (the Mosaic Law or Covenant) became the law of the land, the laws upon which the returned exiles were basing their society and government:

OUTLINE	SCRIPTURE	SCRIPTURE	OUTLINE

1. A binding commitment to follow God, to obey His Word totally, see 28-29
  a. The decision of the leaders: To write out their commitment in a binding document & sign it
 	
  b. The leaders who signed
   1) The two civil leaders: Nehemiah & Zedekiah
 	
   2) The priestly leaders: 21 names (Ezra belonged to the family of Seraiah)
 	
   3) The Levite leaders: 17 names
 	
   4) The political leaders: 44 names
	38 And because of all this we make a sure *covenant,* and write *it;* and our princes, Levites, *and* priests, seal *unto it.*
	
	CHAPTER 10
	
	Now those that sealed *were,* Nehemiah, the Tirshatha, the son of Hachaliah, and Zidkijah,
	2 Seraiah, Azariah, Jeremiah,
	3 Pashur, Amariah, Malchijah,
	4 Hattush, Shebaniah, Malluch,
	5 Harim, Meremoth, Obadiah,
	6 Daniel, Ginnethon, Baruch,
	7 Meshullam, Abijah, Mijamin,
	8 Maaziah, Bilgai, Shemaiah: these *were* the priests.
	9 And the Levites: both Jeshua the son of Azaniah, Binnui of the sons of Henadad, Kadmiel;
	10 And their brethren, Shebaniah, Hodijah, Kelita, Pelaiah, Hanan,
	11 Micha, Rehob, Hashabiah,
	12 Zaccur, Sherebiah, Shebaniah,
	13 Hodijah, Bani, Beninu.
	14 The chief of the people; Parosh, Pahath-moab, Elam,
		Zatthu, Bani,
		15 Bunni, Azgad, Bebai,
		16 Adonijah, Bigvai, Adin,
		17 Ater, Hizkijah, Azzur,
		18 Hodijah, Hashum, Bezai,
		19 Hariph, Anathoth, Nebai,
		20 Magpiash, Meshullam, Hezir,
		21 Meshezabeel, Zadok, Jaddua,
		22 Pelatiah, Hanan, Anaiah,
		23 Hoshea, Hananiah, Hashub,
		24 Hallohesh, Pileha, Shobek,
		25 Rehum, Hashabnah, Maaseiah,
		26 And Ahijah, Hanan, Anan,
		27 Malluch, Harim, Baanah.
		28 And the rest of the people, the priests, the Levites, the porters, the singers, the Nethinims, and all they that had separated themselves from the people of the lands unto the law of God, their wives, their sons, and their daughters, every one having knowledge, and having understanding;
		29 They clave to their brethren, their nobles, and entered into a curse, and into an oath, to walk in God's law, which was given by Moses the servant of God, and to observe and do all the commandments of the LORD our Lord, and his judgments and his stat-
			c. The rest of the people who did not sign: They verbally agreed to follow God & His Word
			   1) They included the wives & the children who were old enough to understand
			   2) They also included converted foreigners
			
			  d. The stated purpose of the binding commitment: To have a written oath
			   1) The people swore they would obey God's law, His commandments
			   2) The people acknowledged God's curse if they disobeyed

a. With a spirit of revival sweeping through the large assembly of people, the leaders of the returnees made a decision to write out the commitment they were making to the LORD in a binding document. Obviously, they felt strongly that a written document of their commitment would be more meaningful and also more likely to be kept than a verbal agreement. Signing any agreement is a serious matter, especially if it is a sworn oath being made to the LORD. Keep in mind that the Jewish returnees, wanting their nation to be richly blessed by God, were adopting the laws of God as the laws of their nation.

b. The legal document was ratified by the following leaders. Most of these leaders represented clans and other bodies of people. Between the two chief civil leaders, the governor Nehemiah was the first to sign; then the other civil leader Zedeciah signed after him. In addition to these two, the other leaders who signed included the following:
⇒ the priestly leaders, which numbered 21 names
⇒ the Levite leaders, which numbered 17 names
⇒ the political leaders, which numbered 44 names

c. The rest of the people did not sign, but verbally agreed to follow God, to make His Holy Word the basic law of their land. Even the children who were old enough to understand gave their verbal agreement to the document of commitment. Also, converted foreigners were allowed to join in the commitment service because they had turned to the LORD by faith and separated themselves from their wicked neighbors (v.28).

d. The stated purpose of the binding agreement was twofold. First, the returnees wanted a sworn oath from every citizen of their community, an oath that they would obey God's law, His Holy Commandments. Second, the returnees wanted every citizen to understand that God's curse would fall upon them if they disobeyed.

Therefore, make absolutely sure that everyone understood the document of commitment, every citizen swore an oath that they would both obey God's law and accept His curse or judgment if they disobeyed or broke the law.

Thought 1. The foundation of human life and society is to be God's Holy Word, His commandments. God expects every one of us and every society to obey Him, to keep His Holy Word. It is the Word of God that instructs us how to live. It is His Word that tells us how to build a successful society, a society that is...

- moral, righteous, and just
- productive and economically sound
- caring and compassionate
- peaceful and secure
- respectful of human life and property

A permanent society of peace and prosperity can be built only if people look to God and His Holy Word for direction. It is God who teaches us to treat one another as we ourselves wish to be treated. It is God who tells us that we should love our neighbors as ourselves. If we love our neighbors, we will respect human life and the property and rights of others. Within a society based upon God's Law, there would be no theft, no murder. There would be no assaults, abuse, prejudice or discrimination, or violation of anyone's rights. Imagine a society without lawlessness and violence, a society where people genuinely cared for one another and looked after the welfare and property of one another. Instead of being selfish, greedy, and covetous, we would be giving and reaching out to help others meet whatever needs they have.

This is the kind of life and society that God's Word structures, the kind of society that Nehemiah and the returnees desired. And this should be the kind of lives and society we crave. But a society of permanent peace and prosperity can come only if we base our lives upon God's Holy Word, His commandments. Listen to what God says about His Word being the foundation of life, the foundation of society:

(1) The Word of God is the foundation for belief and for reproof, correction, and instruction in righteousness and justice.

> "All scripture *is* given by inspiration of God, and *is* profitable for doctrine, for reproof, for correction, for instruction in righteousness" (2 Ti.3:16).
> "Therefore whosoever heareth these sayings of mine, and doeth them, I will liken him unto a wise man, which built his house upon a rock: And the rain descended, and the floods came, and the winds blew, and beat upon that house; and it fell not: for it was founded upon a rock. And every one that heareth these sayings of mine, and doeth them not, shall be likened unto a foolish man, which built his house upon the sand: And the rain descended, and the floods came, and the winds blew, and beat upon that house; and it fell: and great was the fall of it" (Mt.7:24-27).

(2) The Word of God is the way to live a clean, righteous, and just life, a life that rejects immorality, lawlessness, and violence

> "Now ye are clean through the word which I have spoken unto you" (Jn.15:3).
> "Sanctify them through thy truth: thy word is truth" (Jn.17:17).
> "Thy word have I hid in mine heart, that I might not sin against thee" (Ps.119:11).

(3) The Word of God is the instrument Christ used to establish the church within society, the means by which He cleansed and set apart the church within society.

> "Christ also loved the church, and gave himself for it; That he might sanctify and cleanse it with the washing of water by the word" (Ep.5:25-26).

(4) The Word of God is the way to establish a society of respect and brotherly love.

> "Seeing ye have purified your souls in obeying the truth [of God's Word] through the Spirit unto unfeigned love of the brethren, *see that ye* love one another with a pure heart fervently" (1 Pe.1:22).

(5) The Word of God tells a person how to receive life in Christ and how to have the assurance of eternal life.

> "But these are written, that ye might believe that Jesus is the Christ, the Son of God; and that believing ye might have life through his name" (Jn.20:31).
> "These things have I written unto you that believe on the name of the Son of God; that ye may know that ye have eternal life, and that ye may believe on the name of the Son of God" (1 Jn.5:13).
> "Blessed *are* they that do his commandments, that they may have right to the tree of life, and may enter in through the gates into the city" (Re.22:14).

(6) The Word of God tells us how to build hope, endurance, and comfort within people.

> "For whatsoever things were written aforetime were written for our learning, that we through patience and comfort of the scriptures might have hope" (Ro.15:4).

(7) The Word of God builds mature people, which means it builds a mature society.

> "As newborn babes, desire the sincere milk of the word, that ye may grow thereby" (1 Pe.2:2).

(8) The Word of God warns people against breaking the law, spelling out the devastating consequences resulting from a lawless and violent society.

> "Now all these things happened unto them [Old Testament characters] for ensamples: and they are written for our admonition, upon whom the ends of the world are come" (1 Co.10:11).

(9) The Word of God teaches wisdom to the ignorant.

> "The law of the LORD *is* perfect, converting the soul: the testimony of the LORD *is* sure, making wise the simple" (Ps.19:7).
> "Whoso keepeth the law *is* a wise son" (Pr.28:7).

(10) The Word of God delivers people from living carnal, wicked, and lawless lives.

> "Wherefore the law *is* holy, and the commandment holy, and just, and good" (Ro.7:12).
> "For we know that the law is spiritual: but I am carnal, sold under sin" (Ro.7:14).
> "But we know that the law *is* good, if a man use it lawfully" (1 Ti.1:8).

(11) The Word of God lays the foundation for a successful and prosperous society.

> "But whoso looketh into the perfect law of liberty, and continueth *therein,* he being not a forgetful hearer, but a doer of the work, this man shall be blessed in his deed" (Js.1:25).
> "O that there were such an heart in them, that they would fear me, and keep all my commandments always, that it might be well with them, and with their children for ever!" (De.5:29).
> "This book of the law shall not depart out of thy mouth; but thou shalt meditate therein day and night, that thou mayest observe to do according to all that is written therein: for then thou shalt make thy way prosperous, and then thou shalt have good success" (Jos.1:8).

2 **(10:30) Marriage, of Unbelievers, Prohibited—Intermarriage, with Unbelievers—Spiritual Separation, Duty—Worldliness, Duty—Family, Duty—Separation, Spiritual, Duty**: the covenant agreed to was a binding commitment to keep the family holy, set apart to God. No returnee was to marry a person from any of the surrounding nations, that is, an unbeliever. In fact, the Law of God clearly stated that such intermarriage was strictly prohibited:

> "When the LORD thy God shall bring thee into the land whither thou goest to possess it, and hath cast out many nations before thee, the Hittites, and the Girgashites, and the Amorites, and the Canaanites, and the Perizzites, and the Hivites, and the Jebusites, seven nations greater and mightier than thou; And when the LORD thy God shall deliver them before thee; thou shalt smite them, *and* utterly destroy them; thou shalt make no covenant with them, nor show mercy unto them: Neither shalt thou make marriages with them; thy daughter thou shalt not give unto his son, nor his daughter shalt thou take unto thy son. For they will turn away thy son from following me, that they may serve other gods: so will the anger of the LORD be kindled against you, and destroy thee suddenly" (De.7:1-4).
> "Take good heed therefore unto yourselves, that ye love the LORD your God. Else if ye do in any wise go back, and cleave unto the remnant of these nations, *even* these that remain among you, and shall make marriages with them, and go in unto them, and they to you: Know for a certainty that the LORD your God will no more drive out *any of* these nations from before you; but they shall be snares and traps unto you, and scourges in your sides, and thorns in your eyes, until ye perish from off this good land which the LORD your God hath given you" (Jos.23:11-13).

Why was God so forceful in forbidding His people to marry unbelievers? Because the effect of intermarriage is serious. Through intermarriage two distinct people or races become one (Ge.34:16). When two people are married, they separate themselves from all others and commit their lives totally to one another. Throughout the years, they influence one another by attending functions together and by learning to give and take when differences arise. Eventually husband and wife begin to adopt the same beliefs and behaviors, enjoying the same pleasures and focusing their lives on the same goals. Over years and decades husbands and wives somewhat lose their identities, being interwoven together as one person. For this reason true believers were prohibited from marrying unbelievers. If they were allowed to marry their unbelieving neighbors, they would soon turn away from the LORD and His Holy Word. They would lose their distinctiveness as a people of God's Word.

This was a significant decision being made by the returnees. The surrounding nations worshipped false gods, and a continuous flow of traffic would be taking place between the false worshippers and the Jewish returnees due to trade and business transactions. Although the Jewish returnees needed excellent relationships with their unbelieving neighbors, they had to guard themselves against their wicked lifestyle and false worship.

OUTLINE	SCRIPTURE
2. A binding commitment to keep the family holy, set apart to God: Not to intermarry with unbelievers	30 And that we would not give our daughters unto the people of the land, nor take their daughters for our sons:

Thought 1. A believer who marries an unbeliever faces a serious problem, a threatening danger. The believer will be influenced by the unbelief and sinful ways of his or her spouse. God's instructions are clear: we are not to be unequally yoked with unbelievers. Few of us are strong enough to resist the worldly influence of unbelievers. If we are always associating with them, eventually the ways of an unbeliever will wear down our resistance. And we will find ourselves committing spiritual adultery, that is, turning away from the LORD to the gods of this world (the attractions, possessions, and pleasures of the world).

As we walk about day by day, we are constantly bombarded by the seductions of this world, the enticements to give in to the lust of the flesh, the lust of the eyes, and the pride of life (1 Jn.2:15-16). It takes focus and strong effort to control our thoughts and our bodies and to continually seek to grow in Christ. It takes diligence effort to walk faithfully and victoriously, conquering all the temptations and trials of life and being a strong witness for the LORD. We are continually having to wage war against the temptations and trials of life. For these reasons, we need the constant help of other believers, in particular the help of a spouse and other family members who know and love the LORD. This is the reason a believer always needs to marry another believer, never an unbeliever. Listen to what God's Holy Word says:

"I beseech you therefore, brethren, by the mercies of God, that ye present your bodies a living sacrifice, holy, acceptable unto God, *which is* your reasonable service. And be not conformed to this world: but be ye transformed by the renewing of your mind, that ye may prove what is that good, and acceptable, and perfect, will of God" (Ro.12:1-2).

"I wrote unto you in an epistle not to company with fornicators: Yet not altogether with the fornicators of this world, or with the covetous, or extortioners, or with idolaters; for then must ye needs go out of the world. But now I have written unto you not to keep company, if any man that is called a brother be a fornicator, or covetous, or an idolater, or a railer, or a drunkard, or an extortioner; with such an one no not to eat" (1 Co.5:9-11).

"Be ye not unequally yoked together with unbelievers: for what fellowship hath righteousness with unrighteousness? and what communion hath light with darkness? And what concord hath Christ with Belial? or what part hath he that believeth with an infidel? And what agreement hath the temple of God with idols? for ye are the temple of the living God; as God hath said, I will dwell in them, and walk in *them;* and I will be their God, and they shall be my people. Wherefore come out from among them, and be ye separate, saith the Lord, and touch not the unclean *thing;* and I will receive you, And will be a Father unto you, and ye shall be my sons and daughters, saith the Lord Almighty" (2 Co.6:14-18).

"And have no fellowship with the unfruitful works of darkness, but rather reprove *them*" (Ep.5:11).

"Now we command you, brethren, in the name of our Lord Jesus Christ, that ye withdraw yourselves from every brother that walketh disorderly, and not after the tradition which he received of us" (2 Th.3:6).

"Thou shalt not follow a multitude to *do* evil; neither shalt thou speak in a cause to decline after many to wrest *judgment*" (Ex.23:2).

"Enter not into the path of the wicked, and go not in the way of evil *men*" (Pr.4:14).

3 (10:31) **Sabbath, Duty—Sunday, Duty—Worship, Duty—Holy Days, Duty**: the covenant agreed to was a binding commitment to observe the Sabbath and all other holy days. Keeping the Sabbath was a distinctive practice of the Jewish nation, an observance that was not kept by other nations or peoples (9:14; Ex.20:8-11; 31:12-18). To the surrounding nations, the Sabbath was just like any other day. Nothing was distinctive about it. Activity and business continued as usual. Only the Jews followed the Law of God, so only the Jews set aside a day for rest and meditative worship of the LORD. This law was one of the basic Ten Commandments of God (Ex.20:8-11). The leadership of the Jewish returnees knew there would be constant pressure from their unbelieving neighbors to conduct business on the Sabbath. There would be a strong pull to open up their shops and business booths, allowing buying and selling of products. Because of this, the leadership wanted the law governing the Sabbath to be specifically mentioned in the document of commitment.

Note that they also made a commitment to observe all the holy days as well as the Sabbatical year. This was significant, for it meant that the land would be allowed to rest, lie uncultivated every seventh year in order to regenerate itself. Significantly, God's Law established the need for ecology, the protection of the earth and nature (Le.25:1-7).

In addition to the land lying uncultivated, the law of the Sabbatical year spelled out that all Jews who had been forced to become servants due to the death of their major provider were to be released (Ex.21:2-6). Even all debts were to be cancelled (De.15:1-6). Yet despite these advantages, making a commitment to the Sabbatical year would be very costly to the returnees, for many of them were poverty-stricken. In rebuilding their nation, they needed all the commerce they could develop in order to prosper and strengthen their economy. Going a whole year without produce to sell would definitely affect their business contracts with surrounding nations. Faith—a complete and total trust in the LORD—was being demonstrated by the returnees' commitment to the Sabbatical year.

OUTLINE	SCRIPTURE
3. A binding commitment to observe the Sabbath & all other holy days	31 And *if* the people of the land bring ware or any victuals on the sabbath day to sell, *that* we would not buy it
a. To stop all buying & selling	of them on the sabbath, or on
b. To observe the sabbatical year	the holy day: and *that* we would leave the seventh year,
1) Let the land rest, Ex.23:10-11	and the exaction of every
2) Cancel all debts, De.15:1-2	debt.

Thought 1. Are we, genuine Christian believers, to observe these laws today? Scripture is clear about keeping the Sabbath day holy. The New Testament clearly teaches and gives example after example of believers' setting apart one day of the week for rest and worship. However, there is nothing in the New Testament to indicate that we are to observe the Sabbatical year. But we must always remember that the Old Testament is God's Holy Word as much as the New Testament. Therefore its principles are to be applied to our lives. Just as the Old Testament believers committed themselves to the Sabbath and to the Sabbatical year, so we are to commit ourselves to worship one day a week and to practice good cultivation policies, protecting the ecology of the earth and nature. Listen to what God's Holy Word says about keeping the Sabbath, setting aside one day a week for rest and worship:

"How much then is a man better than a sheep? Wherefore it is lawful to do well on the sabbath days" (Mt.12:12).

"And they went into Capernaum; and straightway on the sabbath day he [Christ] entered into the synagogue, and taught" (Mk.1:21).

"And he came to Nazareth, where he had been brought up: and, as his custom was, he went into the synagogue on the sabbath day, and stood up for to read" (Lu.4:16).

"But when they departed from Perga, they came to Antioch in Pisidia, and went into the synagogue on the sabbath day, and sat down" (Ac.13:14).

"And on the sabbath we went out of the city by a river side, where prayer was wont to be made; and we sat down, and spake unto the women which resorted *thither*" (Ac.16:13).

"And Paul, as his manner was, went in unto them, and three sabbath days reasoned with them out of the scriptures" (Ac.17:2).

"Not forsaking the assembling of ourselves together, as the manner of some *is*; but exhorting *one another*: and so much the more, as ye see the day approaching" (He.10:25).

"Remember the sabbath day, to keep it holy. Six days shalt thou labour, and do all thy work: But the seventh day *is* the sabbath of the LORD thy God: *in it* thou shalt not do any work, thou, nor thy son, nor thy daughter, thy manservant, nor thy maidservant, nor thy cattle, nor thy stranger that *is* within thy gates: For *in* six days the LORD made heaven and earth, the sea, and all that in them *is,* and rested the seventh day: wherefore the LORD blessed the sabbath day, and hallowed it" (Ex.20:8-11).

"Six days thou shalt work, but on the seventh day thou shalt rest: in earing time and in harvest thou shalt rest" (Ex.34:21).

"Blessed *is* the man *that* doeth this, and the son of man *that* layeth hold on it; that keepeth the sabbath from polluting it, and keepeth his hand from doing any evil" (Is.56:2).

"If thou turn away thy foot from the sabbath, *from* doing thy pleasure on my holy day; and call the sabbath a delight, the holy of the LORD, honourable; and shalt honour him, not doing thine own ways, nor finding thine own pleasure, nor speaking *thine own* words: Then shalt thou delight thyself in the LORD; and I will cause thee to ride upon the high places of the earth, and feed thee with the heritage of Jacob thy father: for the mouth of the LORD hath spoken *it*" (Is.58:13-14).

4 (10:32-39) **Tithing, Duty—Church, Duty, Support of—Worship, Duty, Support of—Benevolence, Duty, to Support the Church—Temple, Duty, to Support—Giving, Duty, to Support the Church—Ministers, Duty Toward, to Support—Offerings, Duty, to Support the Church—House of God, Duty, to Support**: the covenant agreed to was a binding commitment to financially support the house of God or the rebuilt temple. Scripture spells out six specific ways the house of God was to be supported:

OUTLINE	SCRIPTURE	SCRIPTURE	OUTLINE
4. A binding commitment to support the house of God a. First, to support through the temple tax: Used to cover the expenses of the worship services & the other work of the temple	32 Also we made ordinances for us, to charge ourselves yearly with the third part of a shekel for the service of the house of our God; 33 For the showbread, and for the continual meat offering, and for the continual burnt offering, of the sabbaths, of the new moons, for the set feasts, and for the holy *things,* and for the sin offerings to make an atonement for Israel, and *for* all the work of the house of our God.	times appointed year by year, to burn upon the altar of the LORD our God, as *it is* written in the law: 35 And to bring the first-fruits of our ground, and the firstfruits of all fruit of all trees, year by year, unto the house of the LORD: 36 Also the firstborn of our sons, and of our cattle, as *it is* written in the law, and the firstlings of our herds and of our flocks, to bring to the house of our God, unto the priests that minister in the house of our God:	c. Third, to support through the firstfruit offering: The people were to give the very first & best of their harvest, crops, & fruit, Ex.23:19; Nu.18:13; De.26:1-11; Eze.44:30 d. Fourth, to support through the dedication of the firstborn: They were to dedicate their firstborn son & animals to God, Ex.13:1-6
b. Second, to support through a wood offering: Used to keep the fire going on the brazen altar (Le.6:12-13)	34 And we cast the lots among the priests, the Levites, and the people, for the wood offering, to bring *it* into the house of our God, after the houses of our fathers, at	37 And *that* we should bring the firstfruits of our dough, and our offerings, and the	e. Fifth, to support through a tithe 1) The people committed to

OUTLINE	SCRIPTURE	SCRIPTURE	OUTLINE
give their tithe to support the priests 2) The people also gave a tithe to the Levites who ministered in their local towns • A priest was to witness the tithes being given to the Levites • The Levites were to tithe: Give one tenth to	fruit of all manner of trees, of wine and of oil, unto the priests, to the chambers of the house of our God; and the tithes of our ground unto the Levites, that the same Levites might have the tithes in all the cities of our tillage. 38 And the priest the son of Aaron shall be with the Levites, when the Levites take tithes: and the Levites shall bring up the tithe of the tithes	unto the house of our God, to the chambers, into the treasure house. 39 For the children of Israel and the children of Levi shall bring the offering of the corn, of the new wine, and the oil, unto the chambers, where *are* the vessels of the sanctuary, and the priests that minister, and the porters, and the singers: and we will not forsake the house of our God.	the house of God 3) The Levites were to bring their tithes to the temple like everyone else f. Sixth, never to neglect the House of God

a. First, the house of God was to be supported by an annual temple tax (Ex.30:11-16). When the law was first given, it specified that a "half shekel" or one fifth of an ounce of silver was to be the annual tax. But due to the poverty of the returnees, the leaders set the tax at a third of a shekel which amounted to one eighth of an ounce of silver. The temple tax was used to carry on the daily operations and activities of the temple. These included...

- providing the holy bread or showbread, which included 12 loaves of bread that were placed on the golden table at the beginning of every Sabbath (see outline and note—Le.24:5-9 for more discussion)
- providing for the regular grain offering and burnt offerings (see outline and notes—Ex.29:38-46; Nu.28:3-8 for more discussion)
- providing for the offerings that were made on the Sabbath, the New Moon Festival, and the other appointed festivals (see outline and note—Nu.28:1–29:40 for more discussion)
- providing for all the holy offerings
- providing for the sin offerings that made atonement for the people (see outline and notes—Le.4:1–5:13 for more discussion)
- providing for all the other necessary expenses of the Temple, the House of God

b. Second, they were to support the temple through a wood offering (v.34). The constant flow of daily sacrifices made by people required continuous fire. To keep the fire burning, a constant supply of wood was necessary (Le.6:12-13). Thus each of the returnee families was assigned a set time each year to bring a contribution of wood to the temple. Note that this offering of wood had a biblical basis, for the law stipulated that the fire on the altar was to be kept burning, never to be extinguished (Le.16:12-13).

c. Third, the people were to support the temple through the firstfruit offering (Ex.23:19; see outline and note—De.26:1-15 for more discussion). By firstfruit was meant the very first and best of their harvest, crops, and fruit (Ex.23:19; Nu.18:13; De.26:1-15; Eze.44:30).

d. Fourth, they were to support the house of God through the dedication of the firstborn (see outline and notes—Ex.13:1-16 for more discussion). This simply meant that they were to dedicate their firstborn son and firstborn animals to God. In the case of the firstborn animal, it was taken to the temple and given to the LORD. In the case of the firstborn son, he was to be redeemed by the gift of a substitute lamb (Ex.34:19-20; Le.22–24). As the firstborn child, the child belonged to the LORD. Thus he was to be taken to the temple and dedicated to the LORD by the sacrificial offering. Once the lamb had been offered, the child could return home with his parents.

e. Fifth, the people committed themselves to support the religious workers through a tithe, which meant one-tenth of their produce or income per year. This tithe was to support the priests and also the Levites, including the Levites who ministered out in the local towns and communities (vv.37-39). In receiving the tithe, a priest who had descended from Aaron was to witness the payment being made. Once the Levites had been paid, they themselves were to tithe one-tenth of what they received to the house of God. Like everyone else, the Levites were to pay their tithes to the temple (v.39). Everyone, including the priests and Levites, was responsible to tithe.

f. Sixth, in closing their document of commitment, everyone present promised not to neglect the house of God (v.39). With revival stirring in their hearts, they promised to never rob God of His tithe or offerings.

Thought 1. We must support the house of God, the church of the living LORD. Without financial support the mission of the church is sadly hampered. The needs of people are unmet, people such as...

- the poor
- the homeless
- the hungry
- the orphans
- the lonely
- the widows and widowers
- the dying
- the spiritually lost

Without finances, ministries to help all of these go lacking because there is not enough money to reach out to them. Without finances given to the church, men and women cannot give their full time to the ministries of the church. There would be few ministries and missionaries to fill the pulpits of the world and to carry the gospel to the world. And in most places throughout the world, the church needs lights, heat, and cooling as well as the other basic services needed to provide a meeting place. Listen to what God's Holy Word says about supporting the church:

"And he looked up, and saw the rich men casting their gifts into the treasury. And he saw also a certain poor widow casting in thither two mites. And he said, Of a truth I say unto you, that this poor widow hath cast in more than they all: For all these have of their abundance cast in unto the offerings of God: but she of her penury hath cast in all the living that she had" (Lu.21:1-4).

"Neither was there any among them that lacked: for as many as were possessors of lands or houses sold them, and brought the prices of the things that were sold, And laid *them* down at the apostles' feet: and distribution was made unto every man according as he had need" (Ac.4:34-35).

"Then the disciples, every man according to his ability, determined to send relief unto the brethren which dwelt in Judaea" (Ac.11:29).

"I have showed you all things, how that so labouring ye ought to support the weak, and to remember the words of the Lord Jesus, how he said, It is more blessed to give than to receive" (Ac.20:35).

"Upon the first *day* of the week let every one of you lay by him in store, as *God* hath prospered him, that there be no gatherings when I come" (1 Co.16:2).

"How that in a great trial of affliction the abundance of their joy and their deep poverty abounded unto the riches of their liberality" (2 Co.8:2).

"Every man according as he purposeth in his heart, *so let him give;* not grudgingly, or of necessity: for God loveth a cheerful giver" (2 Co.9:7).

"For even in Thessalonica ye sent once and again unto my necessity" (Ph.4:16).

"And this stone, which I have set *for* a pillar, shall be God's house: and of all that thou shalt give me I will surely give the tenth unto thee" (Ge.28:22).

"And all the tithe of the land, *whether* of the seed of the land, *or* of the fruit of the tree, *is* the LORD's: *it is* holy unto the LORD" (Le.27:30).

"Every man *shall give* as he is able, according to the blessing of the LORD thy God which he hath given thee" (De.16:17).

"Honour the LORD with thy substance, and with the firstfruits of all thine increase" (Pr.3:9).

"Bring ye all the tithes into the storehouse, that there may be meat in mine house, and prove me now herewith, saith the LORD of hosts, if I will not open you the windows of heaven, and pour you out a blessing, that *there shall* not *be room* enough *to receive it*" (Mal.3:10).

CHAPTER 11

D. Step 4—Rebuilding Through Strengthening Both Jerusalem & the Spirit of the People: Three Essentials for a Strong Nation & People, 11:1–12:47

1. The resettling of Jerusalem: A need for the people to settle & serve in the most needed place
a. The need of Jerusalem for population & housing, 7:4
   1) The leaders lived there
   2) Some were selected by lot to move there: One-tenth
   3) Others volunteered to move & were commended

b. The descendants of various family leaders who settled in Jerusalem: A reminder that godly leaders are needed to establish & strengthen any society

   1) The family leaders from the tribe of Judah: Their descendants totaled 468 brave men, 6

   2) The family leaders from the tribe of Benjamin

      • Their descendants totaled 928 men

      • Their chief officer was Joel & his assistant was Judah

c. The priestly families who settled in Jerusalem: A re-

And the rulers of the people dwelt at Jerusalem: the rest of the people also cast lots, to bring one of ten to dwell in Jerusalem the holy city, and nine parts *to dwell* in *other* cities.
2 And the people blessed all the men, that willingly offered themselves to dwell at Jerusalem.
3 Now these *are* the chief of the province that dwelt in Jerusalem: but in the cities of Judah dwelt every one in his possession in their cities, *to wit,* Israel, the priests, and the Levites, and the Nethinims, and the children of Solomon's servants.
4 And at Jerusalem dwelt *certain* of the children of Judah, and of the children of Benjamin. Of the children of Judah; Athaiah the son of Uzziah, the son of Zechariah, the son of Amariah, the son of Shephatiah, the son of Mahalaleel, of the children of Perez;
5 And Maseiah the son of Baruch, the son of Colhozeh, the son of Hazaiah, the son of Adaiah, the son of Joiarib, the son of Zechariah, the son of Shiloni.
6 All the sons of Perez that dwelt at Jerusalem *were* four hundred threescore and eight valiant men.
7 And these *are* the sons of Benjamin; Sallu the son of Meshullam, the son of Joed, the son of Pedaiah, the son of Kolaiah, the son of Maaseiah, the son of Ithiel, the son of Jesaiah.
8 And after him Gabbai, Sallai, nine hundred twenty and eight.
9 And Joel the son of Zichri *was* their overseer: and Judah the son of Senuah *was* second over the city.
10 Of the priests: Jedaiah the son of Joiarib, Jachin.

11 Seraiah the son of Hilkiah, the son of Meshullam, the son of Zadok, the son of Meraioth, the son of Ahitub, *was* the ruler of the house of God.
12 And their brethren that did the work of the house *were* eight hundred twenty and two: and Adaiah the son of Jeroham, the son of Pelaliah, the son of Amzi, the son of Zechariah, the son of Pashur, the son of Malchiah,
13 And his brethren, chief of the fathers, two hundred forty and two: and Amashai the son of Azareel, the son of Ahasai, the son of Meshillemoth, the son of Immer,
14 And their brethren, mighty men of valour, an hundred twenty and eight: and their overseer *was* Zabdiel, the son of *one of* the great men.
15 Also of the Levites: Shemaiah the son of Hashub, the son of Azrikam, the son of Hashabiah, the son of Bunni;
16 And Shabbethai and Jozabad, of the chief of the Levites, *had* the oversight of the outward business of the house of God.
17 And Mattaniah the son of Micha, the son of Zabdi, the son of Asaph, *was* the principal to begin the thanksgiving in prayer: and Bakbukiah the second among his brethren, and Abda the son of Shammua, the son of Galal, the son of Jeduthun.
18 All the Levites in the holy city *were* two hundred fourscore and four.
19 Moreover the porters, Akkub, Talmon, and their brethren that kept the gates, *were* an hundred seventy and two.
20 And the residue of Israel, of the priests, *and* the Levites, *were* in all the cities of Judah, every one in his inheritance.
21 But the Nethinims dwelt in Ophel: and Ziha and Gispa *were* over the Nethinims.
22 The overseer also of the Levites at Jerusalem *was* Uzzi the son of Bani, the son of Hashabiah, the son of Mattaniah, the son of Micha. Of the sons of Asaph, the singers

minder that ministers must be committed, devoted to the LORD & His house, the church

1) The first family totaled 822 priests: These worked at the temple

2) The second family totaled 242 priests

3) The third family totaled 128 priests: These are said to be men of valor, courage

d. The Levite families who settled in Jerusalem: A reminder that associates are essential in the house of God
   1) The families in charge of the outside maintenance work of the temple

   2) The director & his associate who led in thanksgiving & prayer: Mattaniah & Bakbukiah

   3) The total Levites in the Holy City: 284 men

   4) The total Levite gatekeepers who settled in Jerusalem: 172 men

e. The other facts to know about the returned exiles
   1) The rest of the returnees settled on their ancestral property
   2) The temple servants lived on the hill of Ophel

   3) The chief officer or administrator of the Levites in Jerusalem was Uzzi: He was a musician

4) The singers were supported by the Persian king: So they would pray for him, Ezr. 6:8-10; 7:20-24; 1 Ti.2:1-2

5) The king's agent was Pethahiah, who represented the people before the Persian king: A reminder that civil leaders are God's ministers, Ro.13:1-7

f. The list of cities throughout the nation where the rest of the people lived: These were the cities from which one of every ten citizens was selected to repopulate Jerusalem, the holy city

1) The cities of Judah

2) The cities of Benjamin

3) Some Levites who lived in Judah moved to Benjamin: Were more needed there

g. The list of priests & Levites during different generations of the returned exiles

1) The priestly families who returned with the first exiles under Zerubbabel: A reminder that some ministers are *pioneers of faith*

---

were over the business of the house of God. 23 For *it was* the king's commandment concerning them, that a certain portion should be for the singers, due for every day. 24 And Pethahiah the son of Meshezabeel, of the children of Zerah the son of Judah, *was* at the king's hand in all matters concerning the people. 25 And for the villages, with their fields, *some* of the children of Judah dwelt at Kirjath-arba, and *in* the villages thereof, and at Dibon, and in the villages thereof, and at Jekabzeel, and *in* the villages thereof, 26 And at Jeshua, and at Moladah, and at Beth-phelet, 27 And at Hazar-shual, and at Beer-sheba, and *in* the villages thereof, 28 And at Ziklag, and at Mekonah, and in the villages thereof, 29 And at En-rimmon, and at Zareah, and at Jarmuth, 30 Zanoah, Adullam, and *in* their villages, at Lachish, and the fields thereof, at Azekah, and *in* the villages thereof. And they dwelt from Beer-sheba unto the valley of Hinnom. 31 The children also of Benjamin from Geba *dwelt* at Michmash, and Aija, and Bethel, and *in* their villages, 32 *And* at Anathoth, Nob, Ananiah, 33 Hazor, Ramah, Gittaim, 34 Hadid, Zeboim, Neballat, 35 Lod, and Ono, the valley of craftsmen. 36 And of the Levites *were* divisions *in* Judah, *and* in Benjamin.

CHAPTER 12

Now these *are* the priests and the Levites that went up with Zerubbabel the son of Shealtiel, and Jeshua: Seraiah, Jeremiah, Ezra, 2 Amariah, Malluch, Hattush, 3 Shechaniah, Rehum, Meremoth, 4 Iddo, Ginnetho, Abijah, 5 Miamin, Maadiah, Bilgah, 6 Shemaiah, and Joiarib, Jedaiah, 7 Sallu, Amok, Hilkiah, Jedaiah. These *were* the chief

---

of the priests and of their brethren in the days of Jeshua. 8 Moreover the Levites: Jeshua, Binnui, Kadmiel, Sherebiah, Judah, *and* Mattaniah, *which was* over the thanksgiving, he and his brethren. 9 Also Bakbukiah and Unni, their brethren, *were* over against them in the watches. 10 And Jeshua begat Joiakim, Joiakim also begat Eliashib, and Eliashib begat Joiada, 11 And Joiada begat Jonathan, and Jonathan begat Jaddua. 12 And in the days of Joiakim were priests, the chief of the fathers: of Seraiah, Meraiah; of Jeremiah, Hananiah; 13 Of Ezra, Meshullam; of Amariah, Jehohanan; 14 Of Melicu, Jonathan; of Shebaniah, Joseph; 15 Of Harim, Adna; of Meraioth, Helkai; 16 Of Iddo, Zechariah; of Ginnethon, Meshullam; 17 Of Abijah, Zichri; of Miniamin, of Moadiah, Piltai; 18 Of Bilgah, Shammua; of Shemaiah, Jehonathan; 19 And of Joiarib, Mattenai; of Jedaiah, Uzzi; 20 Of Sallai, Kallai; of Amok, Eber; 21 Of Hilkiah, Hashabiah; of Jedaiah, Nethaneel. 22 The Levites in the days of Eliashib, Joiada, and Johanan, and Jaddua, *were* recorded chief of the fathers: also the priests, to the reign of Darius the Persian. 23 The sons of Levi, the chief of the fathers, *were* written in the book of the chronicles, even until the days of Johanan the son of Eliashib. 24 And the chief of the Levites: Hashabiah, Sherebiah, and Jeshua the son of Kadmiel, with their brethren over against them, to praise *and* to give thanks, according to the commandment of David the man of God, ward over against ward. 25 Mattaniah, and Bakbukiah, Obadiah, Meshullam, Talmon, Akkub, *were*

---

2) The Levite families who returned with the first exiles

3) The line of High Priests
  • Jeshua served during the time of Haggai & Zechariah
  • Joiakim served with Ezra; Eliashib with Nehemiah, 10

4) The list of priestly families during the days of Joiakim the High Priest: This was the second generation of priests after the return

5) Additional important facts

  • The Levite family leaders listed here were recorded during the reign of the Persian king, Darius

  • The musicians were organized as prescribed by David, the man of God

  • The gatekeepers who protected the temple & its treasury during the day of Nehemiah are listed

2. The dedication of the wall: A need for the people to have a positive & joyful attitude
a. Nehemiah's summons for the religious personnel to gather & prepare for the dedication celebration
1) The Levites were summoned from everywhere
2) The Levite singers around Jerusalem were summoned: Had built villages around the capital for themselves

3) The priests & Levites dedicated or ceremonially cleansed themselves, the people, the gates, & the wall
b. Nehemiah's division of the leaders & musicians into two processional groups: He led them all to the top of the wall
1) One group walked on top of the wall to the right toward the Dung Gate

• They played musical instruments & sang as they walked in the dedication processional

• They were led by Ezra

• They saw the results of their hard labor: The Dung Gate (31), the Fountain Gate, the steps that led to the city

porters keeping the ward at the thresholds of the gates.
26 These *were* in the days of Joiakim the son of Jeshua, the son of Jozadak, and in the days of Nehemiah the governor, and of Ezra the priest, the scribe.
27 And at the dedication of the wall of Jerusalem they sought the Levites out of all their places, to bring them to Jerusalem, to keep the dedication with gladness, both with thanksgivings, and with singing, *with* cymbals, psalteries, and with harps.
28 And the sons of the singers gathered themselves together, both out of the plain country round about Jerusalem, and from the villages of Netophathi;
29 Also from the house of Gilgal, and out of the fields of Geba and Azmaveth: for the singers had builded them villages round about Jerusalem.
30 And the priests and the Levites purified themselves, and purified the people, and the gates, and the wall.
31 Then I brought up the princes of Judah upon the wall, and appointed two great *companies of them that gave* thanks, *whereof one* went on the right hand upon the wall toward the dung gate:
32 And after them went Hoshaiah, and half of the princes of Judah,
33 And Azariah, Ezra, and Meshullam,
34 Judah, and Benjamin, and Shemaiah, and Jeremiah,
35 And *certain* of the priests' sons with trumpets; *namely,* Zechariah the son of Jonathan, the son of Shemaiah, the son of Mattaniah, the son of Michaiah, the son of Zaccur, the son of Asaph:
36 And his brethren, Shemaiah, and Azarael, Milalai, Gilalai, Maai, Nethaneel, and Judah, Hanani, with the musical instruments of David the man of God, and Ezra the scribe before them.
37 And at the fountain gate, which was over against them, they went up by the stairs of the city of David, at the going up of the wall,

above the house of David, even unto the water gate eastward.
38 And the other *company of them that gave* thanks went over against *them,* and I after them, and the half of the people upon the wall, from beyond the tower of the furnaces even unto the broad wall;
39 And from above the gate of Ephraim, and above the old gate, and above the fish gate, and the tower of Hananeel, and the tower of Meah, even unto the sheep gate: and they stood still in the prison gate.
40 So stood the two *companies of them that gave* thanks in the house of God, and I, and the half of the rulers with me:
41 And the priests; Eliakim, Maaseiah, Miniamin, Michaiah, Elioenai, Zechariah, *and* Hananiah, with trumpets;
42 And Maaseiah, and Shemaiah, and Eleazar, and Uzzi, and Jehohanan, and Malchijah, and Elam, and Ezer. And the singers sang loud, with Jezrahiah *their* overseer.
43 Also that day they offered great sacrifices, and rejoiced: for God had made them rejoice with great joy: the wives also and the children rejoiced: so that the joy of Jerusalem was heard even afar off.
44 And at that time were some appointed over the chambers for the treasures, for the offerings, for the firstfruits, and for the tithes, to gather into them out of the fields of the cities the portions of the law for the priests and Levites: for Judah rejoiced for the priests and for the Levites that waited.
45 And both the singers and the porters kept the ward of their God, and the ward of the purification, according to the commandment of David, *and* of Solomon his son.
46 For in the days of David and Asaph of old *there were* chief of the singers, and songs of praise and thanksgiving unto God.

or house of David, & the Water Gate
2) The second group walked in the opposite direction
• They were led by Nehemiah
• They also saw the results of their diligent labor: The Tower of the Ovens, the Fish Gate, the Tower of Hananel, the Tower of the Hundred, & the Sheep Gate

• They stopped at the Gate of the Guard
c. Nehemiah's worship service: He had ordered the two processional groups to meet at the temple to worship

1) The choirs, officials, priests, & Nehemiah the governor took their places

2) The choirs sang

3) The worshippers offered many sacrifices
4) The people rejoiced greatly—including women & children: Were flooded with joy
5) The celebration was loud: Heard far away
3. The organization for permanent worship: A need for everyone to be faithful, consistent in their duty
a. The appointment of custodians over the offerings & tithes: The people were to provide food & money to support the priests & Levites
b. The ministry of the priests & Levites: Performed their service faithfully
c. The service of the singers & gatekeepers: Faithfully performed their service
1) Followed the duties as outlined by David & Solomon

2) Followed the custom of having choir directors as outlined by David & Asaph

d. The faithfulness of the people in supporting the priests & Levites 1) Were faithful in the days of Zerubbabel &	47 And all Israel in the days of Zerubbabel, and in the days of Nehemiah, gave the portions of the singers and the porters, every day his	portion: and they sanctified *holy things* unto the Levites; and the Levites sanctified *them* unto the children of Aaron.	Nehemiah 2) Were faithful in supporting the Levites in the other cities

DIVISION II

THE REBUILDING OF THE NATION AND THE PEOPLE 8:1–13:31

D. Step 4—Rebuilding Through Strengthening Both Jerusalem and the Spirit of the People: Three Essentials for a Strong Nation and People, 11:1–12:47

(11:1-12:47) **Introduction**: all citizens want to live within some region of a strong nation, a nation whose government truly serves its citizens. A strong nation or government will follow the compass of morality and righteousness, establishing true justice throughout the land. A government controlled by moral and righteous laws will develop a strong economy to provide jobs and a sufficient livelihood for its citizens. Moral and righteous laws will make provision for the strong protection of the nation's citizens, allowing them to live in peace and security. Moral and just laws will also assure that the property and lives of the nation's citizens are protected from destruction and theft.

But in considering what it takes to build a strong nation, it must be remembered that a nation is made up of its citizens. Without people, no nation exists. A nation is its citizens. As go the citizens, so goes the nation. If the citizens are moral, living pure and clean lives, taking a stand for morality and opposing immorality, then the nation becomes a moral nation. Moral people build a moral nation. So it is with righteousness. If the people live righteous lives, taking a stand against evil, wickedness, lawlessness, and violence, then the nation becomes strong and righteous. A righteous people build a righteous nation. If the people treat others as they want to be treated—justly and fairly—then the nation becomes a just society. Only then are the dignity of human life and respect for property honored. Only then is human life no longer abused or destroyed and property no longer damaged or stolen. In summary, what builds a strong nation is a moral and righteous people who execute justice among themselves.

This was the problem confronting Nehemiah: How could Jerusalem and the spirit of the people be strengthened so a strong nation could be structured? The returned exiles were weak, with few assets and resources. In addition, they were bitterly opposed and treated as enemies by the surrounding nations who despised the returned Jews. Nevertheless, Nehemiah had succeeded in leading the people to rebuild the wall of Jerusalem in just 52 days. Immediately after rebuilding the wall, he sought to strengthen the people by focusing their lives upon God's Word, upon obeying the commandments of God. He then led them to seek revival from the LORD. After God had met their need and revived their spirit, Nehemiah led the people to make a renewed commitment to the LORD. Nehemiah and the returned exiles were determined to rebuild their lives and nation by making three very basic commitments.

⇒ First, they sought to rebuild by making a commitment to God's Word (8:1-18).
⇒ Second, they sought to rebuild by making a commitment to seek revival (9:1-37).
⇒ Third, they sought to rebuild through making a covenant, an agreement of commitment to the LORD (9:38–10:39).

Now the returnees sought to strengthen the city of Jerusalem and the spirit of the people by these three definite acts. This is, *Step 4—Rebuilding Through Strengthening Both Jerusalem and the Spirit of the People: Three Essentials for a Strong Nation and People*, 11:1–12:47.

1. The resettling of Jerusalem: a need for the people to settle and serve in the most needed place (11:1–12:26).
2. The dedication of the wall: a need for the people to have a positive and joyful attitude (12:27-43).
3. The organization for permanent worship: a need for everyone to be faithful, consistent in their duty (12:44-47).

1 (11:1-12:26) **Service, Need for, Example—Society, Needs of—Cities, Needs of, Population and Housing—Ministers, Duty, to Be Devoted to God's House—Associates, Need for, in God's House—Government, Need of, Godly Leaders—Politicians, Facts, Are to Be God's Ministers—Leaders, Civil, Facts—Civil Leaders, Facts—Pioneers, of Faith, Example**: the returned Jews rebuilt their nation through the resettling of Jerusalem. Although they had just completed the rebuilding of the city's walls, there were still signs of destruction and debris everywhere. When Nebuchadnezzar conquered Jerusalem, he had destroyed the major structures of the city as well as the walls. As is the case with any city in ruins, some structures were utterly destroyed while others were only partially damaged. Minor structures had probably been left standing, for when the exiles returned, there were a few people living amidst the debris of the city. When surveying the city wall, Nehemiah had been unable to closely follow the barrier because of the rubble (2:14). Now, the massive task of removing tons and tons of rubble and cleaning up the city faced the returned exiles. After the cleanup, the problem of resettling the city with population would confront the leadership. Without a strong Jerusalem, the nation would remain weak. Israel would never again be a vibrant, strong nation, not economically, militarily, judicially, socially, or culturally. Without a strong center of government and authority, Israel would disintegrate into a territory of independent cities and states, with each going its own way. And the LORD's purpose in choosing the Jews to be His witnesses on earth would be lost forever. He would not be able to use them as the people through whom He would send the Messiah, the Savior, into the world. Nor could He use them to give His Word, the Holy Bible to the world. Thus resettling and strengthening Jerusalem and the spirit of the people was an absolute essential. Scripture records how Nehemiah, Ezra, and the other leaders accomplished this impossible task, thus fulfilling the prophecy of Isaiah (Is.10:20-21, 10:33–11:1).

a. Jerusalem was in desperate need of both population and accommodations for its citizens. The city was large and spacious, yet it was lying in utter ruin due to the destruction by the Babylonians over 140 years earlier. Because the construction of the walls had first priority, the houses had not yet been rebuilt. Thus there were few people actually living in Jerusalem. The walls were the main concern because of the enemy nations surrounding the Jewish returnees. They had to complete the wall for protection before they could tackle the cleanup of the city. They never knew when the enemy might attack, so security became Nehemiah's first mission. But now that the wall had been completed, the dire need of Jerusalem was for people to move to the city and for their housing to be constructed. This, of course, necessitated a massive cleanup project due to all the destruction and rubble. Most of the people were living out in the villages and cities of Judah, living on their own property, which had been owned by their families down through the centuries. Scripture says that the leaders already lived in the city (v.1), but they faced the enormous problem of no populace and inadequate housing. In considering the problem and wanting to be fair to all the returned exiles, Nehemiah instituted two policies that guaranteed the repopulation of the city:

1) By casting lots, one out of every 10 citizens would be chosen to live in Jerusalem, while the rest of the population would remain in the other cities and villages (v.1). Lots were usually made out of small stones, metal or wood. These were cast in the lathe and somehow used to determine whatever decision or selection was being made. The result was considered to be the will of the LORD (Pr.16:33).

2) An appeal was made for people to step forth and volunteer to move to Jerusalem (v.2). Some did volunteer, and these were highly commended and recognized in a special way by the people (v.2). Moving is usually a taxing experience, causing apprehension or even fear within some people. When individuals move, they often face a complete change of environment: a new house, new neighbors and friends, new jobs, a different climate, and a host of other unfamiliar surroundings. For these returned exiles, the change must have been even more difficult, for they were having to leave homes and property that in some cases had been in their family for generations. Nevertheless, knowing that a strong nation and capital were essential, these returnees willingly moved into the Holy City. Note that Jerusalem is here called "the holy city" (v.1). The city was considered *holy* because it had been chosen by God as the city where the LORD would place His Name, the city where the temple was built.

OUTLINE	SCRIPTURE	SCRIPTURE	OUTLINE
1. The resettling of Jerusalem: A need for the people to settle & serve in the most needed place a. The need of Jerusalem for population & housing, 7:4	And the rulers of the people dwelt at Jerusalem: the rest of the people also cast lots, to bring one of ten to dwell in Jerusalem the holy city, and nine	parts *to dwell* in *other* cities. 2 And the people blessed all the men, that willingly offered themselves to dwell at Jerusalem.	1) The leaders lived there 2) Some were selected by lot to move there: One-tenth 3) Others volunteered to move & were commended

b. The descendants of various family leaders who settled in Jerusalem are now recorded (vv.3-9). These include the names of the family leaders from the tribe of Judah (vv.4-6). Their descendants totaled 468 brave men. As mentioned above, it was a great sacrifice for these men to leave the land that had been their only home and in their family for so long to move to Jerusalem. In Jerusalem they faced not only the establishment of a new life but also the massive cleanup project and rebuilding of the city. The city had to be rebuilt from the ground up, including homes, shops, civic buildings, and other structures.

The family leaders from the tribe of Benjamin are also listed (vv.7-9). These descendants totaled 928 men who were led by a chief officer named Joel and his assistant Judah.

OUTLINE	SCRIPTURE	SCRIPTURE	OUTLINE
b. The descendants of various family leaders who settled in Jerusalem: A reminder that godly leaders are needed to establish & strengthen any society 1) The family leaders from the tribe of Judah: Their descendants totaled 468 brave men, 6	3 Now these *are* the chief of the province that dwelt in Jerusalem: but in the cities of Judah dwelt every one in his possession in their cities, *to wit,* Israel, the priests, and the Levites, and the Nethinims, and the children of Solomon's servants. 4 And at Jerusalem dwelt *certain* of the children of Judah, and of the children of Benjamin. Of the children of Judah; Athaiah the son of Uzziah, the son of Zechariah, the son of Amariah, the son of Shephatiah, the son of	Mahalaleel, of the children of Perez; 5 And Maseiah the son of Baruch, the son of Col-hozeh, the son of Hazaiah, the son of Adaiah, the son of Joiarib, the son of Zechariah, the son of Shiloni. 6 All the sons of Perez that dwelt at Jerusalem *were* four hundred threescore and eight valiant men. 7 And these *are* the sons of Benjamin; Sallu the son of Meshullam, the son of Joed, the son of Pedaiah, the son of Kolaiah, the son of Maaseiah, the son of Ithiel,	2) The family leaders from the tribe of Benjamin

OUTLINE	SCRIPTURE	SCRIPTURE	OUTLINE
• Their descendants totaled 928 men	the son of Jesaiah. 8 And after him Gabbai, Sallai, nine hundred twenty and eight.	9 And Joel the son of Zichri *was* their overseer: and Judah the son of Senuah *was* second over the city.	• Their chief officer was Joel & his assistant was Judah

Thought 1. Seeing the names of these leaders who tackled the massive problems is a strong reminder that godly leaders are needed to establish and strengthen any city or society. Without strong leadership, no people can thrive, not for long. A people's economy, culture, society, government, and judicial system suffer enormously without strong leadership. Godly leaders are desperately needed within every community, city, state, and nation of this world. Listen to what God's Holy Word says about godly leaders:

"**Masters [leaders], give unto** *your* **servants that which is just and equal; knowing that ye also have a Master in heaven**" (Col.4:1).

"**That which is altogether just shalt thou follow, that thou mayest live, and inherit the land which the** LORD **thy God giveth thee**" (De.16:20).

"**Cursed** *be* **he that perverteth the judgment of the stranger, fatherless, and widow**" (De.27:19).

"**The God of Israel said, the Rock of Israel spake to me, He that ruleth over men** *must be* **just, ruling in the fear of God**" (2 S.23:3).

"**And said to the judges, Take heed what ye do: for ye judge not for man, but for the** LORD, **who is with you in the judgment**" (2 Chr.19:6).

"**Be wise now therefore, O ye kings: be instructed, ye judges of the earth. Serve the** LORD **with fear, and rejoice with trembling**" (Ps.2:10-11).

"**Defend the poor and fatherless: do justice to the afflicted and needy**" (Ps.82:3).

"*It is* **an abomination to kings to commit wickedness: for the throne is established by righteousness**" (Pr.16:12).

"**Mercy and truth preserve the king: and his throne is upholden by mercy**" (Pr.20:28).

"**To do justice and judgment** *is* **more acceptable to the** LORD **than sacrifice**" (Pr.21:3).

"**The king by judgment establisheth the land: but he that receiveth gifts overthroweth it**" (Pr.29:4).

"**The king that faithfully judgeth the poor, his throne shall be established for ever**" (Pr.29:14).

"**Thy princes** *are* **rebellious, and companions of thieves: every one loveth gifts, and followeth after rewards: they judge not the fatherless, neither doth the cause of the widow come unto them. Therefore saith the Lord, the** LORD **of hosts, the mighty One of Israel, Ah, I will ease me of mine adversaries, and avenge me of mine enemies**" (Is.1:23-24).

"**Woe unto them that decree unrighteous decrees, and that write grievousness** *which* **they have prescribed; To turn aside the needy from judgment, and to take away the right from the poor of my people, that widows may be their prey, and** *that* **they may rob the fatherless! And what will ye do in the day of visitation, and in the desolation** *which* **shall come from far? to whom will ye flee for help? and where will ye leave your glory?**" (Is.10:1-3).

c. The names of the priestly families who settled in Jerusalem are recorded in these verses (vv.10-14). Apparently the priests were divided into three family groups who were assigned different tasks in the temple. Interestingly, there were 1,192 priests assigned to the temple, which indicates a large organization even during these days of the returned exiles. Seeing this list of priestly families reminds the reader that ministers must be committed, totally devoted to the LORD and His house, the church.

OUTLINE	SCRIPTURE	SCRIPTURE	OUTLINE
c. The priestly families who settled in Jerusalem: A reminder that ministers must be committed, devoted to the LORD & His house, the church	10 Of the priests: Jedaiah the son of Joiarib, Jachin. 11 Seraiah the son of Hilkiah, the son of Meshullam, the son of Zadok, the son of Meraioth, the son of Ahitub, *was* the ruler of the house of God.	son of Zechariah, the son of Pashur, the son of Malchiah, 13 And his brethren, chief of the fathers, two hundred forty and two: and Amashai the son of Azareel, the son of Ahasai, the son of Meshillemoth, the son of Immer,	2) The second family totaled 242 priests
1) The first family totaled 822 priests: These worked at the temple	12 And their brethren that did the work of the house *were* eight hundred twenty and two: and Adaiah the son of Jeroham, the son of Pelaliah, the son of Amzi, the	14 And their brethren, mighty men of valour, an hundred twenty and eight: and their overseer *was* Zabdiel, the son of *one of* the great men.	3) The third family totaled 128 priests: These are said to be men of valor, courage

"**And he said to** *them* **all, If any** *man* **will come after me, let him deny himself, and take up his cross daily, and follow me**" (Lu.9:23).

"**So likewise, whosoever he be of you that forsaketh not all that he hath, he cannot be my disciple**" (Lu.14:33).

"Then said Jesus to those Jews which believed on him, If ye continue in my word, *then* are ye my disciples indeed" (Jn.8:31).

"If any man serve me, let him follow me; and where I am, there shall also my servant be: if any man serve me, him will *my* Father honour" (Jn.12:26).

"Herein is my Father glorified, that ye bear much fruit; so shall ye be my disciples" (Jn.15:8).

"So when they had dined, Jesus saith to Simon Peter, Simon, *son* of Jonas, lovest thou me more than these? He saith unto him, Yea, Lord; thou knowest that I love thee. He saith unto him, Feed my lambs. He saith to him again the second time, Simon, *son* of Jonas, lovest thou me? He saith unto him, Yea, Lord; thou knowest that I love thee. He saith unto him, Feed my sheep. He saith unto him the third time, Simon, *son* of Jonas, lovest thou me? Peter was grieved because he said unto him the third time, Lovest thou me? And he said unto him, Lord, thou knowest all things; thou knowest that I love thee. Jesus saith unto him, Feed my sheep" (Jn.21:15-17).

"Take heed therefore unto yourselves, and to all the flock, over the which the Holy Ghost hath made you overseers, to feed the church of God, which he hath purchased with his own blood" (Ac.20:28).

"Therefore watch, and remember, that by the space of three years I ceased not to warn every one night and day with tears" (Ac.20:31).

d. The names of the Levite families who settled in Jerusalem are also listed (vv.15-19). Remember that the Levites were assistants to the priests, helping the priests in the performance of their duty. They were also responsible for the maintenance of the temple, for providing music for the worship services, and for guarding the treasuries of the temple as well as the temple property itself.

OUTLINE	SCRIPTURE	SCRIPTURE	OUTLINE
d. The Levite families who settled in Jerusalem: A reminder that associates are essential in the house of God 1) The families in charge of the outside maintenance work of the temple 2) The director & his associate who led in thanksgiving & prayer: Mattaniah & Bakbukiah	15 Also of the Levites: Shemaiah the son of Hashub, the son of Azrikam, the son of Hashabiah, the son of Bunni; 16 And Shabbethai and Jozabad, of the chief of the Levites, *had* the oversight of the outward business of the house of God. 17 And Mattaniah the son of Micha, the son of Zabdi, the son of Asaph, *was* the princi-	pal to begin the thanksgiving in prayer: and Bakbukiah the second among his brethren, and Abda the son of Shammua, the son of Galal, the son of Jeduthun. 18 All the Levites in the holy city *were* two hundred fourscore and four. 19 Moreover the porters, Akkub, Talmon, and their brethren that kept the gates, *were* an hundred seventy and	3) The total Levites in the Holy City: 284 men 4) The total Levite gatekeepers who settled in Jerusalem: 172 men

Thought 1. With all their varied duties, the Levites are a reminder that associates are essential in the house of God. Without assistants, co-workers, or laborers to keep an operation running smoothly, no organization could keep its doors open, not even the church. For this reason, the LORD has given very special gifts to His people. The challenge of the hour is for us to use our gifts and abilities to the fullest in all our efforts, at our jobs, in the church, and in our homes. Every laborer for the LORD, every associate who serves within the church, has been especially gifted with certain abilities. Listen to what God's Holy Word says:

"And unto one he gave five talents, to another two, and to another one; to every man according to his several ability; and straightway took his journey" (Mt.25:15).

"Now there were in the church that was at Antioch certain prophets and teachers; as Barnabas, and Simeon that was called Niger, and Lucius of Cyrene, and Manaen, which had been brought up with Herod the tetrarch, and Saul. As they ministered to the Lord, and fasted, the Holy Ghost said, Separate me Barnabas and Saul for the work whereunto I have called them. And when they had fasted and prayed, and laid *their* hands on them, they sent *them* away" (Ac.13:1-3).

"Having then gifts differing according to the grace that is given to us, whether prophecy, *let us prophesy* according to the proportion of faith; Or ministry, *let us wait* on *our* ministering: or he that teacheth, on teaching; Or he that exhorteth, on exhortation: he that giveth, *let him do it* with simplicity; he that ruleth, with diligence; he that showeth mercy, with cheerfulness" (Ro.12:6-8).

"Now there are diversities of gifts, but the same Spirit. And there are differences of administrations, but the same Lord. And there are diversities of operations, but it is the same God which worketh all in all. But the manifestation of the Spirit is given to every man to profit withal. For to one is given by the Spirit the word of wisdom; to another the word of knowledge by the same Spirit; To another faith by the same Spirit; to another the gifts of healing by the same Spirit; To another the working of miracles; to another prophecy; to another discerning of spirits; to another *divers* kinds of tongues; to another the interpretation of tongues" (1 Co.12:4-10).

"And he gave some, apostles; and some, prophets; and some, evangelists; and some, pastors and teachers; For the perfecting of the saints, for the work of the ministry, for the edifying of the body of Christ: Till we all come in the unity of the faith, and of the knowledge of the Son of God, unto a perfect man, unto the measure of the stature of the fulness of Christ: That we *henceforth* be no more

children, tossed to and fro, and carried about with every wind of doctrine, by the sleight of men, *and* cunning craftiness, whereby they lie in wait to deceive; But speaking the truth in love, may grow up into him in all things, which is the head, *even* Christ" (Ep.4:11-15).

e. Five other facts are recorded about the returned exiles that the reader needs to know (vv.20-24). First, the rest of the returnees settled on their own ancestral property (v.20). They helped rebuild the nation by developing the cities, villages, and farmland of the nation. They also provided the produce and livestock necessary for food and for a robust economy.

Second, the temple servants lived on the hill of Ophel, a hill inside the city wall in the southern section of the capital (v.21). There were so many temple servants that two supervisors had to be appointed to oversee them.

Third, the chief officer or administrator of the Levites in Jerusalem was Uzzi (v.22). He was a descendant of Asaph, the family that had been assigned the task of providing music for the temple.

Fourth, the singers were supported by the Persian king himself (v.23). Note why: so they would pray for him and his family (Ezr.6:8-10; 7:20-24; also see 1 Ti.2:1-2).

Fifth, the king also had a royal agent named Pethahiah stationed in Jerusalem (v.24). This agent was a liaison between the people and the king. When any petitions or complaints arose, it was his responsibility to present them to the king and to relate the king's reply to the people.

OUTLINE	SCRIPTURE	SCRIPTURE	OUTLINE
e. The other facts to know about the returned exiles 1) The rest of the returnees settled on their ancestral property 2) The temple servants lived on the hill of Ophel 3) The chief officer or administrator of the Levites in Jerusalem was Uzzi: He was a musician	20 And the residue of Israel, of the priests, *and* the Levites, *were* in all the cities of Judah, every one in his inheritance. 21 But the Nethinims dwelt in Ophel: and Ziha and Gispa *were* over the Nethinims. 22 The overseer also of the Levites at Jerusalem *was* Uzzi the son of Bani, the son of Hashabiah, the son of Mattaniah, the son of Micha. Of the sons of Asaph,	the singers *were* over the business of the house of God. 23 For *it was* the king's commandment concerning them, that a certain portion should be for the singers, due for every day. 24 And Pethahiah the son of Meshezabeel, of the children of Zerah the son of Judah, *was* at the king's hand in all matters concerning the people.	4) The singers were supported by the Persian king: So they would pray for him, Ezr. 6:8-10; 7:20-24; 1 Ti.2:1-2 5) The king's agent was Pethahiah, who represented the people before the Persian king: A reminder that civil leaders are God's ministers, Ro.13:1-7

Thought 1. Both the king's requests for prayer and his assigning an agent to be stationed in Jerusalem are reminders that civil leaders are to be God's servants. Whether they are aware of the fact or not, they have been appointed by God to serve the citizens under their authority. Being appointed by God, they are as much servants of the people as they are ministers of the gospel. Therefore, civil leaders are to be persons of strong moral and righteous character. They are to encourage righteousness, justice, morality, benevolence, and a caring spirit among their people.

> **"They say unto him, Caesar's. Then saith he unto them, Render therefore unto Caesar the things which are Caesar's; and unto God the things that are God's" (Mt.22:21).**

> **"Let every soul be subject unto the higher powers. For there is no power but of God: the powers that be are ordained of God. Whosoever therefore resisteth the power, resisteth the ordinance of God: and they that resist shall receive to themselves damnation. For rulers are not a terror to good works, but to the evil. Wilt thou then not be afraid of the power? do that which is good, and thou shalt have praise of the same: For he is the minister of God to thee for good. But if thou do that which is evil, be afraid; for he beareth not the sword in vain: for he is the minister of God, a revenger to *execute* wrath upon him that doeth evil. Wherefore *ye* must needs be subject, not only for wrath, but also for conscience sake. For for this cause pay ye tribute also: for they are God's ministers, attending continually upon this very thing. Render therefore to all their dues: tribute to whom tribute *is due;* custom to whom custom; fear to whom fear; honour to whom honour" (Ro.13:1-7).**

> **"Put them in mind to be subject to principalities and powers, to obey magistrates, to be ready to every good work" (Tit.3:1).**

> **"Submit yourselves to every ordinance of man for the Lord's sake: whether it be to the king, as supreme; Or unto governors, as unto them that are sent by him for the punishment of evildoers, and for the praise of them that do well" (1 Pe.2:13-14).**

> **"And whosoever will not do the law of thy God, and the law of the king, let judgment be executed speedily upon him, whether *it be* unto death, or to banishment, or to confiscation of goods, or to imprisonment" (Ezr.7:26).**

> **"*It is* an abomination to kings to commit wickedness: for the throne is established by righteousness" (Pr.16:12).**

f. A list of cities throughout the nation is now recorded, cities where the rest of the people lived (vv.25-36). These were cities from which one of every ten citizens was selected to repopulate Jerusalem, the holy city. Apparently, the bulk of the citizens lived in these cities of Judah (vv.25-30) and Benjamin (vv.21-35). Some Levites who had lived in Judah apparently moved to Benjamin because more Levites were needed there to minister to the people (v.36).

OUTLINE	SCRIPTURE	SCRIPTURE	OUTLINE
f. The list of cities throughout the nation where the rest of the people lived: These were the cities from which one of every ten citizens was selected to repopulate Jerusalem, the holy city 1) The cities of Judah	25 And for the villages, with their fields, *some* of the children of Judah dwelt at Kirjath-arba, and *in* the villages thereof, and at Dibon, and in the villages thereof, and at Jekabzeel, and *in* the villages thereof, 26 And at Jeshua, and at Moladah, and at Beth-phelet, 27 And at Hazar-shual, and at Beer-sheba, and *in* the villages thereof, 28 And at Ziklag, and at Mekonah, and in the villages thereof, 29 And at En-rimmon, and at Zareah, and at Jarmuth, 30 Zanoah, Adullam, and *in*	their villages, at Lachish, and the fields thereof, at Azekah, and *in* the villages thereof. And they dwelt from Beersheba unto the valley of Hinnom. 31 The children also of Benjamin from Geba *dwelt* at Michmash, and Aija, and Bethel, and *in* their villages, 32 *And* at Anathoth, Nob, Ananiah, 33 Hazor, Ramah, Gittaim, 34 Hadid, Zeboim, Neballat, 35 Lod, and Ono, the valley of craftsmen. 36 And of the Levites *were* divisions *in* Judah, *and* in Benjamin.	2) The cities of Benjamin 3) Some Levites who lived in Judah moved to Benjamin: Were more needed there

g. What is now recorded is a list of priests and Levites during different generations of the returned exiles (12:1-26). The scripture and outline are sufficient to show the various groups listed as well as some additional facts important enough to record in Holy Scripture.

OUTLINE	SCRIPTURE	SCRIPTURE	OUTLINE
g. The list of priests & Levites during different generations of the returned exiles 1) The priestly families who returned with the first exiles under Zerubbabel: A reminder that some ministers are *pioneers of faith* 2) The Levite families who returned with the first exiles 3) The line of High Priests • Jeshua served during the time of Haggai & Zechariah • Joiakim served with Ezra; Eliashib with Nehemiah, 10 4) The list of priestly families during the days of	Now these *are* the priests and the Levites that went up with Zerubbabel the son of Shealtiel, and Jeshua: Seraiah, Jeremiah, Ezra, 2 Amariah, Malluch, Hattush, 3 Shechaniah, Rehum, Meremoth, 4 Iddo, Ginnetho, Abijah, 5 Miamin, Maadiah, Bilgah, 6 Shemaiah, and Joiarib, Jedaiah, 7 Sallu, Amok, Hilkiah, Jedaiah. These *were* the chief of the priests and of their brethren in the days of Jeshua. 8 Moreover the Levites: Jeshua, Binnui, Kadmiel, Sherebiah, Judah, *and* Mattaniah, *which was* over the thanksgiving, he and his brethren. 9 Also Bakbukiah and Unni, their brethren, *were* over against them in the watches. 10 And Jeshua begat Joiakim, Joiakim also begat Eliashib, and Eliashib begat Joiada, 11 And Joiada begat Jonathan, and Jonathan begat Jaddua. 12 And in the days of Joiakim were priests, the chief of the fathers: of Seraiah, Me-	raiah; of Jeremiah, Hananiah; 13 Of Ezra, Meshullam; of Amariah, Jehohanan; 14 Of Melicu, Jonathan; of Shebaniah, Joseph; 15 Of Harim, Adna; of Meraioth, Helkai; 16 Of Iddo, Zechariah; of Ginnethon, Meshullam; 17 Of Abijah, Zichri; of Miniamin, of Moadiah, Piltai; 18 Of Bilgah, Shammua; of Shemaiah, Jehonathan; 19 And of Joiarib, Mattenai; of Jedaiah, Uzzi; 20 Of Sallai, Kallai; of Amok, Eber; 21 Of Hilkiah, Hashabiah; of Jedaiah, Nethaneel. 22 The Levites in the days of Eliashib, Joiada, and Johanan, and Jaddua, *were* recorded chief of the fathers: also the priests, to the reign of Darius the Persian. 23 The sons of Levi, the chief of the fathers, *were* written in the book of the chronicles, even until the days of Johanan the son of Eliashib. 24 And the chief of the Levites: Hashabiah, Sherebiah, and Jeshua the son of Kadmiel, with their brethren over against them, to praise *and* to	Joiakim the High Priest: This was the second generation of priests after the return 5) Additional important facts • The Levite family leaders listed here were recorded during the reign of the Persian king, Darius • The musicians were organized as prescribed by David, the man of God

OUTLINE	SCRIPTURE	SCRIPTURE	OUTLINE
	give thanks, according to the commandment of David the man of God, ward over against ward. 25 Mattaniah, and Bak-bukiah, Obadiah, Meshullam, Talmon, Akkub, *were* porters	keeping the ward at the thresholds of the gates. 26 These *were* in the days of Joiakim the son of Jeshua, the son of Jozadak, and in the days of Nehemiah the gover-nor, and of Ezra the priest,	treasury during the day of Nehemiah are listed
• The gatekeepers who pro-tected the temple & its			

Thought 1. In the resettling of Jerusalem, there is a strong lesson for us: we must serve in the most-needed places. Within the church, all kinds of needs exist. There is a need for ministers of the gospel and a host of associate work-ers. There is a constant need for people to count the offerings, to maintain the property and buildings, and to serve as technicians, musicians, and security men. In addition, office staff, ministerial staff, teachers, and volunteers are needed. Think of all who serve on the committees of the church and reach out to visit the shut-ins, the hospitalized, and the lost and unchurched of the community. Just within the local church, a great range of needs exist that must be filled by both volunteers and professional ministers.

Within society in general, the number and diversity of needs are mind-boggling, never-ending. Think of the or-phans, widows, widowers, prisoners, brokenhearted, backslidden, diseased, suffering, hungry, and dying. Think of the lawless, the abusers, and the violent within society. Think of those who are without Christ and have no personal relationship with God. When all the needs within a society are heaped together, the weight is staggering. And the number of people in need makes the task overwhelming. But the needs can be met if enough of us will step forth to serve in the most-needed places. Listen to what God's Holy Word says about reaching out in service to meet the needs of the world:

"Let your light so shine before men, that they may see your good works, and glorify your Father which is in heaven" (Mt.5:16).

"Then saith he unto his disciples, The harvest truly *is* plenteous, but the labourers *are* few; Pray ye therefore the Lord of the harvest, that he will send forth labourers into his harvest" (Mt.9:37-38).

"For I was an hungred, and ye gave me meat: I was thirsty, and ye gave me drink: I was a stranger, and ye took me in: Naked, and ye clothed me: I was sick, and ye visited me: I was in prison, and ye came unto me" (Mt.25:35-36).

"But Jesus called them *to him,* and saith unto them, Ye know that they which are accounted to rule over the Gentiles exercise lordship over them; and their great ones exercise authority upon them" (Mk.10:42).

"But so shall it not be among you: but whosoever will be great among you, shall be your minister: And whosoever of you will be the chiefest, shall be servant of all. For even the Son of man came not to be ministered unto, but to minister, and to give his life a ransom for many" (Mk.10:43-45).

"And Jesus answering said, A certain *man* went down from Jerusalem to Jericho, and fell among thieves, which stripped him of his raiment, and wounded *him,* and departed, leaving *him* half dead. And by chance there came down a certain priest that way: and when he saw him, he passed by on the other side. And likewise a Levite, when he was at the place, came and looked *on him,* and passed by on the other side. But a certain Samaritan, as he journeyed, came where he was: and when he saw him, he had compassion *on him,* And went to *him,* and bound up his wounds, pouring in oil and wine, and set him on his own beast, and brought him to an inn, and took care of him. And on the morrow when he departed, he took out two pence, and gave *them* to the host, and said unto him, Take care of him; and whatsoever thou spendest more, when I come again, I will repay thee. Which now of these three, thinkest thou, was neighbour unto him that fell among the thieves?" (Lu:10:30-36).

"Lift up your eyes, and look on the fields; for they are white already to harvest. And he that reapeth receiveth wages, and gathereth fruit unto life eternal: that both he that soweth and he that reapeth may rejoice together" (Jn.4:35-36).

"If I then, *your* Lord and Master, have washed your feet; ye also ought to wash one another's feet" (Jn.13:14).

"He saith to him again the second time, Simon, *son* of Jonas, lovest thou me? He saith unto him, Yea, Lord; thou knowest that I love thee. He saith unto him, Feed my sheep" (Jn.21:16).

"How God anointed Jesus of Nazareth with the Holy Ghost and with power: who went about doing good, and healing all that were oppressed of the devil; for God was with him" (Ac.10:38).

"Bear ye one another's burdens, and so fulfil the law of Christ" (Ga.6:2).

"As we have therefore opportunity, let us do good unto all *men,* especially unto them who are of the household of faith" (Ga.6:10).

"Charge them that are rich in this world, that they be not highminded, nor trust in uncertain rich-es, but in the living God, who giveth us richly all things to enjoy; That they do good, that they be rich in good works, ready to distribute, willing to communicate [give]; Laying up in store for themselves a good foundation against the time to come, that they may lay hold on eternal life" (1 Ti.6:17-19).

"In all things showing thyself a pattern of good works: in doctrine *showing* uncorruptness, gravity, sincerity" (Tit.2:7).

"And let us consider one another to provoke unto love and to good works" (He.10:24).

"But to do good and to communicate [give] forget not: for with such sacrifices God is well pleased" (He.13:16).

2 (12:27-43) **Thinking, Positive, Need for, Example—Positive Thinking, Need for, Example—Attitude, Positive, Need for, Example—Joy, Need for, Example—Attitude, Joyful, Need for, Example—Jerusalem, Wall of, Dedication—Dedication Service, of Jerusalem's Wall—Service, Dedication, of Jerusalem's Wall**: right after the population and housing crisis had been solved, the dedication of the wall took place. However, remember that the people had already rededicated their lives to the LORD. The people knew that their real security lay in the hands of God, not in the stones and mortar of a protective wall. Once they had made their personal dedication to the LORD, built up the population of the city, and constructed adequate housing, it was now time for the wall to be dedicated to the LORD and His protective hand.

OUTLINE	SCRIPTURE	SCRIPTURE	OUTLINE
2. The dedication of the wall: A need for the people to have a positive & joyful attitude a. Nehemiah's summons for the religious personnel to gather & prepare for the dedication celebration 1) The Levites were summoned from everywhere 2) The Levite singers around Jerusalem were summoned: Had built villages around the capital for themselves 3) The priests & Levites dedicated or ceremonially cleansed themselves, the people, the gates, & the wall b. Nehemiah's division of the leaders & musicians into two processional groups: He led them all to the top of the wall 1) One group walked on top of the wall to the right toward the Dung Gate • They played musical instruments & sang as they walked in the	27 And at the dedication of the wall of Jerusalem they sought the Levites out of all their places, to bring them to Jerusalem, to keep the dedication with gladness, both with thanksgivings, and with singing, *with* cymbals, psalteries, and with harps. 28 And the sons of the singers gathered themselves together, both out of the plain country round about Jerusalem, and from the villages of Netophathi; 29 Also from the house of Gilgal, and out of the fields of Geba and Azmaveth: for the singers had builded them villages round about Jerusalem. 30 And the priests and the Levites purified themselves, and purified the people, and the gates, and the wall. 31 Then I brought up the princes of Judah upon the wall, and appointed two great *companies of them that gave* thanks, *whereof one* went on the right hand upon the wall toward the dung gate: 32 And after them went Hoshaiah, and half of the princes of Judah, 33 And Azariah, Ezra, and Meshullam, 34 Judah, and Benjamin, and Shemaiah, and Jeremiah, 35 And *certain* of the priests' sons with trumpets; *namely,* Zechariah the son of Jonathan, the son of Shemaiah, the son of Mattaniah, the son of Michaiah, the son of Zaccur, the son of Asaph: 36 And his brethren, Shemaiah, and Azarael, Milalai, Gilalai, Maai, Nethaneel,	and Judah, Hanani, with the musical instruments of David the man of God, and Ezra the scribe before them. 37 And at the fountain gate, which was over against them, they went up by the stairs of the city of David, at the going up of the wall, above the house of David, even unto the water gate eastward. 38 And the other *company of them that gave* thanks went over against *them,* and I after them, and the half of the people upon the wall, from beyond the tower of the furnaces even unto the broad wall; 39 And from above the gate of Ephraim, and above the old gate, and above the fish gate, and the tower of Hananeel, and the tower of Meah, even unto the sheep gate: and they stood still in the prison gate. 40 So stood the two *companies of them that gave* thanks in the house of God, and I, and the half of the rulers with me: 41 And the priests; Eliakim, Maaseiah, Miniamin, Michaiah, Elioenai, Zechariah, *and* Hananiah, with trumpets; 42 And Maaseiah, and Shemaiah, and Eleazar, and Uzzi, and Jehohanan, and Malchijah, and Elam, and Ezer. And the singers sang loud, with Jezrahiah *their* overseer. 43 Also that day they offered great sacrifices, and rejoiced: for God had made them rejoice with great joy: the wives also and the children rejoiced: so that the joy of Jerusalem was heard even afar off.	dedication processional • They were led by Ezra • They saw the results of their hard labor: The Dung Gate (31), the Fountain Gate, the steps that led to the city or house of David, & the Water Gate 2) The second group walked in the opposite direction • They were led by Nehemiah • They also saw the results of their diligent labor: The Tower of the Ovens, the Fish Gate, the Tower of Hananel, the Tower of the Hundred, & the Sheep Gate • They stopped at the Gate of the Guard c. Nehemiah's worship service: He had ordered the two processional groups to meet at the temple to worship 1) The choirs, officials, priests, & Nehemiah the governor took their places 2) The choirs sang 3) The worshippers offered many sacrifices 4) The people rejoiced greatly—including women & children: Were flooded with joy 5) The celebration was loud:

a. Nehemiah summoned all the religious personnel together to prepare for the dedication celebration (vv.27-30). The Levites were summoned from throughout Judah to assist in the ceremony. They were to provide the choir and instruments for music. A special invitation was also sent to the Levites within Jerusalem itself and its surrounding villages (vv.28-29). After gathering together, the priests and Levites cleansed themselves ceremonially (v.30). Ritual cleansing included the following activities: bathing, changing into clean clothing, offering sacrifices, praying and rededicating one's life to the LORD (Ge.35:2-3; Le.16:30; 22:4-7; Nu.8:21-22; 2 Chr.29:15; 35:6; Ezr.6:20; Ne.13:22; Mal.3:3). Following their cleansing, the priests and Levites dedicated and purified the people, the gates, and the wall itself. Obviously some of the same ritual activities would have been performed for each of these (1 Chr.23:28; 2 Chr.29:15).

b. With the cleansing ritual fulfilled, Nehemiah divided the leaders and musicians into two processional groups. He then led them to the top of the wall (vv.31-39). One group, placed under Ezra's leadership was instructed to walk in a processional to the right toward the Dung Gate (vv.31-37). As they walked in the dedication processional, they were to play musical instruments and sing. Just as Nehemiah instructed, Ezra led his group in a processional march heading south. By marching along the top of the wall, Ezra's group saw the results of their hard labor. They passed over the Dung Gate (v.31), the Fountain Gate, the steps that led to the city or house of David, and the Water Gate (v.37).

The second group, led by Nehemiah himself, walked in a processional in the opposite direction (vv.38-39). As they marched along they also saw the results of their diligent labor. They marched over the Tower of the Ovens, the Fish Gate, the Tower of Hananel, the Tower of the Hundred, and the Sheep Gate (v.39). When they reached the Gate of the Guard, they stopped. Both processional groups halted when they reached the temple area, for it was there that a worship service was to be held.

Obviously, it was a very wise decision for Nehemiah to dedicate the wall in this way. Having the people walk along the top of the wall caused them to focus on the results of their labor. Realizing that they had accomplished such a massive project would stir them to continue the rebuilding of Jerusalem. Since they had accomplished so much in just 52 days, they would be confident they could achieve any task, even the rebuilding of the city and nation. But there was also another benefit of marching across the top of the wall. The enemy nations surrounding Jerusalem would have had spies observing the festive occasion. Seeing such a joyful experience and the strength of the wall would make the enemy think twice before attacking.

c. When the processionals reached the temple area, Nehemiah gathered them for the dedication worship service (vv.40-43). All the choirs, civil officials, priests, and Nehemiah the governor took their places (vv.40-41). After the music and worship, the worshippers offered their sacrifices (vv.42-43). Afterward, the people rejoiced greatly, including the women and children. Everyone was flooded with joy. In fact, the celebration and rejoicing were so loud that the noise was heard from far away.

Thought 1. In order to continue building the city of Jerusalem and the nation of Judah, Nehemiah needed to arouse a positive and joyful attitude in the people. It was for this reason that he organized the dedication service around a processional on top of the wall and a joyful worship service. What a lesson for us! We, too, must develop a positive and joyful attitude. We must think optimistically, casting all pessimism and negativity out of our minds. Positive thinking is essential in order to live a successful and victorious life. Therefore, we must develop positive thoughts, focusing our minds upon things that are...

- true
- honest and noble
- just and right
- pure and clean
- pleasant and lovely
- excellent and admirable
- good and honorable
- virtuous and praiseworthy

Good and wholesome thoughts are to flood our minds. Nothing else. No negative thought—whether immoral, unjust, lawless, violent, or any other wicked behavior—should ever be harbored or meditated upon. We cannot keep thoughts from flashing across our minds, but we can keep from harboring them and allowing them to nest. We can refuse to think upon negative behavior, instead focusing our minds only upon positive, virtuous, and uplifting behavior. This is the way to develop a joyful attitude. And a joyful attitude based upon the Word of God will always lead to a righteous and fruitful life as well as a righteous and productive society. Listen to what God's Holy Word says about our thoughts:

"And Jesus knowing their thoughts said, Wherefore think ye evil in your hearts?" (Mt.9:4).

"For out of the heart proceed evil thoughts, murders, adulteries, fornications, thefts, false witness, blasphemies" (Mt.15:19).

"These things have I spoken unto you, that my joy might remain in you, and *that* your joy might be full" (Jn.15:11).

"Because that, when they knew God, they glorified *him* not as God, neither were thankful; but became vain in their imaginations, and their foolish heart was darkened" (Ro.1:21).

"This I say therefore, and testify in the Lord, that ye henceforth walk not as other Gentiles walk, in the vanity of their mind" (Ep.4:17).

"Rejoice in the Lord alway: *and* again I say, Rejoice" (Ph.4:4).

"Meditate upon these things [righteousness]; give thyself wholly to them; that thy profiting may appear to all" (1 Ti.4:15).

"We have thought of thy lovingkindness, O God, in the midst of thy temple" (Ps.48:9).

"I thought on my ways, and turned my feet unto thy testimonies" (Ps.119:59).

"The thoughts of the righteous *are* right: *but* the counsels of the wicked *are* deceit" (Pr.12:5).

"For I say, through the grace given unto me, to every man that is among you, not to think *of himself* more highly than he ought to think; but to think soberly, according as God hath dealt to every man the measure of faith" (Ro.12:3).

"Finally, brethren, whatsoever things are true, whatsoever things *are* honest, whatsoever things *are* just, whatsoever things *are* pure, whatsoever things *are* lovely, whatsoever things *are* of good report; if *there be* any virtue, and if *there be* any praise, think on these things" (Ph.4:8).

"And GOD saw that the wickedness of man *was* great in the earth, and *that* every imagination of the thoughts of his heart *was* only evil continually" (Ge.6:5).

"O that they were wise, *that* they understood this, *that* they would consider their latter end!" (De.32:29).

"This book of the law shall not depart out of thy mouth; but thou shalt meditate therein day and night, that thou mayest observe to do according to all that is written therein: for then thou shalt make thy way prosperous, and then thou shalt have good success" (Jos.1:8).

"Only fear the LORD, and serve him in truth with all your heart: for consider how great *things* he hath done for you" (1 S.12:24).

"Hearken unto this, O Job: stand still, and consider the wondrous works of God" (Jb.37:14).

"Blessed *is* the man that walketh not in the counsel of the ungodly, nor standeth in the way of sinners, nor sitteth in the seat of the scornful" (Ps.1:1).

"Stand in awe, and sin not: commune with your own heart upon your bed, and be still. Selah" (Ps.4:4).

"When I consider thy heavens, the work of thy fingers, the moon and the stars, which thou hast ordained; What is man, that thou art mindful of him? and the son of man, that thou visitest him?" (Ps.8:3-4).

"Let the words of my mouth, and the meditation of my heart, be acceptable in thy sight, O LORD, my strength, and my redeemer" (Ps.19:14).

"My heart was hot within me, while I was musing [meditation] the fire burned: *then* spake I with my tongue" (Ps.39:3).

"My soul shall be satisfied as *with* marrow and fatness; and my mouth shall praise *thee* with joyful lips: When I remember thee upon my bed, *and* meditate on thee in the *night* watches" (Ps.63:5-6).

"The LORD knoweth the thoughts of man, that they *are* vanity" (Ps.94:11).

"My meditation of him shall be sweet: I will be glad in the LORD" (Ps.104:34).

"Mine eyes prevent [precede] the *night* watches, that I might meditate in thy word" (Ps.119:148).

"I remember the days of old; I meditate on all thy works; I muse on the work of thy hands" (Ps.143:5).

"These six *things* doth the LORD hate: yea, seven *are* an abomination unto him: A proud look, a lying tongue, and hands that shed innocent blood, An heart that deviseth wicked imaginations, feet that be swift in running to mischief" (Pr.6:16-18; esp.v.18).).

"The thoughts of the wicked *are* an abomination to the LORD: but *the words* of the pure *are* pleasant words" (Pr.15:26).

"For as he thinketh in his heart, so *is* he: Eat and drink, saith he to thee; but his heart *is* not with thee" (Pr.23:7).

"The thought of foolishness *is* sin: and the scorner *is* an abomination to men" (Pr.24:9).

"O Jerusalem, wash thine heart from wickedness, that thou mayest be saved. How long shall thy vain thoughts lodge within thee?" (Je.4:14).

---

3 (12:44-47) **Worship, Duty, to Be Faithful, Consistent—Faithfulness, Duty, in Worship—Consistency, Duty, in Worship—Worship, Organized, by Nehemiah—Organization, of Worship, by Nehemiah—Temple, Organization of, by Nehemiah**: it was at this time at the joyful celebration, that the religious workers were organized to conduct permanent worship services at the temple. Custodians were appointed to be in charge of the offerings, tithes, and storerooms (v.44). Throughout the land the people were to provide food and money to support the priests and Levites.

The priests and Levites had already been appointed, but a significant statement is made about them in these verses: they performed their service faithfully both in personal conduct and in ministry. They lived pure, clean lives, and they faithfully performed their service for the LORD, ministering to the people and helping to meet their spiritual needs (v.30). As a result, the people throughout the nation were well pleased with the priests and Levites.

The singers and gatekeepers also faithfully performed their service for the LORD and His house, the temple (vv.45-46). Two facts in particular are mentioned: they fulfilled their duties exactly as prescribed by David and Solomon, and they followed the custom of having choir directors as described by David and Asaph.

Lastly, all the people were faithful in supporting the priests and Levites (v.47). Under the leadership of both Zerubbabel and Nehemiah, the people proved faithful in supporting the religious workers. Even the Levites scattered throughout the cities and villages of the nation were faithfully supported.

OUTLINE	SCRIPTURE	SCRIPTURE	OUTLINE
3. The organization for permanent worship: A need for everyone to be faithful, consistent in their duty	44 And at that time were some appointed over the chambers for the treasures, for the offerings, for the firstfruits, and for the tithes, to gather into them out of the fields of the cities the portions of the law for the priests and Levites: for Judah rejoiced for the priests and for the Levites that waited.	the commandment of David, *and* of Solomon his son. 46 For in the days of David and Asaph of old *there were* chief of the singers, and songs of praise and thanksgiving unto God. 47 And all Israel in the days of Zerubbabel, and in the days of Nehemiah, gave the portions of the singers and the porters, every day his portion: and they sanctified *holy things* unto the Levites; and the Levites sanctified *them* unto the children of Aaron.	outlined by David & Solomon
a. The appointment of custodians over the offerings & tithes: The people were to provide food & money to support the priests & Levites			2) Followed the custom of having choir directors as outlined by David & Asaph
b. The ministry of the priests & Levites: Performed their service faithfully			d. The faithfulness of the people in supporting the priests & Levites
c. The service of the singers & gatekeepers: Faithfully performed their service	45 And both the singers and the porters kept the ward of their God, and the ward of the purification, according to		1) Were faithful in the days of Zerubbabel & Nehemiah
1) Followed the duties as			2) Were faithful in supporting the Levites in the other cities

205

Thought 1. Everyone of God's people need to be faithful, consistent in their duty. No task ever gets done unless a person diligently works to complete the task. Thus, being loyal and reliable are absolutely essential in order to achieve anything worthwhile in life. No matter who we are, we must be faithful in the task assigned us.

⇒ Ministers and other church workers must be faithful for the Word of God to be carried to the world and for the needs of people to be met.

⇒ Business managers and employees must be faithful for businesses to succeed and for jobs to be available to the people.

⇒ Spouses must be faithful for marriages to survive.

⇒ Friends must be faithful to one another if their friendship is to be maintained.

⇒ Laborers must work diligently if their jobs are to be secure.

⇒ Students must study consistently if they are to pass and graduate and be prepared to secure adequate employment.

⇒ Citizens must be faithful in paying taxes and supporting their nation if the nation is to be economically sound, militarily strong, and able to provide basic services for society.

No matter what the task or who is responsible for the task, faithfulness is demanded if success is to be achieved. Listen to what God's Holy Word says about faithfulness, about being consistently diligent in carrying out our duties:

"Not slothful in business; fervent in spirit; serving the Lord" (Ro.12:11).

"Moreover it is required in stewards, that a man be found faithful" (1 Co.4:2).

"Therefore, my beloved brethren, be ye stedfast, unmovable, always abounding in the work of the Lord, forasmuch as ye know that your labour is not in vain in the Lord" (1 Co.15:58).

"Let him that stole steal no more: but rather let him labour, working with *his* hands the thing which is good, that he may have to give to him that needeth" (Ep.4:28).

"And whatsoever ye do in word or deed, *do* all in the name of the Lord Jesus, giving thanks to God and the Father by him" (Col.3:17).

"Fathers, provoke not your children *to anger,* lest they be discouraged" (Col.3:21).

"And that ye study to be quiet, and to do your own business, and to work with your own hands, as we commanded you; That ye may walk honestly toward them that are without, and *that* ye may have lack of nothing" (1 Th.4:11-12).

"For even when we were with you, this we commanded you, that if any would not work, neither should he eat. For we hear that there are some which walk among you disorderly, working not at all, but are busybodies. Now them that are such we command and exhort by our Lord Jesus Christ, that with quietness they work, and eat their own bread" (2 Th.3:10-12).

"And who *is* he that will harm you, if ye be followers of that which is good? But and if ye suffer for righteousness' sake, happy *are ye:* and be not afraid of their terror, neither be troubled" (1 Pe.3:13-14).

"And the LORD God took the man, and put him into the garden of Eden to dress it and to keep it" (Ge.2:15).

"Go to the ant, thou sluggard; consider her ways, and be wise" (Pr.6:6).

"In all labour there is profit: but the talk of the lips *tendeth* only to penury" (Pr.14:23).

"Whatsoever thy hand findeth to do, do *it* with thy might; for *there is* no work, nor device, nor knowledge, nor wisdom, in the grave, whither thou goest" (Ec.9:10).

CHAPTER 13

E. Step 5—Building Through Discipline, Correcting People's Violation of the Law: Stressing the Need for Continued Reformation, Revival, 13:1-31

1. Violation 1—Evil associations: A need for spiritual separation

a. The discovery of the violation while reading God's Word: No foreigner (unbeliever) was to be allowed in their worship, De.23:3-6
  1) The Ammonites & Moabites had opposed Israel's march to the promised land, Nu.22:1-25:18
  2) The two nations had hired Balaam to curse God's people
b. The correction: Spiritual separation—excluded all foreigners (unbelievers) from their assembly

2. Violation 2—Desecrating the house of God: A need to purify, cleanse the church

a. The violation by the High Priest Eliashib & his close associate Tobiah
  1) The priest had converted a large storage room in the temple & made it available for Tobiah to use as needed, 6:17-19; see 2:10, 19; 4:3; 6:10-12
  2) The two men were desecrating, defiling the temple

b. The discovery of the violation by the governor Nehemiah
  1) He had been absent from Jerusalem, having returned to the palace in the 32nd year of King Artaxerxes' reign
  2) He later secured permission to return to Jerusalem & immediately discovered the abuse of God's house

c. The correction by Nehemiah
  1) He at once threw out all of Tobiah's belongings
  2) He ordered the rooms to be cleansed, purified
  3) He put back all of the temple items that had been removed: The articles &

On that day they read in the book of Moses in the audience of the people; and therein was found written, that the Ammonite and the Moabite should not come into the congregation of God for ever;

2 Because they met not the children of Israel with bread and with water, but hired Balaam against them, that he should curse them: howbeit our God turned the curse into a blessing.

3 Now it came to pass, when they had heard the law, that they separated from Israel all the mixed multitude.

4 And before this, Eliashib the priest, having the oversight of the chamber of the house of our God, was allied unto Tobiah:

5 And he had prepared for him a great chamber, where aforetime they laid the meat offerings, the frankincense, and the vessels, and the tithes of the corn, the new wine, and the oil, which was commanded to be given to the Levites, and the singers, and the porters; and the offerings of the priests.

6 But in all this time was not I at Jerusalem: for in the two and thirtieth year of Artaxerxes king of Babylon came I unto the king, and after certain days obtained I leave of the king:

7 And I came to Jerusalem, and understood of the evil that Eliashib did for Tobiah, in preparing him a chamber in the courts of the house of God.

8 And it grieved me sore: therefore I cast forth all the household stuff of Tobiah out of the chamber.

9 Then I commanded, and they cleansed the chambers: and thither brought I again the vessels of the house of God, with the meat offering and the frankincense.

10 And I perceived that the portions of the Levites had not been given them: for the Levites and the singers, that did the work, were fled every one to his field.

11 Then contended I with the rulers, and said, Why is the house of God forsaken? And I gathered them together, and set them in their place.

12 Then brought all Judah the tithe of the corn and the new wine and the oil unto the treasuries.

13 And I made treasurers over the treasuries, Shelemiah the priest, and Zadok the scribe, and of the Levites, Pedaiah: and next to them was Hanan the son of Zaccur, the son of Mattaniah: for they were counted faithful, and their office was to distribute unto their brethren.

14 Remember me, O my God, concerning this, and wipe not out my good deeds that I have done for the house of my God, and for the offices thereof.

15 In those days saw I in Judah some treading winepresses on the sabbath, and bringing in sheaves, and lading asses; as also wine, grapes, and figs, and all manner of burdens, which they brought into Jerusalem on the sabbath day: and I testified against them in the day wherein they sold victuals.

16 There dwelt men of Tyre also therein, which brought fish, and all manner of ware, and sold on the sabbath unto the children of Judah, and in Jerusalem.

17 Then I contended with the nobles of Judah, and said unto them, What evil thing is this that ye do, and profane the sabbath day?

18 Did not your fathers thus, and did not our God bring all this evil upon us, and upon this city? yet ye bring more wrath upon Israel by profaning the sabbath.

19 And it came to pass, that when the gates of Jerusalem began to be dark before the sabbath, I commanded that the gates should be shut, and charged that they should not

3. Violation 3—Neglecting to tithe: A need to support God's house

a. The violation
  1) The people had stopped tithing, 9:38; 10:32-39
  2) The Levites had to return to secular work
b. The fivefold correction by Nehemiah
  1) He rebuked the officials
  2) He restored the Levites to their duties
  3) He challenged the people to renew their tithes & offerings

  4) He replaced the custodians of the storeroom: This meant removing the High Priest Eliashib from his custodial position as supervisor, 4
    • Appointed trustworthy men
    • Assigned the duty of distribution to new men
  5) He prayed for God's help, that God would preserve him & the service of God's house

4. Violation 4—Working on the Sabbath: A need to honor the Sabbath & keep it holy

a. The violation discovered by Nehemiah, Ex.20:8-11; Ne.10:31
  1) He saw Jews working on the Sabbath throughout Judah & Jerusalem & warned them

  2) He saw foreigners conducting business in Jerusalem on the Sabbath

b. The fivefold correction by Nehemiah
  1) He rebuked the nobles
    • Charged them with perverting the Sabbath
    • Warned them: This was the very sin that had caused their captivity—the sin that would bring wrath upon them again, Je.17:21-27
  2) He ordered the gates of the city to be closed for the Sabbath
  3) He stationed his own guards at the gates so no merchandise could be

brought into the city on the Sabbath

- The merchants camped outside the gates once or twice, tempting the people
- The governor warned the merchants: He would have them arrested
- The merchants stopped trying to do business on the Sabbath

4) He ordered the Levites to purify themselves ceremonially & to guard the gates: To keep the Sabbath day holy

5) He again prayed for God's help in this matter & for God's mercy

5. Violation 5—Compromising, marrying unbelievers: A need to build godly families

a. The violation: Mixed marriages

1) God's people were marrying unbelievers, 10:30; Ezr.9:1-4

2) Sadly, half of the children could not speak Hebrew, the language of God's Word

b. The fourfold correction of guilty parties by Nehemiah

1) He rebuked them

- Asked God to judge them

be opened till after the sabbath: and *some* of my servants set I at the gates, *that* there should no burden be brought in on the sabbath day.

20 So the merchants and sellers of all kind of ware lodged without Jerusalem once or twice.

21 Then I testified against them, and said unto them, Why lodge ye about the wall? if ye do *so* again, I will lay hands on you. From that time forth came they no *more* on the sabbath.

22 And I commanded the Levites that they should cleanse themselves, and *that* they should come *and* keep the gates, to sanctify the sabbath day. Remember me, O my God, *concerning* this also, and spare me according to the greatness of thy mercy.

23 In those days also saw I Jews *that* had married wives of Ashdod, of Ammon, *and* of Moab:

24 And their children spake half in the speech of Ashdod, and could not speak in the Jews' language, but according to the language of each people.

25 And I contended with them, and cursed them, and smote certain of them, and plucked off their hair, and

and made them swear by God, *saying,* Ye shall not give your daughters unto their sons, nor take their daughters unto your sons, or for yourselves.

26 Did not Solomon king of Israel sin by these things? yet among many nations was there no king like him, who was beloved of his God, and God made him king over all Israel: nevertheless even him did outlandish women cause to sin.

27 Shall we then hearken unto you to do all this great evil, to transgress against our God in marrying strange wives?

28 And *one* of the sons of Joiada, the son of Eliashib the high priest, *was* son in law to Sanballat the Horonite: therefore I chased him from me.

29 Remember them, O my God, because they have defiled the priesthood, and the covenant of the priesthood, and of the Levites.

30 Thus cleansed I them from all strangers, and appointed the wards of the priests and the Levites, every one in his business;

31 And for the wood offering, at times appointed, and for the firstfruits. Remember me, O my God, for good.

- Beat some of the men & pulled out their hair, a sign of disgrace, 2 S.10:4; Ezr.9:3; Is.50:6
- Made them renew their oath, 10:30

2) He warned them with reminders from Israel's history

- Reminded them of Solomon's sin in marrying unbelievers: Despite his greatness & God's love for him, the unbelieving women led him into sin
- Warned them that they were repeating the same sins by marrying unbelievers

3) He exiled the most prominent offender: The grandson of the High Priest Eliashib who had married the daughter of Sanballat, an enemy, 2:10; 4:1-6:14

4) He prayed for God to judge the grandson & Sanballat: Had defiled the priesthood

5) The conclusion: Nehemiah held a purification service

- Purified all the priests
- Reassigned the priests
- Reestablished the offerings
- Prayed for God to remember, favor him

DIVISION II

THE REBUILDING OF THE NATION AND THE PEOPLE 8:1-13:31

E. Step 5—Building Through Discipline, Correcting People's Violation of the Law: Stressing the Need for Continued Reformation and Revival, 13:1-31

(13:1-31) **Introduction**: one of the greatest needs of the church is for revival, a continuous spirit of revival. It is not enough to experience revival and then to slip back into a spirit of lethargy, complacency, being "at ease in Zion." Living a life of comfort and indulgence with little concern about the desperate needs of the world—is not the life a believer is to live. God has called us to experience continuous revival, to have our spirits constantly aroused to worship Him daily and to be busy in meeting the needs of the world. But to experience continuous revival, a constant watch is necessary. We must stand guard against complacency, lethargy, indifference, and a dull, inactive mind. We must put a watch over our spirits, arising to worship God daily through Bible study and prayer, learning His commandments and seeking His help. And we must seek opportunities throughout the day to reach out and meet the needs of people as well as to bear witness to the saving grace of Jesus Christ.

A continuous spirit of revival is the call and gift of God to us, but we must daily seek Him to revive our spirits. Stressing the need for continued revival and reformation is the subject of the present Scripture. After Nehemiah had served as governor of Jerusalem for 12 years, he returned to give a report to King Artaxerxes of Persia (13:6). After giving his report, God apparently stirred within his heart a deep longing to return to Jerusalem. He requested permission to return, and his request was granted. Chapter 13 covers his return visit. When Nehemiah arrived in Jerusalem, what he found was both discouraging and upsetting. The spirit of revival that God had so graciously poured out upon the returned exiles had not been nurtured. The people had turned away from their commitment to the LORD, backsliding and violating God's holy commandments. The foundation of their lives and society was no longer the Word of God and its commandments. The behavior and lifestyle of the people had been sadly corrupted. However, Nehemiah was not a leader who was easily discouraged. In fact, he never gave up due to hardship or suffering and never gave in to sin and ungodliness. He took immediate and decisive action: he refocused himself totally upon God's call, the call to rebuild the nation and the people. This necessitated corrective action, correcting the people's violation of God's law. Unless their disobedience was corrected, the LORD's judgment, not His blessing, would fall upon the people. Just as Nehemiah had done during his first 12-year tenure as governor, he sought to refocus the people's attention on rebuilding their nation and their society. During his first term as governor he had taken four steps to achieve this objective:

⇒ First, the people sought to rebuild by making a commitment to God's Word (8:1-18).
⇒ Second, the people sought to rebuild by making a commitment to seek revival (9:1-37).
⇒ Third, the people sought to rebuild through making a covenant of commitment, stressing the importance of total devotion (9:38–10:39).
⇒ Fourth, the people sought to rebuild through strengthening Jerusalem and the spirit of the people (11:1–12:47).

Now, Nehemiah seeks to arouse the returnees to build through discipline, through correcting their violation of the law. This is, *Step 5—Building Through Discipline, Correcting People's Violation of the Law: Stressing the Need for Continued Reformation and Revival*, 13:1-31.

1. Violation 1—evil associations: a need for spiritual separation (vv.1-3).
2. Violation 2—desecrating the house of God: a need to purify, cleanse the church (vv.4-9).
3. Violation 3—neglecting the tithe: a need to support God's House (vv.10-14).
4. Violation 4—working on, breaking the Sabbath: a need to honor the Sabbath and keep it holy (vv.15-22).
5. Violation 5—compromising, marrying unbelievers: a need to build godly families (vv.23-31).

1 **(13:1-3) Evil Associations, Example of, Returned Exiles—Spiritual Separation, Example of, Returned Exiles—Separation, Spiritual, Returned Exiles—Disobedience, Exposure of, by God's Word—Word of God, Power and Work of, Reveals Sin—Church, Discipline of, Expelling Unbelievers—Jews, Returned Exiles, Reforms of, Expelled Foreigners (Unbelievers) from Worship—Ammonites, Unbelief of, Results—Moabites, Unbelief of, Results**: the first violation of God's Word was that of forming evil associations with foreigners or unbelievers. Interestingly, this violation was discovered one day while the people were worshipping and listening to the Word of God being read aloud. Most likely it was Ezra who was reading the Word of God to the congregation. The passage he read stipulated that no Ammonite or Moabite (no unbeliever) was to be allowed to join the congregation of God's people as they worshipped the LORD. No unbeliever was even to be allowed in the temple where the LORD was worshipped. This prohibition was taken from Deuteronomy:

> **"An Ammonite or Moabite shall not enter into the congregation of the LORD; even to their tenth generation shall they not enter into the congregation of the LORD for ever: Because they met you not with bread and with water in the way, when ye came forth out of Egypt; and because they hired against thee Balaam the son of Beor of Pethor of Mesopotamia, to curse thee. Nevertheless the LORD thy God would not hearken unto Balaam; but the LORD thy God turned the curse into a blessing unto thee, because the LORD thy God loved thee. Thou shalt not seek their peace nor their prosperity all thy days for ever" (De.23:3-6).**

Down through the centuries the Ammonites and Moabites had been bitter enemies of the LORD and His people. These two nations were the descendants of Lot and his two daughters, a result of Lot's drunken, wicked, incestuous behavior (Ge.19:30-38). It had been the Ammonites and Moabites who so bitterly opposed Israel's march to the promised land (Nu.22:1–25:18). These two nations had hired the false prophet Balaam to place a curse on Israel. However, God had turned the curse into a blessing. Nevertheless, these two evil nations continued to press Balaam to devise some scheme that would destroy Israel. Soon thereafter, Balaam came up with a scheme that would have utterly eliminated the Israelites if God had not stepped in to stop the devious plot. Balaam's scheme was for the Moabites to infiltrate Jewish society, forming associations with the people and gradually leading the Israelites to intermarry with their sons and daughters and to participate in their false worship. Using the lust of the flesh, the enemy encouraged the Israelites to join them in seeking financial security through trade, business arrangements, and functions of fellowship and pleasure. When they began to fellowship together, the Moabite women deliberately set out to corrupt the Israelite men by seducing them to have sex. Intermarriage soon began to take place, and the plot to destroy the Israelites as a distinct people was set in motion. As a result, the hand of God's judgment fell upon the Israelites. A plague struck down 24,000 of them (Nu.25:1-8).

In the present situation, when the returnees heard this law read from God's Word, they took immediate corrective action. They made the decision to obey God's law, to spiritually separate themselves from the unbelieving foreigners who had infiltrated the congregation. Identifying the unbelievers, they excluded them from the temple. Unbelieving foreigners were prohibited from joining the congregation of believers in the worship of the LORD. It should be noted that this is not racial prejudice or discrimination. It was an act of spiritual separation due to spiritual, doctrinal conviction. Any foreigner could place his trust in the LORD, become a convert, and begin to follow the LORD. And any foreigner who truly trusted the LORD was allowed to join the Israelites in their worship. This is clear from examples such as Ruth and the foreign converts who had joined the Jewish exiles when they returned to Jerusalem (Ru.1:16-17; Ezr.6:21).

OUTLINE	SCRIPTURE	SCRIPTURE	OUTLINE
1. **Violation 1—Evil associations: A need for spiritual separation** a. The discovery of the violation while reading God's Word: No foreigner (unbeliever) was to be allowed in their worship, De.23:3-6 1) The Ammonites & Moabites had opposed Israel's	On that day they read in the book of Moses in the audience of the people; and therein was found written, that the Ammonite and the Moabite should not come into the congregation of God for ever; 2 Because they met not the children of Israel with	bread and with water, but hired Balaam against them, that he should curse them: howbeit our God turned the curse into a blessing. 3 Now it came to pass, when they had heard the law, that they separated from Israel all the mixed multitude.	march to the promised land, Nu.22:1-25:18 2) The two nations had hired Balaam to curse God's people b. The correction: Spiritual separation—excluded all foreigners (unbelievers) from their assembly

Thought 1. God's Word commands us to be spiritually separated from the wicked of this world. No believer is to compromise with evil, no matter who is committing the wickedness. No young lady should ever compromise her morality with a boyfriend. And no employee should ever compromise his or her honesty by stealing from an employer. None of us should ever dirty our mouths nor the ear of any listener with foul language, in particular by taking the name of God or Christ in vain. We should never violate the truthfulness of our words nor the trust people put in us.

When any person lives a wicked life, we are to separate ourselves from that person, never participating in the sinful behavior. If we develop close friendships and associations with wicked unbelievers, their sinful influence will eventually wear us down. We will then begin to participate in their sinful behavior. Of course, we are not to isolate ourselves, but we are not to form close bonds or alliances with the wicked unbelievers of this world. We are to be friendly, kind, and neighborly to every human being—the wicked and vile as well as the pure and righteous; but we are to be spiritually separated. We are to help and even reach out in understanding and compassion to the wicked of the earth, but we are not to participate in their false worship and sinful behavior. Listen to what God's Holy Word says:

"**And take heed to yourselves, lest at any time your hearts be overcharged with surfeiting, and drunkenness, and cares of this life, and so that day come upon you unawares**" (Lu.21:34).

"**And be not conformed to this world: but be ye transformed by the renewing of your mind, that ye may prove what is that good, and acceptable, and perfect, will of God**" (Ro.12:2).

"**I wrote unto you in an epistle not to company with fornicators: Yet not altogether with the fornicators of this world, or with the covetous, or extortioners, or with idolaters; for then must ye needs go out of the world. But now I have written unto you not to keep company, if any man that is called a brother be a fornicator, or covetous, or an idolater, or a railer, or a drunkard, or an extortioner; with such an one no not to eat**" (1 Co.5:9-11).

"**Be ye not unequally yoked together with unbelievers: for what fellowship hath righteousness with unrighteousness? and what communion hath light with darkness? And what concord hath Christ with Belial? or what part hath he that believeth with an infidel? And what agreement hath the temple of God with idols? for ye are the temple of the living God; as God hath said, I will dwell in them, and walk in them; and I will be their God, and they shall be my people**" (2 Co.6:14-16).

"**Wherefore come out from among them, and be ye separate, saith the Lord, and touch not the unclean thing; and I will receive you, And will be a Father unto you, and ye shall be my sons and daughters, saith the Lord Almighty**" (2 Co.6:17-18).

"**And have no fellowship with the unfruitful works of darkness, but rather reprove them**" (Ep.5:11).

"**Now we command you, brethren, in the name of our Lord Jesus Christ, that ye withdraw yourselves from every brother that walketh disorderly, and not after the tradition which he received of us**" (2 Th.3:6).

"**Thou shalt not follow a multitude to do evil; neither shalt thou speak in a cause to decline after many to wrest judgment**" (Ex.23:2).

"**Take heed to thyself, lest thou make a covenant with the inhabitants of the land whither thou goest, lest it be for a snare in the midst of thee**" (Ex.34:12).

"**Blessed is the man that walketh not in the counsel of the ungodly, nor standeth in the way of sinners, nor sitteth in the seat of the scornful. But his delight is in the law of the LORD; and in his law doth he meditate day and night**" (Ps.1:1-2).

"**My son, if sinners entice thee, consent thou not**" (Pr.1:10).

"**My son, walk not thou in the way with them; refrain thy foot from their path**" (Pr.1:15).

"**Enter not into the path of the wicked, and go not in the way of evil men**" (Pr.4:14).

"**Make no friendship with an angry man; and with a furious man thou shalt not go: Lest thou learn his ways, and get a snare to thy soul**" (Pr.22:24-25).

"**Eat thou not the bread of him that hath an evil eye, neither desire thou his dainty meats: For as he thinketh in his heart, so is he: Eat and drink, saith he to thee; but his heart is not with thee**" (Pr.23:6-7).

"**Be not thou envious against evil men, neither desire to be with them**" (Pr.24:1).

"**Depart ye, depart ye, go ye out from thence, touch no unclean thing; go ye out of the midst of her; be ye clean, that bear the vessels of the LORD**" (Is.52:11).

2 (13:4-9) **Church, Duty, to Purify, Cleanse—House of God, Duty, to Purify, Cleanse—Desecration, of the Church, Example—Purity, Duty, to Cleanse the Church—Cleanse, Duty, to Cleanse the Church—Temple, Desecration of, Example—High Priest, Eliashib, Desecrated the Temple—Tobiah, Evil of, Desecrated the Temple—Nehemiah, Reforms of, the Temple—Temple, Cleansing of, by Nehemiah**: the second violation discovered was that the temple was being desecrated. Unbelievably, the Ammonite Tobiah had been given a large room in the temple to use as he needed. Some commentators even state that he was living in the temple. Sadly, it had been the High Priest Eliashib who had provided this room for Tobiah. Remember, Tobiah had been one of the fiercest opponents of Nehemiah and the Jews who were rebuilding the wall of Jerusalem (2:10, 19; 4:3; 6:10-12, 17-19). By allowing Tobiah to use one of the storage rooms for his own personal use, the High Priest had given this enemy of Nehemiah a foothold in the business and political contacts of the returned Jews. Thus Tobiah, this major enemy, gained more and more influence all because of the compromise of the High Priest. Most likely the High Priest had become entangled in some kind of business contract or payoff by Tobiah. Scripture clearly says they were closely associated, which means they were either related through business dealings or through marriage. Whatever the case, the two men were desecrating, defiling the temple.

In the 32nd year of King Araxerxes' reign, Nehemiah returned to the palace to report to the king (vv.6-7). Just how long Nehemiah was away is not known, perhaps for one or two years. But it was during his absence that the violations of God's Word mentioned in this chapter took place. When Nehemiah returned to the palace, he had been governor of Jerusalem for a period of 12 years (445–433 B.C.). After giving his report to the king, he obviously felt the call of God to return to Jerusalem. He secured permission from Artaxerxes. Immediately after returning, he discovered the abuse of God's house. Deeply distressed, he at once corrected the defilement. He threw all of Tobiah's belongings out of the temple and ordered the rooms to be immediately cleansed and purified. All the temple items that had been removed were to be put back into the storage rooms.

OUTLINE	SCRIPTURE	SCRIPTURE	OUTLINE
2. Violation 2—Desecrating the house of God: A need to purify, cleanse the church a. The violation by the High Priest Eliashib & his close associate Tobiah 1) The priest had converted a large storage room in the temple & made it available for Tobiah to use as needed, 6:17-19; see 2:10, 19; 4:3; 6:10-12 2) The two men were desecrating, defiling the temple b. The discovery of the violation by the governor Nehemiah	4 And before this, Eliashib the priest, having the oversight of the chamber of the house of our God, *was* allied unto Tobiah: 5 And he had prepared for him a great chamber, where aforetime they laid the meat offerings, the frankincense, and the vessels, and the tithes of the corn, the new wine, and the oil, which was commanded *to be given* to the Levites, and the singers, and the porters; and the offerings of the priests. 6 But in all this *time* was not I at Jerusalem: for in the two and thirtieth year of Ar-	taxerxes king of Babylon came I unto the king, and after certain days obtained I leave of the king: 7 And I came to Jerusalem, and understood of the evil that Eliashib did for Tobiah, in preparing him a chamber in the courts of the house of God. 8 And it grieved me sore: therefore I cast forth all the household stuff of Tobiah out of the chamber. 9 Then I commanded, and they cleansed the chambers: and thither brought I again the vessels of the house of God, with the meat offering and the frankincense.	1) He had been absent from Jerusalem, having returned to the palace in the 32nd year of King Artaxerxes' reign 2) He later secured permission to return to Jerusalem & immediately discovered the abuse of God's house c. The correction by Nehemiah 1) He at once threw out all of Tobiah's belongings 2) He ordered the rooms to be cleansed, purified 3) He put back all of the temple items that had been removed: The articles & offerings of grain

Thought 1. Desecrating the house of God is a very serious offense. The house of God is to be sanctified, set apart for the worship and praise of God and for the study of His Holy Word. It is not to be used as a place for worldly functions and behavior, a place...
• where business transactions and dealings, trades, buying or selling are allowed
• where smoking, dancing, drinking alcohol, or taking drugs is allowed
• where divisiveness, bitterness, and hatred are allowed
• where gossip, slander, rumors, profanity, and cursing are allowed
• where suggestive, indecent, immodest, and immoral dress and behavior are allowed

Scripture clearly teaches that the house of God, His Holy Church, is sanctified, set apart as a place to worship and serve Him. God's Holy Spirit lives within both the human body and the local church. Both have been set apart as places where God is to be worshipped and praised and His Holy Word taught.
⇒ God teaches us that the human body is designed to be the very temple of the Holy Spirit, designed to be a temple that glorifies God.

> **"What? know ye not that your body is the temple of the Holy Ghost *which is* in you, which ye have of God, and ye are not your own? For ye are bought with a price: therefore glorify God in your body, and in your spirit, which are God's" (1 Co.6:19-20).**

⇒ God teaches that the church as a whole—the congregation of believers—is the temple of God. When believers gather together in a congregation, they become the very sanctuary in which the Spirit of God dwells. This is taught in the third chapter of First Corinthians, where the word "you" is plural. Scripture is saying that all the

Corinthian believers are the temple and sanctuary of God where God's very own Spirit lives. The stress is upon the presence of God dwelling within the sanctuary, within the shrine proper, which is a picture of the temple. The point is powerful: the Spirit of God dwells within the church—among all the believers of the church, in a very, very special sense—no matter where they meet. The church itself, the body of believers, is the sanctuary of God's presence.

> "Know ye not that ye are the temple of God, and *that* the Spirit of God dwelleth in you? If any man defile the temple of God, him shall God destroy; for the temple of God is holy, which *temple* ye are" (1 Co.3:16-17).

Note the warning of verse 17 above. If any man defiles the temple of God, that man will face the judgment of God's hand and perish. Why? Because the temple of God, the congregation of God's people, is holy.

> "At that day ye shall know that I *am* in my Father, and ye in me, and I in you" (Jn.14:20).
> "And what agreement hath the temple of God with idols? for ye are the temple of the living God; as God hath said, I will dwell in them, and walk in *them;* and I will be their God, and they shall be my people" (2 Co.6:16).
> "And are built upon the foundation of the apostles and prophets, Jesus Christ himself being the chief corner *stone;* In whom all the building fitly framed together groweth unto an holy temple in the Lord: In whom ye also are builded together for an habitation of God through the Spirit" (Ep.2:20-22).
> "But Christ as a son over his own house; whose house are we, if we hold fast the confidence and the rejoicing of the hope firm unto the end" (He.3:6).
> "Ye also, as lively stones, are built up a spiritual house, an holy priesthood, to offer up spiritual sacrifices, acceptable to God by Jesus Christ" (1 Pe.2:5).
> "And he that keepeth his commandments dwelleth in him, and he in him. And hereby we know that he abideth in us, by the Spirit which he hath given us" (1 Jn.3:24).

3 (13:10-14) **God's House, Support of, Failure—Church, Support of, Failure—Neglect, of the Church, Failure to Support—Tithe, Neglect of—Giving, Neglect of—Nehemiah, Reforms**: the third violation was the failure to support God's house. While Nehemiah was having the storerooms ritually cleansed, he apparently discovered that the temple and religious workers were short of funds. The people had stopped tithing and giving to the temple. Earlier, they had made a definite commitment that they would not forsake the house of God, even putting their commitment in writing (9:38; 10:32-39). But during Nehemiah's absence they had broken their commitment and become lax in their support of the temple. As a result, some of the work of the temple was suffering, and the Levites were forced to return to secular work in order to survive (v.10). This was a very serious offense, for the LORD had warned the Israelites never to forsake the support of the Levites:

> "Take heed to thyself that thou forsake not the Levite as long as thou livest upon the earth" (De.12:19).
> "And the Levite that *is* within thy gates; thou shalt not forsake him; for he hath no part nor inheritance with thee" (De.14:27; also see De.18:1-8).

Nehemiah took immediate corrective action (vv.11-14). He did five things:
1) He rebuked the government officials, held them personally accountable for not encouraging the people to support God's house. They had failed to do what they had pledged: "We will not forsake the house of God" (10:39). Consequently, they had broken their covenant or vow to God, a very serious offense.
2) After the rebuke, Nehemiah recalled the forsaken Levites (ministers) back to Jerusalem to reinstate them in their various duties (v.11). Since they had been forced to scatter out over the county to earn a living, this step obviously took some time. The Levites had to make whatever arrangements were necessary to move back to Jerusalem. After returning, they were once again stationed at their posts in the temple and reassigned to their former duties.
3) Nehemiah then challenged the people to renew their tithes and offerings (v.12). Responding favorably, the people began once more to support the temple, bringing their tithes and offerings and generously taking care of God's house. They began to provide an adequate livelihood for the priests and their associates, the Levites.
4) Nehemiah also replaced the custodians of the storeroom (v.13). He even removed the High Priest Eliashib from his supervisory authority over the storerooms and treasury of the temple. Replacing the custodians with trustworthy men, Nehemiah assigned the duty of distribution to the new appointees.
5) Feeling deep disappointment over the corruption he was finding and sensing a deep inadequacy in the task of instituting these reforms, Nehemiah cried out for God's help. He asked the LORD to preserve him and the service of God's house. He wanted God to arouse the people to be faithful in obeying God's Word and His Holy commandments. They desperately needed...
   - to live lives of spiritual separation (vv.1-3)
   - to keep the church pure, never desecrating the House of God (vv.4-9)
   - to be faithful in supporting God's house and the temple staff (vv.10-13)

OUTLINE	SCRIPTURE	SCRIPTURE	OUTLINE

3. Violation 3—neglecting the tithe: A need to support God's house
a. The violation
  1) The people had stopped tithing, 9:38; 10:32-39
  2) The Levites had to return to secular work
b. The fivefold correction by Nehemiah
  1) He rebuked the officials
  2) He restored the Levites to their duties
  3) He challenged the people to renew their tithes & offerings
	10 And I perceived that the portions of the Levites had not been given *them*: for the Levites and the singers, that did the work, were fled every one to his field.
	11 Then contended I with the rulers, and said, Why is the house of God forsaken? And I gathered them together, and set them in their place.
	12 Then brought all Judah the tithe of the corn and the new wine and the oil unto the treasuries.
		13 And I made treasurers over the treasuries, Shelemiah the priest, and Zadok the scribe, and of the Levites, Pedaiah: and next to them *was* Hanan the son of Zaccur, the son of Mattaniah: for they were counted faithful, and their office *was* to distribute unto their brethren.
		14 Remember me, O my God, concerning this, and wipe not out my good deeds that I have done for the house of my God, and for the offices thereof.
			4) He replaced the custodians of the storeroom: This meant removing the High Priest Eliashib from his custodial position as supervisor, 4
			• Appointed trustworthy men
			• Assigned the duty of distribution to new men
			
			5) He prayed for God's help, that God would preserve him & the service of God's house

Thought 1. Neglecting the support of God's house is a terrible offense, a very serious sin. When the church is neglected, the proclamation of God's Word is seriously hindered. People without Christ are not reached. They die in their sins, doomed to spend eternity separated from God—all because the money is not available to send forth laborers. Far too often money is not available to support the gospel, mission work, distribution of the Holy Bible, and other Bible materials. Far too often the means of radio, television, computer, and other forms of media cannot be utilized for the spread of God's Word due to a shortage of funds.

Yet it is not only the spread of the gospel and the support of ministers that are neglected. Meeting the needs of people in general is often neglected. Instead of being compassionate in giving, far too many of us hoard our money and build large bank accounts. Instead of reaching out and giving, we allow people to continue in their pain and suffering, people such as...

• the orphans
• the poverty-stricken
• the single mother who has little income is exhausted as she tries to rear her children
• the lonely widow or widower who lacks enough income to buy desperately needed medicine
• the homeless or mentally ill who have been forsaken
• the hungry who lack money or resources to feed themselves
• the children who are abandoned, ignored, abused, or assaulted
• the uneducated and untrained of this world

Failing to provide for people's needs is a serious offense in the eyes of God. God is deeply offended by our banking and hoarding up money while so many are suffering all around us. Neglecting God's church and its mission to spread the gospel around the world and neglecting to meet the needs of the suffering are serious violations of God's Holy Word. Listen to what God's Holy Word says about tithing and giving generously:

"**Give to him that asketh thee, and from him that would borrow of thee turn not thou away**" (Mt.5:42).

"**Give, and it shall be given unto you; good measure, pressed down, and shaken together, and running over, shall men give into your bosom. For with the same measure that ye mete withal it shall be measured to you again**" (Lu.6:38).

"**Sell that ye have, and give alms; provide yourselves bags which wax not old, a treasure in the heavens that faileth not, where no thief approacheth, neither moth corrupteth**" (Lu.12:33).

"**And he looked up, and saw the rich men casting their gifts into the treasury. And he saw also a certain poor widow casting in thither two mites. And he said, Of a truth I say unto you, that this poor widow hath cast in more than they all: For all these have of their abundance cast in unto the offerings of God: but she of her penury hath cast in all the living that she had**" (Lu.21:1-4).

"**Neither was there any among them that lacked: for as many as were possessors of lands or houses sold them, and brought the prices of the things that were sold, And laid *them* down at the apostles' feet: and distribution was made unto every man according as he had need**" (Ac.4:34-35).

"**Then the disciples, every man according to his ability, determined to send relief unto the brethren which dwelt in Judaea**" (Ac.11:29).

"**I have showed you all things, how that so labouring ye ought to support the weak, and to remember the words of the Lord Jesus, how he said, It is more blessed to give than to receive**" (Ac.20:35).

"**Distributing to the necessity of saints; given to hospitality**" (Ro.12:13).

"**Upon the first *day* of the week let every one of you lay by him in store, as *God* hath prospered him, that there be no gatherings when I come**" (1 Co.16:2).

"How that in a great trial of affliction the abundance of their joy and their deep poverty abounded unto the riches of their liberality" (2 Co.8:2).

"But this *I say,* He which soweth sparingly shall reap also sparingly; and he which soweth bountifully shall reap also bountifully" (2 Co.9:6).

"Every man according as he purposeth in his heart, *so let him give;* not grudgingly, or of necessity: for God loveth a cheerful giver" (2 Co.9:7).

"As we have therefore opportunity, let us do good unto all *men,* especially unto them who are of the household of faith" (Ga.6:10).

"For even in Thessalonica ye sent once and again unto my necessity" (Ph.4:16).

"Every man *shall give* as he is able, according to the blessing of the LORD thy God which he hath given thee" (De.16:17).

"Honour the LORD with thy substance, and with the firstfruits of all thine increase" (Pr.3:9).

"The liberal soul shall be made fat: and he that watereth shall be watered also himself" (Pr.11:25).

"He that hath a bountiful eye shall be blessed; for he giveth of his bread to the poor" (Pr.22:9).

"*Is* not this the fast that I have chosen? to loose the bands of wickedness, to undo the heavy burdens, and to let the oppressed go free, and that ye break every yoke? *Is it* not to deal thy bread to the hungry, and that thou bring the poor that are cast out to thy house? when thou seest the naked, that thou cover him; and that thou hide not thyself from thine own flesh?" (Is.58:6-7).

"And *if* thou draw out thy soul to the hungry, and satisfy the afflicted soul; then shall thy light rise in obscurity, and thy darkness *be* as the noonday" (Is.58:10).

"Bring ye all the tithes into the storehouse, that there may be meat in mine house, and prove me now herewith, saith the LORD of hosts, if I will not open you the windows of heaven, and pour you out a blessing, that *there shall* not *be room* enough *to receive it*" (Mal.3:10).

4 **(13:15-22) Sabbath, Duty, to Honor—Sunday Worship, Duty, to Keep—Worship, Sunday, Duty, to Honor and Keep—Sabbath, Violation of, Example—Sunday Worship, Violation of, Example**: the fourth violation was that of breaking the Sabbath. Many of the people were working on the Sabbath, failing to keep it holy, set apart as a day of rest and worship. Remember the returned exiles had promised to honor the Sabbath, not to do any business on the day of worship among themselves or with businessmen from other nations. No buying or selling whatsoever was to be done on this special day. The people had even written their commitment in a legal, binding document before the LORD (9:38; 10:31). Nevertheless, when Nehemiah returned to Jerusalem, one of the first things he saw was the violation of God's day. Jewish farmers and merchants were bringing their produce and products from the countryside into Jerusalem, obviously buying and selling on the Sabbath. Nehemiah also observed foreigners conducting business within Jerusalem on the holy day. The Sabbath day had become nothing more than any other day to the Jewish people.

Nehemiah immediately took five steps to correct the abuse of the Sabbath (vv.17-22). First, he rebuked everyone involved, including the government officials, merchants and businessmen, and all the people who were involved in buying and selling on the Sabbath. He charged them with perverting the holy day that had been set aside for rest and worship of the LORD (vv.17-18). He warned them that this was the very sin that had caused their captivity. Now that they were free, they were choosing to commit the very same sin (Je.17:21-27). The point was clear and forceful: if they failed to observe the Sabbath, they would again bring the hand of God's judgment upon themselves.

Second, Nehemiah ordered the gates of the city to be closed right before the Sabbath began; they were not to be reopened until the Sabbath was over (v.19). Of course, this act immediately stopped products from being transported in and out of Jerusalem. This would not have solved the problem out in the countryside, but it did within the city of Jerusalem. As long as Nehemiah was around, the Sabbath would be observed by the people.

Third, Nehemiah stationed his own guards at the gates to make sure no merchandise could be brought into the city on the Sabbath (v.19). Apparently the guards had earlier been bribed to begin letting business traffic and products flow in and out of Jerusalem. Eventually, most if not all of the merchants and buying public yielded to the temptation to buy and sell on the Sabbath. As a result, the day had become totally corrupt, and few if any were observing the day of rest and worship. Even after Nehemiah had shut the gates, the merchants camped outside the gates, hoping to tempt the people to come outside to buy and sell their needed products. But Nehemiah issued a stern warning to them: they would be arrested if they continued to camp outside the gates. After his warning, they no longer came on the Sabbath.

Fourth, Nehemiah ordered the Levites to purify themselves ceremonially and to guard the gates in order to keep the Sabbath day holy (v.22). The Levites were to set the example for all the people by encouraging them to obey the command of the governor. Having been appointed by God to live out among the people and to minister to them, the Levites were the logical choice to keep watch over the people, encouraging them to obey God's commandment to keep the Sabbath day holy.

Last, Nehemiah again prayed for God's help in this matter, begging for God's mercy and love (v.22). Correcting so many abuses of the people could have led to a revolt against him. This was especially true when dealing with the specific abuses he was being forced to handle. Correcting the violations cost the merchants a significant sum of money. Imagine having to give up doing business one day out of every seven and losing the income of that day. What effect did this have on the businesses and relationships of the Jews with merchants from other nations? It was bound to have a significant impact that could have easily aroused a revolt against Nehemiah. Because of this possibility, Nehemiah sensed the deep need for God's help. He cried out for God to have mercy on him, to infuse him with His great love.

OUTLINE	SCRIPTURE	SCRIPTURE	OUTLINE
4. Violation 4—Working on the Sabbath: A need to honor the Sabbath & keep it holy a. The violation discovered by Nehemiah, Ex.20:8-11; Ne.10:31 　1) He saw Jews working on the Sabbath throughout Judah & Jerusalem & warned them 　2) He saw foreigners conducting business in Jerusalem on the Sabbath b. The fivefold correction by Nehemiah 　1) He rebuked the nobles 　• Charged them with perverting the Sabbath 　• Warned them: This was the very sin that had caused their captivity—sin that would bring the wrath upon them again, Je.17:21-27 　2) He ordered the gates of the city to be closed for	15 In those days saw I in Judah *some* treading winepresses on the sabbath, and bringing in sheaves, and lading asses; as also wine, grapes, and figs, and all *manner of* burdens, which they brought into Jerusalem on the sabbath day: and I testified *against them* in the day wherein they sold victuals. 16 There dwelt men of Tyre also therein, which brought fish, and all manner of ware, and sold on the sabbath unto the children of Judah, and in Jerusalem. 17 Then I contended with the nobles of Judah, and said unto them, What evil thing *is* this that ye do, and profane the sabbath day? 18 Did not your fathers thus, and did not our God bring all this evil upon us, and upon this city? yet ye bring more wrath upon Israel by profaning the sabbath. 19 And it came to pass, that when the gates of Jerusalem	began to be dark before the sabbath, I commanded that the gates should be shut, and charged that they should not be opened till after the sabbath: and *some* of my servants set I at the gates, *that* there should no burden be brought in on the sabbath day. 20 So the merchants and sellers of all kind of ware lodged without Jerusalem once or twice. 21 Then I testified against them, and said unto them, Why lodge ye about the wall? if ye do *so* again, I will lay hands on you. From that time forth came they no *more* on the sabbath. 22 And I commanded the Levites that they should cleanse themselves, and *that* they should come *and* keep the gates, to sanctify the sabbath day. Remember me, O my God, *concerning* this also, and spare me according to the greatness of thy mercy.	the Sabbath 　3) He stationed his own guards at the gates so no merchandise could be brought into the city on the Sabbath 　• The merchants camped outside the gates once or twice, tempting the people 　• The governor warned the merchants: He would have them arrested 　• The merchants stopped trying to do business on the Sabbath 　4) He ordered the Levites to purify themselves ceremonially & to guard the gates: To keep the Sabbath day holy 　5) He again prayed for God's help in this matter & for God's mercy

Thought 1. Keeping the Sabbath is one of the important commandments of God, so important that God included it in the Ten Commandments. God is the Creator of the universe and of all human life, so He knows the importance of rest and worship. Understanding our bodies perfectly, God knows that we get tired and worn out, both mentally and physically. Working continuously without any break or change of activity tears down the human body and eventually destroys it whereas, when we change activities and rest, we become more efficient and productive in our labor.

Yet resting from work and employment is not the only concern of God. He is also concerned about our worship. He has made the human soul to be restless until it finds its rest in God. Our souls are vacuums, empty of God unless we worship and fellowship with Him. In fact, Scripture says that the human soul is actually dead, lacking life and energy unless it has been regenerated by the Spirit of God (Jn.3:6-7; Ep.4:22-24). For these reasons, God commands that we set aside one day a week for rest and worship. Listen to what God's Holy Word says:

"**Remember the sabbath day, to keep it holy. Six days shalt thou labour, and do all thy work: But the seventh day *is* the sabbath of the LORD thy God: *in it* thou shalt not do any work, thou, nor thy son, nor thy daughter, thy manservant, nor thy maidservant, nor thy cattle, nor thy stranger that *is* within thy gates: For *in* six days the LORD made heaven and earth, the sea, and all that in them *is,* and rested the seventh day: wherefore the LORD blessed the sabbath day, and hallowed it**" (Ex.20:8-11).

"**Six days thou shalt work, but on the seventh day thou shalt rest: in earing time and in harvest thou shalt rest**" (Ex.34:21).

"**And they went into Capernaum; and straightway on the sabbath day he entered into the synagogue, and taught**" (Mk.1:21).

"**And he came to Nazareth, where he had been brought up: and, as his custom was, he went into the synagogue on the sabbath day, and stood up for to read**" (Lu.4:16).

"**But when they [Paul and others] departed from Perga, they came to Antioch in Pisidia, and went into the synagogue on the sabbath day, and sat down**" (Ac.13:14).

"**And on the sabbath we went out of the city by a river side, where prayer was wont to be made; and we sat down, and spake unto the women which resorted *thither***" (Ac.16:13).

"**And Paul, as his manner was, went in unto them, and three sabbath days reasoned with them out of the scriptures**" (Ac.17:2).

"**Not forsaking the assembling of ourselves together, as the manner of some *is;* but exhorting *one another:* and so much the more, as ye see the day approaching. For if we sin wilfully after that we have received the knowledge of the truth, there remaineth no more sacrifice for sins, But a certain fearful looking for of judgment and fiery indignation, which shall devour the adversaries**" (He.10:25-27).

"**Upon the first *day* of the week let every one of you lay by him in store, as *God* hath prospered him, that there be no gatherings when I come**" (1 Co.16:2).

5 (13:23-31) **Families, Godly, Duty, to Build—Marriage, Duty—Marriage, Dangers Confronting, Marrying Unbelievers—Intermarriage, Dangers Confronting, Marrying Unbelievers—Compromise, Duty, Not to Marry Unbelievers—Nehemiah, Reforms of, Correcting Mixed Marriages—Marriage, Mixed, Dangers of**: the fifth violation was compromising and marrying unbelievers. Nehemiah immediately noticed the violation regarding mixed marriage when he returned to Jerusalem. Some Jewish men had married unbelievers, women from three of the surrounding nations: Ashdod, Ammon, and Moab (v.23). Just how widespread this compromise was is not known; perhaps it involved only a few cases.

Even worse, half the children could not speak Hebrew, the very language of God's Word (v.24). This meant these children would not be able to read and understand the Law. Unless the situation could be corrected, the compromise of mixed marriages would only grow. Eventually a whole generation of children would not speak Hebrew, which meant they would be ignorant of God's Word and of the laws that were to govern their nation.

Knowing the seriousness of this state of affairs, Nehemiah took immediate action to stop the damage resulting from this corruption. As governor, it was his duty to execute justice throughout the land. For this reason he made a decision to discipline the offenders. First, Nehemiah summoned all the guilty parties and rebuked them. He called down curses upon them, asking God to execute judgment upon them for their terrible compromise. After expressing his horror at their shocking disobedience, Nehemiah had some of the men disciplined through beatings and by having their hair either pulled out or shaven, which was a sign of disgrace (2 S.10:4; Ezr.9:3; Is.50:6). Apparently this was a form of discipline executed against lawbreakers of that day. Nehemiah then challenged these men to renew their oath to the LORD, their commitment to not compromise with unbelievers through mixed marriages (10:30).

Second, Nehemiah warned them of past history, reminding them of Solomon's sin in marrying unbelievers (v.26; 1 K.11:4-8). Despite Solomon's greatness and God's love for him, the unbelieving women led him into sin and false worship. And because of his compromise and wickedness, Solomon brought destruction upon the nation. Thus Nehemiah warned these offenders: they were repeating the same sins by marrying unbelievers (v.27). The implication was clear: through their mixed marriages, they were a threat to the community of returned exiles. They could bring destruction upon Jerusalem through the hand of God's discipline. They could stop the progress or success of rebuilding Jerusalem that the returnees had begun.

Third, Nehemiah exiled the most prominent offender, the grandson of the High Priest Eliashib. This grandson had married the daughter of Sanballat, the archenemy of Nehemiah (2:10; 4:1–6:14).

Fourth, Nehemiah prayed for God to judge Eliashib and his grandson because they had defiled the priesthood. Judgment was necessary because of the seriousness of the offense. The grandson was a priest who had married an unbeliever, an unholy alliance that was similar to treason. The very purity of the priesthood had been compromised and defiled.

Fifth, Nehemiah held a purification service for the priests and the Levites (vv.30-31). Knowing that the priesthood had been tarnished, he felt that the entire priesthood needed to be cleansed of the defilement. The priests should have stepped forth to boldly rebuke the sin when they first became aware of it. But because they lacked courage and loyalty to God's Word, Nehemiah felt compelled to take four very specific actions:

⇒ he purified the priesthood
⇒ he reassigned the priests, spelling out once again their specific duties and assigning each to his specific task (13:10-13)
⇒ he reestablished the contributions of wood that were to be provided for the temple (10:34)
⇒ he prayed once again for God to remember, favor him with His mercy and love

OUTLINE	SCRIPTURE	SCRIPTURE	OUTLINE
5. Violation 5—Compromising, marrying unbelievers: A need to build godly families a. The violation: Mixed marriages 1) God's people were marrying unbelievers, 10:30; Ezr.9:1-4 2) Sadly, half of the children could not speak Hebrew, the language of God's Word b. The fourfold correction of guilty parties by Nehemiah 1) He rebuked them • Asked God to judge them • Beat some of the men & pulled out their hair, a sign of disgrace, 2 S.10:4; Ezr.9:3; Is.50:6 • Made them renew their oaths, 10:30 2) He warned them with reminders about Israel's history • Reminded them of Solomon's sin in marrying unbelievers: Despite his greatness & God's	23 In those days also saw I Jews *that* had married wives of Ashdod, of Ammon, *and* of Moab: 24 And their children spake half in the speech of Ashdod, and could not speak in the Jews' language, but according to the language of each people. 25 And I contended with them, and cursed them, and smote certain of them, and plucked off their hair, and made them swear by God, *saying,* Ye shall not give your daughters unto their sons, nor take their daughters unto your sons, or for yourselves. 26 Did not Solomon king of Israel sin by these things? yet among many nations was there no king like him, who was beloved of his God, and God made him king over all Israel: nevertheless even him	did outlandish women cause to sin. 27 Shall we then hearken unto you to do all this great evil, to transgress against our God in marrying strange wives? 28 And *one* of the sons of Joiada, the son of Eliashib the high priest, *was* son in law to Sanballat the Horonite: therefore I chased him from me. 29 Remember them, O my God, because they have defiled the priesthood, and the covenant of the priesthood, and of the Levites. 30 Thus cleansed I them from all strangers, and appointed the wards of the priests and the Levites, every one in his business; 31 And for the wood offering, at times appointed, and for the firstfruits. Remember me, O my God, for good.	love for him, the unbelieving women led him into sin • Warned them that they were repeating the same sins by marrying unbelievers 3) He exiled the most prominent offender: The grandson of the High Priest Eliashib who had married the daughter of Sanballat, an enemy, 2:10; 4:1-6:14 4) He prayed for God to judge the grandson & Sanballat: Had defiled the priesthood 5) The conclusion: Nehemiah held a purification service • Purified the priesthood • Reassigned the priests • Reestablished the offerings • Prayed for God to remember, favor him

Thought 1. There is a dire need for godly families, families where both husband and wife have trusted Christ as their Savior and are living righteous lives, obeying God's Holy Word. When a believer marries an unbeliever, the family starts off on the wrong foot. The very beginning of the marriage relationship is built upon mixed beliefs and mixed behavior. A genuine believer follows Christ and His righteousness but an unbeliever does not know Christ or His ways. Hence the very principles and behaviors of a mixed marriage differ. The believer is supposed to be going in one direction, seeking to become a stronger follower of the LORD, while the unbelieving spouse is oftentimes indifferent to spiritual matters, seeking the pleasures and possessions of this world. In a mixed marriage, what usually happens is that the unbeliever eventually corrupts the believer. The believer slowly gives in to a little compromise here and there, and eventually the little compromises add up, with the believer sinking into the worldly lifestyle of his or her spouse. Listen to what God's Holy Word says about the need for believers to marry other believers, never an unbeliever:

> **"I beseech you therefore, brethren, by the mercies of God, that ye present your bodies a living sacrifice, holy, acceptable unto God, *which is* your reasonable service. And be not conformed to this world: but be ye transformed by the renewing of your mind, that ye may prove what *is* that good, and acceptable, and perfect, will of God" (Ro.12:1-2).**
>
> **"I wrote unto you in an epistle not to company with fornicators: Yet not altogether with the fornicators of this world, or with the covetous, or extortioners, or with idolaters; for then must ye needs go out of the world. But now I have written unto you not to keep company, if any man that is called a brother be a fornicator, or covetous, or an idolater, or a railer, or a drunkard, or an extortioner; with such an one no not to eat" (1 Co.5:9-11).**
>
> **"Be ye not unequally yoked together with unbelievers: for what fellowship hath righteousness with unrighteousness? and what communion hath light with darkness? And what concord hath Christ with Belial? or what part hath he that believeth with an infidel? And what agreement hath the temple of God with idols? for ye are the temple of the living God; as God hath said, I will dwell in them, and walk in *them;* and I will be their God, and they shall be my people. Wherefore come out from among them, and be ye separate, saith the Lord, and touch not the unclean *thing;* and I will receive you, And will be a Father unto you, and ye shall be my sons and daughters, saith the Lord Almighty" (2 Co.6:14-18).**
>
> **"When the LORD thy God shall bring thee into the land whither thou goest to possess it, and hath cast out many nations before thee, the Hittites, and the Girgashites, and the Amorites, and the Canaanites, and the Perizzites, and the Hivites, and the Jebusites, seven nations greater and mightier than thou; And when the LORD thy God shall deliver them before thee; thou shalt smite them, *and* utterly destroy them; thou shalt make no covenant with them, nor show mercy unto them: Neither shalt thou make marriages with them; thy daughter thou shalt not give unto his son, nor his daughter shalt thou take unto thy son. For they will turn away thy son from following me, that they may serve other gods: so will the anger of the LORD be kindled against you, and destroy thee suddenly" (De.7:1-4).**
>
> **"Take good heed therefore unto yourselves, that ye love the LORD your God. Else if ye do in any wise go back, and cleave unto the remnant of these nations, *even* these that remain among you, and shall make marriages with them, and go in unto them, and they to you: Know for a certainty that the LORD your God will no more drive out *any of* these nations from before you; but they shall be snares and traps unto you, and scourges in your sides, and thorns in your eyes, until ye perish from off this good land which the LORD your God hath given you" (Jos.23:11-13).**

Thought 2. In closing the great book of *Nehemiah,* several commentators make excellent comments that are well worth quoting:

(1) Mervin Breneman in *The New American Commentary* says this:

> *We can learn many practical lessons in Christian leadership from Nehemiah. Nehemiah reminds us that the tolerance of evil leads to spiritual stagnation, which leads to indifference on doctrinal matters; the final result is moral and spiritual degeneration.*
>
> *In order to have lasting results, reform and revival require constant renewal and constant courage. It takes work to maintain the correct priorities....CERTAINLY Ezra and Nehemiah had a lasting influence on the Jewish community of faith. God did answer Nehemiah's prayer: "Remember me with favor, O my God." The Book of Nehemiah begins with prayer and closes with prayer. For lasting results, ministry can never be separated from prayer.*[1]

(2) Gene A. Getz in *The Bible Knowledge Commentary* says this:

> *This book underscores the importance of physical protection for God's people in Jerusalem but, more importantly, it stresses the need for His people to obey His Word, not giving in to sin through neglect, compromise, or outright disobedience.*[2]

---

[1] Mervin Breneman. *Ezra, Nehemiah, Esther*, pp.275-276.

[2] John F. Walvoord and Roy B. Zuck, Editors. *The Bible Knowledge Commentary, Old Testament*, p.696.

(3) Warren W. Wiersbe says this:

> Nehemiah closes with two prayers (Neh.13:29, 31) that God would remember him for his faithful service. His conscience was clear, for he knew he had done everything for the good of the people and the glory of God. There would probably be little appreciation from the people in spite of his sacrifices; but he knew that God would reward him accordingly. May those who come behind us find us faithful![3]

(4) The *Nelson Study Bible* says this:

> Nehemiah's testimony was that he had done everything he knew how to bring about righteousness in the priesthood and among the Levites, including their offerings and service. Nehemiah's last recorded words (see 5:19), **Remember me, O my God for good,** would serve well as the last words of any person of faith.[4]

(5) Mark Roberts in *The Preacher's Commentary* asks two questions and then gives excellent answers to the questions that are applicable to all of our lives:

> What was Israel's fundamental problem? Why did the reforms of Ezra and Nehemiah fail, at least in part? In Nehemiah 13 we see God's people allowing the world to invade what should be holy, set apart for God alone. They failed to live holy lives with respect to the Temple, the Sabbath, and marriage; Eliashib invited the gentile Tobiah to operate within the Temple; foreign traders tempted the Jews to dishonor the Sabbath; and men of Judah married foreign wives, only to bear children who could not even speak Hebrew. Even though adultery with pagan nations had repeatedly brought national destruction, God's people still abandoned their holy status to join with the world.
>
> We contemporary Christians face similar pressures to compromise our holiness. In our efforts to be accepted by the world we allow nonbiblical values to "live within the church." We want preachers to stop talking about sin because "it is offensive to modern ears." The idea of keeping the Sabbath rarely enters our minds. We fill our lives to the brim, rushing from one thing to another, filling the Lord's day with shopping, chores, and extra hours in the office. Then we wonder why we are so exhausted and "stressed out." Whereas the Bible teaches us to honor marriage and keep the bed "undefiled" (Hebrews 13:4), marital infidelity seems commonplace today, even among Christians—not to mention Christian leaders.
>
> Time and again, Israel allowed the world and its fallen idols to invade her life. In Paul's words, she became "conformed to this world" (Rom. 12:2). Though our offenses differ, we Christians regularly come up short in the same way. Surely we need to hear once again Paul's call to holy living, and to respond in gracious obedience. [5]
>
> > I beseech you therefore, brethren, by the mercies of God, that you present your bodies a living sacrifice, holy, acceptable to God, which is your reasonable service. And do not be conformed to this world, but be transformed by the renewing of your mind, that you may prove what is that good and acceptable and perfect will of God.
> >
> > ROMANS 12:1-2
>
> Notice that true transformation requires more than coerced holiness; it begins with an inner transformation that flows out into tangible acts of faithfulness. Notice also that Paul's request is based on God's mercies, which are revealed through the death of Christ on the cross, in which God establishes a new covenant with his people.

(6) Edwin M. Yamauchi in *The Expositor's Bible Commentary* says this:

> Nehemiah provides us with one of the most vivid patterns of leadership in Scriptures.
> 1. He was a man of responsibility, *as shown by his position as the royal cupbearer.*
> 2. He was a man of vision, *confident of who God was and what he could do through his servants. He was not, however, a visionary but a man that planned and then acted.*
> 3. He was a man of prayer, *who prayed spontaneously and constantly even in the presence of the king (2:4-5).*
> 4. He was a man of action and cooperation, *who realized what had to be done, explained it to others, and enlisted their aid. Nehemiah, a layman, was able to cooperate with his contemporary, Ezra the scribe and priest, in spite of the fact that these two leaders were of entirely different temperaments.*
> 5. He was a man of compassion, *who was moved by the plight of the poorer members of society so that he renounced even the rights he was entitled to (5:18) and denounced the greed of the wealthy (5:8).*
> 6. He was a man who triumphed over opposition. *His opponents tried ridicule (4:3), attempted slander (6:4-7), and spread misleading messages (6:10-14). But through God's favor Nehemiah triumphed over all difficulties.*[6]

---

3 Warren W. Wiersbe. *Be Determined*, p.149.
4 *The Nelson Study Bible, New King James Version.* (Nashville, TN: Thomas Nelson Publishers, Inc., 1997), Nch.13:30, 31.
5 Mark Roberts. *The Preacher's Commentary on Ezra, Nehemiah, Esther.* (Dallas, TX: Word Publishing, 1993), pp.304-305.
6 Edwin Yamauchi. *Ezra, Nehemiah*, pp.767-768.

RESOURCES

NEHEMIAH

TYPES, SYMBOLS, AND PICTURES
THE BOOK OF NEHEMIAH

ALPHABETICAL OUTLINE

What is a biblical type or symbol? Simply put, a *biblical type* is a *foreshadowing* of what was to come at a later time in history. Through a person, place, or thing, a biblical type points toward a New Testament fulfillment.

In addition to biblical types, there are what we may call *biblical pictures*. A biblical picture is a lesson that we can see in the Scriptures *without distorting the truth*. The study of biblical types and pictures is a valuable tool in that it helps us apply the truth of the Scriptures in our lives. Scripture itself tells us this:

> **"Now all these things happened unto them for examples: and they are written for our admonition, upon whom the ends of the world are come" (1 Co.10:11).**

> **"For whatsoever things were written aforetime were written for our learning, that we through patience and comfort of the scriptures might have hope" (Ro.15:4).**

PERSON/PLACE/THING	SCRIPTURE, OUTLINE AND DISCUSSION
EGYPT. *Exodus from*. A symbol of being saved from the world's enslavements.	Ne.9:9
FEAST. *Of booths*. A symbol of God's provision in this temporary, fleeting world.	Ne.8:14-18
HINNOM. *Valley of*. A picture of hell.	Ne.3:14
JERUSALEM. *Gates of*.	
Dung Gate. A reminder that we must cleanse our lives and homes of all garbage and filth.	Ne.3:14
East Gate. Pictures God's glory returning to the temple at the coming again of Jesus Christ.	Ne.3:29
Fish Gate. A reminder of Christ's challenge to bring people into the kingdom.	Ne.3:3
Fountain Gate. A reminder that Jesus Christ is the Living Water of Life.	Ne.3:15
Horse Gate. A reminder that believers must prepare to stand against the evil, wicked forces of this world.	Ne.3:28
Inspection Gate. A picture that every person is to be judged by God.	Ne.3:31
Old Gate. A reminder that believers have a great treasure in old things as well as in new things.	Ne.3:6
Sheep Gate. Reminds us of the sacrificial death of Jesus Christ, the Lamb of God.	Ne.3:1
Valley Gate. Can teach us that we are to walk humbly before others, following the pattern of humility Christ set for us.	Ne.3:13
Can teach us that we will walk through the valley of the shadow of death, but the LORD will be with us. He will personally comfort us as we walk through the final valley on earth. And we will dwell in the house of the LORD, in heaven, forever.	Ne.3:13
Water Gate. A reminder that Christ (His Word is the water of life.	Ne.3:26
JERUSALEM. *Walls of*. *Building of*. *By Hanun and Malchijah*. A picture of humble service within the church.	Ne.3:13-14
By the men of Jericho and Zaccur. A picture of cooperation and unity within the church.	Ne.3:1-12
By the priests and the Levites. A picture of hard and diligent workers filled with zeal in the church.	Ne.3:15-32
Living within. A clear picture of spiritual separation for the believer.	Ne.3:1-32
Represented security, protection from enemies.	Ne.3:1-32
OPPRESSION. *Of the poor and needy. By the wealthy*. A picture of greed, covetousness, and insensitivity.	Ne.5:1
PILLAR. *Of cloud and fire. During the wilderness journeys*. A symbol of God's guidance to heaven.	Ne.9:12
PROMISED LAND. A symbol of spiritual rest.	Ne.9:5-31
A type of heaven.	Ne.7:1-4, Thgt.1; 9:8

Types, Symbols, and Pictures
The Book of Nehemiah
Chronological Outline

What is a biblical type or symbol? Simply put, a *biblical type* is a *foreshadowing* of what was to come at a later time in history. Through a person, place, or thing, a biblical type points toward a New Testament fulfillment.

In addition to biblical types, there are what we may call *biblical pictures*. A biblical picture is a lesson that we can see in the Scriptures *without distorting the truth*. The study of biblical types and pictures is a valuable tool in that it helps us apply the truth of the Scriptures in our lives. Scripture itself tells us this:

"**Now all these things happened unto them for examples: and they are written for our admonition, upon whom the ends of the world are come" (1 Co.10:11).**

"**For whatsoever things were written aforetime were written for our learning, that we through patience and comfort of the scriptures might have hope" (Ro.15:4).**

PERSON/PLACE/THING	SCRIPTURE, OUTLINE AND DISCUSSION
JERUSALEM. *Walls of.* *Living within.* *A clear picture of spiritual separation for the believer.*	Ne.3:1-32
Represented security, protection from enemies.	Ne.3:1-32
Building of. **By the men of Jericho and Zaccur.** *A picture of cooperation and unity within the church.*	Ne.3:1-12
By Hanun and Malchijah. *A picture of humble service within the church.*	Ne.3:13-14
By the priests and the Levites. *A picture of hard and diligent workers filled with zeal in the church.*	Ne.3:15-32
JERUSALEM. *Gates of.* *Sheep Gate. Reminds us of the sacrificial death of Jesus Christ, the Lamb of God.*	Ne.3:1
Fish Gate. A reminder of Christ's challenge to bring people into the kingdom.	Ne.3:3
Old Gate. A reminder that believers have a great treasure in old things as well as in new things.	Ne.3:6
Valley Gate. *Can teach us that we are to walk humbly before others, following the pattern of humility Christ set for us.*	Ne.3:13
Can teach us that we will walk through the valley of the shadow of death, but the LORD will be with us. He will personally comfort us as we walk through the final valley on earth. And we will dwell in the house of the LORD, in heaven, forever.	Ne.3:13
Dung Gate. A reminder that we must cleanse our lives and homes of all garbage and filth.	Ne.3:14
HINNOM. *Valley of. A picture of hell.*	Ne.3:14
JERUSALEM. *Gates of.* *Fountain Gate. A reminder that Jesus Christ is the Living Water of Life.*	Ne.3:15
Water Gate. A reminder that Christ (His Word is the water of life.	Ne.3:26
Horse Gate. A reminder that believers must prepare to stand against the evil, wicked forces of this world.	Ne.3:28
East Gate. Pictures God's glory returning to the temple at the coming again of Jesus Christ.	Ne.3:29
Inspection Gate. A picture that every person is to be judged by God.	Ne.3:31
OPPRESSION. *Of the poor and needy.* **By the wealthy.** *A picture of greed, covetousness, and insensitivity.*	Ne.5:1
PROMISED LAND. *A type of heaven.*	Ne.7:1-4, Thgt.1; 9:8
FEAST. *Of booths. A symbol of God's provision in this temporary, fleeting world.*	Ne.8:14-18
EGYPT. *Exodus from. A symbol of being saved from the world's enslavements.*	Ne.9:9
PILLAR. *Of cloud and fire.* **During the wilderness journeys.** *A symbol of God's guidance to heaven.*	Ne.9:12

INDEX — NEHEMIAH

REMEMBER: When you look up a subject and turn to the Scripture reference, you have not just the Scripture but also an outline and a discussion (commentary) of the Scripture and subject.

This is one of the GREAT FEATURES of *The Preacher's Outline & Sermon Bible*®. Once you have all the volumes, you will have not only what all other Bible indexes give you, that is, a list of all the subjects and their Scripture references, but in addition you will have...

- an outline of every Scripture and subject in the Bible
- a discussion (commentary) on every Scripture and subject
- every subject supported by other Scripture, already written out or cross referenced

DISCOVER THE UNIQUE VALUE for yourself. Quickly glance below to the first subject of the Index. It is:

ACCESS
Into God's presence. Fact. Is by
Christ alone. 2:1-8, Thgt.1

Turn to the first reference. Glance at the Scripture and the outline, then read the commentary. You will immediately see the TREMENDOUS BENEFIT of the INDEX of *The Preacher's Outline & Sermon Bible*®.

OUTLINE AND SUBJECT INDEX

ACCESS
Into God's presence. Fact. Is by
Christ alone. 2:1-8, Thgt.1

ACCUSATION (See **PERSECUTION**)

ADMONISH (See **EXHORTATION**)

AMMONITES
Enemy. Of the Jews. 13:1
Excluded. From the assembly. 13:3
Unbelief of. Result. Were excluded
from the Israelite people. 13:1

ANGER
Cause. Wickedness and oppression.
5:6-13
Example. Nehemiah. Against oppression. 5:6-13

APATHY (See **LAZINESS**)

ARTAXERXES
Commission by. Of Nehemiah. To
rebuild the walls of Jerusalem.
2:1-8
King. Of Persia. 2:1; 5:14; 13:6
Letter by. For Nehemiah. To receive
supplies and safe passage. 2:8-9
Reign of. Dates. 465-423 B.C. 1:1
Request to. By Nehemiah. Reaction.
Was sympathetic. 2:8

ASSOCIATES (See **MINISTERS**,
Associates)

ASSOCIATIONS
Evil.
Example. Some of the Jews had
married unbelieving wives.
13:1-3
Forbidden. By Scripture. 13:1-3,
Thgt.1

With the world.
Caution in. Must avoid wicked-
ness. 13:1-3, Thgt.1
Goal in. To win to Christ. 13:1-3,
Thgt.1

ASSYRIA

ATONEMENT (See **SALVATION**)
Day of. Celebrated. After hearing
Ezra read about it. 8:8-12

ATTACK (See **PERSECUTION**)
Against believers. Reasons for. Dis-
cussed. 4:11-23, Thgt.1
Against the Jews. (See **JEWS**, Op-
position to)
Of Satan (See **SATAN**, Attack of)

ATTITUDE, Positive (See **THINK-
ING**, Positive)

AUTHORITY
Approaching. How to. By asking the
Lord to grant favor. 1:11

BARUCH
Example set by. **B.** excelled in zeal
among the workers rebuilding Jerusalem. 3:20

BELIEF (See **BELIEVER**; **FAITH**;
TRUST)

BELIEVER
Attacks against. By unbelievers.
Motive for. Discussed. 4:11-23,
Thgt.1
Blessings to. (See **GOD**, Blessings by)
Duty.
Fact. Requires much persever-
ance. 6:15-19, Tght.1
To God.
To avoid worldly entangle-
ments. 10:30, Thgt.1

To follow Christ faithfully.
2:9-20, Thgt.1
To honor the Sabbath once a
week. 10:31, Thgt.1
To keep the body holy. 13:4-9,
Thgt.1
To not act cowardly. 6:10-14,
Thgt.1
To obey God's Word. 9:38-
10:29, Thgt.1
To pray often and much. 1:5-
11, Thgt.1
To stay separate from the
wickedness of the world.
10:30, Thgt.1; 13:1-3,
Thgt.1
To take proper care of the
earth. 10:31, Thgt.1
To others.
In family. To remain spiritual-
ly separate. 10:30, Thgt.1
In work. (See **LABORERS**,
Duty)
To be faithful in the tasks as-
signed to us. 12:44-47,
Thgt.1
To give to needs of the world.
13:10-14, Thgt.1
To have concern for their
needs. 1:1-4, Thgt.1
To love. 4:1-23, Intro.; 5:1-19,
Intro.
To the church.
To be in unity. 3:1-12
To give monetary support.
10:32-39, Thgt.1
To serve where needed. 11:1-
12:26, note 7, Thgt.1
To work diligently. 3:15-32;
11:1-12:26, note 4, Thgt.1
To work with humility. 3:13-14
Fact. Is the temple of the Holy Spir-
it. 13:4-9, Thgt.1
Protection of. See **GOD**, Protection
by.

223

Security of. See **GOD**, Protection by.
Testimony of. Must be strong. 2:9-20, Thgt.1

BENEVOLENCE (See **GIVING**)

BIBLE (See **WORD OF GOD**)

BLESSINGS (See **GOD**, Blessings by)

BOLDNESS
Example. Nehemiah was a **b.** leader. 2:1-20
Need for. In leadership. 2:1-20, Intro.
Source. Trust in the Lord. 2:1-8, Thgt.1

CARE (See **COMPASSION**)

CENSUS
Of the Jews. Conducted by Nehemiah. 7:5-73

CHALLENGE (See **EXHORTATION**)

CHARGES (See **PERSECUTION**)

CHRIST (See **JESUS CHRIST**)

CHURCH
Attendance. Required. 10:31, Thgt.1
Duty.
To keep the **c.** holy. 13:4-9, Thgt.1
To purify. 13:4-9, Thgt.1
Fact. Is the temple of the Holy Spirit. 13:4-9, Thgt.1
Needs in. Revival. 13:1-31, Intro.
Support of. Fact. Is the duty of every believer. 10:32-39, Thgt.1; 13:10-14, Thgt.1

COERCION (See **PLOTTING**)

COMMISSION
Example.
By Nehemiah. Of Hanani and Hananiah. To head security for Jerusalem. 7:2-3
Of Nehemiah. By King Artaxerxes. To rebuild Jerusalem. 2:1-8

COMMITMENT
Example.
Nehemiah.
Sought only to serve the LORD. 5:15, 19
Used his position only to help the people. 5:14-19
The Jews.
Made a binding **c.**
To keep their families holy. 10:30
To obey God's Word totally. 9:38-10:29

To observe the holy days. 10:31
To support the house of God. 10:32-39
Were totally **c.** to rebuild Jerusalem. 3:6-32
Who first returned to the Promised Land. 7:6-73
Need for. Discussed. 3:15-32, Thgt.1
To giving. Example. The Jews **c.** to give regularly to the house of God. 10:32-39

COMPASSION (See **LOVE; SALVATION**)
Duty toward. Of the believer. To have deep **c.** for those in need. 1:1-4, Thgt.1
Example. Nehemiah. Used his authority only to help the people. 5:14-19
Need for. In the world. Because there is so much desperate need. 1:1-11, Intro.; 5:14-19, Thgt.1

COMPLACENCY (See **COMMITMENT; DILGENCE; FAITHFULNESS; LAZINESS**)

COMPROMISE
Discussed. By prayer. 6:1-4, Thgt.1
Fact.
A common tactic of the enemy. 6:1-4
Can be good. 6:1-4, Thgt.1
Sin of. Result. Discredits the believer's testimony. 6:1

CONCERN (See **COMPASSION**)

CONFESSION
Of praise and worship. By the Jews. Listed and discussed. 9:5-31
Of sin.
Example. The Jews. **C.** the sins of disobedience by their ancestors. 9:16, 26
Fact. Is essential for revival. 9:1-4, Thgt.1

CONFIDENCE (See **BOLDNESS**)

CONQUERING (See **OVERCOMING**)

CONSPIRACY (See **PLOTTING**)

COOPERATION (See **UNITY**)
Example. Clergy and laymen **c.** to rebuild Jerusalem. 3:1-12
Need for. In any job. 3:1-12, Thgt.1
With unbelievers. Example. Nehemiah **c.** enough to allow the enemy to have a change of heart. 6:1-4

COUNTING (See **CENSUS**)

COURAGE
Duty. Of believers. To serve the Lord with **c.** 2:9-20, Thgt.1
Need for. In our tasks. 2:1-8, Thgt.1
Source. Knowing that the Lord will guide, deliver and protect. 2:1-8, Thgt.1

COVENANT
Of the Jews. After Jerusalem was restored. Showed a total commitment to God. 9:38-10:39

COVETOUSNESS (See **GREED**)

COWARDICE (See **FEAR**)
Duty against. To obey God in all circumstances. 6:10-14, Thgt.1
Examples of. Listed. 6:10-14, Thgt.1

CRITICISM (See **PERSECUTION**)

CUPBEARER
Definition of. Tasted wine to protect the king from poisoning. 1:1-4
Position.
Of Nehemiah. 1:11
Very high in the kingdom. 1:1-4

DEDICATION (See **COMMITMENT; DEVOTION; FAITHFULNESS**)
Of the wall of Jerusalem (See **JERUSALEM**, Wall of, Dedication of)

DEFEAT
Cause. Giving in to ridicule. 4:1-6, Thgt.1

DEPRAVITY (See **EVIL; SIN; WICKEDNESS**)

DESECRATION
Of the church. Seriousness of. Discussed. 13:4-9, Thgt.1
Of the temple. By Eliashib and Tobiah. 13:4-5

DETERMINATION (See **DILIGENCE; FAITHFULNESS; PERSEVERANCE**)

DEVIL (See **SATAN**)

DEVOTION
Definition of. Totally committed and completely loyal. 9:38-10:39, Intro.
Importance of. Stressed through making a covenant of commitment. 9:38-10:39

DILIGENCE (See **FAITHFUL-NESS**; **PERSEVERANCE**)
Example. The Jews worked with great **d.** to rebuild the wall of Jerusalem. 6:15-19
Of the Jews. Fact. Did not stop after the wall was rebuilt. 7:1-4

DISCOURAGEMENT
Answer to. Perseverance. 4:10, Thgt.1
Example. The Jews were **d.** from building because of the heavy work. 4:10

DISOBEDIENCE (See **EVIL**; **OBE-DIENCE**; **SIN**; **WICKEDNESS**)
Confession of. Example. By the Jews for their **d.** history. 9:16, 26
Duty against. Even in the face of danger. 6:10-14, Thgt.1
Exposed. By God's Word. 13:1-3

DISSENSION (See **DIVISION**)

DIVISION
Result. Discussed. 3:1-12, Thgt.1

DUTY, Of the believer. (See **BE-LIEVER**, Duty)

ECBATANA
Capital. Of Persia. In the summer months. 6:2

ECOLOGY
Duty toward. By believers. Discussed. 10:31, Thgt.1

EGYPT
Exodus from. A symbol of being saved from the world's enslavement. 9:9

ELIASHIB
High priest. 13:4-7
Sins of. Desecrated the temple. 13:4-5

EMPLOYEES (See **LABORERS**)

EMPTINESS
Feeling of. Source. Lack of diligent, hard work. 3:1-32, Intro.

ENDURANCE (See **FAITHFUL-NESS**; **PERSEVERANCE**)

ENEMIES
Attacks of.
Example. The **e.** of Nehemiah and the Jews to try to prevent them from rebuilding the wall of Jerusalem. 4:1-6:14
Overcome. Example. Nehemiah withstood all the attacks of the **e.** and rebuilt the wall of Jerusalem. 6:15-7:4

Of believers.
The devil. Will use every possible strategy to attack. 4:1-23, Intro.
Unbelievers. Who do not want anything to do with righteousness. 4:1-23, Intro.
Of the Jews.
Motive. Did not want to lose influence and power. 4:1-23, Intro.
Opposing the rebuilding of Jerusalem. Sanballat, Tobiah, Geshem and the Ashdodites. 2:10, 19-20; 4:7-9; 6:1-19
Response to.
Example. Nehemiah. Overcame by prayer, endurance, being armed and trusting in God's power. 4:1-23
Proper. To love. 4:1-23, Intro.
Spiritual. Tactics of. Gossip. 6:5-9

EVANGELISM (See **WITNESSING**)

EVIL (See **SIN**; **WICKEDNESS**; **WORLDLINESS**)

EXHAUSTION
Example. The Jews were **e.** from building because of the heavy work. 4:10

EXHORTATION
Duty. Of ministers. 2:9-20, Thgt.1
Example. Nehemiah. **E.** the others to take up the work of rebuilding. 2:17-18
Need for. In leadership. 2:1-20, Intro.

EXILES (See **JEWS**)

EXODUS
From Egypt. A symbol of being saved from the world's enslavement. 9:9

EZRA
Acts of.
Stirred revival. 8:6, 12, 15-17
Taught God's Word. 8:2-8
Priest. 8:2
Scribe. 8:1
Teaching of. Facts about. 8:9-12

FAITH
Inspiration for. By the pioneers who went before us. 7:5-73, Thgt.1
Pioneers of.
Example. Returned exiles who first returned from captivity under Zerubbabel. Listed. 7:6-73
Fact. Are a dynamic example for us to follow. 7:5-73, Thgt.1
Required. To receive salvation and God's blessings. 7:5-73, Thgt.1

FAITHFULNESS (See **DILI-GENCE**; **PERSEVERANCE**)
Need for. By everyone. 12:44-47, Thgt.1
Of God. (See **GOD**, Faithfulness of)
Required. For every believer. 2:9-20, Thgt.1; 12:44-47, Thgt.1

FAMILY
Commitment to. Example. The Jews made a total commitment to keep their **f.** holy. 10:30
Duty toward. To keep spiritually separate from the world. 10:30; 13:23-31, Thgt.1

FATIGUE (See **EXHAUSTION**)

FEAR (See **COURAGE**)
Acts of. Duty against. To obey even in **f.** situations. 6:10-14
Answer to. Arm ourselves and trust God's power. 4:11-23, Thgt.1
Cause. Intimidation by enemies. 4:11-23

FEASTS
Celebrated. After hearing Ezra read about them. 8:9-12
Listed. 8:2-3
Of booths.
Celebration of. After hearing Ezra read about it. 8:13-18
Symbol of God's provision. 8:14-18

FESTIVAL (See **FEASTS**)

FORGIVENESS (See **SALVATION**)

FOUNDATION
Of life. Fact. Should be based on the Word of God. 8:1-18, Intro.
Of society. Fact. Should be based on obeying God's Word. 8:1-18, Intro.

FULFILLMENT
Feeling of. Source. Diligence. 3:1-32, Intro.

GASHMU (See **GESHEM**)

GATES (See **JERUSALEM**, Gates of)

GESHEM
Arab. 2:19; 6:1
Enemy.
Of Nehemiah. 6:1-14
Of the Jews. 2:19; 6:1-2
Opposition by. Tried to stop the rebuilding of Jerusalem. 2:19; 6:1-2

GIVING
Duty toward. By every believer. To support the house of God. 10:32-39, Thgt.1; 13:10-14, Thgt.1
Of the Jews. To support the temple. Offerings. Listed and explained. 10:32-39

GOD

Blessings by. Requirement for. Believing and trusting in Him. 7:5-73, Thgt.1

Faithfulness of. God. always keeps His promises. 9:32-37, Thgt.1

Favor of. Example. Toward Nehemiah so that the king would be sympathetic toward him. 2:1-8

Guidance by. Pictured by the pillar of cloud and fire during the wilderness journeys. 9:12

Judgment by.
Cause. Wickedness. 5:6-13, Thgt.1
Escape from. Way to. Repentance of sin. 5:6-13, Thgt.1
Fact. Does not strike the rich only. 5:6-13, Thgt.1

Mercy of. (See **MERCY**, Of God)
Plead for. Example. By the Jews. 9:32-37
Seeking. Importance of. For the Jews. To rebuild. 9:1-37, Intro.

Presence of. Access to. Fact. Is by Christ alone. 2:1-8, Thgt.1

Promises of. To guide, deliver and protect the believer. 2:1-8, Thgt.1

Protection by.
Need for. To stand against temptations and trials. 7:1-4, Thgt.1
Picture of. 3:1-32, DS #1
Promise of. 2:1-8, Thgt.1

Sovereignty of. Example. God. moved on the heart of King Artaxerxes to help with the rebuilding of Jerusalem. 2:1-8

Trust in. Result. A spirit of boldness to carry out our tasks. 2:1-8, Thgt.1

GODLINESS

In families. Need for. 13:23-31, Thgt.1

In leadership.
Example. Nehemiah. 1:1-11, Intro.; 2:1-20; 5:14-19; 13:1-31
Need for. 2:1-20, Intro.; 11:1-12:26, note 2, Thgt.1

GOODNESS

Definition. Discussed. 9:1-37, Intro.
Of God. Seeking. Importance of. For the Jews. To rebuild. 9:1-37, Intro.
Works of. Described. 9:1-37, Intro.

GOSPEL (See **WITNESSING**)

GOSSIP

Answer to. Explained. 6:5-9, Thgt.1

Example. By enemies of the Jews. About an attack to cause fear. 4:11-12
That the Jews were trying to rebel against Persia. To discredit Nehemiah. 6:5-9

Fact. Is the tool of the devil. 4:11-23, Thgt.1

Guarding against. How to. By being a person of integrity in the first place. 6:5-9, Thgt.1

Motives for. Listed. 4:11-23, Thgt.1

Results. Discussed. 6:5-9, Thgt.1

Sin of. Fact. Is one of the most terrible evils that can be committed. 6:5-9, Thgt.1

GOVERNMENT (See **LEADERSHIP**)

Burden of.
To provide housing and jobs. 11:1-12:26
To provide justice. 11:1-12:26, note 2, Thgt.1

Desires for. By the people. Discussed. 11:1-12:47, Intro.

Needs of.
Discussed. 11:1-12:47, Intro.
Godly leaders. 11:1-12:26, note 2, Thgt.1

GREED

Example. The rich Jews charged interest of the poor. 5:1-5

Pictured. By the oppression of the poor by the wealthy. 5:1

GUIDANCE (See **GOD**, Guidance by)

HALFHEARTEDNESS (See **COMMITMENT**)

Result. A sense of emptiness and no purpose in life. 3:1-32, Intro.

HANANI

Brother. Of Nehemiah. 1:2; 7:2

Commission of. Put over security for half of Jerusalem. 7:2-3

HANANIAH

Character of.
Faithful. 7:2
Feared God greatly. 7:2

Commission of. Put over security for half of Jerusalem. 7:2-3

HARDNESS OF HEART (See **HEART**, Hard)

HARDSHIP (See **PERSECUTION**; **SUFFERING**; **TRIALS**)

HEART

Hard.
Example. The wealthy who oppressed their Jewish brothers. 5:2-4
Problem of. Discussed. 5:1-5, Thgt.1
Result.
All kinds of evil. 5:1-5, Thgt.1
Ruins the economy. 5:1-5, Thgt.1

Tender. Example. Nehemiah. 1:4

HEAVEN

Fact. Is a place of spiritual rest. 9:5-31

Type of. The Promised Land. 7:1-4, Thgt.1; 9:8

HELL

Pictured. By the Valley of Hinnom. 3:14

HINNOM

Valley of. A picture of hell. 3:14

HOLINESS (See **GODLINESS**)

HONOR (See **WORSHIP**)

HOPE (See **TRUST**)

HOUSE OF GOD (See **CHURCH**; **TEMPLE**)

HUMANITY (See **SOCIETY**; **WORLD**)

Desires of. In government. Discussed. 11:1-12:47, Intro.

HUMILITY

Duty. To work with **h**. 3:13-14

Example. Nehemiah. **H**. prayed, confessing his sins. 1:7

INSENSITIVITY (See **HEART**, Hard)

INSTRUMENTS (See **MUSIC**)

INSULT (See **RIDICULE**)

INTERMARRIAGE (See **MARRIAGE**, Of unbelievers)

By the Jews. Of other nations. Reasons forbidden. 10:30; 13:23-25

INTIMIDATION

Answer to. Arming oneself and prayer. 4:11-23, Thgt.1

Example. The enemies of the Jews used **i**. to try to stop the work. 4:11-13

ISRAEL (See **JEWS**)

JERUSALEM

Concern for. By Nehemiah. Because of the distressful situation. 1:1-4

Condition of. Reported to Nehemiah. Was distressful. 1:1-4

Gates of.
Rebuilt. Section by section with great zeal. 3:1-32
Listed and explained. 3:1-32, DS #2

Leadership of. Organized by Nehemiah. 7:1-4

Overseers. Once the wall was complete. Joel and Judah. 11:9

Rebuilding of.
   Commission for. To Nehemiah.
      By King Artaxerxes. 2:8
   Needs.
      Cooperation. 3:1-12
      Diligence. 3:15-32
      Humble workers. 3:13-14
      Population and housing. 11:1-2
   Projects of. By Nehemiah. Re-
      building the gates, the walls
      and his own residence. 2:8
   Request concerning.
      Building materials. 2:8
      Military protection. 2:7
   Sections of. Listed. 3:1-32
Resettling of.
   Circumstances of. 11:1-12:26
   Important facts about. Listed and
      explained. 11:20-24
Security of. Organization for. Once
   the wall was rebuilt. 7:1-4
Wall of. (See also, Rebuilding of,
   Above)
   Completion of. Despite all at-
      tacks of the enemy. 6:15-7:4
   Dedication of. Ceremony. A
      very joyous celebration.
      12:27-43
   Rebuilt.
      Time. In 52 days. 6:15
      Under Nehemiah's leadership.
      1:1-7:73
   Symbolism of. Explained. 3:1-
      32, DS #1

JESUS CHRIST
Fact.
   Is the answer to the world's
      problems. 5:1-19, Intro.
   Is the only way into God's pres-
      ence. 2:1-8, Thgt.1
Followers of. (See **BELIEVERS**)
Following.
   Fact. Is the duty of every be-
      liever. 2:9-20, Thgt.1
   Result. Persecution by the world.
      4:1-6, Thgt.1
Intercession by.
   Function of. 1:5-11, Thgt.1
   Illustrated by Nehemiah's
      prayers. 1:4-11
Names-Titles.
   Advocate. 1:5-11, Thgt.1
   Intercessor. 1:5-11, Thgt.1
   Representative. 1:5-11, Thgt.1

JEWS (Returned from exile)
Census of. By Nehemiah. 7:5-73
Cities of. Resettled in. Listed.
   11:25-36
Completion by. Of the wall of Jeru-
   salem. Despite all the attacks of
   the enemy. 6:15-7:4
Condition of. In Jerusalem.
   Defenseless. 1:3
   Description of. In detail. 1:1-4
   In great economic difficulty. 5:1-3
   Reported to Nehemiah in Susa.
      In great despair. 1:1-4

Reproached and disgraced. 1:2-3
Confession of. For their history of
   disobedience. 9:16, 26
Descendants. Recorded. 11:3-9
Enemies of. (See also **ENEMIES**,
   Of the Jews)
   Ammonites. 13:1
   Geshem. The Arab. 2:19
   Moabites. 13:1
   Sanballat. The Horonite. 2:10,
      19-20
   Tobiah. The Ammonite. 2:10,
      19-20
Exhorted. By Nehemiah. To rebuild
   Jerusalem. 2:17-18
Feasts of. (See **FEASTS**)
   Celebrated. After hearing Ezra
      read about them. 8:9-12
   Listed. 8:2-3
Heads of. Of Benjamin. Overseeing
   Jerusalem. Joel and Judah. 11:9
Important facts about. Listed and
   explained. 11:20-24
Opposition to.
   Overcoming. How they did.
      Being armed and trusting in
         God's power. 4:11-23
      Endurance. 4:10
      Prayer and perseverance. 4:1-6
      Standing watch and praying.
         4:7-9
   Purpose. To stop the rebuilding
      of Jerusalem. 4:1-23, Intro.
   Source.
      Foreign. (See Enemies of,
         above)
      From within. Some Judeans
         workers were secretly co-
         operating with the opposi-
         tion. 4:10
   Strategies of.
      Conspiracy. 4:7-9
      Discouragement. 4:10
      Ridicule. 4:1-6
      Threats. 4:11-23
Persecution of. By ridicule of their
   work. 4:1-6
Reforms by. (See **NEHEMIAH**,
   Reforms by)
Returned
   With Nehemiah. 3:1-32
   With Zerubbabel. 7:6-73
Revival of. Led by Nehemiah and
   Ezra. 8:6, 12, 15-17
Sins of.
   Breaking the Sabbath. 13:15-22
   Desecrating the house of God.
      13:4-9
   Evil Associations. 13:1-3
   Greed. 5:1-5
   Marriage with unbelievers.
      13:23-31
   Neglecting the tithe. 13:10-14
Songs of. Listed and discussed. 9:5-31
Worship by.
   For God's great delivering
      power. 9:9-31
   Listed and described. 9:5-38

Of God. For His greatness. 9:5-
   8, 32-38

JOBS (See **LABORERS**; **WORK**)

JOY
Example. The Jews were filled with
   j. at the dedication of the wall of
   Jerusalem. 12:27-43
Need for. To be positive and victo-
   rious. 12:27-43, Thgt.1

JUDAH (The Southern Kingdom)
(See **JEWS**)

JUDGMENT
Certainty of. Against wickedness.
   5:6-13, Thgt.1
Of God. (See **GOD**, Judgment of)

JUSTICE (See **JUDGMENT**)

KILLING (See **MURDER**)

KINDNESS (See **MERCY**; **SALVA-
TION**)

LABORERS (See **COMMITMENT**;
DILIGENCE; **LAZINESS**;
ZEAL)
Diligent. Pictured. By the l. on the
   east wall of Jerusalem.
Duty.
   To cooperate. 3:1-12, Thgt.1
   To work hard. 3:15-32, Thgt.1
   To work humbly. 3:13-14,
      Thgt.1
Example. The Jews who l. to re-
   build the walls of Jerusalem.
Humility of. Pictured. By the l. on
   the west wall of Jerusalem. 3:13-14
Need for. Example. Nehemiah
   needed a diligent, hard l. to
   complete the wall of Jerusalem.
   3:1-32
Rebuilding Jerusalem. Were a dy-
   namic example to all workers.
   3:15-32, Thgt.1
Sins of. Refusing to work. 3:5
Unity of. Pictured. By the l. on the
   north wall of Jerusalem. 3:1-12

LAW (See **WORD OF GOD**)
Reading of. By Ezra. Caused a
   great revival. 8:1-36
Violations of. By the Jews. Discov-
   ered by Nehemiah.
   Breaking the Sabbath. 13:15-22
   Desecrating the house of God.
      13:4-9
   Evil Associations. 13:1-3
   Marriage with unbelievers.
      13:23-31
   Neglecting the tithe. 13:10-14

LAZINESS
Answer to. Exhorting people to follow Christ. 2:9-20, Thgt.1

Example. The nobles would not
help rebuild Jerusalem. 3:5
Problem of. Discussed. 2:9-20,
Thgt.1; 3:15-32, Thgt.1

LEADERSHIP
Boldness in. Need for. But must be
tempered with righteousness.
2:1-20, Intro.
Civil. (See **GOVERNMENT**)
Compassionate. Example. Nehe-
miah. Used his authority only to
help the people. 5:14-19
Duty.
To dispense justice. 11:1-12:26,
note 2, Thgt.1
To provide means of housing.
11:1-9
To serve the people. 11:1-12:26,
note 5, Thgt.1
Needs in.
Boldness, righteousness, vision
and exhortation. 2:1-20, Intro.
Godly l. 11:1-12:26, note 2,
Thgt.1
Nehemiah. (See **NEHEMIAH**,
Leadership)
Obedience to. Example. The Jews
followed the spiritual l. of Ezra
and Nehemiah. 8:1-13:31
Of Jerusalem. Organized by Nehe-
miah. 7:1-4
Unselfishness in.
Example. Nehemiah. Only used
his authority to help the peo-
ple. 5:14-19
Need for. 5:14-19, Thgt.1

LETHARGY (See **LAZINESS**)

LEVITES
Duties. In the temple.
To know the Law. 8:7-13
To lead the worship. 9:5; 11: 22-
23; 12:27-30, 44-47; 13:22
Head of. Uzzi. 11:22
Listed. 7:43; 9:5; 10:9-27; 11:15-
18; 12:9-26
Music of. Choirs. 12:31-40
Purification of.
By Nehemiah. By removing evil
practices. 13:22, 30
At the dedication of the wall of
Jerusalem. 12:30, 45
Support for.
Described. 10:34-39; 13:5, 30-31
Neglected. Discovered by Ne-
hemiah. 13:10

LIES (See **GOSSIP**)

LIFE
Foundation of. Fact. Should be
based on the Word of God. 8:1-
18, Intro.
Purpose in. Feeling of. Source.
Hard work. 3:1-32, Intro.

LOST
How to win. By showing God's
love. 5:1-19, Intro.

LOVE (See **COMPASSION**)
Duty to. Regardless of how others
act. 4:1-23, Intro.
Need for. In the world. Discussed.
4:1-23, Intro.; 5:1-19, Intro.
True. Definition. L. everyone in
the name of Jesus Christ. 4:1-23,
Intro.

MARRIAGE
By the Jews. With other nations.
Reasons forbidden. Causes idola-
try and wickedness. 10:30;
13:23-25
Of unbelievers.
Consequences. Discussed. 13:23-
31, Thgt.1
Problem of. Discussed. 10:30,
Thgt.1; 13:23-31, Thgt.1

MERCY (See **SALVATION**)
Need for. By the Jews. Because of
their desperate situation. 9:32-37
Of God.
Fact. Is very great. 9:32-37,
Thgt.1
Plead for. Example. By the
Jews. 9:32-37
Seeking. Importance of. For the
Jews. To rebuild. 9:1-37, Intro.

MINISTERS
Associates. Need for. To keep
things running smoothly. 11:1-
12:26, note 4, Thgt.1
Duty. To be devoted to the house of
God. 11:10-14
Support of. Should be from the giving to the church treasury.
10:32-39, Thgt.1

MOABITES
Enemy. Of the Jews. 13:1
Excluded. From the assembly. 13:3
Unbelief of. Result. Were excluded
from the Israelite people. 13:1

MOCKERY (See **RIDICULE**)

MOTIVATE (See **EXHORTATION**)

MURDER
Plot to. Example. Against Nehemiah. 6:1-4

MUSIC
Example.
By the priests. With trumpets.
12:35
Of choirs. Nehemiah appointed
two choirs to sing at the dedication of the wall of Jerusalem. 12:31-43
Purpose of. To lead the people to
worship. 12:42-43

NEEDS
Of the world. (See **WORLD**,
Needs of)
Specific. Can be prayed for. 1:11

NEGATIVE THINKING (See
THINKING, Negative)

NEHEMIAH
Acts of. Stirred revival. 8:6, 12,
15-17
Attack. By the enemy. Response.
Explained. 2:19-20
Character.
Bold leader. 2:1-20
Compassionate. 5:14-19
Man of deep concern and prayer.
1:1-11, Intro.
Righteous. 2:1-20, Intro.
Commission.
By. Of Hanani and Hananiah to
head security for Jerusalem.
7:2-3
To. By King Artaxerxes. To re-
build Jerusalem. 2:1-8
Devotion of. Only sought to please
the Lord. 5:15, 19
Enemies of. Sanballat, Geshem, To-
biah, Shemaiah, Nodaiah. 6:1-14
Heart of. Was tender. 1:4-11
Inspection by. Of the walls of Jeru-
salem. Wisely done in secret at
night. 2:12-16
Journey of. To Jerusalem. To pre-
pare to rebuild. 2:9-20
Leadership of.
Built through discipline. 13:1-31
Did not give in. 13:1-3
Needs of. Hard workers. 3:1-32
Strong example. Only used his
authority to help the people.
5:14-19
Opposition to. 2:10, 19-20; 6:1-14
Perseverance of. N. persevered
through all attacks to complete
the rebuilding of the wall of Je-
rusalem. 6:17-19
Plots against. Personal. By the ene-
mies of the Jews. 6:1-14
Prayer of. Illustrated Christ's inter-
cession. 1:4-11
Preparations of. To rebuild Jerusa-
lem. Knew exactly what he
needed before he petitioned the
king. 2:9-20
Rebuke by. Of the wealthy. For
oppressing the needy. 5:6-13
Reforms by.
Against corruption. 13:25-31
Cleansed the temple. 13:8-9
Forbid intermarriage with unbelievers. 13:25-28
Ordered the Sabbath to be kept.
13:19, 21
Restored the tithe. 13:11-13
Unbelieving foreigners were excluded from the community.
13:3

Report to. Concerning Jerusalem.
Reaction.
    Broke his heart. 1:4
    Fasted and prayed for many
    days. 1:5-11
    Was very bad news. 1:1-4
Service of. Cupbearer in the palace
of King Artaxerxes of Persia.
1:11-2:1
Son. Of Hacaliah. 1:1
Strategy of. To counter the enemy.
Explained. 4:13-23; 6:8-9
Struggle of.
    Against external opposition. 4:1-23
    Against personal plots. 6:1-14
Testimony of. Was strong. 2:8
Trust of. In God. Prayed before
acting. 2:4
Wisdom of. Evidenced in his han-
dling of the personal plots
against him. 6:1-14
Works of.
    Brought spiritual reform. 8:1-
    9:38; 13:1-31
    Organized security for Jerusa-
    lem. 7:1-4
    Rebuilt the wall of Jerusalem.
    2:17-6:15
    Served as governor of the Jews.
    1:9-13:31

NOADIAH
Evil of. Tried to frighten Nehemiah
into giving up his work on the
wall of Jerusalem. 6:14
False prophet. 6:14

NUMBERING (See **CENSUS**)

OBEDIENCE (See **COMMIT-
MENT; DEVOTION; FAITH-
FULNESS**)
Of God's Word.
    Benefits. Discussed. 9:38-10:29,
    Thgt.1
    Example. The Jews made a total
    commitment to o. God's
    Word. 9:38-10:29
    Need for. Discussed. 8:13-18,
    Thgt.1
Of leadership. (See **LEADER-
SHIP**, Obedience to)

OFFERING (See **GIVING; SACRI-
FICE**)

OFFICIALS (See **GOVERNMENT;
LEADERSHIP**)

OPPOSITION (See **PERSECU-
TION**)
Of the Jews (See **JEWS**, Opposi-
tion to)

OPPRESSION
Anger against. Example. Nehe-
miah. 5:6-13
Answer to.
    A call to fear God. 5:8
    A call to repentance. 5:11

Example. By the wealthy Jews. Of
the poor. 5:2-4
Of the poor. By the wealthy. A picture of greed, covetousness and
insensitivity. 5:1
Sin of. Is based in greed. 5:1-5

OVERCOMING
Example.
    Jews. **O**. much opposition to
    complete the wall of Jerusa-
    lem. 6:15-7:4
    Nehemiah. **O**. the enemy by
    praying and not giving up.
    4:1-23
Fact. Is a constant struggle as long
as we are on this earth. 7:1-4,
Thgt.1
How to.
    Being armed and trusting in
    God's power. 4:11-23
    By God's protection. 7:1-4,
    Thgt.1
    Endurance. 4:10
    Prayer and perseverance. 4:1-6
    Standing watch and praying. 4:7-9
    Vigilance. 6:15-7:73, Intro.
Ridicule. How to. By persevering
and by prayer. 4:1-6, Thgt.1
Source of strength. The power of
the Lord. 4:14-23

PAIN (See **SUFFERING**)

PEER PRESSURE (See **RIDICULE**,
Giving in to)

PEOPLE (See **HUMANITY; SOCI-
ETY; WORLD**)

PERSECUTION
Example. By the enemies of the
Jews. To try to prevent the re-
building of Jerusalem. 2:10, 19-
20; 6:1-19
Responses to. By Nehemiah (See
JEWS, Opposition to, Over-
coming)

PERSEVERANCE
Answer.
    To discouragement. 4:10, Thgt.1
    To ridicule. 4:1-6
Duty in. To complete one's task.
6:15-19, Tght.1
Example. The Jews continued to
rebuild Jerusalem in the face of
much ridicule and persecution.
4:1-23; 6:15-7:4

PERSIA
Capital of.
    Ecbatana. In the summer. 6:2
    Susa. In the winter. 1:1
King of. Artaxerxes. 2:1; 5:14;
13:6

PERSISTANCE (See **COMMIT-
MENT; DILIGENCE; FAITH-
FULNESS; PERSEVERANCE**)

PETITION (See **PRAYER**)
Example. Nehemiah. Of King Artaxerxes. For help to rebuild Jerusalem. 2:5-7

PILLAR
Of cloud and fire. During the wil-
derness journeys. A symbol of
God's guidance to heaven. 9:12

PIONEERS
Example by. Inspires us to follow
the Lord. 7:5-73, Thgt.1
Of faith. Example. The Jews who
first returned to the Promised
Land. 7:6-73

PLOTTING
Example. Against Nehemiah. By
the enemies of the Jews. 6:1-14

POOR
Oppression of. By the wealthy. A
picture of greed, covetousness
and insensitivity. 5:1

POSITIVE ATTITUDE (See
THINKING, Positive)

POSITIVE THINKING (See
THINKING, Positive)

PRAISE (See **WORSHIP**)

PRAYER
Answer. To ridicule. 4:1-6
Example. By Nehemiah. Seeking
God on behalf of the Jews in Je-
rusalem. 1:5-11
How to.
    Asking for specific needs. 1:11
    Confessing sins. 1:6-7
    Pleading for mercy. 1:8-11
    Worshiping God. 1:5
Imprecatory.
    Definition. 4:4-6
    Interpreting. How to. 4:4-6
In the Book of Nehemiah. Mostly
by Nehemiah himself. 1:5-11;
2:4; 4:4-5, 9; 5:19; 6:9, 14; 9:5-
37; 13:14, 22, 29, 31
Intercessory.
    Example. Nehemiah. On behalf
    of the Jews. 1:5-11
    Function. Of Christ. 1:5-11,
    Thgt.1
Power of.
    Delivers from trouble. 9:32-37
    Enables us to conquer trials. 4:1-
    6, Thgt.1
Time to. Often and much. 1:5-11,
Thgt.1
What to pray for. Mercy. 9:32-37

PREPARATION
Example. Nehemiah.
  P. carefully before rebuilding Jerusalem. 2:9-20
  Took four months to **p.** to make request to the king. 1:1; 2:1

PRESENCE OF GOD (See **GOD**, Presence of.)

PRIDE
Example. Some of the Jews had too much **p.** to work on the wall of Jerusalem. 3:5

PRIESTS
Head. Eliashib. 13:4-7
Lists of. 10:1-8; 11:10-14; 12:1-7, 12-21, 41-44
Musicians. 12:35
Purification of. At the dedication of the wall of Jerusalem. 12:30, 45
Shemaiah. Enemy of Nehemiah. 6:10-14
Sons of Jedaiah. 7:39
Sons of Hobaiah. 7:63
Support of. Example. 10:32-39

PROMISED LAND
Commitment to. By the returned exiles. They were true pioneers of faith. 7:6-73
Symbol. Of spiritual rest. 9:5-31
Type. Of heaven. 7:1-4, Thgt.1; 9:8

PROMISES, Of God (See **GOD**, Promises of)

PROPHETS
False.
  Noadiah. Tried to frighten Nehemiah into giving up his work on the wall of Jerusalem. 6:14
  Shemaiah. Hired by Sanballat to bring an evil report about Nehemiah. 6:12-13
  Unnamed. Who tried to stop Nehemiah from rebuilding the wall of Jerusalem. 6:14
True. Message of. Ignored.
  By the Jews before the exile. 9:26-33
  Repentance concerning. By the Jews after the exile. 9:33-38

PROTECTION
By God. (See **GOD**, Protection by)
Of Jerusalem. Organization for. Once the wall was rebuilt. 7:1-4
Pictured. By the walls of Jerusalem. 3:1-32, DS#1
Securing. Example. The Jews posted guards to **p.** Jerusalem. 7:1-4

PURIFICATION
Of the Levites.
  At the dedication of the wall of Jerusalem. 12:30, 45
  By Nehemiah. By removing evil practices. 13:22, 30
Of the priests. At the dedication of the wall of Jerusalem. 12:30, 45

PURPOSE
Feeling of. Source. Diligence. 3:1-32, Intro.

QUICKENING (See **EXHORTATION**)

REBELLION (See **DISOBEDIENCE; SIN; WICKEDNESS**)

REBUILDING
Of Israel. By the Jews. How.
  Through a revived spirit. 9:1-37
  Through discipline. 13:1-31
  Through God's Word. 8:1-18
  Through making a covenant of commitment. 9:38-10:39
  Through strengthening. 11:1-12:47
Of Jerusalem (See **JERUSALEM**, Rebuilding of)

REBUKE
Example. Nehemiah **r.** the wealthy for oppressing the needy. 5:8-13

REFORM
Economic. Example. Nehemiah. To rid the land of oppression. 5:7-13
Spiritual. By Nehemiah. (See **NEHEMIAH**, Reforms by)

REJOICING (See **JOY**)

RENEWAL (See **REVIVAL**)

REPENTANCE
Example. The rich **r.** from charging interest of those in need. 5:6-13
Fact. Is essential for revival. 9:1-4, Thgt.1
Need for. To rid ourselves of wickedness. 5:6-13, Thgt.1

REQUEST (See **PRAYER**)
Example. Nehemiah. Of King Artaxerxes. For help to rebuild Jerusalem. 2:5-7

RESPONSIBILITY (See **BELIEVERS**, Duty; **LABORERS; LAZINESS**)

RESTORATION

RETURNEES (See **JEWS**)

REVIVAL
Example. Of the Jews. Nehemiah and Ezra stirred **r.** 8:6, 12, 15-17; 9:38-10:39
Need for. In the church. Discussed. 13:1-31, Intro.
Requirements for.
  Confession of sin. 9:1-4, Thgt.1
  Repentance. 9:1-4, Thgt.1
  Seeking God's goodness and mercy. 9:1-37
  Worship. Including praise and thanksgiving. 9:5-31

RICHES (See **WEALTH**)

RIDICULE
Example. The enemies of the Jews **r.** the work on Jerusalem. 4:1-6
Giving in to. Result.
  Defeat. 4:1-6, Thgt.1
  Sin. 4:1-6, Thgt.1
How to conquer. By prayer and perseverance. 4:1-6

RIGHTEOUSNESS
Desire for. Fact. Is rare. 4:1-23, Intro.
Need for.
  In leadership. 2:1-20, Intro.
  In nations. 11:1-12:47, Intro.
Response to. By the world. Persecution of believers. 4:1-23, Intro.; 4:11-23, Thgt.1

RUMORS (See **GOSSIP**)

SABBATH
Breaking of.
  Consequences. 13:10-14, Thgt.1
  Example. Merchants were doing business in Jerusalem on the Sabbath. 13:15-16
Duty toward. To keep it holy. 10:31
Observance of. Example. The Jews made a total commitment to keep the **S.** 10:31
Reasons for. Discussed. 13:10-14, Thgt.1
Sanctity of. Guarded by Nehemiah. How he did it. 13:71-22

SACRIFICE
Of self. Required. By Christ. 2:1-20, Intro.

SALVATION
How to. By believing in the Lord and trusting in Him. 7:5-73, Thgt.1
Requirements for. Sacrifice of selfish desires. 2:1-20, Intro.

SANBALLAT
Attack of. Details of. 4:2
Horonite. 2:10, 19; 13:28

Enemy.
Of Nehemiah. 6:1-14
Of the Jews. 2:10, 19-20; 6:1-14
Opposition by. Tried to stop the rebuilding of Jerusalem. 2:10, 19-20; 6:1-14

SANCTIFICATION (See **GODLINESS; PURIFICATION**)

SATAN
Attack of. Overcoming. How to.
Being armed and trusting in God's power. 4:11-23
Endurance. 4:10
Prayer and perseverance. 4:1-6
Standing watch and praying. 4:7-9
Strategies of.
Conspiring. 4:7-9
Discouragement. 4:10
Gossip. 6:5-9
Ridicule. 4:1-6
Threats and intimidation. 4:11-23

SCORN (See **RIDICULE**)

SCRIPTURE (See **WORD OF GOD**)

SECURITY (See **PROTECTION**)

SEEKING
God. Importance of. To have true revival. 9:1-37
Revival. Requirements. Discussed. 9:1-4, Thgt.1

SELFISHNESS (See **GREED**)

SEPARATION
Of duties. By Nehemiah. To complete the wall in a timely manner. 3:1-32
Spiritual.
Duty toward.
By believers. 10:30, Thgt.1; 13:1-3, Thgt.1
By the Jews. 10:30
Example. The Jews excluded the unbelieving foreigners. 13:3

SERVICE
Dedication. Of the wall of Jerusalem (See **JERUSALEM**, Wall of, Dedication of)
Need for. Example. To remove the tons of rubble left from war in Jerusalem. 11:1-2

SHEMAIAH
Enemy. Of Nehemiah. 6:10-14
Men with that name. Four others.
Levite and musician. 12:36, 42
Keeper of the east gate. 3:29
Priest in the lineage of Asaph. 12:35
Priest in Zerubbabel's time. 10:8; 12:6, 18, 24
Plot of. Tried to get Nehemiah to act in fear to discredit him. 6:10-14

Priest. 6:10-14
Son. Of Delaiah. 6:10

SIN (See **EVIL; SALVATION; WICKEDNESS; WORLDLINESS**)
Escape from. How to. By believing in the Lord and trusting in Him. 7:5-73, Thgt.1
Listed. Refusing to work and cooperate. 3:5

SLANDER (See **GOSSIP**)

SLOTHFULNESS (See **LAZINESS**)

SLUGGISHNESS (See **LAZINESS**)

SOCIETY (See **HUMANITY; WORLD**)
Foundation of. Fact. Should be based on the Word of God. 8:1-18, Intro.; 9:38-10-29, Thgt.1
Needs of.
Compassion. 1:1-11, Intro.; 5:14-19, Thgt.1
Fact. Are many. 11:1-12:26, note 7, Thgt.1
Service. 11:1-12:26, note 7, Thgt.1
To study God's Word. 8:1-12, Thgt.1
Strong. Fact. Is based on obeying God's Word. 8:1-18, Intro.; 9:38-10-29, Thgt.1

SOUL-WINNING (See **WITNESSING**)

SOVEREIGNTY (See **GOD**, Sovereignty of)

SPIRITUAL REFORM (See **NEHEMIAH**, Reform by)

SPIRITUAL SEPARATION (See **SEPARATION**, Spiritual)

STANDING WATCH (See **WATCHING**)

STEADFASTNESS (See **DILIGENCE; FAITHFULNESS; PERSEVERANCE**)

STIRRING (See **EXHORTATION**)

STRATEGY
Of Nehemiah. (See **NEHEMIAH**, Strategy of)
Of Satan. (See **SATAN**, Strategy of)

SUCCESS
Keys to.
Faithfulness. 12:44-47, Thgt.1
Joy. 12:27-43, Thgt.1

SUFFERING (See **PERSECUTION, TEMPTATION, TRIALS**)
Deliverance from. How to have. By pleading for God's mercy. 9:32-37
Response to. Should be one of compassion and action. 1:1-4, Thgt.1

SUPPORT, Financial (See **CHURCH**, Support of)

SUSA
Capital. Of Persia. In the winter months. 1:1

SYMPATHY
Example. By Artaxerxes. Toward Nehemiah and the Jews. 2:8

TACTICS
Of Satan. (See **SATAN**, Strategy of)

TAUNTING (See **RIDICULE**)

TAXES
Example. The temple t. was set at one-third shekel per year. 10:32

TEMPLE
Fact.
The believer is the t. of the Holy Spirit. 13:4-9, Thgt.1
The church is the t. of the Holy Spirit. 13:4-9, Thgt.1
Support of.
Failure to.
Corrective action taken by Nehemiah. Explained. 13:11-13
Discovered by Nehemiah. 13:10
The Jews made a total commitment to support the house of God. 10:32-39
Tax for. Set by the Jews. At one-third shekel per year. 10:32
Worship in. Organized. By Nehemiah. 12:44-47

TEMPTATION (See **TRIALS**)
Fact. Are many and constant. 7:1-4, Thgt.1
Overcoming. How to.
By God's protection. 7:1-4, Thgt.1
By staying vigilant. 6:15-7:73, Intro.
Sources.
Close association with the wickedness of the world. 10:30, Thgt.1
Marriage to an unbeliever. 10:30, Thgt.1
To compromise. A common tactic of the enemy. 6:1-4
War against. Fact. Is a constant battle. 10:30, Thgt.1

TESTIMONY, Of the believer (See **BELIEVER**, Testimony of)
Strong. Example. Nehemiah. 2:8

THANKSGIVING (See **WORSHIP**)

THINKING
Negative.
Danger of. Can lead to wicked behavior. 12:27-43, Thgt.1
Definition. Harboring thoughts of wicked behavior. 12:27-43, Thgt.1
Positive.
Definition. Focusing on righteousness and productivity. 12:27-43, Thgt.1
Example. Nehemiah had the people focus on dedication to the Lord as they dedicated the wall of Jerusalem. 12:27-43
Need for. To be joyful and victorious. 12:27-43, Thgt.1

TIRED (See **EXHAUSTION**)

TITHING (See **GIVING**)

TOBIAH
Ammonite. 2:10, 19; 4:3
Enemy.
Of Nehemiah. 6:1-14
Of the Jews. 2:10, 19-20; 6:1-19; 13:4-8
Evil of. Desecrated the temple. 13:4-5
Opposition by. Tried to stop the rebuilding of Jerusalem. 2:10, 19-20; 6:1-19
Punishment of. By Nehemiah. Eviction by force from the temple. 13:8-9

TRANSGRESSION (See **DISOBEDIENCE; SIN; WICKEDNESS**)

TRIALS (See **PERSECUTION; SUFFERING**)
Fact. Are a part of life. 7:1-4, Thgt.1
Deliverance from. How to have. By pleading for God's mercy. 9:32-37
Overcoming. How to.
By God's protection. 7:1-4, Thgt.1
By prayer. 4:1-6, Thgt.1
With wisdom. 6:1-14, Intro.

TRIUMPH (See **OVERCOMING**)

TROUBLE (See **SUFFERING; TRIALS**)

TRUST
In God. Example. Nehemiah. Put his t. in God before he made request of the king. 2:4

UNBELIEVERS (See **LOST; WORLD**)

UNITY (See **COOPERATION**)
Example. Clergy and laymen worked together to rebuild Jerusalem. 3:1-12
Need for. In any job. 3:1-12, Thgt.1

UZZI
Genealogy of. 11:22-23
Levite. Head of. 11:22

VICTORY (See **OVERCOMING**)
How to have. By obeying God's Word. 8:1-18, Intro.

VIGILANCE
Definition of. 6:15-7:73, Intro.
Need for. Reasons. 6:15-7:73, Intro.
Results. Guards against temptation and trials. 6:15-7:73, Intro.

VISION
Need for. In leadership. 2:1-20, Intro.

VOW (See **COVENANT**)

WALL, Of Jerusalem (See **JERUSALEM**, Wall of)

WATCHING
And praying. Answer. To trials and temptations from the enemy. 4:7-9, Thgt.1
Example. Nehemiah. **W**. and prayed when he heard of the plot against the Jews. 4:7-9
With prayer. The answer to plots against us. 4:9

WEALTH
Temptations because of. To be greedy. 5:1-5

WHISPERING (See **GOSSIP**)

WHOLEHEARTEDNESS (See **COMMITMENT; DILIGENCE; FAITHFULNESS**)

WICKEDNESS (See **EVIL; SIN; WORLDLINESS**)
Cause. Hard hearts. 5:1-5, Thgt.1
Judgment of. Fact. Is certain. 5:6-13, Thgt.1
Of humankind. Because they have rejected God's Word. Discussed. 8:1-12, Thgt.1
Separation from. Fact. Is a command of the Scripture for every believer. 13:1-3, Thgt.1

WISDOM
Example. Nehemiah. 6:1-14
Need for.
To overcome enemies. 6:1-14, Intro.
To overcome trials and temptations. 6:1-14, Intro.

WITNESSING
Duty. Of the church. 13:1-31, Intro.
How to.
By avoiding wicked behavior. 13:1-3, Thgt.1
By showing God's love. 5:1-19, Intro.

WORD OF GOD
Hunger for. Example. The Jews listened closely to the **W.o.G**. as Ezra read. 8:1-12
Importance of.
Fact. Cannot be overstressed. 8:1-18, Intro.
Should be the foundation of every, society and nation. 8:1-18, Intro.
Tells us how to live in victory. 8:1-18, Intro.
Obeying. Results.
Establishes society. 8:1-18, Intro.; 9:38-10-29, Thgt.1
Example. The Jews made a total commitment to obey the **W.o.G**. 9:38-10:29
God helps those who obey. 8:1-18, Intro.
Need for. Discussed. 8:13-18, Thgt.1
Power of.
Draws people to obey. 8:1-12, Thgt.1
Exposes sin. 13:1-3
Rejection of. By humankind. Discussed. 8:1-12, Thgt.1
Study of. Need for. 8:1-12

WORK
Diligence in. Fact. Gives a sense of purpose and fulfillment. 3:1-32, Intro.
Privilege of. Discussed. 3:1-32, Intro.
Spirit needed. Humility. 3:13-14

WORKERS (See **LABORERS**)

WORLD (See **HUMANITY**)
How to win.
By avoiding wicked behavior. 13:1-3, Thgt.1
By showing God's love. 5:1-19, Intro.
Needs of.
Compassion. 1:1-11, Intro.; 5:14-19, Thgt.1
Fact. Are desperate. 1:1-11, Intro.
Listed. 1:1-4, Thgt.1; 13:10-14, Thgt.1
Love. 4:1-23, Intro.; 5:1-19, Intro.
Problems of.
Answer to. Jesus Christ. 5:1-19, Intro.
Listed. 5:1-19, Intro.; 5:14-19, Thgt.1
Response to. Proper.

Avoiding the wickedness of the world. 13:1-3, Thgt.1
Compassion and meeting needs. 1:1-4, Thgt.1; 13:1-3, Thgt.1

WORLDLINESS (See **EVIL**; **SIN**; **WICKEDNESS**)
Avoidance.
Example. By the Jews. 10:30
Reason. To remain spiritually separate. 10:30
Defined. 13:4-9, Thgt.1
Duty. Of believers. To avoid. 10:30, Thgt.1

WORSHIP (See **SACRIFICE**)
Definition.
Acknowledging God for His Person and His works. 1:5
Celebrating what God has done. 8:1-12
Duty. To be faithful. 12:44-47
Example.
By Nehemiah. 1:5
By the Jews. Described. 9:5-37
Organized. By Nehemiah. 12:44-47
Reasons for.
Because God can deliver. 9:9-31
Because God is great. 9:5-8, 32-38
Because God is worthy. 8:1-12
Listed and described. 9:5-38

Required.
For true revival. 9:5-31
On a weekly basis. 10:31, Thgt.1

YOM KIPPUR (See **ATONEMENT**, Day of)

ZEAL (See **COMMITMENT**; **DILIGENCE**; **FAITHFULNESS**)
Example. Baruch. Excelled in **z.** among the workers rebuilding Jerusalem. 3:20

ESTHER

ESTHER

THE BOOK OF
ESTHER

AUTHOR: the book of *Esther* makes no claim whatsoever about who the author is. However, it was clearly written by a Jew who was very familiar with the Persian kingdom, especially the empire's customs and law. Also, the author obviously had access to official records of the king of Persia. Suggestions from various commentators regarding the author include Mordecai, Ezra, and Nehemiah. However, it is simply impossible to know who penned the great book of *Esther*.

Although the human author cannot be known, the Divine Author is clearly known. The Holy Spirit of God *breathed* or *inspired* the great book of *Esther*. Through His inspiration, the Holy Spirit has given to the world an inspiring account of the very events God wanted recorded about His sovereign power and faithfulness to deliver His people from their enemies.

DATE: about 465 B.C., toward the end, or after, the reign of King Ahasuerus of Persia.

TO WHOM WRITTEN: to Jews everywhere, especially those living in foreign lands, and to the human race in general. Imagine being forced to live in a different country, under strange laws and customs far from home. Doubt and despair would strike the hearts of most people. Many of the Jewish captives in the pagan land of Persia began to wonder if God had abandoned them. Some even doubted the existence of the one true God. The Jews in the book of *Esther* were facing a life and death situation, but God's sovereign hand moved to deliver them. This message of hope and the power of God is needed by so many today. The great book of *Esther* gives hope to all who are in desperate circumstances, wondering if God can help them. The message is clear: the LORD is sovereign. He will help all who humble themselves and call on His name.

PURPOSE:
1. The *Historical* Purpose:
   a. To document the rise of Esther to power in the Persian kingdom.
   b. To document a large portion of the reign of King Ahasuerus of Persia.
   c. To record the attempt to exterminate the Jews.
   d. To record the deliverance of the Jews by the sovereign hand of God.
   e. To document the institution of the feast of Purim.
   f. To record Mordecai's rise to prominence.
2. The *Doctrinal* or *Spiritual* Purpose:
   a. To remind the returned Jewish exiles that God is faithful. He will protect His true followers in any situation.
   b. To show the sovereignty of God, His powerful hand intervening in circumstances for the good of those who fear Him.
   c. To teach that God will judge every person according to his works.
   d. To teach that God's judgment is certain. What a person sows, he will reap.
   e. To display what it means to be a godly person.
   f. To condemn hatred. Whether discrimination against a person or a family, or prejudice against an entire race, God will not tolerate hatred. The rod of judgment will strike all who harbor hatred in their hearts.
   g. To celebrate God's power to deliver His people from death.
3. The *Christological* or *Christ-Centered* Purpose: to teach that every person needs an intercessor like Esther who risked her life to go before the king to intercede for her people. Jesus Christ is the Advocate, the great Intercessor for the human race. Having died for the sins of all mankind, Christ presents Himself before the Father, asking Him to accept those who fully trust Christ for salvation. Just as King Ahasuerus granted Esther's request, so God grants the requests of Christ. God accepts the person who fully trusts in Christ to cover his sins.

SPECIAL FEATURES:
1. *Esther* is "The Great Book That Tells of the Vast Wealth of the Persian Empire" (1:1-9).
2. *Esther* is "The Great Book That Warns Against Extravagant Living and Drunkenness" (1:10-22).
3. *Esther* is "The Great Book That Shows the Godly Examples of Mordecai and Esther" (2:1-23).
4. *Esther* is "The Great Book That Pictures the Horrifying Evil of Prejudice and Hatred" (3:1-15).
5. *Esther* is "The Great Book That Teaches of the Sovereignty of God and His Protecting Hand" (4:1-6:14; 8:9-17).
6. *Esther* is "The Great Book That Displays True Wisdom in the Actions of Esther to Save Her People" (4:13-5:14; 7:1-6; 8:1-8).
7. *Esther* is "The Great Book That Teaches the Inescapable Law of Sowing and Reaping, the Certainty of Judgment" (7:7-10).
8. *Esther* is "The Great Book That Explains the Establishment of the Feast of Purim" (9:1-32).
9. *Esther* is "The Great Book That Teaches How God Lifts Up His People in Due Time" (10:1-3).

OUTLINE OF ESTHER

THE PREACHER'S OUTLINE AND SERMON BIBLE® is *unique*. It differs from all other Study Bibles and Sermon Resource Materials in that every Passage and Subject is outlined right beside the Scripture. When you choose any *Subject* below and turn to the reference, you have not only the Scripture but also an outline of the Scripture and Subject *already prepared for you—verse by verse*.

For a quick example, choose one of the subjects below and turn over to the Scripture; you will find this to be a marvelous help for more organized and streamlined study.

In addition, every point of the Scripture and Subject is *fully developed in a Commentary with supporting Scripture* at the end of each point. Again, this arrangement makes sermon preparation much simpler and more efficient.

Note something else: the Subjects of *Esther* have titles that are both Biblical and *practical*. The practical titles are often more appealing to people. This *benefit* is clearly seen for use on billboards, bulletins, church newsletters, etc.

A suggestion: for the *quickest* overview of *Esther*, first read *all the Division titles* (I, II, III, etc.), then come back and read the individual outline titles.

OUTLINE OF ESTHER

I. **THE ELEVATION OF ESTHER TO A POSITION OF PROMINENCE, THE QUEEN OF PERSIA, 1:1–2:23**

    A. The Persian King Ahasuerus (Xerxes) Dethroned His Queen: A Picture of Unrestrained Appetites, 1:1-22

    B. The Persian King Chooses Esther to Become His New Queen: A Picture of Morally Corrupt Man Contrasted with True Believers of Strong Character, 2:1-23

II. **THE JEWS MARKED FOR EXTERMINATION BY HAMAN: A PICTURE OF EXTREME PREJUDICE AND HORRIFYING EVIL, 3:1-15**

III. **THE JEWS SAVED BY THE COURAGEOUS ACTION OF ESTHER, 4:1–10:3**

    A. The Courageous Decision of Esther: A Look at Two Desperate Needs, 4:1-17

    B. The Courageous Approach of Esther into the King's Presence: A Contrast Between a Believer's Trust in God and an Unbeliever's Pride, 5:1-14

    C. The Unexpected Honor Bestowed Upon Mordecai: A Picture of God's Providence, Guidance, and Love for His People, 6:1-14

    D. The Suspenseful Exposure and Downfall of Haman: A Picture of Reaping Exactly What One Sows—Justice, Measure for Measure, 7:1-10

    E. The Desperate Intercession of Esther for the Deliverance of the Jews: A Picture of Being Delivered Through Prayer, 8:1-17

    F. The Triumph of the Jews and the Celebration of Purim: A Picture of Victory Over One's Enemy, 9:1–10:3

DIVISION I — ESTHER

THE ELEVATION OF ESTHER TO A POSITION OF PROMINENCE, THE QUEEN OF PERSIA, 1:1–2:23

(1:1–2:23) **DIVISION OVERVIEW**: the account of Esther opens with an impressive look into the grand palace of King Ahasuerus. The reader is given a beautiful picture of great luxury; but a dark picture of the pagan king quickly emerges. Extravagant banquets and uncontrolled drunkenness paint an ugly picture of blatant immorality and degradation. King Ahasuerus was a man of unrestrained appetites. He was so morally corrupt that he had no respect for women, not even for Queen Vashti, his own wife. Queen Vashti was summoned to display her dazzling beauty before a drunken crowd of party guests, but she refused. In a moment of burning anger, King Ahasuerus rejected and dethroned Queen Vashti, banning her from his presence. Almost immediately, the search began for a new queen. All the beautiful young virgins throughout the empire were brought to the capital. Then the process began to see who would be chosen as the new queen.

Among the young women brought to the palace was Esther, a strikingly attractive young woman. However, it was her godly character that stood out and drew attention, causing her to gain favor in the eyes of the king. Soon thereafter, Esther was chosen and elevated to the position of queen. Because the nation was in such a time of uncertainty and instability, her cousin Mordecai, who had reared her since she was a child, wisely warned Esther not to reveal her Jewish heritage. This fact proved critical in the dramatic story of the deliverance of the Jews from destruction.

Remember that the book of *Esther* was written primarily to returned exiles and to the future generations who may be living in a foreign land. In times of uncertainty and discouragement, those hearing the story of *Esther* could gather strength and trust in the LORD. When situations seem hopeless and destruction near, the inspiring account of the great book of *Esther* reminds true believers that God is sovereign. He is at work in every circumstance to uphold the believer.

As the reader studies the elevation of Esther to the position of queen of Persia, this fact should be kept in mind: God's sovereign power is at work in every facet of the believer's life. God knows every circumstance before it happens. He is able to take care of His people. God's sovereign hand is at work, preparing the way for escape and deliverance, even before the trial begins.

> **"And the king loved Esther above all the women, and she obtained grace and favour in his sight more than all the virgins; so that he set the royal crown upon her head, and made her queen instead of Vashti" (Est.2:17).**

THE ELEVATION OF ESTHER TO A POSITION OF PROMINENCE, THE QUEEN OF PERSIA, 1:1–2:23

A. The Persian King Ahasuerus (Xerxes) Dethroned His Queen: A Picture of Unrestrained Appetites, 1:1-22

B. The Persian King Chooses Esther to Become His New Queen: A Picture of Morally Corrupt Man Contrasted with True Believers of Strong Character, 2:1-23

CHAPTER 1

I. THE ELEVATION OF ESTHER TO A POSITION OF PROMINENCE, THE QUEEN OF PERSIA, 1:1–2:23

A. The Persian King Ahasuerus (Xerxes) Dethroned His Queen: A Picture of Unrestrained Appetites, 1:1-22

1. The king's vast kingdom & wealth: A picture of pride & self-exaltation

a. The king's massive empire described

1) Ruled over 127 provinces: From India to Ethiopia

2) Ruled from the fortress city of Susa, the winter palace of the king

b. The king's substantial wealth & power celebrated at a lavish banquet

1) The guests included all the nation's nobles as well as business, political, & military leaders

2) The six-month celebration of the king's opulent wealth & power

3) The celebration ended with a lavish banquet
- It lasted seven days
- It was held in the enclosed garden of the palace

4) The king's vast wealth & dazzling luxury were pridefully displayed
- Beautiful, costly drapes hung on marble pillars
- Couches were made of gold & silver
- Mosaic pavement of costly stone lay throughout the huge courtyard
- Gold goblets were used for wine, each uniquely designed
- An abundance of royal wine was served

5) The king's liberality was shown by allowing everyone to drink as much wine as he wished

Now it came to pass in the days of Ahasuerus, (this *is* Ahasuerus which reigned, from India even unto Ethiopia, *over* an hundred and seven and twenty provinces:)

2 *That* in those days, when the king Ahasuerus sat on the throne of his kingdom, which *was* in Shushan the palace,

3 In the third year of his reign, he made a feast unto all his princes and his servants; the power of Persia and Media, the nobles and princes of the provinces, *being* before him:

4 When he showed the riches of his glorious kingdom and the honour of his excellent majesty many days, *even* an hundred and fourscore days.

5 And when these days were expired, the king made a feast unto all the people that were present in Shushan the palace, both unto great and small, seven days, in the court of the garden of the king's palace;

6 *Where were* white, green, and blue, *hangings,* fastened with cords of fine linen and purple to silver rings and pillars of marble: the beds *were of* gold and silver, upon a pavement of red, and blue, and white, and black, marble.

7 And they gave *them* drink in vessels of gold, (the vessels being diverse one from another,) and royal wine in abundance, according to the state of the king.

8 And the drinking *was* according to the law; none did compel: for so the king had appointed to all the officers of his house, that they should do according to every man's pleasure.

9 Also Vashti the queen made a feast for the women *in* the royal house which *belonged* to king Ahasuerus.

10 On the seventh day, when the heart of the king was merry with wine, he commanded Mehuman, Biztha, Harbona, Bigtha, and Abagtha, Zethar, and Carcas, the seven chamberlains that served in the presence of Ahasuerus the king,

11 To bring Vashti the queen before the king with the crown royal, to show the people and the princes her beauty: for she *was* fair to look on.

12 But the queen Vashti refused to come at the king's commandment by *his* chamberlains: therefore was the king very wroth, and his anger burned in him.

13 Then the king said to the wise men, which knew the times, (for so *was* the king's manner toward all that knew law and judgment:

14 And the next unto him *was* Carshena, Shethar, Admatha, Tarshish, Meres, Marsena, *and* Memucan, the seven princes of Persia and Media, which saw the king's face, *and* which sat the first in the kingdom;)

15 What shall we do unto the queen Vashti according to law, because she hath not performed the commandment of the king Ahasuerus by the chamberlains?

16 And Memucan answered before the king and the princes, Vashti the queen hath not done wrong to the king only, but also to all the princes, and to all the people that *are* in all the provinces of the king Ahasuerus.

17 For *this* deed of the queen shall come abroad unto all women, so that they shall despise their husbands in their eyes, when it shall be reported, The king Ahasuerus commanded Vashti the queen to be brought in before him, but she came not.

18 *Likewise* shall the ladies of Persia and Media say this day unto all the king's princes, which have heard of the deed of the queen. Thus *shall there arise* too much contempt and wrath.

6) The king's wife, Queen Vashti, held a separate banquet for the wives of the nation's leaders

2. The king's shameful order to display the queen's beauty: A picture of loose morals & drunkenness

a. The demand of the drunken, lustful king

1) He ordered seven eunuchs to bring Queen Vashti to the celebration

2) He wanted to display Vashti's dazzling beauty to all the guests: So they could gaze upon her & envy him

b. The refusal by Queen Vashti

1) She defied the king's order

2) The king became furious, burned with anger

3. The king's divorce & dethroning of the queen: A picture of unbridled anger & revenge

a. The consultation between the drunken king & his advisors

1) He sought their legal counsel
- Their names
- Their position: They were the highest ranking & closest advisors to the king

2) He charged the queen with insubordination, defying the direct order of the king

b. The counsel of the advisors: Presented by Memucan

1) The queen's defiance had wronged not only the king but also all Persians

- Her defiance would encourage all women to rebel against their husbands

- The defiance of women would spread throughout the nation: There would be no way to stop the disrespect & contempt of women for men

2) The king should issue a royal decree that could not be repealed or revoked • That Queen Vashti be dethroned & banished forever from the king's presence • That the king choose another queen more worthy than Vashti 3) The desired result would be achieved: Throughout the empire, all the women would honor & respect their husbands	19 If it please the king, let there go a royal commandment from him, and let it be written among the laws of the Persians and the Medes, that it be not altered, That Vashti come no more before king Ahasuerus; and let the king give her royal estate unto another that is better than she. 20 And when the king's decree which he shall make shall be published throughout all his empire, (for it is great,) all the wives shall	give to their husbands honour, both to great and small. 21 And the saying pleased the king and the princes; and the king did according to the word of Memucan: 22 For he sent letters into all the king's provinces, into every province according to the writing thereof, and to every people after their language, that every man should bear rule in his own house, and that *it* should be published according to the language of every people.	c. The royal decree issued by the king 1) He accepted the counsel of the advisors 2) He issued the royal decree • That dethroned & banished Queen Vashti from his presence forever, v.19 • That every man should be the ruler over his own household

DIVISION I

THE ELEVATION OF ESTHER TO A POSITION OF PROMINENCE, THE QUEEN OF PERSIA, 1:1–2:23

A. The Persian King Ahasuerus (Xerxes) Dethroned His Queen: A Picture of Unrestrained Appetites, 1:1-22

(1:1-22) **Introduction**: unrestrained appetites are one of the major problems within society. People—both men and women—often exercise no control over their cravings. Instead they allow the cravings to control them. When they have an urge to do something or get something, they simply give in to it regardless of the consequences. Just think of the people who are enslaved to their uncontrolled cravings, cravings such as...

- food
- sex
- pornography
- money, riches

- power, authority, or position
- recognition, honor, or fame
- pleasure or entertainment
- possessions

The appetites—the cravings and urges of our flesh—can have power over us—if we let them. They can lead to lawless and violent behavior, gluttony and obesity, sexual abuse, child abuse, wrecked marriages, moral corruption, and ruined careers. The present Scripture introduces a man who was gripped by unbridled cravings, carnal and fleshly lusts, and unrestrained appetites: this man is the Persian king Ahasuerus who was also known as Xerxes. He inherited the great Persian Empire from his illustrious grandfather, Cyrus, and his father, Darius. He ruled over the vast Persian empire from 486–465 B.C. The story begins with King Xerxes becoming very angry at Queen Vashti, so furious that he removes her from the throne and banishes her from his presence forever. In her removal from the throne, the stage is set for the story of Esther and for her part in the deliverance of God's people from total annihilation. This is, *The Persian King Ahasuerus (Xerxes) Dethroned His Queen: A Picture of Unrestrained Appetites*, 1:1-22.

1. The king's vast kingdom and wealth: a picture of pride and self-exaltation (vv.1-9).
2. The king's shameful order to display the queen's beauty: a picture of loose morals and drunkenness (vv.10-12).
3. The king's divorce and dethroning of the queen: a picture of unbridled anger and revenge (vv.13-22).

[1] (1:1-9) **Pride, Example of—Self-Exaltation, Example of—Ahasuerus (Xerxes), Pride and Self-Exaltation of—Xerxes, Ahasuerus (King of Persia), Pride and Self-Exaltation—Extravagance, Example of—Wealth, Misuse of, Example—Neglect, Evil of, Misusing Wealth**: Xerxes ruled over a vast kingdom with enormous wealth. A glimpse of his kingdom and wealth is given in the opening scene of Esther:

OUTLINE	SCRIPTURE	SCRIPTURE	OUTLINE
1. **The king's vast kingdom & wealth: A picture of pride & self-exaltation** a. The king's massive empire described 1) Ruled over 127 provinces: From India to Ethiopia 2) Ruled from the fortress city of Susa, the winter palace of the king	Now it came to pass in the days of Ahasuerus, (this *is* Ahasuerus which reigned, from India even unto Ethiopia, *over* an hundred and seven and twenty provinces:) 2 *That* in those days, when the king Ahasuerus sat on the throne of his kingdom, which *was* in Shushan the palace,	3 In the third year of his reign, he made a feast unto all his princes and his servants; the power of Persia and Media, the nobles and princes of the provinces, *being* before him: 4 When he showed the riches of his glorious kingdom and the honour of	b. The king's substantial wealth & power celebrated at a lavish banquet 1) The guests included all the nation's nobles as well as business, political, & military leaders 2) The six-month celebration of the king's opulent wealth & power

OUTLINE	SCRIPTURE	SCRIPTURE	OUTLINE
3) The celebration ended with a lavish banquet • It lasted seven days • It was held in the enclosed garden of the palace 4) The king's vast wealth & dazzling luxury were pridefully displayed • Beautiful, costly drapes hung on marble pillars • Couches were made of gold & silver • Mosaic pavement of	his excellent majesty many days, *even* an hundred and fourscore days. 5 And when these days were expired, the king made a feast unto all the people that were present in Shushan the palace, both unto great and small, seven days, in the court of the garden of the king's palace; 6 *Where were* white, green, and blue, *hangings,* fastened with cords of fine linen and purple to silver rings and pillars of marble: the beds *were of* gold and silver, upon a pavement of red, and blue, and white, and black,	marble. 7 And they gave *them* drink in vessels of gold, (the vessels being diverse one from another,) and royal wine in abundance, according to the state of the king. 8 And the drinking *was* according to the law; none did compel: for so the king had appointed to all the officers of his house, that they should do according to every man's pleasure. 9 Also Vashti the queen made a feast for the women *in* the royal house which *belonged* to king Ahasuerus.	costly stone lay throughout the huge courtyard • Gold goblets were used for wine, each uniquely designed • An abundance of royal wine was served 5) The king's liberality was shown by allowing everyone to drink as much wine as he wished 6) The king's wife, Queen Vashti, held a separate banquet for the wives of the nation's leaders

a. Xerxes inherited the great empire of Persia from his father, Darius I (520–486 B.C.) and his grandfather, Cyrus the Great (550–530 B.C.). He himself ruled from 485 to 465 B.C. The vast empire stretched all the way from India, which included the land of Pakistan, over to Cush or Ethiopia, which is now the northern part of the Sudan. Up to this point in history Persia was the largest empire ever formed through military conquest. In the opening scenes of *Esther*, King Xerxes is ruling from the fortress city of Susa, which was the winter palace of the kingdom. Other royal palaces were located in Babylon, Ecbatana, and Persepolis. Susa was located in territory held by modern Iran, just across the border from modern Iraq. The throne of the kingdom, or *citadel* is distinguished from the city itself. For military purposes, a citadel (the palace complex and government buildings) was always built upon the highest point of a city and was known as the Acropolis or the upper fortified part of a city.

To govern such a vast empire it was necessary for the Persians to divide the territory into smaller areas called provinces and larger divisions called satrapes. There were either 20 or 31 political satrapes and 127 political provinces within Persia.

b. In the third year of his reign Xerxes threw a lavish banquet to celebrate his enormous wealth and power (vv.3-9). In antiquity, rulers used lavish banquets to secure the loyalty of their leadership, to lay plans and strategies for ruling the nation, and for launching military campaigns. The guests included all the nation's nobles (businessmen) and political leaders, as well as the military leaders of both Persia and Media. Years before, Cyrus the Great had conquered Media and formed an alliance with the Medes. Together the Medes and Persians conquered the vast empire that was then being ruled over by Cyrus' grandson Xerxes. Thus the military leaders of both Persia and Media were invited to the lavish banquet being held by King Xerxes. Most likely Xerxes used these six months during the celebrations (v.4) to plan his military campaign against Greece. Some years earlier, Xerxes' father had invaded Greece and been soundly defeated (490 B.C.). Before he could rebuild his economy and army enough to mobilize another invasion, Darius died (486 B.C.). The secular historian Herodotus tells us that Xerxes was driven to conquer Greece as revenge for his father and to conquer all of Europe in order to unite the world into *one empire* under Persian rule.[1] Thus, Xerxes' purpose during the six month celebration was twofold:

⇒ To plan the strategy for the Grecian and European invasions.
⇒ To show the leadership, both military and political, that the empire was strong enough to launch the campaign—economically and militarily.[2]

These historical facts are not covered by Scripture because they are not important to the story of Esther. However knowing the facts helps the reader to better understand the background to Xerxes' daring ambition and to the six-month celebration, which was held primarily for the purpose of planning a massive military campaign.

Scripture says that the celebration of Xerxes' economic wealth and power lasted for a full six months or 180 days (v.4). Most likely this means that the leadership rotated in and out for planning sessions while experiencing the great wealth and power of the empire. If all the leadership had been away from their posts for a period of six months, the empire would have been weakened and subject to attack or uprisings. The probable scenario was that Xerxes summoned his leadership to the capital on a rotating basis. Then, at the end of six months, he threw a lavish banquet to celebrate their planning and the great power of the empire, a celebration that lasted for seven days.

Holding the banquet in the enclosed garden of the palace, the king pridefully displayed his vast wealth and dazzling luxury (vv.6-7). Beautiful, costly drapes were hung on marble pillars, woven out of the most expensive and beautiful white and blue linen and fastened by purple ribbons attached to silver rings. Mosaic pavement of the most costly stones had been laid throughout the courtyard. Gold goblets for wine, each uniquely designed, were passed out to the guests (v.7). And the king provided an abundance of royal wine with the clear instructions that everyone was to be allowed to drink as much wine as he wished (vv.7-8).

---

1 Herodotus. *The History*, Book VII, Section 8.

2 Keil-Delitzsch. *Ezra, Nehemiah, Esther.* "Commmentary on the Old Testament." Vol.3. (Grand Rapids, MI: Eerdmans Publishing Co., n.d.), pp.324-325.

While King Xerxes was holding his banquet for the leadership of the nation, Queen Vashti held a separate banquet for the wives (v.9). It should be noted that Persian law did not require the separation of the sexes at feasts. However, for some reason at this particular celebration, King Xerxes had his wife plan a separate banquet for the wives of the leadership.

Thought 1. King Xerxes was a man of enormous wealth whose life was one of extravagance, pleasure, luxury, comfort, and ease. Having an inflated sense of importance, he delighted and boasted in showing off his wealth and in demonstrating his authority and power over others.

God warns us against living lives of extravagance, indulgence, and excess, of hoarding and piling up wealth. He warns us against selfishness, against neglecting the desperate needs of the world when so many people are crying out for help. Even within our own communities, cities, and nation many are desperate for financial assistance, support, comfort, relief, rest, consolation, reassurance, or understanding.

In addition to all who are in desperate need, there are millions who have never heard a clear-cut, simple explanation of the gospel of the Lord Jesus Christ. People are lost and dying without hope and without Christ, doomed to eternal separation from God forever. All these needs exist around us. Therefore, if a person lives a life of extravagance, hoarding, comfort, and ease while so many are suffering and doomed, what kind of reception will God give this person in the day of judgment? Listen to what God's Holy Word says:

"Lay not up for yourselves treasures upon earth, where moth and rust doth corrupt, and where thieves break through and steal" (Mt.6:19).

"When the Son of man shall come in his glory, and all the holy angels with him, then shall he sit upon the throne of his glory: And before him shall be gathered all nations: and he shall separate them one from another, as a shepherd divideth *his* sheep from the goats: And he shall set the sheep on his right hand, but the goats on the left. Then shall the King say unto them on his right hand, Come, ye blessed of my Father, inherit the kingdom prepared for you from the foundation of the world: For I was an hungred, and ye gave me meat: I was thirsty, and ye gave me drink: I was a stranger, and ye took me in: Naked, and ye clothed me: I was sick, and ye visited me: I was in prison, and ye came unto me. Then shall the righteous answer him, saying, Lord, when saw we thee an hungred, and fed *thee?* or thirsty, and gave *thee* drink? When saw we thee a stranger, and took *thee* in? or naked, and clothed *thee?* Or when saw we thee sick, or in prison, and came unto thee? And the King shall answer and say unto them, Verily I say unto you, Inasmuch as ye have done *it* unto one of the least of these my brethren, ye have done *it* unto me. Then shall he say also unto them on the left hand, Depart from me, ye cursed, into everlasting fire, prepared for the devil and his angels: For I was an hungred, and ye gave me no meat: I was thirsty, and ye gave me no drink: I was a stranger, and ye took me not in: naked, and ye clothed me not: sick, and in prison, and ye visited me not. Then shall they also answer him, saying, Lord, when saw we thee an hungred, or athirst, or a stranger, or naked, or sick, or in prison, and did not minister unto thee? Then shall he answer them, saying, Verily I say unto you, Inasmuch as ye did *it* not to one of the least of these, ye did *it* not to me. And these shall go away into everlasting punishment: but the righteous into life eternal" (Mt.25:31-46).

"And the cares of this world, and the deceitfulness of riches, and the lusts of other things entering in, choke the word, and it becometh unfruitful" (Mk.4:19).

"And he spake a parable unto them, saying, The ground of a certain rich man brought forth plentifully: And he thought within himself, saying, What shall I do, because I have no room where to bestow my fruits? And he said, This will I do: I will pull down my barns, and build greater; and there will I bestow all my fruits and my goods. And I will say to my soul, Soul, thou hast much goods laid up for many years; take thine ease, eat, drink, *and* be merry. But God said unto him, *Thou* fool, this night thy soul shall be required of thee: then whose shall those things be, which thou hast provided? So *is* he that layeth up treasure for himself, and is not rich toward God" (Lu.12:16-21).

"And that servant, which knew his lord's will, and prepared not *himself*, neither did according to his will, shall be beaten with many *stripes*" (Lu.12:47).

"There was a certain rich man, which was clothed in purple and fine linen, and fared sumptuously every day: And there was a certain beggar named Lazarus, which was laid at his gate, full of sores, And desiring to be fed with the crumbs which fell from the rich man's table: moreover the dogs came and licked his sores. And it came to pass, that the beggar died, and was carried by the angels into Abraham's bosom: the rich man also died, and was buried; And in hell he lift up his eyes, being in torments, and seeth Abraham afar off, and Lazarus in his bosom. And he cried and said, Father Abraham, have mercy on me, and send Lazarus, that he may dip the tip of his finger in water, and cool my tongue; for I am tormented in this flame. But Abraham said, Son, remember that thou in thy lifetime receivedst thy good things, and likewise Lazarus evil things: but now he is comforted, and thou art tormented. And beside all this, between us and you there is a great gulf fixed: so that they which would pass from hence to you cannot; neither can they pass to us, that *would come* from thence. Then he said, I pray thee therefore, father, that thou wouldest send him to my father's house: For I have five brethren; that he may testify unto them, lest they also come into this place of torment. Abraham saith unto him, They have Moses and the prophets; let them hear them. And he said, Nay, father Abraham: but if one went unto them from the dead, they will repent. And he said unto him, If they hear not Moses and the prophets, neither will they be persuaded, though one rose from the dead" (Lu.16:19-31).

"But godliness with contentment is great gain. For we brought nothing into *this* world, *and it is* certain we can carry nothing out. And having food and raiment let us be therewith content" (1 Ti.6:6-8).

245

"But they that will be rich fall into temptation and a snare, and *into* many foolish and hurtful lusts, which drown men in destruction and perdition" (1 Ti.6:9).

"For he shall have judgment without mercy, that hath showed no mercy; and mercy rejoiceth against judgment. What *doth it* profit, my brethren, though a man say he hath faith, and have not works? can faith save him? If a brother or sister be naked, and destitute of daily food, And one of you say unto them, Depart in peace, be ye warmed and filled; notwithstanding ye give them not those things which are needful to the body; what *doth it* profit? Even so faith, if it hath not works, is dead, being alone. Yea, a man may say, Thou hast faith, and I have works: show me thy faith without thy works, and I will show thee my faith by my works" (Js.2:13-18).

"Go to now, *ye* rich men, weep and howl for your miseries that shall come upon *you*. Your riches are corrupted, and your garments are motheaten. Your gold and silver is cankered; and the rust of them shall be a witness against you, and shall eat your flesh as it were fire. Ye have heaped treasure together for the last days. Behold, the hire of the labourers who have reaped down your fields, which is of you kept back by fraud, crieth: and the cries of them which have reaped are entered into the ears of the Lord of sabaoth. Ye have lived in pleasure on the earth, and been wanton; ye have nourished your hearts, as in a day of slaughter. Ye have condemned *and* killed the just; *and* he doth not resist you. Be patient therefore, brethren, unto the coming of the Lord. Behold, the husbandman waiteth for the precious fruit of the earth, and hath long patience for it, until he receive the early and latter rain. Be ye also patient; stablish your hearts: for the coming of the Lord draweth nigh" (Js.5:1-8).

"But whoso hath this world's good, and seeth his brother have need, and shutteth up his bowels *of compassion* from him, how dwelleth the love of God in him?" (1 Jn.3:17).

"If there be among you a poor man of one of thy brethren within any of thy gates in thy land which the LORD thy God giveth thee, thou shalt not harden thine heart, nor shut thine hand from thy poor brother" (De.15:7).

"The increase of his house shall depart, *and his goods* shall flow away in the day of his wrath" (Jb.20:28).

"One *thing* have I desired of the LORD, that will I seek after; that I may dwell in the house of the LORD all the days of my life, to behold the beauty of the LORD, and to enquire in his temple" (Ps.27:4).

"Surely every man walketh in a vain show: surely they are disquieted in vain: he heapeth up *riches,* and knoweth not who shall gather them" (Ps.39:6).

"For he seeth *that* wise men die, likewise the fool and the brutish person perish, and leave their wealth to others" (Ps.49:10).

"Whoso stoppeth his ears at the cry of the poor, he also shall cry himself, but shall not be heard" (Pr.21:13).

"As the partridge sitteth *on eggs,* and hatcheth *them* not; *so* he that getteth riches, and not by right, shall leave them in the midst of his days, and at his end shall be a fool" (Je.17:11).

"By thy great wisdom *and* by thy traffick hast thou increased thy riches, and thine heart is lifted up because of thy riches: Therefore thus saith the Lord GOD; Because thou hast set thine heart as the heart of God; Behold, therefore I will bring strangers upon thee, the terrible of the nations: and they shall draw their swords against the beauty of thy wisdom, and they shall defile thy brightness. They shall bring thee down to the pit, and thou shalt die the deaths of *them that are* slain in the midst of the seas. Wilt thou yet say before him that slayeth thee, I *am* God? but thou *shalt be* a man, and no God, in the hand of him that slayeth thee. Thou shalt die the deaths of the uncircumcised by the hand of strangers: for I have spoken *it,* saith the Lord GOD" (Eze.28:5-10).

"And when ye did eat, and when ye did drink, did not ye eat *for yourselves,* and drink *for yourselves?*" (Zec.7:6).

2 (1:10-12) **Morality, Weak, Example of—Drunkenness, Example of—Lust, Example of—Morals, Loose, Example of—Beauty, Abuse of, Example—Abuse, of Wife, Example—Wife, Abuse of, Example—Women, Abuse of, Example—Men, Abuses by, Example**: on the seventh day of the feast, the king and no doubt his guests were drunk and filled with lust from watching the slave girls' seductive dancing. In the passion of the moment, the king decided he wanted to display the beauty of his queen so the guests could gaze upon her. Seeing such an appealing, beautiful woman, they would envy him and his prize possession. Most unwisely, he ordered seven eunuchs to bring Queen Vashti to the feast (vv.10-11). Eunuchs were placed in charge of the kings' wives and concubines because there would be no threat of a sexual relationship developing between them. Note that the king instructed the queen to wear her royal crown. He wanted her to look her best to show off her dazzling beauty to all the guests.

But Queen Vashti refused the order of the king, for she knew that the throng of drunken men would be gazing and lusting after her. For this reason, the queen refused the order of the king, defying his command (v.12). Upon receiving news of her defiance, King Xerxes at once became furious and burned with anger.

OUTLINE	SCRIPTURE	SCRIPTURE	OUTLINE
2. The king's shameful order to display the queen's beauty: A picture of loose morals & drunkenness a. The demand of the drunken, lustful king	10 On the seventh day, when the heart of the king was merry with wine, he commanded Mehuman, Biztha, Harbona, Bigtha, and Abagtha, Zethar, and Carcas, the seven cham-	berlains that served in the presence of Ahasuerus the king, 11 To bring Vashti the queen before the king with the crown royal, to show the	1) He ordered seven eunuchs to bring Queen Vashti to the celebration 2) He wanted to display Vashti's dazzling beauty to all the guests: So they

OUTLINE	SCRIPTURE	SCRIPTURE	OUTLINE
could gaze upon her & envy him b. The refusal by Queen Vashti 1) She defied the king's order	people and the princes her beauty: for she *was* fair to look on. 12 But the queen Vashti refused to come at the	king's commandment by *his* chamberlains: therefore was the king very wroth, and his anger burned in him.	2) The king became furious, burned with anger

Thought 1. Drunkenness led King Xerxes to commit a terrible evil, that of abusing, demeaning, and degrading his wife. Imagine a man being so drunk that he would want to parade his wife before drunken men so they would lust after her and envy him!

Drunkenness is a terrible evil, for it causes a person to lose control of his or her reason and behavior. Despite the great power of alcohol to enslave people and the tragic disasters that result from drunkenness, society accepts and even promotes *social drinking*. In practically every form of advertisement, attractive people are pictured drinking in comfortable, appealing, and exciting settings. The psychological suggestion is that *social drinking* is one of the natural enjoyments of life and actually helps a person achieve success and acceptance among his or her peers. But this is simply not the case, not in reality, not in day-to-day life. Alcohol is a narcotic that leads to addiction and enslavement for millions of people. Furthermore, alcoholic beverages damage the human body and destroy human lives by the millions. Think of the people killed due to drunken driving, the abuse of spouses and children, the wrecked marriages and families, the shattered careers and lost jobs, the sexual and immoral behavior and even assaults that result from a drunken state. Think of the damaged and diseased bodies and minds that are caused by excessive drinking. Among all the millions of alcoholics throughout the world, every single alcoholic began by taking that first drink and they began because of peer pressure or to fit in with what society calls *social drinking*. God's Holy Word warns us against drunkenness:

"**And take heed to yourselves, lest at any time your hearts be overcharged with surfeiting, and drunkenness, and cares of this life, and *so* that day come upon you unawares**" (Lu.21:34).

"**Let us walk honestly, as in the day; not in rioting and drunkenness, not in chambering and wantonness, not in strife and envying. But put ye on the Lord Jesus Christ, and make not provision for the flesh, to *fulfil* the lusts *thereof***" (Ro.13:13-14).

"**But now I have written unto you not to keep company, if any man that is called a brother be a fornicator, or covetous, or an idolater, or a railer, or a drunkard, or an extortioner; with such an one no not to eat**" (1 Co.5:11).

"**Know ye not that the unrighteous shall not inherit the kingdom of God? Be not deceived: neither fornicators, nor idolaters, nor adulterers, nor effeminate, nor abusers of themselves with mankind, Nor thieves, nor covetous, nor drunkards, nor revilers, nor extortioners, shall inherit the kingdom of God**" (1 Co.6:9-10).

"**And be not drunk with wine, wherein is excess; but be filled with the Spirit**" (Ep.5:18).

"**For the time past of *our* life may suffice us to have wrought the will of the Gentiles, when we walked in lasciviousness, lusts, excess of wine, revellings, banquetings, and abominable idolatries: Wherein they think it strange that ye run not with *them* to the same excess of riot, speaking evil of *you*: Who shall give account to him that is ready to judge the quick and the dead**" (1 Pe.4:3-5).

"**Wine *is* a mocker, strong drink *is* raging: and whosoever is deceived thereby is not wise**" (Pr.20:1).

"**He that loveth pleasure *shall be* a poor man: he that loveth wine and oil shall not be rich**" (Pr.21:17).

"**Be not among winebibbers; among riotous eaters of flesh: For the drunkard and the glutton shall come to poverty: and drowsiness shall clothe *a man* with rags**" (Pr.23:20-21).

"**Who hath woe? who hath sorrow? who hath contentions? who hath babbling? who hath wounds without cause? who hath redness of eyes? They that tarry long at the wine; they that go to seek mixed wine. Look not thou upon the wine when it is red, when it giveth his colour in the cup, *when* it moveth itself aright. At the last it biteth like a serpent, and stingeth like an adder. Thine eyes shall behold strange women, and thine heart shall utter perverse things. Yea, thou shalt be as he that lieth down in the midst of the sea, or as he that lieth upon the top of a mast. They have stricken me, *shalt thou say, and* I was not sick; they have beaten me, *and* I felt *it* not: when shall I awake? I will seek it yet again**" (Pr.23:29-35).

"**Woe unto them that rise up early in the morning, *that* they may follow strong drink; that continue until night, *till* wine inflame them!**" (Is.5:11).

3 (1:13-22) **Anger, Unjustified, Example—Revenge, Example—Vindictiveness, Example of—Women, Abuse of, Example—Women, Example—Vashti, Queen of Persia, Dethroned—Xerxes, Traits of, Anger and Revenge**: in a moment of unbridled anger and revenge, King Xerxes divorced and dethroned Queen Vashti. He flew into a rage over the queen's refusal to make an appearance at the banquet and immediately consulted with his chief advisers (vv.13-15). Because the queen had committed a very serious offense against the throne by defying a direct order of the king, he sought their legal counsel. The seven advisors Xerxes summoned were the highest ranking officials in the empire, the closest advisors to the king. They were the only officials in the kingdom who had open access to the king in handling matters of state. Their importance to the king is seen in that all seven names are listed in Scripture.

OUTLINE	SCRIPTURE	SCRIPTURE	OUTLINE
3. The king's divorce & dethroning of the queen: A picture of unbridled anger & revenge a. The consultation between the drunken king & his advisors 1) He sought their legal counsel • Their names • Their position: They were the highest ranking & closest advisors to the king 2) He charged the queen with insubordination, defying the direct order of the king b. The counsel of the advisors: Presented by Memucan 1) The queen's defiance had wronged not only the king but also all Persians • Her defiance would encourage all women to rebel against their husbands • The defiance of women	13 Then the king said to the wise men, which knew the times, (for so *was* the king's manner toward all that knew law and judgment: 14 And the next unto him *was* Carshena, Shethar, Admatha, Tarshish, Meres, Marsena, *and* Memucan, the seven princes of Persia and Media, which saw the king's face, *and* which sat the first in the kingdom;) 15 What shall we do unto the queen Vashti according to law, because she hath not performed the commandment of the king Ahasuerus by the chamberlains? 16 And Memucan answered before the king and the princes, Vashti the queen hath not done wrong to the king only, but also to all the princes, and to all the people that *are* in all the provinces of the king Ahasuerus. 17 For *this* deed of the queen shall come abroad unto all women, so that they shall despise their husbands in their eyes, when it shall be reported, The king Ahasuerus commanded Vashti the queen to be brought in before him, but she came not. 18 *Likewise* shall the ladies	of Persia and Media say this day unto all the king's princes, which have heard of the deed of the queen. Thus *shall there arise* too much contempt and wrath. 19 If it please the king, let there go a royal commandment from him, and let it be written among the laws of the Persians and the Medes, that it be not altered, That Vashti come no more before king Ahasuerus; and let the king give her royal estate unto another that is better than she. 20 And when the king's decree which he shall make shall be published throughout all his empire, (for it is great,) all the wives shall give to their husbands honour, both to great and small. 21 And the saying pleased the king and the princes; and the king did according to the word of Memucan: 22 For he sent letters into all the king's provinces, into every province according to the writing thereof, and to every people after their language, that every man should bear rule in his own house, and that *it* should be published according to the language of every people.	would spread throughout the nation: There would be no way to stop the disrespect & contempt of women for men 2) The king should issue a royal decree that could not be repealed or revoked • That Queen Vashti be dethroned & banished forever from the king's presence • That the king choose another queen more worthy than Vashti 3) The desired result would be achieved: Throughout the empire, all the women would honor & respect their husbands c. The royal decree issued by the king 1) He accepted the counsel of the advisors 2) He issued the royal decree • That dethroned & banished Queen Vashti from his presence forever, v.19 • That every man should be the ruler over his own household

Once the seven legal advisors had been summoned, the king charged Queen Vashti with insubordination, defying the direct order of the king (v.15). The queen had embarrassed the king before his guests, a serious offense in and of itself. But in light of the fact that the guests were the highest officials and leaders of the nation, her defiance was even more shocking and could have very grave repercussions. If the queen was allowed to defy the king's order, others might feel they too had the right to defy his orders. And if her defiance was not punished, others might be encouraged to disobey the king's commands. The result could easily be disorder and perhaps chaos throughout the nation. The king's word was the law, the bond that held the nation together. For that reason, his word must be upheld as the law of the land in order to preserve the unity of the empire. Thus he sought the advice of his legal counsel to see what the law said about the offense of Queen Vashti.

After consulting and discussing the issue among themselves, the legal counselors reported back to the king and the leaders of the nation (vv.16-20). The spokesman for the counselors was probably the chief counsel, an advisor named Memucan. In the opinion of the counselors, the queen's defiance had wronged not only the king himself but also all Persians throughout the entire nation (vv.16-18). Why such a harsh conclusion? Because once the queen's noncompliance became known, other women would be encouraged to despise and rebel against their husbands. All the wives of the nation's officials would hear about the queen's refusal to obey a direct order and begin to follow her example. There would be no way to stop the disrespect and contempt of women for men throughout the nation. Consequently, the advisors counseled the king to issue a royal decree that could not be repealed or revoked, a royal decree declaring that...

- Queen Vashti would be dethroned and banished forever from the king's presence
- the king would choose another queen more worthy than she (v.19)

Once the decree had been proclaimed throughout the nation, women would know that they must honor and respect their husbands. Moreover, everyone would know that they must obey the orders of the king.

The advice pleased the king and his leaders, so Xerxes issued a royal decree that Queen Vashti was to be dethroned and banished from his presence forever (vv.21-22). Furthermore, every man should be the recognized authority and ruler over his own household.

Thought 1. In a drunken state, King Xerxes abused his wife. Showing no respect or honor for her whatsoever—totally ignoring how she would her feel—he sought to parade her beauty like an ornament before his drunken friends. To him his wife existed for pleasure, not for love. She was his wife; therefore she was to do as he wished and asked.

Just as King Xerxes abused his wife, many women are abused in the same way today. Many women are still treated just as they have been down through history, as nothing more than chattel, possessions, and objects of beauty. And shamefully, society stresses that a woman's sexual appeal is more important than her character, knowledge, or abilities. Movies, magazines, television, books, beauty contests, swimsuit issues of sports magazines, promotional ads for nearly every product sold to the public—all of these bombard us daily with the message that beauty and sex appeal are at the root of everything that is good, successful, desirable, satisfying, and worthwhile. The result is tragic. Many young women grow up thinking that looks matter more than character, knowledge, or ability. And many young men grow up thinking that women are mere sex objects to be sought after and used for personal gratification. Society has turned from God and morality. It is sending the message that a woman's value lies in how beautiful or attractive she is rather than in the quality of her being. It is failing to respect and value women as persons of worth. But listen to what God's Holy Word says:

"**And why take ye thought for raiment? Consider the lilies of the field, how they grow; they toil not, neither do they spin: And yet I say unto you, That even Solomon in all his glory was not arrayed like one of these**" (Mt.6:28-29).

"**And Mary said, My soul doth magnify the Lord**" (Lu.1:46).

"**Judge not according to the appearance, but judge righteous judgment**" (Jn.7:24).

"**I commend unto you Phebe our sister, which is a servant of the church which is at Cenchrea**" (Ro.16:1).

"**Salute Tryphena and Tryphosa, who labour in the Lord. Salute the beloved Persis, which laboured much in the Lord**" (Ro.16:12).

"**Do ye look on things after the outward appearance? If any man trust to himself that he is Christ's, let him of himself think this again, that, as he *is* Christ's, even so *are* we Christ's**" (2 Co.10:7).

"**In like manner also, that women adorn themselves in modest apparel, with shamefacedness and sobriety; not with broided hair, or gold, or pearls, or costly array; But (which becometh women professing godliness) with good works**" (1 Ti.2:9-10).

"**Whose adorning let it not be that outward *adorning* of plaiting the hair, and of wearing of gold, or of putting on of apparel; But *let it be* the hidden man of the heart, in that which is not corruptible, *even the ornament* of a meek and quiet spirit, which is in the sight of God of great price**" (1 Pe.3:3-4).

"**And Hannah answered and said, No, my lord, I *am* a woman of a sorrowful spirit: I have drunken neither wine nor strong drink, but have poured out my soul before the LORD**" (1 S.1:15).

"**For the LORD taketh pleasure in his people: he will beautify the meek with salvation**" (Ps.149:4).

"**A gracious woman retaineth honour: and strong *men* retain riches**" (Pr.11:16).

"**As a jewel of gold in a swine's snout, *so is* a fair woman which is without discretion**" (Pr.11:22).

"**A virtuous woman *is* a crown to her husband: but she that maketh ashamed *is* as rottenness in his bones**" (Pr.12:4).

"**Who can find a virtuous woman? for her price *is* far above rubies. The heart of her husband doth safely trust in her, so that he shall have no need of spoil. She will do him good and not evil all the days of her life**" (Pr.31:10-12 (see also Pr.31:13-31).

"**Favour *is* deceitful, and beauty *is* vain: *but* a woman *that* feareth the LORD, she shall be praised**" (Pr.31:30).

"**Moreover the LORD saith, Because the daughters of Zion are haughty, and walk with stretched forth necks and wanton eyes, walking and mincing *as* they go, and making a tinkling with their feet: Therefore the LORD will smite with a scab the crown of the head of the daughters of Zion, and the LORD will discover their secret parts. In that day the Lord will take away the bravery of *their* tinkling ornaments *about their feet,* and *their* cauls, and *their* round tires like the moon, The chains, and the bracelets, and the mufflers, The bonnets, and the ornaments of the legs, and the headbands, and the tablets, and the earrings, The rings, and nose jewels, The changeable suits of apparel, and the mantles, and the wimples, and the crisping pins, The glasses, and the fine linen, and the hoods, and the vails. And it shall come to pass, *that* instead of sweet smell there shall be stink; and instead of a girdle a rent; and instead of well set hair baldness; and instead of a stomacher a girding of sackcloth; *and* burning instead of beauty**" (Is.3:16-24).

CHAPTER 2

B. The Persian King Chooses Esther to Become His New Queen: A Picture of a Morally Corrupt Man Contrasted with True Believers of Strong Character, 2:1-23

1. **The proposal for a new queen: A picture of selfishness & moral corruption in seeking true love**
   a. The king's emotions: Missed Vashti, longing for true love
   b. The concern of the king's personal attendants & their proposal: To secure a new wife
      1) By appointing agents in each province to search for beautiful young virgins
      2) By bringing the beautiful virgins into the king's harem at Susa, his palace
      3) By placing the virgins under Hegai's care & giving them beauty treatments

      4) By seeing which virgin pleased the king the most & making her queen
   c. The sensual, fleshly proposal accepted by the king
2. **The selection of Esther to be queen: A picture of moral purity & strong character**
   a. The background of Mordecai & Esther

      1) Mordecai was a Jew, the great-grandson of Kish: Kish had been taken captive by the Babylonians in 597 B.C., about 120 years earlier, 2 K.24:1-16

      2) Esther was adopted by Mordecai when her mother & father died
         • She & Mordecai were cousins
         • She grew to be a beautiful & shapely young woman

   b. The taking of Esther into the king's palace
      1) She & many other virgins were placed under the care of Hegai: He was the eunuch in charge of the king's harem

After these things, when the wrath of king Ahasuerus was appeased, he remembered Vashti, and what she had done, and what was decreed against her.
2 Then said the king's servants that ministered unto him, Let there be fair young virgins sought for the king:
3 And let the king appoint officers in all the provinces of his kingdom, that they may gather together all the fair young virgins unto Shushan the palace, to the house of the women unto the custody of Hege the king's chamberlain, keeper of the women; and let their things for purification be given *them:*
4 And let the maiden which pleaseth the king be queen instead of Vashti. And the thing pleased the king; and he did so.
5 *Now* in Shushan the palace there was a certain Jew, whose name *was* Mordecai, the son of Jair, the son of Shimei, the son of Kish, a Benjamite;
6 Who had been carried away from Jerusalem with the captivity which had been carried away with Jeconiah king of Judah, whom Nebuchadnezzar the king of Babylon had carried away.
7 And he brought up Hadassah, that *is,* Esther, his uncle's daughter: for she had neither father nor mother, and the maid *was* fair and beautiful; whom Mordecai, when her father and mother were dead, took for his own daughter.
8 So it came to pass, when the king's commandment and his decree was heard, and when many maidens were gathered together unto Shushan the palace, to the custody of Hegai, that Esther was brought also unto the king's house, to the custody

of Hegai, keeper of the women.
9 And the maiden pleased him, and she obtained kindness of him; and he speedily gave her her things for purification, with such things as belonged to her, and seven maidens, *which were* meet to be given her, out of the king's house: and he preferred her and her maids unto the best *place* of the house of the women.
10 Esther had not showed her people nor her kindred: for Mordecai had charged her that she should not show *it.*
11 And Mordecai walked every day before the court of the women's house, to know how Esther did, and what should become of her.
12 Now when every maid's turn was come to go in to king Ahasuerus, after that she had been twelve months, according to the manner of the women, (for so were the days of their purifications accomplished, *to wit,* six months with oil of myrrh, and six months with sweet odours, and with *other* things for the purifying of the women;)
13 Then thus came *every* maiden unto the king; whatsoever she desired was given her to go with her out of the house of the women unto the king's house.
14 In the evening she went, and on the morrow she returned into the second house of the women, to the custody of Shaashgaz, the king's chamberlain, which kept the concubines: she came in unto the king no more, except the king delighted in her, and that she were called by name.
15 Now when the turn of Esther, the daughter of Abihail the uncle of Mordecai, who had taken her for his daughter, was come to go in unto the king, she required nothing but what Hegai the king's chamberlain, the keeper of the women, appointed. And Esther obtained favour in the sight of all them that looked upon her.
16 So Esther was taken unto king Ahasuerus into his house royal in the tenth month, which *is* the month Tebeth, in the seventh year of

2) She impressed Hegai with her lovely, gracious character: He immediately gave Esther special care
   • Additional attention, beauty treatments, & choice food
   • Seven maids
   • The best room in the harem

3) She had kept her nationality & family a secret since childhood (v.20): Mordecai had warned her not to risk discrimination, anti-Semitism
4) She was deeply loved by Mordecai: Daily he walked by the courtyard of the harem to find out how she was

c. The procedure used to please the sensual, lustful cravings of the king
   1) Each girl was given 12 months of beauty treatments

   2) Each girl was then selected to spend a night with the king: Each was given whatever clothing or jewelry she wanted
   3) Each girl was then transferred to the permanent harem where the king's wives lived: She never again returned to the king unless she was summoned by him

d. The selection of Esther to be queen
   1) Esther was summoned to go to the king
      • She asked for nothing other than what Hegai suggested, trusting his judgment
      • Her graciousness & humility as well as her beauty impressed everyone
   2) Esther was taken to the king: The 10th month, the month of Tebeth (Dec-Jan), in the 7th year of the king's reign

3) Esther's striking beauty, poise, & behavior attracted the king more so than did any of the other young ladies: She was sweet, kind, & loving
4) Esther was crowned as the new queen of the Persian empire
5) Esther was given a great banquet to celebrate her coronation
  • A holiday was proclaimed
  • Gifts were generously distributed
e. The nationality of Esther still kept secret
1) She kept it secret even after Mordecai sat at the king's gate, that is, was appointed a palace official
2) She was even now warned by Mordecai: She must
	his reign.
	17 And the king loved Esther above all the women, and she obtained grace and favour in his sight more than all the virgins; so that he set the royal crown upon her head, and made her queen instead of Vashti.
	18 Then the king made a great feast unto all his princes and his servants, *even* Esther's feast; and he made a release to the provinces, and gave gifts, according to the state of the king.
	19 And when the virgins were gathered together the second time, then Mordecai sat in the king's gate.
	20 Esther had not *yet* showed her kindred nor her people; as Mordecai had charged her: for Esther
		did the commandment of Mordecai, like as when she was brought up with him.
		21 In those days, while Mordecai sat in the king's gate, two of the king's chamberlains, Bigthan and Teresh, of those which kept the door, were wroth, and sought to lay hand on the king Ahasuerus.
		22 And the thing was known to Mordecai, who told it unto Esther the queen; and Esther certified the king *thereof* in Mordecai's name.
		23 And when inquisition was made of the matter, it was found out; therefore they were both hanged on a tree: and it was written in the book of the chronicles before the king.
			still fear discrimination, anti-Semitism, 10
			3) She had been an obedient child—all her life
			3. The forewarning of death given to the king by Mordecai: A picture of believers warning others to prepare for death
			a. Mordecai overheard two officers plotting to assassinate King Ahasuerus or Xerxes
			
			b. Mordecai informed Queen Esther
			1) Esther told the king
			2) Esther gave credit to Mordecai
			
			c. Mordecai's report was investigated
			1) It was found to be true
			2) It was the basis for hanging the guilty
			3) It was recorded in the king's records

DIVISION I

THE ELEVATION OF ESTHER TO A POSITION OF PROMINENCE, THE QUEEN OF PERSIA, 1:1–2:23

B. The Persian King Chooses Esther to Become His New Queen: A Picture of Morally Corrupt Man Contrasted with True Believers of Strong Character, 2:1-23

(2:1-23) **Introduction**: men and women of strong moral character are desperately needed in every group and organization within society. But what is often found are men and women who are morally corrupt, insincere, dishonest, corrupt, unjust, abusive, overbearing, wicked, or evil. The only hope for society—for controlling the immorality, lawlessness, and violence of this world—is for us to become men and women of strong character. We must develop the character traits of...

- truth and integrity
- righteousness and justice
- kindness and goodness
- compassion and care
- generosity and service
- faith and trust

This is the practical subject of the present Scripture. This is, *The Persian King Chooses Esther to Become His New Queen: A Picture of Morally Corrupt Man Contrasted with True Believers of Strong Character*, 2:1-23.

1. The proposal for a new queen: a picture of selfishness and moral corruption in seeking true love (vv.1-4).
2. The selection of Esther to be queen: a picture of moral purity and strong character (vv.5-20).
3. The forewarning of death given to the king by Mordecai: a picture of believers warning others to prepare for death (vv.21-23).

1 (2:1-4) **Corruption, Moral—Immorality, Example of—Love, True, Longing for—Xerxes, King of Persia, Moral Corruption of—Carnality, Example of**: about four years after Queen Vashti had been deposed as queen, the king's personal attendants suggested he seek a new queen. He had divorced and removed Queen Vashti in the third year of his reign (1:3), and he did not marry Esther until the seventh year (2:16). Why the search was postponed three to four years is not stated, but it was during this time that King Xerxes launched his disastrous campaign against the Greeks and returned home in humiliation instead of honor. Suffering such a humiliating defeat was bound to take its toll upon King Xerxes. Evidently the personal attendants noticed the dejected and despondent spirit of the king, his despair and anguish. During these days he began to think about Queen Vashti and the events that had led to her removal as queen. He began to long for true companionship and love, a close relationship where he could share his deepest emotions as well as find comfort and encouragement.

In light of the king's downcast spirit and realizing his need for close companionship, the personal attendants made a proposal that he begin to search for a new wife and queen (vv.2-4). They suggested that he secure a new wife...

- by appointing agents in each province of the empire to search for beautiful young virgins
- by bringing the beautiful virgins into the king's harem at the citadel of Susa
- by placing the virgins under the care of Hegai, the king's eunuch, and giving them beauty treatments
- by seeing which one of the virgins pleased him the most and making her queen (v.4)

The king's personal attendants no doubt felt this was the answer to the king's dejection, for they knew he had strong sexual urges. They thought that a new group of virgin concubines would help ease the king's misery until he could find a woman who pleased him and met his needs for a new queen. Once this woman was found, he could crown her as queen and have her at his disposal as needed and desired.

Note that these young virgins were to be searched for throughout the entire empire, and they were to be brought against their will, having no choice whatsoever in the matter. They were to become one of the many wives and concubines in the king's harem, available for his sexual pleasure as he wished. Such a practice in the ancient world was normal for a king but still it was morally corrupt and most tragic. Once a young virgin had been placed in the king's harem, she belonged to him permanently and could never marry anyone else. In reality, the king's harem became a prison, a confinement for the young virgins. After spending one night with the king, they were sometimes doomed to permanent widowhood, for the king was constantly having new virgins brought into the harem for his pleasure. Note, only eunuchs were trusted with the care of the king's concubines because they would be no threat sexually to the women.

The sensual, fleshly proposal pleased the king. He accepted the suggestion of his personal attendants (v.4). No doubt he felt that sexual pleasure with a new group of women would help lift his spirits while he was searching for a queen. Having the power to take any young woman he wanted, he issued a decree to bring all the young beautiful virgins throughout the entire empire to the king's harem.

OUTLINE	SCRIPTURE	SCRIPTURE	OUTLINE
1. **The proposal for a new queen: A picture of selfishness & moral corruption in seeking true love** a. The king's emotions: Missed Vashti, longing for true love b. The concern of the king's personal attendants & their proposal: To secure a new wife 1) By appointing agents in each province to search for beautiful young virgins	**A**fter these things, when the wrath of king Ahasuerus was appeased, he remembered Vashti, and what she had done, and what was decreed against her. 2 Then said the king's servants that ministered unto him, Let there be fair young virgins sought for the king: 3 And let the king appoint officers in all the provinces of his kingdom, that they may	gather together all the fair young virgins unto Shushan the palace, to the house of the women unto the custody of Hege the king's chamberlain, keeper of the women; and let their things for purification be given *them*: 4 And let the maiden which pleaseth the king be queen instead of Vashti. And the thing pleased the king; and he did so.	2) By bringing the beautiful virgins into the king's harem at Susa, his palace 3) By placing the virgins under Hegai's care & giving them beauty treatments 4) By seeing which virgin pleased the king the most & making her queen c. The sensual, fleshly proposal accepted by the king

Thought 1. Some people are just like King Xerxes: they are morally corrupt and they engage in one sexual exploit after another. One-night stands matter little to these persons because sexual pleasure is their only pursuit. Others develop long-term relationships that are sexual in nature but nothing more. However in all cases of morally corrupt people, they either refuse to make a permanent, monogamous, marital commitment or else they make a commitment that is easily broken or disregarded. In both cases they reject God and His holy commandments that forbid adultery and illicit sex and that demand marriage between a man and a woman. A person chooses a morally corrupt lifestyle for any of several reasons:

⇒ experimentation
⇒ pure pleasure of the flesh
⇒ ego, a sense of conquest
⇒ emotional problems, attempting to fill a sense of emptiness or loneliness
⇒ a desire to be acceptable and to fit in with one's peers
⇒ seeking a meaningful relationship, true love

All morally corrupt people have one serious flaw in common: they either fail to realize; or simply do not care, that sex is only one part of many that make up the total relationship between man and woman. Men and women experience unity and pleasure on many levels and in many ways. Therefore attention must be given to all areas of the relationship if it is to grow, thrive, succeed, and stand the test of time. A healthy relationship must be built upon…

- companionship, being together and sharing with each other
- common desires and purposes, wanting the same things and making the commitment to strive for the same goals
- establishing a life and home together, loving, nurturing, helping, and nourishing one another in every area of life, which includes the sexual aspect of the relationship
- diligent and consistent work
- tolerance and patience, forgiving one another when facing shortcomings or failure
- healthy social relationships, respecting each other's family, friends, and co-workers as well as developing mutual friends
- Christ and the church, making a joint commitment to follow and obey the LORD and to become active in a local church

God warns us: we must guard against becoming morally corrupt. We must turn away from adultery, fornication and all other forms of illicit sex. Listen to what God's Holy Word says:

"For the wrath of God is revealed from heaven against all ungodliness and unrighteousness of men, who hold the truth in unrighteousness; Because that which may be known of God is manifest in them; for God hath shewed *it* unto them. For the invisible things of him from the creation of the world are clearly seen, being understood by the things that are made, *even* his eternal power and Godhead; so that they are without excuse: Because that, when they knew God, they glorified *him* not as God,

neither were thankful; but became vain in their imaginations, and their foolish heart was darkened. Professing themselves to be wise, they became fools, And changed the glory of the uncorruptible God into an image made like to corruptible man, and to birds, and fourfooted beasts, and creeping things. Wherefore God also gave them up to uncleanness through the lusts of their own hearts, to dishonour their own bodies between themselves" (Ro.1:18-24).

"I speak after the manner of men because of the infirmity of your flesh: for as ye have yielded your members servants to uncleanness and to iniquity unto iniquity; even so now yield your members servants to righteousness unto holiness" (Ro.6:19).

"Who being past feeling [all sensitivity] have given themselves over unto lasciviousness [unbridled sensuality, immoral ways], to work all uncleanness with greediness" (Ep.4:19).

"But fornication, and all uncleanness, or covetousness, let it not be once named among you, as becometh saints" (Ep.5:3).

"Mortify therefore your members which are upon the earth; fornication, uncleanness, inordinate affection, evil concupiscence, and covetousness, which is idolatry" (Co.3:5).

"For this is the will of God, *even* your sanctification, that ye should abstain from fornication: That every one of you should know how to possess his vessel in sanctification and honour; Not in the lust of concupiscence, even as the Gentiles which know not God: That no *man* go beyond and defraud his brother in *any* matter: because that the Lord *is* the avenger of all such, as we also have forewarned you and testified" (1 Th.4:3-6).

"For God hath not called us unto uncleanness, but unto holiness" (1 Th.4:7).

"Marriage *is* honourable in all, and the bed undefiled: but whoremongers and adulterers God will judge" (He.13:4).

"But chiefly them that walk after the flesh in the lust of uncleanness, and despise government. Presumptuous *are they,* selfwilled, they are not afraid to speak evil of dignities" (2 Pe.2:10).

2 (2:5-20) **Character, Strong, Example—Morality, Sexual, Example—Purity, Sexual, Example—Esther, Character of—Esther, Appointed Queen—Mordecai, Adopted and Reared Esther—Mordecai, Background of—Esther, Background of—Queens, of Persia, Esther**: Scripture now tells how a beautiful young Jewish woman became the wife of King Xerxes and the queen of the great Persian Empire. It is a dramatic story. Esther was a young woman of strong character, a morally pure woman, a virgin. Her moral purity is a strong example for young girls and women of all generations. As the story of Esther's rise to power is read, note how the hand of God works through human events to save His people.

OUTLINE	SCRIPTURE	SCRIPTURE	OUTLINE
2. The selection of Esther to be queen: A picture of moral purity & strong character a. The background of Mordecai & Esther 1) Mordecai was a Jew, the great-grandson of Kish: Kish had been taken captive by the Babylonians in 597 B.C., about 120 years earlier, 2 K.24:1-16 2) Esther was adopted by Mordecai when her mother & father died • She & Mordecai were cousins • She grew to be a beautiful & shapely young woman b. The taking of Esther into the king's palace 1) She & many other virgins were placed under the care of Hegai: He was the eunuch in charge of the king's harem 2) She impressed Hegai with	5 *Now* in Shushan the palace there was a certain Jew, whose name *was* Mordecai, the son of Jair, the son of Shimei, the son of Kish, a Benjamite; 6 Who had been carried away from Jerusalem with the captivity which had been carried away with Jeconiah king of Judah, whom Nebuchadnezzar the king of Babylon had carried away. 7 And he brought up Hadassah, that *is,* Esther, his uncle's daughter: for she had neither father nor mother, and the maid *was* fair and beautiful; whom Mordecai, when her father and mother were dead, took for his own daughter. 8 So it came to pass, when the king's commandment and his decree was heard, and when many maidens were gathered together unto Shushan the palace, to the custody of Hegai, that Esther was brought also unto the king's house, to the custody of Hegai, keeper of the women. 9 And the maiden pleased	him, and she obtained kindness of him; and he speedily gave her her things for purification, with such things as belonged to her, and seven maidens, *which were* meet to be given her, out of the king's house: and he preferred her and her maids unto the best *place* of the house of the women. 10 Esther had not showed her people nor her kindred: for Mordecai had charged her that she should not show *it.* 11 And Mordecai walked every day before the court of the women's house, to know how Esther did, and what should become of her. 12 Now when every maid's turn was come to go in to king Ahasuerus, after that she had been twelve months, according to the manner of the women, (for so were the days of their purifications accomplished, *to wit,* six months with oil of myrrh, and six months with sweet odours, and with *other* things for the	her lovely, gracious character: He immediately gave Esther special care • Additional attention, beauty treatments, & choice food • Seven maids • The best room in the harem 3) She had kept her nationality & family a secret since childhood (v.20): Mordecai had warned her not to risk discrimination, anti-Semitism 4) She was deeply loved by Mordecai: Daily he walked by the courtyard of the harem to find out how she was c. The procedure used to please the sensual, lustful cravings of the king 1) Each girl was given 12 months of beauty treatments

OUTLINE	SCRIPTURE	SCRIPTURE	OUTLINE

2) Each girl was then selected to spend a night with the king: Each was given whatever clothing or jewelry she wanted
 	
3) Each girl was then transferred to the permanent harem where the kings' wives lived: She never again returned to the king unless she was summoned by him
 	
d. The selection of Esther to be queen
  1) Esther was summoned to go to the king
    • She asked for nothing other than what Hegai suggested, trusting his judgment
    • Her graciousness & humility as well as her beauty impressed everyone
  2) Esther was taken to the king: The 10th month, the
	purifying of the women;)
	13 Then thus came *every* maiden unto the king; whatsoever she desired was given her to go with her out of the house of the women unto the king's house.
	14 In the evening she went, and on the morrow she returned into the second house of the women, to the custody of Shaashgaz, the king's chamberlain, which kept the concubines: she came in unto the king no more, except the king delighted in her, and that she were called by name.
	15 Now when the turn of Esther, the daughter of Abihail the uncle of Mordecai, who had taken her for his daughter, was come to go in unto the king, she required nothing but what Hegai the king's chamberlain, the keeper of the women, appointed. And Esther obtained favour in the sight of all them that looked upon her.
	16 So Esther was taken unto king Ahasuerus into his
		house royal in the tenth month, which *is* the month Tebeth, in the seventh year of his reign.
		17 And the king loved Esther above all the women, and she obtained grace and favour in his sight more than all the virgins; so that he set the royal crown upon her head, and made her queen instead of Vashti.
		18 Then the king made a great feast unto all his princes and his servants, *even* Esther's feast; and he made a release to the provinces, and gave gifts, according to the state of the king.
		19 And when the virgins were gathered together the second time, then Mordecai sat in the king's gate.
		20 Esther had not *yet* showed her kindred nor her people; as Mordecai had charged her: for Esther did the commandment of Mordecai, like as when she was brought up with him.
			month of Tebeth (Dec-Jan), in the 7th year of the king's reign
			
			3) Esther's striking beauty, poise, & behavior attracted the king more so than did any of the other young ladies: She was sweet, kind, & loving
			4) Esther was crowned as the new queen of the Persian empire
			5) Esther was given a great banquet to celebrate her coronation
			  • A holiday was proclaimed
			  • Gifts were generously distributed
			e. The nationality of Esther still kept secret
			  1) She kept it secret even after Mordecai sat at the king's gate, that is, was appointed a palace official
			  2) She was even now warned by Mordecai: She must still fear discrimination, anti-Semitism, 10
			  3) She had been an obedient child—all her life

a. Mordecai and Esther are now introduced to the reader (vv.5-7). Mordecai was a Jew, the great grandson of Kish (vv.5-6). Kish had been taken captive by the Babylonians when they conquered Judah about 120 years earlier in 597 B.C., (2 K.24:1-16). When the Jews were allowed by King Cyrus to return under the leadership of Zerubbabel, about 50,000 Jews made the decision to go back to the promised land. But not Mordecai. He chose to remain in Persia. Even when other exiles chose to return in subsequent years, Mordecai still chose to remain behind in Persia. He had obviously become very successful and politically active. Scripture indicates that he held some official position in the citadel of Susa. The citadel was a fortress within the city where the palace was located and where the king and his officials lived and carried on the functions of government (2:5, 21).

Esther was a younger cousin of Mordecai whom he had adopted when Esther's mother and father died. As she grew through the years, she matured into a beautiful, shapely, and lovely young woman (v.7). Note that her Hebrew name was Hadassah which means "Myrtle," and her Persian name was Esther, which means "Star."

b. Because of Esther's striking beauty, she was one of the young ladies taken to Xerxes' palace and placed in the king's harem (vv.8-11). As mentioned earlier, all of the beautiful young women were placed under the care of Hegai, who was the eunuch in charge of the king's harem. Just how many young ladies there were Scripture does not say. However the Jewish historian Josephus says there were 400.[1] Among all the ladies, Esther stood out, impressing and catching the eye of Hegai. Since all of the ladies were attractive, it could not have been Esther's beauty alone that caught his eye. It was bound to be the sweet, gracious, lovely, and kind spirit that flowed from Esther's heart. As will be seen, Esther was a young woman of strong character. She was not only a virgin, a young woman who had kept herself morally pure, but she was also a woman of grace and humility. Because of her lovely spirit as well as her striking beauty, Hegai gave her special attention and care (v.9). She was given additional beauty treatments, choice food, seven maids, and the best room in the harem.

Note that Esther had kept her nationality and family background a secret since her childhood (vv.10, 20). Mordecai had warned her to conceal the fact that she was a Jew because of discrimination, anti-Semitism. Of course, Mordecai did this for safety purposes. Their silence was not a sin, for they were not lying, not telling an untruth. They were merely saying nothing, for no one was asking about their nationality. In the words of Matthew Henry, "[Mordecai] only told her not to proclaim her country. All truths are not to be spoken at all times, though an untruth is not to be spoken at any time. She being born in Shushan (Susa), and her parents being dead, all took her to be of Persian extraction."[2]

Note also that Esther was deeply loved by Mordecai (v.11). Daily he walked by the courtyard of the harem to inquire about her welfare, to ask how she was doing.

c. The procedure used to please the sensual, lustful cravings of the king included three steps (vv.12-14). First, each girl was given twelve months of beauty treatments, with six months of oil baths and massages and six months of perfume and cosmetic applications. No doubt, a course on court etiquette was also given to the beautiful young ladies.

---

1 Josephus. *Antiquities of the Jews*, Book 11, Ch.6, Para.2, p.238.
2 *Matthew Henry's Commentary*, Vol.2, p.1127.

Second, at the end of the year's preparation, each girl was then selected to spend one night with the king (v.13). In order to look her best and be on her best behavior, the young woman was given whatever clothing or jewelry she wanted and anything else she needed to provide additional pleasure for the king (v.13).

Third, after spending one night with the king, each girl was then transferred to the permanent harem where the king's wives lived (v.14). This permanent harem was under the care of a eunuch named Shaashgaz, who was in charge of the concubines. Never again would the young ladies return to the king unless summoned by him. By entertaining new virgins night after night, month after month, the unbridled sexual exploits of the king were bound to make him insensitive to true love. No doubt, by ravaging a different virgin each night throughout the months, the king was unable to remember one lady from another. As a result, most of the beautiful young woman were doomed to spend their young lives as widows. They were sentenced to a life of loneliness and unfulfilled desires for sex and children. In the words of the commentator Warren Wiersbe:

> Such unbridled sensuality eventually would have so bored Ahasuerus that he was probably unable to distinguish one maiden from another. This was not love. It was faceless anonymous lust that craved more and more; and the more the king indulged, the less he was satisfied.[3]

The commentator Mervin Brenenam says this:

> There was no guarantee that the king would call them [young women] again, so many were confined to virtual widowhood. Again we see how one person, the king, could use so many other human beings just to satisfy his personal desire. Xerxes' abuse of power is evident in the demise of so many innocent women for his physical pleasure. Even today those who have no fear of God sometimes can satisfy their desires without limit.[4]

d. Finally, Esther was summoned to go to the king, and after spending a single night with him, she soon learned she was the one to be selected as queen of the great empire of King Xerxes (vv.15-18). After she was summoned, Esther asked for no other clothing or jewelry other than what Hegai suggested. She trusted his judgment entirely. After she was fully dressed and prepared for the king, her stately appearance, as well as her gracious, kind, and humble spirit, impressed everyone who saw her (v.15).

Esther was taken to the palace and presented to the king in the tenth month of Tebeth, in the seventh year of King Xerxes' reign (v.16). Her striking beauty, poise, and behavior attracted the king more so than did any of the other young ladies (v.17). Clearly her sweet, kind, and loving spirit also struck the heart of King Xerxes. He was so delighted with Esther that he set the royal crown upon her head and proclaimed her queen of the great Persian Empire. To celebrate the event, King Xerxes gave a great banquet in honor of Esther to celebrate her coronation (v.18). A holiday was proclaimed throughout the entire empire and gifts were generously distributed by the king to all his princes and servants.

e. Note that the nationality of Esther, the fact that she was a Jew, was still kept secret (vv.19-20). She kept it a secret even after a second group of virgins was brought into the king's harem. She kept it a secret despite the fact that Mordecai sat at the king's gate serving as one of the officials of the city. Despite Esther's being queen, Mordecai still felt that she needed to protect her nationality. The king would never have chosen her as one of his wives if he had known that she was a Jew and not a Persian. Note the reference to the fact that Esther had always been an obedient child—all her life (v.20).

Thought 1. Esther was a beautiful young woman, but her beauty was far more than just physical. The fact that King Xerxes chose her from among hundreds of beautiful women shows this fact. She undoubtedly had some qualities beyond beauty that attracted the king. Her real beauty arose from within, from a gracious, lovely spirit and a strong character. The following character traits in Esther can be gleaned:

⇒ First, she pleased Hegai and King Xerxes. This points to the traits of kindness, graciousness, humility and love.
⇒ Second, Esther was a woman of wisdom. Keeping her nationality a secret demonstrated wisdom. Esther knew that if her neighbors were aware that she was a Jew, she would be persecuted and become the object of prejudice and discrimination.
⇒ Third, the reference to Esther's being an obedient child (v.20) demonstrates that she was trustworthy, dependable, faithful, and loyal.
⇒ Fourth, being chosen by King Xerxes to become the queen points to her being an intelligent and industrious woman. Xerxes must have detected these traits, for he knew that she would be capable of handling the official duties of the queen, which were bound to be many (see 1:9 as an example).

How desperately these traits are needed by all women—young and old alike—today. Imagine the strength of a young lady who is...

- kind
- gracious
- humble
- loving
- wise
- virtuous
- obedient
- trustworthy
- dependable
- loyal
- faithful
- intelligent
- industrious

These traits should be a part of every young woman's life. Listen to what God's Holy Word says:
(1) Young women should be kind and gracious.

> **"Be kindly affected one to another with brotherly love; in honour preferring one another"** (Ro.12:10).

---

3 Warren W. Wiersbe, *Be Committed*. (Colorado Springs, CO: Victor Books, 1993), p.89.
4 Mervin Breneman. *New American Commentary, Ezra, Nehemiah, Esther*, pp.317-318.

"And be ye kind one to another, tenderhearted, forgiving one another, even as God for Christ's sake hath forgiven you" (Ep.4:32).
"A gracious woman retaineth honour" (Pr.11:16).

(2) Young women should be loving.

"Thou shalt love thy neighbour as thyself" (Mt.22:39).
"*Let* love be without dissimulation [without hypocrisy]. Abhor that which is evil; cleave to that which is good" (Ro.12:9).

(3) Young women should be virtuous and wise.

"Every wise woman buildeth her house: but the foolish plucketh it down with her hands" (Pr.14:1).
"Who can find a virtuous woman? for her price *is* far above rubies" (Pr.31:10).
"Favour *is* deceitful, and beauty *is* vain: *but* a woman *that* feareth the LORD, she shall be praised" (Pr.31:30).

(4) Young women should be obedient to their parents.

"Children, obey your parents in the Lord: for this is right" (Ep.6:1).
"Children, obey *your* parents in all things: for this is well pleasing unto the Lord" (Co.3:20).
"Honour thy father and thy mother: that thy days may be long upon the land which the LORD thy God giveth thee" (Ex.20:12).
"Cursed *be* he that setteth light by his father or his mother. And all the people shall say, Amen" (De.27:16).

(5) Young women should be humble, acknowledging the gifts God has given them but also acknowledging the gifts God has given others and esteeming others highly.

"Whosoever therefore shall humble himself as this little child, the same is greatest in the kingdom of heaven" (Mt.18:4).
"But ye *shall* not *be* so: but he that is greatest among you, let him be as the younger; and he that is chief, as he that doth serve" (Lu.22:26).
"For I say, through the grace given unto me, to every man [woman] that is among you, not to think *of himself* more highly than he ought to think; but to think soberly, according as God hath dealt to every man [woman] the measure of faith" (Ro.12:3).
"*Let* nothing *be done* through strife or vainglory; but in lowliness of mind let each esteem other better than themselves. Look not every man [woman] on his own things, but every man [woman] also on the things of others. Let this mind be in you, which was also in Christ Jesus" (Ph.2:3-5).
"Put on therefore, as the elect of God, holy and beloved, bowels of mercies, kindness, humbleness of mind, meekness, longsuffering" (Co.3:12).
"By humility *and* the fear of the LORD *are* riches, and honour, and life" (Pr.22:4).
"A man's [woman's] pride shall bring him [her] low: but honour shall uphold the humble in spirit" (Pr.29:23).

(6) Young women should always be studying and learning, gaining knowledge and intelligence.

"Study to shew thyself approved unto God, a workman that needeth not to be ashamed, rightly dividing the word of truth" (2 Ti.2:15).
"And beside this, giving all diligence, add to your faith virtue; and to virtue knowledge" (2 Pe.1:5).
"Yea, if thou criest after knowledge, *and* liftest up thy voice for understanding; If thou seekest her as silver, and searchest for her as *for* hid treasures; Then shalt thou understand the fear of the LORD, and find the knowledge of God" (Pr.2:3-5).
"Happy *is* the man [woman] *that* findeth wisdom, and the man [woman] *that* getteth understanding" (Pr.3:13).
"Get wisdom, get understanding: forget *it* not; neither decline from the words of my mouth" (Pr.4:5).
"The heart of him [her] that hath understanding seeketh knowledge: but the mouth of fools feedeth on foolishness" (Pr.15:14).
"Buy the truth, and sell *it* not; *also* wisdom, and instruction, and understanding" (Pr.23:23).

(7) Young women should be industrious, diligent, never slothful or lazy.

"In the which ye also walked some time, when ye lived in them" (Co.3:7).
"And whatsoever ye do, do *it* heartily, as to the Lord, and not unto men" (Co.3:23).
"He becometh poor that dealeth *with* a slack hand: but the hand of the diligent maketh rich" (Pr.10:4).

256

"Whatsoever thy hand findeth to do, do *it* with thy might; for *there is* no work, nor device, nor knowledge, nor wisdom, in the grave, whither thou goest" (Ec.9:10).

Thought 2. Standing opposite the strong character and moral purity of Esther is all the immoral, illicit sexual behavior of young women and men today. Esther guarded her virginity and remained sexually pure until her marriage. Yet the opposite is true of so many today. Immorality and premarital sex are being engaged in by so many young people who simply ignore God's commandments and/or the advice of their parents, mentors, or counselors. It is no surprise then, that the average age of sexual activity is dropping every year, dipping down even into the childhood years. If there has ever been a day when women of strong character and moral purity are needed, it is today. Listen to what God's Holy Word says:

"But I say unto you, That whosoever looketh on a woman to lust after her hath committed adultery with her already in his heart" (Mt.5:28).

"Now concerning the things whereof ye wrote unto me: *It is* good for a man not to touch a woman. Nevertheless, *to avoid* fornication, let every man have his own wife, and let every woman have her own husband. Let the husband render unto the wife due benevolence: and likewise also the wife unto the husband. The wife hath not power of her own body, but the husband: and likewise also the husband hath not power of his own body, but the wife. Defraud ye not one the other, except *it be* with consent for a time, that ye may give yourselves to fasting and prayer; and come together again, that Satan tempt you not for your incontinency" (1 Co.7:1-5).

"But fornication, and all uncleanness, or covetousness, let it not be once named among you, as becometh saints" (Ep.5:3).

"Mortify therefore your members which are upon the earth; fornication, uncleanness, inordinate affection, evil concupiscence, and covetousness, which is idolatry" (Co.3:5).

"For this is the will of God, *even* your sanctification, that ye should abstain from fornication: That every one of you should know how to possess his vessel in sanctification and honour; Not in the lust of concupiscence, even as the Gentiles which know not God" (1 Th.4:3-5).

"For God hath not called us unto uncleanness, but unto holiness" (1 Th.4:7).

"The aged women likewise, that *they be* in behaviour as becometh holiness, not false accusers, not given to much wine, teachers of good things; That they may teach the young women to be sober, to love their husbands, to love their children, *To be* discreet, chaste, keepers at home, good, obedient to their own husbands, that the word of God be not blasphemed" (Tit.2:3-5).

"Marriage *is* honourable in all, and the bed undefiled: but whoremongers and adulterers God will judge" (He.13:4).

"These are they which were not defiled with women; for they are virgins. These are they which follow the Lamb whithersoever he goeth. These were redeemed from among men, *being* the firstfruits unto God and to the Lamb" (Re.14:4).

"Thou shalt not commit adultery" (Ex.20:14).

"I made a covenant with mine eyes; why then should I think upon a maid?" (Jb.31:1).

"And why wilt thou, my son, be ravished with a strange woman, and embrace the bosom of a stranger?" (Pr.5:20).

3 (2:21-23) **Assassination, Warning of—Death, Warning of—Xerxes, King, Saved by Mordecai—Mordecai, Saved King Xerxes**: King Xerxes was saved by Mordecai's warning of an assassination plot. Sitting at the king's gate, Mordecai overheard two officers plotting to assassinate King Xerxes. Keep in mind that the king's gate was the place where city officials conducted civil, legal, and business affairs. Thus it was the central place of gathering within the city, a common area that bustled with commotion and busy activity. Overhearing the plot to assassinate the king, Mordecai immediately informed Queen Esther. She in turn rushed to inform the king. Significantly, she gave credit to Mordecai for having uncovered the plot (v.22). Of course, the king immediately had the report investigated and found it to be true. After arresting the two instigators, the king had them executed by hanging. This probably means they were impaled and hung on a large, tall stake. This was one of the major forms of capital punishment used by the Persians.

Note that the king forgot to recognize or reward Mordecai for uncovering the assassination plot (v.23). This fact will later prove to be vitally important (see outline and note—Est.6:1-14 for more discussion).

OUTLINE	SCRIPTURE	SCRIPTURE	OUTLINE
3. The forewarning of death given to the king by Mordecai: A picture of believers warning others to prepare for death	21 In those days, while Mordecai sat in the king's gate, two of the king's chamberlains, Bigthan and Teresh, of those which kept the door, were wroth, and sought to lay hand on the king Ahasuerus.	Esther the queen; and Esther certified the king *thereof* in Mordecai's name.	1) Esther told the king
a. Mordecai overheard two officers plotting to assassinate King Ahasuerus or Xerxes	22 And the thing was known to Mordecai, who told it unto	23 And when inquisition was made of the matter, it was found out; therefore they were both hanged on a tree: and it was written in the book of the chronicles before the king.	2) Esther gave credit to Mordecai
b. Mordecai informed Queen Esther			c. Mordecai's report was investigated
			1) It was found to be true
			2) It was the basis for hanging the guilty
			3) It was recorded in the king's records

Thought 1. King Xerxes' life was spared from assassination because he was warned by Mordecai ahead of time. And because he was warned, he had time to prepare, time to protect himself from his enemies. As believers there are two strong lessons for us in Mordecai's warning to King Xerxes.

(1) As followers of Christ, we too must warn people to prepare for death. Death is inevitable, unstoppable, and inescapable. And our great enemy Satan is always lying in wait.

But there is wonderful news. If we prepare in time, we can be delivered from death through Jesus Christ. We never have to face or experience death. Quicker than the eye can blink, when the moment comes for our departure, God will transfer us right into His presence. God will save us from experiencing death if we will simply trust Jesus Christ as our Savior.

But as stated, being followers of Christ we must warn other people to prepare for death and the judgment to come as well. It is even our responsibility to warn them, to carry out the Great Commission. Once warned, the way they can prepare is for death is to call upon the Lord Jesus Christ to save them and to give them eternal life. Jesus Christ has vanquished death for the believer. Listen to what God's Holy Word says:

> "Even as the Son of man came not to be ministered unto, but to minister, and to give his life a ransom for many" (Mt.20:28).
> "For the Son of man is come to seek and to save that which was lost" (Lu.19:10).
> "And as Moses lifted up the serpent in the wilderness, even so must the Son of man be lifted up: That whosoever believeth in him should not perish, but have eternal life" (Jn.3:14-15).
> "For God so loved the world, that he gave his only begotten Son, that whosoever believeth in him should not perish, but have everlasting life. For God sent not his Son into the world to condemn the world; but that the world through him might be saved" (Jn.3:16-17).
> "He that believeth on the Son hath everlasting life: and he that believeth not the Son shall not see life; but the wrath of God abideth on him" (Jn.3:36).
> "Verily, verily, I say unto you, He that heareth my word, and believeth on him that sent me, hath everlasting life, and shall not come into condemnation; but is passed from death unto life" (Jn.5:24).
> "The thief cometh not, but for to steal, and to kill, and to destroy: I am come that they might have life, and that they might have *it* more abundantly" (Jn.10:10).
> "Jesus said unto her, I am the resurrection, and the life: he that believeth in me, though he were dead, yet shall he live" (Jn.11:25).
> "But these are written, that ye might believe that Jesus is the Christ, the Son of God; and that believing ye might have life through his name" (Jn.20:31).
> "For the wages of sin *is* death; but the gift of God *is* eternal life through Jesus Christ our Lord" (Ro.6:23).
> "That if thou shalt confess with thy mouth the Lord Jesus, and shalt believe in thine heart that God hath raised him from the dead, thou shalt be saved. For with the heart man believeth unto righteousness; and with the mouth confession is made unto salvation" (Ro.10:9-10).
> "The last enemy *that* shall be destroyed *is* death...So when this corruptible shall have put on incorruption, and this mortal shall have put on immortality, then shall be brought to pass the saying that is written, Death is swallowed up in victory" (1 Co.15:26, 54).
> "For he that soweth to his flesh shall of the flesh reap corruption; but he that soweth to the Spirit shall of the Spirit reap life everlasting" (Ga.6:8).
> "But is now made manifest by the appearing of our Saviour Jesus Christ, who hath abolished death, and hath brought life and immortality to light through the gospel" (2 Ti.1:10).
> "Forasmuch then as the children are partakers of flesh and blood, he also himself likewise took part of the same; that through death he might destroy him that had the power of death, that is, the devil; And deliver them who through fear of death were all their lifetime subject to bondage" (He.2:14-15).
> "And God shall wipe away all tears from their eyes; and there shall be no more death, neither sorrow, nor crying, neither shall there be any more pain: for the former things are passed away" (Re.21:4).

(2) As followers of Christ we must serve those in authority. No matter our position or status in life, or whether or not we agree with our political leaders or others to whom we report, God commands us to respect, obey, and serve those in power or authority. His Holy Word is clear:

> "Thou shalt not revile the gods [God, R.S.V.], nor curse the ruler of thy people" (Ex.22:28).
> "I counsel thee to keep the king's commandment, and that in regard of the oath of God" (Ec.8:2).
> "They say unto him, Caesar's. Then saith he unto them, Render therefore unto Caesar the things which are Caesar's; and unto God the things that are God's" (Mt.22:21).
> "Then said Paul, I wist [knew] not, brethren, that he was the high priest: for it is written, Thou shalt not speak evil of the ruler of thy people" (Ac.23:5).
> "Let every soul be subject unto the higher powers. For there is no power but of God: the powers that be are ordained of God" (Ro.13:1).
> "Put them in mind to be subject to principalities and powers, to obey magistrates, to be ready to every good work" (Tit.3:1).
> "Submit yourselves to every ordinance of man for the Lord's sake" (1 Pe.2:13).
> "Honour all men. Love the brotherhood. Fear God. Honour the king" (1 Pe.2:17).

CHAPTER 3

II. THE JEWS MARKED FOR EXTERMINATION BY HAMAN: A PICTURE OF EXTREME PREJUDICE & HORRIFYING EVIL, 3:1-15 **

1. Haman's anger against Mordecai & the Jews: A picture of extreme prejudice & hatred
  a. The background of Haman
    1) He was an Agagite
    2) He was promoted to prime minister
    3) He was honored by all royal officials: By order of the king they were to bow when Haman passed by
  b. The defiance of Mordecai: He refused to bow lest he dishonor the LORD
  c. The officials' questioning of Mordecai about his disrespect
    1) They encouraged him to honor Haman: He refused because he was a Jew—such reverence belonged to God alone, for no man was divine
    2) They informed Haman that Mordecai was a Jew

  d. The violent rage of Haman: He decided to take revenge

    1) To kill Mordecai

    2) To slaughter all the Jews throughout the entire Persian empire

2. Haman's plot to exterminate the Jews: A picture of brutality & horrifying evil
  a. The day chosen for the attack against the Jews
    1) Was chosen by lot
    2) Fell on the 12th month, a year later
  b. The plan of extermination presented to King Ahasuerus (Xerxes)
    1) Haman charged the Jews with a false—but very serious—offense: Rebellion, breaking the king's laws

After these things did king Ahasuerus promote Haman the son of Hammedatha the Agagite, and advanced him, and set his seat above all the princes that *were* with him.
2 And all the king's servants, that *were* in the king's gate, bowed, and reverenced Haman: for the king had so commanded concerning him. But Mordecai bowed not, nor did *him* reverence.
3 Then the king's servants, which *were* in the king's gate, said unto Mordecai, Why transgressest thou the king's commandment?
4 Now it came to pass, when they spake daily unto him, and he hearkened not unto them, that they told Haman, to see whether Mordecai's matters would stand: for he had told them that he *was* a Jew.
5 And when Haman saw that Mordecai bowed not, nor did *him* reverence, then was Haman full of wrath.
6 And he thought scorn to lay hands on Mordecai alone; for they had showed him the people of Mordecai: wherefore Haman sought to destroy all the Jews that *were* throughout the whole kingdom of Ahasuerus, *even* the people of Mordecai.
7 In the first month, that *is,* the month Nisan, in the twelfth year of king Ahasuerus, they cast Pur, that *is,* the lot, before Haman from day to day, and from month to month, *to* the twelfth *month, that is,* the month Adar.
8 And Haman said unto king Ahasuerus, There is a certain people scattered abroad and dispersed among the people in all the provinces of thy kingdom; and their laws *are* diverse from all people; neither keep they the king's laws: therefore it *is* not for the king's profit to suffer them.
9 If it please the king, let it be written that they may be destroyed: and I will pay ten thousand talents of silver to the hands of those that have the charge of the business, to bring *it* into the king's treasuries.
10 And the king took his ring from his hand, and gave it unto Haman the son of Hammedatha the Agagite, the Jews' enemy.
11 And the king said unto Haman, The silver *is* given to thee, the people also, to do with them as it seemeth good to thee.
12 Then were the king's scribes called on the thirteenth day of the first month, and there was written according to all that Haman had commanded unto the king's lieutenants, and to the governors that *were* over every province, and to the rulers of every people of every province according to the writing thereof, and *to* every people after their language; in the name of king Ahasuerus was it written, and sealed with the king's ring.
13 And the letters were sent by posts into all the king's provinces, to destroy, to kill, and to cause to perish, all Jews, both young and old, little children and women, in one day, *even* upon the thirteenth *day* of the twelfth month, which *is* the month Adar, and *to* take the spoil of them for a prey.
14 The copy of the writing for a commandment to be given in every province was published unto all people, that they should be ready against that day.
15 The posts went out, being hastened by the king's commandment, and the decree was given in Shushan the palace. And the king and Haman sat down to drink; but the city Shushan was perplexed.

  2) Haman proposed a decree to exterminate the Jews
    • He promised the king 375 tons of silver
    • He expected to secure the money & more from the plunder

  3) The king gave his royal permission
    • Handed his ring to Haman, a symbol of his authority
    • Politely rejected the money, expecting Haman to insist: An Oriental custom, 4:7; 7:4

  c. The decree of extermination formulated by Haman
    1) Haman summoned the royal secretaries
      • He dictated the decree to all the leaders of every province in all the necessary languages
      • He sealed the decree with the king's ring

    2) Haman sent the decree by couriers to all the provinces: Ordered the people to kill all the Jews, including women & children
      • To kill them on a single day: The 13th day of the 12th month
      • To plunder their goods

    3) Haman had copies sent & published in every district: So all the people would be ready to carry out the decree

  d. The apathy of Haman & the king
    1) They sat down to drink: Callous, insensitive, uncaring
    2) The people of Susa were perplexed, bewildered

** Because Division II consists of only one chapter (Ch.3), no Divisional Overview is needed. The *Introduction* to Chapter 3 should suffice.

DIVISION II

THE JEWS MARKED FOR EXTERMINATION BY HAMAN: A PICTURE OF EXTREME PREJUDICE AND HORRIFYING EVIL, 3:1-15

(3:1-15) **Introduction**: prejudice and discrimination are serious problems within every society. Prejudice leads to dissension and division, and at times to rebellion or uprisings against authority. When a person has feelings of animosity, bigotry, or contempt against others, there is prejudice in his or her heart. When a person has negative opinions about others and feels disgust or displeasure in the company of others, there is intolerance and small-mindedness within. The victims of such behavior feel ashamed, embarrassed, and degraded. And well they should. They have been prejudged and treated unfairly by a narrow-minded, intolerant person.

Prejudice has led to segregation of whole races of people, causing one social class or race to treat another as inferior. Prejudice generally victimizes minorities—those who are of a different color, race, or religion—and judges them as being second-rate or undeserving. Extreme prejudice and bitter hatred against a race of people is the subject of the present Scripture. A sudden and alarming threat now enters the suspenseful story of Esther. A villain steps onto the scene at this point, a man named Haman. In the words of the commentator Mark Roberts:

> *Each year during the holiday of Purim, Jewish leaders around the world read the Book of Esther to excited crowds in the synagogues. Adults, and especially children, wait eagerly for the reading of Chapter 3 because with this chapter their fun begins. Verse 1 introduces Haman, the villain of the story, and each time the reader mentions his name—53 times throughout Esther—the synagogue erupts with raucous noise. Horns blow. Rattles shake. Children shout. Adults jeer. With zealous glee synagogue members try to drown out his name with their uproar. They do so because in the book of Esther, he is, without a doubt, the "villain," the archetypal enemy of the Jews. His evil deeds in chapter 3 create the central conflict of the book, which can only be resolved by Queen Esther's courageous acts to save her people.[1]*

In this chapter Haman's conflict with Mordecai begins. He is able to use this conflict as the basis for launching his plot to exterminate the entire Jewish race. The story that follows can be compared to two stories in the book of Daniel: the story of the three young Hebrew men who refused to bow down to the golden image of Nebuchadnezzar (Da.3); and the story of the officials who plotted against Daniel for praying to God instead of bowing to King Darius (Da.6). This is, *The Jews Marked for Extermination by Haman: A Picture of Extreme Prejudice and Horrifying Evil,* 3:1-15.

1. Haman's anger against Mordecai and the Jews: a picture of extreme prejudice and hatred, (vv.1-6).
2. Haman's plot to exterminate the Jews: a picture of brutality and horrifying evil, (vv.7-15).

---

1 (3:1-6) **Prejudice, Example of, Haman—Hatred, Example of—Anger, Example of—Discrimination, Example of—Jews, Prejudice Against, Example—Anti-Semitism, Example of—Holocaust, Plot for—Haman, Plotted to Exterminate the Jews—Mordecai, Hated by Haman**: Haman is unquestionably the evil villain of the story. His anger was aroused against Mordecai and the Jews because he was a man of extreme prejudice and bitter hatred toward the Jewish race. This high-ranking Persian official was about to erupt into a violent rage. He planned a diabolical scheme to exterminate all the Jews throughout the entire Persian Empire. Filled with bitterness and hatred, he did the unthinkable: he sought to slaughter an entire race of people. In a horrifying picture, Scripture has recorded the event for all generations to remember and guard against:

OUTLINE	SCRIPTURE	SCRIPTURE	OUTLINE
1. Haman's anger against Mordecai & the Jews: A picture of extreme prejudice & hatred	After these things did king Ahasuerus promote Haman the son of Hammedatha the Agagite, and advanced	when they spake daily unto him, and he hearkened not unto them, that they told Haman, to see whether Mor-	such reverence belonged to God alone, for no man was divine
a. The background of Haman	him, and set his seat above all	decai's matters would stand:	2) They informed Haman
1) He was an Agagite	the princes that *were* with	for he had told them that he	that Mordecai was a Jew
2) He was promoted to prime minister	him.	*was* a Jew.	
3) He was honored by all royal officials: By order of the king, they were to bow when Haman passed by	2 And all the king's servants, that *were* in the king's gate, bowed, and reverenced Haman: for the king had so	5 And when Haman saw that Mordecai bowed not, nor did him reverence, then was Haman full of wrath.	d. The violent rage of Haman: He decided to take revenge
b. The defiance of Mordecai: He refused to bow lest he dishonor the LORD	commanded concerning him. But Mordecai bowed not, nor did *him* reverence.	6 And he thought scorn to lay hands on Mordecai alone; for they had showed him the	1) To kill Mordecai
c. The officials' questioning of Mordecai about his disrespect	3 Then the king's servants, which *were* in the king's gate, said unto Mordecai,	people of Mordecai: wherefore Haman sought to destroy all the Jews that *were*	2) To slaughter all the Jews throughout the entire Persian empire
1) They encouraged him to honor Haman: He refused because he was a Jew—	Why transgressest thou the king's commandment? 4 Now it came to pass,	throughout the whole kingdom of Ahasuerus, *even* the people of Mordecai.	

---

1 Mark Roberts. *Ezra, Nehemiah, Esther*, p.363.

a. Three facts are mentioned about Haman's background. First, he is identified as "the Agagite," which probably means that he was a descendant of the Amalekite king *Agag*. Down through the centuries the Amalekites and Jews had been bitter enemies. This enmity between the two peoples stretched all the way back to the Exodus, when the Israelites were first formed into a nation. During the Israelites' journey to the promised land of Canaan, the Amalekites had attacked and slaughtered the handicapped and helpless, including the children, aged, sick, and weary who had lagged behind the main body of travelers (Ex.17:8-9; De.25:17-19). The deep hostility that grew between the two groups can be seen in the war fought against the Amalekites during the reign of King Saul (see outline and notes—1 S.15:1-35 for more discussion). Because of the brutal depravity of the Amalekites, God had commanded Saul to execute judgment against this terrorizing nation of people. Saul failed to carry out the commandment of God, but the prophet Samuel stepped in and did what he could, executing King Agag. Although this event had taken place 600 years earlier, Haman obviously knew the history of his people and was as gripped with bitter hatred for the Jews as his ancestors were.

It should be noted that "Agag" was also the name of a particular district or province of Persia. Consequently, some commentators believe that the reference to Haman as an Agagite simply means that he was from that particular district.

Second, Haman was promoted by King Xerxes to be prime minister of the Persian Empire (v.1). No doubt, he earned the position in the eyes of the king, for no person would be exalted to such a high position of authority unless the king felt he was capable and could make a significant contribution to the government. As prime minister, Haman was the second highest-ranking official in the government, second only to the king himself.

Third, Haman was honored by all the royal officials of the empire (v.2). By order of the king himself, all the officials were to bow in honor and reverence before Haman when he passed by.

b. But in defiance, Mordecai, Esther's guardian, cousin, and a government official, refused to bow before the prime minister (v.2). Obviously, he was a man of strong principle and courageous determination, for he adamantly refused to give Haman the reverence due to God alone.

c. Deeply concerned over Mordecai's defiance, a number of officials questioned his refusal to honor the prime minister (vv.3-4). Time and again they encouraged him to obey the king's command lest he be imprisoned and perhaps even executed. Nevertheless Mordecai still refused. Just why is not clearly stated by Scripture, but it is strongly indicated. Up until this time, Mordecai had never revealed the fact that he and Esther were Jews (2:10, 20). However, now it was necessary to reveal the fact, for he was being forced to take a stand for the LORD. The commandments of God prohibited giving honor or reverence to any man who claimed to be divine (Ex.20:2-6). It was the practice of Jews to bow before kings and other superiors (Ge.23:7; 27:29; 2 S.14:4; 18:28; 24:8; 1 K.1:16). But they were never allowed to bow before any person who claimed to be divine. Apparently the Persians regarded the king as a divine being, as a human incarnation of their false god Oromasdes.[2]

The very fact that Mordecai revealed his Jewish heritage strongly implies that he was taking a religious stand by refusing to pay homage to Haman. However, some commentators think that his persistent defiance was due to the extreme prejudice and bitter hatred he held for the Amalekites. In the Douay version of the Bible, the apocryphal chapters of Esther record a prayer of Mordecai during this period of his life. He appeals to the LORD in the following words:

> *Thou knowest, LORD, that it was neither in contempt nor pride, nor for any desire of glory, that I did not bow to proud Haman, for I could have been content with good will, for the salvation of Israel, to kiss the souls of his feet; but I did this that I might not prefer the glory of man above the glory of God, neither will I worship any but thee (13:12-14).*

Once the other officials learned that Mordecai was a Jew, they immediately informed Haman. They also related the fact of Mordecai's defiance in paying homage to him. By becoming informants against Mordecai, these officials were no doubt seeking the favor of the prime minister.

d. When Haman observed for himself Mordecai's bold refusal to honor him, the prime minister was filled with a violent rage. Thus, with bitter hatred flooding his heart, he made a deliberate decision to take revenge not only on Mordecai but also on the Jewish people as a whole. His plan was to slaughter all the Jews throughout all the Persian Empire (vv.5-6). Having made the decision, he began to look for a way to launch the holocaust, the extermination of the Jews. Note that the atrocity was to be launched throughout the kingdom of Persia, which included the land of Palestine, the promised land itself. This meant that the true surviving believers who had returned under Zerubbabel to rebuild the temple and nation were also to be slaughtered. Haman's diabolical heart was exposed in his shameless plot against the Jews.

Thought 1. Haman's attempt to exterminate the Jews is the basic plot of the book of *Esther*. Guarding ourselves against extreme prejudice and bitter hatred is the lesson for us. Discriminating against other people because of their race, color, appearance, ability or beliefs is wrong. Just because a person is different—whether handicapped, physically deformed, less educated or any other dissimilarity—is no reason for harsh feelings or acts of discrimination. As followers of the Lord Jesus Christ, we are not to open our hearts to prejudice or bitter hatred. When people do wrong and commit atrocities, we are to legally execute justice and hold them accountable. However, justice is never to be executed out of personal bitterness but, rather, out of a sense of righteousness.

No person is ever to be degraded, reacted against, falsely charged, or given fewer rights because he or she differs from the rest of us. We are never to treat others as though they are of less value and worth than we are. We have all been created by the hand of God, and God considers every human being to be of equal value and worth.

(1) The Bible gives example after example of people who have given their hearts over to prejudice and hatred of others.

"Is not this the carpenter, the son of Mary, the brother of James, and Joses, and of Juda, and Simon? and are not his sisters here with us? And they were offended at him [Jesus Christ]" (Mk.6:3).

---

2 Keil-Delitzsch. *Commentary on the Old Testament*, Vol.3, pp.333-334.

"And John answered him, saying, Master, we saw one casting out devils in thy name, and he followeth not us: and we forbad him, because he followeth not us. But Jesus said, Forbid him not: for there is no man which shall do a miracle in my name, that can lightly speak evil of me. For he that is not against us is on our part. For whosoever shall give you a cup of water to drink in my name, because ye belong to Christ, verily I say unto you, he shall not lose his reward" (Mk.9:38-41).

"And he said, Verily I say unto you, No prophet is accepted in his own country" (Lu.4:24).

"And they did not receive him [Jesus Christ], because his face was as though he would go to Jerusalem" (Lu.9:53).

"And when they saw it, they all murmured, saying, That he [Jesus Christ] was gone to be guest with a man that is a sinner" (Lu.19:7).

"And Nathanael said unto him, Can there any good thing come out of Nazareth? Philip saith unto him, Come and see" (Jn.1:46).

"Then saith the woman of Samaria unto him, How is it that thou [Jesus], being a Jew, askest drink of me, which am a woman of Samaria? for the Jews have no dealings with the Samaritans" (Jn.4:9).

"They answered and said unto him, Art thou also of Galilee? Search, and look: for out of Galilee ariseth no prophet" (Jn.7:52).

"And he said unto them, Ye know how that it is an unlawful thing for a man that is a Jew to keep company, or come unto one of another nation; but God hath showed me that I should not call any man common or unclean" (Ac.10:28).

"Saying, Thou [Peter] wentest in to men uncircumcised, and didst eat with them" (Ac.11:3).

"And I [Paul] punished them oft in every synagogue, and compelled them to blaspheme; and being exceedingly mad against them, I persecuted them even unto strange cities" (Ac.26:11).

"For before that certain came from James, he [Peter] did eat with the Gentiles: but when they were come, he withdrew and separated himself, fearing them which were of the circumcision" (Ga.2:12).

"And they set on for him by himself, and for them by themselves, and for the Egyptians, which did eat with him, by themselves: because the Egyptians might not eat bread with the Hebrews; for that is an abomination unto the Egyptians" (Ge.43:32).

(2) In God's eyes all people are of equal value and worth.

"But be not ye called Rabbi: for one is your Master, even Christ; and all ye are brethren" (Mt.23:8).

"And whosoever shall exalt himself shall be abased; and he that shall humble himself shall be exalted" (Mt.23:12).

"And he said unto them, Ye know how that it is an unlawful thing for a man that is a Jew to keep company, or come unto one of another nation; but God hath showed me that I should not call any man common or unclean" (Ac.10:28).

"For there is no difference between the Jew and the Greek: for the same Lord over all is rich unto all that call upon him" (Ro.10:12).

"There is neither Jew nor Greek, there is neither bond nor free, there is neither male nor female: for ye are all one in Christ Jesus" (Ga.3:28).

"Let nothing be done through strife or vainglory; but in lowliness of mind let each esteem other better than themselves. Look not every man on his own things, but every man also on the things of others" (Ph.2:3-4).

"So God created man in his own image, in the image of God created he him; male and female created he them" (Ge.1:27).

"This is the book of the generations of Adam. In the day that God created man, in the likeness of God made he him" (Ge.5:1).

"The rich and poor meet together: the LORD is the maker of them all" (Pr.22:2).

"Though thou exalt thyself as the eagle, and though thou set thy nest among the stars, thence will I bring thee down, saith the LORD" (Ob.4).

(3) God condemns and warns us against hatred and malice.

"Now the works of the flesh are manifest, which are these; Adultery, fornication, uncleanness, lasciviousness, Idolatry, witchcraft, hatred, variance, emulations, wrath, strife, seditions, heresies, Envyings, murders, drunkenness, revellings, and such like: of the which I tell you before, as I have also told you in time past, that they which do such things shall not inherit the kingdom of God." (Ga.5:19-21 note the word "hatred")

"Let all bitterness, and wrath, and anger, and clamour, and evil speaking, be put away from you, with all malice" (Ep.4:31).

"But now ye also put off all these; anger, wrath, malice, blasphemy, filthy communication out of your mouth" (Co.3:8).

"Wherefore laying aside all malice, and all guile, and hypocrisies, and envies, and all evil speakings" (1 Pe.2:1).

"He that saith he is in the light, and hateth his brother, is in darkness even until now" (1 Jn.2:9).

"Whosoever hateth his brother is a murderer: and ye know that no murderer hath eternal life abiding in him" (1 Jn.3:15).
"Thou shalt not hate thy brother in thine heart" (Le.19:17).
"Hatred stirreth up strifes: but love covereth all sins" (Pr.10:12).

2 (3:7-15) **Evil, Depth of—Imaginations, Kind of, Wicked and Evil—Thoughts, Kinds of, Wicked and Evil—Evil, Epitome of—Holocaust, of the Jews—Extermination, of the Jews—Jews, Extermination of—Haman, Plotted to Exterminate the Jews—Ahasuerus (Xerxes), King of Persia, Decreed the Extermination of the Jews—Persia, Decreed the Extermination of the Jews**: after making the personal decision to exterminate the Jews, prime minister Haman immediately began to plan just how to carry out his devious plot. His scheming behavior exposed him as a man of horrifying evil, filled with wicked imaginations and thoughts, a man who epitomizes the depth of evil and wickedness.

OUTLINE	SCRIPTURE	SCRIPTURE	OUTLINE

2. Haman's plot to exterminate the Jews: A picture of brutality & horrifying evil
a. The day chosen for the attack against the Jews
  1) Was chosen by lot
  2) Fell on the 12th month, a year later
b. The plan of extermination presented to King Ahasuerus (Xerxes)
  1) Haman charged the Jews with a false—but very serious—offense: Rebellion, breaking the king's laws
 	
  2) Haman proposed a decree to exterminate the Jews
  • He promised the king 375 tons of silver
  • He expected to secure the money & more from the plunder
 	
  3) The king gave his royal permission
  • Handed his ring to Haman, a symbol of his authority
  • Politely rejected the money, expecting Haman to insist: An Oriental custom, 4:7; 7:4
c. The decree of extermination formulated by Haman
	7 In the first month, that is, the month Nisan, in the twelfth year of king Ahasuerus, they cast Pur, that is, the lot, before Haman from day to day, and from month to month, to the twelfth month, that is, the month Adar.
	8 And Haman said unto king Ahasuerus, There is a certain people scattered abroad and dispersed among the people in all the provinces of thy kingdom; and their laws are diverse from all people; neither keep they the king's laws: therefore it is not for the king's profit to suffer them.
	9 If it please the king, let it be written that they may be destroyed: and I will pay ten thousand talents of silver to the hands of those that have the charge of the business, to bring it into the king's treasuries.
	10 And the king took his ring from his hand, and gave it unto Haman the son of Hammedatha the Agagite, the Jews' enemy.
	11 And the king said unto Haman, The silver is given to thee, the people also, to do with them as it seemeth good to thee.
	12 Then were the king's scribes called on the thir-
		teenth day of the first month, and there was written according to all that Haman had commanded unto the king's lieutenants, and to the governors that were over every province, and to the rulers of every people of every province according to the writing thereof, and to every people after their language; in the name of king Ahasuerus was it written, and sealed with the king's ring.
		13 And the letters were sent by posts into all the king's provinces, to destroy, to kill, and to cause to perish, all Jews, both young and old, little children and women, in one day, even upon the thirteenth day of the twelfth month, which is the month Adar, and to take the spoil of them for a prey.
		14 The copy of the writing for a commandment to be given in every province was published unto all people, that they should be ready against that day.
		15 The posts went out, being hastened by the king's commandment, and the decree was given in Shushan the palace. And the king and Haman sat down to drink; but the city Shushan was perplexed.
			1) Haman summoned the royal secretaries
			  • He dictated the decree to all the leaders of every province in all the necessary languages
			  • He sealed the decree with the king's ring
			
			2) Haman sent the decree by couriers to all the provinces: Ordered the people to kill all the Jews, including women & children
			  • To kill them on a single day: The 13th day of the 12th month
			  • To plunder their goods
			
			3) Haman had copies sent & published in every district: So all the people would be ready to carry out the decree
			
			d. The apathy of Haman & the king
			  1) They sat down to drink: Callous, insensitive, uncaring
			  2) The people of Susa were perplexed, bewildered

a. First, Haman needed to choose the day when the holocaust against the Jews was to be launched (v.7). In choosing the day, Haman wanted the guidance of his false god(s). So he went to the priests of his false religion and had them cast a lot (Pur) in order to select the best day and month to take action against the Jews. It was the twelfth year of King Xerxes' reign, the first month (the month of Nissan) when the lot was cast. This was...

- five years after Esther became queen
- over one hundred years after the first return of the Jewish exiles under Zerubbabel's leadership
- sixteen years before the second return of Jewish exiles under Ezra

When the religious leaders cast the dice-like lot, it fell on the twelfth month, the month of Adar, which was a year later.

The fact that Haman cast the lot in order to choose the day for his attack against the Jews shows just how superstitious he was. Many of the people of that day and time were superstitious, following religions that stressed fate and chance, magic and astrology. People followed these false religions to determine their future and the steps they should take in making decisions and governing their lives. They allowed the stars and the omens of their religions to govern their lives and determine their fate.

Because of his extreme superstitions, prime minister Haman was allowing the casting of lots to dictate the date of his attack against the Jewish people. Little did he know that the true and living God was in control of the situation. The LORD who created and controlled the universe was in control of the lot casting.

Keep in mind that the LORD had made two great promises that had yet to be fulfilled: the promise that both the Messiah and the written Word of God would come through the Jewish people. If Haman had been allowed to exterminate the Jews, these two major promises of God would never have been fulfilled. Thus the LORD was moving behind the scenes to defeat the wicked plot of Haman. In causing the lot to fall on the twelfth month, the LORD was giving the Jews a whole year to get ready for the attack, a year in which events would bring about the deliverance of the Jews and the death of their arch-enemy Haman.

b. After the date had been determined, Haman took his plan of extermination to King Xerxes (vv.8-11). He falsely charged the Jews with a very serious offense, that of rebellion, breaking the king's laws (v.8). Note that he did not identify the people, not at first. He simply informed the king that there was a certain race of people scattered throughout the empire who had laws that were different from the Persian law. And these people were placing the importance of their own laws above the Persian law, obeying their laws and disobeying the Persian law. For these reasons, there was a danger of political disturbance and uprising. It was not in the best interest of the king or the empire to allow this rebellion to continue. If the Jews were allowed to proceed, placing their laws above Persian law, widespread rebellion could extend throughout the entire empire.

Of course, Haman was lying. The Jews had not rebelled against the law of the Persians. In fact, the prophet Jeremiah had encouraged God's people to settle down and build a new life, being good citizens in the land to which they had been taken captive (Je.29:4-7). They were not to cause disturbances. Nonetheless, because of his extreme prejudice, Prime Minister Haman was willing to lie about Mordecai and the Jews, making one false accusation after another in order to carry out his horrific plan of extermination. Note that Haman is called "the enemy of the Jews," five different times throughout the book of Esther (3:10; 7:6; 8:1; 9:10, 24).

After presenting the false charge of rebellion, Haman asked the king for a decree to exterminate the Jews (vv.9-11). To entice King Xerxes, the prime minister offered to personally undergo the cost of the extermination campaign. He himself would put into the treasury 10,000 talents of silver, which was about 375 tons—an enormous amount of money. Not only would this amount cover the cost of the extermination campaign, but it would add significant wealth to the government's treasury, a fact that would help the government greatly. No doubt, the treasury had been depleted because of the Greek wars that Xerxes had launched in his European campaign. Therefore the offer of such a large sum of money was a strong incentive for Xerxes to grant the prime minister's proposal. And this is exactly what the king did. King Xerxes handed his royal signet ring to Haman, which was a symbol of the king's authority (v.10).

Following the Oriental custom of that day, King Xerxes politely rejected the money. But it was the custom for the person who had made the offer to insist that he be allowed to pay or follow through with what he had discussed (4:7; 7:4). Simply stated, King Xerxes was bargaining with Prime Minister Haman, stating that he would accept the money and that Haman could go and do what he wished with the Jewish people.

c. Having received the king's permission, Haman set about to formulate the decree to exterminate the entire Jewish race from the face of the earth (vv.12-14). Summoning the royal secretaries, Haman dictated the decree to all the leaders of every district in all the necessary languages. Once the decree was finished, he sealed it with the king's royal ring. Haman then sent the decree by courier to all the provinces throughout the empire. The message of the decree was stunning, savage and brutal. The Persian population was to destroy—totally annihilate—all the Jews, both young and old, men, women, children, and babies. And note: this holocaust, this horrifying evil was to take place on a single day, the thirteenth day of the twelfth month. After the Jews were slaughtered, the Persians were instructed to plunder their goods.

Haman had become so gripped by prejudice, hatred, and his own evil plan that he left nothing to chance. He sent a copy of the decree to every district. He made sure that all the people of every nationality within the empire knew about the decree, so that they would be prepared to take action against the Jews.

d. The horrible state to which a human heart can sink is now depicted. Look at the apathy of Haman and the king (v.15). Having just issued the decree to exterminate a whole race of people, the two men sat down to drink. They were totally callous, insensitive, and uncaring about the action just taken. But in contrast, the people of the royal city of Susa were perplexed, bewildered by the decree that ordered the extermination of the Jews. No doubt, all the minority populations throughout the empire questioned the decree and worried if they might be the next group of the land to be exterminated. Would they also be targeted as enemies of the state? What had brought about such a change of policy within the Persian government? Confusion and alarm were bound to be setting in among the many minority populations.

Thought 1. Haman is the epitome of wickedness. He shows the depth of evil to which the human heart can sink. Down through history, rulers and governments have passed laws to oppress certain people under their authority. And, sadly, in some cases, they have sought to exterminate whole races of people. Specific examples are...

- the early laws of America that allowed the oppression of Indians and Orientals and the enslavement of the black race
- the German holocaust against the Jews
- the extermination of millions of Russians by certain of their rulers, such as Stalin
- the slaughter of the Kurds by the oppressive and brutal Iraqi dictator Sadam Hussein

Brutality, savagery, and horrific evil did not take place only in past history. Scripture is clear: man's heart is basically sinful, filled with wicked imaginations and thoughts. And unless man controls his selfish desires and lusts, he too is capable of unspeakable atrocities. Every act of lawlessness, violence, and sinful behavior is evidence of man's sinful heart. Thus the human heart needs to be changed, converted, made new.

(1) God's Holy Word says that the human heart is sinful, filled with wicked imaginations and thoughts.

"And Jesus knowing their thoughts said, Wherefore think ye evil in your hearts?" (Mt.9:4).
"For out of the heart proceed evil thoughts, murders, adulteries, fornications, thefts, false witness, blasphemies" (Mt.15:19).

"Woe unto you, scribes and Pharisees, hypocrites! for ye make clean the outside of the cup and of the platter, but within they are full of extortion and excess" (Mt.23:25).

"And he said, That which cometh out of the man, that defileth the man. For from within, out of the heart of men, proceed evil thoughts, adulteries, fornications, murders, Thefts, covetousness, wickedness, deceit, lasciviousness, an evil eye, blasphemy, pride, foolishness: All these evil things come from within, and defile the man" (Mk.7:20-23).

"Because that, when they knew God, they glorified *him* not as God, neither were thankful; but became vain in their imaginations, and their foolish heart was darkened" (Ro.1:21).

"And even as they did not like to retain God in *their* knowledge, God gave them over to a reprobate mind, to do those things which are not convenient" (Ro.1:28).

"What then? are we better *than they?* No, in no wise: for we have before proved both Jews and Gentiles, that they are all under sin; As it is written, There is none righteous, no, not one: There is none that understandeth, there is none that seeketh after God. They are all gone out of the way, they are together become unprofitable; there is none that doeth good, no, not one. Their throat *is* an open sepulchre; with their tongues they have used deceit; the poison of asps *is* under their lips: Whose mouth *is* full of cursing and bitterness: Their feet *are* swift to shed blood: Destruction and misery *are* in their ways: And the way of peace have they not known: There is no fear of God before their eyes" (Ro.3:9-18).

"For they that are after the flesh do mind the things of the flesh; but they that are after the Spirit the things of the Spirit. For to be carnally minded *is* death; but to be spiritually minded *is* life and peace. Because the carnal mind *is* enmity against God: for it is not subject to the law of God, neither indeed can be. So then they that are in the flesh cannot please God" (Ro.8:5-8).

"Take heed, brethren, lest there be in any of you an evil heart of unbelief, in departing from the living God" (He.3:12).

"Having eyes full of adultery, and that cannot cease from sin; beguiling unstable souls: an heart they have exercised with covetous practices; cursed children" (2 Pe.2:14).

"And GOD saw that the wickedness of man *was* great in the earth, and *that* every imagination of the thoughts of his heart *was* only evil continually" (Ge.6:5).

"They also that seek after my life lay snares *for me:* and they that seek my hurt speak mischievous things, and imagine deceits all the day long" (Ps.38:12).

"The LORD knoweth the thoughts of man, that they *are* vanity" (Ps.94:11).

"An heart that deviseth wicked imaginations, feet that be swift in running to mischief" (Pr.6:18).

"The thoughts of the wicked *are* an abomination to the LORD: but *the words* of the pure *are* pleasant words" (Pr.15:26).

"For as he thinketh in his heart, so *is* he: Eat and drink, saith he to thee; but his heart *is* not with thee" (Pr.23:7).

"The thought of foolishness *is* sin: and the scorner *is* an abomination to men" (Pr.24:9).

"O Jerusalem, wash thine heart from wickedness, that thou mayest be saved. How long shall thy vain thoughts lodge within thee?" (Je.4:14).

"The heart *is* deceitful above all *things,* and desperately wicked: who can know it?" (Je.17:9).

"They say still unto them that despise me, The LORD hath said, Ye shall have peace; and they say unto every one that walketh after the imagination of his own heart, No evil shall come upon you" (Je.23:17).

"Then said he unto me, Son of man, hast thou seen what the ancients of the house of Israel do in the dark, every man in the chambers of his imagery? for they say, The LORD seeth us not; the LORD hath forsaken the earth" (Eze.8:12).

(2) God's Holy Word says that the human heart must be converted, changed, made new.

"And said, Verily I say unto you, Except ye be converted, and become as little children, ye shall not enter into the kingdom of heaven" (Mt.18:3).

"But that on the good ground are they, which in an honest and good heart, having heard the word, keep *it,* and bring forth fruit with patience" (Lu.8:15).

"But I have prayed for thee, that thy faith fail not: and when thou art converted, strengthen thy brethren" (Lu.22:32).

"But as many as received him, to them gave he power to become the sons of God, *even* to them that believe on his name: Which were born, not of blood, nor of the will of the flesh, nor of the will of man, but of God" (Jn.1:12-13).

"Jesus answered and said unto him, Verily, verily, I say unto thee, Except a man be born again, he cannot see the kingdom of God. Nicodemus saith unto him, How can a man be born when he is old? can he enter the second time into his mother's womb, and be born? Jesus answered, Verily, verily, I say unto thee, Except a man be born of water and *of* the Spirit, he cannot enter into the kingdom of God. That which is born of the flesh is flesh; and that which is born of the Spirit is spirit. Marvel not that I said unto thee, Ye must be born again. The wind bloweth where it listeth, and thou hearest the sound thereof, but canst not tell whence it cometh, and whither it goeth: so is every one that is born of the Spirit" (Jn.3:3-8).

"Repent ye therefore, and be converted, that your sins may be blotted out, when the times of refreshing shall come from the presence of the Lord" (Ac.3:19).

"Therefore if any man *be* in Christ, *he is* a new creature: old things are passed away; behold, all things are become new" (2 Co.5:17).

"That ye put off concerning the former conversation [behavior, conduct] the old man, which is corrupt according to the deceitful lusts; And be renewed in the spirit of your mind; And that ye put on the new man, which after God is created in righteousness and true holiness" (Ep.4:22-24).

"Not by works of righteousness which we have done, but according to his mercy he saved us, by the washing of regeneration, and renewing of the Holy Ghost; Which he shed on us abundantly through Jesus Christ our Saviour; That being justified by his grace, we should be made heirs according to the hope of eternal life" (Tit.3:5-7).

"Brethren, if any of you do err from the truth, and one convert him; Let him know, that he which converteth the sinner from the error of his way shall save a soul from death, and shall hide a multitude of sins" (Js.5:19-20).

"A new heart also will I give you, and a new spirit will I put within you: and I will take away the stony heart out of your flesh, and I will give you an heart of flesh" (Eze.36:26).

"The law of the LORD *is* perfect, converting the soul: the testimony of the LORD *is* sure, making wise the simple" (Ps.19:7).

"Restore unto me the joy of thy salvation; and uphold me *with thy* free spirit. *Then* will I teach transgressors thy ways; and sinners shall be converted unto thee" (Ps.51:12-13).

266

DIVISION III — ESTHER

THE JEWS SAVED BY THE COURAGEOUS ACTION OF ESTHER, 4:1–10:3

(4:1–10:3) **DIVISION OVERVIEW**: the Jews were in desperate straits because of the evil plan of Prime Minister Haman to exterminate them. Haman hated Mordecai the Jew, hated him so much that he obtained permission from King Ahasuerus to wipe out all the Jews. Once Mordecai reported Haman's evil plot to Queen Esther, a decision had to be made. Esther could take safe harbor in the palace as the queen and try to keep her Jewish heritage a secret, or, she could risk her life by approaching the king about the situation. Mordecai urged Esther to do what she could to save the Jews from destruction. After much prayer, Esther made the courageous decision to approach the king. Much was at stake. If she did not find favor as she approached, she would be executed immediately, and the hope of intercession for the Jews would be gone. The situation could not have been more serious.

At this point, the account of Esther takes several dramatic turns. Esther informed the king that she had a request to ask of him, but she first wanted him and the prime minister to come to a banquet. Earlier, the king had approved Haman's request to eliminate the Jewish race, but he still had no idea that Esther was Jewish. At the banquet, instead of presenting her request to the king, Esther surprisingly asked the king and Haman to come to another banquet on the following night. Why did she delay her request to save her people? Perhaps she was studying Haman and the situation further. Or perhaps she was looking for the right moment, trying to gather her courage. All that is known is that somehow, God caused her to delay her request.

The next day, Mordecai the Jew, who was bitterly hated by Haman, was suddenly honored by the king. It had just been discovered that Mordecai had saved the king's life from an assassination plot years earlier. This, of course, changed the situation dramatically. What happened next reaches the pinnacle of suspense and drama. At the second banquet, Esther informed the king that Haman wanted to exterminate her people, which meant that she also would be killed. The king exploded in wrath. Haman and his ten sons were immediately executed. By law, the decree of extermination could not be changed. But another decree was issued by the king. This second decree gave the Jews the right to defend themselves against their attackers. On the day of the battle, the Jews won an overwhelming victory, and they were granted another day of battle in order to completely defeat their enemies. The Feast of Purim was established to celebrate the great deliverance of the Jews. Esther was greatly esteemed, and Mordecai was elevated by King Ahasuerus to replace Haman as prime minister of Persia.

Remember that the book of *Esther* was written primarily to the returned exiles and to the future generations who may be facing threatening enemies or suffering affliction or hardship. In times of uncertainty and discouragement, those hearing the story of *Esther* can gather strength and trust in the LORD. When situations seem hopeless and destruction near, the inspiring account of the great book of *Esther* is a reminder that God is sovereign. He will not forsake His people nor leave them without hope. He will protect, deliver, strengthen, and carry them through any difficult trial.

As the reader studies God's great deliverance of the Jews, this fact should be kept in mind: God will deliver the believer from difficult circumstances or else give the believer strength to walk through the hardship or affliction.

"The Jews had light, and gladness, and joy, and honour" (Est.8:16).

THE JEWS SAVED BY THE COURAGEOUS ACTION OF ESTHER, 4:1–10:3

A. The Courageous Decision of Esther: A Look at Two Desperate Needs, 4:1-17

B. The Courageous Approach of Esther into the King's Presence: A Contrast Between a Believer's Trust in God and an Unbeliever's Pride, 5:1-14

C. The Unexpected Honor Bestowed Upon Mordecai: A Picture of God's Providence, Guidance, and Love for His People, 6:1-14

D. The Suspenseful Exposure and Downfall of Haman: A Picture of Reaping Exactly What One Sows—Justice, Measure for Measure, 7:1-10

E. The Desperate Intercession of Esther for the Deliverance of the Jews: A Picture of Being Delivered Through Prayer, 8:1-17

F. The Triumph of the Jews and the Celebration of Purim: A Picture of Victory Over One's Enemy, 9:1-10:3

CHAPTER 4

III. THE JEWS SAVED BY THE COURAGEOUS ACTION OF ESTHER, 4:1–10:3

A. The Courageous Decision of Esther: A Look at Two Desperate Needs, 4:1-17

1. The deep anguish of Mordecai over the *Decree of Extermination* & his appeal to Queen Esther: A picture of the desperate need for an intercessor who can plead for mercy

a. Mordecai & the Jews' intense grief
1) Mordecai put on sackcloth & ashes & walked into the city, crying loudly & bitterly: Went to the palace gate
2) The Jews mourned deeply throughout the empire
   • They fasted, wept, & prayed
   • Many lay in sackcloth & ashes

b. Esther's concern over news of Mordecai's deep distress
1) She sent Mordecai clothing to allow him to enter the palace, 2
2) Mordecai refused to change

c. Esther's distress over her adoptive father's grief
1) She sent her trusted aide Hathach to find out what was troubling Mordecai

2) Hathach found Mordecai in the open square of the city: Was in front of the palace gate

d. Mordecai's explanation of the decree & his appeal to Esther
1) He stated that money—the plunder of Jewish property—was one of reasons for the decree

2) He gave the aide a copy of the royal decree so Esther could see the proof herself

When Mordecai perceived all that was done, Mordecai rent his clothes, and put on sackcloth with ashes, and went out into the midst of the city, and cried with a loud and a bitter cry;
2 And came even before the king's gate: for none *might* enter into the king's gate clothed with sackcloth.
3 And in every province, whithersoever the king's commandment and his decree came, *there was* great mourning among the Jews, and fasting, and weeping, and wailing; and many lay in sackcloth and ashes.
4 So Esther's maids and her chamberlains came and told *it* her. Then was the queen exceedingly grieved; and she sent raiment to clothe Mordecai, and to take away his sackcloth from him: but he received *it* not.
5 Then called Esther for Hatach, *one* of the king's chamberlains, whom he had appointed to attend upon her, and gave him a commandment to Mordecai, to know what it *was,* and why it *was.*
6 So Hatach went forth to Mordecai unto the street of the city, which *was* before the king's gate.
7 And Mordecai told him of all that had happened unto him, and of the sum of the money that Haman had promised to pay to the king's treasuries for the Jews, to destroy them.
8 Also he gave him the copy of the writing of the decree that was given at Shushan to destroy them, to

show *it* unto Esther, and to declare *it* unto her, and to charge her that she should go in unto the king, to make supplication unto him, and to make request before him for her people.
9 And Hatach came and told Esther the words of Mordecai.
10 Again Esther spake unto Hatach, and gave him commandment unto Mordecai;
11 All the king's servants, and the people of the king's provinces, do know, that whosoever, whether man or woman, shall come unto the king into the inner court, who is not called, *there is* one law of his to put *him* to death, except such to whom the king shall hold out the golden sceptre, that he may live: but I have not been called to come in unto the king these thirty days.
12 And they told to Mordecai Esther's words.
13 Then Mordecai commanded to answer Esther, Think not with thyself that thou shalt escape in the king's house, more than all the Jews.
14 For if thou altogether holdest thy peace at this time, *then* shall there enlargement and deliverance arise to the Jews from another place; but thou and thy father's house shall be destroyed: and who knoweth whether thou art come to the kingdom for *such* a time as this?
15 Then Esther bade *them* return Mordecai *this answer,*
16 Go, gather together all the Jews that are present in Shushan, and fast ye for me, and neither eat nor drink three days, night or day: I also and my maidens will fast likewise; and so will I go in unto the king, which *is* not according to the law: and if I perish, I perish.
17 So Mordecai went his way, and did according to all that Esther had commanded him.

3) He instructed the aide to urge Esther to seek an audience with the king, to plead for mercy for her people

e. Mordecai's message delivered to Esther by Hathach

2. The courageous decision of Esther to risk her life: A picture of the desperate need for courage, prayer, & fasting
a. Esther's dilemma & her desire for Mordecai's guidance
1) Persian law prohibited anyone from approaching the king without first being summoned, upon penalty of death
2) Esther had not been summoned for 30 days: Perhaps he no longer favored her

b. Mordecai's insistence that Esther be courageous
1) Because being queen would not protect her, for she too was a Jew

2) Because if she kept silent during this crisis, God would raise up another deliverer: Still she & her family would perish
3) Because God had raised her up for this very purpose

c. Esther's courageous decision sent to Mordecai
1) He must mobilize the Jews to fast & pray for her for three days—night & day
2) She would then disobey the law & go to the king: She would risk her life to save her people

d. Esther's request for prayer & fasting carried out by Mordecai

DIVISION III

THE JEWS SAVED BY THE COURAGEOUS ACTION OF ESTHER, 4:1–10:3

A. The Courageous Decision of Esther: A Look at Two Desperate Needs, 4:1-17

(4:1-17) **Introduction**: throughout life we all face crises from time to time. Sometimes the crises are severe, threatening the stability and security of our lives. Other times the situations are less critical. But whether the crisis is financial difficulty or bankruptcy, marital problems or divorce, disobedient or rebellious children, failing grades or unemployment, assault or rape, severe disease or accident, terminal illness or death, in such times we stand in desperate need of help.

In this present Scripture, Mordecai and the Jews were facing the crisis of their lives, a *Decree of Extermination* that had been issued by the Persian Empire. A whole race of people had been decreed by law to be slaughtered. Millions of Jews—every man, woman, child, and even babies—were to be killed. The Jews stood in desperate need of help, and only two people could help them: Mordecai and his daughter Esther. For this very purpose, Esther had been raised up by God to sit on the throne as queen to King Xerxes (4:14). This is, *The Courageous Decision of Esther: A Look at Two Desperate Needs*, 4:1-17.

1. The deep anguish of Mordecai over the *Decree of Extermination* and his appeal to Queen Esther: a picture of the desperate need for an intercessor who can plead for mercy (vv.1-9).
2. The courageous decision of Esther to risk her life: a picture of the desperate need for courage, prayer, and fasting (vv.10-17).

1 (4:1-9) **Anguish, Example of—Need, for What, an Intercessor—Mercy, Need for, Example—Jews, Oppression of, Persian Decree of Extermination—Mordecai, Example of, Anguish—Extermination, of the Jews, Effects of—Intercessor, Need for**: as soon as Mordecai heard about the decree of extermination, he was gripped with fear and trembling. He immediately knew that the best hope of deliverance lay with his adopted daughter, Queen Esther. As queen, she stood the best chance of appealing to King Xerxes for mercy. Somehow, some way, he had to get an urgent message to Esther, informing her of the *Decree of Extermination* against the Jews and appealing to her for help. She alone could intercede and plead for mercy before the king. In this dramatic story, God meets the Jews' desperate need for an intercessor, a deliverer, and a savior through the obedience and courage of Esther.

OUTLINE	SCRIPTURE	SCRIPTURE	OUTLINE

1. The deep anguish of Mordecai over the *Decree of Extermination* & his appeal to Queen Esther: A picture of the desperate need for an intercessor who can plead for mercy
a. Mordecai & the Jews' intense grief
  1) Mordecai put on sackcloth & ashes & walked into the city, crying loudly & bitterly: Went to the palace gate
  2) The Jews mourned deeply throughout the empire
  • They fasted, wept, & prayed
  • Many lay in sackcloth & ashes
b. Esther's concern over news of Mordecai's deep distress
  1) She sent Mordecai clothing to allow him to enter the palace, v.2
  2) Mordecai refused to change
 	
c. Esther's distress over her adoptive father's grief
	When Mordecai perceived all that was done, Mordecai rent his clothes, and put on sackcloth with ashes, and went out into the midst of the city, and cried with a loud and a bitter cry;
	2 And came even before the king's gate: for none *might* enter into the king's gate clothed with sackcloth.
	3 And in every province, whithersoever the king's commandment and his decree came, *there was* great mourning among the Jews, and fasting, and weeping, and wailing; and many lay in sackcloth and ashes.
	4 So Esther's maids and her chamberlains came and told *it* her. Then was the queen exceedingly grieved; and she sent raiment to clothe Mordecai, and to take away his sackcloth from him: but he received *it* not.
	5 Then called Esther for Hatach, *one* of the king's
		chamberlains, whom he had appointed to attend upon her, and gave him a commandment to Mordecai, to know what it *was*, and why it *was*.
		6 So Hatach went forth to Mordecai unto the street of the city, which *was* before the king's gate.
		7 And Mordecai told him of all that had happened unto him, and of the sum of the money that Haman had promised to pay to the king's treasuries for the Jews, to destroy them.
		8 Also he gave him the copy of the writing of the decree that was given at Shushan to destroy them, to show *it* unto Esther, and to declare *it* unto her, and to charge her that she should go in unto the king, to make supplication unto him, and to make request before him for her people.
		9 And Hatach came and told Esther the words of Mordecai.
			1) She sent her trusted aide Hatach to find out what was troubling Mordecai
			
			2) Hatach found Mordecai in the open square of the city: Was in front of the palace gate
			d. Mordecai's explanation of the decree & his appeal to Esther
			  1) He stated that money—the plunder of Jewish property—was one of reasons for the decree
			
			2) He gave the aide a copy of the royal decree so Esther could see the proof herself
			3) He instructed the aide to urge Esther to seek an audience with the king, to plead for mercy for her people
			
			e. Mordecai's message delivered to Esther by Hatach

a. When Mordecai and the Jews heard about the *Decree of Extermination*, they reacted just as any people would: with deep, intense grief and mourning (vv.1-3). Knowing that Queen Esther could approach King Xerxes in behalf of the Jews, believing that perhaps she could convince him to reverse the decree of extermination, Mordecai rushed out into the city dressed in sackcloth and ashes. Crying loudly and bitterly, he made his way to the palace gate (vv.1-2). However, he could not enter the palace grounds because Persian law prohibited anyone clothed in sackcloth to go beyond the gate. No doubt the law had been instituted as a protection for the king, his family, and royal officials.

In the midst of the Jews' weeping and wailing, they began to fast and pray. Many even prostrated themselves in sackcloth and ashes, a clear indication of repentance and prayer before the LORD (Ne.9:1-2; Da.9:3-4; Jona.3:1-10).

b. Eventually, Esther received news of Mordecai's deep distress, and she became very concerned (v.4). Although her servants did not know that the relationship between the queen and Mordecai was like that of a father and daughter, they did know that they were acquainted. In view of that, when some of the servants noticed Mordecai mourning at the palace gate, they reported his distress to Queen Esther. Apparently, she immediately became fearful, for if the king happened to hear Mordecai mourning so loudly and bitterly at the palace gate, he might have Mordecai arrested due to the disturbance he was causing. As quickly as she could, she gathered up clothing to send to him so he could enter the palace grounds to meet and share his problem with her. But, shockingly, he refused to accept the clothing. No doubt, Mordecai wanted to protect Esther all he could. To be identified with him now would have been most unwise, for he could have exposed the fact that she too was a Jew. Since she was queen, exposure could endanger her life immediately. Consequently, he refused to accept the clean clothing and chose not to enter the palace courtyard. Knowing that Queen Esther loved him, he knew that she would send a trusted servant to find out what the problem was.

c. Just as Mordecai expected, Esther became extremely distressed over her adoptive father (vv.5-6). She promptly sent her trusted aide Hathach to find out what was troubling him. Hathach found Mordecai in the open square of the city in front of the palace gate.

d. After explaining the *Decree of Extermination* to this trusted servant, Mordecai made his appeal to Esther (vv.7-8). He explained that money—the plunder of Jewish property—was one of the reasons for the decree. Prime Minister Haman had promised to use the plunder to build up the depleted treasury of the Persian Empire (3:9). After sharing all the facts about the decree of extermination, Mordecai gave the aide a copy of the royal decree so Esther could see the proof for herself and know that the situation was critical. Finally he instructed the aide to urge Esther to seek an audience with the king. She must become a mediator for the Jewish people. She must plead with the king for mercy, plead with him to reverse the sentence of death upon her people.

e. The trusted aide Hathach returned to Esther and reported Mordecai's message to her.

Thought 1. Only Queen Esther stood in the gap between the king and the extermination of the Jews. She alone could mediate in their behalf. She alone could approach the king and cry out for mercy in behalf of her people.

This is a clear picture of our desperate need for an intercessor, for a person who can stand before God and plead for mercy in our behalf. There is an enormous gap between God and us, an impassable gulf that separates God from man. This gap or gulf exists between God's perfection and our imperfection. Only perfection is acceptable to God. Only a perfect person can approach God, and we are anything but perfect. We are sinful because we have committed wickedness and evil, both in thought and in behavior.

Our only hope is for a mediator—a perfect person—to stand between God and us and to plead for mercy in our behalf. The wonderful news is this: there is such a person, a perfect person, the Lord Jesus Christ. Jesus Christ is our Intercessor, the perfect Savior and Deliverer who is accepted by God the Father. Standing before the Father, Jesus Christ pleads for God to have mercy when we trust and call out to him. And when we call in the name of Christ, God hears. He hears because Jesus Christ is the Perfect Intercessor, the Perfect Mediator who brings us to God. Listen to what God's Holy Word says:

"Who *is* he that condemneth? *It is* Christ that died, yea rather, that is risen again, who is even at the right hand of God, who also maketh intercession for us" (Ro.8:34).

"For this *is* good and acceptable in the sight of God our Saviour; Who will have all men to be saved, and to come unto the knowledge of the truth. For *there is* one God, and one mediator between God and men, the man Christ Jesus" (1 Ti.2:3-5).

"Wherefore in all things it behoved him to be made like unto *his* brethren, that he might be a merciful and faithful high priest in things *pertaining* to God, to make reconciliation for the sins of the people" (He.2:17).

"Seeing then that we have a great high priest, that is passed into the heavens, Jesus the Son of God, let us hold fast *our* profession. For we have not an high priest which cannot be touched with the feeling of our infirmities; but was in all points tempted like as *we are, yet* without sin" (He.4:14-15).

"For every high priest taken from among men is ordained for men in things *pertaining* to God, that he may offer both gifts and sacrifices for sins: Who can have compassion on the ignorant, and on them that are out of the way; for that he himself also is compassed with infirmity. And by reason hereof he ought, as for the people, so also for himself, to offer for sins. And no man taketh this honour unto himself, but he that is called of God, as *was* Aaron. So also Christ glorified not himself to be made an high priest; but he that said unto him, Thou art my Son, to day have I begotten thee" (He.5:1-5).

"Which *hope* we have as an anchor of the soul, both sure and stedfast, and which entereth into that within the veil; Whither the forerunner is for us entered, *even* Jesus, made an high priest for ever after the order of Melchisedec" (He.6:19-20).

"Wherefore he is able also to save them to the uttermost that come unto God by him, seeing he ever liveth to make intercession for them. For such an high priest became us, *who is* holy, harmless, undefiled, separate from sinners, and made higher than the heavens; Who needeth not daily, as those high priests, to offer up sacrifice, first for his own sins, and then for the people's: for this he did once, when he offered up himself" (He.7:25-27).

"Now of the things which we have spoken *this is* the sum: We have such an high priest, who is set on the right hand of the throne of the Majesty in the heavens" (He.8:1).

"But Christ being come an high priest of good things to come, by a greater and more perfect tabernacle, not made with hands, that is to say, not of this building; Neither by the blood of goats and calves, but by his own blood he entered in once into the holy place, having obtained eternal redemption *for us.* For if the blood of bulls and of goats, and the ashes of an heifer sprinkling the unclean, sanctifieth to the purifying of the flesh: How much more shall the blood of Christ, who through the eternal Spirit offered himself without spot to God, purge your conscience from dead works to serve the living God? And for this cause he is the mediator of the new testament, that by means of death, for the redemption of the transgressions *that were* under the first testament, they which are called might receive the promise of eternal inheritance" (He.9:11-15).

"For Christ is not entered into the holy places made with hands, *which are* the figures of the true; but into heaven itself, now to appear in the presence of God for us" (He.9:24).

"And *having* an high priest over the house of God; Let us draw near with a true heart in full assurance of faith, having our hearts sprinkled from an evil conscience, and our bodies washed with pure water" (He.10:21-22).

"My little children, these things write I unto you, that ye sin not. And if any man sin, we have an advocate with the Father, Jesus Christ the righteous: And he is the propitiation for our sins: and not for ours only, but also for *the sins of* the whole world" (1 Jn.2:1-2).

"Therefore will I divide him *a portion* with the great, and he shall divide the spoil with the strong; because he hath poured out his soul unto death: and he was numbered with the transgressors; and he bare the sin of many, and made intercession for the transgressors" (Is.53:12).

2 **(4:10-17) Courage, Example—Prayer, Need for—Fasting, Example of—Esther, Courage of:** Esther was faced with the decision of her life, with one of the most difficult decisions ever faced by a man or woman. She alone could step forth to save the Jewish people from extermination, but she needed a deep-seated courage. Thankfully, such courage existed within her heart. Thereby Esther made a momentous and extraordinary decision. She determined to risk her life by appearing before King Xerxes to plead for mercy for her people. Yet note: at first, Esther's courage was dormant. It needed to be stirred by Mordecai. Through Hathach the queen's trusted aide, Mordecai and Esther exchanged message after message until the courage was aroused within her to risk her life to save the Jewish people from annihilation.

OUTLINE	SCRIPTURE	SCRIPTURE	OUTLINE
2. **The courageous decision of Esther to risk her life: A picture of the desperate need for courage, prayer, & fasting**	10 Again Esther spake unto Hatach, and gave him commandment unto Mordecai;	holdest thy peace at this time, *then* shall there enlargement and deliverance arise to the Jews from another	2) Because if she kept silent during this crisis, God would raise up another deliverer: Still she & her family would perish
a. Esther's dilemma & her desire for Mordecai's guidance	11 All the king's servants, and the people of the king's provinces, do know, that	place; but thou and thy father's house shall be destroyed: and who knoweth	3) Because God had raised her up for this very purpose
1) Persian law prohibited anyone from approaching the king without first being summoned, upon penalty of death	whosoever, whether man or woman, shall come unto the king into the inner court, who is not called, *there is* one law of his to put *him* to death, except such to whom the king shall hold out the golden sceptre, that he may live: but I have not been called to come in unto the king these thirty days.	whether thou art come to the kingdom for *such* a time as this?	
2) Esther had not been summoned for 30 days: Perhaps he no longer favored her		15 Then Esther bade *them* return Mordecai *this answer,*	c. Esther's courageous decision sent to Mordecai
		16 Go, gather together all the Jews that are present in Shushan, and fast ye for me, and neither eat nor drink three days, night or day: I also and my maidens will fast likewise; and so will I go in unto the king, which *is* not according to the law: and if I perish, I perish.	1) He must mobilize the Jews to fast & pray for her for three days—night & day
b. Mordecai's insistence that Esther be courageous	12 And they told to Mordecai Esther's words.		2) She would then disobey the law & go to the king: She would risk her life to save her people
1) Because being queen would not protect her, for she too was a Jew	13 Then Mordecai commanded to answer Esther, Think not with thyself that thou shalt escape in the king's house, more than all the Jews.	17 So Mordecai went his way, and did according to all that Esther had commanded him.	d. Esther's request for prayer & fasting carried out by Mordecai
	14 For if thou altogether		

a. Because of Persian law, Esther faced a serious dilemma, so she sent her trusted aide Hathach back to Mordecai in order to seek her adoptive father's advice (v.11). Persian law prohibited anyone from approaching the king without first being summoned. Such a law was necessary in order to protect the king from potential assassins and from being interrupted while conducting important business. Esther simply saw no way to secure an audience with the king, for she had not been summoned by him for 30 days. There was the possibility that she was no longer favored by him. Hence, she knew she might never again be summoned into his presence.

b. When Esther's dilemma was reported to Mordecai, he insisted that she be courageous and figure out some way to approach the king (vv.12-14). Her reaching the king and pleading the case of the Jews was an absolute essential. She could not make excuses nor shrink from this responsibility. Seeking to arouse her courage, Mordecai gave three reasons why she had to figure out a way to approach the king to lead him to reverse the decree.

　1) Esther herself was a Jew and would not escape execution. Being queen was meaningless in the face of Persian law, for Persian law could not be reversed, not even by the king himself. Although she was the wife and queen of King Xerxes, she too was doomed to death unless she could arouse King Xerxes to figure out a way to reverse the decree.

　2) Esther had been placed upon the throne as queen for this very purpose: to save the Jews (v.14). If she failed in her mission by keeping silent during this crisis, God would raise up another deliverer. But she and her family, including her adoptive father Mordecai, would perish.

Note how Mordecai believed that God would protect His people from annihilation, either through his adopted daughter Esther or through some other agent. He knew that God would fulfill His promises to Abraham (see outline and notes—Ge.12:1-3 for more discussion). Keep in mind that the name of the LORD is not mentioned anywhere in the book of *Esther*. However, there is no doubt that this is a veiled reference to God. Although God's name is not mentioned, Mordecai was suggesting that God stands behind human affairs and He would somehow save his people. Keep in mind that the book of *Esther* was written soon after these events occurred, before Ezra's return to Jerusalem, which would have been somewhere between 450 and 400 B.C. The plot of extermination was launched because of Mordecai's faithful stand for the LORD (3:1-15). Because of the extreme prejudice and bitter hatred of the Jews by the public, the author apparently eliminated any direct reference to the LORD in order to protect the Jews. They were still citizens of Persia, a secular society while this book was being written and circulated. Whatever the case, the author records the fact of Mordecai's strong faith in the LORD through this veiled reference to God (v.14).

3) Esther had definitely been placed on the throne as queen to be the liberator, the savior of her people. Moreover, Mordecai had a deep conviction that God had moved world events in order to place her upon the throne with King Xerxes. The LORD would fulfill His promise to Abraham, which meant that He would save the Jewish people from annihilation. For this very purpose, God had raised up Esther. She was to be used by the LORD as the deliverer, the savior, the liberator of the Jewish people.

c. Esther responded to Mordecai's challenge. She made the courageous decision to go to the king to plead for mercy for her people, the Jews (v.15). But note her challenge to Mordecai: he had to mobilize the Jews to fast and pray for her for three days, both night and day. She and her maids would join in the fast and, then, at the end of the three days, she would disobey the law of the land. Risking her life, she would go to the king and plead for him to seek a way to reverse the *Decree of Extermination*.

A momentous decision! Esther was risking her life out of conviction that she had been raised up by God *for a time such as this*. If she perished, then she would perish, but she would have fulfilled God's purpose for her life. And by fulfilling His purpose, even if she failed, she was convinced that God would make another way to save His people, the Jews. She would do all she could, so no matter what the outcome, she could rest in peace.

d. Note that Esther's request for prayer and fasting was carried out by her adoptive father Mordecai (v.17). Sending word to all the Jews throughout the royal city of Susa, he encouraged and challenged them to fast and pray in behalf of Esther.

Thought 1. In facing any desperate situation, there is a need for courage, prayer, and fasting. When we face the crises of life, we must be courageous. But we must also seek the face of God, for only God can give us permanent help.

⇒ Only God can place permanent peace within our hearts, a peace that will never leave us as long as we are trusting Him.

⇒ Only God can give us permanent power, the power that can triumph over all trials and temptations of life.

⇒ Only God can give us continued victory over the terrifying crises that may confront us, crises that can leave us frightened and confused, wondering what we can do to overcome the problem. The crisis may be separation or divorce, accident or disease, financial difficulty or bankruptcy, or even the terrifying prospect of death, hell, and eternal separation from God.

No matter what the crises in life, there is hope in the LORD. If we turn to the LORD in prayer and fasting, seeking His face for help, He will help us. This is the clear declaration of God's Holy Word.

(1) In facing the crises of life we must be courageous.

"Only let your conversation [conduct, behavior] be as it becometh the gospel of Christ: that whether I come and see you, or else be absent, I may hear of your affairs, that ye stand fast in one spirit, with one mind striving together for the faith of the gospel; And in nothing terrified by your adversaries: which is to them an evident token of perdition, but to you of salvation, and that of God" (Ph.1:27-28).

"Be strong and of a good courage, fear not, nor be afraid of them: for the LORD thy God, he *it is* that doth go with thee; he will not fail thee, nor forsake thee" (De.31:6).

"Be strong and of a good courage: for unto this people shalt thou divide for an inheritance the land, which I sware unto their fathers to give them" (Jos.1:6).

"And Joshua said unto them, Fear not, nor be dismayed, be strong and of good courage: for thus shall the LORD do to all your enemies against whom ye fight" (Jos.10:25).

"Be ye therefore very courageous to keep and to do all that is written in the book of the law of Moses, that ye turn not aside therefrom *to* the right hand or *to* the left; That ye come not among these nations, these that remain among you; neither make mention of the names of their gods, nor cause to swear *by them,* neither serve them, nor bow yourselves unto them: But cleave unto the LORD your God, as ye have done unto this day" (Jos.23:6-8).

"Be of good courage, and let us play the men for our people, and for the cities of our God: and the LORD do that which seemeth him good" (2 S.10:12).

"Be of good courage, and let us behave ourselves valiantly for our people, and for the cities of our God: and let the LORD do *that which is* good in his sight" (1 Chr.19:13).

"Then shalt thou prosper, if thou takest heed to fulfil the statutes and judgments which the LORD charged Moses with concerning Israel: be strong, and of good courage; dread not, nor be dismayed" (1 Chr.22:13).

"And David said to Solomon his son, Be strong and of good courage, and do *it:* fear not, nor be dismayed: for the LORD God, *even* my God, *will be* with thee; he will not fail thee, nor forsake thee, until thou hast finished all the work for the service of the house of the LORD" (1 Chr.28:20).

"I will not be afraid of ten thousands of people, that have set *themselves* against me round about" (Ps.3:6).

"The LORD *is* my light and my salvation; whom shall I fear? the LORD *is* the strength of my life; of whom shall I be afraid? When the wicked, *even* mine enemies and my foes, came upon me to eat up my flesh, they stumbled and fell. Though an host should encamp against me, my heart shall not fear: though war should rise against me, in this *will* I *be* confident" (Ps.27:1-3).

"I will say of the LORD, *He is* my refuge and my fortress: my God; in him will I trust. Surely he shall deliver thee from the snare of the fowler, *and* from the noisome pestilence. He shall cover thee with his feathers, and under his wings shalt thou trust: his truth *shall be thy* shield and buckler. Thou shalt not be afraid for the terror by night; *nor* for the arrow *that* flieth by day; *Nor* for the pestilence *that* walketh in darkness; *nor* for the destruction *that* wasteth at noonday" (Ps.91:2-6).

"The LORD *is* on my side; I will not fear: what can man do unto me?" (Ps.118:6).

"Behold, God *is* my salvation; I will trust, and not be afraid: for the LORD JEHOVAH *is* my strength and *my* song; he also is become my salvation" (Is.12:2).

(2) In facing the crises of life we must fast and seek the face of the LORD.

"But thou, when thou fastest, anoint thine head, and wash thy face; That thou appear not unto men to fast, but unto thy Father which is in secret: and thy Father, which seeth in secret, shall reward thee openly" (Mt.6:17-18).

"Ask, and it shall be given you; seek, and ye shall find; knock, and it shall be opened unto you" (Mt.7:7).

"And Jesus rebuked the devil; and he departed out of him: and the child was cured from that very hour. Then came the disciples to Jesus apart, and said, Why could not we cast him out? And Jesus said unto them, Because of your unbelief: for verily I say unto you, If ye have faith as a grain of mustard seed, ye shall say unto this mountain, Remove hence to yonder place; and it shall remove; and nothing shall be impossible unto you. Howbeit this kind goeth not out but by prayer and fasting" (Mt.17:18-21).

"And the prayer of faith shall save the sick, and the Lord shall raise him up; and if he have committed sins, they shall be forgiven him. Confess *your* faults one to another, and pray one for another, that ye may be healed. The effectual fervent prayer of a righteous man availeth much. Elias was a man subject to like passions as we are, and he prayed earnestly that it might not rain: and it rained not on the earth by the space of three years and six months. And he prayed again, and the heaven gave rain, and the earth brought forth her fruit" (Js.5:15-18).

"But if from thence thou shalt seek the LORD thy God, thou shalt find *him,* if thou seek him with all thy heart and with all thy soul" (De.4:29).

"If my people, which are called by my name, shall humble themselves, and pray, and seek my face, and turn from their wicked ways; then will I hear from heaven, and will forgive their sin, and will heal their land" (2 Chr.7:14).

"He shall call upon me, and I will answer him: I *will be* with him in trouble; I will deliver him, and honour him" (Ps.91:15).

"Therefore also now, saith the LORD, turn ye *even* to me with all your heart, and with fasting, and with weeping, and with mourning" (Joel 2:12).

CHAPTER 5

B. The Courageous Approach of Esther into the King's Presence: A Contrast Between a Believer's Trust in God & an Unbeliever's Pride, 5:1-14

1. Esther's daring, forbidden approach before the king: A bold example of a believer's trust in the Lord

a. Esther's entrance into the royal court of the king: She stood right at the entrance, in the palace's inner court

b. The king's favor & pardon
1) He saw Queen Esther & was pleased
2) He held out his scepter, pardoning the queen: She approached & touched the tip of the scepter

3) He asked Queen Esther what she wanted: Assured her she could receive whatever she wanted

c. Esther's request: An invitation for the king to attend a banquet she had prepared for him & Haman that very day

d. The king's quick acceptance of the invitation
1) He ordered Haman to be summoned
2) He & the prime minister went to the banquet
   • He & Haman finished eating & were relaxing, drinking wine
   • He again asked Esther what her request was, politely assuring her that it would be granted
e. Esther's reverence for the king & her surprising,

Now it came to pass on the third day, that Esther put on *her* royal *apparel,* and stood in the inner court of the king's house, over against the king's house: and the king sat upon his royal throne in the royal house, over against the gate of the house.
2 And it was so, when the king saw Esther the queen standing in the court, *that* she obtained favour in his sight: and the king held out to Esther the golden sceptre that *was* in his hand. So Esther drew near, and touched the top of the sceptre.
3 Then said the king unto her, What wilt thou, queen Esther? and what *is* thy request? it shall be even given thee to the half of the kingdom.
4 And Esther answered, If *it seem* good unto the king, let the king and Haman come this day unto the banquet that I have prepared for him.
5 Then the king said, Cause Haman to make haste, that he may do as Esther hath said. So the king and Haman came to the banquet that Esther had prepared.
6 And the king said unto Esther at the banquet of wine, What *is* thy petition? and it shall be granted thee: and what *is* thy request? even to the half of the kingdom it shall be performed.
7 Then answered Esther, and said, My petition and my

request *is;*
8 If I have found favour in the sight of the king, and if it please the king to grant my petition, and to perform my request, let the king and Haman come to the banquet that I shall prepare for them, and I will do to morrow as the king hath said.
9 Then went Haman forth that day joyful and with a glad heart: but when Haman saw Mordecai in the king's gate, that he stood not up, nor moved for him, he was full of indignation against Mordecai.
10 Nevertheless Haman refrained himself: and when he came home, he sent and called for his friends, and Zeresh his wife.
11 And Haman told them of the glory of his riches, and the multitude of his children, and all *the things* wherein the king had promoted him, and how he had advanced him above the princes and servants of the king.
12 Haman said moreover, Yea, Esther the queen did let no man come in with the king unto the banquet that she had prepared but myself; and to morrow am I invited unto her also with the king.
13 Yet all this availeth me nothing, so long as I see Mordecai the Jew sitting at the king's gate.
14 Then said Zeresh his wife and all his friends unto him, Let a gallows be made of fifty cubits high, and to morrow speak thou unto the king that Mordecai may be hanged thereon: then go thou in merrily with the king unto the banquet. And the thing pleased Haman; and he caused the gallows to be made.

suspense-filled request
1) That if she pleased the king, let him & Haman attend another banquet with her the next day
2) That she would then make her request known

2. Haman's wicked pride & malice: A shameful example of an unbeliever's boasting

a. Haman's anger at Mordecai
1) He was in high spirits leaving the banquet
2) He saw Mordecai not bowing & became furious
3) He restrained himself & went home

b. Haman's social gathering with his wife & friends: His pride, arrogance, & boasting
1) About his vast wealth
2) About his children
3) About the honor given him
4) About his promotion: His position, authority, & power

5) About the distinctive recognition & honor given him by the queen

c. Haman's only stated disappointment in life: Mordecai's refusal to honor him

1) His wife & friend's counsel
   • To build gallows
   • To ask the king the next day to hang Mordecai upon the gallows
   • To then go to the dinner & be happy
2) His pleasure with the idea

DIVISION III

THE JEWS SAVED BY THE COURAGEOUS ACTION OF ESTHER, 4:1–10:3

B. The Courageous Approach of Esther into the King's Presence: A Contrast Between a Believer's Trust in God and an Unbeliever's Pride, 5:1-14

(5:1-14) **Introduction**: in life, there are basically two attitudes toward the LORD. There is the attitude that God is our Provider and that our sufficiency is found in Him alone. Therefore, we must trust the LORD as we walk about day by day. Then, there is the attitude that takes great pride in self, believing that we are self-sufficient and perfectly capable of handling all of the circumstances of life through the power, wisdom, and technology of man. The first attitude is that of humility before God, and the second attitude is that of pride before God. The first attitude confesses a person's need for God, whereas the second attitude confesses no need for God.

The Holy Bible has a message for people with both attitudes. The person who trusts God is given wonderful promises by the Holy Scripture, promises of God's guidance, protection, provision, strength, help, and wisdom. But for the person who relies only upon self and what man can do, who is stiff-necked and stubborn toward the LORD, God's Word says he will reap exactly what he sows. The LORD gives the person exactly what he wants. If his attitude is that of unbelief, of trusting only the arm of the flesh and technology, then the LORD leaves the person in the hands of his flesh and earthly technology. He receives no help from the LORD. Throughout life…

- he does not want God's guidance, so God does not guide him
- he does not want God's protection, so God does not protect him
- he does not want God's strength or help, so God does not strengthen or help him
- he does not want God's wisdom, so God withholds His wisdom from him

The subject of the present Scripture is a contrast between a believer who trusted God and an unbeliever who shamefully looked only to self for answers. This man's pride kept him from ever surrendering his life to the LORD.

Remember that a decree to exterminate the Jews had been issued throughout the Persian Empire. Every Jew—the entire race—was to be slaughtered and wiped off the face of the earth. Mordecai had encouraged Esther to seek an audience with King Xerxes to plead for mercy for the Jewish people. But Esther faced a dilemma, for Persian law prohibited anyone from approaching the king without first being summoned, upon penalty of death. Also of concern, the king had not requested her presence for 30 days, an entire month. Perhaps he no longer desired her presence or favored her. She simply did not know. Therefore, to approach the king under these circumstances was to place her life in danger. The king could react against her, commanding her execution for having broken the Persian law. Nevertheless, Esther became convinced that she had been placed upon the throne as queen for this very purpose: to be the liberator, savior, and deliverer of her people. She sensed deeply that God had appointed her to rescue the Jews from extermination. Holding this conviction down deep within her soul, Esther was willingly ready to risk her life by unlawfully approaching the king. This is, *The Courageous Approach of Esther into the King's Presence: A Contrast Between a Believer's Trust in God and an Unbeliever's Pride*, 5:1-14.

1. Esther's daring, forbidden approach before the king: a bold example of a believer's trust in the Lord (vv.1-8).
2. Haman's wicked pride and malice: a shameful example of an unbeliever's boasting (vv.9-14).

1 (5:1-8) **Trust, in the LORD, Example—Faith, in the LORD's Guidance, Example—Xerxes, King of Persia, Approached by Esther—Esther, Trust of, in the Lord—Esther, Courage of, Approached King Xerxes**: after praying and fasting for three days, Esther made her bold and unlawful approach before King Xerxes. With all her heart she trusted the LORD to guide, protect, strengthen, and give her wisdom as she approached the king. She was unquestionably a person of strong faith in the LORD, and her trust in Him was now being proven. Now it was time for her to act, and she must do so immediately. Her brave but illegal approach before King Xerxes was both suspenseful and dramatic:

OUTLINE	SCRIPTURE	SCRIPTURE	OUTLINE
1. Esther's daring, forbidden approach before the king: A bold example of a believer's trust in the Lord a. Esther's entrance into the royal court of the king: She stood right at the entrance, in the palace's inner court b. The king's favor & pardon 1) He saw Queen Esther & was pleased 2) He held out his scepter, pardoning the queen: She approached & touched the tip of the scepter 3) He asked Queen Esther what she wanted: Assured her she could receive whatever she wanted c. Esther's request: An invitation for the king to attend a	Now it came to pass on the third day, that Esther put on *her* royal *apparel,* and stood in the inner court of the king's house, over against the king's house: and the king sat upon his royal throne in the royal house, over against the gate of the house. 2 And it was so, when the king saw Esther the queen standing in the court, *that* she obtained favour in his sight: and the king held out to Esther the golden sceptre that *was* in his hand. So Esther drew near, and touched the top of the sceptre. 3 Then said the king unto her, What wilt thou, queen Esther? and what *is* thy request? it shall be even given thee to the half of the kingdom. 4 And Esther answered, If *it seem* good unto the king, let the king and Haman come	this day unto the banquet that I have prepared for him. 5 Then the king said, Cause Haman to make haste, that he may do as Esther hath said. So the king and Haman came to the banquet that Esther had prepared. 6 And the king said unto Esther at the banquet of wine, What *is* thy petition? and it shall be granted thee: and what *is* thy request? even to the half of the kingdom it shall be performed. 7 Then answered Esther, and said, My petition and my request *is;* 8 If I have found favour in the sight of the king, and if it please the king to grant my petition, and to perform my request, let the king and Haman come to the banquet that I shall prepare for them, and I will do to morrow as the king hath said.	banquet she had prepared for him & Haman that very day d. The king's quick acceptance of the invitation 1) He ordered Haman to be summoned 2) He & the prime minister went to the banquet • He & Haman finished eating & were relaxing, drinking wine • He again asked Esther what her request was, politely assuring her that it would be granted e. Esther's reverence for the king & her surprising, suspense-filled request 1) That if she pleased the king, let him & Haman attend another banquet with her the next day 2) That she would then make her request known

a. Esther put on her beautiful royal robes, walked out of the queen's quarters into the inner court of the palace, and stood right at the entrance of the king's hall (v.1). Sitting on the throne in all his royal splendor as Persian king, Xerxes actually faced the entrance where Queen Esther suddenly appeared.

b. When the king saw her standing at the entrance of the royal court, instead of being offended, he was very pleased (vv.2-3). Remember, he had not seen her for over a month (4:11). No doubt he was once again stricken with her beauty and stately appearance. But he also knew that she had a matter of urgency that needed his attention, for she had broken one of the major laws of Persia by approaching him without having been summoned. Thus to protect her, he held out his scepter, which indicated that she had permission to approach him. When she approached, she touched the tip of the scepter and expressed gratitude for the privilege of an audience. As would be expected, he asked what she wanted, what her request was. And to show his extreme pleasure with her, he stated that she could request up to half the kingdom and it would be given her (v.3). Of course, this offer was not to be taken literally. It was apparently an oriental custom for kings of that day to show their pleasure in someone by making this statement, which simply meant that the person would be granted what they requested if the request was within reason.

c. Rather surprisingly, Esther did not bring up the *Decree of Extermination* that she wanted the king to revoke. Instead, she made a very simple request that the king attend a banquet that she had prepared for him and his prime minister, Haman (v.4). As soon as the king could free himself, she wanted him to spend some time with her. The implication was that she would make her request known at that time. Two questions need to be asked at this point:

First, why did Esther not grasp this opportunity to intercede for the Jews, begging Xerxes to have mercy upon them by revoking the *Decree of Extermination*? Commentators have various explanations. But regardless, Esther obviously sensed the leadership of the LORD, for her delay was to prove a wise decision. Time was needed for other events to take place before her requests were made. It definitely was not God's timing, not yet. Xerxes' heart needed to be prepared, made tender and soft and favorable toward her before she could make an accusation against Prime Minister Haman. The royal court was not the place to make a charge of conspiracy being plotted against the Jews by the prime minister. She needed to confront the king and Haman alone, without anyone else present. By Esther's standing alone with them, the king was far more likely to accept her charge against the prime minister for plotting evil against her and her people.

Second, why would Esther want Haman present when she exposed the evil plot of the prime minister? No doubt, she wanted to hear what Haman himself had to say. In case the prime minister attempted to defend himself with seemingly justifiable arguments, she wanted to be present to refute these arguments. She wanted to argue the case against him.

d. Indicating his pleasure with Queen Esther, King Xerxes quickly accepted her invitation (vv.5-6). The meal had already been prepared, so he immediately ordered Haman to be summoned. When Haman arrived, the king and prime minister walked together to the banquet in Esther's quarters. After King Xerxes and the prime minister finished eating, they relaxed and drank wine. At some point during the conversation, the king again asked Esther what her request was, politely assuring her that it would be granted.

e. In response, Esther showed reverence to the king and then made another surprising, suspense-filled request (vv.7-8). If the king was really pleased with her and wanted to grant her request, she wanted him and Haman to attend another banquet with her the very next day. At that time she would make her request known. By requesting another banquet with her husband the king, Esther was showing a desire to be in his presence more. This, of course, was bound to build up his ego and at the same time show great reverence for him. She did not want him to think that her request was more important than her desire for his attention and love. By delaying her request one more day and requesting his presence at a second banquet, the king would sense that she desired him as a man as well as the provider of her needs. Thus he was bound to accept the second invitation, giving his wife and queen the honor of his attention once again.

But behind Esther's request was an effort to soften his spirit and to make him tender toward her. By showing how much she valued his presence and company, she hoped to please him beyond measure. If he was deeply pleased, he would be more likely to accept her charge against Haman, the charge that he was devising an evil plot against her and her people.

Thought 1. Throughout this entire drama, Esther is seen trusting the LORD. By approaching the king without being summoned, she broke the law of the land. Her unauthorized approach to the king could have been interpreted by one of the guards as a threat to his safety and against his life. Also, the king could have been involved in a critically important state matter that demanded privacy. Had that been the case, Esther could have been executed on the spot. Yet Esther risked her life, knowing she had only one source of help available to her. And that source was not a man. It was the LORD God Himself. Imagine what Esther was facing: she had to be accepted by the king and forgiven for having broken the law; she had to have very persuasive powers. She had to trust the LORD to change or convince the king about Haman's evil plot. In addition, the king's heart needed to be stirred to revoke, reverse, or counteract the horrendous decree against the Jews. All of this could be worked out only by the LORD God Himself. Therefore Esther's only hope was to trust the LORD. She had to relinquish her desires, instincts, and fears and turn to the LORD for guidance, protection, strength, health, and wisdom.

When we are facing difficult circumstances in life, we too must turn to the LORD and place our trust in Him. Often there is no help available other than the LORD. During those times, we are foolish if we do not call upon Him. The LORD is always available to help us, and no matter how bad our circumstances are, the LORD loves us and longs to help us. Listen to what God's Holy Word says:

(1) In difficult circumstances, we can trust the LORD for guidance.

> "Through the tender mercy of our God; whereby the dayspring from on high hath visited us, To give light to them that sit in darkness and *in* the shadow of death, to guide our feet into the way of peace" (Lu.1:78-79).

> "Howbeit when he, the Spirit of truth, is come, he will guide you into all truth: for he shall not speak of himself; but whatsoever he shall hear, *that* shall he speak: and he will show you things to come" (Jn.16:13).

"Lead me, O LORD, in thy righteousness because of mine enemies; make thy way straight before my face" (Ps.5:8).

"The LORD is my shepherd; I shall not want. He maketh me to lie down in green pastures: he leadeth me beside the still waters. He restoreth my soul: he leadeth me in the paths of righteousness for his name's sake. Yea, though I walk through the valley of the shadow of death, I will fear no evil: for thou art with me; thy rod and thy staff they comfort me. Thou preparest a table before me in the presence of mine enemies: thou anointest my head with oil; my cup runneth over. Surely goodness and mercy shall follow me all the days of my life: and I will dwell in the house of the LORD for ever" (Ps.23:1-6).

"The meek will he guide in judgment: and the meek will he teach his way" (Ps.25:9).

"Teach me thy way, O LORD, and lead me in a plain path, because of mine enemies" (Ps.27:11).

"For this God is our God for ever and ever: he will be our guide even unto death" (Ps.48:14).

"Thou shalt guide me with thy counsel, and afterward receive me to glory" (Ps.73:24).

"If I take the wings of the morning, and dwell in the uttermost parts of the sea; Even there shall thy hand lead me, and thy right hand shall hold me" (Ps.139:9-10).

"And thine ears shall hear a word behind thee, saying, This is the way, walk ye in it, when ye turn to the right hand, and when ye turn to the left" (Is.30:21).

"And I will bring the blind by a way that they knew not; I will lead them in paths that they have not known: I will make darkness light before them, and crooked things straight. These things will I do unto them, and not forsake them" (Is.42:16).

(2) In difficult circumstances, we must trust the LORD for protection.

"But there shall not an hair of your head perish" (Lu.21:18).

"The LORD shall fight for you, and ye shall hold your peace" (Ex.14:14).

"The eternal God is thy refuge, and underneath are the everlasting arms: and he shall thrust out the enemy from before thee; and shall say, Destroy them" (De.33:27).

"O Jerusalem, wash thine heart from wickedness, that thou mayest be saved. How long shall thy vain thoughts lodge within thee?" (Je.4:14).

"The heart is deceitful above all things, and desperately wicked: who can know it?" (Je.17:9).

"They say still unto them that despise me, The LORD hath said, Ye shall have peace; and they say unto every one that walketh after the imagination of his own heart, No evil shall come upon you" (Je.23:17).

"For in the time of trouble he shall hide me in his pavilion: in the secret of his tabernacle shall he hide me; he shall set me up upon a rock" (Ps.27:5).

"Thou shalt hide them in the secret of thy presence from the pride of man: thou shalt keep them secretly in a pavilion from the strife of tongues" (Ps.31:20).

"Our soul waiteth for the LORD: he is our help and our shield" (Ps.33:20).

"The angel of the LORD encampeth round about them that fear him, and delivereth them" (Ps.34:7).

"God is our refuge and strength, a very present help in trouble" (Ps.46:1).

"Be thou my strong habitation, whereunto I may continually resort: thou hast given commandment to save me; for thou art my rock and my fortress" (Ps.71:3).

"He shall cover thee with his feathers, and under his wings shalt thou trust: his truth shall be thy shield and buckler" (Ps.91:4).

"O Israel, trust thou in the LORD: he is their help and their shield" (Ps.115:9).

"As the mountains are round about Jerusalem, so the LORD is round about his people from henceforth even for ever" (Ps.125:2).

"In the fear of the LORD is strong confidence: and his children shall have a place of refuge" (Pr.14:26).

"The name of the LORD is a strong tower: the righteous runneth into it, and is safe" (Pr.18:10).

"Every word of God is pure: he is a shield unto them that put their trust in him" (Pr.30:5).

"For the eyes of the LORD run to and fro throughout the whole earth, to show himself strong in the behalf of them whose heart is perfect toward him. Herein thou hast done foolishly: therefore from henceforth thou shalt have wars" (2 Chr.16:9).

"For I, saith the LORD, will be unto her a wall of fire round about, and will be the glory in the midst of her" (Zec.2:5).

(3) In difficult circumstances, we must trust the LORD for strength and help.

"Let your conversation [conduct, behavior] be without covetousness; and be content with such things as ye have: for he hath said, I will never leave thee, nor forsake thee. So that we may boldly say, The Lord is my helper, and I will not fear what man shall do unto me" (He.13:5-6).

"But I am poor and needy; yet the Lord thinketh upon me: thou art my help and my deliverer; make no tarrying, O my God" (Ps.40:17).

"Fear thou not; for I *am* with thee: be not dismayed; for I *am* thy God: I will strengthen thee; yea, I will help thee; yea, I will uphold thee with the right hand of my righteousness" (Is.41:10).

"Fear not: for I have redeemed thee, I have called *thee* by thy name; thou *art* mine. When thou passest through the waters, I *will be* with thee; and through the rivers, they shall not overflow thee: when thou walkest through the fire, thou shalt not be burned; neither shall the flame kindle upon thee" (Is.43:1-2).

"I will go before thee, and make the crooked places straight" (Is.45:2).

4) In difficult circumstances, we must trust the LORD for wisdom.

"Therefore whosoever heareth these sayings of mine, and doeth them, I will liken him unto a wise man, which built his house upon a rock: And the rain descended, and the floods came, and the winds blew, and beat upon that house; and it fell not: for it was founded upon a rock. And every one that heareth these sayings of mine, and doeth them not, shall be likened unto a foolish man, which built his house upon the sand: And the rain descended, and the floods came, and the winds blew, and beat upon that house; and it fell: and great was the fall of it" (Mt.7:24-27).

"For I will give you a mouth and wisdom, which all your adversaries shall not be able to gainsay nor resist" (Lu.21:15).

"O the depth of the riches both of the wisdom and knowledge of God! how unsearchable *are* his judgments, and his ways past finding out!" (Ro.11:33).

"Because the foolishness of God is wiser than men; and the weakness of God is stronger than men" (1 Co.1:25).

"If any of you lack wisdom, let him ask of God, that giveth to all *men* liberally, and upbraideth not; and it shall be given him" (Js.1:5).

"But the wisdom that is from above is first pure, then peaceable, gentle, *and* easy to be intreated, full of mercy and good fruits, without partiality, and without hypocrisy" (Js.3:17).

"For *God* giveth to a man that *is* good in his sight wisdom, and knowledge, and joy: but to the sinner he giveth travail, to gather and to heap up, that he may give to *him that is* good before God. This also *is* vanity and vexation of spirit" (Ec.2:26).

"Daniel answered and said, Blessed be the name of God for ever and ever: for wisdom and might are his" (Da.2:20).

"And he changeth the times and the seasons: he removeth kings, and setteth up kings: he giveth wisdom unto the wise, and knowledge to them that know understanding" (Da.2:21).

"And unto man he said, Behold, the fear of the Lord, that *is* wisdom; and to depart from evil *is* understanding" (Jb.28:28).

2 (5:9-14) **Boasting, Example—Position, Boasting in, Example—Power, Boasting in, Example—Wealth, Boasting in, Example—Pride, Example—Anger, Sinful, Example—Haman, Sin and Evil of, Pride and Anger**: the true nature of Haman's heart is exposed in dramatic fashion. His heart was full of shameful pride and bitter anger against the Jews. In these six verses he is pictured as a man of extreme boasting, a man who took great pleasure in bragging about his position, power, and wealth. Scripture exposes the truth of his sinful, evil heart:

OUTLINE	SCRIPTURE	SCRIPTURE	OUTLINE

2. Haman's pride & malice: A shameful example of an unbeliever boasting
a. Haman's anger at Mordecai
  1) He was in high spirits leaving the banquet
  2) He saw Mordecai not bowing & became furious
  3) He restrained himself & went on home
b. Haman's social gathering with his wife & friends: His pride, arrogance, & boasting
  1) About his vast wealth
  2) About his children
  3) About the honor given him
  4) About his promotion: His position, authority, & power
  5) About the distinctive
	9 Then went Haman forth that day joyful and with a glad heart: but when Haman saw Mordecai in the king's gate, that he stood not up, nor moved for him, he was full of indignation against Mordecai.
	10 Nevertheless Haman refrained himself: and when he came home, he sent and called for his friends, and Zeresh his wife.
	11 And Haman told them of the glory of his riches, and the multitude of his children, and all *the things* wherein the king had promoted him, and how he had advanced him above the princes and servants of the king.
	12 Haman said moreover,
		Yea, Esther the queen did let no man come in with the king unto the banquet that she had prepared but myself; and to morrow am I invited unto her also with the king.
		13 Yet all this availeth me nothing, so long as I see Mordecai the Jew sitting at the king's gate.
		14 Then said Zeresh his wife and all his friends unto him, Let a gallows be made of fifty cubits high, and to morrow speak thou unto the king that Mordecai may be hanged thereon: then go thou in merrily with the king unto the banquet. And the thing pleased Haman; and he caused the gallows to be made.
			recognition & honor given him by the queen
			
			c. Haman's only stated disappointment in life: Mordecai's refusal to honor him
			
			  1) His wife & friend's counsel
			  • To build gallows
			  • To ask the king the next day to hang Mordecai upon the gallows
			  • To then go to the dinner & be happy
			  2) His pleasure with the idea

a. Haman was extremely happy and in high spirits as he left the banquet given by Esther (vv.9-10). The queen had shown him the highest honor by inviting him to join her and the king at the banquet. And by being the only invited guest to join the king and queen, he presumed that Esther held him in high esteem. In light of that and because of the honor granted him, Haman's ego soared. But suddenly, as he walked alone, he saw Mordecai at the palace gate. Haman noticed that he neither stood up in honor of the prime minister nor trembled nervously due to the *Decree of Extermination*. This caused a raging fury to arise within Haman's heart. But he restrained himself and went home.

b. After reaching his house, Haman summoned his friends to a social gathering so he could share the day's joyful events with them. In his sharing, Scripture exposes the shameful depth of his prideful, arrogant heart. Sitting with his wife and friends and looking forward to the second banquet the next evening, Haman began to focus attention solely upon himself. Flooded with euphoria and pride, he boasted...

- about his vast wealth
- about his ten sons (9:7-10)
- about the honors the king had bestowed upon him
- about his promotion to be prime minister—the position, authority, and power the king had granted him
- about the distinctive recognition and honor given him by the queen, clearly seen in her invitation to join her and the king at the two banquets

c. Nevertheless, despite his position, wealth, and power, there was still one disappointment in Haman's life. This disappointment was Mordecai's refusal to honor him (vv.13-14). After hearing Haman express his disappointment, his wife and friends offered counsel. What they recommended would immediately remove Mordecai from the scene. They suggested Haman build gallows 75 feet high and then inform the king in the morning of Mordecai's contempt. The king's command had been to bow and show reverence for the prime minister, which Mordecai had clearly violated. Thus on hearing of Mordecai's contempt, the king would have him executed on the gallows immediately. The irritation caused by Mordecai would finally be removed. Haman's heart could be at peace and he could go about his daily affairs. In addition, he would be able to attend the queen's banquet free of irritation and disturbance. Hearing this suggestion pleased Haman immensely, and he immediately ordered that the gallows be built.

Thought 1. All of us—men and women, boys and girls, young and old—must guard against shameful pride and boasting, against a spirit of hostility and revenge. How many people do we know who talk about themselves, constantly, using the word "I," "me," and "mine" over and over again? How many of us brag about our wealth, children, promotions, or honors? When bragging about our wealth, we expose the hardness of our hearts, for it shows that our thoughts are focused on accumulating wealth not on meeting the desperate needs of the world. When boasting about our children, we are being insensitive to those who cannot have children, who have lost children, or those whose children don't measure up to our standards—whether in intelligence, education, looks, talents, abilities, or even health. The pain this causes is immeasurable and long-lasting. Think of any area of life where a person can brag and it is wrong, sinful, and wicked.

Our hearts should be thankful for God's blessings not boastful, for every good and perfect gift comes from Him (Js.1:17). We should be thankful for the honors and promotions given to us, but we should not boast in these things. Boasting always hurts someone, and at the same time it makes us appear obnoxious. Any boasting we do is distasteful, causing people to shy away and want little to do with us. This is particularly true if we continue to boast, giving little attention, recognition, or respect to others.

(1) Listen to what God's Holy Word says about boasting.

> **"And he spake a parable unto them, saying, The ground of a certain rich man brought forth plentifully: And he thought within himself, saying, What shall I do, because I have no room where to bestow my fruits? And he said, This will I do: I will pull down my barns, and build greater; and there will I bestow all my fruits and my goods. And I will say to my soul, Soul, thou hast much goods laid up for many years; take thine ease, eat, drink, *and* be merry. But God said unto him, *Thou* fool, this night thy soul shall be required of thee: then whose shall those things be, which thou hast provided? So *is* he that layeth up treasure for himself, and is not rich toward God"** (Lu.12:16-21).
>
> **"For who maketh thee to differ *from another?* and what hast thou that thou didst not receive? now if thou didst receive *it,* why dost thou glory, as if thou hadst not received *it?"*** (1 Co.4:7).
>
> **"Even so the tongue is a little member, and boasteth great things. Behold, how great a matter a little fire kindleth!"** (Js.3:5).
>
> **"But now ye rejoice in your boastings: all such rejoicing is evil"** (Js.4:16).
>
> **"For the wicked boasteth of his heart's desire, and blesseth the covetous, *whom* the LORD abhorreth"** (Ps.10:3).
>
> **"They that trust in their wealth, and boast themselves in the multitude of their riches; None *of them* can by any means redeem his brother, nor give to God a ransom for him"** (Ps.49:6-7).
>
> **"Pride *goeth* before destruction, and an haughty spirit before a fall"** (Pr.16:18).
>
> **"Whoso boasteth himself of a false gift *is like* clouds and wind without rain"** (Pr.25:14).
>
> **"Boast not thyself of to morrow; for thou knowest not what a day may bring forth"** (Pr.27:1).

(2) Listen to what God's Word says about hatred and malice.

> **"For the wrath of God is revealed from heaven against all ungodliness and unrighteousness of men, who hold the truth in unrighteousness....Being filled with all unrighteousness, fornication,**

wickedness, covetousness, maliciousness; full of envy, murder, debate, deceit, malignity; whisperers, Backbiters, haters of God, despiteful, proud, boasters, inventors of evil things, disobedient to parents" (Ro.1:18, 29-30; note the phrase "haters of God").

"Therefore let us keep the feast, not with old leaven, neither with the leaven of malice and wickedness; but with the unleavened bread of sincerity and truth" (1 Co.5:8).

"Brethren, be not children in understanding: howbeit in malice be ye children, but in understanding be men" (1 Co.14:20).

"Now the works of the flesh are manifest, which are these; Adultery, fornication, uncleanness, lasciviousness, Idolatry, witchcraft, hatred, variance, emulations, wrath, strife, seditions, heresies, Envyings, murders, drunkenness, revellings, and such like: of the which I tell you before, as I have also told you in time past, that they which do such things shall not inherit the kingdom of God" (Ga.5:19-21; note the word "hatred").

"Let all bitterness, and wrath, and anger, and clamour, and evil speaking, be put away from you, with all malice: And be ye kind one to another, tenderhearted, forgiving one another, even as God for Christ's sake hath forgiven you" (Ep.4:31-32).

"But now ye also put off all these; anger, wrath, malice, blasphemy, filthy communication out of your mouth" (Col.3:8).

"Wherefore laying aside all malice, and all guile, and hypocrisies, and envies, and all evil speakings, As newborn babes, desire the sincere milk of the word, that ye may grow thereby" (1 Pe.2:1-2).

"He that saith he is in the light, and hateth his brother, is in darkness even until now" (1 Jn.2:9).

"Whosoever hateth his brother is a murderer: and ye know that no murderer hath eternal life abiding in him" (1 Jn.3:15).

"Thou shalt not hate thy brother in thine heart" (Le.19:17).

"Hatred stirreth up strifes: but love covereth all sins" (Pr.10:12).

CHAPTER 6

C. The Unexpected Honor Bestowed Upon Mordecai: A Picture of God's Providence, Guidance, & Love for His People, 6:1-14

1. **Mordecai unexpectedly honored: God moves, uses human events to save His people**
   a. The king's sleepless night
   b. The king's decision to read the royal records
   c. The king's choice of records to be read

   d. The king's delay in rewarding Mordecai, 2:21-23

   e. Haman's early, timely arrival at the palace

   f. The king's vague question asked of Haman
      1) His question did not identify who the king wished to reward
      2) His question stirred the prideful, evil Haman to think he was to be honored
   g. Haman's selfish, ambitious answer: The man should be second only to the king
      1) Should be given a royal robe & stallion: The very

On that night could not the king sleep, and he commanded to bring the book of records of the chronicles; and they were read before the king. 2 And it was found written, that Mordecai had told of Bigthana and Teresh, two of the king's chamberlains, the keepers of the door, who sought to lay hand on the king Ahasuerus. 3 And the king said, What honour and dignity hath been done to Mordecai for this? Then said the king's servants that ministered unto him, There is nothing done for him. 4 And the king said, Who is in the court? Now Haman was come into the outward court of the king's house, to speak unto the king to hang Mordecai on the gallows that he had prepared for him. 5 And the king's servants said unto him, Behold, Haman standeth in the court. And the king said, Let him come in. 6 So Haman came in. And the king said unto him, What shall be done unto the man whom the king delighteth to honour? Now Haman thought in his heart, To whom would the king delight to do honour more than to myself? 7 And Haman answered the king, For the man whom the king delighteth to honour, 8 Let the royal apparel be brought which the king useth

to wear, and the horse that the king rideth upon, and the crown royal which is set upon his head: 9 And let this apparel and horse be delivered to the hand of one of the king's most noble princes, that they may array the man withal whom the king delighteth to honour, and bring him on horseback through the street of the city, and proclaim before him, Thus shall it be done to the man whom the king delighteth to honour. 10 Then the king said to Haman, Make haste, and take the apparel and the horse, as thou hast said, and do even so to Mordecai the Jew, that sitteth at the king's gate: let nothing fail of all that thou hast spoken. 11 Then took Haman the apparel and the horse, and arrayed Mordecai, and brought him on horseback through the street of the city, and proclaimed before him, Thus shall it be done unto the man whom the king delighteth to honour. 12 And Mordecai came again to the king's gate. But Haman hasted to his house mourning, and having his head covered. 13 And Haman told Zeresh his wife and all his friends every thing that had befallen him. Then said his wise men and Zeresh his wife unto him, If Mordecai be of the seed of the Jews, before whom thou hast begun to fall, thou shalt not prevail against him, but shalt surely fall before him. 14 And while they were yet talking with him, came the king's chamberlains, and hasted to bring Haman unto the banquet that Esther had prepared.

authority of the king himself

   2) Should be presented to the people as a member of royalty with royal authority, second only to the king

   h. The king's shocking order that reversed the fate, the destiny of both Haman & Mordecai
      1) The king stunned & horrified Haman: Charged him to so honor Mordecai the Jew
      2) The king warned Haman: Neglect nothing

2. **Haman unexpectedly humiliated: God humbles the prideful of this world**
   a. Haman's obedience to the king: His humiliating experience, being forced to exalt the man he had despised

   b. Haman's disgrace: Rushed home with his head covered

   c. Haman's future predicted: By his wife & friends
      1) His downfall had started
      2) His plot against the Jews was doomed to failure

   d. Haman's call to attend the queen's second banquet

DIVISION I

THE JEWS SAVED BY THE COURAGEOUS ACTION OF ESTHER, 4:1–10:3

C. The Unexpected Honor Bestowed Upon Mordecai: A Picture of God's Providence, Guidance, and Love for His People, 6:1-14

(6:1-14) **Introduction**: How often has a small event changed our lives? Some seemingly insignificant circumstance, experience, problem, or joyful occasion took place, and our lives were twisted and turned completely around. What we expected did not happen. Instead, a complete reversal of our plans took place and our lives changed dramatically. In some cases our fate and destiny were completely changed.

When life-changing events take place in our lives—whether good or bad—this is known as *divine providence*, God's providential care and guidance in our lives. God loves us and wants to save us so that we can know the fullness of life. As we walk about day by day, God wants us to live victorious lives, conquering all the trials and temptations that confront us and living life to the fullest. He wants us to experience the fullness of love, joy, and peace. But because of the wickedness of the human heart and all the evil and violence on the earth, God has to use human events to arouse our hearts to turn to Him for salvation. God wants our hearts stirred to live for Him and to worship Him. He wants us to live righteous and just lives, treating others as we want them to treat us. He wants us to love others just as we love ourselves. Divine providence simply means that God loves and cares for this world. Through His providential care, moving and using human events, He saves, guides, protects, and sustains His people.

God's providential care is the subject of the present Scripture. The story of Esther is one that suddenly and unexpectedly twists and turns. What is expected does not happen. The unexpected does. A complete reversal of events takes place. The story changes dramatically as honor is bestowed upon Mordecai and dishonor upon Haman. Mordecai is not hung upon the gallows, but Haman is (Ch.7).

Through the providence of God, Mordecai is saved from the gallows and the Jews from extermination. This is, *The Unexpected Honor Bestowed Upon Mordecai: A Picture of God's Providence, Guidance, and Love for His People*, 6:1-14.

1. Mordecai unexpectedly honored: God moves, uses human events to save His people (vv.1-10).
2. Haman unexpectedly humiliated: God humbles the prideful of this world (vv.11-14).

---

1 (6:1-10) **Providence, of God, His Guidance and Care—Guidance, of God, Example—Care, of God, Example—Protection, of God, Example—Preservation, of God, Example—Sustaining Providence, of God, Example—Overshadowing, Providence of God, Example—Sovereignty, of God, Example—Mordecai, Honored by King Xerxes—Xerxes, King of Persia, Honored Mordecai—Haman, Pride and Ambition of, Example—God, Guidance of**: in a surprising and quick succession of events, Mordecai was unexpectedly honored by King Xerxes. Instead of being executed upon the gallows built by Haman, Mordecai was exalted. God moved human events to save His people from the holocaust of extermination. During the very night of Esther's banquet, eight very simple yet incredible circumstances pointed to God's providential care for His people, His guiding the circumstances to save the Jewish race from annihilation.

OUTLINE	SCRIPTURE	SCRIPTURE	OUTLINE
1. Mordecai unexpectedly honored: God moves, uses human events to save His people a. The king's sleepless night b. The king's decision to read the royal records c. The king's choice of records to be read	On that night could not the king sleep, and he commanded to bring the book of records of the chronicles; and they were read before the king. 2 And it was found written, that Mordecai had told of Bigthana and Teresh, two of the king's chamberlains, the keepers of the door, who sought to lay hand on the king Ahasuerus.	man whom the king delighteth to honour? Now Haman thought in his heart, To whom would the king delight to do honour more than to myself? 7 And Haman answered the king, For the man whom the king delighteth to honour,	tify who the king wished to reward 2) His question stirred the prideful, evil Haman to think he was to be honored g. Haman's selfish, ambitious answer: The man should be second only to the king
d. The king's delay in rewarding Mordecai, 2:21-23	3 And the king said, What honour and dignity hath been done to Mordecai for this? Then said the king's servants that ministered unto him, There is nothing done for him.	8 Let the royal apparel be brought which the king *useth* to wear, and the horse that the king rideth upon, and the crown royal which is set upon his head: 9 And let this apparel and horse be delivered to the hand of one of the king's most noble princes, that they may array the man *withal* whom the	1) Should be given a royal robe & stallion: The very authority of the king himself
e. Haman's early, timely arrival at the palace	4 And the king said, Who *is* in the court? Now Haman was come into the outward court of the king's house, to speak unto the king to hang Mordecai on the gallows that he had prepared for him.	king delighteth to honour, and bring him on horseback through the street of the city, and proclaim before him, Thus shall it be done to the man whom the king delighteth to honour.	2) Should be presented to the people as a member of royalty with royal authority, second only to the king
f. The king's vague question asked of Haman 1) His question did not iden-	5 And the king's servants said unto him, Behold, Haman standeth in the court. And the king said, Let him come in. 6 So Haman came in. And the king said unto him, What shall be done unto the	10 Then the king said to Haman, Make haste, *and* take the apparel and the horse, as thou hast said, and do even so to Mordecai the Jew, that sitteth at the king's gate: let nothing fail of all that thou hast spoken.	h. The king's shocking order that reversed the fate, the destiny of both Haman & Mordecai 1) The king stunned & horrified Haman: Charged him to so honor Mordecai the Jew 2) The king warned Haman: Neglect nothing

a. After enjoying Queen Esther's presence at her banquet, King Xerxes returned to his own quarters. But he had a very sleepless night (v.1). What kept him from sleeping? Was it the pleasure of Esther's company once again? Had he begun to long for her presence? Or was it a matter of state business that weighed heavily on his mind? Or did he perhaps eat and drink too much at the banquet? Or was the mystery of Esther's request confounding him, wondering what her petition would be?[1]

The fact that King Xerxes could not sleep after a dinner of wine is surprising, a clear evidence that God was keeping him awake. The LORD had begun to work in the king's heart, so He could arouse Xerxes to save the Jewish people. Because of the king's sleepless night, a series of events were to take place that would change the course of Jewish history. The Jews would not be exterminated as a race; instead, they would be saved. And God would continue to fulfill the covenant promises He had made to Abraham, Moses, and David.

b. Unable to sleep, the king ordered the royal records to be brought in and read to him (v.1). For a man who wanted to sleep, this was a strange solution to insomnia. It would have made far more sense to have ordered music or have a simple, relaxing story read. Or, he could have easily summoned a concubine to massage and spend time with him helping him to relax. But instead, he ordered the royal records, which is clear evidence that God's providence was moving and using even the king's decision to save His people.

c. The third event used by God was the king's choice of records to be read (v.2). Of all the royal records that could have been read, the one chosen by the servant recorded the uncovering of the assassination plot by Mordecai (2:21-23). No doubt there were many volumes of the royal records in the king's library, but the one chosen happened to include the fact that Mordecai had saved the king's life several years earlier. A sleepless night, a decision to read the royal records, choosing the very record that included Mordecai's having saved the king's life—three simple events, all taking place just hours before Haman was planning to execute Mordecai. God's providence was moving and using events to save His people. Warren Wiersbe gives an excellent application of this point.

> *Can God direct in the books that people pick up and read? Yes, He can. Late in February 1916, a British student bought a book at a used-book stall in a railway station. He had looked at that book and rejected it at least a dozen times before, but that day he purchased it. It was Phantastes by George MacDonald, and the reading of that book eventually led to that young man's conversion. Who was he? C.S. Lewis, perhaps the greatest and most popular apologist for the Christian faith of the middle-twentieth century. He wrote to a friend that he had picked up the book "by hazard" but I believe God had directed his choice.*
>
> *God can even direct what we read in a book. A young man in North Africa sought peace, first in sensual pleasures and then in philosophy, but only became more miserable. One day he heard a neighbor child playing a game and saying, "Take it and read! Take it and read!" The young man immediately picked up the Scriptures and "happened" to open to Romans 13:13-14; and those verses brought him to faith in Christ. We know that young man today as Augustine, Bishop of Hippo, and author of numerous Christian classics.*
>
> *The king's servant picked out the very book that told about Mordecai's good deed and read that section to Ahasuerus. How marvelous is the providence of God!*[2]

d. Fourth, God's providence moved and used the king's delay in rewarding Mordecai to save His people. It had been five years since Mordecai had uncovered the plot and saved the king's life. If Mordecai had been immediately rewarded, the event now about to take place would have never happened. Most likely Mordecai would have been executed and the Jews exterminated. Thus the hand of God's providential guidance and care for His people can be clearly seen in the king's delay in rewarding Mordecai. Again, Warren W. Wiersbe gives an excellent practical application to this point that is well worth quoting:

> *Is God in charge of schedules? He certainly is! After befriending Pharaoh's butler, Joseph thought it would lead to his being released from prison; but Joseph had to wait two more years until the time God had chosen for him to become second ruler in Egypt (Gen. 40:23–41:1). God had a specific day selected for the Jews to leave Egypt (Ex. 12:40-42); see Gen. 15:13-16), and even the birth of Jesus Christ in Bethlehem occurred "when the fullness of the time was come" (Gal. 4:4, KJV). In the midst of a confused and troubled world, the dedicated believer is able to say, "My times are in Thy hand" (Ps. 31:15, KJV) and find peace in God's will.*[3]

e. Fifth, God moved and used the early, timely arrival of Haman to the palace in order to save Mordecai and His people (vv.4-5). Remember, the previous evening Haman had made the decision to approach the king to suggest the immediate execution of Mordecai (5:14). Anxious to secure the warrant of execution from the king as soon as day broke, Haman rushed to the palace.

Not having slept all night, the king apparently heard Haman when he entered the outer court. Not knowing who it was, the king asked his attendants for the identity of the person. When they mentioned that it was Haman standing in the court, the king ordered them to bring him in. Evidently the king was still in his bedchamber. Whatever the case, the king was most anxious to honor Mordecai who had saved his life.

Even in the early arrival of Haman to the palace, we can see the hand of God's providence. He used Haman's bitter hatred against Mordecai to arouse him to be the first royal official to arrive at the palace on this particular morning.

f. Sixth, when Haman entered the king's presence, the LORD moved and used the wording of the king's question to Haman (v.6). Note that the king's question did not identify the man whom the king wished to reward. Addressing Haman, the king asked what should be done for the man whom the king wishes to honor?

The question stirred Haman's prideful, evil heart, for he believed the king was planning to honor him. Within his mind, he was asking himself: Just who is the king going to honor? It must be me, for no one deserves it as much as I do.

---

[1] Warren W. Wiersbe. *Be Committed*, p.128.
[2] Ibid., pp.129-130.
[3] Ibid., pp.130-131.

After all, I am the closest advisor and counselor to the king. The king's vague question is clear evidence of God's sovereign power, for He used the exact words of the king's question to help His people.

g. Seventh, God moved and used the selfish, ambitious answer of Haman to save Mordecai and the Jews (vv.7-9). Thinking that he was the one to be honored by the king, Haman suggested the highest honor that could be given to a person. The man would be second only to the king.

1) The man should be given a royal robe, one of the same robes the king himself had worn (v.8). He should also be given one of the royal stallions the king had ridden, and the stallion should have the royal crest placed on its head.

2) The man should be presented to the people as a member of royalty with royal authority, second only to the king (v.9). In all the pomp and ceremony of the king himself, he should be led through the city streets by one of the king's most noble officials, proclaiming that this man was honored by the king and was to be honored as second only to the king. Even in Haman's self-centered and determined answer, God was moving to save Mordecai and His people from Haman's evil plot. The prime minister had just spelled out the honor that was soon to be bestowed upon Mordecai.

h. Finally, God used the king to give the shocking order that reversed the fate, the destiny of Haman and Mordecai (v.10). Pleased with the suggestion of Haman, the king ordered the prime minister to immediately secure the king's robe and horse and then to do exactly as he had prepared—for Mordecai the Jew. Utterly shocked and horrified, Haman's spirit no doubt crumpled. Above all others throughout the empire, Haman never would have expected Mordecai to be the man the king wished to honor. Continuing his command, the king warned Haman: he must not neglect anything he had recommended. Every honor suggested by the prime minister was to be bestowed upon Mordecai the Jew.

Thought 1. Divine providence simply means God's guidance and care. He sustains and guides human destiny. He moves and uses human events to save people, to arouse people to awaken out of their sins and turn to Him. He longs for people to worship and serve Him and to live righteous lives while on earth. Through His providential care, God guides, provides, protects, sustains, and preserves His people, all who turn to him through faith in the Lord Jesus Christ (Ep.2:8-9). Listen to what God's Holy Word says about His providence.

(1) God's providential care provides for His people.

"**But seek ye first the kingdom of God, and his righteousness; and all these things shall be added unto you**" (Mt.6:33).

"**But my God shall supply all your need according to his riches in glory by Christ Jesus**" (Ph.4:19).

"**And ye shall serve the LORD your God, and he shall bless thy bread, and thy water; and I will take sickness away from the midst of thee**" (Ex.23:25).

"**That I will give *you* the rain of your land in his due season, the first rain and the latter rain, that thou mayest gather in thy corn, and thy wine, and thine oil**" (De.11:14).

"**Thou preparest a table before me in the presence of mine enemies: thou anointest my head with oil; my cup runneth over**" (Ps.23:5).

"***Oh* how great *is* thy goodness, which thou hast laid up for them that fear thee; *which* thou hast wrought for them that trust in thee before the sons of men!**" (Ps.31:19).

"**Thou visitest the earth, and waterest it: thou greatly enrichest it with the river of God, *which* is full of water: thou preparest them corn, when thou hast so provided for it**" (Ps.65:9).

"**Blessed *be* the Lord, *who* daily loadeth us *with benefits, even* the God of our salvation. Selah**" (Ps.68:19).

"***It is* vain for you to rise up early, to sit up late, to eat the bread of sorrows: *for* so he giveth his beloved sleep**" (Ps.127:2).

(2) God's providential care protects his people.

"**But even the very hairs of your head are all numbered. Fear not therefore: ye are of more value than many sparrows**" (Lu.12:7).

"**But there shall not an hair of your head perish**" (Lu.21:18).

"**For the which cause I also suffer these things: nevertheless I am not ashamed: for I know whom I have believed, and am persuaded that he is able to keep that which I have committed unto him against that day**" (2 Ti.1:12).

"**Who are kept by the power of God through faith unto salvation ready to be revealed in the last time**" (1 Pe.1:5).

"**Casting all your care upon him; for he careth for you**" (1 Pe.5:7).

"**Now unto him that is able to keep you from falling, and to present *you* faultless before the presence of his glory with exceeding joy**" (Jude 24).

"**And, behold, I *am* with thee, and will keep thee in all *places* whither thou goest, and will bring thee again into this land; for I will not leave thee, until I have done *that* which I have spoken to thee of**" (Ge.28:15).

"**For the eyes of the LORD run to and fro throughout the whole earth, to shew himself strong in the behalf of *them* whose heart *is* perfect toward him. Herein thou hast done foolishly: therefore from henceforth thou shalt have wars**" (2 Chr.16:9).

"**The angel of the LORD encampeth round about them that fear him, and delivereth them**" (Ps.34:7).

"Be merciful unto me, O God, be merciful unto me: for my soul trusteth in thee: yea, in the shadow of thy wings will I make my refuge, until *these* calamities be overpast" (Ps.57:1).

"He shall cover thee with his feathers, and under his wings shalt thou trust: his truth *shall be thy* shield and buckler" (Ps.91:4).

"Behold, he that keepeth Israel shall neither slumber nor sleep" (Ps.121:4).

"As the mountains *are* round about Jerusalem, so the LORD *is* round about his people from henceforth even for ever" (Ps.125:2).

"For thou hast been a strength to the poor, a strength to the needy in his distress, a refuge from the storm, a shadow from the heat, when the blast of the terrible ones *is* as a storm *against* the wall" (Is.25:4).

(3) God's providential care sustains His people.

"So that we may boldly say, The Lord *is* my helper, and I will not fear what man shall do unto me" (He.13:6).

"Ye have seen what I did unto the Egyptians, and *how* I bare you on eagles' wings, and brought you unto myself" (Ex.19:4).

"The eternal God *is thy* refuge, and underneath *are* the everlasting arms: and he shall thrust out the enemy from before thee; and shall say, Destroy *them*" (De.33:27).

"Thou hast also given me the shield of thy salvation: and thy right hand hath holden me up, and thy gentleness hath made me great" (Ps.18:35).

"The LORD *is* my strength and my shield; my heart trusted in him, and I am helped: therefore my heart greatly rejoiceth; and with my song will I praise him" (Ps.28:7).

"But I *am* poor and needy; *yet* the Lord thinketh upon me: thou *art* my help and my deliverer; make no tarrying, O my God" (Ps.40:17).

"Fear thou not; for I *am* with thee: be not dismayed; for I *am* thy God: I will strengthen thee; yea, I will help thee; yea, I will uphold thee with the right hand of my righteousness" (Is.41:10).

"I have redeemed thee, I have called *thee* by thy name; thou *art* mine When thou passest through the waters, I *will be* with thee; and through the rivers, they shall not overflow thee: when thou walkest through the fire, thou shalt not be burned; neither shall the flame kindle upon thee" (Is.43:1-2).

"And *even to your* old age I *am* he; and *even* to hoar [gray] hairs will I carry *you:* I have made, and I will bear; even I will carry, and will deliver *you*" (Is.46:4).

"Behold, the Lord GOD will help me; who *is* he *that* shall condemn me? lo, they all shall wax old as a garment; the moth shall eat them up" (Is.50:9).

(4) God's providential care preserves His people.

"And the Lord shall deliver me from every evil work, and will preserve *me* unto his heavenly kingdom: to whom *be* glory for ever and ever. Amen" (2 Ti.4:18).

"And the LORD commanded us to do all these statutes, to fear the LORD our God, for our good always, that he might preserve us alive, as *it is* at this day" (De.6:24).

"For the LORD our God, he *it is* that brought us up and our fathers out of the land of Egypt, from the house of bondage, and which did those great signs in our sight, and preserved us in all the way wherein we went, and among all the people through whom we passed" (Jos.24:17).

"And the LORD preserved David whithersoever he went" (2 S.8:6).

"O love the LORD, all ye his saints: *for* the LORD preserveth the faithful, and plentifully rewardeth the proud doer" (Ps.31:23).

"For the LORD loveth judgment, and forsaketh not his saints; they are preserved for ever: but the seed of the wicked shall be cut off" (Ps.37:28).

"The LORD openeth *the eyes of* the blind: the LORD raiseth them that are bowed down: the LORD loveth the righteous. The LORD preserveth the strangers; he relieveth the fatherless and widow: but the way of the wicked he turneth upside down. The LORD shall reign for ever, *even* thy God, O Zion, unto all generations. Praise ye the LORD" (Ps.146:8-10).

"He keepeth the paths of judgment, and preserveth the way of his saints" (Pr.2:8).

"Thou, *even* thou, *art* LORD alone; thou hast made heaven, the heaven of heavens, with all their host, the earth, and all *things* that *are* therein, the seas, and all that *is* therein, and thou preservest them all; and the host of heaven worshippeth thee" (Ne.9:6).

---

2 (6:11-14) **Humiliation, Example of—Embarrassment, Example of—Abased - Abasement, Example of—Disgrace, Example of—Dishonor, Example of—Shame, Example of—Degraded, Example of—Haman, Humiliation of**: quickly, unexpectedly, Haman was humiliated before the public while Mordecai was honored. The honorable prime minister was to suffer the most embarrassing, disgraceful act of his life. His experience clearly shows how God humbles the prideful of the world and exalts the humble.

OUTLINE	SCRIPTURE	SCRIPTURE	OUTLINE

2. Haman unexpectedly humiliated: God humbles the prideful of this world
  a. Haman's obedience to the king: His humiliating experience, being forced to exalt the man he had despised
 	
  b. Haman's disgrace: Rushed home with his head covered
	11 Then took Haman the apparel and the horse, and arrayed Mordecai, and brought him on horseback through the street of the city, and proclaimed before him, Thus shall it be done unto the man whom the king delighteth to honour.
	12 And Mordecai came again to the king's gate. But Haman hasted to his house mourning, and having his head covered.
	13 And Haman told Zeresh
		his wife and all his friends every *thing* that had befallen him. Then said his wise men and Zeresh his wife unto him, If Mordecai *be* of the seed of the Jews, before whom thou hast begun to fall, thou shalt not prevail against him, but shalt surely fall before him.
		14 And while they *were* yet talking with him, came the king's chamberlains, and hasted to bring Haman unto the banquet that Esther had prepared.
			c. Haman's future predicted: By his wife & friends
			  1) His downfall had started
			  2) His plot against the Jews was doomed to failure
			
			d. Haman's call to attend the queen's second banquet

a. Haman's pride was crushed by the command of the king, for he was forced to exalt the man he had personally despised and plotted to execute, the Jew Mordecai. In a state of shock and shameful humiliation, Haman went out to the city gate to get Mordecai to bring him into the palace. Cringing at the very thought of what he was being forced to do, Haman placed the king's royal robe on Mordecai and led him through the city streets on the king's royal horse shouting out that the people were to honor Mordecai. What irony! Bowing down before the prime minister was the very thing Mordecai had refused to do. Now Haman was being forced to demand that the public bow before Mordecai.

b. Imagine Haman's utter disgrace in view of the fact many of his friends and royal officials knew of his bitter hatred toward Mordecai. Everyone also knew of his extreme prejudice and malice toward the Jews. Naturally—and deservedly—his spirit was crushed. Therefore when Haman and Mordecai returned to the palace gate, the disgraced prime minister covered his head in shame and rushed home. He just could not bear the embarrassment.

c. When Haman arrived home, he found that all his friends, not knowing what had just transpired, had gathered to encourage him. But after he related the disgrace he had suffered, he again received a shock. His wife and friends did not give him comforting advice but, rather, a prediction of his downfall. They warned that he could not stand against Mordecai since he was a Jew. And because the king had so highly honored Mordecai, Haman was running a dangerous risk in continuing with his plot to exterminate the Jews. His *Decree of Extermination* was doomed to fail, for the king would now be sympathetic to the Jews.

There is far more meaning than meets the eye in this prediction by Haman's wife and friends. God stands behind his people, guaranteeing their survival. No person or nation will ever stand who opposes God's dear people. Just as the LORD protected the Jewish nation down through the years, so the LORD will protect all who truly put their trust in Him.

d. While Haman's wife and friends were still talking with him, several of the king's attendants arrived and rushed him to the queen's second banquet (v.14). Earlier in the day Haman's plans were to enjoy the banquet with a free and joyful spirit. If the events had happened as he planned, by this time he would have already executed his archenemy Mordecai. But now he was forced to go to the banquet with a crushed spirit and with fear flooding his heart, for his wife had predicted the start of his downfall. With these thoughts in mind as well as the utter disgrace he had suffered, he no doubt cringed at the thought of having to attend the banquet. But because it was a banquet prepared by Queen Esther herself, Haman had no choice.

Thought 1. God humbles the prideful of this world, those who exalt themselves above others. A prideful person feels more important than others and lifts himself up above others. He loves himself, regards himself, and respects himself more than he does others. A prideful person esteems himself more highly than others and is often smug, cocky, bigheaded, conceited, and condescending toward others. Self-centered pride is a terrible evil upon this earth. It puts other people down, often degrading belittling, shaming, humiliating, and weakening them.

God commands us to love one another, not to walk around in a spirit of haughtiness or arrogance toward others. For this reason God declares that He will humble the prideful of this world. Listen to what God's Holy Word says:

> **"And whosoever shall exalt himself shall be abased; and he that shall humble himself shall be exalted" (Mt.23:12).**

> **"*Be* of the same mind one toward another. Mind not high things, but condescend to men of low estate. Be not wise in your own conceits" (Ro.12:16).**

> **"And if any man think that he knoweth any thing, he knoweth nothing yet as he ought to know" (1 Co.8:2).**

> **"*Let* nothing *be* done through strife or vainglory; but in lowliness of mind let each esteem other better than themselves. Look not every man on his own things, but every man also on the things of others" (Ph.2:3-4).**

> **"But he giveth more grace. Wherefore he saith, God resisteth the proud, but giveth grace unto the humble" (Js.4:6).**

> **"Love not the world, neither the things *that are* in the world. If any man love the world, the love of the Father is not in him. For all that *is* in the world, the lust of the flesh, and the lust of the eyes, and the pride of life, is not of the Father, but is of the world" (1 Jn.2:15-16).**

"They are exalted for a little while, but are gone and brought low; they are taken out of the way as all *other,* and cut off as the tops of the ears of corn" (Jb.24:24).

"He divideth the sea with his power, and by his understanding he smiteth through the proud" (Jb.26:12).

"The wicked in *his* pride doth persecute the poor: let them be taken in the devices that they have imagined" (Ps.10:2).

"An high look, and a proud heart, *and* the plowing of the wicked, *is* sin" (Pr.21:4).

"Therefore pride compasseth them about as a chain; violence covereth them *as* a garment" (Ps.73:6).

"Thou hast rebuked the proud *that are* cursed, which do err from thy commandments" (Ps.119:21).

"These six *things* doth the LORD hate: yea, seven *are* an abomination unto him: A proud look, a lying tongue, and hands that shed innocent blood, An heart that deviseth wicked imaginations, feet that be swift in running to mischief, A false witness *that* speaketh lies, and he that soweth discord among brethren" (Pr.6:16-19).

"*When* pride cometh, then cometh shame: but with the lowly *is* wisdom" (Pr.11:2).

"Only by pride cometh contention: but with the well advised *is* wisdom" (Pr.13:10).

"Pride *goeth* before destruction, and an haughty spirit before a fall" (Pr.16:18).

"He loveth transgression that loveth strife: *and* he that exalteth his gate seeketh destruction" (Pr.17:19).

"For thou wilt save the afflicted people; but wilt bring down high looks" (Ps.18:27).

"Seest thou a man wise in his own conceit? *there is* more hope of a fool than of him" (Pr.26:12).

"He that is of a proud heart stirreth up strife: but he that putteth his trust in the LORD shall be made fat" (Pr.28:25).

"A man's pride shall bring him low: but honour shall uphold the humble in spirit" (Pr.29:23).

"And I will punish the world for *their* evil, and the wicked for their iniquity; and I will cause the arrogancy of the proud to cease, and will lay low the haughtiness of the terrible" (Is.13:11).

"Thy pomp is brought down to the grave, *and* the noise of thy viols: the worm is spread under thee, and the worms cover thee" (Is.14:11).

"For thou hast said in thine heart, I will ascend into heaven, I will exalt my throne above the stars of God: I will sit also upon the mount of the congregation, in the sides of the north: I will ascend above the heights of the clouds; I will be like the most High. Yet thou shalt be brought down to hell, to the sides of the pit" (Is.14:13-15).

"The LORD of hosts hath purposed it, to stain the pride of all glory, *and* to bring into contempt all the honourable of the earth" (Is.23:9).

"For he bringeth down them that dwell on high; the lofty city, he layeth it low; he layeth it low, *even* to the ground; he bringeth it *even* to the dust" (Is.26:5).

"And I will bring an everlasting reproach upon you, and a perpetual shame, which shall not be forgotten" (Je.23:40).

"Thy terribleness hath deceived thee, *and* the pride of thine heart, O thou that dwellest in the clefts of the rock, that holdest the height of the hill: though thou shouldest make thy nest as high as the eagle, I will bring thee down from thence, saith the LORD" (Je.49:16).

"They shall bring thee down to the pit, and thou shalt die the deaths of *them that are* slain in the midst of the seas" (Eze.28:8).

"And the pride of Israel testifieth to his face: and they do not return to the LORD their God, nor seek him for all this" (Ho.7:10).

"Though they dig into hell, thence shall mine hand take them; though they climb up to heaven, thence will I bring them down" (Am.9:2).

"Though thou exalt *thyself* as the eagle, and though thou set thy nest among the stars, thence will I bring thee down, saith the LORD" (Obad.4).

"Behold, his soul *which* is lifted up is not upright in him: but the just shall live by his faith" (Hab.2:4).

CHAPTER 7

D. The Suspenseful Exposure & Downfall of Haman: A Picture of Reaping Exactly What One Sows—Justice, Measure for Measure, 7:1-10

1. **Esther's exposure of Haman's evil: A surety—all sin will be exposed by God**
   a. The queen's banquet
      1) The guests were drinking wine following the meal
      2) The king again asked for Esther's request & repeated his offer to grant anything she wished, 5:6

   b. The queen's startling & perplexing request: That her life & the lives of her people be spared

   c. The queen's explanation
      1) She reminded the king of his horrific decree, 3:1-15
      2) She charged that a man—without mentioning his name—had committed a conspiracy against her & her people: Had sold them for extermination
   d. The bewildered king's question: Who is the man? Who would dare touch the queen?

So the king and Haman came to banquet with Esther the queen.
2 And the king said again unto Esther on the second day at the banquet of wine, What *is* thy petition, queen Esther? and it shall be granted thee: and what *is* thy request? and it shall be performed, *even* to the half of the kingdom.
3 Then Esther the queen answered and said, If I have found favour in thy sight, O king, and if it please the king, let my life be given me at my petition, and my people at my request:
4 For we are sold, I and my people, to be destroyed, to be slain, and to perish. But if we had been sold for bondmen and bondwomen, I had held my tongue, although the enemy could not countervail the king's damage.
5 Then the king Ahasuerus answered and said unto Esther the queen, Who is he,

and where is he, that durst presume in his heart to do so?
6 And Esther said, The adversary and enemy *is* this wicked Haman. Then Haman was afraid before the king and the queen.
7 And the king arising from the banquet of wine in his wrath *went* into the palace garden: and Haman stood up to make request for his life to Esther the queen; for he saw that there was evil determined against him by the king.
8 Then the king returned out of the palace garden into the place of the banquet of wine; and Haman was fallen upon the bed whereon Esther *was*. Then said the king, Will he force the queen also before me in the house? As the word went out of the king's mouth, they covered Haman's face.
9 And Harbonah, one of the chamberlains, said before the king, Behold also, the gallows fifty cubits high, which Haman had made for Mordecai, who had spoken good for the king, standeth in the house of Haman. Then the king said, Hang him thereon.
10 So they hanged Haman on the gallows that he had prepared for Mordecai. Then was the king's wrath pacified.

   e. The queen's abrupt response: The culprit was present
      1) Identified Haman as the man
      2) Struck terror in Haman

2. **Haman's execution: A surety—there is no escape from God's judgment**
   a. The king's burning rage: He hastily walked out to get alone
   b. Haman's plea to Esther for his life

   c. The king's return & verdict of death
      1) He saw Haman, shockingly, at the feet of Esther where she was reclining on a couch
      2) He angrily charged Haman with molesting his wife
      3) The king's guards covered Haman's face: Signaled his doom
   d. The eunuch's report to the king: Informed him about the gallows built by Haman
      1) That it was 75 feet high
      2) That it had been built for Mordecai

   e. The king's order for Haman to be executed on the gallows
      1) The order was carried out
      2) The king's fury calmed down

DIVISION III

THE JEWS SAVED BY THE COURAGEOUS ACTION OF ESTHER, 4:1–10:3

D. The Suspenseful Exposure and Downfall of Haman: A Picture of Reaping Exactly What One Sows—Justice, Measure for Measure, 7:1-10

(7:1-10) **Introduction**: a person reaps exactly what he has sown. If we sow friendship and love in this life, we will reap friendship and love. If we sow a life of commitment, hard work, and diligence, we will reap some material reward. But if we sow laziness and slothfulness, we will reap unemployment and little material provisions. Within a marriage, if we sow true love, care, tenderness, and morality, we will reap faithfulness and a growing love and commitment. But if we sow immorality, we will reap hurt, pain and divorce. If we sow lawlessness and violence, we will reap due punishment. As a society, if we sow justice and peace, we will reap justice and peace throughout our nation.

Sowing and reaping is the theme and lesson of this Scripture. The king now favored the Jew Mordecai because Moredecai had saved the king's life. In addition, Haman had just been utterly humiliated and publicly shamed by this unexpected honor bestowed upon Mordecai, his avowed enemy. After the unsettling incident, Haman was warned by his wife and friends to turn away from his enmity against the Jews and stop his plot to exterminate them. They warned him that his downfall had already started. In fact, while Haman's friends were still talking with him, the king's attendants arrived to rush him to the banquet Queen Esther had prepared for the king and his prime minister. Rushing to the banquet with a heavy heart and broken spirit, Haman had absolutely no idea what was to come. This is, *The Suspenseful Exposure and Downfall of Haman: A Picture of Reaping Exactly What One Sows—Justice, Measure for Measure*, 7:1-10.

1. Esther's exposure of Haman's evil: a surety—all sin will be exposed by God (vv.1-6).
2. Haman's execution: a surety—there is no escape from God's judgment (vv.7-10).

1 (7:1-6) **Sin, Exposure of, a Surety—Exposure, of Sin, a Surety—Hidden, Facts, Sin Cannot be—Haman, Exposure of His Evil—Esther, Exposure of Haman's Evil—Xerxes, King of Persia, Informed of Haman's Evil—Sowing, Reaping of—Reaping, What One Sows**: Esther's exposure of Haman's evil plot against the Jews was about to take place. While the king and Haman were having dinner with Esther, the king would receive one of the biggest shocks of his life. Esther would expose the evil conspiracy of his prime minister, a conspiracy that involved the killing of Queen Esther as well as all the Jewish people. In a scene of high drama and suspense, Scripture paints the picture of what happened:

OUTLINE	SCRIPTURE	SCRIPTURE	OUTLINE

1. Esther's exposure of Haman's evil: A surety—all sin will be exposed by God
a. The queen's banquet
  1) The guests were drinking wine following the meal
  2) The king again asked for Esther's request & repeated his offer to grant anything she wished, 5:6
 	
b. The queen's startling & perplexing request: That her life & the lives of her people be spared
	So the king and Haman came to banquet with Esther the queen.
	2 And the king said again unto Esther on the second day at the banquet of wine, What *is* thy petition, queen Esther? and it shall be granted thee: and what *is* thy request? and it shall be performed, *even* to the half of the kingdom.
	3 Then Esther the queen answered and said, If I have found favour in thy sight, O king, and if it please the king, let my life be given me at my petition, and my people at my request:
		4 For we are sold, I and my people, to be destroyed, to be slain, and to perish. But if we had been sold for bondmen and bondwomen, I had held my tongue, although the enemy could not countervail the king's damage.
		5 Then the king Ahasuerus answered and said unto Esther the queen, Who is he, and where is he, that durst presume in his heart to do so?
		6 And Esther said, The adversary and enemy *is* this wicked Haman. Then Haman was afraid before the king and the queen.
			c. The queen's explanation
			  1) She reminded the king of his horrific decree, 3:1-15
			  2) She charged that a man—without mentioning his name—had committed a conspiracy against her & her people: Had sold them for extermination
			d. The bewildered king's question: Who is the man? Who would dare touch the queen?
			
			e. The queen's abrupt response: The culprit was present
			  1) Identified Haman as the man
			  2) Struck terror in Haman

a. After eating their meal, the king and Haman were sitting around drinking wine just as they had done at the banquet the evening before. Ever since the queen first approached him regarding a very special request, King Xerxes had been wondering with some expectation what her request was. But each time he had asked, she had delayed making her petition. But not this night. Esther had promised to reveal her request at this second banquet. So while sitting there drinking wine, Xerxes asked for the third time what Esther's request was, and he repeated his offer to grant any wish she made (5:6).

At long last Esther had the opening she was waiting for. The king's heart was soft and tender toward her, and she sensed that within him. If the king was ever going to grant her request to reverse the *Decree of Extermination*, it would be now. If he accepted her plea for mercy upon herself and the Jews, God's people would be delivered. But if the king rejected her plea, she herself would be executed.

b. Risking her life, Queen Esther made a stunning yet perplexing request of the king: that her life be spared as well as the lives of her people (v.3). "Spare my life—this is my petition. And spare the lives of my people—this is my request" (v.3).

No doubt the king had expected Esther to ask for some material possession or for extra time with him or perhaps for the right to take some journey. Therefore having anticipated a certain type of request only increased his utter shock at her actual petition. Who would dare endanger the life of his queen? And for what reason would they seek to kill Queen Esther and her people?

c. Obviously shocked by Esther's petition, the king was unable to say anything before Esther continued speaking to explain what she meant (v.4). She reminded the king of the *Decree of Extermination* (3:1-15). She then charged that a man had committed a conspiracy against her and her people. This man had sold them for extermination. Note that she spelled out the extermination in the very words that were included in the decree: this man had sold them to be *killed, slaughtered,* and *annihilated* (3:13). In hearing these words, the king would have remembered the decree and realized what Esther meant by sparing her life. Esther does not mention the Jews by name, but she personally identifies with them by saying that she too will be killed. To stress the seriousness of the conspiracy, Esther tells the king that she would not have disturbed him if she and her people had only been sold as slaves. She would have kept quiet for being enslaved was a matter too trivial to justify disturbing the king. Of course, the king knew as she did that slavery was not a trivial, meaningless event in a person's life. Slavery was very serious for the person being enslaved. But the king understood her point. The plot to take her and her people's lives was far more serious than being enslaved. Cold-blooded, unjustifiable murder is most tragic because it snuffs out an innocent person's life carelessly and senselessly. And slaughtering an entire race of people is of course a far more serious offense.

d. Stunned and outraged that any man would attempt to kill the queen, the king managed to calm himself enough to ask a multifaceted question: Who is this man? Where is he who would dare touch the queen? Who would dare injure the king by killing his queen? These were the very questions Esther needed the king to ask. The providential care of God was guiding the conversation between the king and his queen.

e. In a brief but pointed statement, Queen Esther exposed the evil man (v.6). The adversary and enemy was wicked Haman. Terror paralyzed Haman when he heard his name mentioned and panic rushed through his body. He was utterly helpless and hopeless before the king.

Thought 1. Just as Haman's evil was exposed, so all sin will be exposed by God. We may attempt to hide drugs and alcohol from family, but it will eventually be exposed. We may have premarital sex or adultery behind closed doors, but our immorality will be exposed. We may steal when no one else is looking, but our theft will eventually be known. We may lie and deceive, but the truth will eventually come out. We may abuse, assault, commit lawless or criminal acts and even escape punishment for a while, but eventually we will be caught and suffer just punishment for our illegal behavior.

All acts of sin, wickedness, and evil will be exposed, brought out into the light. This is the surety of God's Holy Word:

"For there is nothing covered, that shall not be revealed; neither hid, that shall not be known" (Lu.12:2).

"And again, The Lord knoweth the thoughts of the wise, that they are vain" (1 Co.3:20).

"Therefore judge nothing before the time, until the Lord come, who both will bring to light the hidden things of darkness, and will make manifest the counsels of the hearts: and then shall every man have praise of God" (1 Co.4:5).

"Neither is there any creature that is not manifest in his sight: but all things *are* naked and opened unto the eyes of him with whom we have to do" (He.4:13).

"For if our heart condemn us, God is greater than our heart, and knoweth all things" (1 Jn.3:20).

"Talk no more so exceeding proudly; let *not* arrogancy come out of your mouth: for the LORD *is* a God of knowledge, and by him actions are weighed" (1 S.2:3).

"And thou, Solomon my son, know thou the God of thy father, and serve him with a perfect heart and with a willing mind: for the LORD searcheth all hearts, and understandeth all the imaginations of the thoughts: if thou seek him, he will be found of thee; but if thou forsake him, he will cast thee off for ever" (1 Chr.28:9).

"If I sin, then thou markest me, and thou wilt not acquit me from mine iniquity" (Jb.10:14).

"For now thou numberest my steps: dost thou not watch over my sin?" (Jb.14:16).

"The heaven shall reveal his iniquity; and the earth shall rise up against him" (Jb.20:27).

"Hell *is* naked before him, and destruction hath no covering" (Jb.26:6).

"Doth not he see my ways, and count all my steps?" (Jb.31:4).

"For his eyes *are* upon the ways of man, and he seeth all his goings" (Jb.34:21).

"Great *is* our Lord, and of great power: his understanding *is* infinite" (Ps.147:5).

"He that hateth dissembleth with his lips, and layeth up deceit within him; When he speaketh fair, believe him not: for *there are* seven abominations in his heart. *Whose* hatred is covered by deceit, his wickedness shall be showed before the *whole* congregation" (Pr.26:24-26).

"For God shall bring every work into judgment, with every secret thing, whether *it be* good, or whether *it be* evil" (Ec.12:14).

"For though thou wash thee with nitre, and take thee much sope, *yet* thine iniquity is marked before me, saith the Lord GOD" (Je.2:22).

"For mine eyes *are* upon all their ways: they are not hid from my face, neither is their iniquity hid from mine eyes" (Je.16:17).

"I the LORD search the heart, *I* try the reins, even to give every man according to his ways, *and* according to the fruit of his doings" (Je.17:10).

"Can any hide himself in secret places that I shall not see him? saith the LORD. Do not I fill heaven and earth? saith the LORD" (Je.23:24).

"And the Spirit of the LORD fell upon me, and said unto me, Speak; Thus saith the LORD; Thus have ye said, O house of Israel: for I know the things that come into your mind, *every one of* them" (Eze.11:5).

"He revealeth the deep and secret things: he knoweth what *is* in the darkness, and the light dwelleth with him" (Da.2:22).

"And they consider not in their hearts *that* I remember all their wickedness: now their own doings have beset them about; they are before my face" (Ho.7:2).

"For I know your manifold transgressions and your mighty sins: they afflict the just, they take a bribe, and they turn aside the poor in the gate *from their right*" (Am.5:12).

2 (7:7-10) **Judgment, Surety of—Surety, of Judgment, Example of—No Escape, from Judgment, Example— Haman, Execution of**: Haman's execution is a clear picture of the surety of judgment. No matter who the person is, even if he is the prime minister of a nation, he will face the judgment of God for the deeds he has done. Note the downfall of this prime minister, the highest-ranking official of Persia whose power was superceded only by that of the king. As soon as Xerxes heard Esther's identification of Haman as the culprit, the king jumped to his feet in a rage and abruptly walked into the palace garden to get alone (v.7). No doubt he needed time to collect his thoughts, time to think through the conspiracy. Esther had just exposed Haman's deception in leading him to issue the *Decree of Extermination*. Xerxes' anger burned toward Haman...

* because Haman had been so deceptive
* because Haman had misled him into issuing the decree of extermination
* because Haman's conspiracy meant that his own dear wife and her adoptive father, who had saved the king's life, would also be killed
* because he had personally misjudged Haman's character and promoted him to be prime minister
* because he had made Haman the closest and most trusted advisor to the king
* because Haman had betrayed the trust he had put in him as prime minister
* because Haman had worked his way into the king's heart, seemingly becoming the closes friend to the king[1]

---

[1] Some of the statements are taken from Warren W. Wiersbe's *Be Committed*, p.140.

Haman quickly realized that the king had already determined his fate and that his only hope was to plead with Esther for his life (v.7). Therefore as soon as the king left the room, Haman arose and walked over to Esther to beg for mercy. Just as Haman reached her the king returned and saw Haman, shockingly, fall at the feet of Esther where she was reclining on a couch (v.8). Angrily, he charged the prime minister with molesting his wife. He then immediately ordered the guards to cover Haman's face and escort him out, away from both him and the queen. By covering Haman's face, the king was signaling his doom. He was to be executed. Standing nearby was a eunuch named Harbona who attended the king. He informed the king that Haman had constructed a gallows 75 feet high by the side of his house. The gallows had been built for the execution of Mordecai. Without a moment's hesitation, the king ordered Haman to be executed upon the gallows. The order was promptly carried out, after which the king's fury calmed down.

OUTLINE	SCRIPTURE	SCRIPTURE	OUTLINE
2. Haman's execution: A surety—there is no escape from God's judgment	7 And the king arising from the banquet of wine in his wrath *went* into the palace garden: and Haman stood up to make request for his life to Esther the queen; for he saw that there was evil determined against him by the king.	went out of the king's mouth, they covered Haman's face. 9 And Harbonah, one of the chamberlains, said before the king, Behold also, the gallows fifty cubits high, which Haman had made for Mordecai, who had spoken good for the king, standeth in the house of Haman. Then the king said, Hang him thereon.	3) The king's guards covered Haman's face: Signaled his doom
a. The king's burning rage: He hastily walked out to get alone			d. The eunuch's report to the king: Informed him about the gallows built by Haman
b. Haman's plea to Esther for his life			1) That it was 75 feet high
c. The king's return & verdict of death			2) That it had been built for Mordecai
1) He saw Haman, shockingly, at the feet of Esther where she was reclining on a couch	8 Then the king returned out of the palace garden into the place of the banquet of wine; and Haman was fallen upon the bed whereon Esther *was*. Then said the king, Will he force the queen also before me in the house? As the word		e. The king's order for Haman to be executed on the gallows
			1) The order was carried out
2) He angrily charged Haman with molesting his wife		10 So they hanged Haman on the gallows that he had prepared for Mordecai. Then was the king's wrath pacified.	2) The king's fury calmed down

Thought 1. The same evil that Haman had planned for Mordecai was turned against him. Haman reaped what he had sown. The principle of sowing and reaping is one of the great principles of life, a strong teaching of God's Holy Word. Whatever a person sows, he will reap, and whatever a person measures, it will be measured back to him. God's justice will be exact. We will bear exactly what we have sown, nothing more and nothing less. Whatever we dish out and measure in life, the same portion will be doled out and measured to us. Nothing more and nothing less. Justice will be perfectly executed by God. There will be no opportunity in the day of judgment to accuse God of judging someone unfairly, too lightly or too severely. Judgment will be completely accurate and precise. And there will be no escape from God's judgment. The surety of judgment is guaranteed by God.

(1) Listen to what God's Holy Word says about sowing and reaping:

> **"For with what judgment ye judge, ye shall be judged: and with what measure ye mete, it shall be measured to you again" (Mt.7:2).**

> **"For the wages of sin *is* death; but the gift of God *is* eternal life through Jesus Christ our Lord" (Ro.6:23).**

> **"Be not deceived; God is not mocked: for whatsoever a man soweth, that shall he also reap. For he that soweth to his flesh shall of the flesh reap corruption; but he that soweth to the Spirit shall of the Spirit reap life everlasting" (Ga.6:7-8).**

> **"Even as I have seen, they that plow iniquity, and sow wickedness, reap the same" (Jb.4:8).**

> **"He that soweth iniquity shall reap vanity: and the rod of his anger shall fail" (Pr.22:8).**

> **"They have sown wheat, but shall reap thorns: they have put themselves to pain, *but* shall not profit: and they shall be ashamed of your revenues because of the fierce anger of the LORD" (Je.12:13).**

(2) Listen to what God's Holy Word says about the judgment of our works and deeds:

> **"For the Son of man shall come in the glory of his Father with his angels; and then he shall reward every man according to his works" (Mt.16:27).**

> **"But after thy hardness and impenitent heart treasurest up unto thyself wrath against the day of wrath and revelation of the righteous judgment of God; Who will render to every man according to his deeds: To them who by patient continuance in well doing seek for glory and honour and immortality, eternal life: But unto them that are contentious, and do not obey the truth, but obey unrighteousness, indignation and wrath, Tribulation and anguish, upon every soul of man that doeth evil, of the Jew first, and also of the Gentile" (Ro.2:5-9).**

> **"For we must all appear before the judgment seat of Christ; that every one may receive the things *done* in *his* body, according to that he hath done, whether *it be* good or bad" (2 Co.5:10).**

> **"And if ye call on the Father, who without respect of persons judgeth according to every man's work, pass the time of your sojourning *here* in fear" (1 Pe.1:17).**

> **"Behold, I will cast her [Jezebel] into a bed, and them that commit adultery with her into great tribulation, except they repent of their deeds. And I will kill her children with death; and all**

the churches shall know that I am he which searcheth the reins and hearts: and I will give unto every one of you according to your works" (Re.2:22-23).

"And I saw a great white throne, and him that sat on it, from whose face the earth and the heaven fled away; and there was found no place for them. And I saw the dead, small and great, stand before God; and the books were opened: and another book was opened, which is *the book* of life: and the dead were judged out of those things which were written in the books, according to their works. And the sea gave up the dead which were in it; and death and hell delivered up the dead which were in them: and they were judged every man according to their works. And death and hell were cast into the lake of fire. This is the second death. And whosoever was not found written in the book of life was cast into the lake of fire" (Re.20:11-15).

"And, behold, I come quickly; and my reward *is* with me, to give every man according as his work shall be" (Re.22:12).

"Also unto thee, O Lord, *belongeth* mercy: for thou renderest to every man according to his work" (Ps.62:12).

"If thou forbear to deliver *them that are* drawn unto death, and *those that are* ready to be slain; If thou sayest, Behold, we knew it not; doth not he that pondereth the heart consider *it?* and he that keepeth thy soul, doth *not* he know *it?* and shall *not* he render to *every* man according to his works?" (Pr.24:11-12).

"I the LORD search the heart, *I* try the reins, even to give every man according to his ways, *and* according to the fruit of his doings" (Je.17:10).

"Great in counsel, and mighty in work: for thine eyes *are* open upon all the ways of the sons of men: to give every one according to his ways, and according to the fruit of his doings" (Je.32:19).

"Therefore I will judge you, O house of Israel, every one according to his ways, saith the Lord GOD. Repent, and turn *yourselves* from all your transgressions; so iniquity shall not be your ruin" (Eze.18:30).

CHAPTER 8

E. The Desperate Intercession of Esther for the Deliverance of the Jews: A Picture of Being Delivered Through Prayer, 8:1-17

1. The reward given to Esther & the promotion of Mordecai by the king: A picture of the believer being rewarded for faithful service
a. Esther given Haman's estate
b. Mordecai promoted to be prime minister
   1) The king gave him the signet ring (full authority) of the king
   2) Esther appointed him head of Haman's estate

2. The anguish & plea of Esther for her people: A picture of the believer's intercession
a. Esther's second approach & request of the king: To stop the evil scheme of Haman
   1) She fell at his feet

   2) He accepted, extended the gold scepter to her
   3) She arose to present her request
b. Esther's humble request
   1) She based her request upon their relationship & the king's wisdom
      • If he favors her
      • If he thought the request wise
   2) She asked him to write a second decree to save her people: To reverse Haman's *Decree of Extermination*

   3) She shared her intense grief

3. The proclamation assuring the Jews' deliverance: A picture of proclaiming the salvation of God's people
a. The king's answer to his dear wife's plea: He immediately ordered a new decree
   1) He gave Esther & Mordecai a free hand in its wording
   2) He reminded them of Persian law: That no decree signed & sealed with his ring could ever be revoked

On that day did the king Ahasuerus give the house of Haman the Jews' enemy unto Esther the queen. And Mordecai came before the king; for Esther had told what he *was* unto her.

2 And the king took off his ring, which he had taken from Haman, and gave it unto Mordecai. And Esther set Mordecai over the house of Haman.

3 And Esther spake yet again before the king, and fell down at his feet, and besought him with tears to put away the mischief of Haman the Agagite, and his device that he had devised against the Jews.

4 Then the king held out the golden sceptre toward Esther. So Esther arose, and stood before the king,

5 And said, If it please the king, and if I have found favour in his sight, and the thing *seem* right before the king, and I *be* pleasing in his eyes, let it be written to reverse the letters devised by Haman the son of Hammedatha the Agagite, which he wrote to destroy the Jews which *are* in all the king's provinces:

6 For how can I endure to see the evil that shall come unto my people? or how can I endure to see the destruction of my kindred?

7 Then the king Ahasuerus said unto Esther the queen and to Mordecai the Jew, Behold, I have given Esther the house of Haman, and him they have hanged upon the gallows, because he laid his hand upon the Jews.

8 Write ye also for the Jews, as it liketh you, in the king's name, and seal *it* with the king's ring: for the writing which is written in the king's name, and sealed with the king's ring, may no man reverse.

9 Then were the king's scribes called at that time in the third month, that *is,* the month Sivan, on the three and twentieth *day* thereof; and it was written according to all that Mordecai commanded unto the Jews, and to the lieutenants, and the deputies and rulers of the provinces which *are* from India unto Ethiopia, an hundred twenty and seven provinces, unto every province according to the writing thereof, and unto every people after their language, and to the Jews according to their writing, and according to their language.

10 And he wrote in the king Ahasuerus' name, and sealed *it* with the king's ring, and sent letters by posts on horseback, *and* riders on mules, camels, *and* young dromedaries:

11 Wherein the king granted the Jews which *were* in every city to gather themselves together, and to stand for their life, to destroy, to slay, and to cause to perish, all the power of the people and province that would assault them, *both* little ones and women, and *to* take the spoil of them for a prey,

12 Upon one day in all the provinces of king Ahasuerus, *namely,* upon the thirteenth *day* of the twelfth month, which *is* the month Adar.

13 The copy of the writing for a commandment to be given in every province *was* published unto all people, and that the Jews should be ready against that day to avenge themselves on their enemies.

14 So the posts that rode upon mules *and* camels went out, being hastened and pressed on by the king's commandment. And the decree was given at Shushan the palace.

15 And Mordecai went out from the presence of the king in royal apparel of blue and white, and with a great crown of gold, and with a garment of fine linen and purple: and the city of Shushan rejoiced and was glad.

16 The Jews had light, and gladness, and joy, and

b. The proclamation prepared by the new prime minister, Mordecai
   1) Mordecai immediately summoned the royal secretaries: The 23rd day of Sivan
      • He dictated the decree to them: Was then sent to the Jews & the leaders of Persia, to all 127 provinces stretching from India to Cush (Ethiopia)

      • He wrote in the full authority of King Ahasuerus (Xerxes): Signed his name & sealed the letters with his ring
      • He sent them by courier

c. The contents of the proclamation
   1) It granted *the right of self-defense* to the Jews: They could assemble & protect themselves against any armed force of any nationality who attacked them

   2) It limited the time conflict could be waged within the empire to just one day, the 13th day of Adar

   3) It was to be issued as law in every province throughout the empire: So the Jews would be ready to defend themselves

d. The proclamation rushed out to the whole empire by couriers (messengers): They were stirred by the king's command

e. The response to the proclamation: Great joy
   1) The Jews rejoiced over Mordecai's promotion: He now represented them
   2) The Jews in Susa rejoiced

   3) The Jews throughout the empire rejoiced & celebrated

4) The deliverance of the Jews struck fear in the hearts of some people: They converted to Judaism	honour. 17 And in every province, and in every city, whithersoever the king's commandment and his decree came, the	Jews had joy and gladness, a feast and a good day. And many of the people of the land became Jews; for the fear of the Jews fell upon them.	• Some were genuine • Some probably just pretended for safety

DIVISION III

THE JEWS SAVED BY THE COURAGEOUS ACTION OF ESTHER, 4:1–10:3

E. The Desperate Intercession of Esther for the Deliverance of the Jews: A Picture of Being Delivered Through Prayer, 8:1-17

(8:1-17) **Introduction**: we live in a world filled with danger and evil every day. As we travel from place to place, we risk our lives through exposure to inexperienced, careless, or drunk drivers. A young woman out on a date can be seduced, attacked, or raped. A wife, child, or husband can be abused. Drugs or alcohol can be pushed upon us or our children. People can steal from us, lie, deceive, or mislead us. Husbands and wives can commit adultery or totally neglect each other. Children can disobey parents, and parents can abuse children, provoking them to wrath and rebellion. Business partners can split up and politicians can lie and deceive the public. Nations can abuse their citizens through unjust laws, overtaxation, and unnecessary wars caused by power struggles. Evil leaders and their followers can plot terrorist attacks and cause enormous destruction of property and life. Things can go terribly wrong for any of us due either to the evil in the world or to the normal problems that arise in life.

In the present Scripture, a serious problem confronted the Jews. A *Decree of Extermination* had been issued against them. Every Jew throughout the Persian Empire was to be slaughtered, wiped off the face of the earth. In the former chapter, Queen Esther had just informed King Xerxes of the plot to exterminate the Jews, a plot that had been schemed by the prime minister, Haman. Filled with extreme prejudice and bitter hatred toward the Jews, Haman had led King Xerxes to issue the *Decree of Extermination*. When Esther exposed the plot, Haman was immediately executed. And although Esther and Mordecai were now safe under the protection of the king, all the remaining Jews were still doomed. The *Decree of Extermination* was irrevocable, so unless Esther could intercede before the king and lead him to put an end to the evil plot, there was no hope. Intercession was the answer to save the Jews. And intercession is the answer to protect us from the threats and evil of this world. This is, *The Desperate Intercession of Esther for the Deliverance of the Jews: A Picture of Being Delivered Through Prayer*, 8:1-17.

1. The reward given to Esther and the promotion of Mordecai by the king: a picture of the believer being rewarded for faithful service (vv.1-2).
2. The anguish and plea of Esther for her people: a picture of the believer's intercession (vv.3-6).
3. The proclamation assuring the Jews' deliverance: a picture of proclaiming the salvation of God's people (vv.7-17).

[1] (8:1-2) **Faithfulness, to God, Rewards of—Rewards, Based Upon, Faithful Service—Faithfulness, Example of—Esther, Rewarded by King Xerxes—Mordecai, Rewarded by King Xerxes**: on the very same day of Esther's banquet and the hanging of Haman, Esther was greatly rewarded and Mordecai promoted by the king. King Xerxes actually gave Haman's estate to Esther. Most likely, the gift was compensation for the fear she had been suffering, the horror of thinking that she and all her people were to be killed due to the decree to exterminate the Jews. By law, the estate of a traitor was confiscated by the state. Thus King Xerxes had the legal right to give Haman's estate to his wife, and the estate must have been enormous. Some months earlier Haman had paid the king 375 tons of silver to cover the cost of exterminating the Jews. The contribution also helped build up the depleted treasury of Persia resulting from the cost of war against the coalition of Grecian forces.

In conversation with the king, Queen Esther informed Xerxes that Mordecai and she were related, that he was her cousin and had adopted and reared her after her parents' death. Hearing this and remembering that Mordecai had uncovered a plot to assassinate him, Xerxes summoned Mordecai to the palace. When he was brought before the king, Xerxes promoted him to be prime minister of the empire. Moredecai was given the signet ring of the king and given full authority to act in behalf of the king. Furthermore, Esther appointed him to be the steward or manager over Haman's vast estate.

Mordecai is a strong example of a believer who was rewarded for faithful service to the LORD and His people. He was a man of deep conviction, a responsible man with a tender and loving heart. He was also a courageous, just, humble, and modest man dedicated to serving all nationalities as well as his own people, the Jews. These traits are clearly seen in his faithful walk throughout life. He walked faithfully before the LORD, helping and serving people. Note the good deeds of his life mentioned in Scripture:

⇒ He adopted Esther after her parents' death (2:5-7).
⇒ He reared and protected Esther, even to the point of instructing her to keep her Jewish nationality a secret because of the prejudice of the people against the Jews (2:10, 20).
⇒ He served the people of the city through his position as a city official (2:19).
⇒ He saved the life of the king by uncovering the plot to assassinate Xerxes (2:21-23).
⇒ He took a strong stand for the LORD by refusing to bow before Haman, which would have given the prime minister the reverence due to God alone (3:1-4).
⇒ He courageously took a public stand for the Jews after the *Decree of Extermination* had been issued. (4:1-3).
⇒ He aroused Esther to save the Jews by pleading with the king for mercy (4:4-13).
⇒ He was a man who believed in fasting and prayer before the Lord (4:15-17).

⇒ He willingly accepted the enormous responsibility of prime minister, second only to the king in authority and duty (8:1-2).

⇒ He willingly took on the responsibility of overseeing Esther's estate, serving as manager or steward (8:1-2).

⇒ He along with Esther saved the Jews from extermination (8:7–9:19).

⇒ He instituted the Festival of Purim as a permanent festival, one that celebrated the wonderful deliverance of the Jews from their enemies (9:20-32).

⇒ He had a strong testimony of good works, of working for the benefit of people and of speaking up for their welfare (10:3).

OUTLINE	SCRIPTURE	SCRIPTURE	OUTLINE
1. The reward given to Esther & the promotion of Mordecai by the king: A picture of the believer being rewarded for faithful service a. Esther given Haman's estate	On that day did the king Ahasuerus give the house of Haman the Jews' enemy unto Esther the queen. And Mordecai came before the king; for Esther had told what he *was* unto	her. 2 And the king took off his ring, which he had taken from Haman, and gave it unto Mordecai. And Esther set Mordecai over the house of Haman.	b. Mordecai promoted to be prime minister 1) The king gave him the signet ring (full authority) of the king 2) Esther appointed him head of Haman's estate

Thought 1. If we know the LORD, are worshipping and serving the LORD, and are truly faithful in living righteous lives, God promises to reward us. And the rewards are great. In truth, they are beyond our comprehension or imagination.

For example, Scripture declares that the believer is a *joint-heir* with Christ (Ro.8:17). This is an astounding truth and promise. We will inherit all that God has and all that Christ is and has. We will be given the privilege of sharing in all things with the Son of God Himself. However, note this fact: to be a joint-heir with Christ does not mean that we will receive an equal amount of the inheritance with Christ. Rather, it means that believers are fellow-heirs with Christ; that is, we will *share in* the inheritance of Christ or we will *share* Christ's inheritance with Him.

Being a fellow-heir with Christ means at least three glorious things: it means that we will share in the *nature, position,* and *responsibility* of Christ. The following chart shows this with a quick glance:

FELLOW HEIRS BY NATURE

Christ is the Son of God, the very being and energy of life and perfection. Therefore, we share in the inheritance of His nature. We receive...

- adoption as a son or daughter of God (Ga.4:4-7; 1 Jn.3:1).
- a sinless and blameless nature (Ph.2:15).
- eternal life (Jn.1:4; 3:16; 10:10; 17:2-3; 1 Ti.6:19).
- lasting possessions (He.10:34).
- a glorious body (1 Co.15:42-44; Ph.3:21).
- eternal glory and honor and peace (Ro.2:10).
- eternal rest and peace (He.4:9; Re.14:13).
- a crown that will last forever, an incorruptible body (1 Co.9:25; 1 Pe.1:3-4; 15:42).
- a righteous being (2 Ti.4:8).

FELLOW HEIRS BY POSITION

Christ is the exalted Lord, the Sovereign Majesty of the universe, the King of kings and Lord of lords. Therefore, we share in the inheritance of His position. We receive...

- the position of an exalted being (Re.7:9-12).
- a citizenship in the Kingdom of God (Mt.25:34; Js.2:5).
- enormous treasures in heaven (Mt.19:21; Lu.12:33).
- unsearchable riches (Ep.3:8).
- the right to surround the throne of God (Re.7:9-13; 20:4).
- the position of a king (Re.1:5; 5:10).
- the position of a priest (Re.1:5; 5:10; 20:6).
- the position of glory (1 Pe.5:4).

FELLOW HEIRS BY RESPONSIBILITY

Christ is the Sovereign Majesty of the Universe, the One who is ordained to rule and oversee all. Therefore, we share in the inheritance of His responsibility. We receive...

- rulership over many things (Mt.25:23).
- the right to rule and hold authority (Lu.12:42-44; 22:28-29).
- eternal responsibility and joy (Mt.25:21, 23).
- rule and authority over cities (Lu.19:17, 19).
- thrones and the privilege of reigning forever (Re.20:4; 22:5).

2 (8:3-6) **Intercession, Example of—Jews, Love for, Example—Esther, Intercession of, for the Jews**: Esther was experiencing deep anguish and she pleaded for the lives of her people. Although Esther and Mordecai were now protected from the *Decree of Extermination*, their fellow Jews were not. Many throughout the Persian Empire hated the Jews and were anxiously waiting for the day when they could take up arms against them. The decree not only called for the slaughter of the Jews, but it also allowed the public to plunder the property and wealth of the Jews. In light of this, greed entered the picture. Many of the citizens would be taking up arms just to steal the wealth of the Jews. The very fate of the entire Jewish population had been doomed by the legal document and the decree was still in force because once a Persian decree had been issued, it was legally irrevocable.

Realizing that the king's heart was tender toward her, Esther decided to seize the moment and approach the king a second time. Again, she entered the king's court without being summoned and approached the king. Falling at his feet weeping, she begged him to stop Haman's evil scheme (v.3). In tenderness, Xerxes again accepted her unlawful approach by extending the golden scepter toward her, symbolizing that she was accepted and was not to be removed by the guards. Rising to her feet, Esther made a humble request of the king. Note that she based her request on their relationship and the king's wisdom: if he favored her and if he thought the request was wise, then she begged him to grant her wish (v.5). She then stated her request, asking him to write a second decree to save her people. She wanted the king to reverse Haman's *Decree of Extermination*. Concluding her plea, she asked the king how she could bear the pain of seeing her people and family slaughtered.

OUTLINE	SCRIPTURE	SCRIPTURE	OUTLINE
2. The anguish & plea of Esther for her people: A picture of the believer's intercession a. Esther's second approach & request of the king: To stop the evil scheme of Haman 1) She fell at his feet	3 And Esther spake yet again before the king, and fell down at his feet, and besought him with tears to put away the mischief of Haman the Agagite, and his device that he had devised against the Jews.	and the thing *seem* right before the king, and I *be* pleasing in his eyes, let it be written to reverse the letters devised by Haman the son of Hammedatha the Agagite, which he wrote to destroy the Jews which *are* in all the king's provinces:	the king's wisdom • If he favors her • If he thought the request wise 2) She asked him to write a second decree to save her people: To reverse Haman's *Decree of Extermination*
2) He accepted, extended the gold scepter to her 3) She arose to present her request b. Esther's humble request 1) She based her request upon their relationship &	4 Then the king held out the golden sceptre toward Esther. So Esther arose, and stood before the king, 5 And said, If it please the king, and if I have found favour in his sight,	6 For how can I endure to see the evil that shall come unto my people? or how can I endure to see the destruction of my kindred?	3) She shared her intense grief

Thought 1. For the believers, the story of Esther is a strong example of the power of intercession. Esther and Mordecai would be safe from the *Decree of Extermination* because of the king's protection. But Esther could not rest in the comfort, provision, pleasure, and security of the palace, not while so many people were living under the weight of fear, insecurity, uncertainty, distress, hatred, and discrimination.

How *unlike* so many of us! While we live in comfort, plenty, and security, and have the freedom to enjoy recreation and other pleasurable events, so many in the world are living lives that are the very opposite. They are suffering from…

- poverty
- hunger
- unclean drinking water
- unsanitary living conditions
- inadequate or total lack of housing

- disease
- imprisonment
- hatred or discrimination
- depression
- abuse

- financial difficulties
- unemployment
- oppression
- tyranny
- enslavement

Instead of serving the LORD, we are serving ourselves, ever seeking for newer and bigger and better possession, pleasures and recreation. Not that possessions and recreations are wrong. They are not. God expects us to enjoy life to the fullest. But enjoying life is not the problem for most of us. Most of us live self-centered lives, serving ourselves and giving little time in service to the LORD. Few of us bear strong testimony and witness for the LORD. Far too many of us think that attending and supporting the church financially on occasions makes us a true follower of Christ, that this fulfills our responsibilities to the LORD. And few of us spend much time in prayer and intercession for others. When so many people are hurting, too few of us have a heavy burden for their souls and for ministering to their needs. How desperately true prayer warriors and intercessors are needed. Listen to God's Word as He encourages us to pray and intercede for other people.

"After this manner therefore pray ye: Our Father which art in heaven, Hallowed be thy name. Thy kingdom come. Thy will be done in earth, as *it is* in heaven. Give us this day our daily bread. And

forgive us our debts, as we forgive our debtors. And lead us not into temptation, but deliver us from evil: For thine is the kingdom, and the power, and the glory, for ever. Amen" (Mt.6:9-13).

"Again I say unto you, That if two of you shall agree on earth as touching any thing that they shall ask, it shall be done for them of my Father which is in heaven" (Mt.18:19).

"I pray for them: I pray not for the world, but for them which thou hast given me; for they are thine. And all mine are thine, and thine are mine; and I am glorified in them. And now I am no more in the world, but these are in the world, and I come to thee. Holy Father, keep through thine own name those whom thou hast given me, that they may be one, as we *are*. While I was with them in the world, I kept them in thy name: those that thou gavest me I have kept, and none of them is lost, but the son of perdition; that the scripture might be fulfilled. And now come I to thee; and these things I speak in the world, that they might have my joy fulfilled in themselves. I have given them thy word; and the world hath hated them, because they are not of the world, even as I am not of the world. I pray not that thou shouldest take them out of the world, but that thou shouldest keep them from the evil....Neither pray I for these alone, but for them also which shall believe on me through their word; That they all may be one; as thou, Father, *art* in me, and I in thee, that they also may be one in us: that the world may believe that thou hast sent me. And the glory which thou gavest me I have given them; that they may be one, even as we are one: I in them, and thou in me, that they may be made perfect in one; and that the world may know that thou hast sent me, and hast loved them, as thou hast loved me. Father, I will that they also, whom thou hast given me, be with me where I am; that they may behold my glory, which thou hast given me: for thou lovedst me before the foundation of the world" (Jn.17:9-15, 20-24).

"Peter therefore was kept in prison: but prayer was made without ceasing of the church unto God for him" (Ac.12:5).

"Likewise the Spirit also helpeth our infirmities: for we know not what we should pray for as we ought: but the Spirit itself maketh intercession for us with groanings which cannot be uttered. And he that searcheth the hearts knoweth what *is* the mind of the Spirit, because he maketh intercession for the saints according to *the will of* God" (Ro.8:26-27).

"For this cause I bow my knees unto the Father of our Lord Jesus Christ, Of whom the whole family in heaven and earth is named, That he would grant you, according to the riches of his glory, to be strengthened with might by his Spirit in the inner man; That Christ may dwell in your hearts by faith; that ye, being rooted and grounded in love, May be able to comprehend with all saints what *is* the breadth, and length, and depth, and height; And to know the love of Christ, which passeth knowledge, that ye might be filled with all the fulness of God. Now unto him that is able to do exceeding abundantly above all that we ask or think, according to the power that worketh in us, Unto him *be* glory in the church by Christ Jesus throughout all ages, world without end. Amen" (Ep.3:14-21).

"Praying always with all prayer and supplication in the Spirit, and watching thereunto with all perseverance and supplication for all saints" (Ep.6:18).

"And the prayer of faith shall save the sick, and the Lord shall raise him up; and if he have committed sins, they shall be forgiven him. Confess *your* faults one to another, and pray one for another, that ye may be healed. The effectual fervent prayer of a righteous man availeth much. Elias was a man subject to like passions as we are, and he prayed earnestly that it might not rain: and it rained not on the earth by the space of three years and six months. And he prayed again, and the heaven gave rain, and the earth brought forth her fruit" (Ja.5:15-18).

"And Abraham drew near, and said, Wilt thou also destroy the righteous with the wicked? Peradventure there be fifty righteous within the city: wilt thou also destroy and not spare the place for the fifty righteous that *are* therein? That be far from thee to do after this manner, to slay the righteous with the wicked: and that the righteous should be as the wicked, that be far from thee: Shall not the Judge of all the earth do right? And the LORD said, If I find in Sodom fifty righteous within the city, then I will spare all the place for their sakes. And Abraham answered and said, Behold now, I have taken upon me to speak unto the Lord, which *am but* dust and ashes: Peradventure there shall lack five of the fifty righteous: wilt thou destroy all the city for *lack of* five? And he said, If I find there forty and five, I will not destroy *it*. And he spake unto him yet again, and said, Peradventure there shall be forty found there. And he said, I will not do *it* for forty's sake. And he said *unto him,* Oh let not the Lord be angry, and I will speak: Peradventure there shall thirty be found there. And he said, I will not do *it*, if I find thirty there. And he said, Behold now, I have taken upon me to speak unto the Lord: Peradventure there shall be twenty found there. And he said, I will not destroy *it* for twenty's sake. And he said, Oh let not the Lord be angry, and I will speak yet but this once: Peradventure ten shall be found there. And he said, I will not destroy *it* for ten's sake. And the LORD went his way, as soon as he had left communing with Abraham: and Abraham returned unto his place" (Ge.18:23-33).

"For this child I prayed; and the LORD hath given me my petition which I asked of him" (1 S.1:27).

"If my people, which are called by my name, shall humble themselves, and pray, and seek my face, and turn from their wicked ways; then will I hear from heaven, and will forgive their sin, and will heal their land" (2 Chr.7:14).

"And at the evening sacrifice I arose up from my heaviness; and having rent my garment and my mantle, I fell upon my knees, and spread out my hands unto the LORD my God. And said, O my God, I am ashamed and blush to lift up my face to thee, my God: for our iniquities are increased over *our* head, and our trespass is grown up unto the heavens" (Ezr.9:5-6).

"And I set my face unto the Lord God, to seek by prayer and supplications, with fasting, and sackcloth, and ashes: And I prayed unto the LORD my God, and made my confession, and said, O Lord, the great and dreadful God, keeping the covenant and mercy to them that love him, and to them that keep his commandments; We have sinned, and have committed iniquity, and have done wickedly, and have rebelled, even by departing from thy precepts and from thy judgments" (Da.9:3-5).

3 (8:7-17) **Witnessing, Example of—Proclamation, of Good News—Jews, Deliverance of, Proclaimed—Esther, Intercession of, Saved the Jews—Mordecai, Saved the Jews from Annihilation—Jews, Deliverance, by Esther—Xerxes, King of Persia, Saved the Jews**: the Jews' deliverance from extermination was assured in the new proclamation. As already stated, Persian law was irrevocable. Consequently, the *Decree of Extermination* against the Jews could not be cancelled. Today, in democratic societies, laws can be reversed by legislative action or by being overridden by the Supreme Court. But this was not true in ancient Persia. Once a decree had been signed by the king, it was a law never to be revoked. In light of this fact and despite the tenderness of the king's heart toward Esther, Xerxes was handicapped? How was he going to respond to his dear wife's broken heart and to her fearful request for mercy upon her people? Note the Scripture and outline:

OUTLINE	SCRIPTURE	SCRIPTURE	OUTLINE
3. The proclamation assuring the Jews' deliverance: A picture of proclaiming the salvation of God's people a. The king's answer to his dear wife's plea: He immediately ordered a new decree 1) He gave Esther & Mordecai a free hand in its wording 2) He reminded them of Persian law: That no decree signed & sealed with his ring could ever be revoked b. The proclamation prepared by the new prime minister, Mordecai 1) Mordecai immediately summoned the royal secretaries: The 23rd day of Sivan • He dictated the decree to them: Was then sent to the Jews & the leaders of Persia, to all 127 provinces stretching from India to Cush (Ethiopia) • He wrote in the full authority of King Ahasuerus (Xerxes): Signed his name & sealed the letters with his ring • He sent them by courier c. The contents of the proclamation 1) It granted *the right of self-defense* to the Jews:	7 Then the king Ahasuerus said unto Esther the queen and to Mordecai the Jew, Behold, I have given Esther the house of Haman, and him they have hanged upon the gallows, because he laid his hand upon the Jews. 8 Write ye also for the Jews, as it liketh you, in the king's name, and seal *it* with the king's ring: for the writing which is written in the king's name, and sealed with the king's ring, may no man reverse. 9 Then were the king's scribes called at that time in the third month, that *is,* the month Sivan, on the three and twentieth *day* thereof; and it was written according to all that Mordecai commanded unto the Jews, and to the lieutenants, and the deputies and rulers of the provinces which *are* from India unto Ethiopia, an hundred twenty and seven provinces, unto every province according to the writing thereof, and unto every people after their language, and to the Jews according to their writing, and according to their language. 10 And he wrote in the king Ahasuerus' name, and sealed *it* with the king's ring, and sent letters by posts on horseback, *and* riders on mules, camels, *and* young dromedaries: 11 Wherein the king granted the Jews which *were* in every city to gather themselves together, and to stand for their	life, to destroy, to slay, and to cause to perish, all the power of the people and province that would assault them, *both* little ones and women, and *to* take the spoil of them for a prey, 12 Upon one day in all the provinces of king Ahasuerus, *namely,* upon the thirteenth *day* of the twelfth month, which *is* the month Adar. 13 The copy of the writing for a commandment to be given in every province *was* published unto all people, and that the Jews should be ready against that day to avenge themselves on their enemies. 14 *So* the posts that rode upon mules *and* camels went out, being hastened and pressed on by the king's commandment. And the decree was given at Shushan the palace. 15 And Mordecai went out from the presence of the king in royal apparel of blue and white, and with a great crown of gold, and with a garment of fine linen and purple: and the city of Shushan rejoiced and was glad. 16 The Jews had light, and gladness, and joy, and honour. 17 And in every province, and in every city, whithersoever the king's commandment and his decree came, the Jews had joy and gladness, a feast and a good day. And many of the people of the land became Jews; for the fear of the Jews fell upon them.	They could assemble & protect themselves against any armed force of any nationality who attacked them 2) It limited the time conflict could be waged within the empire to just one day, the 13th day of Adar 3) It was to be issued as law in every province throughout the empire: So the Jews would be ready to defend themselves d. The proclamation rushed out to the whole empire by couriers (messengers): They were stirred by the king's command e. The response to the proclamation: Great joy 1) The Jews rejoiced over Mordecai's promotion: He now represented them 2) The Jews in Susa rejoiced 3) The Jews throughout the empire rejoiced & celebrated 4) The deliverance of the Jews struck fear in the hearts of some people: They converted to Judaism • Some were genuine • Some probably just pretended for safety

a. The king gave a positive answer to Esther's plea for mercy in behalf of the Jews. Granting exactly what she requested, he immediately ordered a new decree. He also gave Esther and Mordecai a freehand in wording the document. Assuring them of his full support, he instructed them to seal the new decree with his signet ring. No decree signed and sealed with the royal ring could ever be revoked.

b. The new prime minister, Mordecai, summoned the royal secretaries immediately to begin preparing the new proclamation. This new decree would hopefully save the Jews from extermination (vv.9-10). It was the 23rd day of the 3rd month, the month of Sivan, which was a little over two months after Haman had issued the original *Decree of Extermination*. This meant that the Jews would have about nine months' notice regarding the new decree. As Mordecai dictated, the secretaries made copies for each province in the various languages of the people, including the Jewish or Hebrew language. Writing under the full authority of King Xerxes, Mordecai signed his name and sealed the letter with his ring. He then sent the new decree by couriers to the farthest points of the empire.

c. The new decree granted the right of self-defense to the Jews (vv.11-13). The Jews were given the right to assemble and protect themselves against any armed force or nationality that might attack them (v.11). Note that the exact language used by Haman's *Decree of Extermination* is repeated in this second decree. The Jews were given the right of self-defense, the right "to kill, slaughter, and annihilate" anyone who attacked them. Moreover, they were given the right to plunder the property of any of their attackers.

This second decree also limited the time that actual conflict could be waged within the empire. The time was limited to just one day, the 13th day of the 12th month, the month of Adar (v.12). A copy of the *Decree of Self-Defense* was to be issued in every province or district throughout the empire (v.13). Within the cities of the nation, the Jews were allowed to band together to defend themselves against any citizen or group of citizens who attacked them. Anti-Semitism was everywhere throughout the empire, but this *Decree of Self-Defense* meant that the Jews would at least be able to stop the extermination of their race. Most likely only a few of them would die. Most of the citizens throughout the empire would now know that the king supported the Jews and that the prime minister was Mordecai, a Jew himself. Few citizens would be willing to oppose the wishes of the king and the Jewish prime minister despite the irrevocable law that gave them the right to annihilate the Jews. Moreover, the citizens knew that the king and prime minister could find some way to take vengeance on them in the future if they chose to go against the desires of the king.

d. As soon as the decree was finished, Mordecai had it rushed out to the empire by couriers or messengers (v.14). Because of the time it would take to reach the farthest points of the empire, he no doubt ordered them to rush as quickly as they could. It would take a good deal of time to reach the outposts of the nation, and the Jews needed all the time they could get to prepare for their defense. Note the descriptive words used to convey the urgency sensed by the couriers: they "went out" or were "urged on"—"hastened" or "rode swiftly"—"pressed on." The idea is that of total commitment to the king's command, the command to carry the message of hope and deliverance to the condemned Jews. Knowing that the Jews were condemned, the messenger sensed the urgency of the hour. In view of this, they rushed as quickly as they could with the good news of salvation for those who were condemned.

e. As would be expected, the response to the proclamation was that of great joy (vv.15-17). When the Jews read that Mordecai was now the prime minister of the Persian Empire, they rejoiced over his promotion. This meant that they had a representative in the government, a Jew who was second only to the king himself. In fact, when Mordecai left the palace after completing the *Decree of Self-Defense*, he was wearing the royal clothes of blue and white, which indicated that he had been appointed prime minister. He was also wearing a large gold crown and an outer purple robe made of fine linen. When the Jews in the city of Susa saw him walking about the streets, they knew immediately that they had strong representation in the government. Over this, they joyfully celebrated. And when the Jews throughout the empire received the *Decree of Self-Defense,* joy, relief, thankfulness, and praise to God were naturally stirred within their hearts. They could now legally defend themselves against the expected holocaust (vv.16-17a).

Among the other nationalities throughout the empire, fear began to grip many of their hearts. For many of them had been extremely prejudiced toward the Jews and heavily discriminated against them. But now the decree seemed to indicate that King Xerxes favored the Jews, which could pose a threat to them because of their hostility toward the Jewish race. As a result of this fear, many people throughout Persia converted to Judaism. However, their conversion for the most part was due primarily to fear, not out of conviction and commitment to the LORD.

On the other hand, some of those who turned to Judaism may have actually been converted. They had witnessed a complete turnaround for the Jews, a twisting of their fate from the threat of being exterminated to being accepted and even favored by the king himself. Any intelligent and honest person could see the hand of God working out the deliverance of the Jews. It was clearly evident that God was protecting them. Thus some unbelievers probably did begin to fear, reverence, and trust God as well as worship Him. These later became known as *God-fearers* or *worshippers of God* (Ac.10:2; 16:14; 17:4; 18:7). There is also the likelihood that some throughout the empire were fed up with the wicked lifestyle and the pagan religions that accepted any and all gods as being true. These people would have been attracted by the truth proclaimed by the Jews, that there is only one true and living God who demands that people live righteously.

Thought 1. Mordecai, Esther, and the couriers rushed as swiftly as they could to get the good news out to the condemned Jews, the good news of the *Decree of Self-Defense*. The same should be true with us: we should be quick to get the good news of the gospel of Jesus Christ out to the world. Just as the Jews were condemned to death, so any person without Christ is condemned to death, eternally separated from God. Just think about the *good news* of the gospel. A person can be set free, liberated from sin, death, and hell. No person has to be enslaved by the sins of this world, held in bondage to the addictions that captivate our flesh. We can be set free from the enslavement of drugs, tobacco, alcohol, gluttony, immorality, evil thoughts, sexual bondage, habitual stealing and a host of other emotional, mental and physical enslavements. No person has to be enslaved by the sins of the flesh or the mind. The good news of Jesus Christ can set us free from the bondage of sin.

But this is not all. Jesus Christ can set us free from the enslavement of death. And the human race is enslaved by death in that we will all die. But we can escape this terrifying bondage, for God never created us to die. We die because of sin. Therefore when God delivers us from sin, He saves us from death. We are free, delivered from death by faith in the Lord Jesus Christ.

But even this is not the only liberty we have in Christ. Jesus Christ delivers, sets us free from hell. Once we receive Christ, we never have to face the judgment of God. Christ Himself bore the judgment of God for us. He sets us free from judgment, making us acceptable to God through His righteousness and perfection.

Such good news, the gospel of Christ, must be carried to the world. Just as the messengers of Esther's day rushed the good news to the condemned Jews, so we must rush the good news of Christ to the condemned of this world. Listen to what God's Holy Word says:

"Go ye therefore, and teach all nations, baptizing them in the name of the Father, and of the Son, and of the Holy Ghost: Teaching them to observe all things whatsoever I have commanded you: and, lo, I am with you alway, *even* unto the end of the world. Amen" (Mt.28:19-20).

"And he said unto them, Go ye into all the world, and preach the gospel to every creature" (Mk.16:15).

"And ye also shall bear witness, because ye have been with me from the beginning" (Jn.15:27).

"Then said Jesus to them again, Peace *be* unto you: as *my* Father hath sent me, even so send I you" (Jn.20:21).

"But ye shall receive power, after that the Holy Ghost is come upon you: and ye shall be witnesses unto me both in Jerusalem, and in all Judaea, and in Samaria, and unto the uttermost part of the earth" (Ac.1:8).

"For we cannot but speak the things which we have seen and heard" (Ac.4:20).

"Go, stand and speak in the temple to the people all the words of this life" (Ac.5:20).

"And we are his witnesses of these things; and *so is* also the Holy Ghost, whom God hath given to them that obey him" (Ac.5:32).

"And he said, The God of our fathers hath chosen thee, that thou shouldest know his will, and see that Just One, and shouldest hear the voice of his mouth. For thou shalt be his witness unto all men of what thou hast seen and heard" (Ac.22:14-15).

"We having the same spirit of faith, according as it is written, I believed, and therefore have I spoken; we also believe, and therefore speak" (2 Co.4:13).

"Be not thou therefore ashamed of the testimony of our Lord, nor of me his prisoner: but be thou partaker of the afflictions of the gospel according to the power of God" (2 Ti.1:8).

"These things speak, and exhort, and rebuke with all authority. Let no man despise thee" (Tit.2:15).

"But sanctify the Lord God in your hearts: and *be* ready always to *give* an answer to every man that asketh you a reason of the hope that is in you with meekness and fear" (1 Pe.3:15).

"Feed the flock of God which is among you, taking the oversight *thereof,* not by constraint, but willingly; not for filthy lucre, but of a ready mind" (1 Pe.5:2).

"I have set watchmen upon thy walls, O Jerusalem, *which* shall never hold their peace day nor night: ye that make mention of the LORD, keep not silence" (Is.62:6).

"The LORD hath brought forth our righteousness: come, and let us declare in Zion the work of the LORD our God" (Je.51:10).

"Son of man, I have made thee a watchman unto the house of Israel: therefore hear the word at my mouth, and give them warning from me" (Eze.3:17).

1. The successful defense of the Jews: Being prepared for the attack of the enemy
a. The date of the fighting: 13th day of Adar
b. The attack by the enemies: They were overpowered by the Jews

1) Because the Jews had mobilized & were prepared in city after city
2) Because fear gripped the hearts of the enemies as well as all the other people
3) Because the Persian nobles & political leaders helped the Jews
• They feared Mordecai, their superior

• Mordecai had become more & more powerful since becoming prime minister

c. The summary of the Jews' great victory against their enemies: They survived the holocaust launched against them
d. The defense of the Jews in Susa
1) They killed 500 men
2) They killed the 10 sons of Haman

3) They did not plunder the property of those they killed
4) The number of the slain in Susa was reported to the king

e. The grant of the king for one more day as a mopping up

CHAPTER 9

F. The Triumph of the Jews & the Celebration of Purim: A Picture of Victory Over One's Enemy, 9:1–10:3

Now in the twelfth month, that is, the month Adar, on the thirteenth day of the same, when the king's commandment and his decree drew near to be put in execution, in the day that the enemies of the Jews hoped to have power over them, (though it was turned to the contrary, that the Jews had rule over them that hated them;)
2 The Jews gathered themselves together in their cities throughout all the provinces of the king Ahasuerus, to lay hand on such as sought their hurt: and no man could withstand them; for the fear of them fell upon all people.
3 And all the rulers of the provinces, and the lieutenants, and the deputies, and officers of the king, helped the Jews; because the fear of Mordecai fell upon them.
4 For Mordecai was great in the king's house, and his fame went out throughout all the provinces: for this man Mordecai waxed greater and greater.
5 Thus the Jews smote all their enemies with the stroke of the sword, and slaughter, and destruction, and did what they would unto those that hated them.
6 And in Shushan the palace the Jews slew and destroyed five hundred men.
7 And Parshandatha, and Dalphon, and Aspatha,
8 And Poratha, and Adalia, and Aridatha,
9 And Parmashta, and Arisai, and Aridai, and Vajezatha,
10 The ten sons of Haman the son of Hammedatha, the enemy of the Jews, slew they; but on the spoil laid they not their hand.
11 On that day the number of those that were slain in Shushan the palace was brought before the king.
12 And the king said unto Esther the queen, The Jews

have slain and destroyed five hundred men in Shushan the palace, and the ten sons of Haman; what have they done in the rest of the king's provinces? now what is thy petition? and it shall be granted thee: or what is thy request further? and it shall be done.
13 Then said Esther, If it please the king, let it be granted to the Jews which are in Shushan to do to morrow also according unto this day's decree, and let Haman's ten sons be hanged upon the gallows.
14 And the king commanded it so to be done: and the decree was given at Shushan; and they hanged Haman's ten sons.
15 For the Jews that were in Shushan gathered themselves together on the fourteenth day also of the month Adar, and slew three hundred men at Shushan; but on the prey they laid not their hand.
16 But the other Jews that were in the king's provinces gathered themselves together, and stood for their lives, and had rest from their enemies, and slew of their foes seventy and five thousand, but they laid not their hands on the prey,
17 On the thirteenth day of the month Adar; and on the fourteenth day of the same rested they, and made it a day of feasting and gladness.
18 But the Jews that were at Shushan assembled together on the thirteenth day thereof; and on the fourteenth thereof; and on the fifteenth day of the same they rested, and made it a day of feasting and gladness.
19 Therefore the Jews of the villages, that dwelt in the unwalled towns, made the fourteenth day of the month Adar a day of gladness and feasting, and a good day, and of sending portions one to another.
20 And Mordecai wrote these things, and sent letters unto all the Jews that were in all the provinces of the king Ahasuerus, both nigh and far,
21 To stablish this among them, that they should keep the fourteenth day of the month Adar, and the fifteenth

operation in Susa
1) He shared the report on the fighting with Esther
2) He was so pleased he asked her if she had any other requests:
• She requested the additional day to assure that all enemies were defeated
• She requested that Haman's 10 sons be hanged on gallows as a warning, a deterrent to the public

3) He granted her requests

f. The resistance by the Jews on the additional day of fighting
1) They killed 300 more men in Susa
2) They again did not plunder the enemies' property
g. The resistance by the Jews in the provinces throughout the rest of the empire
1) They killed 75,000 enemies
2) They did not plunder their property

h. The celebration of the Jews' deliverance: Was celebrated the day after the victory

1) The Jews in Susa celebrated on the 15th day of Adar

2) The Jews in the provinces celebrated on the 14th day of Adar

2. The celebration of the deliverance (the Festival of Purim): Rejoicing over God's wonderful deliverance

a. The letters of Mordecai establishing the festival

1) To be celebrated annually, the 14-15th day of Adar
2) To be celebrated in honor of their wonderful deliverance from the enemies
   • As a day of feasting & joy
   • As a day for giving gifts to one another, including to the poor
b. The festival agreed to & instituted by the Jews

1) The reasons
   • Because Haman had plotted to exterminate the Jews

   • Because Esther had informed the king of the plot: He had issued a proclamation that caused Haman's plot to fail & resulted in a great deliverance of the Jews

2) The name given to the Festival was Purim

3) The declaration of the Jews
   • They would observe the celebration of Purim within every city & province or district

   • They & their descendants would never fail to observe these two days

day of the same, yearly,
22 As the days wherein the Jews rested from their enemies, and the month which was turned unto them from sorrow to joy, and from mourning into a good day: that they should make them days of feasting and joy, and of sending portions one to another, and gifts to the poor.
23 And the Jews undertook to do as they had begun, and as Mordecai had written unto them;
24 Because Haman the son of Hammedatha, the Agagite, the enemy of all the Jews, had devised against the Jews to destroy them, and had cast Pur, that *is,* the lot, to consume them, and to destroy them;
25 But when *Esther* came before the king, he commanded by letters that his wicked device, which he devised against the Jews, should return upon his own head, and that he and his sons should be hanged on the gallows.
26 Wherefore they called these days Purim after the name of Pur. Therefore for all the words of this letter, and *of that* which they had seen concerning this matter, and which had come unto them,
27 The Jews ordained, and took upon them, and upon their seed, and upon all such as joined themselves unto them, so as it should not fail, that they would keep these two days according to their writing, and according to their *appointed* time every year;
28 And *that* these days *should be* remembered and kept throughout every generation, every family, every

province, and every city; and *that* these days of Purim should not fail from among the Jews, nor the memorial of them perish from their seed.
29 Then Esther the queen, the daughter of Abihail, and Mordecai the Jew, wrote with all authority, to confirm this second letter of Purim.
30 And he sent the letters unto all the Jews, to the hundred twenty and seven provinces of the kingdom of Ahasuerus, *with* words of peace and truth,
31 To confirm these days of Purim in their times *appointed,* according as Mordecai the Jew and Esther the queen had enjoined them, and as they had decreed for themselves and for their seed, the matters of the fastings and their cry.
32 And the decree of Esther confirmed these matters of Purim; and it was written in the book.

CHAPTER 10

And the king Ahasuerus laid a tribute upon the land, and *upon* the isles of the sea.
2 And all the acts of his power and of his might, and the declaration of the greatness of Mordecai, whereunto the king advanced him, *are* they not written in the book of the chronicles of the kings of Media and Persia?
3 For Mordecai the Jew *was* next unto king Ahasuerus, and great among the Jews, and accepted of the multitude of his brethren, seeking the wealth of his people, and speaking peace to all his seed.

   • They would never let the memory of their deliverance fade

c. The festival confirmed by Esther
1) She wrote a letter to put her full authority as queen behind the Festival of Purim

2) Mordecai sent a second round of letters to the Jews throughout the empire—all 127 provinces

   • The festival was also to include fasting & mourning

   • The decree of Esther confirmed these regulations as well

c. The greatness of Mordecai
1) He was prime minister, next to the king in authority
2) He was held in high esteem by the Jews
3) He served his people:
   • Worked for their good
   • Spoke up for them

3. **The greatness of King Ahasuerus & Mordecai: The steps to true greatness**
a. The tax imposed by the king, 1
b. The power & wealth of the king & the greatness of Mordecai: Recorded in the official records, *The History of the Kings of Media & Persia*

c. The greatness of Mordecai
1) He was prime minister, next to the king in authority
2) He was held in high esteem by the Jews
3) He served his people:
   • Worked for their good
   • Spoke up for them

DIVISION III

THE JEWS SAVED BY THE COURAGEOUS ACTION OF ESTHER, 4:1–10:3

F. **The Triumph of the Jews and the Celebration of Purim: A Picture of Victory Over One's Enemy, 9:1–10:3**

(9:1–10:3) **Introduction**: as we walk throughout life, we will meet people who oppose us. No matter who we are, we will encounter some who dislike us. Perhaps our personalities do not match theirs, rubbing them the wrong way. Our looks, facial expressions, speech, or behavior may irritate others. All of us have misbehaved in life and done wrong, in some instances arousing anger against us. As a result, a number of us are hated, even despised. Others of us have a strong testimony of righteousness for the cause of Christ. Consequently, many of those who live for the world—for its pleasures, power, and possessions—ridicule and persecute the individuals who take a stand for the LORD.

In other cases, people are prejudiced and do all they can to degrade and tear down those of a different race, color, religion, or belief.

But there is wonderful hope for all of us, for the entire human race: the hope of Jesus Christ, God's only Son. Jesus Christ came to this earth to preach the glorious gospel of deliverance. We can be delivered from the hatred, prejudice, discrimination, and divisions of this earth. Our hearts can be set free, liberated from all the sin, wickedness, and evil within the human heart. This is the glorious message of the present passage of Scripture.

Remember, a decree of extermination had been issued throughout the Persian Empire by Haman the prime minister. The entire Jewish race was to be exterminated, wiped off the face of the earth (3:1-15). But through the courageous action of Queen Esther, Haman's evil plot was exposed. Afterward, King Xerxes issued a second decree that granted the Jews the right of self-defense (8:1-17). The present Scripture covers the great victory of the Jews over this holocaust, the slaughter launched against them by some of the citizens of the Persian Empire. This is: *The Triumph of the Jews and the Celebration of Purim: A Picture of Victory Over One's Enemy*, 9:1–10:3.

1. The successful defense of the Jews: being prepared for the attack of the enemy (9:1-19).
2. The celebration of the deliverance as (the Festival of Purim): rejoicing over God's wonderful deliverance (9:20-32).
3. The greatness of King Ahasuerus and Mordecai: the steps to true greatness (10:1-3).

1 (9:1-19) **Spiritual Warfare, Duty, to Be Prepared—Warfare, Spiritual, Duty—Preparation, for Spiritual Warfare, Duty—War, Duty—Government, Duty—Defense, Duty—Jews, Discrimination Against—Anti-Semitism, Example of—Jews, Victory of, Over Holocaust—Holocaust, Against the Jews**: the Jews successfully defended themselves against their enemies and achieved significant victories over all who attacked them. Exactly what happened is graphically described by the Scripture:

OUTLINE	SCRIPTURE	SCRIPTURE	OUTLINE
1. The successful defense of the Jews: Being prepared for the attack of the enemy a. The date of the fighting: 13th day of Adar b. The attack by the enemies: They were overpowered by the Jews	Now in the twelfth month, that *is,* the month Adar, on the thirteenth day of the same, when the king's commandment and his decree drew near to be put in execution, in the day that the enemies of the Jews hoped to have power over them, (though it was turned to the contrary, that the Jews had rule over them that hated them;)	Dalphon, and Aspatha, 8 And Poratha, and Adalia, and Aridatha, 9 And Parmashta, and Arisai, and Aridai, and Vajezatha, 10 The ten sons of Haman the son of Hammedatha, the enemy of the Jews, slew they; but on the spoil laid they not their hand.	of Haman 3) They did not plunder the property of those they killed
1) Because the Jews had mobilized & were prepared in city after city 2) Because fear gripped the hearts of the enemies as well as all other nationalities 3) Because the Persian nobles & political leaders helped the Jews • They feared Mordecai, their superior • Mordecai had become more & more powerful since becoming prime minister	2 The Jews gathered themselves together in their cities throughout all the provinces of the king Ahasuerus, to lay hand on such as sought their hurt: and no man could withstand them; for the fear of them fell upon all people. 3 And all the rulers of the provinces, and the lieutenants, and the deputies, and officers of the king, helped the Jews; because the fear of Mordecai fell upon them. 4 For Mordecai *was* great in the king's house, and his fame went out throughout all the provinces: for this man Mordecai waxed greater and greater.	11 On that day the number of those that were slain in Shushan the palace was brought before the king. 12 And the king said unto Esther the queen, The Jews have slain and destroyed five hundred men in Shushan the palace, and the ten sons of Haman; what have they done in the rest of the king's provinces? now what *is* thy petition? and it shall be granted thee: or what *is* thy request further? and it shall be done. 13 Then said Esther, If it please the king, let it be granted to the Jews which *are* in Shushan to do to morrow also according unto this day's decree, and let Haman's ten sons be hanged upon the gallows.	4) The number of the slain in Susa was reported to the king e. The grant of the king for one more day as a mopping up operation in Susa 1) He shared the report on the fighting with Esther 2) He was so pleased he asked her if she had any other requests: • She requested the additional day to assure that all enemies were defeated • She requested that Haman's 10 sons be hanged on gallows as a warning, a deterrent to the public
c. The summary of the Jews' great victory against their enemies: They survived the holocaust launched against them d. The defense of the Jews in Susa 1) They killed 500 men 2) They killed the 10 sons	5 Thus the Jews smote all their enemies with the stroke of the sword, and slaughter, and destruction, and did what they would unto those that hated them. 6 And in Shushan the palace the Jews slew and destroyed five hundred men. 7 And Parshandatha, and	14 And the king commanded it so to be done: and the decree was given at Shushan; and they hanged Haman's ten sons. 15 For the Jews that *were* in Shushan gathered themselves together on the fourteenth day also of the month	3) He granted her requests f. The resistance by the Jews on the additional day of fighting a) They killed 300 more men

303

OUTLINE	SCRIPTURE	SCRIPTURE	OUTLINE
in Susa b) They again did not plunder the enemies' property	Adar, and slew three hundred men at Shushan; but on the prey they laid not their hand.	of feasting and gladness. 18 But the Jews that *were* at Shushan assembled together on the thirteenth *day* thereof; and on the fourteenth thereof; and on the fifteenth *day* of the same they rested, and made it a day of feasting and gladness.	1) The Jews in Susa celebrated on the 15ᵗʰ day of Adar
g. The resistance by the Jews in the provinces throughout the rest of the empire 1) They killed 75,000 enemies 2) They did not plunder their property	16 But the other Jews that *were* in the king's provinces gathered themselves together, and stood for their lives, and had rest from their enemies, and slew of their foes seventy and five thousand, but they laid not their hands on the prey,	19 Therefore the Jews of the villages, that dwelt in the unwalled towns, made the fourteenth day of the month Adar *a day of* gladness and feasting, and a good day, and of sending portions one to another.	2) The Jews in the provinces celebrated on the 14th day of Adar
h. The celebration of the Jews' deliverance: Was celebrated the day after the victory	17 On the thirteenth day of the month Adar; and on the fourteenth day of the same rested they, and made it a day		

a. The appointed day for the extermination of the Jews finally came, the 13ᵗʰ day of the 12ᵗʰ month, the month of Adar (v.1). Ever since the announcement of the *Decree of Extermination*, the enemies of the Jews had hoped to erase them from the face of the earth. But presently the tables were turned against them because King Xerxes had issued a second decree that allowed the Jews to defend themselves.

b. The Jews now were permitted to defend themselves to gain the upper hand over all who attacked them. Three reasons are given for their successful defense:

1) Because of King Xerxes's second decree, the *Decree of Defense*, the Jews had time to prepare and mobilize themselves against all adversaries. In city after city throughout the empire, the Jews banded together to defend themselves against all who sought their death. If each family had stood alone, they would have been easy prey. But by banding together in cities, they were able to successfully defend themselves when attacked.

2) Because of God's love for the Israelites. He aroused fear within the hearts of the anti-Semites (v.2; 8:17). None of them were successful in attacking the Jews because they were too apprehensive, too afraid. Once again the LORD, through His sovereignty, had protected the Jews. He had long ago appointed them to be the people through whom He would give the Word of God (the Holy Bible) to the world and through whom He would send the Messiah, the LORD Jesus Christ, to save the world.

3) Because the Persian nobles and political leaders threw their weight behind the Jews, the Jews were able to successfully defend themselves (v.3). Within the cities throughout the empire, the political officials took their stand with the Jews. This was to be expected, for King Xerxes had thrown his weight behind the Jews. Furthermore, he had appointed the Jew Mordecai to be the prime minister of the nation. In fact, Scripture says that the governors and political officials actually *feared* Mordecai. Thus they were bound to support the Jews against their attackers. If they had actually supported the aggressors, they themselves would have been executed.

c. For the above three reasons, the Jews gained a great victory against the citizens who attacked them. They survived the attempted holocaust launched by those who so despised the Jews. Instead of being slaughtered, they were actually able to defend themselves and to kill the aggressors. Moreover, they were apparently strong and confident in their defense. For the most part they were able to do as they pleased, gaining an easy and complete victory over those who assaulted them (v.5).

d. In the fortress of Susa the Jews killed 500 men. In addition, they killed the ten sons of Haman, the former prime minister who had so bitterly despised the Jews and who had deceived King Xerxes into signing the decree of extermination. But note this fact: the Jews did not plunder the property of those they killed (vv.6-10). This fact is so important that it is repeated three times (v.10, 15-16). The only motive of the Jews was to defend and protect their lives, not to steal property. They had as much a right to live and to defend themselves as any other people. At some point during the day, the number of the slain in Susa was reported to the king (v.11).

e. Pleased with the report of the Jews' success, Xerxes shared the news of the fighting with Queen Esther. He then asked if she had any other requests that might help the Jews against their attackers (v.12). To assure a complete victory over the brutal enemies, Esther made two additional requests:

⇒ That the Jews in Susa be given one more day to continue pursuing the attackers who sought to slaughter them (v.13).

⇒ That the bodies of Haman's ten sons be hanged on gallows as a warning and deterrent to any future aggressor seeking to slaughter the Jews.

King Xerxes granted the request of his beloved wife and queen (v.14). He immediately issued a decree in Susa that extended the right of the Jews to pursue and execute those who had so viciously attacked them, seeking to slaughter their families and steal their property. He also hung the bodies of Haman's ten sons in public as a warning, to bring a halt to any future aggressor who might wish to slaughter the Jews.

f. In the additional day, the Jews were able to track down and kill 300 more of their attackers in the city of Susa. But again note, they did not plunder the enemy's property.

g. Throughout the rest of the empire, the Jews were able to successfully defend themselves. They killed 75,000 of their aggressors (v.16). But for a third time: they did not plunder their property. They sought only to protect themselves and to live peacefully without oppression.

h. As a result of their great victory, the Jews celebrated their deliverance from the aggressors (vv.17-19). Celebrations were held all over the empire on the day after their triumphant stand. In the city of Susa the Jews celebrated on the 15th day of Adar, which was the 12th month (v.18). But out in the provinces or districts, where they had not been given an extra day, the Jews celebrated on the 14th day of Adar (v.19).

Thought 1. The Jews were able to help save themselves from extermination by preparing for the attacks of the enemy. If they had not prepared themselves, the Persian citizens who despised and oppressed them would have tried to wipe them off the face of the earth. Who knows how many would have survived. As pointed out earlier, God's sovereignty worked out the circumstances to preserve the Jews. However, the Jews were still required to prepare—not just sit around and expect God to miraculously wipe out the enemy. God could have done so but, instead, He required them to prepare.

In facing any enemy, preparation is essential. As Christian believers we must be prepared to stand against the attack of any foe. And there are many. When we stand for righteousness and the claims of Christ, all who live for the world—its pleasures, power, and possessions—will oppose us. Few people are willing to give all they are and have for the cause of Christ. Yet this is just what Christ demands: total commitment. We are to give our all so the gospel can be taken to the whole world and the needs of people everywhere can be met—both in our own local communities and throughout the world. When we proclaim that righteousness and total commitment are demanded by Christ, the world opposes us. Unbelievers seek to stop our witness. Sometimes they simply ridicule or mock us, but at other times they seek to persecute or even kill us.

For these reasons, the LORD tells us to prepare ourselves for opposition and persecution. Preparation is an absolute essential if we are to be triumphant, victorious. To help us, the LORD tells us exactly how to prepare. The following steps are to be taken in preparing for the attack of the enemy:

(1) We must put on the armor of God.

"Finally, my brethren, be strong in the Lord, and in the power of his might. Put on the whole armour of God, that ye may be able to stand against the wiles of the devil. For we wrestle not against flesh and blood, but against principalities, against powers, against the rulers of the darkness of this world, against spiritual wickedness in high *places*. Wherefore take unto you the whole armour of God, that ye may be able to withstand in the evil day, and having done all, to stand. Stand therefore, having your loins girt about with truth, and having on the breastplate of righteousness; And your feet shod with the preparation of the gospel of peace; Above all, taking the shield of faith, wherewith ye shall be able to quench all the fiery darts of the wicked. And take the helmet of salvation, and the sword of the Spirit, which is the word of God: Praying always with all prayer and supplication in the Spirit, and watching thereunto with all perseverance and supplication for all saints" (Ep.6:10-18).

(2) We must be ready to give an answer to every person who asks us about the hope that is in us.

"But sanctify the Lord God in your hearts: and *be* ready always to *give* an answer to every man that asketh you a reason of the hope that is in you with meekness and fear" (1 Pe.3:15).

(3) We must not hate our enemies but, rather, love them for the cause of Christ.

"But I say unto you, Love your enemies, bless them that curse you, do good to them that hate you, and pray for them which despitefully use you, and persecute you" (Mt.5:44).

(4) We must endure hardship as a good soldier of Jesus Christ, not entangling ourselves with the affairs of this life.

"Thou therefore endure hardness, as a good soldier of Jesus Christ. No man that warreth entangleth himself with the affairs of *this* life; that he may please him who hath chosen him to be a soldier" (2 Ti.2:3-4).

(5) We must be angry about and hate sin and evil, but not the sinner, the one who does evil against us.

"Be ye angry, and sin not: let not the sun go down upon your wrath: Neither give place to the devil" (Ep.4:26-27).

(6) We must pursue, follow peace with all men.

"Flee also youthful lusts: but follow righteousness, faith, charity, peace, with them that call on the Lord out of a pure heart" (2 Ti.2:22).
"Follow peace with all *men*, and holiness, without which no man shall see the Lord: Looking diligently lest any man fail of the grace of God; lest any root of bitterness springing up trouble *you*, and thereby many be defiled" (He.12:14-15).

(7) We must avoid foolish and stupid arguments because they will cause divisions and strife.

"But foolish and unlearned questions avoid, knowing that they do gender strifes. And the servant of the Lord must not strive; but be gentle unto all *men*, apt to teach, patient, In meekness instructing those that oppose themselves; if God peradventure will give them repentance to the acknowledging of the truth; And *that* they may recover themselves out of the snare of the devil, who are taken captive by him at his will" (2 Ti.2:23-26).

(8) We must be constantly aware that the world will persecute us and that evil men and deceivers will grow from bad to worse.

"And ye shall be hated of all *men* for my name's sake: but he that endureth to the end shall be saved" (Mt.10:22).
"And in nothing terrified by your adversaries: which is to them an evident token of perdition, but to you of salvation, and that of God" (Ph.1:28).
"Yea, and all that will live godly in Christ Jesus shall suffer persecution. But evil men and seducers shall wax worse and worse, deceiving, and being deceived" (2 Ti.3:12-13).

(9) We must follow the example of those who have withstood persecution in the past.

"By faith Moses, when he was come to years, refused to be called the son of Pharaoh's daughter; Choosing rather to suffer affliction with the people of God, than to enjoy the pleasures of sin for a season; Esteeming the reproach of Christ greater riches than the treasures in Egypt: for he had respect unto the recompence of the reward" (He.11:24-26).
"Take, my brethren, the prophets, who have spoken in the name of the Lord, for an example of suffering affliction, and of patience" (Js.5:10).

(10) We must keep our eyes on the reward.

"And ye shall be hated of all *men* for my name's sake: but he that endureth to the end shall be saved" (Mt.10:22).
"Therefore, my beloved brethren, be ye stedfast, unmovable, always abounding in the work of the Lord, forasmuch as ye know that your labour is not in vain in the Lord" (1 Co.15:58).
"But watch thou in all things, endure afflictions, do the work of an evangelist, make full proof of thy ministry. For I am now ready to be offered, and the time of my departure is at hand. I have fought a good fight, I have finished *my* course, I have kept the faith: Henceforth there is laid up for me a crown of righteousness, which the Lord, the righteous judge, shall give me at that day: and not to me only, but unto all them also that love his appearing" (2 Ti.4:5-8).

(11) We must know, be fully convinced that the LORD will strengthen us to stand against those who attack us.

"At my first answer no man stood with me, but all *men* forsook me: *I pray God* that it may not be laid to their charge. Notwithstanding the Lord stood with me, and strengthened me; that by me the preaching might be fully known, and *that* all the Gentiles might hear: and I was delivered out of the mouth of the lion. And the Lord shall deliver me from every evil work, and will preserve *me* unto his heavenly kingdom: to whom *be* glory for ever and ever. Amen" (2 Ti.4:16-18).
"*Let your* conversation [behavior, conduct] *be* without covetousness; *and be* content with such things as ye have: for he hath said, I will never leave thee, nor forsake thee. So that we may boldly say, The Lord *is* my helper, and I will not fear what man shall do unto me" (He.13:5-6).
"The LORD *is* my strength and my shield; my heart trusted in him, and I am helped: therefore my heart greatly rejoiceth; and with my song will I praise him" (Ps.28:7).
"But I *am* poor and needy; *yet* the Lord thinketh upon me: thou *art* my help and my deliverer; make no tarrying, O my God" (Ps.40:17).
"Fear thou not; for I *am* with thee: be not dismayed; for I *am* thy God: I will strengthen thee; yea, I will help thee; yea, I will uphold thee with the right hand of my righteousness" (Is.41:10).
"Fear not: for I have redeemed thee, I have called *thee* by thy name; thou *art* mine. When thou passest through the waters, I *will be* with thee; and through the rivers, they shall not overflow thee: when thou walkest through the fire, thou shalt not be burned; neither shall the flame kindle upon thee" (Is.43:1-2).

(12) We must honor the rulers of this world and the leaders who have authority over us. We must work for the good of the society in which we live.

"Let every soul be subject unto the higher powers. For there is no power but of God: the powers that be are ordained of God. Whosoever therefore resisteth the power, resisteth the ordinance of God: and they that resist shall receive to themselves damnation. For rulers are not a terror to good works, but to the evil. Wilt thou then not be afraid of the power? do that which is good, and thou shalt have praise of the same" (Ro.13:1-3).

"Put them in mind to be subject to principalities and powers, to obey magistrates, to be ready to every good work, To speak evil of no man, to be no brawlers, *but* gentle, showing all meekness unto all men" (Tit.3:1-2).

"Submit yourselves to every ordinance of man for the Lord's sake: whether it be to the king, as supreme; Or unto governors, as unto them that are sent by him for the punishment of evildoers, and for the praise of them that do well" (1 Pe.2:13-14).

(13) We must take a stand and defend ourselves against those who would assault or kill us. We must not indulge nor give license to evil, allowing it to run rampant through our neighborhoods, communities, states, nations, and all the earth. We must take a stand for righteousness, justice and the execution of justice within society.

"Let every soul be subject unto the higher powers. For there is no power but of God: the powers that be are ordained of God. Whosoever therefore resisteth the power, resisteth the ordinance of God: and they that resist shall receive to themselves damnation. For rulers are not a terror to good works, but to the evil. Wilt thou then not be afraid of the power? do that which is good, and thou shalt have praise of the same: For he is the minister of God to thee for good. But if thou do that which is evil, be afraid; for he beareth not the sword in vain: for he is the minister of God, a revenger to *execute* wrath upon him that doeth evil. Wherefore *ye* must needs be subject, not only for wrath, but also for conscience sake. For for this cause pay ye tribute also: for they are God's ministers, attending continually upon this very thing. Render therefore to all their dues: tribute to whom tribute *is due;* custom to whom custom; fear to whom fear; honour to whom honour" (Ro.13:1-7).

"Submit yourselves to every ordinance of man for the Lord's sake [the laws of justice]: whether it be to the king, as supreme; Or unto governors, as unto them that are sent by him for the punishment of evildoers, and for the praise of them that do well" (1 Pe.2:13-14).

"Put them in mind to be subject to principalities and powers, to obey magistrates, to be ready to every good work [obeying the laws of justice]" (Tit.3:1).

"That which is altogether just shalt thou follow, that thou mayest live, and inherit the land which the LORD thy God giveth thee" (De.16:20).

"Defend the poor and fatherless: do justice to the afflicted and needy" (Ps.82:3).

"To do justice and judgment *is* more acceptable to the LORD than sacrifice" (Pr.21:3).

"Thus saith the LORD, Keep ye judgment, and do justice: for my salvation *is* near to come, and my righteousness to be revealed" (Is.56:1).

2 (9:20-32) **Deliverance, Rejoicing Over—Rejoicing, for What, Deliverance—Festival, of Purim, Institution of—Purim, Festival of, Instituted**: the great deliverance of the Jews was instituted as a permanent festival. The date of the wonderful victory was placed on the Jewish calendar to be celebrated year after year as a reminder that God had delivered His people from extermination. Just how the celebration came to be established as a permanent festival is described in detail by the Scripture:

OUTLINE	SCRIPTURE	SCRIPTURE	OUTLINE
2. The celebration of the deliverance (the Festival of Purim): Rejoicing over God's wonderful deliverance a. The letters of Mordecai establishing the festival 1) To be celebrated annually, the 14-15th day of Adar 2) To be celebrated in honor of the wonderful deliverance from their enemies • As a day of feasting & joy • As a day for giving gifts to one another, including to the poor b. The festival agreed to & instituted by the Jews 1) The reasons	20 And Mordecai wrote these things, and sent letters unto all the Jews that *were* in all the provinces of the king Ahasuerus, *both* nigh and far, 21 To stablish *this* among them, that they should keep the fourteenth day of the month Adar, and the fifteenth day of the same, yearly, 22 As the days wherein the Jews rested from their enemies, and the month which was turned unto them from sorrow to joy, and from mourning into a good day: that they should make them days of feasting and joy, and of sending portions one to another, and gifts to the poor. 23 And the Jews undertook to do as they had begun, and as Mordecai had written unto them; 24 Because Haman the son	of Hammedatha, the Agagite, the enemy of all the Jews, had devised against the Jews to destroy them, and had cast Pur, that *is,* the lot, to consume them, and to destroy them; 25 But when *Esther* came before the king, he commanded by letters that his wicked device, which he devised against the Jews, should return upon his own head, and that he and his sons should be hanged on the gallows. 26 Wherefore they called these days Purim after the name of Pur. Therefore for all the words of this letter, and *of that* which they had seen concerning this matter, and which had come unto them, 27 The Jews ordained, and took upon them, and upon	• Because Haman had plotted to exterminate the Jews • Because Esther had informed the king of the plot: He had issued a proclamation that caused Haman's plot to fail & resulted in a great deliverance of the Jews 2) The name given to the Festival was Purim 3) The declaration of the Jews

OUTLINE	SCRIPTURE	SCRIPTURE	OUTLINE
• They would observe the celebration of Purim within every city & province or district	their seed, and upon all such as joined themselves unto them, so as it should not fail, that they would keep these two days according to their writing, and according to their *appointed* time every year;	all authority, to confirm this second letter of Purim. 30 And he sent the letters unto all the Jews, to the hundred twenty and seven provinces of the kingdom of Ahasuerus, *with* words of peace and truth,	her full authority as queen behind the Festival of Purim
• They & their descendants would never fail to observe these two days • They would never let the memory of their deliverance fade	28 And *that* these days *should be* remembered and kept throughout every generation, every family, every province, and every city; and *that* these days of Purim should not fail from among the Jews, nor the memorial of them perish from their seed.	31 To confirm these days of Purim in their times *appointed,* according as Mordecai the Jew and Esther the queen had enjoined them, and as they had decreed for themselves and for their seed, the matters of the fastings and their cry.	2) Mordecai sent a second round of letters to the Jews throughout the empire—all 127 provinces • The festival was also to include fasting & mourning
c. The festival confirmed by Esther 1) She wrote a letter to put	29 Then Esther the queen, the daughter of Abihail, and Mordecai the Jew, wrote with	32 And the decree of Esther confirmed these matters of Purim; and it was written in the book.	• The decree of Esther confirmed these as well

a. It was Mordecai himself who established the Festival of Purim (vv.20-22). Sending letters to all the Jews throughout the provinces of Persia, Mordecai instructed the people to celebrate their wonderful deliverance from extermination annually, on the 14th and 15th day of Adar. It was to be a day of joyful festivities, a day when gifts were exchanged. To assure that every Jew could participate, food and gifts were to be distributed to the poor.

b. Throughout the empire the Jews readily agreed with Mordecai's suggestion. Hence they instituted the festival as an annual celebration. They agreed for two reasons:
⇒ They knew that Haman had plotted to exterminate them as a race, that he would have succeeded if the LORD had not raised up Esther as queen to King Xerxes.
⇒ They knew that Esther had informed the king of Haman's plot and that the king had issued a proclamation that caused Haman's plot to fail. In addition, Haman's evil scheme brought about his own death as well as the great deliverance of the Jews (v.25).

The name given to the festival was Purim, which is taken from the Babylonian word *pur* meaning "lot." The name *Purim* was chosen because Haman had actually cast lots to determine the days when the Jews would be exterminated (3:7). In establishing the Festival of Purim, the Jews made three significant declarations (vv.27-28):
⇒ They and their descendants would never fail to observe these two days.
⇒ They would observe the celebration of Purim within every city and province or district.
⇒ They would never let the account of their deliverance fade from their memory nor from the memory of their descendants.

c. The Festival of Purim was also confirmed by Esther (vv.29-32). Some years after the institution of the festival, Mordecai sent a second letter apparently to encourage faithfulness in the celebration of Purim. He wanted his message to carry as much weight as possible to ensure the people's faithful participation. For this reason, he encouraged Esther to write a letter also, putting her full authority as queen behind the festival. Sending his letter of encouragement to all 127 provinces, he reemphasized the importance of making the day a period of fasting and mourning (v.31). Esther's decree confirmed the instructions included in Mordecai's letter. Also note that the institution of Purim as a permanent festival and the guidelines that were to control it were recorded in the official records.

Thought 1. The Jews praised God for His wonderful deliverance from extermination. We too should praise God for the wonderful deliverance He has given us. God has delivered us from sin, death, and judgment to come. No longer are we held in bondage to the sins of this world. No longer do we have to fear death and its consequences. We do not even have to fear the judgment to come, not if we have accepted Jesus Christ as our Savior and are living faithfully and obediently to Him. Christ has delivered us from every bondage, every enslavement of this world, including the bondage of death. We have been set free to live with God eternally. Because of God's great salvation, we must praise Him for His wonderful deliverance.

> "What? know ye not that your body is the temple of the Holy Ghost *which is* in you, which ye have of God, and ye are not your own? For ye are bought with a price: therefore glorify God in your body, and in your spirit, which are God's" (1 Co.6:19-20).
> "Giving thanks unto the Father, which hath made us meet to be partakers of the inheritance of the saints in light" (Col.1:12).
> "Wherefore Jesus also, that he might sanctify the people with his own blood, suffered without the gate. Let us go forth therefore unto him without the camp, bearing his reproach. For here have we no continuing city, but we seek one to come. By him therefore let us offer the sacrifice of praise to God continually, that is, the fruit of *our* lips giving thanks to his name" (He.13:12-15).

"But ye *are* a chosen generation, a royal priesthood, an holy nation, a peculiar people; that ye should show forth the praises of him who hath called you out of darkness into his marvellous light: Which in time past *were* not a people, but *are* now the people of God: which had not obtained mercy, but now have obtained mercy" (1 Pe.2:9-10).

"Sing praises to the LORD, which dwelleth in Zion: declare among the people his doings....That I may show forth all thy praise in the gates of the daughter of Zion: I will rejoice in thy salvation" (Ps.9:11, 14).

"Rejoice in the LORD, O ye righteous: *for* praise is comely for the upright. Praise the LORD with harp: sing unto him with the psaltery *and* an instrument of ten strings. Sing unto him a new song; play skilfully with a loud noise....Behold, the eye of the LORD *is* upon them that fear him, upon them that hope in his mercy; To deliver their soul from death, and to keep them alive in famine. Our soul waiteth for the LORD: he *is* our help and our shield. For our heart shall rejoice in him, because we have trusted in his holy name. Let thy mercy, O LORD, be upon us, according as we hope in thee" (Ps.33:1-3, 18-22).

"I will bless the LORD at all times: his praise *shall* continually *be* in my mouth. My soul shall make her boast in the LORD: the humble shall hear *thereof,* and be glad. O magnify the LORD with me, and let us exalt his name together. I sought the LORD, and he heard me, and delivered me from all my fears....The LORD redeemeth the soul of his servants: and none of them that trust in him shall be desolate" (Ps.34:1-4, 22).

"Blessed *be* God, which hath not turned away my prayer, nor his mercy from me" (Ps.66:20).

"Let them give glory unto the LORD, and declare his praise in the islands....And I will bring the blind by a way *that* they knew not; I will lead them in paths *that* they have not known: I will make darkness light before them, and crooked things straight. These things will I do unto them, and not forsake them" (Is.42:12, 16).

Thought 2. Warren W. Wiersbe gives a description of the Jewish celebration of Purim that is worth quoting:

> *Today, the Jews begin their celebration with a fast on the 13th day of the month (v.31), commemorating the date on which Haman's evil decree was issued (3:12). They go to the synagogue and hear the Book of Esther publicly read; and whenever the name of Haman is mentioned, they cry out, "May he be accursed!" or "May his name perish!" Children bring a special Purim rattle called a "gregar" and use it to make a noise every time they hear Haman's name read.*
>
> *On the morning of the 14th day of the month, the Jews again go to the synagogue where the Esther story is read again and the congregation engages in prayer. The story about Moses and the Amalekites (Ex.17:8-16) is also read. Then the celebrants go home to a festive holiday meal with gifts and special foods, and the celebrating continues on the next day. They also send gifts to the poor and needy so that everybody can rejoice together.* [1]

3 (10:1-3) **Greatness, True, Steps to—Mordecai, Life of, Summarized—Ahasuerus, Life of, Summarized—Xerxes, King of Persia, Summary of**: in closing the great book of *Esther,* the significance of King Ahasuerus (Xerxes) and Mordecai is summarized. At some point during his reign King Xerxes imposed a tax upon the people throughout the empire, a tax that was enforced to the distant shores of the nation (v.1). Note the emphasis on the vast territory controlled by the Persian Empire. By pointing out this system of taxation and the enormous territory of the empire, the author was likely stressing the substantial power and wealth of King Xerxes. Whatever the case, an account of his power, wealth, and achievements were recorded in the official records, *The History of the Kings of Media and Persia* (v.2). Mordecai's greatness was also recorded in these records. In summarizing Mordecai's importance, the author stresses three facts:

⇒ He was prime minister, second only to the king himself in authority.
⇒ He was held in high esteem by many of his fellow Jews.
⇒ He served the king and the people of the nation by working for the good of all the people and by speaking up for the welfare of the Jews (v.3).

OUTLINE	SCRIPTURE	SCRIPTURE	OUTLINE
3. The greatness of King Ahasuerus & Mordecai: The steps to true greatness	And the king Ahasuerus laid a tribute upon the land, and *upon* the isles of the sea.	of the chronicles of the kings of Media and Persia?	*of the Kings of Media & Persia*
a. The tax imposed by the king, 1	2 And all the acts of his power and of his might, and	3 For Mordecai the Jew *was* next unto king Ahasuerus, and great among the	c. The greatness of Mordecai
b. The power & wealth of the king & the greatness of Mordecai: Recorded in the official records, *The History*	the declaration of the greatness of Mordecai, whereunto the king advanced him, *are* they not written in the book	Jews, and accepted of the multitude of his brethren, seeking the wealth of his people, and speaking peace to all his seed.	1) He was prime minister, next to the king in authority 2) He was held in high esteem by the Jews 3) He served his people: • Worked for their good • Spoke up for them

Thought 1. Mordecai is a strong example of greatness in that he lived his life *serving* other people. Only those who build up, help, and nurture other people are truly great. Any person who is self-centered—who seeks only to build up himself and to increase his own honor, wealth, position, authority, or power—is anything but great. He is an

---

1 Warren W. Wiersbe. *Be Committed,* pp.160-161.

egotist, looking out for his own welfare, not the welfare of others. No man is an island unto himself. No person is to be focused only upon himself or herself, paying no attention whatsoever to the needs of others. God has put us on earth to serve others, to help others when they have needs, to edify others and esteem them better than ourselves. Loving one another, caring for and helping one another, nurturing and encouraging one another—this is the will of God *for* us. It is the way to greatness. It was this that Mordecai acknowledged and practiced. And it is this—serving others—is to be the major focus of our lives. Listen to what God's Holy Word says:

"Let your light so shine before men, that they may see your good works, and glorify your Father which is in heaven" (Mt.5:16).

"Even as the Son of man came not to be ministered unto, but to minister, and to give his life a ransom for many" (Mt.20:28).

"But Jesus called them *to him,* and saith unto them, Ye know that they which are accounted to rule over the Gentiles exercise lordship over them; and their great ones exercise authority upon them. But so shall it not be among you: but whosoever will be great among you, shall be your minister: And whosoever of you will be the chiefest, shall be servant of all. For even the Son of man came not to be ministered unto, but to minister, and to give his life a ransom for many" (Mk.10:42-45).

"And Jesus answering said, A certain *man* went down from Jerusalem to Jericho, and fell among thieves, which stripped him of his raiment, and wounded *him,* and departed, leaving *him* half dead. And by chance there came down a certain priest that way: and when he saw him, he passed by on the other side. And likewise a Levite, when he was at the place, came and looked *on him,* and passed by on the other side. But a certain Samaritan, as he journeyed, came where he was: and when he saw him, he had compassion *on him,* And went to *him,* and bound up his wounds, pouring in oil and wine, and set him on his own beast, and brought him to an inn, and took care of him. And on the morrow when he departed, he took out two pence, and gave *them* to the host, and said unto him, Take care of him; and whatsoever thou spendest more, when I come again, I will repay thee. Which now of these three, thinkest thou, was neighbour unto him that fell among the thieves?" (Lu.10:30-36).

"If I then, *your* Lord and Master, have washed your feet; ye also ought to wash one another's feet" (Jn.13:14).

"He saith to him again the second time, Simon, *son* of Jonas, lovest thou me? He saith unto him, Yea, Lord; thou knowest that I love thee. He saith unto him, Feed my sheep" (Jn.21:16).

"How God anointed Jesus of Nazareth with the Holy Ghost and with power: who went about doing good, and healing all that were oppressed of the devil; for God was with him" (Ac.10:38).

"Bear ye one another's burdens, and so fulfil the law of Christ" (Ga.6:2).

"As we have therefore opportunity, let us do good unto all *men,* especially unto them who are of the household of faith" (Ga.6:10).

"With good will doing service, as to the Lord, and not to men" (Ep.6:7).

"Charge them that are rich in this world, that they be not highminded, nor trust in uncertain riches, but in the living God, who giveth us richly all things to enjoy; That they do good, that they be rich in good works, ready to distribute, willing to communicate; Laying up in store for themselves a good foundation against the time to come, that they may lay hold on eternal life" (1 Ti.6:17-19).

"In all things showing thyself a pattern of good works: in doctrine *showing* uncorruptness, gravity, sincerity" (Tit.2:7).

"And let us consider one another to provoke unto love and to good works" (He.10:24).

"But to do good and to communicate [give] forget not: for with such sacrifices God is well pleased" (He.13:16).

"Even so faith, if it hath not works, is dead, being alone. Yea, a man may say, Thou hast faith, and I have works: show me thy faith without thy works, and I will show thee my faith by my works" (Js.2:17-18).

"Therefore to him that knoweth to do good, and doeth *it* not, to him it is sin" (Js.4:17).

"Trust in the LORD, and do good; *so* shalt thou dwell in the land, and verily thou shalt be fed" (Ps.37:3).

"They that sow in tears shall reap in joy. He that goeth forth and weepeth, bearing precious seed, shall doubtless come again with rejoicing, bringing his sheaves *with him*" (Ps.126:5-6).

Thought 2. King Xerxes and Mordecai eventually brought peace and prosperity to the Persian Empire. In speaking about this Matthew Henry says:

Thanks be to God, [for] *such a government as this we are blessed with, which* seeks the welfare of our people, speaking peace to all their seed. *God continue it long, very long, and grant us, under the happy protection of it, to* live quiet and peaceable lives, in godliness, honesty, and charity [love]![2]

---

2 *Matthew Henry's Commentary.* Vol.2, p.1153.

Thought 3. In closing the book of *Esther,* the commentator John A. Martin says this:

> As the original Jewish readers read this account they would have been struck by the way God was sovereignly protecting them, often when they did not even know it. Many things in the Book of Esther happened that were beyond anyone's control except that of God, who oversees history. And the book of Esther is filled with irony, with ways in which events turned out unexpectedly and in favor of God's people. Queen Vashti, a Persian, was deposed so that Esther, a Jewess, could become queen and save her people. Haman, once exalted, was brought low, and **Mordecai** and **the Jews**, once hated, were exalted and honored. A decree that would have wiped out the Jews was overruled by one which led to the destruction of nearly 76,000 enemies of the Jews. No wonder Purim was celebrated yearly with such rejoicing: to help the Jews remember that God is in control and that people should faithfully worship and serve their great God.[3]

Thought 4. In closing his excellent commentary on the book of *Esther,* Mervin Breneman says this:

> The book closes with a picture of peace and prosperity for the Jews. The author did not mention God even one time in the book. But it is evident that he wanted his readers to see God's hand in preserving the Jews. The Feast of Purim celebrates a historical event and has been repeated many times over two thousand years. Over that time period, the Jews have often been in danger of annihilation by their enemies, but God has "miraculously" preserved them. In many cases, for example the Holocaust, many Jews died while others were saved from such an end. God is still faithful to his promise to Abraham and his descendants: "I will bless those who bless you, and whoever curses you I will curse; and all peoples on earth will be blessed through you" (Gen 12:3). The challenge the Book of Esther presents is that we must recognize when our "time" has come to act (Esth 4:14). Upon such recognition we must immediately proceed in doing God's will, trusting in God's presence and favor.
>
> There are few books of the Old Testament more relevant to life in a society hostile to the gospel. Believers are scattered throughout the world, awaiting the Lord's return. Although he is present and active now as much as ever, he is usually "hidden" behind the events of life that he is directing for his own glory and the benefit of his children. Although unbelievers can refuse to acknowledge him, those "who have eyes to see" are able to recognize his hand at work in the affairs of life. "In a world in which hostility to the household of faith seems to flourish naturally, and indeed in which atheistic explanations of the universe grow more strident, 'scientific' and apparently convincing, it belongs to faith to 'hold fast' nevertheless to our hope—now specifically in Christ—'for he who promised is faithful.'"[4]

Thought 5. In closing his commentary on the book of *Esther,* Warren W. Wiersbe says this:

> The exciting drama of Esther is over, but the blessings go right on. God preserved the Jewish nation so that we today can have a Bible and a Savior. Now it's our job to tell the whole world about this Savior and seek to win as many as we can to the Lord. We are the king's couriers, and we dare not fail.
>
> ...Esther reach[s] across the centuries, join[s] hands, and say[s] to the church today: **BE COMMITTED!**[5]

---

[3] F. Walvoord and Roy B. Zuck, Editors. *The Bible Knowledge Commentary,* p.713.
[4] Mervin Breneman. *Ezra, Nehemiah, Esther,* p.370.
[5] Warren W. Wiersbe. *Be Committed,* p.163.

RESOURCES

ESTHER

TYPES, SYMBOLS, AND PICTURES
THE BOOK OF ESTHER

ALPHABETICAL OUTLINE

What is a biblical type or symbol? Simply put, a *biblical type* is a *foreshadowing* of what was to come at a later time in history. Through a person, place, or thing, a biblical type points toward a New Testament fulfillment.

In addition to biblical types, there are what we may call *biblical pictures*. A biblical picture is a lesson that we can see in the Scriptures *without distorting the truth*. The study of biblical types and pictures is a valuable tool in that it helps us apply the truth of the Scriptures in our lives. Scripture itself tells us this:

> **"Now all these things happened unto them for examples: and they are written for our admonition, upon whom the ends of the world are come" (1 Co.10:11).**
> **"For whatsoever things were written aforetime were written for our learning, that we through patience and comfort of the scriptures might have hope" (Ro.15:4).**

PERSON/PLACE/THING	SCRIPTURE, OUTLINE AND DISCUSSION
AHASUERUS. *Decrees of. That the Jews could fight against the enemy. A picture of proclaiming the salvation of God's people.*	Est.8:7-17
To divorce Queen Vashti. A picture of unbridled anger and revenge.	Est.1:13-22
To find a new queen. A picture of selfishness and moral corruption in seeking true love.	Est.2:1-4
Immorality of. Order a fleshly, carnal display of the queen's beauty. A picture of loose morals and drunkenness.	Est.1:10-12
Marriage. To Esther. A picture of a morally corrupt man contrasted with a true believer of strong character.	Est.2:1-23
Wealth of. A picture of pride and self-exaltation.	Est.1:1-9
ESTHER. *Character of. A picture of moral purity and strong character.*	Est.2:5-20
Courage of. Risking her life to save her people. A picture of the desperate need for courage, prayer, and fasting.	Est.4:10-17
Desperate intercession of. For the life of the Jews. A picture of being delivered through prayer.	Est.8:1-17
Plea of. For her people. A picture of the believer's intercession.	Est.8:3-6
Rewarded. By King Ahasuerus. A picture of the believer being rewarded for faithful service.	Est.8:1-2
HAMAN. *Anger of. Against Mordecai and the Jews. A picture of extreme prejudice and hatred.*	Est.3:1-6
Execution of. A clear picture of the surety of judgment.	Est.7:7-10
Exposure and downfall of. A picture of reaping exactly what one sows.	Est.7:1-10
Humiliation of. In public. Because Mordecai was honored instead of him. A clear picture of God humbling the prideful and exalting the humble.	Est.6:11-14
Plot of. To exterminate the Jews. A picture of brutality and horrifying evil.	Est.3:7-15
JEWS. *Preparation of. For war. A picture of the believer being fully prepared for the attack of the enemy.*	Est.9:1-19
MORDECAI. *Anguish of. Reason. The decree to kill all the Jews. A picture of the desperate need for an intercessor who can plead for mercy.*	Est.4:1-9
Honor bestowed upon. Unexpectedly. A picture of God's providence, guidance, and love for His people.	Est.6:1-14
Warning by. To King Ahasuerus. Of the assassination plot against him. A picture of believers warning others to prepare for death.	Est.2:21-23
PURIM. *Feast of. Celebration of. A picture of the believer's victory in spiritual warfare.*	Est.9:1–10:3
Institution of. A picture of the believer celebrating and rejoicing over God's wonderful deliverance.	Est.9:20-32

TYPES, SYMBOLS, AND PICTURES
THE BOOK OF ESTHER

CHRONOLOGICAL OUTLINE

What is a biblical type or symbol? Simply put, a *biblical type* is a *foreshadowing* of what was to come at a later time in history. Through a person, place, or thing, a biblical type points toward a New Testament fulfillment.

In addition to biblical types, there are what we may call *biblical pictures*. A biblical picture is a lesson that we can see in the Scriptures *without distorting the truth*. The study of biblical types and pictures is a valuable tool in that it helps us apply the truth of the Scriptures in our lives. Scripture itself tells us this:

"Now all these things happened unto them for examples: and they are written for our admonition, upon whom the ends of the world are come" (1 Co.10:11).

"For whatsoever things were written aforetime were written for our learning, that we through patience and comfort of the scriptures might have hope" (Ro.15:4).

PERSON/PLACE/THING	SCRIPTURE, OUTLINE AND DISCUSSION
AHASUERUS. *Wealth of. A picture of pride and self-exaltation.*	Est.1:1-9
Immorality of. Ordered a fleshly, carnal display of the queen's beauty. A picture of loose morals and drunkenness.	Est.1:10-12
Decrees of. To divorce Queen Vashti. A picture of unbridled anger and revenge.	Est.1:13-22
Marriage. To Esther. A picture of a morally corrupt man contrasted with a true believer of strong character.	Est.2:1-23
Decrees of. To find a new queen. A picture of selfishness and moral corruption in seeking true love.	Est.2:1-4
ESTHER. *Character of. A picture of moral purity and strong character.*	Est.2:5-20
MORDECAI. *Warning by. To King Ahasuerus. Of the assassination plot against him. A picture of believers warning others to prepare for death.*	Est.2:21-23
HAMAN. *Anger of. Against Mordecai and the Jews. A picture of extreme prejudice and hatred.*	Est.3:1-6
Plot of. To exterminate the Jews. A picture of brutality and horrifying evil.	Est.3:7-15
MORDECAI. *Anguish of. Reason. The decree to kill all the Jews. A picture of the desperate need for an intercessor who can plead for mercy.*	Est.4:1-9
ESTHER. *Courage of. Risking her life to save her people. A picture of the desperate need for courage, prayer, and fasting.*	Est.4:10-17
MORDECAI. *Honor bestowed upon. Unexpectedly. A picture of God's providence, guidance, and love for His people.*	Est.6:1-14
HAMAN. *Humiliation of. In public. Because Mordecai was honored instead of him. A clear picture of God humbling the prideful and exalting the humble.*	Est.6:11-14
Exposure and downfall of. A picture of reaping exactly what one sows.	Est.7:1-10
Execution of. A clear picture of the surety of judgment.	Est.7:7-10
ESTHER. *Desperate intercession of. For the life of the Jews. A picture of being delivered through prayer.*	Est.8:1-17
Rewarded. By King Ahasuerus. A picture of the believer being rewarded for faithful service.	Est.8:1-2
Plea of. For her people. A picture of the believer's intercession.	Est.8:3-6
AHASUERUS. *Decrees of. That the Jews could fight against the enemy. A picture of proclaiming the salvation of God's people.*	Est.8:7-17
PURIM. *Feast of. Celebration of. A picture of the believer's victory in spiritual warfare.*	Est.9:1–10:3
JEWS. *Preparation of. For war. A picture of the believer being fully prepared for the attack of the enemy.*	Est.9:1-19
PURIM. *Feast of. Institution of. A picture of the believer celebrating and rejoicing over God's wonderful deliverance.*	Est.9:20-32

REMEMBER: When you look up a subject and turn to the Scripture reference, you have not just the Scripture but also an outline and a discussion (commentary) of the Scripture and subject.

This is one of the GREAT FEATURES of *The Preacher's Outline & Sermon Bible*®. Once you have all the volumes, you will have not only what all other Bible indexes give you, that is, a list of all the subjects and their Scripture references, but in addition you will have...

- an outline of every Scripture and subject in the Bible
- a discussion (commentary) on every Scripture and subject
- every subject supported by other Scripture, already written out or cross referenced

DISCOVER THE UNIQUE VALUE for yourself. Quickly glance below to the following subject of the Index. It is:

> **ACCUSATION**
> Example. By Haman. Against
> the Jews. Of being lawbreakers.
> 3:8-11

Turn to the first reference. Glance at the Scripture and the outline, then read the commentary. You will immediately see the TREMENDOUS BENEFIT of the INDEX of *The Preacher's Outline & Sermon Bible*®.

OUTLINE AND SUBJECT INDEX

ABASEMENT (See HUMILIATION)

ACCUSATIONS (See CHARGES; PERSECUTION)
Example. By Haman. Against the Jews. Of being lawbreakers. 3:8-11

ADVICE (See COUNSEL)
Example. To King Ahasuerus.
By Haman. On how to honor a citizen. 6:7-9
By his counselors.
To dethrone Queen Vashti. 1:19-20
To search for a new queen. 2:2-4

AHASUERUS
Advisors of. Listed. 1:14
Anger of. Against Haman. Reasons for. 7:7-10
Approach of. By Esther. Was given favor. 5:1-8
Character.
A man of unrestrained appetites. 1:1-22
Anger. 1:12
Morally Corrupt. 1:10-12
Ungrateful. Did not think to reward Mordecai immediately for saving his life. 2:23
Vengeful. 1:13-15, 19-21
Decrees of.
Called for a new queen. 1:19-22
Divorced Queen Vashti. A picture of unbridled anger and revenge. 1:19-22
Extermination. To allow the slaughter of the Jews. 3:10-15
Honored Mordecai. For saving his life. 6:7-11
Levied a tax. 10:1
Ordered the execution of Haman. 7:7-10

Self-Defense.
That the Jews could fight against the enemy. A picture of proclaiming the salvation of God's people. 8:7-17
To find a new queen. A picture of selfishness and moral corruption in seeking true love. 2:1-4
Immorality of. Ordering the sexual display of Queen Vashti. A picture of loose morals and drunkenness. 1:10-12
King. Of Persia. 1:1
Kingdom of. Was very large. 1:1-9
Life of. Summarized. 10:1-3
Marriage. To Esther. A picture of a morally corrupt man contrasted with a true believer of strong character. 2:1-23
Plot against. To assassinate him.
Foiled. Because Mordecai overheard the plot and reported it to Queen Esther. 2:21-23
Pride of. Held great banquets to honor his kingdom and himself. 1:3-8
Reign. Time of. 486-465 B.C. 1:1-22, Intro.
Wealth of. A picture of pride and self-exaltation. 1:1-9

ALCOHOL (See DRUNKENNESS)

ANGER
Sinful. Example. Haman. Had tremendous **a.** against Mordecai. 3:1-6; 5:13-14
Unjustified. Example. King Ahasuerus sought revenge against Queen Vashti. 1:13-22

ANGUISH (See SORROW)

ANNIHILATION (See HOLOCAUST)

ANTI-SEMITISM
Example.
By Haman. 3:1-6
By many enemies in Susa. 9:5, 16

APPETITES (See DESIRES)

APPROACHING
God (See GOD, Approaching)
The king. Example. By Esther. 5:1-2

ARROGANCE (See PRIDE)

ASSASSINATION
Attempt. Against King Ahasuerus.
By two of his officers. 2:21
Found out by Mordecai. 2:22-23

ATTACK (See PERSECUTION; WAR)

BATTLE (See WAR)

BELIEF (See BELIEVERS; GOD, Trust in)

BELIEVER
Care for. By God. 6:1-10, Thgt.1
Duty.
To God.
To be prepared for spiritual warfare. 9:1-19, Thgt.1
To be thankful for His blessings. 5:9-14, Thgt.1
To bear a strong, testimony. 8:3-6, Thgt.1
To guard against boasting and pride. 5:9-14, Thgt.1
To others.
To never allow hatred or prejudice within. 3:1-6, Thgt.1
To serve. 10:1-3, Thgt.1

To serve. 10:1-3, Thgt.1

To use extra resources to help meet the needs of the world. 1:1-9, Thgt.1; 8:3-6, Thgt.1

To the church.
 To make intercession for other believers. 8:3-6, Thgt.1
 To support the church financially. 8:3-6, Thgt.1

Persecution of. Reason. Because they stand for righteousness and the cause of Christ. 9:1-10:3, Intro.

Position of. Fellow-heirs with Jesus Christ. 8:1-2, Thgt.1

Preparation by. For spiritual warfare. How to. 9:1-19, Thgt.1

Promises to. (See GOD, Promises by)

Rewards of. For being faithful. Are many. 8:1-2, Thgt.1

Trust by. In God. Pictured by Esther's courage in time of crisis. 4:16-5:2

BIBLE (See WARNINGS, In Scripture)

BIGTHAN
Execution of. For his assassination plot. 2:23
Official. Of the palace of King Ahasuerus. 2:21
Plotted. To kill King Ahasuerus. 2:21

BLAME (See ACCUSATIONS; PERSECUTION)

BOASTING
Consequences of. Discussed. 5:9-14, Thgt.1
Duty toward. By every believer. To guard against. 5:9-14, Thgt.1
Example. Haman. B. about his wealth and position. 5:10-12

BONDAGE
To sin. Fact. Can be broken by Jesus Christ. 8:7-17, Thgt.1

BRAGGING (See BOASTING; PRIDE)

CAPITAL PUNISHMENT (See EXECUTION)

CARNALITY (See IMMORALITY)

CHARACTER
Immoral. Fact. Is common in the world. 2:1-4, Thgt.1
Strong.
 Defined. 2:1-23, Intro.
 Example. Esther. 2:5-20

CHARGES (See ACCUSATIONS)

CHRIST (See JESUS CHRIST)

CIRCUMSTANCES
Bad. How to handle. 5:1-8, Thgt.1
Facing of. (See CRISIS)

COMMITMENT (See FAITHFULNESS)

COMPASSION (See SALVATION)

CONCEIT (See PRIDE)

CONFLICT (See PERSECUTION; WAR)

CONQUERING (See VICTORY)

CONQUEST (See VICTORY)

CONSPIRACY (See PLOTTING)

CORRUPTION
Moral. (See IMMORALITY)

COURAGE
Example. Esther. Risked her life to save her people, the Jews. 7:3-6

CRAVINGS (See DESIRES)

CRISIS
Answer to. Trusting in the Lord. 4:10-17, Thgt.1
Example. The Jews were marked for death by the king. 4:7
Facing of. In life.
 Discussed. 4:1-17, Intro.
 How to. 5:1-14, Intro.
Severe. Kinds of. Listed. 4:1-17, Intro.

CRITICISM (See PERSECUTION)

DEATH
Danger of.
 Example.
  Ahasuerus' servants plotted to kill him. 2:21
  The Jews were to be killed at the end of the year by decree of the king. 3:10-14
 Warning against. By Mordecai. 3:22-23
Decree concerning. The Jews were to be killed at the end of the year by decree of the king. 3:10-14

DEDICATION (See FAITHFULNESS)

DEGRADATION (See HUMILIATION)

DELIVERANCE
Example. The Jews.
 Through the intercessory work of Esther. 7:3-6, 8:3-17

Were allowed to defend themselves from the decree of death. 8:9-9:17
From sin. By Jesus Christ. Fact. Is available to all. 8:7-17, Thgt.1; 9:1-10:3, Intro.
Rejoicing over. Example. By the Jews after their great victory over the enemy. 9:20-32
Through prayer. Pictured by the d. of the Jews from death. 8:1-17

DEPRAVITY (See EVIL; SIN)

DESIRES
Unrestrained. Fact. Causes major problems in the world today. 1:1-22, Intro.

DETERMINATION (See FAITHFULNESS)

DILIGENCE (See FAITHFULNESS)

DISCRIMINATION (See ANTISEMITISM; PREJUDICE)

DISGRACE (See HUMILIATION)

DISHONOR (See HUMILIATION)

DRUNKENNESS
Example. Ahasuerus. 1:10
Sin of. How it enslaves a person. Discussed. 1:10-12, Thgt.1

DUTY
Of believers. (See BELIEVERS, Duty)

ELIMINATION (See HOLOCAUST)

EMBARASSMENT (See HUMILIATION)

ENDURANCE (See FAITHFULNESS)

ENEMIES
In life. Fact. There will be people who oppose us. 9:1-10:3, Intro.
Of the Jews.
 Destruction of. 9:1-19
 Haman. 3:1-15
 Those prejudiced against the Jews. 9:5-16

ESTHER
Appeals.
 By.
  To King Ahasuerus. For her and her people to be saved. 7:3-6
  To Mordecai. For support with fasting and prayer. 4:16
  To. By Mordecai. For her to help save the Jews. 4:10-17

Book of. Plot. The attempted extermination of the Jews. 3:1-6, Thgt.1
Character.
A picture of moral purity and strong character.
Brave. Risked her life to save her people. 4:1-10:3
Good example to all women. 2:5-20
Morally pure. 2:9
Not presumptuous. 2:15
Strong. 2:5-20
Courage of.
Approached the king without being summoned. 5:1-2
Demonstrated trust in God. 4:16-5:2
Risked her life to save her people. A picture of the desperate need for courage, prayer and fasting. 4:10-17
Cousin. Of Mordecai. 2:7
Daughter. Of Abihail. 2:15
Elevation of. To queen. 1:1-2:23
Exposure by. Of Haman and his evil plot. 7:1-6
Heritage of.
Concealed. 2:10
Jewish. 2:5-7
Intercession by. To the king.
A picture of being delivered through prayer. 8:1-17
To save her people, the Jews. 7:3-6; 8:3-6
Name.
Hebrew. Hadassah. 2:7
Persian. Esther. 2:5-7
Plea of. For her people. A picture of the believer's intercession. 8:3-6
Raising of. By Mordecai, her cousin, because E. was an orphan. 2:7
Rewarded. By King Ahasuerus. Because she was a faithful servant. 8:1-2
Trust. In God. Seen over and over again in her life. 5:1-8, Thgt.1

EVIL (See **SIN**)
Depth of. Example. Haman.
Filled with hate. 3:5
Wanted to eliminate all Jews. 3:7-15
Of the human heart. Discussed. 3:7-15, Thgt.1

EXECUTION
Example.
Haman. 7:10
Haman's sons. 9:6-10
The assassins, Bigthan and Teresh. 2:23

EXTERMINATION (See **HOLO-CAUST**)

EXTRAVAGANCE
Example. King Ahasuerus held great banquets to honor his kingdom and himself. 1:3-8
Warnings against. **E.** while ignoring the needs of the world will be judged by God severely. 1:1-9, Thgt.1

FAITH
In the Lord's guidance. Example. Esther. 5:1-8

FAITHFULNESS
Example.
Esther. 8:1-2
Mordecai. 8:1-2
To God. Rewards of. Fact. Are great. 8:1-2, Thgt.1

FASTING
Example.
Esther and her servants. 4:16
Mordecai and the Jews in Susa. 4:16-17
Need for. Discussed. 4:10-17, Thgt.1

FEASTS
Of Purim.
Established. To celebrate the great deliverance of the Jews from their enemies and the attempted holocaust. 9:20-32
Name. Meaning of. Lots. Because God providentially oversaw the casting of the lots. 9:23-28

FESTIVAL (See **FEASTS**)

FLESH
Desires of. Fact.
Can enslave us. 1:1-22, Intro.
Leads to lawless and violent behavior. 1:1-22, Intro.

FORGIVENESS (See **SALVATION**)

GENOCIDE (See **HOLOCAUST**)

GOD
Attitudes toward. By all people. Whether they trust God. 5:1-14, Intro.
Care of. For those who trust in Him. Discussed. 6:1-10, Thgt.1
Guidance by.
Example.
Esther. Took just the right steps at the right time to save her people. 5:1-4
Mordecai. Was honored by the intervening work of God. 6:1-10
Fact. Is promised to the believer. 5:1-14, Intro.
Need for. In bad circumstances. 5:1-8, Thgt.1

Judgment by. Fact. God will humble the prideful. 6:11-14, Thgt.1
Love of. Of every person. Discussed. 6:1-14, Intro.
Promises by. To those who trust in Him. Listed and discussed. 5:1-14, Intro.
Protection by.
Example.
Of Mordecai. God. caused Mordecai to be honored by the king. 6:1-10
Of the Jews. God. worked circumstances about so that the Jews were saved extermination. 7:1-9:28
Providence. (See Sovereignty of, below)
Seeking. Result. Gives peace even in time of crisis. 4:10-17, Thgt.1
Sovereignty of.
Definition of. God's guidance and care. 6:1-10, Thgt.1
Example.
Kept King Ahasuerus from sleeping. 6:1
Moved on King Ahasuerus' hard heart to honor Mordecai. 6:3-11
Moved on King Ahasuerus' mind to read how Mordecai had saved his life. 6:2
Was moving behind the scenes to protect the Jews from Haman. 3:7
Fact.
Does not relieve us of our duty. 9:1-19, Thgt.1
God. does intervene in our lives. 6:1-14, Intro.
Pictured. In the honoring of Mordecai by King Ahasuerus. 6:1-14
Trusting in.
Example. Esther. 5:1-8
Result. Peace. 4:10-17, Thgt.1
Warnings by. (See **WARNINGS**)

GOVERNMENT (See **PERSIA**)

GREATNESS
How to become. By serving others. 10:1-3, Thgt.1

GUIDANCE
By God (See **GOD**, Guidance by)

HAMAN
Acts of. Secured an order to exterminate the Jews. 3:6-15
Anger of. Against Mordecai and the Jews. A picture of extreme prejudice and hatred. 3:1-6
Character.
Angry. 3:5; 5:13
Arrogant. 3:5
Boastful. 5:11-12
Evil. 3:6-15

Extremely prejudiced against the Jews. 3:1-15

Superstitious. 3:7

Conflict. With Mordecai. Mordecai would not bow down to him. 3:2-5

Evil of.

Depth of. Was willing to wipe out an entire people because of his hatred for one man. 3:7-15

Lied. Against the Jews. Accusing them of breaking the law. 3:8-11

Murderous. Would not be satisfied until Mordecai was dead. 5:13-14

Execution of.

A clear picture of the surety of judgment. 7:7-10

Reasons. 7:7-10

Exposure of. His evil. A picture of reaping exactly what one sows. 7:1-10

Foolishness of. Knew nothing of the One True God. 3:7

Hate of. Hated Mordecai so much that he could not be satisfied with life. 3:5; 5:13

Heritage. Agagite. 3:1

Humiliation of. In public. Because Mordecai was honored instead of him. A clear picture of God humbling the prideful and exalting the humble. 6:10-14

Judgment of. Was forced to honor Mordecai, whom he hated. 6:10-11

Plot of. To exterminate the Jews. A picture of brutality and horrifying evil. 3:7-15

Promotion of. By King Ahasuerus. Ordered everyone to bow down to **H**. 3:1-3

Over all the other princes. 3:1

Sons of.

Execution of. 9:6-10

Listed. 9:7-9

Public display. Of their bodies. 9:13

HATE

Example.

Citizens of Susa. Against the Jews. 9:5, 16

Haman. Had tremendous **h**. against Mordecai. 3:1-6; 5:13

Warning against. Is condemned by God. 3:1-6, Thgt.1

HAUGHTINESS (See PRIDE)

HEART

Depravity of. Discussed. 3:7-15, Thgt.1

Evil of. Examples. Of history. Listed. 3:7-15, Thgt.1

HOARDING

Sin of. Discussed. 1:1-9, Thgt.1

HOLOCAUST

Defeated. In a great victory by the Jews. 9:1-25

Plot for. By Haman. To exterminate the Jews. 3:7-15

HONOR (See WORSHIP)

HUMANITY (See SOCIETY; WORLD)

Equality of. Reason all **h**. is equal. Discussed. 3:1-6, Thgt.1

Needs of. Jesus Christ. To intercede for mercy. 4:1-9, Thgt.1

HUMILIATION

Example.

Haman. Was **h**. by having to parade Mordecai around in the streets. 6:10-11

Haman's sons. Dead bodies were placed on the execution stakes, because they were enemies of the state. 9:13

IMAGINATIONS

Wicked. Worst kind of. Example. Haman. Tried to eliminate all the Jews. 3:7-15

IMMORALITY

Example. King Ahasuerus. 1:10-12; 2:1-4

Problem of.

Fact. Is common in the world. 2:1-23, Intro.

In women. Discussed. 2:5-20, Thgt.1

Reasons for. Discussed. 2:1-4, Thgt.1

Warnings against. In Scripture. 2:1-4, Thgt.1

INTERCESSION

Answer. To the many dangers of the world. 8:1-17, Intro.

Example. Esther. For the life of her people. 7:3-6; 8:3-6

For humanity. For mercy from God. Fact. Can only be found in Jesus Christ. 4:1-9, Thgt.1

Need for.

By humanity. To be saved. Fact. Is found only in Jesus Christ. 4:1-9, Thgt.1

Example. The Jews. To avoid being eliminated. 4:1-9; 7:3-6; 8:3-6

JEHOVAH (See GOD)

JESUS CHRIST

Names-Titles.

Deliverer. 4:1-9, Thgt.1

Intercessor. 4:1-9, Thgt.1

Perfect One. 4:1-9, Thgt.1

Savior. 4:1-9, Thgt.1

Need for. By humanity. To be saved. 4:1-9, Thgt.1

Power of. Delivers from.

All hate and prejudice. 9:1-10:3, Intro.

Death. 8:7-17, Thgt.1

The bondage of sin. 8:7-17, Thgt.1

Works of.

Intercedes on behalf of those who trust in Him. 4:1-9, Thgt.1

Vanquished death for all believers. 2:21-23, Thgt.1; 8:7-17, Thgt.1

JEWS

Deliverance of.

From the decree of death. Were allowed to fight back. 8:7-17

Proclamation of. 8:16-17

Discrimination against. By many in Susa. 9:5, 16

Enemies of.

Haman. 3:7-15

Many in Susa. 9:5, 16

Feasts of. Purim. Established when they were delivered from the death decree. 9:26-28

Plot against.

By Haman. To exterminate them. 3:7-15

Stopped.

By the intercession of Esther. 7:1-4

By the victory in battle by the Jews. 9:1-25

Prejudice against. Example. By Haman. 3:1-6

Preparation of. For war. A picture of the believer being fully prepared for the attack of the enemy. 9:1-19

Triumph of. Over the enemy, ending the potential holocaust. 9:1-10:3

Wars of. Fought against the enemies who tried to annihilate them. 9:1-25

JOY

Reasons for. Victory over the enemy. 9:20-32

JUDGMENT (See JUSTICE)

By God. Fact. God will humble the prideful. 6:11-14, Thgt.1

Surety of. By God.

According to our works. 7:7-10, Thgt.1

Example. The execution of Haman. 7:7-10

JUSTICE (See JUDGMENT)

KINGS (See PERSIA, King)

LAW OF GOD (See REAPING)

LAWLESSNESS
Reason for. Unrestrained desires. 1:1-22, Intro.

LIFE
Changes in. Fact. Is due to divine providence. 6:1-14, Intro.

LORD, The (See GOD)

LOST (See UNBELIEVERS; WORLD)

LOTS
Casting of. Example. By Haman. To determine the day to carry out his evil plan to exterminate the Jews. 3:7

LOVE
True. Longing for. Fact. Is the need immoral people are trying to fulfill. 2:1-4, Thgt.1

LOYALTY (See FAITHFULNESS)

LUST
Example. King Ahasuerus and his guests were filled with l. passion. 1:10-12

LYING
Example. Haman. L. about the Jews, accusing them of being lawbreakers. 3:8-11

MEDIATOR (See INTERCESSOR)

MEN
Abuses by. Of women. Example. King Ahasuerus. 1:10-12

MERCY (See SALVATION)
Need for. From God. Discussed. 4:10-19, Thgt.1

MESSIAH (See JESUS CHRIST)

MORALITY
Strong. Need for. Discussed. 2:1-23, Intro.
Weak.
Commonness of. Fact. Is a problem in the world. 2:1-23, Intro.
Example. King Ahasuerus and his guests engaged in an immoral feast. 1:10-12

MORALS (See MORALITY)

MORDECAI
Acts of. Overheard an assassination plot against the king and reported it, saving the life of the king. 2:21-23

Anguish of.
Discovered. By Esther. 4:10-17
Reason. The decree to kill all the Jews. A picture of the desperate need for an intercessor who can plead for mercy. 4:1-9
Conflicts of. Hated by Haman. 3:5
Cousin. To Esther. 2:7
Faithfulness of. Discussed. 8:1-2
Greatness of. Was obtained because he served others. 10:1-3, Thgt.1
Heritage. Benjamite. Of the Jews. 2:5
Honor bestowed upon. Unexpectedly. A picture of God's providence, guidance, and love for His people. 6:1-14
Kindness of. Adopted and raised the Esther, because she was an orphan. 2:5-7
Life of. Summarized. 10:1-3
Sorrow of. (See Anguish of, above)
Warning by. To King Ahasuerus. Of the assassination plot against him. A picture of believers warning others to prepare for death. 2:21-23
Wisdom of.
Advised Esther not to reveal her Jewish heritage. 2:10
Found out a conspiracy against the king and reported it. 2:21-23

NEEDS
For God. Confession of. Fact. Is required for salvation. 5:1-14, Intro.
Of humankind. For an intercessor. 4:1-9, Thgt.1

OFFICIALS (See PERSIA, Officials)

OPPOSITION (See ACCUSATIONS; PERSECUTION; WAR)

OPPRESSION (See PERSECUTION)

OVERCOMING (See VICTORY)

PEACE
Source. Trust in God. 4:10-17, Thgt.1

PERSECUTION
Of believers. Reason. Because they stand for righteousness and the cause of Christ. 9:1-10:3, Intro.
Of the Jews. Example. The Persian decree of extermination. 3:10-14

PERSEVERANCE (See FAITHFULNESS)

PERSIA
Government of. Described. 1:1-9
Kings.
Ahasuerus. 1:1

Former.
Cyrus the Great. 550-530 B.C. 1:1-9
Darius the Mede. 520-486 B.C. 1:1-9
Officials.
Advisors. Listed. 1:14
Assassins. Bigthan and Teresh. Found out and executed due to Mordecai's quick action. 2:21-23
Keeper. Of the women.
After selected by the king. Shaashgaz. 2:14
Before selected by the king. Hegai. 2:3, 8, 15
Princes. Over each of the 127 provinces. 1:1-2
Policies of. Concerning decrees of the king. Could not be cancelled. 8:5-8
Queen.
Esther. Elevated to that position. 1:1-2:23
Search for. To replace Vashti. 2:2-17
Vashti. Dethroned. 1:19-21
Wealth of. Described. 1:5-7

PERSISTANCE (See FAITHFULNESS)

PETITION (See PRAYER)

PLOTTING
Example.
Bigthan and Teresh. P. to kill King Ahasuerus. 2:21
Haman. P. to eliminate the Jews. 3:7-15

POSITION
Boasting about. Example. Haman boasted about his wealth and p. 5:10-12

PRAISE (See WORSHIP)

PRAYER
Need for. Example. Esther asked Mordecai to have everyone p. before she made request of the king. 4:16
With fasting. Need for. In desperate situations. 4:10-17, Thgt.1

PREJUDICE
Evil of. Discussed. 3:1-6, Thgt.1
Example. Haman. Was p. against the Jews because of his hatred for Mordecai. 3:1-6
Problem of. Fact. Is in every society. 3:1-15, Intro.

PREPARATION
For spiritual warfare. How to. 9:1-19, Thgt.1

PRESERVATION
Example.
Of Mordecai. God caused Mordecai to be honored, protecting him from Haman. 6:1-10
Of the Jews. God worked circumstances about so that the Jews were saved extermination. 7:1-9:28

PRIDE
Duty toward. By every believer. To guard against. 5:9-14, Thgt.1
Evil of. Discussed. 6:11-14, Thgt.1
Example.
Haman.
Assumed the king would honor him. 6:6
Bragged about his wealth and position. 5:10-12
King Ahasuerus. Held great banquets to honor his kingdom and himself. 1:3-8
Fact. Prevents a person from being saved from sin. 5:1-14, Intro.
Judgment of. Fact. God will humble the **p.** 6:11-14, Thgt.1

PROCLAMATION (See **WITNESSING**)

PROMINENCE
Elevation to. Example. Esther was elevated to the **p.** position of queen of Persia. 1:1-2:23

PROVIDENCE (See **GOD**, Sovereignty of)

PURIM
Feast of.
Celebration of. A picture of the believer's victory in spiritual warfare. 9:1-10:3
Instituted. By Mordecai and Queen Esther. A picture of the believer celebrating and rejoicing over God's wonderful deliverance. 9:20-32
Meaning of. To celebrate the great deliverance of the Jews from their enemies and the attempted holocaust. 9:20-32
Name. Meaning of. Lots. Because God providentially oversaw the casting of the lots. 9:23-28

QUEEN (See **PERSIA**, Queen)

RANSOM (See **SALVATION**)

REAPING
Fact. A person will **r.** what he sows. 7:1-10, Intro.
What one sows. Pictured. In Haman's execution on the gallows he had prepared for someone else. 7:10

REBELLION (See **EVIL; SIN**)

RECONCILIATION (See **SALVATION**)

REDEMPTION (See **SALVATION**)

REJOICING (See **JOY**)

REQUEST (See **PRAYER**)

RESCUE (See **DELIVERANCE; SALVATION**)

REVENGE
Example. By King Ahasuerus. Against Queen Vashti. 1:13-22

REWARDS
Basis of. Faithful service. 8:1-2, Thgt.1

RICHES (See **WEALTH**)

RULERS (See **PERSIA**)

SALVATION
Requirement for. Trusting in God. 5:1-14, Intro.

SAVIOR (See **JESUS CHRIST**)

SCRIPTURE (**WARNINGS**, Of Scripture)

SEEKING GOD (See **GOD**, Seeking)

SELF-CENTEREDNESS (See **PRIDE**)

SELF-EXALTATION (See **PRIDE**)

SELF-SUFFICIENCY
Fact. Prevents a person from being saved from sin. 5:1-14, Intro.

SELFISHNESS
Example. King Ahasuerus. Held great extravagant banquets to honor his kingdom and himself. 1:3-8
Sin of. Discussed. 1:1-9, Thgt.1

SERVICE
Example. Mordecai. 10:2-3
Fact. Is a requirement by God. 10:1-3, Thgt.1
Result. Greatness. 10:1-3, Thgt.1

SHAME (See **HUMILIATION**)

SIN (See **EVIL**)
Binding power of. Fact. Can be broken by Jesus Christ. 8:7-17, Thgt.1
Exposure of. Surety of. 7:1-6, Thgt.1
Of drinking. Enslavement by. Discussed. 1:10-12, Thgt.1

Of hoarding. Discussed. 1:1-9, Thgt.1
Of pride. Will inevitably be judged by humbling the person. 6:11-14, Thgt.1

SOCIETY (See **HUMANITY; WORLD**)
Problems of. Reasons for. Discussed. 1:1-22, Intro.

SORROW
Example. Mordecai. Over the decree to kill all the Jews. 4:1-9
Source. Crises in life. 4:1-17, Intro.

SOUL-WINNING (See **WITNESSING**)

SOVEREIGNTY (See **GOD**, Sovereignty of)

SOWING AND REAPING (See **REAPING**)

SPIRITUAL WARFARE (See **WAR**, Spiritual)

STEADFASTNESS (See **FAITHFULNESS**)

SUPPLICATION (See **PRAYER**)

TERESH
Execution of. For his assassination plot. 2:23
Official. Of the palace of King Ahasuerus. 2:21
Plotted. To kill King Ahasuerus. 2:21

THOUGHTS (See **IMAGINATIONS**)

TRANSGRESSION (See **EVIL; SIN**)

TRIUMPH (See **VICTORY**)

TRUTH
Quality of. Will eventually come out. 7:1-6, Thgt.1

UNBELIEVER
Definition. One who does not trust in God. 5:1-14, Intro.
Trust by. Fact.
Is in human strength and ability. 5:1-14, Intro.
Is not in God; therefore God will withhold His blessings. 5:1-14, Intro.

URGES (See **DESIRES**)

VASHTI
Appearance of. Was very beautiful. 1:11

Dethroned. Because she refused to be put on display. 1:19-21
Queen. Of Persia. 1:9, 11, 16

VICTORY
Over the enemy. By the Jews. Was a triumphal celebration. 9:1–10:3

VINDICTIVENESS (See **REVENGE**)

VIOLENCE
Reasons for. Unrestrained desires. 1:1-22, Intro.

WAR (See **PERSECUTION**)
Of the Jews. Fought against the enemies who tried to annihilate them. 9:1-25
Spiritual. Preparation for. How to. 9:1-19, Thgt.1

WARFARE (See **WAR**)

WARNINGS
Of God. Condemns hatred and malice. 3:1-6, Thgt.1
Of Scripture. Against.
Boasting. 5:9-14, Thgt.1
Extravagance. 1:1-9, Thgt.1
Hate. 5:9-14, Thgt.1
Immorality. 2:1-4, Thgt.1
Pride. 5:9-14, Thgt.1; 6:11-14, Thgt.1
Sin. Will eventually be exposed. 7:1-6, Thgt.1

WEALTH
Boasting about. Haman. Boasted about his **w.** and position. 5:10-12

Misuse of. Example. King Ahasuerus held great banquets to honor his kingdom and himself. 1:3-8
Of Persia.
Exhibited. By King Ahasuerus. 1:5-7
Was enormous. 1:3-8

WHOLEHEARTEDNESS (See **FAITHFULNESS**)

WICKEDNESS (See **EVIL**; **SIN**)

WIFE
Abuse of. Example. By King Ahasuerus. Demanded that Vashti to put on a sexual display for his guests. 1:11

WITNESSING
Definition. Telling others.
Jesus Christ can deliver them from death. 8:7-17, Thgt.1
They can be set free from the bondage of the world. 8:7-17, Thgt.1
Example. The Jews were w. to God's delivering power, causing many to convert to Judaism. 8:16-17
Of good news. By the Jews. Of their deliverance. 8:16

WOMEN
Abuse of.
Discussed. 1:10-12, Thgt.1; 1:13-22, Thgt.1
Example. By Ahasuerus, Demanded that the w. put on a sexual display for his guests. 1:11

Character.
Immoral. Problem of. 2:5-20, Thgt.1
Needed. Discussed. 2:5-20, Thgt.1

WORLD (See **HUMANITY**; **SOCIETY**; **UNBELIEVERS**)
Dangers in.
Answer to. Intercession. 8:1-17, Intro.
Fact. Are many. 8:1-17, Intro.
Desires of. Unrestrained. Fact. Causes major problems. 1:1-22, Intro.
Needs of.
Listed. 1:1-9, Thgt.1
Duty toward. Must be met by those who have more than they need. 1:1-9, Thgt.1
Problems of.
Drunkenness. 1:13-22, Thgt.1
Help with. Fact. Is the responsibility of every believer. 8:3-6, Thgt.1
Listed. 8:3-6, Thgt.1
Loose morals. 2:1-23, Intro.
Pride. 5:1-14, Intro.

WORSHIP
Example. By the Jews. After their great deliverance from the enemy. 9:23-32
Reasons for. Because God delivers us from death and its consequences. 9:20-32, Thgt.1

XERXES (See **AHASUERUS**)

YAHWEH (See **GOD**)

PRACTICAL BIBLE HELPS & RESOURCES*

---

* A comprehensive chart of all Biblical Prophets—their times and places of ministry, their messages and practical application—may be found in *The Preacher's Outline & Sermon Bible®, Isaiah* Volumes 1 and 2. The Prophets Chart is also available as a separate booklet to compliment all POSB volumes, especially those containing a book or books written by these dear servants of God. It is our hope that you will access this invaluable tool as you preach, teach, or study about any of God's true prophets.

THE PERSIAN EMPIRE

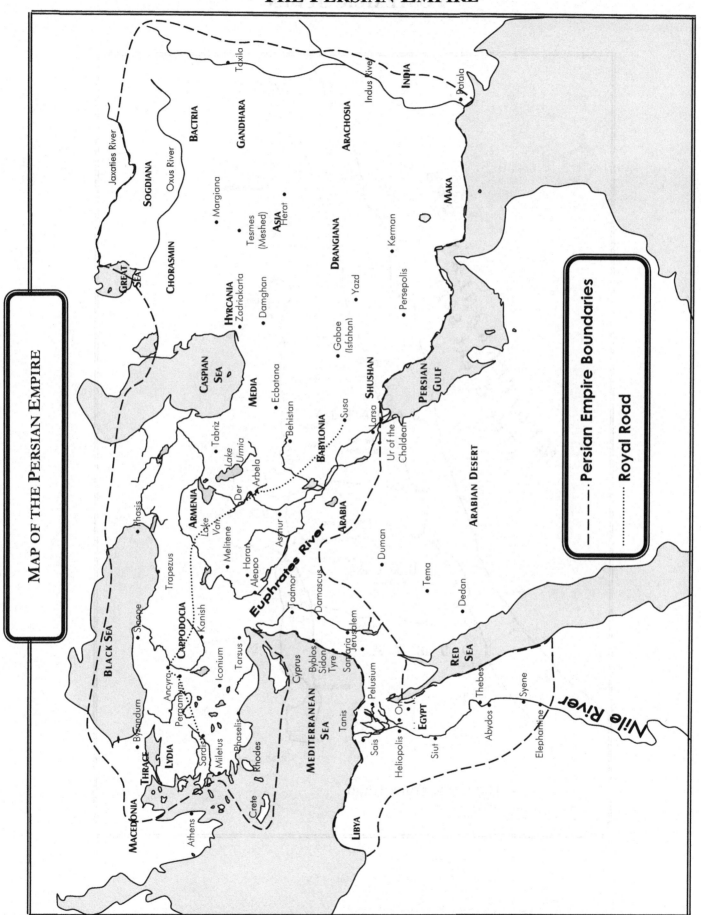

MAP OF THE PERSIAN EMPIRE

Persian Empire Boundaries

Royal Road

INDIA
Taxila
Indus River
Patala
BACTRIA
GANDHARA
ARACHOSIA
Jaxartes River
Oxus River
SOGDIANA
MAKA
Margiana
CHORASMIN
Tesmes (Meshed)
ASIA
Herat
DRANGIANA
Kerman
GREAT SEA
Zadriakarta
Damghan
Yazd
Persepolis
HYRCANIA
CASPIAN SEA
MEDIA
Ecbatana
Gabae (Isfahan)
SHUSHAN
PERSIAN GULF
Tabriz
Behistan
Susa
Lake Urmia
Arbela
BABYLONIA
Larsa
Ur of the Chaldean
ARABIAN DESERT
ARMENIA
Lake Van
Der
Ashur
ARABIA
Phasis
Melitene
Duman
Harah
Aleppo
Euphrates River
Trapezus
Tadmor
Damascus
Tema
Dedan
CAPPODOCIA
Kanish
Samaria
Jerusalem
BLACK SEA
Sinope
Iconium
Tarsus
Cyprus
Byblos
Sidon
Tyre
RED SEA
Thebes
Syene
Ancyra
Pergamum
Phaselis
Pelusium
On
Abydos
Byzandum
MEDITERRANEAN SEA
Tanis
EGYPT
Elephantine
THRACE
LYDIA
Sardis
Miletus
Rhodes
Crete
Sais
Heliopolis
Siut
Nile River
MACEDONIA
Athens
LIBYA

327

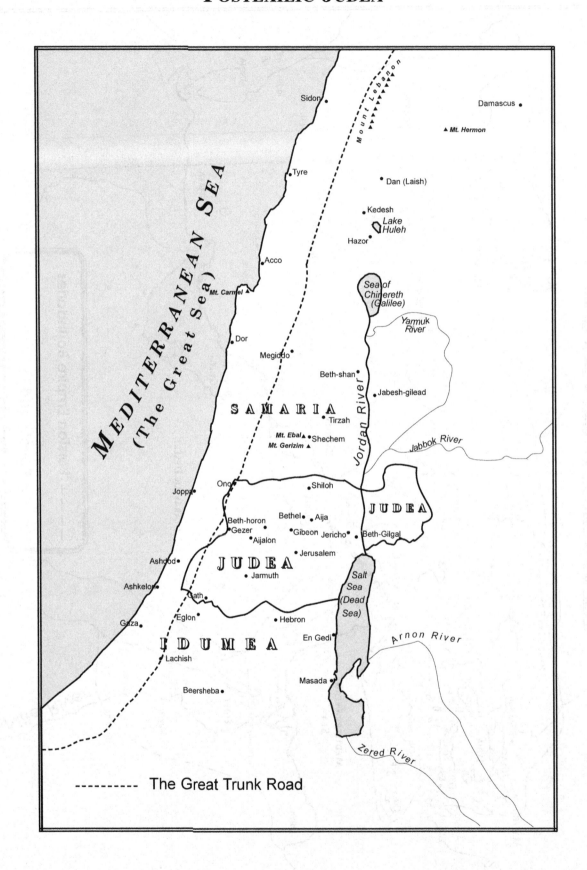

The Great Trunk Road

NEHEMIAH'S WALL

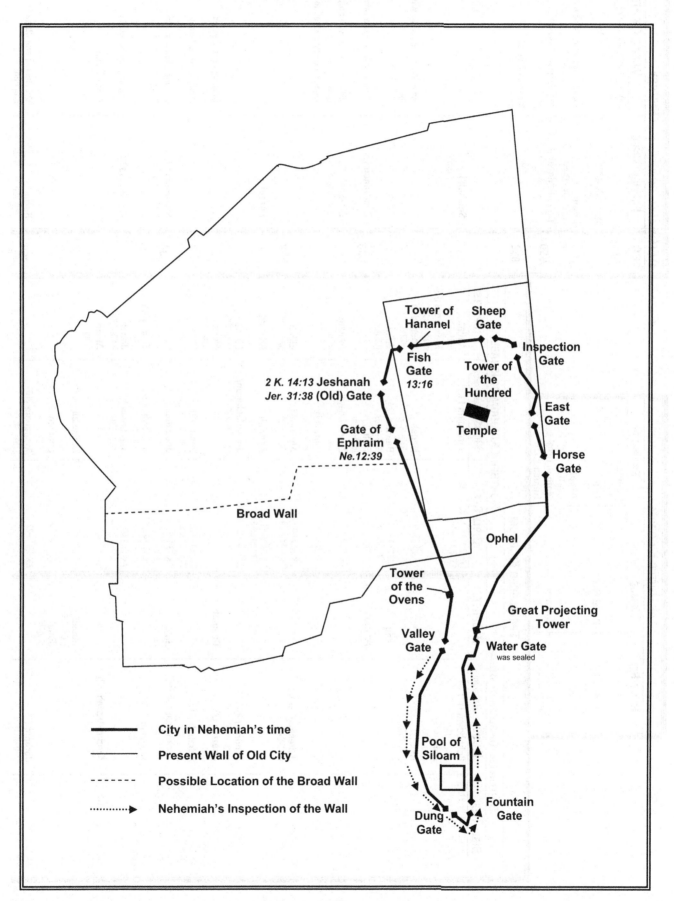

Tower of Hananel

Sheep Gate

Inspection Gate

Fish Gate 13:16

Tower of the Hundred

East Gate

2 K. 14:13 Jeshanah
Jer. 31:38 (Old) Gate

Temple

Gate of Ephraim
Ne. 12:39

Horse Gate

Broad Wall

Ophel

Tower of the Ovens

Great Projecting Tower

Valley Gate

Water Gate
was sealed

Pool of Siloam

Fountain Gate

Dung Gate

City in Nehemiah's time

Present Wall of Old City

Possible Location of the Broad Wall

Nehemiah's Inspection of the Wall

TIMELINE OF KINGS, PROPHETS AND HISTORY*

HISTORY

DATE BC	FOREIGN KINGS	WORLD EVENTS
1000	Ashur-Rabi II (1010–970) (Assyria) Hiram (1003–966) (Tyre) Tiglath-Pileser II (960–935) (Assyria)	David captures Jerusalem (1004) Foundation for the Temple (966) 22nd Egyptian Dynasty (945)
950		
930		Kingdom Divided (930)
	Shishak I (945–924) (Egypt)	Assyria makes peace with Babylon (915)
900	Ben-Hadad I (900) (Syria) Eth-Baal (887–856) (Sidon)	Jehoshaphat leads a revival (865) Elijah's contest with prophets of Baal (857)
850	Hazael (840) (Syria)	Elijah's mantle passed to Elisha (845)
800	Ben-Hadad II (798) (Syria) Ben-Hadad III (773) (Syria)	Carthage established (814) Joash repairs Temple (812) 23rd Egyptian dynasty (800) Olympic games begin (776) Rome founded (753)
750	Rezin (750) (Syria)	Babylonian and Chinese calendar (750)

THE UNITED KINGDOM

BIBLE REF.	KINGS (YEARS REIGNED)	PROPHETS
1 S.16:1-1 K.2:11; 1 Chr.11:1-30	David (40) (1011–971)	Samuel (1095–1015) Gad (1015–950) Asaph (1004) Nathan (1003–931) Heman (971)
1 K.2:12-11:43; 1 Chr.28:1-2 Chr.9:31	Solomon (40) (971–931)	

THE DIVIDED KINGDOM

NORTHERN KINGDOM OF ISRAEL

BIBLE REF.	KINGS (YEARS REIGNED)	PROPHETS
1 K.12:1-24; 12:25-14:20; 2 Chr.10:1-16	Jeroboam I (22) (931–910)	Abijah (931–910) Man from Judah (930) Shemaiah (927)
1 K.15:25-31	Nadab (2) (910–909)	
1 K.15:16-16:7; 2 Chr.16:1-6	Baasha (24) (909–886)	Jehu (886)
1 K.16:6-14	Elah (2) (886–885)	
1 K.16:9-20	Zimri (7 days) (885)	
1 K.16:21-28	Omri (12) (885–874)	Hanani (870)
1 K.16:28-22:40; 2 Chr.18:1-34	Ahab (22) (874–853)	Elijah (860–845)
1 K.22:49-51; 2 K.1:1-18; 2 Chr.20:35-37; 22:1-11	Ahaziah (2) (853–852)	Micaiah (853)
2 K.1:17; 3:1-8:15	Joram/Jehoram (12) (852–841)	Elisha (850–795) Eliezer (849–48)
2 K.9:1-10:36; 2 Chr.22:7-9	Jehu (28) (841–814)	
2 K.13:1-9	Jehoahaz (17) (814–798)	
2 K.13:9-25; 14:8-16	Jehoash (16) (798–782)	
2 K.14:23-29	Jeroboam II (41) (793–753)	Zechariah (797) Jonah (780–765) Amos (750)
2 K.15:8-12	Zechariah (6 mos) (753)	
2 K.15:13-15	Shallum (1 mo) (752)	
2 K.15:16-22	Menahem (10) (752–742)	

SOUTHERN KINGDOM OF JUDAH

BIBLE REF.	KINGS (YEARS REIGNED)	PROPHETS
1 K.12:1-24; 14:21-31; 2 Chr.9:31-12:16	Rehoboam (17) (931–913)	
1 K.15:1-8; 2 Chr.12:16-14:1	Abijah (3) (913–911)	
1 K.15:9-24; 2 Chr.14:1-16:14	Asa (3) (911–870)	Iddo (910) Azariah (896)
1 K.22:41-50; 2 Chr.3:6-14; 2 Chr.17:1-21:1	Jehoshaphat (25) (873–848)	
2 K.8:16-24; 2 Chr.21:1-20	Jehoram (8) (853–841)	Obadiah (845)
2 K.8:25-29; 9:27-29; 2 Chr.22:1-10	Ahaziah (2) (841)	
2 K.11:1-16; 2 Chr.22:10-23:21	Athaliah (7) (841–835)	
2 K.11:17-12:21; 2 Chr.22:11-12; 24:1-27	Joash/Jehoash (40) (835–796)	Joel (830)
2 K.14:1-20; 2 Chr.24:27-25:28	Amaziah (29) (796–767)	
2 K.14:21-22; 15:1-7; 2 Chr.26:1-23	Azariah/Uzziah (52) (792–740)	Hosea (788–723) Jonah (780–765)
2 K.15:32-38; 2 Chr.26:23-27:9	Jotham (16) (750–731)	

THE DIVIDED KINGDOM

SOUTHERN KINGDOM OF JUDAH

BIBLE REF.	KINGS (Years Reigned)	PROPHETS
2 K.15:38-16:20; 2 Chr.27:9-27; Is.7:1-9:1	Ahaz (16) (735-715)	Isaiah (740-690)
		Micah (735-725)
		Oded (733)
2 K.18:1-20:21; 2 Chr.28:27-32:33; Pr.25:1; Is.36:1-39:8	Hezekiah (29) (729-686)	
2 K.20:21-21:18; 2 Chr.32:33-33:20	Manasseh (55) (696-642)	Nahum (663-612)
2 K.21:18-26; 2 Chr.33:20-25	Amon (2) (642-640)	
2 K.21:26-23:30; 2 Chr.33:25-35:27	Josiah (31) (640-609)	Zephaniah (640-609)
		Jeremiah (627-562)
2 K.23:31-33; 2 Chr.36:1-4	Jehoaz/Jehoahaz (3 mos) (609)	Habakkuk (615-598)
2 K.23:34-24:7; 2 Chr.36:5-8	Jehoiakim (11) (608-598)	Daniel (605-535)
2 K.24:8-17; 25:27-30; 2 Chr.36:8-10;	Jehoiachin (3 mos) (598-597)	Ezekiel (593-571)
2 K.24:18-25:21; 2 Chr.36:10-14; Je.21:1-52:11	Zedekiah/Mattaniah (11) (597-586)	
2 K.25:22-26; Je.40:5-41:18	Gedaliah (2 mos) (Appointed by Nebuchadnezzar) (586)	
		Haggai (520)
		Zechariah (520-518)
		Malachi (430)

NORTHERN KINGDOM OF ISRAEL

PROPHETS	KINGS (Years Reigned)	BIBLE REF.
	Pekahiah (2) (742-740)	2 K.15:23-26
	Pekah (20) (752-732) (752-740) (ruled only in Gilead) (740-732) (ruled in Samaria)	2 K.15:27-31
	Hoshea (9) (732-722)	2 K.17:1-23

DATE BC

700 · 650 · 600 · 550 · 500 · 450

HISTORY

FOREIGN KINGS	WORLD EVENTS
Tiglath-Pil[n]eser III [or Pul] (745-727) (Assyria)	Assyria takes control of Northern Kingdom (745-627)
Shalmaneser V (727-722) (Assyria)	Assyria invades Northern Israel (732)
So (727-716) (Egypt)	Fall of Northern Kingdom (722)
Sargon II (710-705) (Assyria)	
Sennacherib (705-681) (Assyria)	Sennacherib defeats Egypt (701) Hezekiah's tunnel (701)
Merodach-Baladan (721-710, 705-704) (Assyria)	185,000 Assyrians killed by God (701)
Tirhakah (690-664) (Egypt)	Sennacherib destroys Babylon (689)
Esarhaddon (681-669) (Assyria)	Josiah's reform (621) Nineveh destroyed (612)
Nabopolassar (626-605) (Assyria)	Battle of Carchemish (605) 1st group of exiles from Judah taken to Babylon (605)
Neco (610-595) (Egypt)	
Nebuchadnezzar II (605-562) (Babylon)	2nd group of exiles from Judah taken to Babylon (597) Fall of Judah—Third group of exiles from Judah taken to Babylon (586)
Evil-Merodach (562-560) (Babylon)	Fall of Babylon to Medo-Persian Empire (539)
Cyrus II (559-530) (Medo-Persia)	Cyrus II decrees that the Jews may return to the Holy Land (538) 1st exiles return to Holy Land with Zerubbabel (537)
Belshazzar (552-539) (Babylon)	1st Temple foundation laid (536) 2nd Temple foundation laid (520) Temple completed (516) Republic of Rome est. (509)
Darius I (521-486) (Medo-Persia)	2nd return under Ezra (458)
Artaxerxes (465-425) (Persia)	3rd return under Nehemiah (445)

*Some dates are approximate.

The resources used for the Timeline are as follows:

1 The Bible
2 Archer, Gleason L. *Encyclopedia of Bible Difficulties.* (Grand Rapids, Michigan: Zondervan Publishing House), 1982.
3 Freedman, David Noel, ed., et. al. *The Anchor Bible Dictionary.* (New York: Doubleday), 1992.
4 Grun, Bernard. *The Timetables of History.* 3rd ed. (New York: Simon & Schuster), 1991.
5 Kaiser, Walter C. *A History of Israel.* (Nashville, Tennessee: Broadman & Holman Publishers), 1998.
6 Silverman, David P., ed. *Ancient Egypt.* (New York: Oxford University Press), 1997.

SACRED DAYS IN THE HEBREW CALENDAR
AND THEIR PROPHETIC SYMBOLISM

NAME OF FEAST OR EVENT	OLD TESTAMENT PURPOSE	NEW TESTAMENT SYMBOLISM	CALENDAR TIME	FARM SEASON (Crops/ Weather)
The Festival of Passover	To remember God's judgment and deliverance from Egyptian bondage. (Le.23:6; Nu.9:5; Jos.5:10; 2 K.23:22; 2 Chr.35:1)	A symbol of Christ our Passover who was sacrificed to deliver us from the judgment of God. (Mt.26:17; Lu.2:41; Lu.22:15; He.11:28)	*Hebrew Time*: The 1st Month [Abib or Nisan], 14th Day *Secular Equivalent*: March - April	Harvesting barley & flax; Later Spring rains.***
The Festival of Unleavened Bread	To recall the need and urgency to leave Egypt (a symbol of the world). (Ex.12:17-18; Ex.13:6-7; Ex.23:15; Ex.34:18; Le.23:6; Nu.28:17; De.16:3; De.16:16; 2 Chr.8:13; 2 Chr.30:13)	A symbol of the urgency for God's people to escape the enslavement of the world and immediately begin their march to the promised land of heaven. (Mt.26:17; Mk.14:1)	*Hebrew Time*: The 1st Month [Abib or Nisan], 15th thru the 21st Day *Secular Equivalent*: March - April	Harvesting barley & flax; Later Spring rains.
The Festival of Firstfruits	To thank God for the crops, the first harvest of the season that sustained life. (Ex.34:22; Le.23:10; Nu.28:26)	A symbol of Christ's resurrection and of the believers hope: Christ is the first of the harvest, the first to arise from the dead. (Ro.8:23; 1 Co.15:23)	*Hebrew Time*: The 1st Month [Abib or Nisan], 16th Day *Secular Equivalent*: March - April	Harvesting barley & flax; Later Spring rains
The Festival of Pentecost or Harvest or Weeks	To give thanks for the harvest and to dedicate one's life anew to God This festival took place fifty days after the Festival of Firstfruits. (Ex.23:16; Ex.34:22; Le.23:16; Nu.28:26; De.16:10)	A symbol of Pentecost... • of the great harvest of souls • of people giving their lives to God • of the coming of the Holy Spirit & the birth of the church (Ac.2:1-47; Ac.20:16; 1 Co.16:8)	*Hebrew Time*: The 3rd Month [Sivan], the 6th Day *Secular Equivalent*: May - June	Wheat harvest; other crops—grapes and almonds begin to open.
The Festival of Trumpets	To focus upon God, learning to trust God more and more and to proclaim the message of joy over the atonement or reconciliation with God. (Le.23:24; Nu.29:1; Ne.8:2)	A symbol of salvation and of the rapture, the glorious day when Christ will return and take believers—both the living and the dead—to with Him forever.	*Hebrew Time*: 7th Month, [Ethanim or Tishri **], the 1st Day *Secular Equivalent* September - October	Plowing of the fields: Early autumn rains.
The Day of Atonement	To focus upon the only way to approach God and be forgiven—through the shed blood of the atoning sacrifice. Celebrated yearly, it was a national day of repentance. (Ex.30:10; Le.16:30; Le.23:27; Nu.29:7)	A symbol of being reconciled with God through the atonement, through the substitute sacrifice of Christ. (He.9:7)	*Hebrew Time*: 7th Month, [Ethanim or Tishri **], the 10th Day *Secular Equivalent*: September - October	Plowing of the fields: Early autumn rains.
The Feast of Tabernacles or Booths	To celebrate the wilderness wanderings when the people lived in tents on their way to the promised land and to thank God for the harvest. (Le.23:34, 39; Nu.29:12; De.16:13; 2 Chr.8:13; Ezr.3:4; Ne.8:14; Zec.14:16)	A symbol of the believer's march through this world to heaven, a symbol of how temporary our world is as believers march to heaven. (Jn.7:2)	*Hebrew Time*: 7th Month, [Ethanim or Tishri **], the 15th thru the 21st Day *Secular Equivalent*: September - October	Plowing of the fields: Early autumn rains.
The Feast of Purim	To remember God's deliverance from Israel's enemies during the time of Esther. Purim was a time of sharing with one's neighbor and with the poor. (Est.9:18-32)	Not mentioned in the New Testament.	*Hebrew Time*: The 12th Month [Adar *], the 14th & 15th Day *Secular Equivalent*: February - March	Blooming of almond trees; Harvesting of citrus fruit; the later rains begin.

* Note: An additional month (Second Adar or Adar Sheni or Veadar) was added to the Hebrew calendar about every three years. This was how the lunar calendar corresponded to the solar year.

** Hebrew names of the month that are not in the Bible are marked with two stars (**). These are known as "Post-exilic" names, from the period of history known as "The Babylonian Exile."

*** The idea for listing the Farm Seasons was stirred by *The NIV Study Bible*, Grand Rapids, MI: Zondervan Bible Publishers, 1985, pp.102-103.

OTHER SACRED DAYS IN THE HEBREW CALENDAR

NAME OF FEAST OR EVENT	OLD TESTAMENT PURPOSE	NEW TESTAMENT SYMBOLISM	CALENDAR TIME	FARM SEASON (Crops/ Weather)
The Sabbath Day	To have a day of rest and worship (Ex.20:8-11; Ex.31:12-17; Le.23:3; De.5:12-15)	The Sabbath is a symbol of the spiritual rest that God promises to those who believe and follow him. The Sabbath rest is a symbol of redemption, of God's deliverance from the heavy burdens and trials of this life. (Mt.12:1-14; Mt.28:1; Lu. 4:16; Jn.5:9; Ac.13:42; Col.2:16; He.4:1-11)	*Hebrew Time*: Celebrated on the seventh day of each week *Secular Equivalent*: Same as above	Not Applicable.
The Sabbatical Year	The Sabbatical Year was celebrated every seven years. During the seventh year the land was given rest from agricultural use and debts were forgiven (Ex.23:10-11; Le. 25:1-7; De.15:1)	Not mentioned in the New Testament.	*Hebrew Time*: Celebrated every seven years *Secular Equivalent*: Same as above	Not Applicable.
The Year of Jubilee	The Year of Jubilee was celebrated at the end of every forty-ninth year on the Day of Atonement. On this special day, the trumpet would sound out the message of freedom to all the inhabitants of the land who had been held in bondage. In addition, all property was to be returned to the original owners who had been forced to sell because of poverty. This meant that all prices in the economy throughout the forty-nine years were to be fairly adjusted according to the closeness to The Year of Jubilee. (Le.25:8-17; Le. 27:17-24; Nu.36:4)	Not mentioned in the New Testament.	*Hebrew Time*: Celebrated at the end of every forty-ninth year on the Day of Atonement. *Secular Equivalent*: Same as above	Not Applicable.
The Sacred Assembly	To celebrate the end of the final feast. The sacred assembly was a day of sacrifice and then rest. (Le.23:36; Nu.29:35-38)	Not mentioned in the New Testament.	*Hebrew Time*: The 7th Month [Ethanim or Tishri **], on the 22nd Day. *Secular Equivalent*: September – October	Plowing of the fields; early autumn rains.

LEADERSHIP MINISTRIES WORLDWIDE

PURPOSE STATEMENT

LEADERSHIP MINISTRIES WORLDWIDE exists to equip ministers, teachers, and laypersons in their understanding, preaching, and teaching of God's Word by publishing and distributing worldwide *The Preacher's Outline & Sermon Bible*® and derivative works to reach & disciple all people for Jesus Christ.

MISSION STATEMENT

1. To make the Bible so understandable – its truth so clear and plain – that men and women everywhere, whether teacher or student, preacher or hearer, can grasp its message and receive Jesus Christ as Savior, and…

2. To place the Bible in the hands of all who will preach and teach God's Holy Word, verse by verse, precept by precept, regardless of the individual's ability to purchase it.

The Preacher's Outline & Sermon Bible and derivative works have been given to LMW as LMW Resources for printing and distribution worldwide at/below cost, by those who remain anonymous. One fact, however, is as true today as it was in the time of Christ:

THE GOSPEL IS FREE, BUT THE COST OF TAKING IT IS NOT

LMW depends on the generous gifts of believers with a heart for Him and a love for the lost. They help pay for the printing, translating, and distributing of LMW Resources into the hands of God's servants worldwide, who will present the Gospel message with clarity, authority, and understanding beyond their own.

LMW was incorporated in the state of Tennessee in July 1992 and received IRS 501 (c)(3) non-profit status in March 1994. LMW is an international, nondenominational mission organization. All proceeds from USA sales, along with donations from donor partners, go directly to underwrite translation and distribution projects of LMW Resources to preachers, church and lay leaders, and Bible students around the world.

LMW RESOURCES

This material, like similar works, has come from imperfect man and is thus susceptible to human error. We are nevertheless grateful to God for both calling us and empowering us through His Holy Spirit to undertake this task. Because of His goodness and grace, *The Preacher's Outline & Sermon Bible*® New Testament and the Old Testament volumes have been completed.

LMW Resources include *The Minister's Personal Handbook, The Believer's Personal Handbook,* and other helpful resources available in printed form as well as electronically on various digital platforms.

God has given the strength and stamina to bring us this far. Our confidence is that as we keep our eyes on Him and remain grounded in the undeniable truths of the Word, we will continue to produce other helpful resources for God's dear servants to use in their Bible study and discipleship.

We offer this material, first, to Him in whose name we labor and serve and for whose glory it has been produced and, second, to everyone everywhere who studies, preaches, and teaches the Word.

Our daily prayer is that each volume will lead thousands, millions, yes even billions, into a better understanding of the Holy Scriptures and a fuller knowledge of Jesus Christ the Incarnate Word, of whom the Scriptures so faithfully testify.

You will be pleased to know that Leadership Ministries Worldwide partners with Christian organizations, printers, and mission groups around the world to make LMW Resources available and affordable in many countries and foreign languages. It is our goal that *every* leader around the world, both clergy and lay, will be able to understand God's holy Word and present God's message with more clarity, authority, and understanding—all beyond his or her own power.

LEADERSHIP MINISTRIES WORLDWIDE
1928 Central Avenue • Chattanooga, TN 37408
1(800) 987-8790
Email: info@lmw.org
lmw.org

11/22

Product Listing

THE PREACHER'S OUTLINE & SERMON BIBLE® (POSB)   *Available in KJV (44 vols) & NIV (40 vols)*

OLD TESTAMENT

- Genesis I: Chs. 1–11
- Genesis II: Chs. 12–50
- Exodus I: Chs. 1–18
- Exodus II: Chs. 19–40
- Leviticus
- Numbers
- Deuteronomy
- Joshua
- Judges, Ruth
- 1 Samuel
- 2 Samuel
- 1 Kings
- 2 Kings
- 1 Chronicles
- 2 Chronicles
- Ezra, Nehemiah, Esther
- Job
- Psalms I: Chs. 1-41
- Psalms II: Chs. 42-106
  Psalms III: Chs. 107-150
- Proverbs
- Ecclesiastes, Song of Solomon
- Isaiah I: Chs. 1-35
- Isaiah II: Chs. 36-66
- Jeremiah I: Chs. 1-29
- Jeremiah II: Chs. 30-52, Lamentations
- Ezekiel
- Daniel, Hosea Joel, Amos, Obadiah, Jonah, Micah, Nahum
- Habakkuk, Zephaniah, Haggai, Zechariah, Malachi

NEW TESTAMENT

- Matthew I: Chs. 1–15
- Matthew II: Chs. 16–28
- Mark
- Luke
- John
- Acts
- Romans
- 1 & 2 Corinthians
- Galatians, Ephesians, Philippians, Colossians
- 1 & 2 Thessalonians, 1 & 2 Timothy, Titus, Philemon
- Hebrews, James
- 1 & 2 Peter, 1, 2, & 3 John, Jude
- Revelation
- Master Outline & Subject Index

Handbooks

- **What the Bible Says to the Believer** —
  The Believer's Personal Handbook
  11 Chapters. – Over 500 Subjects, 300 Promises, & 400 Verses Expounded - Gift leatherette or paperback options

- **What the Bible Says to the Minister** —
  The Minister's Personal Handbook
  12 Chapters. - 127 Subjects - 400 Verses Expounded - Gift leatherette or paperback options

- **What the Bible Says to the Business Leader**—The Business Leader's Personal Handbook
  12 Chapters – Over 100 topics plus hundreds of scriptural values for conducting business in a 21st-century world — Paperback

- **What the Bible Says About Series** —
  Various Subjects

everyWORD

Scripture, Outline, Commentary of the Gospels with ESV Scripture

- everyWORD: Matthew 1–16:12

- everyWORD: Matthew 16:13–28:20

- everyWORD: Mark

- everyWORD: Luke 1–13:21

- everyWORD: Luke 13:22–24:53

- everyWORD: John

- **The Teacher's Outline & Study Bible™** - Various New Testament Books
  Complete 30 - 45 minute lessons – with illustrations and discussion questions
- *Practical Illustrations — Companion to the POSB Arranged by topic and Scripture reference*
- *LMW Resources on various digital platforms Learn more on our website at lmw.org*
- *Contact for resources in other languages*

Contact Us

LEADERSHIP MINISTRIES WORLDWIDE
1928 Central Avenue • Chattanooga, TN 37408
1(800) 987-8790 • E-mail - info@lmw.org
Order online at lmw.org

Made in the USA
Columbia, SC
31 January 2025

52864655R00196